International Terrorism in the 1980s

A Chronology of Events

International Terrorism in the 1980s

A Chronology of Events

VOLUME I

1980–1983

Edward F. Mickolus, Todd Sandler, and Jean M. Murdock

Iowa State University Press / Ames

EDWARD F. MICKOLUS is President of Vinyard Software, Inc.
TODD SANDLER is Professor of Economics, Iowa State University.
JEAN M. MURDOCK is a research associate of Todd Sandler.

Manufactured in the United States of America

First edition, 1989

Library of Congress Cataloging-in-Publication Data

Mickolus, Edward F.
    International terrorism in the 1980s : a chronology of events / Edward F. Mickolus, Todd Sandler, and Jean M. Murdock. — 1st ed.
      p. cm.
    Bibliography: p.
    Contents: v. 1. 1980–1983.
    ISBN 0–8138–0024–2
    1. Terrorism — Chronology.   I. Sandler, Todd.   II. Murdock, Jean M. (Jean Marie),
1955–   .   III. Title.
HV6431.M494   1989
909.82′8 — dc19
                                                                      88–19891
                                                                      CIP

CONTENTS

Preface

ALTHOUGH INTERNATIONAL TERRORISM leveled off slightly in 1986 after showing marked increases in 1984 and 1985, it indicates no signs of disappearing. Authorities have become better at thwarting incidents, but at the same time, terrorists have become more efficient at countering the authorities' measures. Terrorism in the 1980s is marked by a number of characteristics: (1) A large portion of terrorist events are directed at Western democracies, their people and property. (2) Terrorist acts are becoming increasingly bloody with deaths and injuries rising in the 1980s as compared with the two preceding decades. (3) The bulk of terrorist acts are the result of turmoil in the Middle East. (4) Terrorist groups, such as Direct Action, the Combatant Communist Cells, the Italian Red Brigades, are beginning to coordinate acts. (5) Intergovernmental cooperation is increasing in the fight against terrorism.

The present volume chronicles terrorist events in the 1980–83 period; a companion volume chronicles events in the 1984–87 period. It is our hope that these two volumes will assist researchers, scholars, and policymakers in understanding the threat posed by international terrorism.

To concentrate our efforts, the three of us have divided our writing tasks. Ed was responsible for the 1980–82 period and the October 1986–December 1987 period (see the next volume). Jean and I were responsible for the January 1983–September 1986 period. An astute reader will surely note some differences in writing style among these sections. We have, however, tried to coordinate our efforts and maintain consistency throughout both volumes.

We are indebted to a number of people who have helped in this volume's preparation. Lynn Nyhus did an excellent job in typing the chronology material for the first volume. Without her cheerful and intelligent assistance, the book would have taken much longer to prepare. Sue Streeter did a fine job in typing the Preface and Introduction.

Manus I. Midlarsky from the University of Colorado at Boulder provided invaluable reader's comments on an earlier draft. We also appreciate the many fine professionals at Iowa State University (ISU) Press who assisted with the manuscript's publication. Arne Hallam from the Department of Economics at ISU helped Jean with computer-related inquiries. Finally, we express our gratitude to Richard Kinney, the Director of ISU Press.

Introduction

IN RECENT YEARS terrorism has come increasingly to the attention of the public; hardly a week passes without the news media reporting an aerial hijacking, a dramatic hostage incident, a destructive car bombing, or the assassination of a diplomat. During the summer of 1987, the so-called Irangate Hearings reminded us daily that terrorist acts can impose great costs and moral dilemmas upon governments. Since 1968 governments and businesses have been forced to allocate more resources, in terms of time and money, to thwarting terrorism and to managing terrorist crises when they occur. Thus, most industrial nations maintain a terrorist commando squad (e.g., Delta Force in the United States) that can be airlifted to deal with hostage-taking incidents. Following the United States bombing of Libya in April 1986 and a terrorist's failed attempt to place a bomb on board an El Al plane departing London in April 1986, airport security has been increased worldwide. In the last two years, the United States has publicized the names of airports that United States officials view as inadequate in their provision of security against terrorist attack. Even if terrorists do not achieve their political goals, they have managed to divert a large quantity of the authorities' resources to the struggle to deal effectively with terrorist threat. Terrorists have also been successful in gaining media exposure. This exposure has caused citizens to feel at risk, and many have heeded the threat. After some highly publicized events in 1986, approximately one out of four Americans who had intended to travel to Europe took vacations in the United States instead. Apparently, the terrorists succeeded in creating an atmosphere of fear. Even Greece felt it necessary in 1987 to air commercials on United States television in an effort to entice American vacationers.

Many authorities have formulated definitions of terrorism. Quite simply, terrorism is the premeditated "threatened or actual use of force or violence to attain a political goal through fear, coercion, or intimidation" (Russell et al., 1979). In any definition of political terrorism, emphasis must be placed on the political goal. Terrorists often unleash their violence and threats at a target group who is not directly involved in the political decision-making process that the terrorists seek to influence; for example, innocent people at the Rome and Vienna airports are murdered by Palestinian terrorists who want a homeland in territory occupied by Israel.

International or transnational terrorism concerns terrorist activities involving terrorists or government participants from two or more nations. Incidents originating in one country and terminating in another are transnational in character, as are incidents involving the demands made of a nation other than the one where the incident occurs. Any terrorist incident that includes the governments, the citizens, or the institutions of two or more countries is considered transnational. In short, transnational terrorist incidents have ramifications that spill over national borders by involving participants or territories of two or more nations. A detailed working definition for transnational terrorism appears later in this Introduction.

This book provides comprehensive descriptions of worldwide terrorist incidents for 1980–83. A companion volume in preparation gives descriptions of terrorist incidents for 1984–87. These two volumes carry on the work begun in Edward F. Mickolus (1980), *Transnational Terrorism: A Chronology of Events, 1968–1979.* Where information has become available since 1980, these two volumes will provide updates of incidents included in the earlier Mickolus chronology for 1968–79. These updates will be placed in the current chronology according to the date on which the additional information became available. Thus, if a terrorist, who took part in an incident on April 8, 1978, is convicted and sentenced on May 1, 1981, the update will be listed under this latter date.

Although other chronologies exist, our chronology is the only comprehensive, publicly available one. Rand maintains a chronology of international terrorist events; however, the Rand chronology includes very brief descriptions highlighting only the most important aspects of an incident. Moreover, Rand charges subscribers a substantial fee for the complete chronology. Paul Wilkinson of the University of Aberdeen, United Kingdom, has put together a chronology that his associates draw upon in their scholarly writings. The Aberdeen chronology has not been made available to researchers elsewhere; hence, we cannot comment on its form. From time to time, the United States Department of State and the United States Central Intelligence Agency (CIA) have published a selected chronology of significant incidents. These chronologies are not comprehensive in their coverage; they include only a fraction of terrorist incidents.

The descriptions of the terrorist incidents in our chronology are based upon publicly available materials that have appeared in the world press. Key sources include the Associated Press, United Press International, Reuters tickers, the *Washington Post, New York Times, Washington Times,* the *Foreign Broadcast Information Service (FBIS) Daily Reports,* and ABC,

NBC, and CBS evening news. Of this group, the items available through the regional *FBIS Daily Reports* have been invaluable: FBIS draws from hundreds of world print and electronic media sources and is the best single source of material on foreign coverage of terrorist incidents. We also utilized chronologies provided by the Nuclear Regulatory Commission, the Federal Bureau of Investigation (FBI), and several foreign embassies.

The chronology includes more than transnational terrorist incidents; this volume and its companion also survey key domestic terrorist events. The inclusion of these events enables the interested readers to construct their own list of transnational events if their definition of transnational event is somewhat broader than the one used here. A comparison of the summary statistics (e.g., the annual number of terrorist events) reported by the University of Aberdeen, the United States Department of State, Rand, and Mickolus (1980) indicates some variation owing to different working definitions. Even though number counts have differed somewhat, the trends depicted by the various chronologies have shown a marked similarity. The interested reader should consult the United States Department of State (1986), *Patterns of Global Terrorism: 1985,* for the most recent official United States views on terrorism trends. The publication is issued annually. Cordes et al. (1984) depict some recent trends in transnational terrorism derived from the Rand chronology.

Interwoven with the terrorist incidents is a partial listing of threats and acts of violence against nuclear facilities. This list came about as a result of Mickolus's research on the likelihood of terrorist exploitation of nuclear weapons or facilities in the future. The chronology here also contains important policy announcements relevant to the fight against terrorism. In particular, new laws enacted to combat terrorism are included, as are intergovernment agreements to cooperate in thwarting terrorism. Noteworthy terrorist actions, such as meetings between group leaders, are also reported. We have also attempted to include all aerial hijackings, whatever their location and the motive of the perpetrators.

The remainder of the Introduction contains five sections designed to aid the reader in using the chronology. First, we provide the working definition used to classify terrorist events as transnational. Illustrative examples demonstrate how we distinguish terrorist events from nonterrorist events, and domestic terrorist events from transnational terrorist events. Second, we briefly characterize theoretical models of terrorism, whose verification depends on data such as that contained in the chronology. Third, we present some empirical applications of the Mickolus (1980) chronology to assist the reader in seeing the wide uses made of the previous chronology. Fourth, we describe computer diskettes that we are developing with the raw data of the chronology. Finally, we present concluding remarks. The Introduction of the 1984–87 volume will contain summary statistics and trends of events for the entire 1980–87 period.

DEFINITIONS, CONVENTIONS, AND OTHER PRELIMINARIES

On Terrorism and Nonterrorism

The working definition of international/transnational terrorism employed by the chronology is the use, or threat of use, of anxiety-inducing, extranormal violence for political purposes by any individual or group, whether acting for or in opposition to established governmental authority, when such action is intended to influence the attitudes and behavior of a target group wider than the immediate victims and when, through the nationality or foreign ties of its perpetrators, through its location, through the nature of its institutional or human victims, or through the mechanics of its resolution, its ramifications transcend national boundaries. For a definition of terrorism per se, one can place a period after the words "immediate victims" in the previous definition. Acts of a purely criminal nature with no political motivation whatsoever are not considered terrorism. For example, a group that kidnaps the son of a wealthy individual solely for the ransom is not engaged in an act of terrorism. Similarly, threats issued to a candy manufacturer in Japan in the hopes of securing extortion payments do not constitute political terrorism. If, however, there is clear evidence that the kidnappers or extortionists intend to use their ransoms to further a political goal or cause, then the act is considered a terrorist incident. In these instances, the people responsible usually go to great lengths to publicize the group's name, symbol, and political message. Moreover, the kidnappers or extortionists often choose victims who are symbolic of the elements that they oppose. Thus, the Sudanese People's Liberation Army (SPLA) kidnaps foreign workers who lend technical assistance to projects that the SPLA opposes; the Hezbollah kidnaps Americans living in Beirut; and the Italian Red Brigades abduct former Premier Aldo Moro.

The chronology does not classify incidents as terrorism that relate to declared wars or major military interventions by governments, or guerrilla attacks on military targets conducted as internationally recognized acts of belligerency. If, however, the guerrilla attacks were against civilians or the dependents of military personnel in an attempt to create an atmosphere of fear to foster political objectives, then the attacks are considered terrorism. Official, government-sanctioned military acts in response to terrorist attacks, such as the United States bombing of Libya or the United States seizure of an Egyptian plane carrying the terrorists from the Achille Lauro incident, are not themselves coded.

We also exclude unintended acts from our definition of terrorism. If, for example, a foreign newspaper reporter is killed in the cross fire between government troops and guerrillas, the reporter's death is not considered a terrorist assassination. When guerrillas attempt to hit a military convoy with a mortar but hit a civilian school instead, the act is not termed a terrorist incident even though civilian deaths have resulted. We also exclude bombings that occur near a political target — an embassy, for example — but were intended for a nonpolitical target even if the damage spills over to a political target.

Since terrorism involves the use or the threatened use of violence, we exclude all peaceful protests that remain so. Thus, peaceful marches and demonstrations are not terrorist acts. A peaceful occupation of an embassy that ends with no arrests or confrontations with authorities is not classified as a terrorist act. If the occupiers destroy property, take hostages, or fail to heed a request to leave, then the occupation is listed as a terrorist act.

In the chronology, we write up all political threats, even very general, all-encompassing ones — for instance, a threat against Italian interests worldwide. A threat must, however, be credible, specific, and transnational in substance to be classified as a transnational terrorist act. Hence, the almost daily threats by the Islamic Jihad to crush America are not sufficiently credible or specific to be counted as terrorist acts. Nevertheless, a threat by the Islamic Jihad to blow up the United States embassy in Beirut or elsewhere is all too credible and quite specific.

When a "victim's" claim cannot be believed or substantiated, the incident is listed but is not counted as a terrorist act. If, for example, a United States soldier claims to have been kidnapped by a group of West German terrorists, but no corroborating evidence exists, then the incident is not included in the tally of transnational terrorist events. Wherever possible, the motivation of the participants is considered when forming judgments about the legitimacy of a terrorist incident.

On Domestic and Transnational Terrorism

Since we have already indicated our distinction between domestic and transnational terrorism, we need only present some specific conventions used in the harder-to-call cases. When a terrorist group from West Germany attacks an Italian embassy in Bonn, the event is clearly transnational even though a border has not been crossed. In fights of self-determination for a province, island protectorates, or territory, the question is not always so clear-cut and a convention must be established. For this chronology, we classify events as transnational when the terrorist executes the act on the ruling country's own soil. If, for example, an Irish Republican Army (IRA) terrorist plants a bomb on Oxford Street, London, then the incident is classified as transnational. If, however, the IRA terrorist plants the bomb in the path of a British military convoy in Londonderry, Northern Ireland, then the act is considered domestic. Similarly, when the Armed Front for National Liberation (FALN) brings their operations to the steps of the United States Capitol, the incidents are transnational; but FALN terrorist attacks performed in Puerto Rico are classified as domestic. A similar distinction involves the Caribbean Revolutionary Army (ARC), which seeks autonomy for French Martinique and Guadeloupe, and the Corsican National Liberation Front, which seeks autonomy for Corsica.

Although the crossing of a border by a terrorist group is sufficient for an act to be transnational, the border crossing is not a necessary condition. South American terrorists who threaten to kill a domestically held hostage unless United States newspapers run advertisements publicizing their cause are engaged in transnational terrorism since another country's institutions are involved. A domestic act that attempts to pressure a second country into changing its policies is a transnational event; however, the same act when employed to make the home country alter its foreign policies is a domestic terrorist incident. Thus, Japanese terrorists who perpetrate acts of arson to force the Japanese government to prohibit United States nuclear ships from docking in Japan are performing domestic terrorism.

We must also make a distinction between domestic and transnational events in regard to the numerous incidents in the Basque region during the 1980-87 period. Basque Separatists, including the Basque Fatherland and Liberty (ETA) group, seek an autonomous state carved out of France and Spain. Basque Separatist events that take place in Spain (France) and that affect French (Spanish) persons, property, or interests are counted as transnational terrorist incidents. When the terrorist incident in Spain (France) is directed at Spanish (French) interests, the event is domestic.

Even though terrorist attacks against an occupying military force — such as Israel in Lebanon, the Soviets in Afghanistan — are not classified as terrorist acts, attacks on peacekeeping forces are considered transnational terrorist acts. During 1983–85 numerous terrorist incidents in Lebanon involved the peacekeeping forces from the United States, France, and Italy. We also classify terrorist attacks as transnational when launched against the personnel or property of an ally's forces stationed on a foreign soil. An operation by the Combatant Communist Cells (CCC), Direct Action (AD), or some other terrorist group against United States troops stationed in a European country constitutes a transnational terrorist incident, as does an attack against a NATO headquarters, airstrip, or pipeline. In fact, all terrorist attacks against an international institution — for example, the United Nations, the United States–Peruvian Cultural Center — are listed as transnational terrorist incidents.

On Numbering Events

An eight-digit code number is assigned to all transnational events and all skyjackings and follows the descriptions of these incidents in the chronology. Domestic terrorist acts are not given a code number unless they are skyjackings. The first two digits of the code number indicate the year; the third and fourth digits denote the month; the fifth and sixth digits refer to the day; and the final two digits indicate the event number for the date. That is, 83010202 corresponds to the second event on January 2, 1983, while 80040604 denotes the fourth event on April 6, 1980. These code numbers will be used in both the index to the 1984–87 volume and the *International Terrorism: Attributes of Terrorist Events* (ITERATE 3) data files that we plan to market through Vinyard Software at a later date.

In counting events, we interpret three threats made in, say, a single phone call as one event. When three threats are made in three separate phone calls, each threat is counted as a separate event. Similarly, the kidnapping of three foreigners (or a planeload of passengers) by a terrorist group in a single attack is handled as a single event. In contrast, the abduction of three foreigners by the same group in three separate operations is counted as three events.

Of all terrorist incidents, skyjackings represent some of the most publicized and spectacular events. A skyjacking incident, such as the diversion of Trans World Airline flight 847 in June 1985, receives a great deal of media attention and is not easily forgotten. In order to keep better track of these events, we assign them a code number even when they do not constitute a transnational terrorist incident. Thus, we include a complete list of aerial hijackings for the periods surveyed, whatever the motivation of the attacker or the location of the incident. Nonterrorist skyjackings are listed to illustrate the environment of violence that terrorists may believe exists. These incidents serve as a research tool for those readers who wish to investigate the possible diffusion of violence by criminals, psychopaths, and terrorists who utilize the same forms of violent expression. We do not assign a code number to incidents where individuals have stolen a plane or a military aircraft and have flown it to another country for political asylum, provided that no threats of violence have been issued and no hostages have been seized.

Other Details of the Chronology

In the chronology, a country or place follows the date. This location refers to the country or place where the event originated. If, for example, an Iranian Airlines plane is hijacked in Tehran and made to fly to Dubai, then to Egypt, and finally to Lebanon, the incident is listed under Iran, the country of origin. Items in the chronology that involve related attacks or events in several countries have all of the relevant countries' names listed after the date. The incident date denotes the onset of the incident.

Whenever information is available as to the time of day when an incident occurs, the local time is given. In long, drawn-out incidents, we include the timing of key events, such as the sequential release of hostages during a hijacking, within the description of the incident. When a hijacking lasts for a number of days and involves multiple landings in different time zones, we list the local time followed by Greenwich mean time (GMT).

News media names are given in capital letters in order to distinguish them from the names of terrorist groups. Unfortunately, some terrorist groups' names show minor variations: the Combatant Communist Cells is sometimes called the Fighting Communist Cells, while the Basque Fatherland and Liberty group is sometimes called Basque Nation and Liberation. This minor variation really does not pose much of a problem since the variations are easy to spot. We have tried to be consistent in our use of these names. A complete list of terrorist groups is given in Appendix 1 at the end of the book. Greater difficulty arises for groups that employ a host of different names. The Abu Nidal Group, headed by Sabri al-Banna, operates under the names of Fatah–Revolutionary Council for Israeli targets, the Arab Revolutionary Army for Persian Gulf targets, the Revolutionary Organization of Socialist Moslems for British attacks, and Black September for Jordanian and Palestinian targets. Abu Nidal has also used the name Black June. Many terrorist groups have letters or acronyms associated with their names—for example, ETA for Basque Fatherland and Liberty and ASALA for the Armenian Secret Army for the Liberation of Armenia. In order to make the description of each incident self-contained, we give the group's acronym in parentheses following the group's name, written out in full. Thereafter, the group's acronym is used in the rest of the description of the incident.

Judgment had to be made concerning the spelling of some proper names. A good example is Qaddafi, whose name has been spelled in literally hundreds of different fashions. For the chronology, we fix on a common spelling and then adhere to it throughout. Wherever possible, we have used the foreign spelling of Chinese and Arabic names for individuals, rather than their Anglicized alternatives.

A final detail involves casualty figures given in the chronology for those incidents resulting in the loss of life or limb. Newspaper accounts often disagree about casualties following shoot-outs or bombings. In a bombing attack, bodies may be sufficiently mutilated to inhibit accurate body counts. Moreover, casualty figures are updated as the search for victims continues and as injured people succumb to their wounds. We utilized the casualty reports issued after a sufficient time had elapsed to allow for the most accurate count possible. If disagreement arises among various sources, we employ every means at our disposal to reconcile differences.

On Terrorist Tactics

Violence-prone groups can engage in numerous types of nonviolent actions to try to publicize their political views; here, however, we are concerned with actions that threaten or cause harm to property or individuals. Table I.1 lists the most common kinds of terrorist attacks.

Table I.1.   *Types of Terrorist Incidents*

01 – Kidnapping
02 – Barricade and hostage seizure
03 – Occupation of facilities without hostage seizure
04 – Letter or parcel bombing
05 – Incendiary bombing, arson, Molotov cocktail
06 – Explosive bombing (dynamite or plastic)
07 – Armed attack employing missiles
08 – Armed attack – other, including mortars, bazookas
09 – Aerial hijacking (skyjacking)
10 – Takeover of nonaerial means of transportation (e.g., a ship or bus)
11 – Assassination, murder
12 – Sabotage not involving explosives or arson
13 – Exotic pollution, including chemical and biological agents
14 – Nuclear-related weapons attack
15 – Threat with no subsequent terrorist action
16 – Theft, break-in of facilities
17 – Conspiracy to commit terrorist action
18 – Hoax
19 – Other actions
20 – Sniping at buildings, other facilities
21 – Shoot-out with police
22 – Arms smuggling
23 – Car bombing
24 – Suicide car bombing

As indicated in Table I.1, we distinguish between different types of bombings. We also differentiate between various kinds of hostage-taking incidents. Kidnappings, for instance, involve the taking of one or more hostages to an unknown location; barricade-and-hostage incidents concern the seizing of hostages in a known location. The latter kind of incident is the more risky for terrorists as they themselves are hostages of the authorities owing to the latter's knowledge of the incident's location. Skyjackings also occur in a known location and represent one of the most risky types of terrorist incidents. Mickolus (1980, pp. xix–xx) and the United States Central Intelligence Agency (1981) have shown that political terrorists rank the tactics that they adopt with respect to such factors as risk, time, and the probability of confrontation with authorities. Such high-risk activities as skyjackings and barricade-and-hostage missions have the smallest frequency; such low-risk activities as bombings and assassinations have the highest. In spite of some highly publicized suicide attacks, the majority of terrorists appear to value their own lives along with their cause.

THEORETICAL MODELS OF TERRORISM

In recent years, Sandler and his colleagues have applied economic methods to the modeling of terrorist behavior. Relevant papers include Sandler, Tschirhart, and Cauley (1983), Lapan and Sandler (1987), Sandler and Scott (1987), Atkinson, Sandler, and Tschirhart (1987), and Im,

Cauley, and Sandler (1987). The message of their research is simple: Terrorists are rational individuals whose behavior can be modeled and predicted. As rational beings, terrorists maximize their goals subject to constraints that include resources and risks imposed by authorities. Changes in these constraints lead to predictable adjustments.

Economics is concerned with optimization in the face of constraints. In particular, economists study the allocation of scarce resources among alternative ends. Thus, the consumer is depicted as maximizing utility subject to a budget constraint and a time constraint; the firm is characterized as maximizing profits subject to the technology constraint or production function; and the production manager is seen as minimizing costs subject to technology constraints. Since the start of classical economic thought in the 18th century, "economic man" has been depicted as a rational being who maximizes beneficial returns and minimizes costs, while responding to constraints. Changes in these constraints, as might arise when prices or success probabilities are deliberately altered by authorities, are hypothesized to produce predictable behavioral responses, in which individuals substitute out of relatively more expensive activities into relatively less expensive ones. If, for example, embassy security is increased, terrorists may choose to kidnap and assassinate embassy personnel once they leave the compound, since these terrorist tactics are relatively cheaper to perform once the embassies are fortified. An economist judges rationality in terms of an individual's response to changes in one's constraints, not in terms of the goals or tastes possessed. Thus, a terrorist group that bombs barracks and kidnaps foreign peacekeeping personnel in the hopes of removing foreign influences from the group's home soil is viewed as rational, provided that it responds appropriately to constraints and that its actions might serve to further the members' goal.

A nice application of the economic choice model applied to terrorism can be found in Landes (1978). In his study of United States aircraft hijackings during 1961–76, Landes indicated with economic statistical techniques that the use of sky marshals and metal detectors had had a significant positive effect on the probability of apprehension and a significant negative influence on the number of offenses committed. The data showed a precipitous drop in skyjackings after these security measures were operational in January 1973: In the United States, there were 27 incidents of skyjackings in 1972 and only 1 in 1973 (Landes, 1978, p. 3). Such a reaction implies terrorist rationality.

A terrorist's willingness to assume a risk of death does not necessarily mean that he or she is irrational. Policemen and firefighters, to name but two occupations, are willing to face a probability of death greater than in other fields, provided that their remuneration compensates them for the added risks that employment entails (Thaler and Rosen, 1976). Since the attacks on the Rome and Vienna airports in December 1985, the perceived probability of death to air travelers has increased somewhat; nevertheless, many people still travel.

Gary Becker (1968) was the first to apply rational-actor models to the study of criminal behavior. In the economic model of crime, a criminal is regarded as choosing between legal activities with certain returns and illegal activities with uncertain returns so as to maximize expected utility. In other words, a criminal is depicted as allocating his or her time and resources among various legal and illegal activities in the hopes of maximizing one's expected return.

As Ehrlich (1975) has shown, the expected return to illegal activities can be made to account for the probability of apprehension, the probability of sentencing when apprehended, and the severity of the sentence through the use of conditional probabilities. The use of these models has produced many interesting theoretical predictions that are not inconsistent with the evidence. For instance, Ehrlich's (1975, 398) empirical analysis of the deterrent effects of capital punishment suggests that "on average the trade-off between the execution of an offender and the lives of potential victims it might have saved was of the order of magnitude of 1 for 8 for the period 1933–67 in the United States." Ehrlich (1973) and Becker (1968) have shown that the deterrent effects of a one-percent increase in the penalty per offense is greater than those of a one-percent increase in the probability of apprehension when criminals are risk averse — that is, they oppose an actuarially fair bet. Knowledge gained from these studies can assist law enforcement agencies in allocating their own scarce resources among alternative criminal-thwarting activities. Similar "deterrent studies" can be performed to investigate terrorist choices. The chronology contains the sentences given to convicted terrorists as well as the amount of time, if any, served in prison. This information can be used to analyze the deterrent effects of sentences on terrorism.

The economics of crime literature has helped examine recidivism by applying career-choice models to the study of criminal choices. For these career-choice models, an individual is hypothesized as comparing alternative expected income streams when deciding to switch out of one career into another. Empirical estimates of "offense functions," which relate the number of offenses to deterrent actions of the police and to self-protecting actions of the criminals, have the potential to assist law enforcement agencies to ascertain the efficacy of their methods. Many other empirical estimates have been derived from economic models of crime.

Once one realizes that terrorism is a choice-theoretic subset of criminal activity, it is easy to conclude that the paradigms of the economics of crime might be fruitfully modified and applied to terrorism. Like the criminal, the terrorist confronts decision making under uncertainty. In modeling terrorist behavior, the researcher must be careful to endow the model with its own unique assumptions so as to capture the environment of the terrorist.

For economic models of terrorism, we refer the readers to the following papers: Sandler, Tschirhart, and Cauley (1983), Lapan and Sandler (1987), Sandler and Scott (1987), Kirk (1983), and Lee (1987). Many of these papers apply game theory so as to model the interactive strategy choices of terrorists and government authorities. Thus, choice variables of the terrorists (government agents) influence the payoffs and choices of the government participants (terrorists).

EMPIRICAL APPLICATIONS

In this section, we draw on some recent papers to describe the application of econometrics (i.e., economic statistical modeling) to the examination of terrorist behavior. All of these econometric exercises attempt to test hypotheses derived from a theoretical model such as the choice-theoretic model described in the last section. In many instances, the researcher used data drawn from Mickolus (1981), *International Terrorism: Attributes of Terrorist Events, 1968–1977,* known as ITERATE 2, which contains coded information given in the Mickolus (1980) chronology. A careful study of the articles cited here will enable the reader to discover the many uses to which the chronology can be applied.

Incidents Involving Bargaining

Although hostage seizures are a small percentage of terrorist incidents, these seizures represent some of the most publicized and influential events. From 1968 through 1982, of the approximate 8,000 reported terrorist events, 7 percent (540 events) constituted hostage-taking acts involving 3,162 hostages (United States Department of State, 1983). The bulk of these acts have been directed at industrialized democracies, particularly the United States and some Western European countries (United States Central Intelligence Agency, 1981). Even though governments are dealing more effectively with these incidents, terrorists have been very successful: (1) In kidnappings, terrorists successfully capture their hostage(s) in 80 percent of the acts and receive their ransom demands in 70 percent of the incidents. (2) In barricade-and-hostage incidents, the terrorists achieve at least a portion of demands in 75 percent of the cases (United States Department of State, 1983).

Atkinson, Sandler, and Tschirhart (1987) have modified the bargaining model of John Cross (1969, 1977) in order to investigate hostage negotiations. Unlike other bargaining models, the Cross model accounts explicitly for the length of the negotiations. In each period of the bargaining process, the terrorists (government officials) are viewed as maximizing the difference between their time-discounted payoffs, which is dependent on their demands (concessions) and the time-discounted costs of bargaining. These costs are incurred in each period of negotiations. Each side perceives that the duration of the incident equals the difference between current demands and concessions divided by the concession rate of the opponent. In deciding demands (concessions) in each period, the terrorists (government officials) can therefore trade off large (small) values of demands (concessions) at the expense of a longer incident with its concomitant greater waiting costs. The incident ends in a settlement when demands equal concessions. If either side is unsatisfied with the progress of the negotiations, refuses to negotiate, or views the final outcome as a stalemate, then the incident can end in violence.

Atkinson, Sandler, and Tschirhart (1987) test three hypotheses derived from the bargaining model: (1) Increases (decreases) in bargaining costs to the terrorists induce them to decrease (increase) their demands. Similarly, increases (decreases) in bargaining costs to the government cause it to raise (reduce) concessions. (2) Increases (decreases) in bargaining costs to either side will shorten (lengthen) the duration of the incident. (3) Bluffing will diminish a terrorist group's payoff.

Empirical analyses of these hypotheses used the data from ITERATE 2. In most instances, the proxies for bargaining costs had the predicted effects on terrorist demands as indicated by (1) and (3). To test the second hypothesis, Atkinson, Sandler, and Tschirhart (1987) used a time-to-failure regression technique, in which the incident's duration is regressed against bargaining cost proxies (e.g., the number of hostages held, the type of hostage, sequential release of prisoners). Most cost proxies were significant with the predicted sign. These researchers also tested for the underlying distribution for the length of negotiated incidents. Their results showed that incidents have a memory: As the incident drags on, the instantaneous probability of the incident ending continually declines. Roughly, the longer an incident goes on, the more difficult it is to end in the ensuing period. Even though the cumulative probability of terminating the incident rises with time, the falling instantaneous probability means that the cumulative probability is rising at a declining rate. Thus, the marginal effects, associated with government actions to end an incident, appear to decline as the incident drags on. In order to allow for time-to-failure analysis, we have included the length of the incident in the incident descriptions. When available, we also indicate the timing of important events within the negotiations (e.g., the release of some hostages).

On Terrorist Substitution between Events

Economic modeling and econometric techniques can be employed to quantify the substitution phenomenon associated with changes in the relative costs of terrorist tactics and to suggest the most efficacious assignment of government resources between terrorist-thwarting activities. Im, Cauley, and Sandler (1987) utilized spectral analysis to examine aspects of the choice-theoretical problem facing terrorists whose constraints are partly determined by government behavior. Mickolus (1980, pp. xviii–xix) has conjectured that there may be cyclical patterns in terrorist activities. Im, Cauley, and Sandler (1987) searched for cycles in the time series data on terrorist events. Spectral analysis is an ideal statistical technique to test for any regular or periodic variations in the data (Gottman, 1981). Spectral analytic tests can provide additional evidence of the rational-actor hypothesis (e.g., the complex attack-counterattack phenomenon) and may serve as a basis for government forecasting of terrorist activity.

In Im, Cauley, and Sandler (1987), spectral analysis was applied to residuals obtained from estimated trend regressions for the following time series: (1) skyjacking (SJ), (2) barricade and hostage taking (BH), (3) kidnapping (KN), (4) all international terrorist events (TL), and (5) all events not involving hostages (OT). Their results indicated that all terrorist events (TL) have a 28-month-long cycle, which is somewhat longer than Mickolus's (1980) hypothesized 24-month cycle. The series for skyjackings has two significant periodicities—4.1 months and 28 months. Only a single significant cycle was associated with BH and KN—72 months and 48 months, respectively.

Im, Cauley, and Sandler (1987) utilized cross-spectral analysis to provide evidence of the substitution phenomenon. In essence, cross-spectral analysis can display the degree of association between two time series at individual frequencies. The precise measure of association is signified by the coherency reading, which, when squared, is analogous to the coefficient of determination in regression analysis. A coherency reading of *1* implies that two time series are exactly associated in terms of amplitude at each frequency. The phase difference estimate denotes angular displacement between two series. For a sinusoidal function that repeats every four years, 360° would correspond to the completion of a four-year cycle. A phase difference estimate of 180° would indicate that two series were completely out of phase (i.e., as one series is increasing, the other is decreasing). For two types of terrorist activities, a phase difference equal to 180° would suggest that the activities are perfect substitutes. In short, the empirical issue of whether two terrorist activities with the same periodicity are substitutes boils down to testing the null hypothesis that the phase difference is 180°. Failure to reject this hypothesis is suggestive of a substitution effect.

Im, Cauley, and Sandler (1987) applied cross-spectral techniques to the six possible pairs of series. Each pair displayed from three to nine statistically significant coherencies. Moreover, they uncovered evidence of orthogonality (i.e., a phase difference of 180°) for five of the six pairs studied. This evidence suggests that terrorists substitute between related events; this substitution primarily showed up in the short run.

On Terrorist Success in Hostage-Taking Incidents

Sandler and Scott (1987) identified factors that helped determine terrorist success in hostage-taking events. Two measures of success were examined: logistical success and negotiated success. A logistical success occurs when the terrorists manage to capture and secure one or more hostages as planned; a negotiated success occurs when the terrorists achieve some of their demands and manage to escape. Both measures of success were related to terrorist resource variables (e.g., the number of terrorists in the attack squad, type of weapon) and negotiation strategies (e.g., did the terrorists permit sequential release of hostages?). Sandler and Scott (1987) employed a logit model, in which the log of the odds ratio was regressed against various sets of explanatory variables. Many of the explanatory variables proved to be significant factors explaining terrorist success. The Sandler and Scott (1987) study can be extended to 1987 by using information contained in the chronology on the incidents' outcome. Whenever the outcome is known, the incident description presents this information. Success probabilities can then be ascertained by computing the ratio of successful incidents to total incidents.

On Policy Effectiveness

In a recent paper, Cauley and Im (1987) have applied the statistical technique of intervention analysis to evaluate three specific antiterrorist policies: (1) increased airport security screening (January 1973), (2) increased security at United States embassies and other diplomatic missions (January 1976), and (3) the institution of the United Nations convention on preventing crimes against diplomatic personnel (February 1977). Important policy decisions such as these are noted in the chronology when they are instituted. In general, intervention analysis provides a means of assessing the impact of a discrete intervention or interruption of a social process created, for example, by implementing a policy. Although Landes (1978) employed more traditional techniques to ascertain the magnitude of an antiskyjacking policy, only intervention analysis allows for an estimate of both the size and the time profile of the policy's impact. Details of this statistical procedure are given in McCleary and Hay (1980) and Cauley and Im (1987).

Cauley and Im (1987) constructed six time series from the Mickolus (1980) chronology. In particular, they computed the monthly total for the following: (1) skyjackings, (2) all nonskyjackings, (3) barricade-and-hostage-taking events, (4) all nonbarricade events, (5) all terrorist acts directed against diplomats, and (6) all acts not directed against diplomats. Intervention analysis also permits tests of the substitution phenomenon.

Cauley and Im found that the installation of metal detectors in airports resulted in a permanent reduction of 2.69 hijackings per month. Unfortunately, evidence was also uncovered that terrorists substituted into other modes of attack; hence, the net impact of the policy is difficult to judge. In the case of embassy security, the policy had an abrupt but transitory influence on the number of attempted embassy takeovers: Within 21 months, the impact had disappeared. Cauley and Im also concluded that the United Nations convention had no impact in either the short run or the long run.

Other policy intervention analyses can be performed with the information provided in this volume and its companion. The 1980–87 period is rich with policy intervention points. The statistical index planned for the 1984–87 volume will facilitate the construction of time series for monthly totals, as required by the intervention analysis technique.

Other Applications

The above applications are illustrative of the uses made of the previous chronology; the large number of incidents in the 1980–87 period provides sufficient data to apply even more sophisticated techniques such as simultaneous-equations estimation. The earlier chronology and the ITERATE 2 dataset have been used by scores of researchers in numerous disciplines. We are aware of works by political scientists, sociologists, psychologists, statisticians, and economists that have relied on the data. Dissertations and conference papers abound. It is beyond the scope of this Introduction to present a comprehensive listing of items that have appeared. In addition to those already mentioned we have found:

Tracking Studies: These include simple annual frequency counts across regions, and by types of events, to trace general patterns in overall terrorist behavior.

Contagion Studies: Heyman and Mickolus (1981) have applied the techniques of Markov chains and contingency maps to look at the types of modeling behavior among terrorist groups and across regions to determine if there are "fads" among terrorists.

Incident-Specific Studies: Mickolus used an early version of the dataset to discuss the policy debate regarding negotiations with terrorists.

ITERATE 3 AND CODE BOOK

We are in the process of quantifying the information of the chronology into a dataset known as *International Terrorism: Attributes of Terrorist Events (ITERATE 3) 1978–1987*. ITERATE 3 updates the coverage of terrorist incidents first reported in ITERATE 1 and 2, which can be obtained from the Inter-University Consortium for Political and Social Research,

Box 1248, Ann Arbor, Michigan, 48106. ITERATE 3 is compatible with the coding categories used in its predecessors, but includes new variables — such as, the length of hostage incidents, the number of female terrorists in the attack squad, the state sponsorship, if any, of an incident. Like its predecessors, ITERATE 3 groups variables into four files: (1) a COMMON file giving the characteristics of the incidents, terrorists, and victims, (2) a FATE file indicating the fate of the terrorists, (3) a HOSTAGE file listing hostage characteristics, terrorists' demands, and the negotiation behavior and outcomes for events with hostages, and (4) a SKYJACK file giving additional pertinent information on hijackings.

The ITERATE 3 codebook is reprinted in Appendix 2 with the kind permission of Vinyard Software, which holds the copyright.

CONCLUDING REMARKS

We hope that this Introduction will give the reader some insights into the many fruitful ways that the information within this book can be applied. The 1980s has experienced a disturbing growth in transnational terrorism as compared with the preceding decade. We believe that the best way to deal with the threat posed by terrorism is, first, to become as informed as possible about terrorist modes of operation, targets, and demands. This chronology provides the public with this kind of information. Second, we believe that rational-actor models should be constructed as a means of predicting terrorist behavior so as to thwart future operations. If theoretical models are to be refined, they must be subjected to empirical tests. Thus, the third step in dealing with terrorism concerns the testing, evaluation, and reformulation of the theoretical models. The data provided in the chronology facilitates these empirical tests. With the application of scientific methods, law enforcement and policy agencies will have a powerful tool when making decisions in fighting terrorism.

Throughout the writing of the chronology, we have exerted every care possible in accurately reporting names, places, firms, and countries. Because we had to rely on newspaper accounts, some errors have undoubtedly, been included. We sincerely apologize to anyone who has been wrongly characterized in the incidents' descriptions; we assure such individuals that any errors were purely accidental.

BIBLIOGRAPHY

Atkinson, Scott E., Todd Sandler, and John Tschirhart. (1987). Terrorism in a bargaining framework. *Journal of Law and Economics 30*:1–21.
Becker, Gary S. (1968). Crime and punishment: An economic approach. *Journal of Political Economy 78*:169–217.

Cauley, Jon and Eric I. Im. (1987). Intervention policy analysis of skyjackings and other terrorist incidents. Unpublished manuscript.

Cordes, Bonnie et al. (1984). *Trends in international terrorism, 1982 and 1983.* Santa Monica, Calif.: Rand.

Cross, John G. (1969). *The economics of bargaining.* New York: Basic Books.

Cross, John G. (1977). Negotiations as a learning process. *Journal of Conflict Resolution 21*:581–606.

Ehrlich, Isaac. (1973). Participation in illegitimate activities: A theoretical and empirical investigation. *Journal of Political Economy 81*:521–65.

Ehrlich, Isaac. (1975). The deterrent effect of capital punishment: A question of life and death. *American Economic Review 65*:397–417.

Gottman, J. M. (1981). *Time-series analysis.* New York: Cambridge University Press.

Heyman, Edward and Edward F. Mickolus. (1981). Imitation by terrorists: Quantitative approaches to the study of diffusion patterns in transnational terrorism. In Yonah Alexander and John M. Gleason (Eds.), *Behavioral and quantitative perspectives on terrorism.* New York: Pergamon Press, 175–91.

Im, Eric I., Jon Cauley, and Todd Sandler. (1987). Cycles and substitutions in terrorist activities: A spectral approach. *Kyklos 40*:238–55.

Kirk, R. M. (1983). Political terrorism and the size of government: A positive institutional analysis of violent political activity. *Public Choice 40*:41–52.

Landes, William M. (1978). An economic study of U.S. aircraft hijackings, 1961–1976. *Journal of Law and Economics 21*:1–31.

Lapan, Harvey E. and Todd Sandler. (1987). To bargain or not to bargain: That is the question. Unpublished manuscript.

Lee, Dwight R. (1987). Free riding and paid riding in the fight against terrorism. Unpublished manuscript.

McCleary, Richard and Richard A. Hay. (1980). *Applied time series analysis for the social sciences.* Beverly Hills, Calif.: Sage Publications.

Mickolus, Edward F. (1980). *Transnational terrorism: A chronology of events 1968–1979.* Westport, Conn.: Greenwood Press.

Mickolus, Edward F. (1981). *International terrorism: Attributes of terrorist events, 1968–1977 (ITERATE 2).* Ann Arbor, Mich.: Inter-University Consortium for Political and Social Research.

Russell, C. A., L. J. Banker, and B. H. Miller. (1979). Out-inventing the terrorist. In Yonah Alexander, D. Carlton, and Paul Wilkinson (Eds.), *Terrorism: Theory and practice.* Boulder, Colo.: Westview Press.

Sandler, Todd and John L. Scott. (1987). Terrorist success in hostage-taking incidents. *Journal of Conflict Resolution 31*:35–53.

Sandler, Todd, John Tschirhart, and Jon Cauley. (1983). A theoretical analysis of transnational terrorism. *American Political Science Review 77*:36–54.

Thaler, R. and Sherwin Rosen. (1976). The value of saving a life: Evidence from the labor market. In N. E. Terleckji (Ed.), *Household production and consumption.* New York: Columbia University Press for National Bureau of Economic Research.

United States Central Intelligence Agency. (1981). *Patterns of international terrorism: 1980.* Springfield, Va.: National Technical Information Service.

United States Department of State. (1983). *International terrorism: Hostage seizures.* Washington, D.C.: Office for Combatting Terrorism.

United States Department of State. (1986). *Patterns of global terrorism: 1985.* Washington, D.C.: Office of the Ambassador at Large for Counter-Terrorism.

International Terrorism in the 1980s

A Chronology of Events

A CHRONOLOGY OF EVENTS

1980

T HIS LISTING should be read in conjunction with Edward F. Mickolus (1980), *Transnational Terrorism: A Chronology of Events, 1968–1979* (Westport, Conn.: Greenwood Press), 969 pp. The present chronology updates the incidents that occurred before 1980 (e.g., subsequent arrests and court processing of offenders, denouements of marathon hostage seizures) and notes attacks and other terrorism-related events that occurred after 1979.

January 1980—LEBANON—A bomb was thrown into the garden of the Soviet consulate, which is located within the embassy compound in Corniche al-Mazra'ah. The bombing may have been to protest the recent Soviet occupation of Afghanistan. 80019901

January 1, 1980—BRAZIL—Farid Semaha, the Lebanese consul in Brasilia, escaped an assassination attempt believed to be a protest of Brazil's recognition of the Palestine Liberation Organization. 80010101

January 2, 1980—TURKEY—Abraham Elazar, the manager of the Istanbul office of El Al, was killed by 15 Kalashnikov rounds while he was driving home during the night. A car blocked his way home on the highway. Two people jumped out of the vehicle and fired, then drove off. Two passersby drove the victim to the hospital. Police later found the terrorists' car 10 kilometers away from the scene, and reported that the getaway car had been stolen. The Marxist-Leninist Armed Propaganda Union, the Anti–Camp David Front, and the Sons of the Land claimed credit for the attack, which the latter group claimed was the execution of a Zionist agent who had planned assassinations of Palestinian guerrilla leaders. 80010201

3

January 2, 1980 — INDIA — One hundred Afghan students took over the Afghan embassy, holding three diplomats and a businessman hostage for six hours, to protest the Soviet occupation of Afghanistan. 80010202

January 2, 1980 — FEDERAL REPUBLIC OF GERMANY — Thirty Afghan students took over the Afghan embassy for an hour to protest the Soviet invasion of Afghanistan.

January 2, 1980 — TRINIDAD AND TOBAGO — A fairly large bomb exploded at the Texaco refinery at Pointe-a-Pierre, causing no injuries and only minor damage. 80010203

January 3, 1980 — TURKEY — Thirty to 40 members of the pro-Albanian People's Path, protesting the Soviet invasion of Afghanistan, threw a grenade at the Soviet consulate general, which is situated in the Tunel section of Istiklal Street in Istanbul. A soldier, Mustafa Dur, was wounded in the leg. Turkish guards fired on the demonstrators, killing Fatih Verligullari, a student at Umraniye High School, who was shot in the head. Mustafa Aydin, a teacher who was passing by the scene, was slightly wounded in the hand. Several people were arrested. Police found 11 empty cartridges, silencers, and parts of weapons at the scene. Elsewhere in Sudan, India, Indonesia, and Iran, Islamic leaders led protests against the Soviet occupation of Afghanistan. 80010301

January 3, 1980 — UNITED KINGDOM — An incendiary bomb was found near the entrance of a building in Glasgow, Scotland, which houses the Scottish Stock Exchange, the South African consulate, KLM Dutch Airlines, and Pakistan Airlines offices. 80010302

January 4, 1980 — FRANCE — Iparretarrak, a Basque autonomist movement, claimed credit for a bomb that injured two workmen at the building site of a new police barracks in Anglet. 80010401

January 5, 1980 — COLOMBIA — A band of 25 to 35 members of the Camilo Torres Front of the National Liberation Army kidnapped British/Colombian citizens Mrs. Telery Jones and her 16-year-old son, Owen, from their ranch in northern Colombia near Chiriguana. The group, reportedly led by Comdr. Gabriel Vera (Vidal), and former priest Manuel Perez, demanded P 20 million (five hundred thousand dollars), but later dropped the figure to P 12 million (three hundred thousand dollars), from ranch owner Cyrus Jones for the release of his family. The family, naturalized Colombians, had lived in Ibague, in the southeast province of Tolima, for the previous 20 years. The guerrillas reportedly had intended to kidnap another British family named Curry, farmers in Chiriguana, who had invited the Jones family to spend the New Year's with them. The two were released on August 9, 1980, after spending most of their captivity in the jungle near the Venezuelan border. They reported the group wore Colombian Army clothing. Owen Jones had symptoms of malaria, but the two hostages were otherwise in good condition. 80010501

January 5, 1980 — IRELAND — Irish police discovered an Irish Republican Army (IRA) bomb factory in Dunleer, on a farm near the northern border, and confiscated thirty 18-inch cylinder bombs.

January 5, 1980 — PHILIPPINES — During the night, a group of men threw a small explosive device at the United States embassy in Manila, causing no injuries and only minor damage. They escaped in their car. 80010502

January 6, 1980 — IRAN — Forty Afghan theological students and workers took over the Afghan embassy, taking 13 persons hostage for four hours, to protest the Soviet takeover of Afghanistan. 80010601

January 7, 1980 — PUERTO RICO — The right-wing Anti-Communist Alliance claimed credit for using converted navy explosives to bomb the offices of the Puerto Rican Bar Association in San Juan, causing minor damage but no injuries. The group said the bombing was to retaliate for the December 3 terrorist attack on a navy bus in which two navy personnel were killed and eight wounded. On January 25, the Federal Bureau of Investigation arrested navy lieutenant Alex De La Zerda, 28, assigned to the Roosevelt Roads Naval Station in Puerto Rico; Robert Lopez, 46, an alleged anti-Castro Cuban; and Rene Fernandez, 28. The former two were arrested on Vieques, while Fernandez, armed with an automatic pistol, was arrested in San Juan. The trio were also charged with conspiring to bomb an airplane operating between San Juan and neighboring islands.

January 9, 1980 — IRELAND — The Irish National Liberation Army (INLA) was believed responsible for kidnapping Mrs. Thomas Scully, the wife of an Allied Irish Bank manager, and their two teenage daughters in Dublin. A $200,000 ransom was demanded. The trio was freed on January 10 after Scully paid $60,000. 80010901

January 9, 1980 — UNITED STATES — An anonymous telephone caller told a Sacramento radio station that "patriotic scuba divers" had mined the 30-mile-long Sacramento ship channel to stop the Soviet freighter *Nicolay Karamzin,* which was taking on corn. The port was closed while a navy minesweeper checked the waters. 80010902

January 11, 1980 — EL SALVADOR — Fifty members of the 28 February Popular League took over the Panamanian embassy in San Salvador, taking hostage Panamanian ambassador David Perez Ramos, Costa Rican ambassador Alejandro Alvarado Piza, Costa Rican charge d'affaires Santo David Lopez, two children of an embassy maid (who were released shortly after the 10:30 A.M. takeover), embassy secretary Maria Teresa Barraza, Salvadoran employees Antonio Villalobos and Guadalupe Gonzalez de Mendez, and several other embassy employees. The group, led by Argueta, demanded the release of 3 political prisoners, a demand reportedly later increased to 9 and then 15 prisoners. Their principal demand was for the release of 7 individuals held in Usulutan Prison, 70 miles east of San Salvador, who had been arrested on December 17 during a clash with guardsmen in a labor dispute at a coffee plantation in Berlin: Amelia Noemi Ozorga, Catalino Reyes, Avilio Cruz, Dionisio Bustillo Macias, Atilio Ruiz, Simon Mercado Pleites, and Francisco Torcios Jimenez. The group also called for a "halt to repression in Las Vueltas, Chalatenango and Morazan," withdrawal of a police station in Las Vueltas, dispersal of a police cordon around the embassy, and the reappearance of 6 people who reportedly were missing. The group asked the Venezuelan and Mexican embassies to mediate, a chore later handled by Nicaraguan charge Aldo Diaz Lacayo. Ambassador Perez offered asylum to the occupants (and the Panamanian government offered asylum to the 7 in prison) but was turned down. The group held interviews with news media representatives from Colombia, Panama, Costa Rica, Nicaragua, Mexico, and El Salvador and permitted the delivery of clothes, food, drugs, personal items for the diplomats, and some aid from the Red Cross. A physician among the occupiers determined that the pulmonary embolism of the Costa Rican ambassador did not merit his early release. On January 14, the government released the 7 prisoners and the occupiers left the embassy in a bus headed for the University of El Salvador. They reported that their group's name came from the February 28, 1977, takeover of the townships of Mejicanos, Pocapansingo, San Marcos, and Soyapango around the capital. 80011101

January 13, 1980 — UNITED STATES — Police dismantled a bomb that had been slipped through a mail slot at a New York City building where a Taiwanese diplomat and his family reside. 80011301

January 13, 1980 — UNITED STATES — A homemade bomb exploded at 12:40 A.M. at the Padron Hand Made Cigars and Pilato Cigars building in the Little Havana section of Miami, Florida, causing significant damage but no injuries. Omega-7, an anti-Castro Cuban group, claimed credit. 80011302

January 13, 1980 — UNITED STATES — A bomb thrown from a street through the windows of Aeroflot in Manhattan at 6:15 P.M. injured two men and a woman who were passing by and shattered the windows at Aeroflot, as well as at the offices of British Airlines and Qantas Airlines across the street. Police chased and captured a man who ran from the scene. More than half an hour later, the Jewish Defense League claimed credit, saying that it was protesting the imprisonment of Soviet dissidents. Fifteen minutes later, the anti-Castro Cuban group Omega-7 said that it had shown "solidarity with the people of Cuba and Afghanistan in their struggle against Soviet imperialism." 80011303

January 14, 1980 — EL SALVADOR — Machine gunners from the Central American Workers Revolutionary Party (PRTC) fired on the Guatemalan embassy, smashing windows but causing only property damage and no casualties. 80011401

January 14, 1980 — ITALY — A lone Tunisian gunman hijacked an Alitalia twin-engined DC-9 flying 83 passengers (23 Italians and 60 North Africans) and 6 crewmen on a flight that began in Rome at 15:20 GMT and was scheduled to end in Tunis. He had intended to divert the plane to Tripoli, Libya, but was prevented by a sandstorm there. Valletta, Malta, airport authorities refused permission to land and refuel, and the hijacker settled for Palermo, Italy. He demanded a flight plan for Tripoli in return for the non-Tunisian passengers and claimed that he was a member of Les Vivants. He called for the release of 25 Tunisian political prisoners and asked for a French- or English-speaking journalist to enter the plane to aid him in writing out a communique. He spoke to Italian reporter Franco Fontana, who was in the control tower, and told him that he would use his explosives if he was not flown to Benghazi or Tunis. Negotiations were directed by phone from Rome by Italian interior minister Virginio Rognoni. On January 15, the gunman surrendered to Palermo police. None of the hostages had been harmed. Initially, two hijackers had been reported. 80011402

January 15, 1980 — CANADA — Havana news media reported a terrorist attack on the Cuban consulate in Montreal during the early morning. 80011501

January 15, 1980 — AUSTRIA — At 5:00 A.M., four bombs exploded at the Asmahan restaurant and night club, an Arab establishment on 24 Bauermarkt in Vienna's first district, damaging the restaurant, cars parked nearby, and other buildings, but causing no injuries. The Organization of Petroleum Exporting Countries (OPEC) conference was scheduled to be held in Vienna the next day. 80011502

January 15, 1980 — SYRIA — Moslem Brotherhood gunmen ambushed 2 senior Soviet officers training the Syrian armed forces in front of their home in Hamah, two hundred kilometers north of Damascus. The duo, identified as

Lt. Col. Barsil Sozlie, a pilot, and Maj. Victor Yodrizenko, died from their wounds shortly thereafter. Security forces rushed the Brotherhood's headquarters in Aleppo, killing 2 and arresting 16 others. 80011503

January 16, 1980 — SYRIA — A Moslem Brotherhood gunman shot and wounded Peter Zabolomel, a Soviet topographical surveyor working at the headquarters of a railroad agency in Aleppo. His attacker was arrested. 80011601

January 16, 1980 — SYRIA — A bomb exploded outside the Aeroflot offices in Damascus, slightly injuring one person. 80011602

January 17, 1980 — UNITED KINGDOM — A powerful bomb exploded at 7:30 A.M. on the fifth floor of London's three-star Mount Royal Hotel, injuring three Germans and killing a 22-year-old man whose Bahraini passport identified him as Mohammed Soltani. The individual had registered as a student. Cairo's MIDDLE EAST NEWS AGENCY identified him as Hasan Ilyas Badr, who had taken part in several fedayeen attacks against Israeli interests in various European capitals. It claimed he had set a timer on a bomb and was working on a second, which exploded and killed him. The second bomb exploded in the rubble five hours later, injuring a policeman. The May 15 Arab Organization claimed credit for the bombing, saying the hotel was a Zionist facility. 80011701

January 17, 1980 — SWEDEN — The United States, Canadian, United Kingdom, and Israeli ambassadors received increased protection after the United States embassy received a threatening letter the previous day that noted the license numbers of embassy cars. 80011702

January 17, 1980 — UNITED KINGDOM — A bomb exploded on a commuter train during the evening rush hour in Belfast, killing 3 and injuring 14. Bombs were defused on two other trains. The 3 deaths raised to 2,007 the official death toll in 10 years of conflict.

January 17, 1980 — FRANCE — Sabri al-Banna's fedayeen group claimed credit for shooting in the head the manager of an Arab bookstore in Paris as he was leaving the store. The gunman escaped on foot. 80011703

January 18, 1980 — LEBANON — A Lebanese Middle East Airlines plane flying from Beirut to Larnaca, Cyprus, was hijacked at 1:45 P.M., 15 minutes after takeoff, by a young gunman who demanded to fly to Tehran. Pilot 'Abshi Andis landed the plane, carrying 72 passengers, at Beirut airport. The hijacker, Fu'ad Hammudah, a Shiite from Khirbat Silm, threatened to blow up the plane. He said he was from the Sons of the South and demanded that the fate of the missing Imam Musa as-Sadr be revealed and that a commission of inquiry be established to look into the matter. He also requested entry of the Lebanese army into the south. He surrendered a few hours later to Beirut police. 80011801

January 18, 1980 — GUATEMALA — The Guatemala City building housing the United Nations offices was badly damaged by a bomb that caused no injuries. 80011802

January 18, 1980 — UNITED STATES — An American member of a New York airport flight control center allegedly tampered with the computer that was controlling the approach of an Aeroflot plane, which landed safely. 80011803

January 19, 1980 — ITALY — The Red Brigades bombed a Rome police barracks at 2:00 A.M., wounding 18 officers engaged in counterterrorist work.

January 19, 1980 — UNITED ARAB EMIRATES — United Arab Emirates minister of petroleum and natural resources Dr. Mani' Sa'id al-'Utaybah escaped a second attempt to poison him. The Japanese ambassador received a parcel from West Germany that contained another parcel and a letter directing him to deliver the parcel to Dr. Utaybah, who became suspicious. Security authorities found that the package contained botanical samples, herbs, and a letter impregnated with a poison that kills upon touch. On December 19, 1979, Dr. Utaybah's food had been poisoned during the Organization of Petroleum Exporting Countries (OPEC) ministerial meeting in Caracas, Venezuela. 80011901

January 19, 1980 — SPAIN — Several people were injured when bombs exploded at the Madrid offices of Trans World Airlines, British Airways, Swissair, and the Belgian airline Sabena. An individual claimed credit for the Commando for Justice for the Genocide of Armenians, saying that the bombs were to protest "against the policy of world imperialism and fascism," and warned of "important operations" to take place in the near future. The next day, another individual said this group was not responsible for the Trans World Airlines bombing. 80011902–05

January 19, 1980 — SYRIA — Gunmen killed three Soviet advisors and three other persons near the Maysalum fire brigade station in Aleppo, according to the VOICE OF LEBANON. 80011906

January 19, 1980 — FRANCE — Yusef Mubarak Hisham, the supervisor of the Arab library in Paris, was shot to death. Sabri al-Banna's splinter fedayeen organization claimed credit, saying that Hisham had been executed because of his "betrayal of the organization, his conveyance of some information about it to Salah Khalaf, the second strongman in Fatah and his refusal to part with funds and arms which belong to the splinter organization." The Palestine Liberation Organization (PLO) had earlier blamed Israeli intelligence agents for the killing, noting that Hisham had taken over from Mahmud Salih, who had previously been assassinated. 80011907

January 21, 1980 — GREECE — Anonymous individuals telephoned Turkish diplomats and said, "We are Armenians. We are going to kill you." Istanbul's TERCUMAN news service reported that the Turkish embassy was being filmed by individuals believed to be Armenians. 80012101

January 22, 1980 — EL SALVADOR — Seven bombs exploded at the Italian embassy. 80012201

January 22, 1980 — UNITED STATES — A small bomb exploded at 3:20 A.M. in a luggage area at Los Angeles International Airport used by the Taiwan-based China Airlines, causing $25,000 damage but no injuries. 80012202

January 22, 1980 — EL SALVADOR — A demonstration by members of the United Popular Action Front around the National Palace was broken up when paramilitary forces fired into the crowd. Local human rights groups claimed 67 persons were shot to death and 250 wounded, including Bruce Douglas Yaeger, an American journalism student from Washington state, who was wounded in the leg. Leftist gunmen among the 50,000 demonstrators returned the fire.

January 23, 1980 — GUATEMALA — The Secret Anti-Communist Army threatened to kill the 52 Jesuit priests in the country a week after the priests signed a document criticizing human rights violations.

January 24, 1980 — TURKEY — A leftist group protesting United States–Turkish cooperation firebombed five banks in Istanbul, burning one branch down but causing no injuries in early morning attacks.

January 24, 1980 — SYRIA — Terrorists killed a "Soviet expert" in Aleppo while he was riding in a car with other Soviets, according to the VOICE OF LEBANON. 80012401

January 24, 1980 — TURKEY — Three men and a woman entered a United States/NATO military motor pool near Yesilkoy Airport in Istanbul's Sefakoy district, poured gasoline on several vehicles and around the building, and ignited it. Several vehicles were damaged, and the building was destroyed, but no injuries were reported, as a Turkish employee was able to escape the building in time. A banner left on a gas pump read Victory for the THKPC (Turkish People's Liberation Party/Front). 80012402

January 25, 1980 — UNITED STATES — A Delta L-1011 flying the Los Angeles–Dallas–Atlanta–New York route with 53 passengers and 15 crewmen was hijacked over Greensboro, North Carolina, by a man brandishing a .25 automatic pistol who demanded to go to Cuba. On the ground for 14 hours in Havana, the hijacker permitted a diabetic female passenger to deplane. While the 3 pilots kept the hijacker's attention, the other hostages escaped the plane by knotting together blankets and sliding down a food shaft. The hijacker claimed to have a (nonexistent) bomb and demanded to be flown to Tehran, claiming he was a Black Muslim. He had also demanded that journalist Jim Nobble, presently in Jamaica, accompany him as a hostage to Iran. He was overpowered by the pilots, who turned him over to Cuban authorities. He was later identified as Samuel Alben Ingram, who had been accompanied by his wife and two children. He apparently had been able to smuggle the pistol through Atlanta's security system by hiding it in a metal baby stroller, a trick that had been described in a recent *Dick Tracy* cartoon strip. Ingram was convicted of hijacking by a United States federal jury on November 19, 1980. 80012501

January 25, 1980 — REPUBLIC OF SOUTH AFRICA — In the first taking of white hostages by black nationalists in South African history, 3 members of the African National Congress (ANC) carrying rifles and hand grenades in handbags took over the Volkskas bank branch in Silverton, a white suburb of Pretoria. Although 35 customers and bank employees escaped, the terrorists held 25 white hostages for six hours, threatening to kill them if several political prisoners, including Nelson Mandela, age 61, president of the ANC, who had been serving a life sentence on Robben Island since 1964, were not released and transported to Angola, where the terrorists claimed they had been trained. Two male hostages had been sent out of the bank with the demands. Police came near to negotiation but later claimed that they never considered granting the demands.

Police reported that they installed listening devices in the bank, and that shortly before 7:00 P.M. they heard the terrorists decide to shoot all the hostages at 7:30. A spokesman announced, "At 7:05, the terrorists began throwing hand grenades and shooting at the hostages with Russian AK-47 machine guns. The police task force stormed the building from all angles." A hostage claimed that the two sides began firing at roughly the same time. The police killed all 3 terrorists, while 2 female hostages died and 22 people, including 4 policemen, were wounded.

On February 6, police fired tear gas to break up a crowd of 2,000 mourners at the Soweto funeral of Wilfred Madela, one of the hostage-takers. On February 9, police teargassed buses that were carrying mourners for Fanie Mafoko, another of the black nationalists.

On November 21, Judge Jaap de Villiers, a white, acquitted 9 black nationalists of treason and murder charges related to the Silverton case, as they were not at the bank. However, they had already been convicted the previous day of separate treason charges based on their ANC membership and other antiregime activities. On November 26, Ncimbithi Johnson Lubisi, 29, Petrus Tsepo Mashigo, 20, and Naphtali Menana, 24, were sentenced to death for attempting to murder 2 black police officers on January 4 during an armed assault on a Soekmekaar police station in rural Transvaal. Those also jailed were Moses Molebatsi, Hlolili Benjamen Tau, Phumulani Grant Shezi, Jeremia Radebe, Boyce Johannes Mogale, and Thomas Mngadi.

January 26, 1980 — SPAIN — A parcel bomb left by an unidentified youth exploded in the Madrid office of Friends of the United Nations Educational, Scientific, and Cultural Organization, seriously injuring the man who opened it, Luis Esteban, and a club waitress. 80012601

January 26, 1980 — UNITED STATES — Three firebombs exploded at the Arlington, Virginia, home of anticommunist Vietnamese refugee Nguyen Thanh Hoang, 59, causing $125,000 damage to his home and $10,000 damage to his car and garage. Hoang was described as a former Saigon journalist who now publishes TIEN PHONG, a Vietnamese publication for Arlington refugees who do not speak English. 80012602

January 26, 1980 — AFGHANISTAN — A sniper shot and seriously wounded a Soviet soldier in Kabul. The attack was believed to be the first daytime sniper attack on Soviets in the capital city.

January 28, 1980 — IRAQ — A Middle East Airlines flight from Baghdad to Beirut carrying 137 passengers and crew was hijacked by a Lebanese man, Ali Issa, 28, whose wife and 4 children were among the passengers. The knife-wielding man demanded publicity for the disappearance of Imam Musa as-Sadr. He surrendered upon being granted a press conference. 80012801

January 29, 1980 — BELGIUM — Emmanuel Desire Ayessa, first secretary at the Congolese embassy, was shot in the head on a Brussels street but survived. 80012901

January 29, 1980 — FRANCE — Two bombs exploded — one on the second floor near the ambassador's office and another on the first floor in the visa office — in the Syrian embassy at 11:30 A.M., killing Marwan Hammami, a Syrian working in the consular section, and injuring nine others. Five of the injured were Syrians: Umaymad al-Hilu (a pregnant diplomat), Habibah Jundi, Intisar Ahmad, Madelaine al-Jidd, and Adnan Masalmah. Three Frenchmen and a Romanian were also injured. Three previously unknown groups—the Palestinian Resistance, the Jewish Brigades, and the Afghan Collectives—claimed responsibility. A witness saw a tall and rotund man, accompanied by a small, Arab-speaking man with curly hair, in the embassy corridors only minutes before the explosion. The two men joined a third man before leaving the premises. The bombs went off three hours before the arrival of Syrian foreign minister Abdel Halim Khaddam, who was scheduled to join the European Council debate on the Middle East in Strasbourg. The Lebanese Front later claimed responsibility. 80012902

January 30, 1980—GERMAN DEMOCRATIC REPUBLIC—The crew and passengers of a German Democratic Republic Interflug IL-18 flying from East Berlin to Erfurt overpowered two men attempting to hijack the plane. 80013001

January 31, 1980—BOLIVIA—Unidentified individuals threw two sticks of dynamite at the doors of the United States embassy, damaging the building but causing no injuries. 80013101

January 31, 1980—LEBANON—Three potential Lebanese hijackers, hoping to publicize the disappearance of Shiite Moslem leader Imam Musa as-Sadr, were arrested at Beirut's airport as they attempted to board an Air France plane. 80013102

January 31, 1980—GUATEMALA—Thirty Ixil-speaking peasants from northern Quiche Province took over the Spanish embassy to request Spanish ambassador Maximo Cajal y Lopez for help in requesting an independent commission to be set up to investigate their charges of murders and disappearances at the hands of military officials who wanted their land. Quiche had been the scene of clashes between the military services and the Guerrilla Army of the Poor (EGP). The previous week, government officials had refused to meet with the peasants to discuss their case. The group briefly took over two local radio stations and had been branded as terrorists.

Approximately 400 police surrounded the embassy as soon as the peasants took it over. Despite Spanish pleas for calm, the police soon stormed the embassy, working their way up to the ambassador's office, where the embassy staff and the occupiers were huddled. When police broke down the office door, one of the peasants threw a gasoline bomb. In the ensuing fire, all but one of the peasants died. Ambassador Cajal escaped by jumping out a window. In all, 39 people died, including former Guatemalan vice president Eduardo Caceres Lenhoff, former foreign minister Rodolfo Molina Orantes, embassy first secretary Ruiz del Arbol, the embassy's personnel manager, and a Spanish woman who was in the building on business. Only one peasant and the ambassador survived, although both were injured. The surviving peasant was later taken away from his hospital bed by 15 heavily armed men who put him into a car and drove off. Shortly thereafter his body was found on the campus of the national university. On February 1, Spain broke relations with Guatemala, claiming that permission had not been granted for the police to enter the embassy. On August 23, 1986, Spain dropped its request for indemnification. 80013103

February 1980 — EGYPT—Cairo's MIDDLE EAST NEWS AGENCY charged that Libyan leader Muammar Qaddafi "sent a Greek ship loaded with poisoned fodder to deliberately run aground on Egyptian shores so that the fodder might be confiscated and provide poisoned food for our livestock."

February 1980 — AFGHANISTAN — A British correspondent for the LONDON OBSERVER was held by Afghan rebels for two weeks.

February 1980 — UNITED KINGDOM — A "Libyan-looking" man set fire to a Park Lane, London, bookshop that had been distributing AL-JIHAD, which is published by the Libyan opposition. London's AL-HAWADITH claimed that the Libyan government had decided to attack exile opposition leaders, beginning with overseas newspapers, and that a seven-thousand-pound fund had been paid to a newspaper distributor to begin these operations. 80029901

February 1, 1980 — FRANCE — Joseph Fontanet, 59, who had served as labor minister between 1969 and 1972 and then education minister until 1974, was shot and critically wounded outside his Paris home by a member of the previously unknown Autonomous Revolutionary Brigade.

February 1, 1980 — SPAIN — Basque Freedom and Homeland (ETA) terrorists attacked a small munitions convoy on a coastal road outside Bilbao in the Basque district, killing six members of the Civil Guard, the Spanish paramilitary police force. The attack apparently was aimed at disrupting local Basque elections scheduled for March 9. The Spanish Armed Groups, a newly formed rightist group, vowed to continue reprisal murders for police killings, noting that they had been responsible for five revenge deaths so far this year.

February 2, 1980 — SYRIA — The Moslem Brotherhood was blamed for a nighttime attack in Aleppo in which Sheik Mohammed Shami, a Moslem scholar and preacher, and his assistant, Sheik Mohammed Qattan, were shot to death and another sheik was wounded.

February 2, 1980 — BELGIUM — The New Armenian Resistance claimed credit for bombing the Brussels offices of Turkish Airlines and Aeroflot, causing considerable damage but no injuries. 80020201–02

February 2, 1980 — FRANCE — The New Armenian Resistance bombed the information bureau of the Soviet embassy in northwest Paris, causing considerable damage but no injuries. The attacks in Brussels and Paris were to mark the announcement on January 30, 1979, that three Armenians had been executed for a bomb attack in the Moscow subway system two years ago. 80020203

February 3, 1980 — ISRAEL — A bomb placed by Palestinians exploded in a garbage can opposite a police station in Rehovot, near Tel Aviv, wounding a young mother and her three-year-old child and four other persons. Several Arabs were held for questioning.

February 3, 1980 — EL SALVADOR — Just before midnight, gunmen fired on a San Salvador church filled with members of the Union of Slum Dwellers, a group that forms part of the Popular Revolutionary Bloc, killing 1 person and injuring 17.

February 3, 1980 — RHODESIA — In the worst breach of a month-old cease-fire, guerrillas fired on a bus 80 miles southeast of Salisbury, killing 13 blacks and injuring 24 others. Elsewhere, a grenade was thrown into a bus of Muzorewa supporters, killing 1 woman and wounding 4 other blacks.

February 4, 1980 — EL SALVADOR — The Revolutionary People's Army machine-gunned the Guatemalan embassy in reprisal for the Guatemalan police's January 31 raid on the Spanish embassy, which led to the death of 39 people. No one was injured in the evening attack. 80020401

February 4, 1980 — LIBYA — Mobs stormed the French and Tunisian embassies in Tripoli, claiming that France had invaded Tunisia. The French ambassador claimed that only two Libyan policemen guarded the embassy and that reinforcements were not sent despite his pleas. The ambassador said the embassy's destruction "could only have been decided" by the Libyan authorities. France ordered all of its diplomatic personnel in Tripoli home the next day, as the French consulate in Benghazi was sacked. 80020402–03

February 5, 1980 — EL SALVADOR — Fifteen members of the January 28 Popular Leagues (LP-28), armed with machine guns and pistols, took over the Spanish embassy and seized 10 hostages, including Spanish ambassador Victor Sanchez Mesas, 3 top aides, 3 secretaries, and 3 persons visiting the embassy. Elsewhere, 50 youths took over the Education Ministry, seizing 100 hostages, including Minister Eduardo Colindre, whose wife, Marina, had been held hostage for a week by another leftist group.

The group initially demanded that the government release four LP-28 members: Rodolfo Vasquez, Adilio Cruz, Hector Canales, and Eduardo Vasques; that Spain break relations with El Salvador; that the Organization of American States (OAS) send a human rights team to visit the country; and that the Red Cross send a committee. They later called for the release of members of the United Popular Action Front (FAPU), who were evicted from two churches they had occupied in San Francisco and San Miguel. Still later, they demanded the release of Mario Rolando Aguinado Carranza, secretary-general of the National Democratic Union. On February 11, they demanded the return of documents, possessions, and C 22,000 taken from a house searched in the Miramonte suburb where Norma Guevara was captured, and the settlement of labor demands of workers in the Spanish Agroman Company.

The government released 7 of 14 prisoners demanded late the first day. Three others were released on February 8, and another on the ninth. Still another escaped while being transferred between prisons. On February 16, the government released 17 jailed militants, but the occupiers demanded the release of 6 others.

Carlos Argueta, leader of the LP-28 occupiers, said on February 7 that he had received a telephoned threat that the embassy would be set on fire unless the hostages were released. Right-wing members of the Organization for the Struggle Against Communism kidnapped 3 communist leaders of the National Democratic Union and threatened to kill them if the leftists did not vacate the embassy by the next day. However, the trio was released the following day without explanation.

The LP-28 occupiers at the Spanish embassy released 3 Salvadoran employees the first evening. On February 10, 2 other Salvadoran hostages were released. On February 14, the group released Elvia Menjivar, the ambassador's Salvadoran secretary; and Sebastian Hernandez and Francisco Nunez, Spanish employees of the Agroman firm. This left Juan Carlos de Ranero, the charge d'affaires; and Manuel de la Helguera, embassy counselor, as the final hostages. The group ended the siege on February 18, thanks to the mediation of Pedro Bermejo, special envoy of the Spanish government; Adriano Righetti, Italy's ambassador; and the ambassadors of Mexico and Ecuador.

West Germany announced on February 7 that it was leaving El Salvador. 80020501

February 6, 1980 — SWITZERLAND — Gunmen of the Commando of

Avengers of Armenian Genocide fired four shots at the Turkish ambassador, Dogam Turkmen, as he was in his car outside the British embassy at 11:00 A.M. Three men were arrested for the attack, which slightly injured the ambassador. The Armenian Genocide Justice Commandos also claimed credit. 80020601

February 6, 1980 — ITALY — Two gunmen shot and killed a policeman guarding the Lebanese embassy. 80020602

February 9, 1980 — THAILAND — Moslem guerrillas were blamed for setting off a bomb at the Hat Yai railway station, killing 4 persons and injuring 40 others.

February 10, 1980 — NORTHERN IRELAND — Betty Williams, 37, resigned from Peace People, the pacifist organization she and Mairead Corrigan organized in August 1976 in an attempt to end the Irish troubles. The third member of the group's original leadership, former student radical Ciaran McKeown, denied that the resignation was due to a factional dispute regarding the political role of the organization.

February 10, 1980 — RHODESIA — Eighty pounds of explosives were remotely detonated under a convoy of cars taking guerrilla leader Robert Mugabe to Fort Victoria Airport. Mugabe was unhurt in the assassination attempt (a bomb had exploded at his home seven days previously), but five members of his Zimbabwe African National Union party were hospitalized.

February 10, 1980 — VENEZUELA — Marko Sunejic, Yugoslavia's ambassador, was shot in the left leg by two individuals as he was stepping out of his car in front of his Caracas home. His assailants had demanded money and valuables.

February 13, 1980 — EL SALVADOR — Fifty members of the 28 February Popular Leagues (LP-28), armed with automatic weapons, seized an undetermined number of hostages in the Panamanian embassy, which they held for a day. The group demanded the release of 23 members of their group who were arrested when police stormed the Christian Democratic party offices, which had been occupied since January 29. The resolution of the siege included a news conference with the terrorists and Panamanian ambassador David Pere. The government agreed to release members of the LP-28, the Popular Revolutionary Bloc (BPR), and the United Popular Action Front (FAPU): Alva Marisol Galindo, Manuel Gerber, Marco Portillo, Alvaro Castillo, Juan Benjamin Lopez, and Raul Cuellar. 80021301

February 14, 1980 — GUATEMALA — Unidentified individuals machine-gunned the Salvadoran embassy at midnight, damaging window glass and office furniture. 80021401

February 14, 1980 — GREECE — Athens police reported breaking up the People's Front Initiative, a small group formed in November 1979 by members of the Marxist-Leninist People's Authority, which had published a leftist newspaper in November. The group had planned to bomb the embassies and assassinate the ambassadors of the United States, Israel, Turkey, Cyprus, and West Germany. The group had received training in the use of automatic weapons in an undisclosed Middle Eastern country and had links with the Popular Front for the Liberation of Palestine and the Marxist-Leninist Organization of Cyprus. The group also planned to sabotage United States military bases in Greece. Police arrested journalist George Economeas, Konstandinos Zirinis (Pappous), 37, Isabella Bertrand (Daphne), 23, Kiriakos Khristofis, Khristina Makridhou, Vasiliki Sokratous, Thomas Kharalambous, Avyi Platsi, Anastasia Boyiatzidhou, Maria Anna Pasevski, Georguia Khatzakou, and Elevtheria Makridhou. 80021402

February 15, 1980 — USSR — A man with a German accent warned Moscow airport authorities that a bomb had been placed on an Air France plane scheduled to fly to Paris. 80021501

February 16, 1980 — ISRAEL — Two bombs placed by Arabs killed 2 Israelis and an Arab and wounded 11 other persons in the Gaza Strip.

February 16, 1980 — FEDERAL REPUBLIC OF GERMANY — Colonel Mark E. Coe, 44, a British senior staff officer at the First Rhine Army Corps in Bielefeld, was killed by three pistol bullets fired at 7:30 P.M. as he was parking his car at his home. The Irish Republican Army (IRA) claimed responsibility for this attack as well as for the March 1979 assassination of British ambassador Sir Richard Sykes in the Netherlands, bombings at British military bases in West Germany during the previous two years, and a bombing in Brussels in August in which 16 persons were injured. A Dublin-born Irishman and a West German woman were held briefly for questioning. 80021601

February 18, 1980 — ITALY — One man was wounded when two homemade bombs exploded during the night outside the Rome offices of El Al, Lufthansa, and Swissair. A spokesman for the Secret Army for the Liberation of Armenia said, "This is the last warning to the Swiss Government that it must not repeat its mistake and jail innocent Armenian citizens. We hit Lufthansa as a punishment for the German Government which helps Turkish fascism and thus helps bury our cause. We must also not forget the role of Zionism together with Turkish fascism in the Armenian genocide of

1915. Our next target will be a painful blow in the heart of Turkey."
80021801

February 18, 1980 — TURKEY— The home of two United States embassy officials was bombed and the cars of two United States soldiers attached to the
NATO headquarters in Izmir were burned. No casualties were reported.
80021802–04

February 18, 1980 — MEXICO — Ten members of the National Independent
Committee for Political Prisoners and Persecuted and Missing Persons
took over the Belgian embassy, holding Ambassador Renald Wateeuw and
14 staffers. Meanwhile, 20 unarmed members of the National Democratic
Popular Front (FPDN) seized the Danish embassy. The groups claimed they
were peacefully occupying the embassies and were not holding hostages.
They demanded freedom for 208 political prisoners, information on 623
people who had disappeared, and better living conditions — primarily more
equitable land distribution — for poor people. On February 20, two people
were released from the Danish embassy, leaving Ambassador Vagn Hoel-
gaard and 6 staffers. The previous day, the groups had shifted their demands, calling for the reinstatement of 25 dismissed workers. On February
20, they released a pregnant Mexican typist and 2 phone company workers
from the Danish embassy. The Danish ambassador and 8 staffers declined
to escape down a ladder raised to the fifth-floor window. Later that day,
the groups reduced the number of political prisoners whose release they
demanded from 133 to 26. However, they now also called for "cessation of
repression in rural zones in Hidalgo and Puebla states" and the withdrawal
of soldiers stationed there. On the 21st, they dropped all demands for
political prisoners, and offered to accept any honorable settlement of the
situation. On the 23d, unarmed female police officers drove the peasants
from the embassies. That day, President Jose Lopez Portillo ordered a
pardon for all occupiers. It was unclear whether this amnesty would include
Felipe Martinez Soriano, leader of the FPDN, who had allegedly orchestra-
ted the occupations and for whom an arrest warrant had been issued.
80021805–06

February 19, 1980 — RHODESIA — Fifteen armed guerrillas shot and
bayoneted to death Rev. Kilian Huesser, 38, a member of the Swiss Mission
Society of Bethlehem, at his mission 40 miles south of Fort Victoria. The
group took several hostages. Two weeks earlier, another priest had been
killed. 80021901

February 20, 1980 — BURUNDI — Arnol Knevels, a Belgian Catholic missionary, was killed by unidentified extremists in Muyange. 80022001

February 21, 1980 — UNITED STATES — A shot was fired at the USSR's United Nations Mission at 3:00 A.M., causing no injuries. 80022101

February 22, 1980 — FEDERAL REPUBLIC OF GERMANY — Frankfurt Judge Johanna Dierks sentenced Baader-Meinhof Gang member Astrid Proll, 32, to 5½ years imprisonment for bank robbery but recommended her release due to time already served. The charge of establishing a terrorist organization was dropped, and she was acquitted of attempting to murder two policemen during a gun battle in Frankfurt in 1971. She was also fined $2,600 for falsifying documents. She escaped to the United Kingdom in 1974 during her original trial after being permitted to attend a medical clinic. She married a London plumber and worked as a garage mechanic until her arrest in September 1978. She claimed British citizenship and fought extradition but agreed to return to West Germany in June 1979 when the interior minister said that repentant terrorists would be given light sentences.

February 22, 1980 — TURKEY — The United States Air Force transient facility in Ankara was bombed, digging a small hole in the ground but causing no injuries. 80022201

February 22, 1980 — EGYPT — A diplomat in the Turkish embassy in Cairo was murdered in the afternoon, according to the JERUSALEM DOMESTIC SERVICE. 80022202

February 23, 1980 — MEXICO — Three armed individuals kidnapped two wealthy Lebanese businessmen, Juan Jabourg and his brother Assad Yabourg, from their Mexico City home, and demanded a $2 million ransom.

February 23, 1980 — LEBANON — A remote-controlled bomb exploded under the Mercedes of Lebanon's top right-wing Christian militia commander, Bashir Gemayel, at 11:00 A.M., killing at least 8 people, including his 18-month-old daughter, and injuring another 20. Unconfirmed reports said that 19 were killed and 55 wounded.

February 23, 1980 — TURKEY — A homemade bomb exploded on the grounds of the Soviet consulate in Istanbul, causing no injuries. 80022301

February 24, 1980 — LEBANON — The owner and editor of Lebanon's London-based weekly magazine AL HAWADESS, Selim Al Lawzi, was kidnapped along with his wife in Beirut at gunpoint while driving to Beirut airport for a flight to London.

February 24, 1980 — FRANCE — Thirty people threw firebombs at the Aeroflot offices in Paris to protest the Soviet occupation of Afghanistan. A man claiming membership in the Afghanistan Islamic Nationalist Revolutionary Council said this was an operation by Gazi, the group's international operations arm. He said the group had also conducted missions against Soviet property in Genoa, Brussels, and Paris. The Assembly for Moral Order and Anti-Communist Youth also claimed credit. 80022401

February 27, 1980 — COLOMBIA — Sixteen members of the April 19 Movement (M-19) seized the Dominican Republic's embassy at 5:40 P.M. during a National Day celebration and took 54 hostages, including numerous diplomats and Colombian officials.

The incident began after two couples among the terrorists, elegantly dressed, entered the party and smuggled in their weapons. Their dozen compatriots stormed the embassy when an ambassador's Mercedes drove up. During the initial attack, Pablo Emilio Olivares, the United States ambassador's bodyguard, was injured (initial reports incorrectly claimed that Ambassador Diego Asencio was hospitalized), as were soldier Hector Gaviria Montoya, the ambassadors from Brazil and Mexico, and a Paraguayan diplomat. A 20-year-old student died when caught in the assault's cross fire, and a 17-year-old terrorist was later reported dead. A woman terrorist, Martha, was examined for head wounds but elected to remain in the embassy. The authorities later announced that F-2 S2c. Rafael Casareas Chavez was also killed in the gun battle, during which the terrorists reportedly used obsolete machine guns. During the fray, a Chilean diplomat and 15 others escaped through a back door. The terrorists quickly announced that they had mined the embassy against any government rescue attempts, an option that was early on ruled out by Bogota. The guerrillas ordered the evacuation of the immediate area by local residents, and a terrorist sniper wounded 3 people during the evacuation. A total of 10 people were reported wounded in the initial takeover.

The list of hostages reads like a who's who of the local diplomatic community. Among them were Brazilian ambassador Geraldo Eulalio do Nascimento de Silva; Austrian ambassador Karl Selzer (who was released March 6 with an embolism); Swiss ambassador Jean Bourgeois; Vatican nuncio Msgr. Angelo Acerbi; Uruguayan ambassador Fernando Gomez; Egyptian ambassador Salah Alluf; Mexican ambassador Virgilio Lovera; United States ambassador Diego Asencio; Dominican ambassador Diogenes Mallol Burgos and his wife, Maria de Mallol; Costa Rican ambassador Maria Elena Chassoul; Guatemalan ambassador Aquiles Pinto Flores; Haitian ambassador Leonard Pierre-Louis; Bolivian charge Reinaldo de Cavero; Israeli ambassador Eliyahu Baraq; Peruvian consul Alfredo Tejada; Costa Rican counselor Rolando Blanco Solis; Venezuelan vice consul Angela de Salazar; and Paraguayan charge Oscar Gorostiaga (who was quickly evacuated because of wounds he suffered in the attack).

The list would have been longer but for the good fortune of some of the invitees. Hungarian ambassador Miklos Vass, the Soviet ambassador, and the ambassadors of two other Eastern European countries left the reception two minutes before the attack to attend a meeting at the East German embassy. Salvadoran ambassador Mauricio Garcia Prieto and British ambassador Kenneth James Uffen arrived late to the party and drove away, avoiding capture.

Saying they were instituting Operation Liberty and Democracy, the Marcos Zambrano Commando Group of the M-19 set an initial deadline of March 28, 10:00 P.M. (which was soon ignored), for the release of 311 prisoners, including 200 members of M-19, plus members of the Revolutionary Armed Forces of Colombia, the National Liberation Army, the Popular Liberation Army, and members of peasant, labor, and student organizations. They also demanded a ransom of $50 million (to be paid by the governments of the hostages), publication of an M-19 manifesto, and a continuing dialogue between the M-19 and the government. President Turbay Ayala claimed the executive branch of the government could not overturn court decisions by releasing prisoners and would not pay ransom but would also not prevent the concerned governments from negotiating with the terrorists. The government offered safe passage to Algeria, Syria, or Libya, but said that the Latin countries that had offered asylum (Mexico, Costa Rica, and Panama—the Venezuelan ambassador also suggested offering "itinerant asylum") were too close to Colombia and were thus unacceptable. The demands were later scaled down to release of 70 prisoners and payment of $10 million and still later were reduced to 20 prisoners, including those charged with the assassination of Dr. Nicolas Escobar, labor leader Jose Raquel Mercado, General Rincon Quinones, and former minister Pardo Buelvas. The government claimed that it never acceded to any of these demands but on April 18 released nine leftists from jail on the grounds that there was "no basis" for the charge that they had participated in a crime. The press reported that $2.5 million was raised by private sources as ransom payments, and still other press sources claimed that several countries had cut private deals with the terrorists.

Negotiations were conducted in a van parked in front of the embassy. Mexican ambassador Ricardo Galan initially accompanied the terrorists and was later replaced by Peruvian consul Alfredo Teuada. Former Colombian foreign minister Alfred Vasquez Carrizosa and Dr. Ernest Martinez Cayon began negotiations for the government. The terrorists refused to meet with Guillermo Rueda Montana, director of the Colombian Red Cross and asked for the mediation of newsmen Jorge Enrique Pulido of the TODELAR network and Yamit Amat of the CARACOL network. Spain's ambassador Emilio Martin Martin offered his services in finding a favorable solution, and a local diplomatic committee of Soviet ambassador Leonid Romanov, Swiss ambassador Hugo Schwalp, and Argentine ambassador Raul Medina Munoz liaised with the Colombian government. Later, Ramiro Zambrano and Camilo Jimenez of Colombia's International Protocol Department handled negotiations, while United States ambassador Diego Asencio led a committee of hostages that aided in the negotiations.

On March 17, Uruguayan ambassador Fernando Gomez, 43, escaped by tying several sheets together and climbing down from the second floor. Several hostages were sequentially released as well. The terrorists allowed the daughter of the Israeli ambassador to visit him in the embassy, but later they cut off visits by relatives. In response to rumors of a planned hunger strike, the terrorists' Commander Uno threatened to kill any hostage who participated in such a strike.

Despite threatening to kill the hostages and blow up the embassy, the terrorists on February 27 released a 16-year-old and 10 women: Aida de Pinto, wife of the Guatemalan ambassador; Judith de Baraq, wife of the Israeli ambassador; Clemencia de Baisel, wife of the Jamaican consul; Pura de Sanchez, wife of the Dominican consul; and Colombians Marta Lucia Ulano, Lucia Guzman de Ulano, Margarita Parra, Arbara Regina Ortiz de Echeverri, Alejandra Maria Gil, and Magda Alvarado de Lozano. Rafael Velez, the honorary consul of Paraguay (but a Colombian citizen), was shot in the left shoulder during the takeover and quickly released to seek medical attention. The terrorists later permitted a police ambulance to take away Venezuelan ambassador Virgilio Lover, 63, who suffered a heart attack. On March 2, they released Roberto Bermudez, the chief of protocol of Colombia's Ministry of Foreign Affairs, Dr. Gustavo Caicedo, and three embassy employees who were later treated for shock. By March 3, the terrorists still held 15 ambassadors, 5 other diplomats, 2 Colombian protocol officers, photographer Jorge Guzman, publisher Jorge Valencia of Colombia's DIPLOMATIC WORLD magazine, and several Dominican employees. By March 5, 23 hostages (of a total of 38 who ultimately would be freed) had been released. On April 3, the terrorists released Mario Guzman, a Dominican citizen; and Edgar Hernandez, a Foreign Ministry official. The next day, they released William Barquero, the former Nicaraguan ambassador; and Spanish citizen Manuel Lozano, a liquor salesman. On April 6, they released Labert Byfield, the honorary Jamaican consul; Tito Livio Tiburcio, a Dominican employee the army believed had helped the terrorists; and Guillermo Triana, the Foreign Ministry's under secretary for protocol. On April 19, Costa Rican consul Roland Blanco was freed. On the 22nd, Tom Tarer (an American professor) and Andres Aguilar (a Venezuelan), representing the Inter-American Human Rights Commission, met with the terrorists and began an Organization of American States (OAS) investigation into M-19 charges of torture by the government. The terrorists later released Dominican consul general Rafael Augusto Sanchez as a "gesture of good will."

On April 27, the terrorists released the diplomats from Venezuela, the Dominican Republic, Israel, and Egypt, before boarding a Cubana Airlines Ilyushin 62 for Havana. Upon landing, they were granted asylum, and they released the ambassadors of the United States, Mexico, Brazil, Switzerland, Guatemala, Haiti, the papal nuncio, the charges of Bolivia and Paraguay, and the consuls of Venezuela, Peru, and Guatemala. Cuba's ambassador had accompanied the flight, as had Eric Kobell of the International Committee of the Red Cross.

The identity of the terrorists was the subject of several conflicting reports. The dead terrorist was initially identified as "#30" among the terrorists (the group identified themselves by numbers rather than names), later identified as Jose Antonio Gomez Feo, 19. However, the real Feo later stepped forth to announce that his identity card had been stolen. The terrorist was later identified as Carlos Arturo Sandoval.

The day before the takeover, authorities had arrested Hondurans Jose Ramon Mata and Pedro Enrique Cardena Sastoque, who admitted during the seige that they were smuggling M-19 communications equipment into the embassy.

The identity of Commander Uno, the leader of the operation, was particularly subject to speculation. Various press reports claimed that he was Carlos Jaime Bateman, 30, or lawyer Everth Bustamante Garcia, 32, or Ernesto Charry Montealegre, educator and founder of the Trotskyite Worker's Self-Defense Movement (MAO). On April 23, the government claimed the group consisted of Rosemberg Pabon Pabon (Commander Uno); Luis Francisco Otero Cifuentes (Commander Tres), 36; Antonio Jose Navarro Wolfe (Commander Cinco); Guillermo Elbecio Ruiz Gomez (William); Jorge Ivan Rojas Sanchez (El Negro); Pompilio Aragon Zamora (Pomponio); Freddy Ramos, (Jorge, Pinana), a law student; Jose Yamil Ramos Riano (Manuel), M-19 financier; Rene Ramos Suarez; Carmenza (also spelled Carmen) Cardona Londono (La Chiqui, Luz Estela, Martha, Commander Nueve), the terrorists' negotiator; Ivon Consuelo Izquierdo (La Medica); Maria Clemencia Sandoval Garcia (Susana, Martha); Amparo Afanador Soto (La Negra); Dr. Gladys Diaz Ospino de Amortequi; Clara Aurora Beltran Gonzalez (Clarita); and Cecilia Maria Garcia Henao (Mariela). Other reports claimed the terrorists included Manuel Osvaldo Leyva Osorio; Consuelo Yvonne Izquierdo; Libio Tiborcio Sadino, 35, a Dominican; and Mary Brigen, 30, a physician and daughter of an Englishman and a Colombian woman. On July 7, 1980, Panama announced that it would consider the extradition request for Rosemberg Pabon, Jaime Bateman, Carlos Toledo Plata, Ivan Marino, and Jose Elbert Merino. On March 19, 1981, Colombia announced the capture after a pitched gun battle of Rosemberg Pabon, and the death of Carmenza Cardona Londono, the female negotiator. 80022701

February 28, 1980 — COLOMBIA — At 7:00 P.M., unknown persons threw two firebombs at the Argentine consulate in Medellin, damaging the facade, but not the interior, of the building. 80022801

February 28, 1980 — PANAMA — Sixteen members of the Revolutionary Student Front seized six hostages at the Salvadoran embassy to protest alleged government repression. Salvadoran charge Manuel Aguirre was among those held for two hours. University deputy rector Ceferino Sanchez, at the students' request, served as a mediator. The students gave reporters a communique demanding the release of two prominent Salvadoran leftists held for possession of dangerous weapons and conspiracy in the occupation of the Panamanian and Spanish embassies and other government buildings in January and February. 80022802

March 2, 1980 — FEDERAL REPUBLIC OF GERMANY — Two Irish Republican Army (IRA) gunmen fired 20 shots at a British Army patrol that had stopped for a traffic signal in Muenster, wounding the driver, a lance corporal. 80030201

March 3, 1980 — COLOMBIA — Bombs went off in the Mexican consulate in Pereira, causing damage but no injuries. 80030301

March 3, 1980 — SPAIN — An Arab terrorist, armed with a hand grenade and firing a submachine gun, shot and killed Spanish lawyer Adolfo Cotelo Villarreal, 50, brother-in-law of the agriculture minister in the first post-Franco cabinet, when he stopped his car for a red light in Madrid. Police arrested a Palestinian carrying an Omani passport made to Said Salman, 27. The local Palestine Liberation Organization (PLO) office condemned the killing. A second suspect, who apparently pointed out the target, was being sought. The killer may have mistaken Cotelo for Max Mazin, Spanish B'nai B'rith president, who lived in the same apartment building. 80030302

March 6, 1980 — KENYA — A bus driving between Mwingi and Garissa was shot at by armed Somalis. 80030601

March 6, 1980 — COLOMBIA — Anonymous callers threatened to bomb the Peruvian, French, and other embassies if they failed to support the group holding hostages in the Dominican embassy. 80030602

March 7, 1980 — WEST BERLIN — The People's Mojahedin of Afghanistan claimed credit for bombing the Soviet consulate general in the Zehlendorf Borough, causing considerable damage. 80030701

March 7, 1980 — FEDERAL REPUBLIC OF GERMANY — A few hours after the Soviet consulate general in West Berlin was bombed, members of the Hesse Criminal Investigation Department defused an explosive device hidden in a plastic bag in the Aeroflot office in Frankfurt. 80030702

March 7, 1980 — FRANCE — Six youths threw gasoline and firebombs at the Phoenix Bookstore in Paris (a concern selling Chinese books and periodicals and run by the president of the Franco-Chinese Friendship Association), injuring the manager and 12 employees. 80030703

March 7, 1980 — UNITED KINGDOM — The Irish National Liberation Army bombed a British Army camp in Netheravon, destroying two huts and injuring two people. 80030704

March 7, 1980 — FEDERAL REPUBLIC OF GERMANY — A bomb went off under a British car in the British military housing area in Laarbrueck, causing no injuries. 80030705

March 8, 1980 — GUATEMALA — Police claimed to have foiled leftist plans to occupy several diplomatic missions. 80030801

March 8, 1980 — SPAIN — The Camilo Torres cell of the Colombian April 19 Movement (M-19) sent a cassette via mail to the office of EFE (a Spanish news service) in Barcelona, threatening "vigorous reprisals" against the governments of France, the United Kingdom, the United States, and West Germany unless commando units surrounding the besieged Dominican embassy in Colombia were withdrawn. 80030802

March 9, 1980 — PHILIPPINES — Grenades were thrown into the orchestra pits from the balconies of two Ozamis City movie theaters, and four splinter hand grenades were lobbed into a public plaza in Iligan City, where an amateur singing contest was in progress. Police reported 31 deaths and 225 injuries and blamed the Moro National Liberation Front (MNLF) and the Maoist New People's Army for the blasts. Four MNLF terrorists were arrested. On March 28, the government claimed that it had cracked a grenade-throwers-for-hire ring, which charged $133 for each attack.

March 10, 1980 — CORSICA — Twelve bombs exploded on the island, apparently set by nationalist rebels.

March 10, 1980 — JORDAN — A 20-year-old Shiite Moslem armed with a toy pistol hijacked a Middle East Airlines B-707 flying from Amman to Beirut with 53 passengers and 8 crew members. The plane landed in Lebanon, where the hijacker said he wanted to focus attention on the missing Imam

Musa as-Sadr. Mustafa Abdel-Kader Hammoud was permitted to address a hastily convened press conference at the airport before surrendering. 80031001

March 10, 1980 — ITALY — Two bombs planted by the Armenian Secret Army for the Liberation of Armenia at the Turkish Airlines office on the Piazza della Repubblica in Rome killed 2 persons (Dante Sena, 64, who was born in New York, lived in Buenos Aires, and most recently resided in Venice; and Domenico Porcellonato, 67, a Roman citizen), and injured 12, including 3 policemen. The casualties occurred when the second bomb, a booby trap, went off after curious onlookers stopped to see the damage caused by the first explosion. A policeman reportedly saw 3 youths running from the scene and fired several shots at them. 80031002

March 10, 1980 — FEDERAL REPUBLIC OF GERMANY — Irish Republican Army (IRA) gunmen shot and wounded a British soldier who was jogging behind his Osnabrueck barracks. 80031003

March 11, 1980 — EL SALVADOR — As they were boarding a bus going from San Salvador to Honduras, Ana Silvia Gonzalez Quintanilla, a Nicaraguan; and Maria Guadalupe Gonzalez, 24, Mexican leader of the Committee of Solidarity with the People of El Salvador, were kidnapped. 80031101

March 11, 1980 — NORTHERN IRELAND — Police discovered the badly decomposed body of Thomas Niedermayer, 45, West German director of a Grundig electronics plant in Belfast and honorary West German consul, who had been kidnapped in 1974. No group ever claimed responsibility for the attack, and no demands for his release were made.

March 11, 1980 — FEDERAL REPUBLIC OF GERMANY — During the early morning, a man and woman, believed to be Irish Republican Army (IRA) members, fired shots from a car at a British Army radio relay station in Bielefeld, causing no injuries. Shots were also reported near the British compound on Meisentr in Bielefeld. 80031102–03

March 12, 1980 — USSR — The Japanese military attache, Koji Hirano of the Japanese Self-Defense Force, was apparently poisoned with tainted vodka offered him in a Tbilisi, Georgia, restaurant. He recovered after three days of treatment, and the Japanese did not issue a formal protest, being unable to produce the poisoned bottle. The action may have been a reprisal after a Japanese police investigation into the action of Col. Yuriy Kozlov, a Soviet military attache in Tokyo, who apparently bought military secrets from retired and present officers of Japan's Defense Agency.

March 12, 1980 — PUERTO RICO — The Machete Wielders claimed credit for shooting at a government car carrying Col. Charles Tucker, chief of the local Reserve Officers Training Corps (ROTC) program, and Lt. Col. Robert L. Davenport and Sgt. Major Mora Audili (a Puerto Rican), ROTC instructors in San Juan. No injuries were reported.

March 12, 1980 — LEBANON — An Armenian terrorist warned press agencies in Beirut that Turkish establishments would be attacked. 80031201

March 13, 1980 — UNITED STATES — The Omega-7 Cuban terrorist group claimed credit for setting off a firebomb at 11:03 A.M. at the Angolan United Nations Mission, starting a two-alarm fire, which caused no injuries. 80031301

March 14, 1980 — VENEZUELA — Ubaldo Calabresi, the papal nuncio, reported that several ambassadors had received telephone threats. 80031401

March 14, 1980 — EL SALVADOR — A Panamanian reporter for UNITED PRESS INTERNATIONAL, Demetrio Olaciregui, was abducted in San Salvador by three men who left him on the Honduran side of the border after robbing him. Rightists were believed responsible. 80031402

March 15, 1980 — UNITED STATES — Members of the Puerto Rican Armed Forces of National Liberation took over the Carter-Mondale campaign headquarters in Chicago, binding and gagging 7 workers. Meanwhile, members of the group bound and gagged 10 in the George Bush campaign headquarters in New York City. The armed and masked terrorists spraypainted slogans on the walls, ripped out phones, scattered papers, and escaped. 80031501-02

March 17, 1980 — UNITED STATES — The Croatian Freedom Fighters claimed credit for setting off a bomb on the 30th-floor stairwell of the skyscraper that houses the Jugobanka Representatives, a major Yugoslav bank. Extensive damage but no injuries were reported. A letter was found in a Port Authority bus terminal locker. 80031701

March 19, 1980 — UNITED STATES — The Puerto Rican Armed Forces of National Liberation sent threatening letters to Carter delegates in Illinois and phoned the Federal Bureau of Investigation's regional office in Manhattan to threaten Carter delegates. 80031901-02

March 21, 1980 — COLOMBIA — The Bogota morning newspaper EL ESPECTADOR ran a joint letter from the Jose Marti Command of the Colombian April 19 Movement (M-19), the Armed Forces for Liberation of

Puerto Rico, and the Dominican 14 June Movement, which announced "to the world and the Colombian people that if the captive ambassadors and the companeros who are inside the Dominican Embassy die because of some military action . . . the only ones responsible will be the US imperialists and their military lackeys." Referring to "counterguerrilla groups from Britain, Germany, the US, and Colombia," the group vowed, "We will respond with armed action in the US itself. You must remember, US gentlemen, that you have never experienced war in your own vitals and that you have many nuclear reactors." The communique was mailed in New York. 80032101

March 22, 1980 — BOLIVIA — Rightists were believed responsible for the murder of Spanish-Bolivian Jesuit Luis Espinal. Bolivian Jesuits later were threatened by ultrarightist commandos, as were progressive-leaning priests. 80032201

March 23, 1980 — PHILIPPINES — Police reported the arrest of eight people, including a Japanese and three other foreigners, who emerged from two flights from the Middle East smuggling submachine guns and hand grenades. Police alleged that they were planning to assassinate Chilean president Augusto Pinochet during his March 24 Manila visit, which was abruptly canceled by the Philippine government. Pinochet threatened to break diplomatic relations. 80032301

March 23, 1980 — LEBANON — Palestine sources in Beirut claimed to have broken up a plot to assassinate Yasir Arafat when he was departing for 'Alayh to participate in the third anniversary of the death of Kamal Junblatt. 80032302

March 23, 1980 — UNITED KINGDOM — An unemployed Italian laborer was arrested for firebombing the London offices of the Italian consulate general. A leaking gas main was ignited, wrecking the offices. 80032303

March 24, 1980 — EL SALVADOR — Archbishop Oscar A. Romero, 1979 Nobel Peace Prize nominee for his human rights work, was assassinated by four gunmen who walked up and shot him during a memorial Mass in San Salvador. The group fled through a side door and into a red Volkswagen. The Salvadoran Proletarian Brigades claimed credit, saying Romero was collaborating with the United States. Judge Atilio Ramirez claimed in a law review article that former National Guard colonel Jose A. Medrano and major Roberto d'Abuisson paid the assassins. Ramirez survived an assassination attempt and fled to Costa Rica.

On March 21, 1985, Col. Roberto Santivanez, who headed the Salvadoran intelligence agency in 1978–79, claimed at a Washington, D.C., news conference that Col. Richard Lau, a prominent anti-Nicaraguan figure, was paid $120,000 by wealthy Salvadoran exiles for training former Nicaraguan national guardsmen who carried out the assassination.

March 25, 1980 — EL SALVADOR — The Revolutionary People's Army bombed the International Telephone and Telegraph building in residential San Salvador. 80032501

March 25, 1980 — UNITED STATES — Explosives were found under the car of Cuban United Nations representative Raul Roa Kouri in New York City. The anti-Castro Cuban group Omega-7 claimed credit. As of February 21, 1984, Eduardo Arocena, alleged Omega-7 leader, was awaiting trial on charges of attempting to murder Roa. 80032502

March 27, 1980 — IRELAND — Bernard McGinn, an Irish Republican Army (IRA) gunman who had threatened to blow up himself and his three hostages, surrendered to Dundalk police after 24 hours. 80032701

March 28, 1980 — FRANCE — Toulon police arrested four members of the Italian Red Brigades. 80032801

March 29, 1980 — UNITED STATES — An extortionist put cyanide in a jar of pickles and a bottle of teriyaki sauce in shelves in separate stores in San Diego. A note from "The Poison Gang" said, "Five other food items loaded with cyanide . . . are now on the shelves of this store. If you comply with our demands, we will give you a list and the exact location of these food items. Otherwise, we will poison the food in every Safeway store in the area." The individual demanded 50 loose diamonds. On April 1, an extortionist told a Safeway employee in Palm Desert, California, that he had laced a bottle of salad dressing with cyanide. It was later revealed that a similar poisoning in Beaverton, Oregon, was made. Police had arrested Richard Q. Williams, 46, a horse trainer, for poisoning food for $100,000 in a Sun City Safeway store in May 1979. A California judge dismissed the charges on June 18, 1980. On April 9, 1980, a can of food was removed from a Colorado Springs, Colorado, supermarket following a similar extortion attempt for $10,000. Allen L. Henderson was charged with criminal extortion.

March 29, 1980 — UNITED STATES — Four Croatian members of OTPOR were arrested in New York for plotting to bomb a Yugoslavian Independence Day celebration when more than hundred foreign diplomats would be on hand. Police found 14 sticks of dynamite, a machine gun, 2 military rifles, and several hand grenades in the hideout. On May 12, 1981, a judge sentenced Ivan Kale, Franjo Ivi, Stipe Ivkosic, and Nejelko Sovulj to 20–35 years for the plot and for planning to bomb a Bronx travel agency and assassinate a political opponent. 80032901

March 29, 1980 — EL SALVADOR — Gunmen fired on the United States Peace Corps office in San Salvador but caused no injuries. 80032902

March 30, 1980 — EL SALVADOR — Snipers killed 40 people participating in the funeral of slain Archbishop Oscar A. Romero.

March 30, 1980 — COLOMBIA — Bombs exploded in the Cali consulates of Costa Rica and Uruguay. The April 19 Movement (M-19) was believed responsible. 80033001–02

April 1980 — SYRIA — The Moslem Brotherhood was blamed for killing a Soviet adviser and seriously wounding his wife. 80049901

April 1980 — LEBANON — Iraq blamed Iran for the bombing of Iraqi Airlines, the trade center, and the IRAQI NEWS AGENCY offices in Beirut. 80049902–04

April 1, 1980 — UNITED STATES — A federal grand jury in Raleigh, North Carolina, indicted Howard B. Brutton, Jr., of Wilson, North Carolina, and Robert Ferraro and George DeMeo of New York City for conspiring to export weapons illegally to Northern Ireland and the Republic of Ireland. 80040101

April 1, 1980 — EL SALVADOR — Five members of the Revolutionary Party of Central American Workers (PRTC) fired submachine guns at Guatemalan ambassador Carlos Lemus Gallardo, slightly cutting his arm. The ambassador and his bodyguard drove off the attackers in a brief gun battle in San Salvador. 80040102

April 1, 1980 — EL SALVADOR — The Popular Liberation Forces bombed and machine-gunned the El Salvador–United States Cultural Center in northeastern San Salvador, causing no casualties. 80040103

April 1, 1980 — IRAQ — Iraqi Prime Minister Tariq Aziz escaped an assassination attempt by an Iranian member of Ayatollah Sadegh Khalkhali's Fedaye Islam group who threw a hand grenade into a student gathering in Baghdad's Al-Mustansiriyah University at 7:00 A.M. Police shot and killed Samir Nur'Ali, and the Iraqi government gave an Iranian diplomat 24 hours to leave the country. Razkar Nuri Muhammad Salih (a sophomore), a woman, and another student were killed in the blast, and several others, including Aziz, were wounded. On April 5, one student was killed and several others injured when a grenade was thrown at the funeral procession for two of the dead students. 80040104

April 2, 1980 — CHAD — Sudanese consul general Ahmed Hamza was killed in an Ndjamena bar which was raked by machine-gun fire at 3:00 A.M. by one of Chad's warring factions. 80040201

April 2, 1980 — CYPRUS — Three members of EOKA, a Cypriot nationalist group, died when a bomb they were planting in an orange grove at a British Air Force base in Nicosia exploded prematurely. 80040202

April 2, 1980 — FRANCE — A Ukrainian nationalist group threw two fire-bombs at two Soviet diplomats' cars in the 16th District in Paris during the night. 80040203–04

April 4, 1980 — UNITED STATES — Evanston, Illinois, police captured 6 men and 5 women believed to be the core of the Puerto Rican Armed Forces of National Liberation (FALN), which has been responsible for over one hundred bombings. Police held Carlos Alberto Torres, 27, FALN's leader and number one on the Federal Bureau of Investigation's (FBI) most wanted list; his wife Marie Haydee Torres, 25, also on the FBI list; Ida Luz Rodriguez, 29; Dylcia Noemi Pagan, 33; Elizam Escobar, 31; and Fred Mendez. Police also found 20 firearms after an armed robbery in which a large truck was stolen from an Evanston rent-a-car office. The 11 were charged with a variety of local weapons, theft, and armed robbery charges. Bond was set at $2 million.

April 4, 1980 — REPUBLIC OF SOUTH AFRICA — Five African National Congress terrorists fired submachine guns and lobbed four grenades into a police station in a white Johannesburg suburb but caused no injuries.

April 4, 1980 — FEDERAL REPUBLIC OF GERMANY — Patrick, a self-proclaimed member of the Irish Republican Army (IRA) Supreme Command, told a DER SPIEGEL interviewer that attacks against British forces in West Germany would continue, and that his group would kill former British ambassador to Washington, Peter Jay, and former chancellor of the exchequer, Denis Healey. 80040401

April 5, 1980 — UNITED STATES — The State Department declared persona non grata two Libyan diplomats identified as Moftah S. Ibrahim, third secretary, and Mohamed S. A. Turhuni, a cultural attache, for distributing leaflets among Libyan students calling for the assassination of opponents of Qaddafi.

April 7, 1980—ISRAEL—The Group of Martyr Commander Kamal Ka'ush of the Arab Liberation Front, apparently made up of a Syrian, an Egyptian, an Iraqi, a Pakistani, and a Palestinian, seized a children's house in the Misgav 'Am kibbutz south of the border town of Metulla. In an initial attempt to free the hostages, kibbutz secretary Sammy Shani was killed by the terrorists. Medical orderly Eliyahu Elad Tzafrir was also killed by machine-gun fire that raked a team truck. The group, which apparently exploited a weakness in an electronic fence, demanded the release of 50 Palestinian prisoners, a plane to fly them out of the country, and the intervention of the Romanian ambassador and a Red Cross representative. Kibbutz members freed 8 children and 3 women on the ground floor, while the terrorists ran to the second floor, seizing Meir Perez, 25, a kibbutz member, and 6 children. The terrorists demanded milk for the children, which was provided. It was later learned that Eyal Gluska, age 2, was killed, apparently during the initial assault. After several deadlines passed, a second army rescue squad was launched, resulting in the deaths of all of the terrorists and injuries to Perez, 10 soldiers, and 4 children. The siege had lasted for 10 hours. 80040701

April 7, 1980—FRANCE—Members of Direct Action raided the Philips Data Systems Company computer center in Toulouse and claimed to have stolen Ministry of Defense and SDECE (French intelligence) tapes. They also sabotaged computers, erased programs, and set fire to the facility, causing extensive damage. They conducted a similar raid on the Toulouse offices of CII-Honeywell-Bull. The group claimed its members were computer workers who know the dangers of such systems. In a press release, they argued, "Computers are the favorite instrument of the powerful. They are used to classify, control and repress. We do not want to be shut up in the ghettos of programs and organizational patterns." Police claimed the group was active in Italy, where it had contacts with the Red Brigades. 80040702

April 8, 1980—GUATEMALA—Gunmen fired from a car at the Japanese embassy, breaking windows but causing no injuries. 80040801

April 9, 1980—UNITED STATES—At 7:58 A.M. Gerald Leland Merity (Mohamed Jalal Akbar), 35, a stocky Black Muslim, jumped a wall at southern California's Ontario Airport and took over an American Airlines B-727 waiting to take on passengers. The hijacker, armed with a .45 caliber pistol, forced the three crewmen and four stewardesses to accompany him to Dallas Airport, then on to Havana, where he surrendered to authorities at 5:18 P.M., about six hours after the hijacking began. The former dental school student requested asylum in a Moslem country. 80040901

April 9, 1980 — INDIA — Police arrested Rajesh Singhal for carrying a loaded pistol in his pants in an attempt to hijack the New Delhi–Bombay Indian Airlines flight to Karachi, Pakistan. 80040902

April 10, 1980 — EL SALVADOR — Policeman Gil Ramos was slightly injured when a bomb exploded near the Brazilian embassy. 80041001

April 10, 1980 — EL SALVADOR — Policeman Carlos Mendes was seriously injured when a rock was thrown through the limousine of Brazilian charge Augusto Esteli Salinas, whom he was protecting from terrorists. 80041002

April 10, 1980 — INDIA — An anonymous caller claimed that a bomb had been planted on the grounds of the American consulate in New Delhi. 80041003

April 10, 1980 — EL SALVADOR — Daisy Zuniga, in charge of consular affairs at the Nicaraguan embassy, received a threatening telephone call telling her that her "time was up." While driving on official business, she noted that she was being followed by two station wagons carrying armed civilians. On her way to Ambassador Francisco Quinonez's residence, she heard two shots ring out in the street. An embassy guard said he had arrested an individual who had fired shots from one of the station wagons. 80041004

April 10, 1980 — AZORES — The British press reported that Egyptian president Anwar Sadat's plane refueled at a United States Air Force base in Mildenhall, Suffolk, rather than make a scheduled landing in the Azores because authorities had learned that Libyan terrorists were planning to rocket the plane with SA-7s. 80041005

April 11, 1980 — UNITED STATES — The Federal Bureau of Investigation (FBI) reported that it had uncovered a plan by the leader of the Armed Forces of National Liberation of Puerto Rico to bomb the Republican and Democratic national conventions. Federal agents in Chicago found a cache of blasting caps hidden by the group, while FBI agents in Jersey City found a "hit list" of one hundred of the nation's leading corporate executives and industrialists. 80041101

April 11, 1980 — UNITED KINGDOM — Libyan dissident journalist Mohammed Mustafa Ramadan, 35, was shot by two Libyan gunmen near a Regent's Park, London, mosque. Police arrested the gunmen, plus two other suspects the following day. Ramadan had received numerous death threats for contributing to anti-Qaddafi leaflets. The gunmen received life sentences in September 1980. 80041102

April 13, 1980—UNITED STATES—Francis Tolbert, the nephew of assassinated Liberian president William Tolbert, received a death threat in Trenton, New Jersey. A General Motors worker and Trenton resident for eight years, he had recently attended Mercer County Community College. Police escorted him to an undisclosed destination after searching his car for bombs. 80041301

April 14, 1980—INDIA—Ram Bulchand Lalwani, 37, a member of the Dalit Panthers, an untouchable group modeled on the American Black Panthers, threw a four-inch switchblade knife at Prime Minister Indira Gandhi, who was entering her car after attending a ceremony for the late untouchable leader B. R. Ambedkar. The knife grazed one of her security inspectors. On April 18, fellow prisoner Khalias Parmar stabbed Lalwani in the stomach. On April 24, eight days after their arrest, the Supreme Court granted bail to Baroda deputy mayor Pratap Ramchandani and four others arrested in connection with the Gandhi assassination attempt.

April 14, 1980—JAMAICA—Shots were fired near Prime Minister Michael Manley while he was campaigning in his Kingston district. Shortly before the attack, rival political gangs had clashed, resulting in injuries to a policeman and a youth.

April 14, 1980—COLOMBIA—Four or five members of the April 19 Movement (M-19) broke into the Uruguayan embassy, hoping to kidnap charge Raul Liar in reprisal for the escape from the besieged Dominican embassy of ambassador Fernando Gomez Gyn. When they discovered that Liar had left the city, they vacated the embassy peacefully. 80041401

April 15, 1980—FRANCE—The Direct Action fired rockets from passing cars at the Paris offices of the Ministry of Transport, an annex of the ministry, and a bank in the 14th District, causing considerable damage but no injuries.

April 15, 1980—LEBANON—Bombs went off in several Iraqi and Iranian offices in Beirut. 80041501–02

April 16, 1980—COSTA RICA—Police arrested five to nine people, including three Nicaraguans, one Chilean, and one Costa Rican, for planning to kill President Rodrigo Carazo Odio with four sticks of dynamite. Police seized a fragmentation grenade, a large quantity of cartridges, and gas masks. Alfonso Ayub, a Costa Rican, was believed the gang's ringleader. 80041601

April 16, 1980—LEBANON—The Iranian Amal Movement fired on the Arab Socialist Baath Party's offices in Burj al-Baranjinah, killing one party member and injuring two others. The group then fired rockets and machine guns at the Arab Liberation Front's offices, killing four ALF members and injuring five others. Later, the group attacked the Iraqi embassy with rocket-propelled grenades (RPGs) and machine guns, but no injuries were reported in a one-hour gun battle. 80041602

April 16, 1980—FEDERAL REPUBLIC OF GERMANY—Two gunmen hiding in shrubs on a Duesseldorf street shot to death Dusan Sedlar, 71, the leader of Serbian exiles in Western Europe. 80041603

April 16, 1980—TURKEY—Kadir Tandogan, Ahmet Taner, and Hakki Kolgu, members of the leftist Marxist-Leninist Armed Propaganda Unit, shot and killed Master Chief Botswain's Mate Sam A. Novello, 56, a United States citizen, and his Turkish driver, Sabri Bayraktar, as they were entering Novello's car at his home at 8:30 A.M. The trio escaped on a motorcycle but, after a clash with police, were arrested. Tandogan was slightly wounded, and Kolgu later died of his wounds. Menderes Ataseven, a gendarme commando; Riza Karabal, a guard; and Adriya Mustaraki, a bystander, were wounded in the gun battle. Police found 4 pistols, 112 rounds of ammunition, 9 clips, and 10 spent cartridges at the scene. An Istanbul military court sentenced the surviving duo to death on October 13. They were executed on the morning of June 25, 1981. 80041604

April 17, 1980—SAINT MARTIN ISLAND, WEST INDIES—Two unsuccessful bank robbers fled to a nearby hotel where they took two hostages, including a United States citizen, and injured another American during a gun battle. After releasing their hostages, they escaped into the hills on the French side of the island.

April 17, 1980—VATICAN CITY—Two young gunmen of the Justice Commandos of the Armenian Genocide stopped the car of Turkish ambassador Vecdi Turel, 62, as he was being driven to work, and fired into the car, wounding the ambassador in the chest and seriously wounding his bodyguard. An anonymous caller told REUTERS in Beirut, "Our only aim is to strike against Turkish personalities and Turkish institutions all over the world." Turel's predecessor as ambassador to the Vatican was shot dead on a Roman street in 1977. 80041701

April 17, 1980—LEBANON—During the afternoon, pro-Iraqi Palestinian gunmen fired on the car of Iranian charge Jawad Yirdajaei, slightly wounding him, his bodyguard, and the embassy accountant. 80041702

April 17, 1980—LEBANON—Members of the Amal movement attacked the AL-MUHARRIR newspaper offices in Beirut, killing 5 Iraqis and taking 9 others prisoner. The building was destroyed by fire. An Amal member, Ghalib, and 3 Arab Liberation Front members were also killed, while 10 Iraqis were injured. 80041703

April 17, 1980—HONDURAS—Six gunmen wearing stocking masks and hiding pistols beneath folded newspapers kidnapped Texaco regional vice president Arnold Quiroz, a Costa Rican-born United States citizen, as he was walking from his car to the Gran Hotel Sula at about 6:15 P.M. The group threw him into a white Toyota van. At 8:00 the next morning, two of the kidnappers took him to the Nicaraguan embassy, where one of them went inside the embassy with Quiroz to ask for the ambassador's aid. As they were walking back to the door of the embassy wall, Quiroz threw the kidnapper into the street, slammed the door, and awaited assistance. No injuries were reported. Police arrested several suspects and were searching for others. 80041704

April 18, 1980—LEBANON—Mahmoud Bazi, a Shiite Moslem villager whose brother died in a clash between United Nations forces and the Christian militia of Maj. Saad Haddad, claimed credit for an attack by six gunmen on an unarmed United Nations convoy near Vint Jbail. The group abducted three Irish soldiers and later killed two of them, one of whom had been sexually assaulted before being shot in the back. The third Irish soldier, Pvt. John O'Mahoney, was shot in the leg and stomach. United Nations forces in two other cars, including American major Harry Klein, French captain Patrick Vincent of the United Nations Truce Supervisory Organization, a reporter, and a photographer for the ASSOCIATED PRESS were briefly detained. The killers claimed the attack was a blood feud for the deaths of two militiamen at the hands of Irish troops the previous week near the village of At Tiri. 80041801

April 18, 1980—ECUADOR—Four hooded male members of the 18 October Movement Astra Revolutionary Action Command took over the Colombian consulate in Quito at 5:00 P.M. and held it for 15 minutes while they delivered a message to the consul to be given to the press. None of the 14 hostages was harmed. 80041802

April 18, 1980—ITALY—Three gunmen killed Abdel Belil Aref, 51, a wealthy Libyan businessman, as he was dining at the Cafe du Paris on the Via Veneto in Rome. Police arrested Libyan Jussef Sallata, 23, and later picked up two other Libyans, Elbai Khalifa and Ahmed Hamad Hamed, 23, who had entered Italy three months previously and were students at the Perugia University for foreigners. On April 26 in Libya, police arrested Francesco Franco Corsi, 42, at the Alitalia terminal at Tripoli Airport and accused him of spying on Libya while posing as the Alitalia manager. Rome police believed this was in retaliation for the April 22 detention of the manager of the Libyan airline in Rome in connection with the Aref assassination.

On October 6, 1986, the Italian government announced that for "humanitarian motives" it had freed the three convicted Libyan gunmen in exchange for four Italians being held in Libya for the last six years. A Red Cross plane for the Libyans flew to Tripoli and returned with the Italians. The exchange was negotiated by Italian foreign minister Guilio Andreotti, and followed the April 1986 incident in which Libya fired two Scud missiles at the Italian island of Lampedusa in the wake of the April 15, 1986, United States bombing of Libya. The freed Libyans included Jussef Uhida, who was serving a 26-year sentence for the murder of Aref. The other two Libyans, Mohammed Sidki Sayed Bous and Juma Mohammed Ali Mezdawi, were serving 15-year sentences for wounding two Lebanese at Fiumincino Airport in 1981, when the terrorists mistook the victims for opponents of Qaddafi whom they had been ordered to kill.

The freed Italians included contractor Edoardo Seliciato and worker Enzo Castelli, who were serving life sentences handed down by a Libyan military court for plotting against Libya following a 1980 uprising in Tobruk. Mauro Piccin and Massimo Caporali were serving 10-year sentences for drug possession. 80041803

April 18, 1980 — EL SALVADOR — Leftists fired on a Texas Instruments plant in San Salvador. 80041804

April 19, 1980 — FRANCE — Four people were injured by a blast at the Paris offices of an antiapartheid group. Several leftist groups had also used the conference center.

April 19, 1980 — FRANCE — The Armenian terrorist organization Avril Noir claimed credit for placing a rocket launcher near the Turkish consulate in Marseilles. A cleaning person noticed the device, which was defused by police seven minutes before it was timed to fire. 80041901

April 20, 1980 — CUBA — Costa Rican consul general Oscar Vargas Bello denied press reports that he had been the victim of a terrorist attack in Havana.

April 21, 1980 — TURKEY — The Armenian Secret Army Struggling for the Liberation of Armenia accused the United States Central Intelligence Agency of infiltrating Armenian groups in an attempt to thwart the group's work.

April 21, 1980 — SWITZERLAND — Arab terrorists hid a bomb in the luggage of a West German boarding an El Al jetliner flying from Zurich to Tel Aviv. After Israeli security agents detained the man, the device exploded in the police lab at the airport before it could be defused but caused no injuries. The man claimed the bomb had been placed without his knowledge, but police noted that he was using a passport in the name of Karl Braun with his picture substituted for Braun's. 80042101

April 22, 1980 — EL SALVADOR — Washington radio correspondent Rene Tamsen, 28, a WHUR staffer, was reported missing for a week on April 29.

April 22, 1980 — YUGOSLAVIA — A bomb was thrown at noon at the Mercedes owned by the chief of the Palestine Liberation Organization office in Belgrade, injuring one of the three people in the car, which had stopped for a traffic light. 80042201

April 23, 1980 — FRANCE — The National Liberation Front of Corsica bombed a post office, an Air France office, a shop, and a revenue office in Paris, causing considerable damage and four injuries. In Nice, a bomb that went off at the general treasurer's office of the Customs Office was an indirect attack at the revenue office. 80042301–06

April 24, 1980 — AFGHANISTAN — Chain Singh, Indian national hockey team coach, and 18 Afghan hockey players were attacked and abducted by Afghan rebels when they landed in Gonduz Province on the way back from the USSR. Their driver drove them into a deserted area, then fled, leaving the team open to attack. Two Soviet guards were killed, as were two fleeing team members. Three other players managed to escape. On July 24, Singh reportedly was to be released.

April 25, 1980 — IRAQ — The government expelled the 32-man delegation of the Popular Front for the Liberation of Palestine three weeks after expelling members of the Democratic Front for the Liberation of Palestine.

April 25, 1980 — FRANCE — The Self-Defense against All Authority bombed the Toulouse office of a United States agricultural equipment company, causing extensive damage but no injuries, "as a reprisal against US intervention in Iran." 80042501

April 25, 1980 — UNITED KINGDOM — Mahmud Abu Salem Nafa, 48, a Libyan lawyer who translated and published Arab legal books and had lived in London for five years, was shot and killed at an Arab legal center. The Arab gunman and an accomplice had asked for him by name at the center.

The duo was apprehended. On September 16, 1980, the duo plus another Libyan were sentenced for this murder and that of Mohammed Mustafa Ramadan, killed earlier in the month. 80042502

April 26, 1980 — LIBYA — Libyan leader Muammar Qaddafi issued a "final warning" to Libyan exiles abroad that they should return home immediately or "be liquidated." Exiles were directed to report to the local popular student bureaus and register for repatriation.

April 26, 1980 — LEBANON — The Mujahidin Iraqis, who Iraq claimed were Iranian agents, bombed the IRAQI NEWS AGENCY offices in Beirut, causing serious damage and wounding two guards. 80042601

April 26, 1980 — FRANCE — Twenty members of the National Youth Front, a right-wing group, firebombed two coaches of a train that was waiting to depart for Moscow in Paris's Gare du Nord station. No injuries were reported, but damage was extensive. The group was protesting the Moscow Olympics. 80042602

April 26, 1980 — FEDERAL REPUBLIC OF GERMANY — Several leftists apparently protesting United States Iranian policy threw three Molotov cocktails into the Hamburg offices of Pan American World Airways, causing minimal damage and no injuries. 80042603

April 28, 1980 — IRAN — The TEHRAN DOMESTIC SERVICE reported three attacks on the besieged United States embassy by unknown individuals.

April 28, 1980 — ITALY — Corrado Alunni, a major Italian terrorist leader, and 15 other prisoners shot their way out of Milan's San Vittore jail, injuring 2 guards. Police immediately recaptured 9 escapees, including 5 wounded prisoners, Alunni among them.

April 29, 1980 — KUWAIT — Unknown gunmen fired machine guns from two cars in an attempt to assassinate Iranian foreign minister Sadegh Ghotbzadeh, 43, as he was being driven to a meeting with Sheik Jaber Ahmad, Kuwait's leader. One of the following cars in Ghotbzadeh's convoy was hit, and a guard was injured. Police later arrested two suspects and found two of the terrorists' cars, loaded with 20 weapons. Iran's news agency claimed that the suspects had escaped into the Iraqi embassy. 80042901

April 30, 1980 — IRAN — TEHRAN DOMESTIC SERVICE reported that a Revolutionary Guard was wounded in an attack on the besieged American embassy.

April 30, 1980 — UNITED KINGDOM — Six Iranians from the Khuzestan (Arabistan) region seized the Iranian embassy in London, taking 26 hostages, including several non-Iranians. They demanded publicity for their cause — autonomy for Arabistan — and the release from Iranian prison of 91 people to be brought to London, then flown with the terrorists to another country. The demand for release was dropped two days later, and the terrorists demanded safe passage out of the United Kingdom. A rumor that they had also offered to swap the 26 hostages for the release of the 52 hostages being held in the United States embassy in Tehran proved false. Iran refused to deal with the terrorists, placing the responsibility on the British. Iran claimed that the Iraqis, Israelis, Americans, and British were behind the raid. Foreign Minister Ghotbzadeh saw no parallel between the holding of the United States hostages and the London takeover, saying, "The occupation in Tehran is in reaction to 25 years of suppression and killings in Iran. We condemn the occupation of our embassy which is totally in a foreign land of foreign people and has nothing to do with the issue."

The terrorists threatened to use their hand grenades to blow up the embassy, but the next day let two deadlines pass. Ghotbzadeh vowed to execute the prisoners if any Iranian embassy staff members were harmed. Fifty demonstrating Iranian students told British police that they wished to become substitute hostages in place of the diplomats, but they were refused. The terrorists initially forced BBC television newsman Chris Cramer to contact the local news media via the embassy's telex machine, then released him on May 1 when he developed severe stomach cramps. Charge Gholam Ali Afrooz tried unsuccessfully to escape by jumping from a second-floor office window but was grabbed by one of the terrorists. On May 4, the terrorists released embassy secretary Mrs. Haydeh Kanji, 23, who was three months pregnant, as well as Pakistani-born Ghanzanfar Ali Gull. A few hours later, the terrorists released a Syrian journalist working for a Lebanese newspaper, Mustafa Karkouti, who also complained of stomach pains. These hostages joined a woman who had been released during the initial assault, when she had fainted from the stress. The terrorists still held non-Iranian hostages, including London police private Trevor Lock, 41, of the Diplomatic Protection Group, who was not able to use his firearm, which had gone undetected by the terrorists; Ronald Morris, a British clerk at the embassy; and BBC news cameraman Sid Harris.

In statements from the embassy, as well as from Beirut, the terrorists were variously identified as belonging to the Political Organization of the Arab People, the Arab Masses Movement, the Movement of the Moslem Arab People Strugglers, the Martyr Muhyi ad-Din an-Nasir Operation, the Group of the Martyr, the Al-Nasir Mojahedin Group, the Arab People's Political Organization, the Arab People's Movement, and the Arab People's Mujahiddin Combatants Movement. The terrorists requested mediation from Iraq, Jordan, Algeria, and the Red Cross, but offered to settle for Libya, Syria, and Kuwait if the first group of diplomats was not available. The Jordanian, Algerian, Kuwaiti, and Syrian ambassadors in London later conferred with the British Foreign Office.

On May 5 at 6:30 P.M., the terrorists announced that they had executed 2 of the hostages and threatened to kill 1 hostage every half hour if their demands were not met. At first the British believed the terrorists were bluffing and brought forward an Islamic religious leader to talk to the terrorists. At 7:00 P.M. the terrorists threw onto the street the body of Iranian embassy press counselor Abbas Levasani, 25. They apparently had also killed the military attache. At 7:30 masked members of the British Special Air Services set off stun and flash grenades in an assault at the elegant five-story townhouse in the West End. During the gun battle, the SAS rescued the surviving 15 men and 4 women, killing 5 of the terrorists and capturing the 6th. Three Iranian hostages, including the charge, were wounded in the cross fire.

The surviving terrorist, Fowzi Badavi Nejad, 23, an Iranian dockworker, was charged with the murder of the 2 hostages, assault, unlawful imprisonment, and several other offenses. During his January 1981 trial, he claimed the attack was planned and organized by the Iraqis. He was sentenced to life in prison.

On May 12, 1980, the British announced that they were searching for a 7th man, Sami Muhammed Ali, who gave a Baghdad address and telephone number when he rented a London apartment for the terrorists before the attack. 80043001

May 1980—SWEDEN—A Croatian accused of assassinating the Yugoslav ambassador to Sweden on April 7, 1971 was extradited to Sweden by the United States. He had been turned over to United States authorities for prosecution on charges of fraudulently applying for a visa to enter the United States in December 1979 but was acquitted.

May 1980—SWITZERLAND—Three Spanish Foreign Legionnaires who had hijacked an airliner from the Canary Islands were found guilty by the Geneva Criminal Court of false imprisonment and were sentenced to 20 months in jail. 80059901

May 1980—LEBANON—A Libyan dissident was believed to have been murdered by Muammar Qaddafi's assassination squads. 80059902

May 1, 1980—LEBANON—The Iranian National Liberation Movement—Red June Organization claimed that "Iraqi fascists under Saddam Husayn in cooperation with British intelligence services and the remnants of SAVAK," the former Iranian regime's intelligence service, conspired to arrange the seizure of the Iranian embassy in London. The group said that if any harm came to the Iranian diplomats, "the British Thatcher government fully responsible" would be held to account. 80050101

May 1, 1980 — IRAN — Jane Woodell, 58, secretary of the Anglican Bishop in Tehran (who himself had escaped an assassination attempt), was shot and seriously wounded by two gunmen who broke into her home. 80050102

May 1, 1980 — UNITED STATES — Steve Bilson, 25, jumped a fence at Stockton California's Metropolitan Airport and attempted to take over a Pacific Southwest B-727 at 6:50 P.M. When Bilson flashed his gun, the pilot and copilot managed to escape, leaving only flight engineer Al Ramatowski, who disarmed the Ceres, California, native while he was claiming that he was going to free the United States hostages by flying to Iran. Police had disabled the plane by letting the air out of its tires. 80050103

May 2, 1980 — UNITED KINGDOM — The French embassy was evacuated after receiving a bomb threat. 80050201

May 2, 1980 — ISRAEL — Arab terrorists fired small arms and threw two grenades at Jewish religious students walking from the Machpela Cave shrine in the West Bank (where Abraham, Isaac, and Jacob are believed to be buried) to the old Hadassah Clinic in Hebron. After killing 5 settlers (Israeli Hannah Kreutheimer later died) and injuring 17, including 2 Americans — Mordechai Shvat, 21, of New York City, and Allon Gasserman — the 4 terrorists fled into a cemetery and escaped. The Palestine Liberation Organization's Unit of the Martyr Ibrahim Abu Safwat claimed responsibility, saying that the attackers killed or wounded more than 50.

On September 16, 1980, Israeli security forces arrested the 4 terrorists plus 6 Fatah accomplices who had been helping them hide in caves in the Hebron hills. The Israelis confiscated two Kalashnikov assault rifles, a Gustave submachine gun, two hand grenades, and six improvised bombs. Those arrested for the murders were identified as squad commander Yasir Husayn Muhamad Saydat, 30, from Bani Na'im; deputy Adnan Jabir, 32, who spoke of training in the Soviet Union with Fatah, the Popular Democratic Front for the Liberation of Palestine, the Arab Liberation Front, Saiqa, and the Popular Front for the Liberation of Palestine; Taysir abu Snayna, 28, from Hebron; and Muhamad Shubaki, who also admitted to the murder of Uriel and Hadassa Baraq, 2 Israeli tourists whose bodies were discovered on March 1, 1980, in the Bet Govrin region. 80050202

May 2, 1980 — LEBANON — Members of the Revolutionary Islamic Organization (RIO), firing from two cars, assassinated an Iranian Shiite clergyman, Imam Hasan Shirazi, in the Ar-Ramlat al-Bayda section of Beirut.

The RIO claimed it backed Iranian religious leader Ayatollah Kazem Shari'at-Madari and accused Shirazi, the leader of the Shiite Ulema in Lebanon, of being a "traitor, known for his persistent contacts with the American ambassador in Lebanon." The Red June Organization, the military wing of the Iranian National Movement, accused the Iraqi mission of the murder. 80050203

May 3, 1980—IRAN—The Revolutionary Islamic Organization (RIO), charging that its leader Ayatollah Kazem Shari'at-Madari had been arrested in Qom, threatened to mount operations against Iranian embassies if he was not released. 80050301

May 4, 1980—AFGHANISTAN—The rebel Islamic Alliance for the Liberation of Afghanistan claimed that two students fired pistols on Soviet ambassador Ahmed Janovitch's car during an anti-Soviet demonstration in Kabul, but caused no damage due to bulletproofing. The bodyguards of the ambassador scuffled with the youths, seriously injuring them. The rebels also claimed that two Russians were killed when a Kabul high school girl fired on Soviet troops guarding the Kabul governor's home. She was killed in the return fire.

May 4, 1980—PAKISTAN—Nine Afghan refugees and two Pakistanis were killed when a bomb exploded at the Peshawar building used by the Afghan rebel group Jamiat-i-Islami. 80050401

May 6, 1980—AUSTRIA—Linz Kepler University physics students who had formed the Committee for Peace and Disarmament claimed that two of them had built an atom bomb, which they would present to the government "in order to draw attention to the dangers of an uncontrolled construction and use of atom bombs." The next day, the students admitted to a hoax.

May 6, 1980—PORTUGAL—Rui Manuel Da Costa Rodrigues, 16, a Portuguese high school student armed with a pistol, hijacked a Portuguese airline TAP B-727 flying from Lisbon to Faro and diverted it to Madrid. He demanded a $10 million ransom and fuel to fly to Switzerland. He released 43 passengers upon landing. He had been flying in the first-class section, feigned illness, and rushed into the cockpit. The next day, he released all other passengers save the Swedish consular office who voluntarily remained on board. Swedes made up 70 percent of the passengers. The plane left Madrid with 7 of its original 11 crewmen and landed in Lisbon at 4:15 A.M. After a 7½ hour ordeal, the mentally deranged hijacker surrendered and was arrested by local police. 80050601

May 6, 1980—IRAN—An unidentified gunman forced Bahram Deghani

Tafti, 24, out of his car in central Tehran and shot him dead. Tafti worked as an interpreter for correspondents and was returning home from lecturing at a local college. His father, Bishop Deghani Tafti, headed Iran's four-thousand-strong Anglican community, but left Iran for Cyprus after escaping an assassination attempt in October. The previous week, the bishop's Scottish secretary, Jane Woodell, was critically wounded by gunshots in her Tehran home. The previous year, the bishop's English-born wife, Margaret, was shot in the hand when gunmen broke into their Isfahan home. The younger Tafti held dual Iranian-British citizenship. 80050602

May 6, 1980 — FRANCE — Paris police arrested five women in the Latin Quarter, including two members of the West German Red Army Faction: Ingrid Barabass, 28, and Sieglinde Hoffmann, 35, both of whom were armed. Police also found gasoline bombs, guns, a thousand rounds of ammunition, and false identity papers. 80050603

May 6, 1980 — FRANCE — The Militant Zionist Resistance Fighters bombed the Libyan embassy annex during the night, damaging doors and nearby cars and shattering windows but causing no injuries. 80050604

May 6, 1980 — CYPRUS — Nicosia's newspaper, O AGON, reported that police had foiled an attempt to free assassins of Yousef as-Sibai. 80050605

May 7, 1980 — UNITED STATES — Claiming that they were behind a Tripoli campaign to harass and assassinate Libyan exiled dissidents and students, the United States State Department ordered the expulsion of Nuri Ahmed Swedan, Ali Ramram, Mohammed Gamudi, and Abdulla Zbedi of the Libyan People's Bureau. The group initially refused to leave, claiming that they had registered as students and thus were technically not diplomats who could be expelled. Libya ultimately recalled the foursome on May 11, and they left for Paris.

May 7, 1980 — NORTHERN IRELAND — A bomb damaged a railway bridge fewer than one hundred yards from the Irish border, halting all cross-border train traffic.

May 7, 1980 — LEBANON — TEHRAN INTERNATIONAL SERVICE claimed that Iraqi elements shelled the Iranian embassy during the night.

May 8, 1980 — GREECE — The Revolutionary Popular Struggle (ELA) fire-bombed 20 cars belonging to foreign missions in Athens, Psikhiko, and Khalandhri. 80050801–20

May 8, 1980 — COLOMBIA — Ten armed members of the April 19 Movement

(M-19) took over the Colombian-American Center in Medellin. After giving anti–United States speeches, handing out literature, and painting the walls with slogans, the group left. No injuries were reported, and only a switchboard and telephone were damaged. 80050821

May 8, 1980 — COLOMBIA — Firebombs went off at the main entrance of the Venezuelan consulate in Maicao, causing minor damage. 80050822

May 9, 1980 — ITALY — "A bandit" claimed to have kidnapped a Swedish geologist from his Nuoro, Sardinia, summer home and demanded $480,000 ransom by October 7.

May 10, 1980 — FEDERAL REPUBLIC OF GERMANY — A Libyan businessman living in Cologne, who had served as a Libyan finance attache in Bonn, was shot four times by a Libyan who was quickly seized by passersby as he attempted to flee. The assailant claimed to work for a Libyan information bureau and said that the victim owed him a debt. Police believe the attack was tied to the recent Libyan calls for "physical liquidation of the enemies of the revolution abroad." The victim had received death threats in April.

On September 21, 1982, a federal grand jury in Alexandria indicted former Central Intelligence Agency employee Edwin P. Wilson on firearms violations charges involving the transport of guns to Libyan officials. One of these guns was the Smith and Wesson .357 used to assassinate the former finance attache. Bond was set at $20 million on the firearms charge, in addition to the $40 million fine already set against Wilson. 80051001

May 10, 1980 — ITALY — Libyan businessman Abdallah Mohamed Kazmi, 37, a foe of Qaddafi, was shot at noon after being lured to a Rome hotel for an appointment with two Libyans. The duo disappeared into a nearby station. Police rounded up 30 suspects, including Mohamed Fadi Kazmi, the victim's cousin, who had arrived in Rome from Tripoli several days previously to attempt to convince his relative to return to Libya. 80051002

May 10, 1980 — FRANCE — A bomb exploded at the Algerian consulate at Aubervilliers, destroying the door. The Charles Martel Club claimed credit. 80051003

May 11, 1980 — COLOMBIA — Gonzalo Sepulveda, 25, engineering student at the University of El Valle, and Ana Maria Rebelledo Collazo, 28, a University of Tolima student, were killed when an April 19 Movement (M-19) bomb they were setting at the United States consulate in Cali exploded prematurely. 80051101

May 12, 1980 — EL SALVADOR — United States Marines lobbed tear gas and drove through a roadblock to break a siege by 30 rightists around the Escalon home of United States ambassador Robert White. Later, unidentified gunmen fired heavy-caliber bullets and threw two bombs into the United States embassy, causing no injuries. 80051201

May 13, 1980 — ISRAEL — Police arrested Rabbi Meir Kahane, 46, founder of the Jewish Defense League, and supporter Karukh Green for planning to retaliate against Arabs for the attack on the West Bank two weeks earlier. The United States-born Kahane said he had nothing to do with the arms found on the roof of Yeshivat Hakotel, a hotel.

May 13, 1980 — GUATEMALA — Rightist gunmen paused from their coffee break in a Santa Lucia Cotzumalguapa cafe to fire 10 shots and kill Victor Voordeckers, a Belgian priest and active associate of the church-sponsored human rights group Justice and Peace Committee. 80051301

May 14, 1980 — ISRAEL — Israeli Defense Force troops killed three Palestine Liberation Front terrorists who had infiltrated from the Lebanese border and intended to take hostages in a house in Kibbutz Hanita in the western Galilee. The group was armed with Kalashnikov rifles, explosives, and leaflets and intended to demand being flown to Tehran.

May 14, 1980 — UNITED KINGDOM — A bomb injured five policemen when it went off at a southeast London police station at 4:20 A.M. after it was left on a counter by a man who had asked directions.

May 14, 1980 — GUINEA — Two grenades were thrown at Guinean president Sekou Toure, as he was attending celebrations at the People's Palace at Conakry marking the 33rd anniversary of the founding of the ruling Guinea Democratic party. One man from the Kankan region was killed, and 30 were injured.

May 14, 1980 — FRANCE — Corsican National Liberation Front gunmen fired submachine gun bursts and threw a bomb at police guarding the Iranian embassy, injuring four policemen. The group said the attack was directed at the police, not the embassy. The previous evening, the State Security Court had handed down to seven Corsican autonomists sentences ranging from three years in jail, suspended, to eight years of hard labor. 80051401

May 15, 1980 — IRAQ — Baghdad's IRAQI NEWS AGENCY reported that Iranian agent Hamid 'Aziz 'Ali admitted that the Ad-Da'wah Party intended to assassinate Iraqi officials and blow up buildings. He claimed he distributed arms smuggled from Iran and had forged identity cards.

May 15, 1980—COSTA RICA—Twenty-two unarmed Cuban refugees in an attempt to go to the United States seized an empty Pan American jetliner during its stopover on its flight to Miami. They relented when San Jose police threatened force to dislodge them. 80051501

May 15, 1980—UNITED KINGDOM/IRELAND—The Irish Republican Army (IRA) withdrew its warning against using the Belfast-to-Dublin railway line.

May 16, 1980—UNITED STATES—James Thomas Wright, 34, a black armed with a .22 caliber rifle, grabbed Scott Anderson, 17, and took over a Chalk's International Airlines Grumman Mallard amphibian, demanding to be flown to South Africa. The plane was being readied for its daily scheduled flights from Miami to the Bahamas and was otherwise unoccupied. Wright claimed he had been cheated out of three thousand dollars in welfare payments by Georgia officials. He surrendered and left the flying boat after eight hours of negotiations. 80051601

May 17, 1980—IRAN—Unidentified gunmen fired Kalashnikovs during the night at a house in Kerman where several of the United States embassy hostages were being held. Revolutionary Guards returned the fire.

May 17, 1980—UNITED STATES—Fifty pounds of arsenic-laced potatoes were stolen off a New York truck loading dock while on the way to a New England laboratory.

May 17, 1980—UNITED KINGDOM—One Iranian man was killed and another injured when a bomb they were assembling exploded in the room in London's Queen's Garden Hotel, across Hyde Park from the Iranian embassy. A third Iranian, uninjured, was arrested in the fourth-floor room. 80051701

May 17, 1980—ITALY—The Red Brigades threatened to attack the economic summit of Western leaders, which would include President Jimmy Carter, scheduled to be held in Venice in June. 80051702

May 18, 1980—LEBANON—A bomb exploded during the evening in the office of the Iraqi Land Transport Company in Beirut, causing some damage but no injuries. The Iraqis blamed Iran. 80051801

May 20, 1980—JAMAICA—Political arsonists were believed responsible for a fire in a Kingston home for the aged and orphans, which killed 171 women and injured 10 others.

May 20, 1980 — ITALY — Mohammed Fuad Buohjar, 55, a lumber trader from Tripoli, was found stabbed and strangled to death under a bed in a Rome boardinghouse. Libyan hit teams were believed responsible, leaving behind a note from the Libyan Revolutionary Committees in Rome. 80052001

May 21, 1980 — ITALY — Monsur Mezaroni Belgazem, 25, was arrested after firing three shots in a restaurant at Salem Mohammed Fezzani, 45, a Libyan restaurant owner and naturalized Italian citizen. All the shots missed. Belgazem said, "I was sent by the people to kill Fezzani." He was believed to be a member of Tripoli's antidissident hit squads. 80052101

May 21, 1980 — GREECE — Abu Bakr Abdel Rahman, 23, a furniture factory worker and Libyan critic of Qaddafi, was found in his apartment in a working-class Athens suburb, virtually decapitated by a sharp instrument. Libyan hit squads were believed responsible. 80052102

May 21, 1980 — KHMER REPUBLIC — Two Vietnamese guards were killed in an attack on the Vietnamese embassy. No casualties were reported in a later firefight outside the Soviet embassy. 80052103–04

May 22, 1980 — UNITED STATES — Marie Haydee Torres, 24, a Puerto Rican Armed Forces of National Liberation terrorist, was found guilty of planting a bomb that killed a man and injured nine others in a Manhattan building in 1977. She was sentenced to life in prison the next day.

May 23, 1980 — FRANCE — Saturnino Montero-Ruiz, 64, former mayor of Buenos Aires, was kidnapped in Paris by three men believed to be Argentine citizens who demanded a $1.2 million ransom. The trio tied him up, threw him into the trunk of his car in the underground parking garage of his apartment, and drove off. Six days later, Jorge Cedron, 38, his son-in-law, committed suicide at police headquarters while being interrogated about the kidnapping. Police do not believe he was involved in the abduction. The hostage was freed on June 3, although the ransom was not paid. 80052301

May 23, 1980 — BANGLADESH — Two bombs exploded at a political rally in an attempt to assassinate former president Dhandoker Mustaq Ahmed, whose Democratic League organized the meeting. The blasts killed 7 and wounded 40, including 8 journalists.

May 23, 1980 — TURKEY — Turkey's supreme military court threw out the death sentences passed by a military tribunal in October on four Palestinian terrorists who had seized the Egyptian embassy the previous July. A retrial in a civilian court was ordered.

May 23, 1980 — NETHERLANDS — Dutch police handed four Basque Fatherland and Liberty (ETA) terrorists over to Spanish police. The foursome had arrived in Amsterdam from South Yemen, where they reportedly received terrorist training with another eight ETA terrorists and a number of Palestine Liberation Organization (PLO) dissidents. One of the ETA members, Jose Manuel Arzallus, was implicated in the murder of a forest ranger, Ramirez Quintero, in Lazarza. 80052302

May 24, 1980 — FEDERAL REPUBLIC OF GERMANY — Bonn police arrested Keni Nusbah Khalafa, 15, and Khaled Tagiuri, 19, in their hotel after arrival from Tripoli. They were believed part of an antidissident Libyan hit team. 80052401

May 26, 1980 — KUWAIT — Two bombs exploded in the Kuwait city offices of Iran Air, causing damage but no injuries. 80052601

May 27, 1980 — GUATEMALA — Unknown gunmen shot and killed the acting secretary-general of the Guatemalan Bottling Company (a Coca-Cola distributor) while he was waiting for his bus near the plant. Two Guatemalan union members connected with the firm and the company's industrial relations manager were previously murdered in May.

May 28, 1980 — SWEDEN — Miro Baressich, a Croatian who killed Yugoslav ambassador to Sweden Vladimir Rolovic in 1971, was imprisoned after extradition by the United States. First imprisoned in Sweden in 1971, he was freed in 1972 as a result of terrorists demands after a Scandinavian Airlines hijacking and moved to Paraguay. Later he was believed by the Yugoslavs to be involved in terrorist activities in the United States.

May 29, 1980 — ASIA — Thailand, Indonesia, Malaysia, Singapore, and the Philippines agreed to form the Association of South East Asian Nations (ASEAN) Association of Chiefs of National Police, which would jointly combat regional terrorism, drug trafficking, hijacking, and smuggling.

May 29, 1980 — IRAN — Gunmen driving a Peugeot fired on a Mashhad house where some of the United States embassy hostages were being held.

May 29, 1980 — INDIA — The Bangladesh Biman office in Calcutta was attacked. 80052901

May 31, 1980 — BOLIVIA — A bomb went off at the Argentine embassy. 80053101

May 31, 1980 — TURKEY — The Revolutionary Way bombed the NATO Rod and Gun Club in Izmir, causing extensive damage but no injuries. 80053102

June 1980 — CANADA — Canadian authorities deported to Lebanon a Lebanese who bragged to friends that he had killed US Ambassador Francis E. Meloy, Jr., on June 16, 1976, in Beirut. Bassam al-Fark appeared before a Lebanese military judge on June 27.

June 1980 — FRANCE — An American Black Panther who hijacked a Western Airlines jet to Algeria on June 2, 1972, was given a five-year suspended sentence by French authorities who had refused a United States request for extradition. His accomplice, a woman who had left France, was expected to be tried in absentia.

June 1980 — SYRIA — Syria began a major crackdown against Moslem Brotherhood terrorists after a grenade was thrown at President Hafez al-Assad as he was escorting Niger's president Seyni Kountche to his airliner. A presidential bodyguard was killed smothering the blast. Also in June, BRITISH BROADCASTING CORPORATION (BBC) correspondent Tim Llewellyn was threatened after he filed stories considered unfriendly by Damascus. 80069901–02

June 1980 — CZECHOSLOVAKIA/GERMAN DEMOCRATIC REPUBLIC — Extra security precautions were taken at Prague Castle and the Niederschoenhausen Palace in Berlin after threats were made against Cypriot president Spyros Kyprianou. Iraqi terrorists were reportedly demanding the release of Samir Khadir and Zayid al-'Ali, two Iraqi Palestinians serving life sentences in Nicosia's central prison for the February 1978 murder of Yousef as-Sibai'i. 80069903–04

June 1980 — GUATEMALA — Leftist guerrillas were believed responsible for the murder of a West German tourist. 80069905

June 1980 — FRANCE — A bomb exploded at the Kuwaiti Airlines offices in Paris. Kuwait's newspaper AL-QABAS blamed the world's oil companies. 80069906

June 1980 — WESTERN SAHARA — Polisario guerrillas kidnapped 15 Portuguese fishermen on the trawler *Rio Vouga*. They were released in Algiers on July 24 following Portugal's "recognition of the rights of the people of the

Western Sahara to independence under the leadership of the Polisario Front." 80069907

June 1, 1980 — REPUBLIC OF SOUTH AFRICA — African National Congress guerrillas attempted to destroy three South African oil-from-coal plants with a daring coordinated series of midnight bombings. Blasts at the SA-SOL I plant at Sasolburg in the Orange Free State set ablaze four tanks, including one that contained butadiene, the raw material for synthetic rubber. A second series of two bombs went off at the SASOL II installation at Secunda in eastern Transvaal. At the Natraf refinery about three kilometers away from the SASOL plant, a guard was wounded in the shoulder from gunfire, which was followed by explosions at three storage tanks, a diesel tank, and two aviation fuel tanks. Damage was estimated at $7 million in the attacks on the highly sensitive South African energy facilities.

June 1, 1980 — UNITED KINGDOM — A 1½ pound bomb exploded at the Kuwait Oil Company's offices in London, blowing out the front of the building but causing no injuries. 80060101

June 1, 1980 — BELGIUM — A bomb was thrown at the Saudi embassy from a car passing by but caused no injuries. 80060102

June 2, 1980 — ISRAEL — The Sons of Zion claimed responsibility for bombs that went off in the cars of Nablus mayor Bassam Shaka and Ramallah mayor Karim Khalaf. Shaka lost both legs, Khalaf a foot, and an Israeli demolitions expert was blinded when a third bomb went off as he was attempting to defuse it in the car of a third West Bank Arab mayor.

June 2, 1980 — FEDERAL REPUBLIC OF GERMANY — Six men and a woman believed to be Red Army Faction members restrained the receptionist in the Amerika House in Frankfurt and broke windows and a glass display case and wrote slogans on the walls. Police speculated that a fire, which started before the incident, was a ruse to delay police response at the facility.

June 3, 1980 — SOUTH YEMEN — According to the Rand Corporation, "An Iraqi professor who was teaching at Aden University was murdered at his home. The ADEN NEWS AGENCY (ANA) reported that two Iraqis were seen leaving the scene in a car with diplomatic plates. ANA accused them of killing the professor and of taking refuge in the Iraqi Embassy. Troops and tanks surrounded the Embassy the next day and threatened to storm the building unless the suspects were handed over. On June 5, the Embassy was stormed and five Iraqis were taken into custody." 80060301

June 3, 1980 — UNITED STATES — The Croatian Freedom Fighters claimed credit for the 4:00 A.M. bombing of the Washington home of acting Yugoslav ambassador Vladimir Sindjelic. The letter demanded an investigation into the case of Miro Baresic, 29, who had been released from a Swedish prison in 1972 in response to demands by Croatian hijackers. Baresic worked for the Paraguayan embassy in Washington in 1977 and 1978 under an assumed name. In 1978, he was extradited by Paraguay to the United States with another Croatian terrorist, spent a year in a New York jail, and was deported to Sweden in May 1980. In April 1971, Baresic had pleaded guilty to the assassination of the Yugoslav ambassador to Sweden earlier that year.

The bomb was placed in a flower box at the front of Sindjelic's home and caused extensive damage but no injuries. 80060302

June 3, 1980 — UNITED STATES — A bomb exploded at 7:25 P.M. in the exhibit area at the base of the Statue of Liberty, damaging three historic items but causing no injuries. Among those who claimed credit for the blast were the Puerto Rican Armed Forces of National Liberation, Cuban Omega-7, Palestine Liberation Army, Jewish Defense League, neo-Nazi National Socialist Movement, and Croatian Freedom Fighters. 80060303

June 4, 1980 — LIBYA — 'Abd as-Salam Jallud, second in command of the Libyan Jamahiriyah's Revolutionary Command Council, categorized the recent series of assassinations of dissident Libyan exiles as acts of individuals. "Al-Qaddafi has never said to kill that one or that one."

June 4, 1980 — UNITED KINGDOM/IRELAND — Irish Republican Army (IRA) gunmen battled with British troops in a 40-minute cross-border firefight near Crossmaglen. No casualties were reported. 80060401

June 4, 1980 — KUWAIT — A hand grenade exploded at 3:30 P.M. at the Iranian embassy, blowing a hole in the wall of the ambassador's office's and breaking glass but causing no injuries. Police said the bomb was either tossed from a car or shot from a grenade launcher. Iran blamed Iraq for the attack. Police searched for a Dodge believed to have been the getaway car. 80060402

June 4, 1980 — ITALY — Two Arabic-speaking gunmen walked into the Iraqi embassy, yelled "Long live Khomeini," and fired at the embassy staff, killing one Iraqi employee and wounding another. The time bomb they left before escaping was defused with three minutes to spare. Embassy guards fired on the gunmen, wounding and capturing one while the other escaped. In Beirut, the Iraqi Mujahidin Islam claimed credit. The captive gunman claimed to be an Iraqi. Police later identified the dead man as the ambassador's chauffeur, while the wounded man was identified as an embassy telephone operator. A dark-skinned man was arrested at noon, an hour after the attack, and detained at the Tratevere police station. 80060403

June 4, 1980—SWAZILAND—Two houses in Manzini rented by the South African National Congress were bombed, killing two people and injuring several others. 80060404–05

June 5, 1980—ITALY—Police announced the arrest of two Argentine members of the Red Brigades: Rafael Eduardo Continanza, 24, a musician from Buenos Aires, and Licia Goldin, 34, of Sante Fe. 80060501

June 6, 1980—GREECE—Spanish Basque terrorists were believed responsible for planting a hand grenade that was found in the freight hold of a Transavia Dutch charter B-737 carrying tourists to Greece after it landed on the Island of Rhodes. 80060601

June 6, 1980—LEBANON—A gunman shot in the back Bernd Debusmann, 37, the REUTERS Beirut bureau chief, as he and his wife left a party. The West German national was reported in satisfactory condition at American University Hospital. The gunman used a silencer-equipped pistol. 80060602

June 7, 1980—ISRAEL—Israeli Army soldiers pursued four Palestinian guerrillas back into Jordan, where they killed two of the terrorists and wounded the other two. The foursome had attempted to cross the border near the Neot Hakikar kibbutz in the Arava region of the Negev Desert, about 10 miles south of Sodom below the Dead Sea. The terrorists carried Kalashnikov assault rifles, hand grenades, binoculars, and medical equipment.

June 7, 1980—LEBANON—At 2:00 A.M., a bomb exploded in the Iranian Airlines office in the As-Sana'i' quarter of western Beirut, causing damage but no injuries. 80060701

June 9, 1980—JAPAN—Police speculated that a letter sent to their homeland's comrades might presage a Japanese Red Army attack on the Venice summit meeting. The leftist PEOPLE'S DAILY printed the letter, dated May 10, but did not indicate from where it was mailed.

June 9, 1980—COLOMBIA—A Bolivian embassy guard fired on five youths who struck a secretary and attempted to enter the building. The guerrillas fled in a waiting automobile. Embassy officials denied rumors that a diplomat was wounded. 80060901

June 10, 1980—ISRAEL—Several leftist Knesset members and the editor of the leftist AL HAMISHMAR daily received phone calls saying, "This is Terror against Terror. You are traitors and you will be liquidated."

June 10, 1980—ISRAEL—A sniper shot and seriously wounded an Israeli border guard outside the walls of the Moslem quarter of the Old City of Jerusalem.

June 10, 1980—LIBYA—In a speech commemorating the 10th anniversary of the evacuation of the United States Wheelus Airbase, Muammar Qaddafi clarified his policy regarding the murders of exiled Libyan dissidents:

> After the revolutionary committees confirmed their capability to oper-ate anywhere in the world and that they were capable of striking with bravery and with a steel fist everywhere, and after the enemies of the revolution became convinced that the hotels of London, the brothels of Italy, and the winehouses of Beirut could not protect them from the verdict passed on them by the revolutionary committees—when all this has been asserted, I want to ask the revolutionary committees some-thing.
>
> But before stating these points I want to observe that hundreds of Libyans who fled from the popular revolution since its beginning and until now, have now returned following the ultimatum addressed to them. Others began preparing for their return and all the base attempts by imperialism and agents of imperialism in the region to lure some . . . to cooperate with them have failed. This spy who fled the country and lost his Libyan nationality for his treason is today a resi-dent of mental hospitals; he has totally collapsed. From the . . . hospi-tal in Egypt, he went to the military hospital in Kuwait, and then to the . . . mental hospital in Tunis.
>
> I want to ask the revolutionary committees to do the following: First, to stop now all the fedayeen operations in all parts of the world. Second, not to carry out the death sentences of the revolutionary com-mittees except on those who are convicted by a revolutionary court. Exceptions to this are those who are proved, in any way—even if this is not by a revolutionary court—to have had dealings with the following: the Egyptian, Israeli, and U.S. authorities. Those who deal with these authorities commit high treason and lose every protection and deserve death everywhere.

June 11, 1980—FEDERAL REPUBLIC OF GERMANY—In an anonymous let-ter to the FRANKFURTER RUNDSCHAU, an individual purporting to speak for the 2 June Movement claimed that the group had dissolved and that its members would join the Red Army Faction.

June 11, 1980—ITALY—A few hours after the midnight deadline set by Muammar Qaddafi for the return of dissident Libyan exiles to their homeland, Abdel Labi Shudi invoked Qaddafi's name twice and shot Mohammed Saad Biget, 33, in a dispute after they lunched together in a Rome suburb. Biget was grazed in the temple by a bullet meant to be fatal. His attacker was arrested. 80061101

June 11, 1980—ITALY—At 6:00 P.M., an unidentified gunman fired five shots that killed Mohammed Azavi Laderi, 56, in Milan's central train station. The dead Libyan was a wholesale industrial machinery dealer who lived in Bolzano. His assailant threw the pistol to the ground before escaping. On October 7, French police arrested Rashid Sa'id Muhammad 'Abdallah, 34, on an Italian warrant for the killing. He was also alleged to have headed "Islamic Courts" that were behind the murders in Europe of several opponents of the Libyan government. On October 9, Libya refused to allow 37 French nationals to leave the country. On October 28, 1983, a French appeals court ordered his release. The French government claimed it had not received an Italian extradition request within the legal time limit of 20 days after the arrest, although Rome officials said that the request had been sent through diplomatic channels on October 18. 'Abdallah was expected to board a flight to Tripoli. 80061102

June 11, 1980—UNITED STATES—A package exploded outside the former Iranian consulate in Beverly Hills, California, but caused no injuries. 80061103

June 12, 1980—GUATEMALA—According to the Rand Corporation,

> The President of a Nestle Company subsidiary in Guatemala was kidnapped by members of the Rebel Armed Forces (FAR), an armed leftist organization. Nestle's offices in Mexico said no negotiations should be held with a subversive organization for the release of company officials. However, on June 26, the Nestle Company and the FAR were negotiating. FAR demanded the publication in Guatemala and abroad of an FAR manifesto and the payment of a "war tax which will help promote the revolutionary struggle." In early September, the hostage was released, after three months of captivity. Guatemalan newspapers reported that the Swiss company paid $4.7 million for his release. In addition to the ransom, Nestle agreed to distribute 1 million cans of powdered milk among children in rural areas of Guatemala, and to publish the FAR manifesto in Bonn, Paris, and London.

80061201

June 12, 1980—FRANCE—The March 27–28 Direct Action Group placed a suitcase containing 4½ pounds of plastic explosives inside a luggage locker at Orly Airport. The bomb went off at 1:00 A.M., injuring seven Portuguese and North African cleaning workers and causing $250,000 damage. 80061202

June 13, 1980 — LIBYA — A firebomb was thrown during an attack by four demonstrators at the British embassy but caused no injuries and little damage. Hours earlier, the British had ordered the expulsion of Musa Kousa, the head of the Libyan diplomatic mission in London, who said he had approved of the latest threat to murder two Libyan dissident exiles. Kousa also warned that Libya might support the Irish Republican Army (IRA) in retaliation. 80061301

June 14, 1980 — FRANCE — Egyptian nuclear scientist Dr. Yahya al-Mashadd, on loan to the Iraqi nuclear program, was found murdered in Paris's Meridien Hotel. Israel denied involvement in the murder.

June 14, 1980 — LEBANON — The VOICE OF LEBANON reported that a member of the Libyan Revolutionary Committee was killed in the south, 20 kilometers from Tyre. No further details were given on the death of the Libyan, who had "secretly arrived in the Lebanese capital two weeks ago."

June 14, 1980 — GUYANA — Dr. Walter Rodney, leader of the opposition Working People's Alliance, was killed during the night when a bomb he was holding in his lap exploded in a car in which he was riding. His two brothers, Donald and Edward, were injured and apprehended, respectively. Police believed the trio planned to detonate the bomb at a prison where 17 members of the group were held for trying to overthrow Prime Minister Forbes Burnham's government.

June 14, 1980 — ITALY — A timed firebomb exploded outside the Jordanian Airlines office in Rome, causing limited damage and no injuries. 80061401

June 14, 1980 — GUATEMALA — Armed masked men set a Hardee's restaurant on fire but caused no injuries, having cleared the area of people. 80061402

June 14, 1980 — EL SALVADOR — Four gunmen fired submachine guns during Mass at a San Juan Nonualco church, 27 miles east of San Salvador, and killed Cosme Spessoto, 60, an Italian priest who had served in the country for 27 years. 80061403

June 16, 1980 — UNITED STATES — Arsonists caused five thousand dollars' damage at 2:40 A.M. to the Washington, D.C., building housing the IRAN TIMES weekly newspaper. 80061601

June 16, 1980 — ISRAEL — An Israeli Navy Debur class high-speed cruiser intercepted a Fatah boat attempting a daylight landing in preparation for a 5:00 A.M. attack on bathers near Achziv, between Rosh Hanaqura and Nahariva, south of the Lebanese border. When the cruiser's officers ordered the fiberglass speedboat to heave to, three Palestinian guerrillas fired a rocket-propelled grenade (RPG), which slightly injured an Israeli crewman. The Israelis returned the fire, killing all on board. Officers recovered an M-16 rifle, a grenade launcher, a pistol with silencer, and Fatah literature. 80061602

June 17, 1980 — ITALY — The VOICE OF PALESTINE (VOP) denied a report that Abu Iyad had visited Tunisia to help a planned Palestinian operation in Venice. The VOP said Abu Iyad was there to talk Muhammad al-Masmudi out of his hunger strike.

June 17, 1980 — LEBANON — A radio-triggered car bomb exploded outside a casino in the Moslem section of west Beirut, killing 2 people and injuring 17 others.

June 17, 1980 — BOLIVIA — The rightist Falange Socialista Boliviana ransacked and torched the United States consular office in Santa Cruz de la Sierra and looted and damaged the Bolivian-American Cultural Center. 80061701

June 19, 1980 — IRAQ — On the eve of the first election since the 1958 overthrow of the monarchy, three terrorists threw grenades and shot their way with automatic weapons into the grounds of the British embassy at 10:15 A.M. The terrorists, members of Al Dawa, a clandestine Iraqi fundamentalist Moslem organization, said they had launched a "punitive operation against a center of British and American plotters." With British approval, Iraqi security men stormed the building an hour later and killed the trio, who had been unable to penetrate the building and were in the garden. No other casualties were reported. There was an unconfirmed report that a fourth terrorist was arrested. 80061901

June 20, 1980 — COLOMBIA — Six young, heavily armed gunmen attempted to kidnap Kenneth H. Reysen, manager of the Cali branch of the Colgate-Palmolive Company, as he was leaving his home in the morning. Reysen's chauffeur, a watchman, and several policemen exchanged fire with the gunmen, one of whom was wounded. All six gunmen escaped after having wounded watchman Jose Ortiz Rodriguez. 80062001

June 20, 1980 — YUGOSLAVIA — The Chilean consulate in Belgrade was bombed in the early morning, causing serious damage but no injuries. 80062002

June 20, 1980—GUATEMALA—Revolutionary Armed Forces (FAR) gunmen machine-gunned to death Francisco Javier Rodas, personnel chief at the Coca-Cola Bottling Company, as he was driving in Guatemala City. 80062003

June 21, 1980—GUATEMALA—In an apparent act of retribution 10 hours after the Rodas killing, several armed men entered the Coca-Cola plant in Guatemala City and shot to death Rene Aldana Pellecer, discipline secretary of the company's labor union. The killers trucked the body several blocks away from the tightly guarded plant. 80062101

June 21, 1980—UNITED STATES—The Iranian Red June organization claimed credit for an attempt to illegally enter the New York home of the former Shah's nephew. Two armed intruders carrying a large box were stopped by a security guard. One of the men was shot by his own gun in the ensuing struggle. Both escaped from the town house, which was owned by the Shah's twin sister, who was to have been killed in the attack. 80062102

June 21, 1980—KUWAIT—Unidentified masked men attempted to enter the home of the Palestine Liberation Organization (PLO) office director, 'Awni Battah, but were repulsed by armed guards. 80062103

June 22, 1980—GREECE—Six persons linked to Palestinian guerrillas were sentenced to prison for plotting to attack the United States embassy and the ambassador's residence. 80062201

June 23, 1980—EL SALVADOR—The Armed Forces of National Resistance (FARN) threatened 215 people with death. Among those threatened were 3 former presidents, Fidel Sanchez Hernandez, Arturo Armando Molina, and Carlos Humberto Romero, and junta members Napoleon Duarte and Antonio Morales Ehrlich, who suffered a mild heart attack. Morales's older son was recently jailed for being a member of the People's Liberation Forces. His other son, 16, joined the group a week before this incident. In addition, FARN threatened foreign correspondents and the editors and reporters of the local PRENSA GRAFICA and DIARIO DE HOY. They warned that "whether they are in El Salvador, in Miami, or in Europe, persons condemned will be pursued so that the people have justice." 80062301

June 24, 1980—GUATEMALA—Heavily armed gunmen from the Central American Workers Revolutionary Party kidnapped two World Health Organization staffers working at night at the Institute of Nutrition for Central America. Carlos Tejada Valenzuela, a Guatemalan, served as the institute's director general, while United States citizen Richard W. Newman was its administrative director. The group left its demands at a fire station and called for publication of a manifesto in local and foreign media that criticized a "repressive plan unleashed by international imperialism, principally American." On August 14, the local news media reported that the United Nations had successfully negotiated in secret for the release of the duo, who left immediately for the United States. 80062401

June 25, 1980 — MOZAMBIQUE — The Ministry of the Interior announced the discovery of a group responsible for several bombings since 1978, including attacks on the Bulgarian agency at Marginal, the Mobil gas station at 1 May Square, the German Democratic Republic embassy, and the Soviet agency at Marginal.

June 25, 1980 — SPAIN — Basque Nation and Liberty (ETA) terrorists set off four bombs at resort areas in Alicante and Javea on the eastern Mediterranean coast during President Jimmy Carter's one-day state visit to Madrid. No injuries were reported. The ETA had threatened to disrupt Spain's tourist industry, as it had the previous year, by a bombing campaign. The group demanded the release of 19 ETA members in jail, the replacement of a prison warden who supervised ETA prisoners, and the absorption of Navarre Province into the existing three Basque provinces. The Basque-Spanish Battalion, a rightist group, threatened to retaliate by bombing northern Basque coastal beaches. 80062501–04

June 26, 1980 — NORTHERN IRELAND — The body of Miriam Daly, 45, a founding member of the leftist Irish Republican Socialist Party, was discovered sprawled on the floor of her West Belfast home. Her legs had been tied together and she had been shot several times in the head.

June 27, 1980 — ZIMBABWE — Minister of State Emerson Mnangagwa announced the foiling of a plan originated in South Africa to kill Zimbabwean leaders during independence celebrations. Police displayed traffic light control boxes loaded with radio-detonated plastic explosives, surface-to-air missiles, and limpet mines allegedly smuggled in by whites.

June 27, 1980 — ITALY — Transport Minister Rino Formica suggested that the Itavia DC-9 that crashed into the Tyrrhenian Sea southwest of Naples, killing 81 persons, was shot down by a missile. A government committee in 1982 claimed that a terrorist bomb was responsible, but later evidence — traces of T-4 explosive and bits of glass found in plane seats and at least two recovered bodies — suggested that the explosion took place outside of the plane. Various observers suggested that the Italian Air Force on NATO maneuvers, French Navy Super Etendards, or Libyan MIG-21s fired the missile.

June 30, 1980 — ARGENTINA — Roberto Atilio de Prinzio, 25, of Mar del Plata, pointed a pistol at stewardess Maria Alejandra Nicolas Mouzo, 19, and hijacked Aerolineas Argentina's flight 601, a B-737 flying 50 passengers and 7 crew members from Mar del Plata to Buenos Aires at 9:40 A.M. He demanded one hundred thousand dollars ransom and a flight to Mexico. He spoke to the passengers, criticizing the economic policy minister Martinez de Hoz. He threatened to kill all on board and commit suicide if his demands were not met but released 45 passengers upon landing. He survived one attempt to storm the plane when tear gas grenades were lobbed into the plane, but he surrendered at 10:30 P.M. Police claimed he was a member of Peronist Youth. 80063001

July 1980 — TURKEY — Eight individuals damaged part of the Turkish-Iraqi crude oil pipeline in July and September. On January 10, 1984, a Diyarbakir martial law court convicted six of the defendants and sentenced them to 12½ years in prison. The other two were sentenced to 5 years and 10 months for the Silopi, Mardin Province, attack. 80079901, 80099901

July 1980 — PHILIPPINES — Moslem rebels were believed responsible for the ransom kidnapping of a Pepsi-Cola sales team in the south. 80079902

July 1980 — CHILE — A Belgian-born priest who lived in Chile for 13 years was kidnapped by armed civilians but later released. The human rights activist was then ordered out of the country. 80079903

July 3, 1980 — LEBANON — An Iraqi commando group claimed responsibility for a bomb that slightly injured the Iraqi press attache in Beirut. 80070301

July 3, 1980 — ANGOLA — The National Union for the Total Independence of Angola was blamed for an attack in the Bata Farta region in which Dr. Laszlo Eosi, a Hungarian veterinary surgeon, was killed, an Angolan priest was injured, and a Vietnamese specialist was reported missing. 80070302

July 5, 1980 — JAMAICA — The home of United States embassy first secretary Richard Kinsman was bombed and machine-gunned during the night, two days after he had been publicly accused of being the Central Intelligence Agency chief of station. No injuries were reported. 80070501

July 7, 1980 — MALTA — A bomb destroyed the Valletta office of Libyan Arab Airlines in the early morning. Elsewhere, the Libyan Arab Cultural Office was damaged and some documents were burned. No injuries were reported. 80070701–02

July 8, 1980 — UNITED STATES — Cathlyn Platt Wilkerson, 35, a founder of the Weather Underground, surrendered to police after being hunted for 10 years. On July 18, she pleaded guilty to a charge of possession of dynamite. In return, the district attorney dropped a charge of criminally negligent homicide stemming from the 1970 explosion of a bomb factory in her father's Greenwich Village town house that killed three other Weathermen.

July 8, 1980 — CANADA — A suspect in the 1970 kidnapping of James Cross, senior United Kingdom trade commissioner in Quebec, was arrested and charged with conspiracy to kidnap, extortion, and forcible detention.

July 8, 1980 — FRANCE — Police arrested seven members of the Italian terrorist group Front Line, which is ideologically allied with the Red Brigades. The group was sought for a series of assaults, robberies, and kidnappings in northern Italy. 80070801

July 8, 1980 — LEBANON — Unknown individuals attempted to assassinate the Iraqi consul and another member of the Iraqi embassy staff during the night. 80070802

July 9, 1980 — LEBANON — Gunmen in a speeding automobile shot and killed Ibrahim Khazaal, a member of the Iraqi embassy staff, and wounded three other Iraqis (embassy staff and students) as they walked near Lebanese University. A Lebanese female student was also reported wounded in an attack blamed on the Iranians. The shooting came a week after unidentified gunmen killed two Iranian students near the campus. 80070901

July 10, 1980 — GUATEMALA — Spanish priest Fausto Villanueva was shot and killed in the parochial house in the town of Joyabaj in El Quiche Province during the night. 80071001

July 11, 1980 — COLOMBIA — Police confiscated a rifle, a shotgun, two revolvers, and a large quantity of ammunition from three United States citizens without identity documents in the Taganga tourist resort. They were presumed to have entered the country illegally. The roundup was part of an arms control drive in an attempt to counter violence in La Guajira and Magdalena. 80071101

July 11, 1980 — UNITED STATES — Glenn Tripp, 17, claiming to have a bomb, seized a Northwest Airlines DC-727 at Seattle-Tacoma International Airport. He released all of the passengers and crew except for two pilots. Claiming to be a professional assassin, he demanded that his boss be killed. He also called for between one hundred thousand and six hundred thousand dollars, two parachutes, and a single-engine Cessna. His demands were later reduced to the plane, one parachute, and one hundred thousand dollars. He was taken into custody without injury 10 hours after the siege began. 80071102

July 11, 1980 — EL SALVADOR — The Committee of Rural Dwellers of the Marxist 28 February Popular League (LP-28) led 115 illiterate peasants, including 58 children and 25 women, in an occupation of the Costa Rican embassy. A Salvadoran policeman was killed in the initial assault. No hostages were held in the incident, which occurred after a wave of political assassinations in which 22 persons were killed in 24 hours. The group said it wanted to present its demands for ending repression to a group of ambassadors from Mexico, Venezuela, Italy, Spain, and Panama. From the ambassadors the LP-28 requested mediation and protection. The group was supposedly led by 5 young peasants and 2 alleged students within the LP-28, one of whom was armed with a .45 caliber pistol. The group demanded an end to violence in the rural areas, an international human rights commission to conduct an on-site investigation of government abuses, asylum in Costa Rica, Venezuela, Panama, Mexico, or the United States, and release of People's Revolutionary Bloc (BPR) leaders captured in the southern highway at the entrance of the San Francisco neighborhood on July 3: Raul (last name unknown), secretary of information of the BPR National Executive directorate; Carlos Gonzalez, secretary of organization of the June 21 National Association of Salvadoran Teachers; and Manuel Pena, secretary-general of the Union of Slum Dwellers. The Red Cross was permitted to deliver food and medicine. On July 14, LP-28 leader Jose Leoncio Pichinte reported that Costa Rica had offered asylum. On July 16, a young girl died from dehydration in the cramped and unsanitary conditions in the small embassy. On July 17, 112 more peasants arrived at the embassy. The next day, despairing of the impasse, Costa Rica gave up its claim to the embassy, and said that it would relocate. Costa Rica sent a plane to airlift those who were offered asylum, but as of July 21, when 10 more peasants entered the crowded former embassy, no one had left. 80071103

July 12, 1980 — KUWAIT — Fatah bombs killed two people at the newspaper AL RAI AL AAM. On November 15, a Kuwaiti court sentenced to death Rauhi Ibrahim Abdul-Latif Nimr, 23, a Jordanian who worked as a guard at the Fatah offices. Wail Abdul-Latif Hassan, 21, a Jordanian mechanic, was sentenced to life imprisonment at hard labor. Jihad Amin, 36, a Jordanian and Fatah official, was acquitted. The trio were charged with murder and possession of explosives. 80071201

July 12, 1980 — IRAN — Following two telephoned threats that three bombs had been planted in the Austrian embassy, Tehran police discovered and defused two bombs. 80071202

July 12, 1980 — UNITED STATES — No injuries were reported when bottles filled with gasoline were hurled through windows and on the roof of a South Salt Lake City duplex housing two Vietnamese families, causing three thousand dollars' damage. 80071203

July 12, 1980 — PHILIPPINES — A Philippine jetliner was hijacked shortly after takeoff from Manila by a man who claimed to have a bomb. He said he would release most of the 124 passengers in Cebu but would hold all Americans for $6 million and a flight to Libya. Manila authorities stormed the plane and arrested him after determining that he was unarmed. 80071204

July 15, 1980 — ISRAEL — The Arab Liberation Front's Group of Struggler 'Abdallah 'Ayyash (who is imprisoned in Nafhah prison in Beersheba) claimed credit for a bungled assassination attempt against Ariel Sharon, the Israeli agriculture minister. Security guards arrested the attackers after a gun battle, which the Palestinians claimed occurred on Sharon's farm.

July 15, 1980 — SWEDEN — The Israeli press reported the foiling of an Arab Liberation Front/Ahmad Jibril group/Popular Front for the Liberation of Palestine (PFLP)–Haddad/PFLP-Habash plot to send young Swedish men and women to Copenhagen to take over a hotel and seize El Al crew members as hostages. 80071501

July 16, 1980 — KUWAIT — Palestine Liberation Organization (PLO) political department chief Faruq Qaddumi denied reports that the PLO had sent a youth to kill President Jimmy Carter.

July 17, 1980 — AUSTRIA — The Austrian Airlines flight from Vienna to Tel Aviv landed in Athens after receiving a bomb threat. No bomb was found. 80071701

July 17, 1980 — LEBANON — A bomb exploded in the Iranian Airlines offices in the As-Sanayi' quarter of western Beirut at 8:00 P.M., causing material damages. 80071702

July 17, 1980 — EL SALVADOR — A powerful bomb exploded at 11:00 P.M. at the Nicaraguan embassy, causing extensive damage but no injuries. 80071703

July 17, 1980 — FRANCE — The Paris offices of Iran Air on the Champs Elysees were bombed at 4:30 A.M. Pictures of the deposed Shah were plastered on the windows. 80071704

July 17, 1980 — FRANCE — The Guards of Islam group claimed credit for the attempted assassination of Shahpour Bakhtiar, 65, the Shah's last prime minister. The attack began at 8:25 A.M. on the corner of Boulevard Bineau and Boulevard d'Inkermann in Neuilly-sur-seine, west of Paris. The four men and one woman passed the guard of Bakhtiar's home by claiming to be reporters sent to interview Bakhtiar. They had cameras around their necks, and one flashed a press pass for the French communist newspaper L'HU-MANITE.

Once inside, the group went to the third floor, where Bakhtiar's sister had her apartment. They began knocking on doors at random looking for Bakhtiar. A neighboring woman, Yvonne Stein, 45, opened her door to complain of the racket and was shot dead with machine guns and pistols by the terrorists. A person inside Bakhtiar's apartment opened the chained door a crack but quickly slammed it as the terrorists fired seven shots at the heavily armored door. Police opened fire on the terrorists as they fled. One policeman who ran up the stairs, Jean-Michel Jamme, 25, was killed. Three other people — another woman tenant and two policemen, including Philippe Jourdain, 25 — were wounded, as were two of the terrorists. Three of the terrorists were apprehended on the spot, and the other two were captured the next day. Police found an apparent getaway car parked nearby, whose trunk contained a large sum of money, passports, ammunition, and a pistol silencer.

The captured trio of men claimed to be in their 20s, and gave their nationalities as Syrian, Lebanese, and Palestinian. They claimed that the wounded Palestinian, Abu Mazem, was their leader and that the other two were Muhammad Lu'ay and Fawzi. Later, AGENCE FRANCE-PRESSE reported that Abu Mazem claimed to be Anis Naqqash, 29, and that Yasir Arafat had ordered the attack. Naqqash said he was a Fatah intelligence officer living in Lebanon who had carried out several missions in Israel and overseas. He claimed to have arrived in France on July 3 and rented the Latin Quarter apartment where the other two commandos were arrested. The Palestine Liberation Organization denied that their Abu Mazin (Mahmud 'Abbas), head of the Syrian branch of Fatah, was involved. The squad later claimed that their names were Fatah Shaddini, Salad-Din al-Q'arah, Muhammad 'Ubayd, and Muhammad Fawzi.

Iranian Ayatollah Sadegh Khalkhali, who had ordered several assassinations of exiled Iranians, claimed to know nothing of the attack or the Guards of Islam. However, Jalaladin Farsi, a prominent member of the Islamic Republican party, said that Khalkhali had foreknowledge and approved of the operation. RADIO IRAN claimed that Libyan leader Qaddafi and European leftists had aided the terrorists.

On March 10, 1982, a Nanterre jury sentenced four of the group, under the names Anis Naccache, Nejad Tabrizi, Faouzi Satari, and Salaheddine Kaara, to life imprisonment; and one, Mohammed Henab, to 20 years in prison. 80071705

July 18, 1980—HONDURAS—A bomb exploded in the Nicaraguan embassy, causing no injuries and minor damage. 80071801

July 18, 1980—LEBANON—Unidentified gunmen armed with explosives exchanged fire with guards at the Iraqi cultural center on Antoine al-Jamayyil street in western Beirut. 80071802

July 19, 1980—UNITED KINGDOM—Welsh demonstrators hurled smoke bombs at a Swansea building where Prime Minister Margaret Thatcher was about to speak.

July 19, 1980—TURKEY—Four extremist leftist gunmen escaped in a car after killing former Turkish premier Nihat Erim at his vacation home near Istanbul.

July 19, 1980—FRANCE—Firebombs were thrown during the night at the Afghan embassy. 80071901

July 19, 1980—SWEDEN—Cairo newspapers reported that Swedish authorities had foiled a Palestinian plot to kidnap Egyptian first lady Jihan as-Sadat while she participated in the world conference of women. The group would demand the return of the Shah to Iran. 80071902

July 19, 1980—IRAN—The Guard Corps of Islam group, which claimed credit for the attempted assassination in France of Shahpour Bakhtiar, warned the French that "unless you free our brothers and deport Bakhtiar from France, we will put your interests in the Middle East in jeopardy." 80071903

July 20, 1980—HONDURAS—Gunmen machine-gunned the Nicaraguan consulate in Danli, just missing Consul Fabio Ponce. 80072001

July 21, 1980—LEBANON—A gas-filled balloon carrying Palestinian guerrillas with automatic weapons, antitank grenades, and plastic explosives was apparently shot down by Christian militiamen as it made its way for the Israeli border near Majdel Islim, about seven miles west of the Israeli town of Kiryat Shemona.

July 21, 1980—FEDERAL REPUBLIC OF GERMANY—'Isam al-'Attar, leader of the Moslem Brotherhood branch in Europe, escaped an assassination attempt in Aachen. 80072101

July 21, 1980 — FRANCE — Former Syrian premier Salah Eddin Bitar, 68, the most prominent Syrian opposition leader in western Europe, was fatally shot in the neck, as he was unlocking his office near L'Arch, by a gunman armed with a silenced pistol. Witnesses saw a man running from the building soon after the noontime shooting. Syrian agents were suspected. Bitar edited the ARAB RENAISSANCE journal. 80072102

July 21, 1980 — HONDURAS — The Patriotic Anticommunist Front (FREPA) claimed credit for throwing a bomb at the Nicaraguan embassy, which caused no damage or injuries. 80072103

July 21, 1980 — EL SALVADOR — The Patriotic Anticommunist Front (FREPA) claimed credit for an attack on the Nicaraguan embassy. 80072104

July 21, 1980 — EL SALVADOR — Police reported that they had foiled an attempt to seize the Italian embassy by 131 peasants led by 6 leaders of the 28 February People's Leagues. 80072105

July 22, 1980 — BRAZIL — Police inspectors Orandir Potassi Lucas (Didi Pedalada) and Joao Augusto da Rosa (Irno) were sentenced to six months imprisonment for the kidnapping of Uruguayan citizens Lilian Celiberti and Universindo Diaz. Two other policemen, Commissioner Pedro Seelig and Inspector Janito Kepler, were released for lack of evidence. 80072201

July 22, 1980 — UNITED STATES — Silvio Mesa Cabrera, a Cuban claiming to be a Puerto Rican, grabbed a stewardess, held her arms behind her back, and forced her into the cockpit, where he diverted the Chicago–Miami–San Juan Delta L-1011 flight with 142 passengers and 14 crew members to Cuba. The hijacker said he had personal problems and wanted to go to Havana, but the Spanish-speaking, jeans-clad male settled for Camaguey. The pilot had to pass the hat among the passengers to pay the thousand-dollar landing fee demanded by the Cubans. 80072202

July 22, 1980 — UNITED STATES — A man posing as a postman with two special delivery packages fired three shots into Ali Akbar Tabatabai, 49, former press attache of the Shah's Iranian embassy, killing him. Tabatabai, who had received numerous death threats over the telephone, was the head of the Iran Freedom Foundation, an anti-Khomeini exile group in the United States. He had obtained political asylum from the United States in May 1979, then began the foundation in his Bethesda home the next month. It was originally believed that the gunman and two other individuals kidnapped a mailman shortly before noon and held him while his mail van was used.

The suspected gunman, Daoud Salahuddin (David Belfield), 29, had worked as a security guard at the Iranian embassy, and later in the Iranian Interests Section of the Algerian embassy. After the assassination, he apparently flew to New York City, was driven to Montreal, then fled to Geneva and on to Iran. He was charged with a federal civil rights violation and a state charge of murder. He had been previously detained on November 4, 1979 — the day that the United States embassy in Tehran was seized — after taking over the Statue of Liberty in an anti-Shah rally.

Ahmed Rauf (Horace Butler), a Washington carpenter accused of aiding in the assassination, was arraigned on December 16, 1980, in District of Columbia Superior Court on charges of conspiracy within the District to commit a crime outside the District. He was held on $50,000 bond.

On January 3, 1981, the Federal Bureau of Investigation said Musa Abdul Majid (Derrick Pritchett), 26, a Takoma Park cabdriver, furnished the gun (described by various sources as either a 9 mm Luger or a Walther P-38) and ammunition for the killing. Pritchett apparently had fled the country. United States District Court judge Oren R. Lewis sentenced him to consecutive three-year terms on each of three counts of fraudulent weapons purchases.

On May 27, 1981, Tyrone Anthony Frazier, 31, a United States mailman, was sentenced to two years probation after pleading guilty to taking a five hundred dollar bribe for the use of his van. Frazier said he was given two hundred dollars down and a promise of three hundred dollars later.

On July 16, 1981, Ahmed Rauf, 36, was indicted for helping to obtain the truck and dispose of the murder weapon. Also indicted were Ali Abdul-Mani (Lee Curtis Manning), 26, who rented the vehicle used for the escape, and William Cafee, Jr., (Kalid), 34, who wiped the car clean of fingerprints and abandoned it near Tabatabai's home. Cafee was already in the District of Columbia corrections system for holding up a Washington liquor store after the shooting. Named as an unindicted coconspirator was Abu Bakr Zaid Sharriff (Al Fletcher Hunter), 27, of Forestville. The indicted foursome were members of the Islamic Guerrillas in America, a small organization with ties to black American Moslems.

On December 3, 1981, a District of Columbia Superior Court jury found Ahmed Rauf and Ali Abdul-Mani guilty in the case. On February 18, 1982, Judge Fred B. Ugast sentenced Rauf to serve 8 to 80 years in prison (with a minimum of 6 years) for being an accessory after the fact to the murder and to serve at least 2 years for grand larceny of the vehicle. He sentenced Manning to serve 6¼ to 25 years on related charges. Abdul-Mani received 5 to 18 years for making a false stolen car report as part of the cover-up a week after the assassination. He lent the rental car to Salahuddin, who used it to escape after the shooting. Abdul-Mani was also sentenced to 15 months to 7 years for lying to a grand jury when he testified that he had never lent the car to Salahuddin. 80072203

July 23, 1980—LEBANON—Riad Taha, 53, president of the Lebanese Publishers Association for the previous 13 years, was machine-gunned to death by four assailants during the day. His chauffeur raced through Beirut's Raouche section in an evasive maneuver, but the car was riddled in front of the Hotel Continental. Several other newsmen had been killed, kidnapped, or threatened in recent years.

July 23, 1980—IRAN—Forqan, an Iranian terrorist group, claimed credit for setting off three bombs in the underground parking garage of Tehran's four-story shopping mall, killing 6 persons and injuring 100.

July 23, 1980—MEXICO—Irate sports fans threatened the Soviet embassy with revenge for the theft of a gold medal from Mexican diver Carlos Giron and the disqualification of Mexican walker Daniel Bautista. Over 250 policemen were deployed.

July 23, 1980—HONDURAS—Three sticks of dynamite were found in the Nicaraguan embassy. 80072301

July 23, 1980—DENMARK—A Mrs. Pak, member of the South Korean delegation to the United Nations World Women's Congress in Copenhagen, reported that a man identifying himself as Yi Myong-su, a Japanese tae kwon do instructor, attempted to persuade her to get into a car with a Swedish license plate at noon. He was later identified as Kim Yong-tu, a North Korean and naturalized Swedish citizen, leader of the Choson Minju Chonson group with North Korean contacts. He was believed involved in the 1979 abduction of a 30-year-old South Korean high school teacher in Oslo, Norway. 80072302

July 23, 1980—UNITED STATES—Jeffrey Ira Cohen, 33, of Tennessee, was arrested by Secret Service police after he placed explosives at the French embassy. He was charged with assault with intent to commit murder and with possession of an unregistered 30.06 semiautomatic rifle. 80072303

July 24, 1980—ZIMBABWE—Forty shots were fired at the home of an aide to Joshua Nkomo, Patriotic Front leader, during the night.

July 24, 1980—LEBANON—Two Palestinian brothers with Jordanian passports, armed with guns, hand grenades, and explosives, hijacked a Kuwait Airlines B-737 flying 80 persons from Beirut to Kuwait. The duo demanded between $750,000 and $2.7 million they claimed was owed them by a Kuwaiti businessman. They released 37 women and children in Kuwait, then flew on to Bahrain, back to Kuwait, on to Abadan (where they freed 2 ill passengers), and back to Kuwait. They released several more women and a

40-day-old baby as the plane's temperature reached 118° F. The British pilot, copilot, and flight engineer escaped after they were allowed to deplane. The rest of the crew was forced back into the plane while the hijackers fired at the escaping hostages. After police surrounded the plane, the hijackers surrendered to Anwi Battache, the Palestine Liberation Organization's local representative. No injuries were reported. Yusuf Miflih and 'Uthman 'Abd al-Karim were imprisoned. 80072401

July 25, 1980—FEDERAL REPUBLIC OF GERMANY—Red Army Faction (RAF) members Juliane Plambeck and Wolfgang Beer died in a car crash near Stuttgart. Police believed Inge Viett was following in a red BMW. The RAF sent a letter to Hamburg police in which it denied that it was planning to assassinate Helmut Schmidt, federal prosecutor-general Kurt Rebmann, or Baden-Wuerttemberg minister-president Lothat Spaeth.

Bundeskriminalamt members believed that the RAF was planning to set a booby trap and blow up Helmut Schmidt's passing car by remote control, based on evidence found in the Paris apartment of five alleged German female terrorists.

July 25, 1980—ITALY—The Chaka II group claimed credit for kidnapping three West German teenaged girls from their Florence vacation home. Letters received by Dieter Kronzucker, journalist father of two of the girls, demanded $6 million ransom for funding a proletarian revolution on the island of Sardinia, and $10,000 for each Sardinian imprisoned in Tuscany. The group, to which the three to four kidnappers may have belonged, also threatened to kidnap five more West German children in Tuscany. The trio was released unharmed. 80072501

July 25, 1980—BELGIUM—Fatah–Revolutionary Council (Abu Nidal's group) claimed credit for assassinating Yosef Halahi, the Israeli commercial attache, whom the group claimed was an intelligence operative. 80072502

July 27, 1980—LEBANON—Kuwait Airways officials denied a report by Abu Dhabi's AL-ITTIHAD newspaper that three Arab gunmen at 5:00 P.M. attempted to hijack a Kuwaiti Airways plane with weapons hidden in their luggage. The paper reported that the trio died in a hand grenade and automatic weapons battle. It suggested that they wanted to bargain for the release of the duo that had hijacked a Kuwaiti plane three days earlier.

July 27, 1980—WEST BERLIN—A car with United States plates in the United States sector was firebombed during the night. A message nearby with a drawing of a skull read, "Amis get out of West Berlin. Tolerable here for the pigs until 1984. Peng." 80072701

July 27, 1980 — BELGIUM — Naser Said Abdel Wahib, who carried a Moroccan identity document but was believed to be Lebanese, threw two hand grenades into a crowd of 40 Jews, most of them teenagers waiting to take a bus to summer camp from the Antwerp Agoudath Israel cultural center to the Ardennes. David Kuhan, 15, of Paris, was killed, and 20 others, including children and adults from Austria, the United Kingdom, France, and the Netherlands, were injured. After a chase by witnesses, police arrested Wahib, who was carrying a pistol and several magazines of ammunition. On August 1, an Antwerp court remanded him to custody, along with Nihad Declas, a Tunisian student who was arrested a few days later. Declas claimed he was to throw a grenade at passengers arriving at Brussels' Zavantem Airport on El Al, coinciding with the attack on the children. The Popular Front for the Liberation of Palestine (PFLP) and Fatah–Revolutionary Council (Abu Nidal's group) claimed credit. 80072702

July 27, 1980 — ABU DHABI — A bomb went off at 7:00 P.M. in the Beirut home of Adnam Hussein, the Iraqi press attache, wounding him, killing Hisan Mohammed (the embassy's second secretary), injuring embassy employee Hikmat Abdul Razzaq Haj, and wounding another 13 passersby. The Martyr Araef Basri Commando claimed the attack was a reprisal for the Iraqi execution of their namesake, but the Iraqi government blamed Iran for the attack. 80072703

July 28, 1980 — AFGHANISTAN — A lone assassin fired a single shot into the Volga of a Russian brigadier general working as a senior adviser at the Ministry of the Interior, killing him at 7:00 A.M. near his residence at Karte Char. The assassin, believed to be an Afghan rebel, escaped in a Volkswagen that had rammed the Soviet's car.

July 28, 1980 — LEBANON — Two pro-Iranian underground Shiite organizations — the Mojahedin Iraq Movement and the Revolutionaries of Mohammed Baqir as-Sadr (a clergyman executed by the Iraqis earlier in the year for involvement in the Al-Dawa organization, which attempted to overthrow the regime of Ayatollah Khomeini) claimed credit for the killing, by unknown gunmen, of pro-Iraqi Shiite politician Moussa Sheib, 42, and his driver in Beirut.

July 28, 1980 — UNITED STATES — A bomb exploded in the Los Angeles home of the son of the mayor of Kaohsiung, Taiwan, killing the visiting brother-in-law of the mayor. The victim apparently moved the booby-trapped box as he entered the front door. The bomb was similar to those previously used by the Taiwanese Independence Movement against Taiwanese offices. 80072801

July 28, 1980 — LIBYA — The Lebanese Amal organization claimed credit for sending an explosives-packed suitcase on a Middle East Airlines flight from Beirut to Baninah Airport, Benghazi, where it exploded in the passenger hall, causing no injuries. 80072802

July 29, 1980 — FRANCE — According to the Rand Corporation, two Armenian Secret Army for the Liberation of Armenian gunmen fired on the Turkish consulate in Lyons, killing two people and seriously wounding two others. 80072901

July 30, 1980 — LEBANON — TEHRAN DOMESTIC SERVICE claimed that gunmen fired various weapons from the Iraqi military attache's office from 10:00 P.M. to 3:00 A.M. at the Iranian embassy. 80073001

July 30, 1980 — AUSTRIA — A bomb exploded at 1:00 P.M. five hundred meters from the Iranian embassy, injuring eight people and shattering the windows of the embassies of West Germany, the USSR, the United Kingdom, and Switzerland. The bomber, an Iraqi Kurd who was previously photographed entering the car of an Iraqi embassy official, was slightly injured. He was arrested after a brief struggle. He claimed that he was given a briefcase by Sami Hanna Attalah, Iraqi second secretary, and ordered to bring it to the Iranian embassy. The Kurd had second thoughts and decided to call police, but the bomb exploded as soon as he put the briefcase down. The Austrians expelled two Iraqi diplomats. On August 1, Iraq expelled Austrian embassy secretary Dr. Josef Litschauer, who was followed three days later by Erich Klaus, Austrian embassy administrative secretary. 80073002

July 31, 1980 — COLOMBIA — Colombia ratified the July 1974 air/sea hijacking agreement with Cuba.

July 31, 1980 — UGANDA — Armed men stopped an American United Nations envoy's car as she was returning to her Entebbe hotel from Kampala, where she was arranging food distribution convoys. They stole her car but left her unharmed.

July 31, 1980 — GREECE — Two gunmen from the Armenian Secret Army for the Liberation of Armenia (ASALA) shot and killed Turkish embassy administrative attache Galip Ozmen and his daughter Neslihan, 19, and seriously wounded his wife and another woman as they sat in a parked car outside their apartment in the Athens suburb of Pangrati. Athens police questioned 150 persons. On August 2, the ASALA warned AGENCE FRANCE-PRESSE, "To the Greek Government — we remind you that all your diplomats are within our reach of fire. Therefore if anything happens to any Armenian in Athens, your diplomats will be our next targets." BAY-RAK RADIO accused Greek Cypriots of the murder, a charge that was denied by the government. 80073101

July 31, 1980 — UNITED STATES — A black man in a jogging suit shot and wounded a 19-year-old Iranian student outside the Los Angeles home of an anti-Khomeini dissident organization leader. The 10:15 P.M. shooting was preceded by telephoned threats. Five shots were fired in front of the home of Cambyse Shah-Rais. 80073102

July 31, 1980 — TURKEY — Several youths threw two Molotov cocktails into the apartment of United States Air Force S. Sgt. Ruminer in Izmir, causing injury to him and igniting a curtain. The sergeant sustained burns on 22 percent of his body. 80073103

August 1980 — TURKEY — One of the terrorists who killed four Americans in Istanbul on December 14, 1979, escaped from prison.

August 1, 1980 — WEST BERLIN — After chasing a Mercedes-Benz with East Berlin diplomatic license plate CD21-09, registered to the Iraqi embassy in East Berlin, West Berlin police arrested two Iraqi embassy employees who had given a suitcase to a 30-year-old Kurd, who was to detonate the en-closed explosives at the congress of the Association of Kurdish Students Abroad. The man claimed he received DM 500 a month from the Iraqis and was promised DM 3,500 for the bombing. Although criminal charges were filed, on September 17 the Germans deported without criminal proceedings First Secretary Khalid Jabir and a member of the Iraqi embassy's technical staff, Hajj 'Ali Mahmud. 80080101

August 2, 1980 — KUWAIT — A Kuwaiti newspaper reported a Palestinian threat to attack the interests of any state that moved its embassy in Israel from Tel Aviv to Jerusalem. 80080201

August 2, 1980 — ITALY — A bomb believed containing two hundred pounds of TNT exploded in the crowded waiting rooms and restaurant of Bo-logna's main rail station, killing 84 and injuring 189. Although most of the victims of the 10:25 A.M. blast were Italians, the bodies of a Japanese man and a Frenchwoman were also found in the rubble. Two American brothers from Provo, Utah, were injured: Jeff Davis, 19, suffered leg wounds, and William S. Davis, 22, received a kidney wound. Callers claimed the Red Brigades were responsible, but later calls denied the charge. The Organized Communist Movements also denied credit. Another caller said the neofas-cist Armed Revolutionary Nuclei set the bomb in retaliation for a Bologna judge's decision that morning to try 8 persons for the August 4, 1974, bombing of a passenger train inside a tunnel between Bologna and Florence, which killed 12 and injured 35. Police suggested that the crash of the Italian domestic airlines DC-9 in the Tyrhenian Sea June 27 may have been caused by a rightist bomb, as was claimed in the same phone call. All 81 on board died.

On August 4, French police arrested Marco Affatigato, 24, an Italian neofascist. He was extradited on September 5. He had been wanted by Rome since 1978 and had been sentenced in absentia the previous month by a Pisa court to 3½ years for helping Mario Tuti, one of the train bombers, escape from prison. (Tuti was recaptured.)

On August 16, an arrest warrant was issued against neo-Nazi Luca de Orazi, 17, who was charged with subversion. On August 29, police raids in Rome and two other cities netted a dozen suspects. Warrants for 16 others were issued. On October 11, 1982, Bolivia expelled to Italy Pier Luigi Tagliari.

On February 17, 1983, Spain arrested 7 people suspected of being involved in the Bologna bombing and the bombing of a Paris synagogue.

On December 12, 1985, Bologna magistrates issued warrants for 16 people, including former chiefs of the Italian Intelligence and Military Security Service (SISMI) (Gen. Pietro Musumeci, former assistant director; Col. Giuseppe Belmonte and Francesco Pazienza, currently imprisoned in the United States) and Licio Gelli, the head of the underground P-2 Masonic Lodge. Gelli, who allegedly was involved in tax frauds and financial scandals that brought down the Christian Democratic government in 1982, escaped from a Swiss prison in 1983. The three service chiefs were sentenced to heavy prison terms in July 1984 in connection with illicit SISMI activities on charges of conspiracy, embezzlement, arms and explosives infringements, and "interference in magistrates' investigations." Police arrested Professor Fabio de Felice, who was believed to be a right-wing terrorism leader who organized the bombing. Others charged with "complicity in a massacre and forming an armed gang" included Paolo Signorelli, leader of the Armed Revolutionary Nuclei (NAR), Italy's principal right-wing terrorist group, and Massimiliano Facchini and Stefano Delle Chiaie, sought abroad for the past 15 years. Some of those charged were already serving prison sentences, including Valerio Fioravanti and Francesca Mambro, who had been recently married in prison. 80080202

August 4, 1980—UNITED STATES—Luis Rosa and Mary Rodriguez, members of the Puerto Rican Armed Forces of National Liberation (FALN), were sentenced in Cook County Circuit Court to 30 years for conspiracy and armed robbery. Rodriguez also received three consecutive 6-month terms and Rosa two consecutive 6-month terms for contempt of court stemming from their outbursts during the trial.

August 5, 1980 — EL SALVADOR — The Secret Anticommunist Army claimed credit for throwing four headless bodies in front of a movie theater in downtown San Salvador. Notes on the bodies said the dead people had been involved in the kidnapping of South African ambassador Archibald Dunn on November 28, 1979.

August 5, 1980 — FRANCE — The Armenian Secret Liberation Army claimed credit for two gunmen who entered the Turkish consulate in Lyons and fired on people sitting in the waiting room. Mehmet Bozdag, a consulate guard, Remazan Sezer, Kadir Akildan, and Huseyin Tokmak were wounded. 80080501

August 5, 1980 — PHILIPPINES — Military authorities announced that 20 members of the Light A Fire Movement — 19 Filipinos and Steve Psinakis, the Californian son-in-law of the late Filipino industrialist Eugenio Lopez, Sr., a Marcos political foe — were charged with plotting a bomb assassination of President Ferdinand Marcos and his wife, attempted assassination of cabinet officials, arson, and conspiracy to commit rebellion. 80080502

August 7, 1980 — ABU DHABI — The newspaper AL-KHALIJ reported receiving several threats to blow up its offices and murder its editors. IRAQI NEWS AGENCY in Baghdad said the threats came from Syrian intelligence agents because of the paper's critical treatment of the assassination of Salah ad-Din al-Bitar.

August 7, 1980 — ITALY — According to the Rand Corporation, "In Rome, a bomb assault took place against SNIA-Techint, the company that had furnished Iraq with nuclear technology. The attack was claimed by the Committee for the Defense of the Islamic Revolution." 80080701

August 7, 1980 — FRANCE — The Committee for the Safeguard of the Islamic Revolution threatened to blow up nuclear power plant construction companies if they delivered a research reactor to Iraq. Four other companies working on the project had received similar threats. The group claimed credit for an attempted July 31 bombing on Jean-Jacques Graf, a senior French atomic scientist working on the Osiraq project. The bomb blew up the home of a bookseller with the same name but caused no injuries. 80080702, 80073104

August 7, 1980 — ABU DHABI — The Islamic Front against Heretics claimed that it had bombed an Iraqi diplomat's residence. A caller said that similar acts would occur at Iraqi embassies in other Gulf states and also threatened the Qatari newspaper AR-RAYAH. 80080703

August 7, 1980—GUATEMALA—A group of unidentified gunmen shot and killed George Frank Rials, 48, a United States citizen and overseer for the Nello Teer Company, which was building roads in the jungles of Peten for petroleum exploitation. He was traveling in a vehicle to a camp in El Zapote. 80080704

August 7, 1980—SYRIA—JERUSALEM DOMESTIC SERVICE reported that 5 Soviet experts were killed and more than 20 wounded in Moslem Brotherhood attacks in Aleppo and Damascus in the preceding two days. 80080705

August 9, 1980—TURKEY—Having aroused suspicion when he arrived at the Palestine Liberation Organization office in Ankara from Athens, Ziyad Saqiti, a Palestinian living in Jerusalem, confessed that he had been ordered by Israeli agents to kill the PLO representative. 80080901

August 10, 1980—UNITED STATES—A 40-year-old Spanish-speaking man hijacked an Air Florida B-737 carrying 28 passengers and 5 crewmen from Miami to Key West, diverting it to Havana. The man carried a package with a wick protruding from it. A bilingual passenger who translated during the incident said it was a bomb, but it turned out to be a box of soap. No injuries were reported. The plane landed safely in Cuba at 11:02 A.M. and departed shortly thereafter. 80081001

August 11, 1980—FRANCE—The Order and New Justice cell of the Friends of Inspector Jacques Mazel bombed the print works of a leftist magazine, ENCRE NOIRE, in Marseilles. Six people, including a five-month-old baby, were injured. Mazel died in an accident during a demonstration by conscientious objectors at a Marseilles fair in April 1979.

August 11, 1980—AFGHANISTAN—Three young rebels armed with rifles killed two Soviet soldiers and three Afghans near a golf course on the outskirts of Kabul, according to a diplomat and businessman.

August 12, 1980—FRANCE—The clandestine FREE VOICE OF IRAN claimed that Mullah Hadi Ghaffair's group planned to occupy the British embassy in Tehran, take 12 British diplomats hostage, and demand the release of 67 Hezbollahis arrested in London. The radio station also claimed that Tehran threatened the directors of five French nuclear firms with death for building the Osiraq nuclear reactor for Iraq.

August 13, 1980—UNITED STATES—Seven Cubans believed to have arrived in the United States via the Freedom Flotilla hijacked an Air Florida B-737 flying from Key West to Miami at 10:30 A.M. and diverted it to Cuba. None of the 61 passengers and 6 crewmen were injured when the hijackers doused the plane's floor with gasoline and pulled out their cigarette lighters. Havana took the 7 into custody. An 8th man, J. Hernandez, had tripped the Key West metal detector while trying to smuggle a toy gun on board. He was convicted of air piracy and conspiracy and sentenced to 20 years in February 1981 by a Florida court. 80081301

August 14, 1980 — UNITED STATES — National Airlines flight 872, a DC-10 flying 211 passengers and 12 crew members from Miami to Puerto Rico, was diverted to Cuba at 7:40 P.M. by 2 men carrying a jar apparently filled with gasoline. No injuries were reported. The Federal Aviation Administration reported that it would revive using its behavioral profile of potential hijackers, because the x-ray devices were not preventing offenders from bringing false weapons on board. 80081401

August 15, 1980 — HONDURAS — Claiming that they were attempting to publicize collaboration by the governments of Honduras and El Salvador in the "genocide of the people of El Salvador," 15 armed leftists seized 6 men and 7 women in the Organization of American States office in the capital city. Two days later, the members of the Revolutionary People's Union (URP) released their hostages and disappeared into a crowd on the grounds of the Honduras National University. 80081501

August 16, 1980 — COLOMBIA — Twelve Colombia Rebel Armed Forces (FARC) members kidnapped United States citizen rancher Ira Hubbard, Jr., and demanded $435,000 ransom (Madrid EFE , a Spanish news agency, set the figure at $5 million). Hubbard was released unharmed on October 28, after his family, according to military authorities, paid a ransom of $160,000 (Madrid EFE set the figure at $2 million). 80081601

August 16, 1980 — UNITED KINGDOM — The Rodos and Victor Gonzalez social clubs, frequented mainly by South Americans and Spaniards, were destroyed in London by a fire apparently set by a man seen running along the sidewalk. At least 37 were killed and 23 injured in what was described as the worst fire in London since World War II. 80081602

August 16, 1980 — UNITED STATES — In the first of the day's three hijackings, 3 men carrying a small bottle of flammable deodorant and a toy gun hijacked an Eastern Airlines B-727 flying from Miami to Orlando with 44 passengers and 6 crewmen and diverted it to Cuba. A psychologist said the Federal Aviation Administration behavioral profile of potential hijackers was not in use at the airport. Havana authorities arrested all of the hijackers. 80081603

August 16, 1980 — UNITED STATES — At 6:35 P.M., four hijackers diverted to Havana a Republic Airlines DC-9 flying from Miami to Orlando with 106 passengers and 5 crew. Cuban authorities arrested the foursome. 80081604

August 16, 1980 — UNITED STATES — At 7:02 P.M., a man hijacked a Delta Airlines Lockheed L-1011 Tristar with 157 passengers and 8 crewmen, flying from Puerto Rico to Los Angeles with a stop in Miami, and diverted it to Cuba. The hijacker was arrested by Cuban authorities. 80081605

August 16, 1980 — UNITED STATES — Tampa police arrested four Cubans from the Freedom Flotilla who were attempting to board an Eastern Airlines flight 115 to Miami while carrying bottles filled with flammable liquid. The four were identified as Antolin Acevedo, 35; Aurelio Acevedo, 38; Eugenio Areu-Del Campo, 29; and Alvarino Nelson-Gonzalez, 30. 80081606

August 17, 1980 — UNITED STATES — Miami airport police arrested two men believed planning to hijack Air Florida's flight 41 en route from Miami to Key West. The duo was found carrying a beer bottle full of gasoline. They were identified as Jose Antonio Pablo-Lugones, 37, and Hector Pinero, 41. 80081701

August 18, 1980 — UNITED STATES — Police in Atlanta arrested a man who told an Eastern Airlines flight crew that he was carrying a bomb. No one was injured. 80081801

August 20, 1980 — AFGHANISTAN — A West German tourist who was stopped at a rebel roadblock three miles from Jalalabad was killed, either by the rebels or by a burst of machine-gun fire from a government helicopter attacking the rebels.

August 20, 1980 — UNITED STATES — The Iranian Liberation Army set off two bombs at a meeting of the pro-Khomeini Iranian Students Association at Berkeley High School in San Francisco, injuring one student. Police had evacuated the building after receiving two warning phone calls. United States District Court judge Spencer Williams sentenced Naser Rahimi Almaneih, 28, an Iranian national, to 50 years in prison on August 23, 1981, saying, "The maximum sentence, including the death penalty where authorized, will be imposed on any terrorist who commits acts of violence." Almaneih, who was charged in a seven-count federal indictment for threatening President Jimmy Carter's life three times, attempting to bomb a pro-Khomeini rally at San Jose State, and making two bombs that exploded during an Iranian cultural event at the University of California-Berkeley, said he was framed by an ex-agent of SAVAK (the Shah's intelligence service), Amir

Ehdaee, 39, who made timing devices for bombs in his glass shop. 80082001

August 22, 1980—PHILIPPINES—The April 6 Liberation Movement bombed nine major government and commercial buildings, including the First National City Bank of New York, the Hong Kong–Shanghai Banking Corporation, the Metro Bank, the Government Service Insurance System, the National Housing Authority, the Metro Manila Commission, the Li Mall shopping center, the Executive Suite firm, and the social security office. Unexploded bombs were found at the Manila Ramada Hotel and the Philippine-American Life Insurance building. The group takes its name from a 1978 protest in which motorists honked horns and people clanged iron sheets in support of then-imprisoned anti-Marcos dissident Benigno Aquino, who resided in the United States until 1983, when he was assassinated upon his return to the Philippines. The four banks are foreign owned. Three injuries were reported. 80082201–04

August 22, 1980—LEBANON—A bomb exploded near the entrance of a Beirut building housing the embassies of the Netherlands, Venezuela, and India, causing minimal damage and no injuries. 80082205

August 22, 1980—COLOMBIA—Five members of the April 19 Movement (M-19) took over the Bolivian consulate in Cali, binding the honorary consul, his wife, children, and receptionist. After threatening the group, the armed terrorists painted anti-Bolivian slogans on the walls. No injuries were reported. 80082206

August 24, 1980—ISRAEL—A Palestine Liberation Organization bomb hidden in a trash can exploded at a Jerusalem gas station, killing a station attendant and wounding several tourists, including seven from the Netherlands, Australia, and West Germany. 80082401

August 26, 1980—UNITED STATES—A Chicago Circuit Court judge sentenced Carlos Alberto Torres and seven other Puerto Rican Armed Forces of National Liberation (FALN) members to eight-year prison terms for possession of a sawed-off shotgun and conspiracy to commit armed robbery.

August 26, 1980—UNITED STATES—Three Spanish-speaking men, spilling liquid from plastic bottles and shouting, "Cuba, Cuba!" diverted an Eastern Airlines plane carrying 228 passengers from New York to Miami. Havana authorities arrested the trio. On January 6, former stewardess Carolanne Ray was reported fighting her dismissal from Eastern for allegedly taking a drink a passenger offered her while in Cuba's Jose Marti Airport. 80082601

August 27, 1980 — LEBANON — Gunmen from the Front for the Liberation of Lebanon from Foreigners attacked the three-car convoy of United States ambassador John Gunther Dean, firing machine guns and lobbing a grenade. Dean's bodyguards returned the fire and drove off the attackers, who abandoned their Mercedes on Beirut's Al-Hazimiyah Road at 8:00 P.M. Elsewhere, the Spanish ambassador, Luis Jordana de Pozas, and his wife were seized at gunpoint by a carload of men who cut off their car at an airport traffic circle. The ambassador was able to summon help from the commander of the Arab peacekeeping force, and troops freed the couple.

Lebanese intelligence officers believed that four gunmen were in the Mercedes, while a fifth, hiding in a clump of woods, fired a rocket-propelled grenade (RPG). The Lebanese Army questioned three men in connection with the attack, which apparently caused no casualties. The VOICE OF PALESTINE claimed that two of those arrested said they were Phalangists. Former President Sham'un denied Lebanese were behind the attack, and the Lebanese newspaper AN-NAHAR suggested Israeli complicity. 80082701–02

August 29, 1980 — PERU — At 1:00 A.M., 168 Cubans forced their way onto a Braniff International Airlines DC-8 set to fly from Lima to Los Angeles, seized 11 passengers and 3 flight attendants, and demanded passage to the United States. Interior Minister Jose Maria de la Jara conducted negotiations and offered himself as a substitute hostage. Four hundred Cubans had approached the plane, which had a seating capacity of only 164, but the boarding ramp was lifted before the rest could board. Three Cubans were injured by police gunfire during the attack on the plane. Three others were cut by glass from doors that were broken in the rush from the terminal. The plane, flight 920, had left Santiago the previous evening and was scheduled to end its route in San Francisco. The Cubans gave up after 22 hours and were returned to a refugee camp to await processing of visas for the United States. None of the passengers, which included 7 Americans, were injured, despite refugee threats to burn the plane if their demands were not met. President Belaunde had rejected the Cubans' demand for a second plane. The refugees apparently were unarmed. The Federal Aviation Administration believed this was the first time anyone had attempted to hijack a plane to the United States. On August 31, the refugees at the Tupac Amaru Camp outside Lima threatened to hijack another plane or capture a ship to reach the United States. 80082901

August 31, 1980 — COLOMBIA — A bomb exploded at the front entrance of a Drug Enforcement Agency office, causing heavy damage but no injuries. 80083101

September 1980 — El SALVADOR — The United States embassy denied Armed

Forces of National Resistance (FARN) claims that it had killed a United States military adviser.

September 3, 1980 — GUATEMALA — Unidentified individuals fired machine guns from a passing car at the United States embassy at 3:00 A.M., causing some damage but no injuries. 80090301

September 5, 1980 — FEDERAL REPUBLIC OF GERMANY — Christof Wackernagel and Gert Schneider, Red Army Faction members, were sentenced to five years in prison for attempted murder in a December 1977 shoot-out in the Netherlands.

September 6, 1980 — PHILIPPINES — Victor B. Lovely, 32, general manager of the California-based Arco Foods International Corporation, was seriously injured when a bomb exploded in his room at the YMCA next to Manila's city hall. His Philippine brother, Romeo, 22, was also injured in the blast. Philippine police arrested the duo, claiming they were manufacturing the bomb for the Light A Fire Movement, and that eight other bombs were found in the apartment. Police also tied the brothers to the April 6 Liberation Movement. 80090601

September 8, 1980 — UNITED STATES — An Eastern Airlines B-727 flying out of John F. Kennedy International Airport at 9:05 A.M. to Tampa and Sarasota was hijacked at 10:00 A.M. by a Spanish-speaking man who threatened to ignite a bottle of liquid he was carrying. The plane landed at Cuba's Jose Marti Airport at 11:52 A.M., where the man was taken into custody. None of the 6 crew members and 82 passengers were injured. 80090801

September 9, 1980 — UNITED STATES — A bomb went off inside a package being unloaded from the baggage compartment of a United Airlines B-727 that had arrived in Sacramento from a flight from Seattle and Portland, carrying 44 passengers. Two freight handlers — Allen Wright and Robert Daye — were injured.

September 11, 1980 — EL SALVADOR — The People's Liberation Forces (FPL) fired on policemen guarding the Guatemalan embassy but caused no injuries. 80091101

September 12, 1980 — NORTH KOREA — Two United Red Army of Japan terrorists, including Takamaro Tamiya, 37, who led the 1970 hijacking of a Japan Air Lines plane, told Motofumi Makieda, chairman of the General Council of Trade Unions of Japan, that they wished to return to Japan and "engage in activities which will be to the benefit of Japan and the people," provided they would not be arrested. They said that they had hijacked the plane to North Korea so that they could study and engage in military training, but they had been prevented from the latter.

September 12, 1980 — UNITED STATES — Guillermo Lima, 24, a Cuban refugee, attempted to hijack an Eastern Airlines flight carrying 6 crew members and 79 passengers from Newark to Miami. A Federal Bureau of Investigation spokesman said, "When the man got up, he was immediately overpowered by passengers and crew members and it's our understanding that they beat him up." Lima was charged with air piracy and jailed with no bond set. 80091201

September 12, 1980 — UNITED STATES — Felix Garcia-Rodriguez, a Cuban United Nations Mission attache, was killed at 6:30 P.M. while driving in a commercial section of Queens when three .45 caliber bullets hit him in the neck. His station wagon collided with another car, injuring another person. Omega-7 claimed responsibility and said that Cuban United Nations ambassador Raul Roa would be next. The NEW YORK DAILY NEWS claimed the victim, apparently the first United Nations diplomat assassinated on United States soil, was a high-level Cuban intelligence operative tasked with surveilling a Cuban drug smuggling ring. 80091202

September 12, 1980 — PORTUGAL — A bomb exploded at the Chilean embassy in Lisbon, causing minor damage. Another bomb exploded at the Chilean consulate in Oporto, injuring a guard. 80091203–04

September 12, 1980 — PHILIPPINES — Bombs exploded at nine locations in downtown Manila, wounding at least 30 Filipinos and killing Annie Kuzmuk, 51, American wife of a Manila-based United States businessman from Newark. She died in an explosion at a supermarket. President Ferdinand Marcos announced that $6.8 million had been budgeted for improved security. Police reported 19 other bomb threats. Kumander Bituin (Commander Star) of the Sandigan (pillar) unit of the April 6 Liberation Movement claimed responsibility for the blasts, which occurred a day after Marcos' 63rd birthday. On November 29, Filipino authorities charged 59 people with rebellion, illegal possession of explosives, attempted murder (including attempted murder of Marcos), arson, and the murder of Kuzmuk. Two Americans — Steve Psinakis, a businessman residing in San Francisco, and Gregory Edward Kandziora, a retired army sergeant from Tucson, Arizona — were among those charged. Authorities said they had recruited Philippine terrorists in the United States and trained them in explosives handling. Others accused included Jesuit priests Romeo Intengan, Jr., and Toti Olaguer; Filipino Dorris Baffrey; former senators Benigno Aquino, Jr., Raul Manglapus, and Sergio Osmena, all of whom lived in the United States. 80091205

September 13, 1980 — UNITED STATES — Two Spanish-speaking males hijacked a Delta Airlines B-727 during a flight from New Orleans to Atlanta, claiming to have bottles of flammable liquid. Cuban authorities arrested the duo upon landing in Havana. None of the 88 passengers were injured. On September 16, Cuba warned Cuban refugees that they had made a "one way trip" to the United States, and that hijackers would be imprisoned or extradited to the United States. 80091301

September 14, 1980 — UNITED STATES — Orlando Airport officials arrested a 43-year-old Cuban refugee who met the Federal Aviation Administration's hijacker profile. He was found attempting to board an Eastern Airlines flight to Miami with a small bottle of gasoline. 80091401

September 14, 1980 — UNITED STATES — Miami airport police arrested Carlos Jesus Figueroa, 45, of Tampa, a Cuban exile who had entered the United States in the early 1960s, when he attempted to hijack an Eastern B-727 to Havana. The pilot called his bluff on the ground. A group of Cubans handed a note to a flight 115 attendant saying that a bomb would be detonated in Tampa if the Tampa-to-Miami flight did not go to Cuba. 80091402

September 15, 1980 — UNITED STATES — The United States Court of Appeals overturned the convictions of Guillermo Novo Sampol, Alvin Ross Diaz, and Ignacio Novo Sampol, three anti-Castro Cubans jailed in the September 1976 car-bombing assassination of Chilean Orlando Letelier. New trials were ordered for the two men convicted of murder.

September 15, 1980 — EL SALVADOR — The People's Liberation Front bombed the office of Siemens (a West German firm) at 2:50 A.M., causing considerable property damage but no injuries. 80091501

September 15, 1980 — GUATEMALA — Unidentified persons threw a hand grenade from a speeding car at the Nicaraguan embassy, causing considerable damage and injuring two policemen, Hilario Hernandez Diaz and Carlos Humberto Aceituno. 80091502

September 16, 1980 — EL SALVADOR — A brief attack was conducted against the Shell Company's Aguacaliente substation in Soyapango. Two bombs exploded at the Shell Company office in Santa Tecla, causing slight damage. 80091601–02

September 16, 1980 — GREECE — Five cars belonging to members of the United States military mission in Athens were firebombed during the night. The Revolutionary Left claimed credit, saying it was protesting alleged

United States support for the Turkish Army takeover. No injuries were reported. 80091603–07

September 16, 1980—EL SALVADOR—The People's Revolutionary Army (ERP) fired three Chinese-made antitank rockets from a building 50 feet away into the United States embassy compound, causing some damage but no injuries. 80091608

September 16, 1980—GUADELOUPE—Police believed the Guadeloupe Liberation Army was responsible for setting bombs under an Air France B-727 at Le Raizet airport. One of the bombs exploded at 10:00 A.M., damaging the plane. An army explosives expert was killed trying to disarm a second bomb. A guerrilla group had demanded that the French leave the island by December 31 or "face physical sanctions." 80091609

September 17, 1980—ABU DHABI—TEHRAN INTERNATIONAL SERVICE reported that Iraqi Ba'thist mercenaries had planned to blow up the Iranian office. Local police arrested one of the individuals, who was carrying a revolver and three ammunition clips. Six others were being sought.

September 17, 1980—VENEZUELA—A military prosecutor withdrew charges against Venezuelans Hernan Ricardo and Freddy Lugo, two CARRILES PUBLICATIONS cameramen, who had been implicated in the bombing of a Cubana plane in Barbados in 1976. The prosecutor said the investigative evidence against them had been refuted by a Scotland Yard report, which indicated that the explosion had occurred in the plane's cargo compartment, to which the accused did not have access.

September 17, 1980—UNITED STATES—Two Cuban refugees who claimed to be "tired of all the robbing and killing" in New York City hijacked a Delta Airlines B-727, flight 470, flying from Atlanta to Charleston, South Carolina, with 104 passengers and 7 crewmen. The plane landed in Columbia, South Carolina, to refuel at 2:30 A.M. before flying on to Havana's Jose Marti Airport. The duo poured gasoline on a stewardess and threatened to ignite it if their demands were ignored. Cuban authorities arrested the hijackers and returned them to the United States the next day, the first time that Cuba had returned Cuban hijackers to the United States. The duo were indicted on air piracy charges in October. In January 1981, Juan Adega-Fresneda, 25, and Crecencio Perez-Perez, 26, pleaded guilty and were sentenced to 40 years in jail. 80091701

September 17, 1980—EL SALVADOR—Eighteen members of the Revolutionary Democratic Front (FDR), led by a woman, took over the San Salvador offices of the Organization of American States (OAS), killing a guard and injuring 4 people. They seized 10 hostages, including Alvino Roman y Vega, a Nicaraguan who headed the OAS mission; 4 other OAS diplomats; 2 secretaries; 2 office boys; and a cleaning woman in the 11:00 A.M. attack. The group demanded demilitarization of all work places, the people's right to self-determination, liberation of 55 political prisoners, an end to the six-month-old state of siege, reopening of the university, and the free flow of information. They named Eduardo Calles, Leoncio Pichinte, Julio Flores, and Enrique Escobar Herrera to negotiate for the Revolutionary Coordinating Board of the Masses (CRM). Negotiations for the OAS were initially conducted by Colombian colonel Julio Cesar Blanco, chief of the OAS military observers, and later by Alberto Salem, a special envoy of the OAS secretary-general. On September 27, the terrorists released Guillermo Pino, 53, the assistant OAS director for the country, when he had heart trouble. The terrorists agreed to end their occupation when the government promised to investigate the status of political prisoners and the disappearance of 300 leftists that year. The hostages were released unharmed on October 8, while the terrorists left in a bus. The occupiers arrived at the office of the Roman Catholic archbishop of El Salvador, where they dispersed. 80091702

September 17, 1980—PARAGUAY—Former Nicaraguan president Anastacio Somoza Debayle, 54; his driver Cesar Gallardo, a Nicaraguan; and Colombian economic adviser Joseph Bertnier were killed in a hail of machine-gun fire in an attack on Somoza's Mercedes in Asuncion. Three men driving a blue Chevrolet pickup truck blocked Somoza's car, while another trio fired two bazooka rounds from a nearby house. Somoza's body was riddled with 25 bullets. The trio ran out of the house and seized the car of a passing Argentine, who said they spoke with Argentine or Uruguayan accents. The pickup truck was found three blocks away from the scene, which itself was seven blocks from Somoza's villa and two blocks from the United States embassy. Police announced that weapons found in a Mitsubishi car, the last the terrorists were seen driving, included two .45 Ingraham M-10 submachine guns, a rocket launcher, a 7.62 mm FAL rifle, and a Colt M-16 carbine.

Police initially said two people who did not participate in the killing were involved in its planning and were members of the Argentine People's Revolutionary Army (ERP), which was believed defunct before the assassination. Hugo Alfredo Yrurzun (Captain Santiago), 30, died in a police raid the next day. Police claimed he owned the pickup truck. He had used a false Uruguayan passport to enter Paraguay and had traveled earlier in 1980 to Costa Rica and Panama. The other conspirator, Silvia Mercedes Hodges (Luisa, Diana, Ana Morales, Ana Aguilar, Alejandra Renata Colombo), 28, rented the house.

On September 22, police said three Montoneros were involved, and that a fourth killer was a member of the Reorganization Committee of Revolutionary Front 17. Authorities named Jorge Alberto Ruiz (Cacho), a rug and lamp peddlar; Jorge Omar Lewinger (Joselito, Wilfredo Delgado); Juan Jose Partinni (Pepe, Jose Gonzalez), all Argentines; Guillermo Victor Thomas (Julian); and Foca, a radio broadcaster. On September 26, police also named Daniel Oscar Raconto (Toto), ERP and PRT (Revolutionary Workers Party) member. That day, Mario Eduardo Firmenich, leader of the Montoneros in exile, denied responsibility for the attack.

On October 23, police released suspect Julio Eduardo Caerbone, an Argentine architect, after questioning.

On January 22, 1981, Paraguayan police said the Sandinista government paid $40,000 to Chilean photographer Alejandro Mella Torres to film the 10:00 A.M. killing. 80091703

September 19, 1980 — GUATEMALA — Gunmen on a motorcycle and in a pickup truck machine-gunned and killed Francisco Alvarado Franco, 29, security chief of the Coca-Cola Company, in the capital city. His wife, Maria Dalila Calderon de Alvarado, was seriously injured. 80091901

September 21, 1980 — HONDURAS — Nicaraguan ambassador Jose Leon Talavera received a death threat. 80092101

September 23, 1980 — PANAMA — Commander Danilo of the Salvadoran Unified Revolutionary Directorate (DRU) Anastasio Aquino Special Brigade said the brigade would not operate in Panama, but only against United States facilities on the banks of the canal. "Our psychological harassment operations against the military and civilian personnel on US posts and bases on this beloved Panamanian soil for now do not include acts of terrorism or sabotage. We have succeeded in smuggling a quantity of arms and ammunition, uniforms and revolutionary insignia from a neighboring country to meet any emergency. I can assure that these supplies are no longer on the Panamanian side, but are at various points in the canal still under the hated Yankee heel." 80092301

September 26, 1980 — SWITZERLAND — A Swiss court sentenced to life imprisonment Rolf Clemens Wagner for murder and attempted murder during a Zurich bank holdup 10 months earlier. West German authorities sought him for the kidnap/murder of industrialist Hanns Martin-Schleyer in 1977.

September 26, 1980 — VENEZUELA — The Caracas Permanent Council of War absolved anti-Castroite leader Orlando Bosch, Luis Posada Cariles, Freddy Lugo, and Hernan Ricardo of charges of homicide and high treason in the 1976 bombing of a Cubana plane, which resulted in the deaths of 73 people.

September 26, 1980 — ARGENTINA — A bomb was defused in a Peugeot parked outside the United States embassy. 80092601

September 26, 1980 — FRANCE — Selcuk Bakkalbasi, Turkish embassy press attache, was wounded by gunmen from the Armenian Secret Army Organization as he was returning home from work in the evening. 80092602

September 26, 1980 — FEDERAL REPUBLIC OF GERMANY — A hand grenade studded with nails went off at 10:18 P.M. in a trash can near the exit from the Munich Oktoberfest beer festival, killing 13, including a Swiss, a Brit, and 2 Austrians, and injuring 215, including 7 Americans. Among the injured Americans were 5 United States Air Force personnel, including A1C. Cynthia Fox, 22, of Loomis, California, who lost a leg; her husband, Sgt. John I. Fox, of Mountain Home, Idaho; A1C. Denise Fowler, of Sparta, New York; Amn. Jim Evans, of Montague, Michigan; and Sgt. Mark Kantenberg, who sustained lesser injuries. The bomber, Gundolf Koehler, 21, was killed in what probably was a premature explosion. He was linked to the banned Military Sports Group Hoffman, a neo-Nazi paramilitary group. Karl-Heinz Hoffman, 42, the group's founder, and 5 of his followers were arrested the next day. Four of the group were caught trying to cross the border to Austria on their way to Yugoslavia in a convoy of cars, including six vehicles allegedly destined for the Middle East. On September 29, 5 of the suspects were released for insufficient evidence of connection to the blast. 80092603

September 26, 1980 — LEBANON — The Forces of Mojahedin claimed credit for firing three rocket-propelled grenades at the United States embassy in Beirut. No injuries were reported, but three large holes were punched in the embassy's walls, causing damage to two offices. The group said the attack was intended to "force American imperialism to raise its hand from the Islamic people of Iran." He claimed the group would attack the United States "everywhere in the Middle East, as long as this policy of the United States continues." 80092604

September 27, 1980 — GREECE — Athens customs officials discovered several weapons — including 2 rifles, 4 revolvers, 10 pistols, 8,300 cartridges, a large stock of powder, 2 boxes of caps, 4 hunting rifles, and a book on how to assemble weapons — in the suitcases of Irene Christakou, 45, a Greek-American woman who was moving to Greece from Chicago. 80092701

September 28, 1980 — FRANCE — The Organization of European Nationalist Groups, a right-wing band, machine-gunned a synagogue, the fifth attack against Jewish targets in Paris in 48 hours. No injuries were reported.

September 29, 1980 — FRANCE — Yeves Stella, 38, Corsica nationalist leader, was sentenced in Paris to 15 years imprisonment for taking part in bombings in Corsica, and for masterminding the bombing campaign from his prison cell for 2 years.

September 29, 1980 — JAPAN — The government filed a $6 million damage suit against five members of the Japanese Red Army who hijacked a Japan Air Lines jet on September 28, 1977. The government had paid that sum for the passengers' safe release. Four of the five were named: Osamu Maruoka, 29, Jun Nishikawa, 30, Kunio Bando, 33, and Norio Sasaki, 32.

September 29, 1980 — PHILIPPINES — The government announced that its troops had killed Commander Mercy, leader of a Moslem rebel group that attacked a college run by Rev. Lloyd G. Van Vactor, an American missionary, nine days previously. No injuries were reported in the rebels' attack. 80092001

September 30, 1980 — FEDERAL REPUBLIC OF GERMANY — Paul Otte, 56, Volker Heidel, 26, Oliver Schreiber, 21, Wolfgang Sachse, 36, and Hans-Dieter Lepzien, 37, members of the neo-Nazi Brunswick Group, went on trial for bombing courts in Hanover and Flensburg and planning attacks on unnamed public figures.

September 30, 1980 — USSR — One man was killed and two others injured around midnight when four shots rang out at No. 13 Kutuzovsky Prospekt, at the entrance to a foreign residential compound a few blocks from the apartment of Soviet premier Leonid Brezhnev. 80093001

September 30, 1980 — WESTERN SAHARA — Polisario guerrillas kidnapped 25 Spanish sailors off fishing boats. News of the attacks came from the engine room chief of one of the boats, the Costa de Terranova, who escaped detection. 80093002

October 1980 — FRANCE — The illustrated weekly NEUE REVUE claimed that in police raids on West German terrorist safe houses in Paris, traces were found of the lethal bacterium clostridium botulinum. Police also seized books on medicine and biology, and handwritten notes by Silke Maier-Witt, Red Army Faction terrorist who had worked as a nurse and who was sought for the September 1977 kidnap/murder of Hanns-Martin Schleyer. Clostridium botulinum gives off a poison that paralyzes the nervous system. It can be cultured with relatively simple means from tainted food. The required technical literature was apparently found in the safe house. 80109901

October 1, 1980 — COLOMBIA — Colombian legislator Olga Duque de Ospina said that the Colombian Revolutionary Armed Forces (FARC) received P 11 million (about $275,000) ransom for the release of American biologist Richard Starr in February. Starr was kidnapped in early 1977.

October 1, 1980 — BOLIVIA — The military government announced the deaths of two foreigners in Santa Cruz, Denis Palmieri, a Brazilian, and Eduardo Bernardini, an Argentine, during a raid on a Montoneros safe house. 80100101

October 2, 1980 — LEBANON — The Amal organization fired rockets and grenades on the Iraqi embassy, causing material damage to the embassy and a nearby building but injuring no one. The Forces of Mujahidin (Quwwat as-Saf al-Mujahid) also claimed credit, demanding the release of Moslem mujahidin in Iraq and an end to the attacks on the Islamic revolution in Iran. The attack came around midnight. 80100201

October 2, 1980 — LEBANON — Apparently in retaliation for the previous incident, at 3:45 A.M., pro-Iraqi elements fired rockets and machine guns at the Iranian embassy, causing no casualties. 80100202

October 2, 1980 — TURKEY — Bombs were discovered in Izmir on the stairs outside the building occupied by the United States Army and in the doorway of the nearby Army post office. The explosions caused no injuries and only minor damage. The leftist Dev Sol claimed credit. Another bomb exploded at a local Pan American Airlines office. 80100203–04

October 3, 1980 — GRENADA — The government announced the death penalty for terrorist attacks leading to death.

October 3, 1980 — FRANCE — A 25-pound plastique bomb hidden under a car outside Paris' most fashionable synagogue on the Rue Coperic exploded, killing 4, including a young Israeli woman, and injuring 12. One of the 4 dead was a 22-year-old motorcyclist who diverted police attention by asking directions while 2 other motorcyclists planted the bomb. It went off, possibly prematurely, when he drove off. A man identifying himself as Alexander Panaryu, and carrying a Cypriot passport, had purchased the motorcycle for one thousand dollars two weeks previously. The Palestine Liberation Organization (PLO) in London denied responsibility, saying that such anti-Semitism "reinforces the Zionist movement, encouraging Jewish emigration from Europe to Palestine and thereby strengthening the movement that has enforced the exile of millions." The attack came in the wake of scores of incidents against Jews in Europe and sparked increased defensive militancy among French Jews. During the summer, 67 prominent southern French Jews received written death threats from the National European Action Federation, which the police believed to have 250 members.

According to the Rand Corporation,

> An anonymous phone call to AGENCE FRANCE-PRESSE claimed responsibility for the neo-Nazi European Nationalist Fascists, a small group of the extreme right. . . . Public opinion and the press attributed the attacks to a rising wave of anti-Semitism from the extreme right within France. Police immediately made dozens of arrests among members of the named group and began intensive questioning. The group's leader, already awaiting trial on another charge, disclaimed the bombing. After interrogating many of the members and releasing them for lack of evidence, the police came upon the 29-year-old author of the phone call. Excited and pleased with himself, he admitted to the call, adding that he was an "agent" from a Jewish organization infiltrating the French neo-Nazi group. "I wanted to ridicule and discredit the European Nationalist Fascists." Subsequent investigations, as reported in the French press, raised doubts that the bombing was the work of European rightwing extremists. In sifting through the debris of the blast, authorities determined the bomb was attached to a moped, the only unclaimed item. From the engine number, the moped was traced to an Arab, believed to be a Palestinian, who had entered the country on a false passport along with four other known Palestinians. With his false identification, he rented a car until October 4 (the day after the bombing). The car was later found abandoned. The five Palestinians, identified as members of a hardline branch of the PLO, were later discovered to have left the country on board a flight to Beirut on October 4.

On February 17, 1983, Spain arrested 7 people suspected of being involved in the synagogue bombing and the August 2 Bologna bombing. 80100301

October 3, 1980 — SWITZERLAND — Armenian-American Suzy K. Mahseredjian, 24, of Canoga Park, California, and Ara Yenikomchian, 25, were injured when a bomb they were fabricating exploded in their Geneva hotel room. Although the Armenian Secret Army for the Liberation of Armenia threatened reprisals, on January 13, 1981, Mahseredjian was given an 18-month suspended sentence for helping extort the equivalent of six thousand dollars from a Geneva businessman. She was acquitted of an explosives charge. The arrests provoked bombing reprisals in Beirut and four European cities by the October 3 Group. Yenikomchian, son of a successful Beirut pediatrician, lost all of one eye and most of the other. The group threatened retaliation against the United States for a Federal Bureau of Investigation interrogation of the woman. 80100302

October 4, 1980—PHILIPPINES—The April 6 Liberation Movement bombed three hotels in Manila and one in Angeles City, injuring 11 persons, including an Australian. The hotels were identified as the Century Park Sheraton and seaside Philippine Plaza in Manila, the Peninsula Hotel in the suburbs, and the Marlim Mansion Hotel in Angeles City. The Sheraton had earlier received a bomb threat. The Oasis Hotel in Angeles City was later bombed. The terrorists said they were warning organizers and delegates to conferences planned by the International Hotels Association and the American Society of Travel Agents. 80100401–02

October 4, 1980—UNITED STATES—The Federal Bureau of Investigation (FBI) arrested Naser Rahimi Almaneih, 28, member of the anti-Khomeini Iranian Free Army, for plotting to bomb a meeting of the Moslem Students Association at San Jose State University. He was held in lieu of $1 million bond after being booked for investigation of possession and manufacture of explosives. The FBI raided his framing and glass shop and confiscated two pipe bombs. 80100403

October 4, 1980—ITALY—The Armenian Secret Army for the Liberation of Armenia bombed the Turkish Airlines office in Milan, causing minor damage and no injuries. The group said this was part of its campaign to stop the flow of Armenian emigrants to the United States. 80100404

October 4, 1980—TURKEY—A Dev Sol note was found in a United States Air Force staff sergeant's car that was firebombed in Izmir. No injuries were reported. 80100405

October 5, 1980—ISRAEL—A bomb blast killed three persons and wounded seven others in the central post office of Givatayim, a Tel Aviv suburb. The Palestine Liberation Organization (PLO) claimed credit.

October 5, 1980—FRANCE—A bomb exploded under a car with Dutch plates on the Boulevard Saint Germain in Paris's Latin Quarter, maiming Carmelia van Puffelen, 33, of the Netherlands and destroying her car. She had just entered her parked car after a dinner celebrating her husband's birthday. Both her legs were amputated. The National Revolutionary Movement, an ultrarightist organization, claimed credit, but another caller later denied responsibility. On October 8, French police charged her husband with attempted murder.

October 5, 1980—LEBANON—A one-kilogram stick of dynamite was thrown from a passing car onto the grounds of the Saudi Arabian embassy in Beirut, causing no injuries and breaking glass. The Martyr Abu Ja'far Group accused the Saudis of supporting Iraq in its war against Iran. According to the VOICE OF LEBANON, "The group said that if no Saudi statement was issued declaring complete neutrality . . . the organization would want to emphasize that a suicide squad stands ready to assassinate Saudi Ambassador Gen. 'Ali ash-Sha'ir and another suicide group will assassinate Prince Fahd in Riyadh." 80100501

October 5, 1980—SPAIN—The Armenian Secret Army for the Liberation of Armenia bombed the Madrid office of Alitalia, injuring 12 but causing minimal damage. 80100502

October 5, 1980—UNITED STATES—A bomb hidden in a car exploded in front of the Turkish Center, which houses the Turkish United Nations Mission, injuring four passersby. The home of the Turkish consul in Los Angeles was also bombed, injuring one person. The Justice Commandos of the Armenian Genocide claimed credit for both blasts. 80100503–04

October 7, 1980—GRENADA—The government announced that terrorists who set off a bomb in the town of Saint Patrick's in northern Grenada on September 27 left a note warning all Cubans to leave the island "or there will be war."

October 8, 1980—NORTH KOREA—Nine members of the Japanese United Red Army, who hijacked a domestic Japanese Air Lines flight 10 years earlier, expressed interest in returning to Japan if they would not be imprisoned. The government refused to offer such a deal, and conservative Japanese Dietmen considered requesting extradition. In an interview with a correspondent of KYODO, a news agency, Takamaro Tamiya and Seiryo Wakabayashi apologized to the Japanese people. They claimed they lived in Pyongyang and did not have any military training.

October 8, 1980—TURKEY—In the first executions since 1972, the military junta hanged Necdet Adali, 24, a leftist terrorist, and Mustafa Phalivanoglu, 22, a rightist terrorist, demonstrating its determination to fight terrorism, which claimed 1,700 lives in 1980 before a September 12 coup.

October 9, 1980—EL SALVADOR—The Farabundo Marti Popular Liberation Forces stated that it had killed South African ambassador Archibald Gardner Dunn, whom it had kidnapped on November 28, 1979, for noncompliance by Dunn's son with their $20 million ransom demand.

October 9, 1980 — LEBANON — The Iraqi Strugglers' Movement bombed the offices of the Jordanian Alia Airlines. 80100901

October 9, 1980 — LEBANON — A bomb wrecked the offices of Iran Air and caused extensive damage to the Beirut headquarters of the REUTERS news agency. 80100902

October 10, 1980 — JAMAICA — Assassins fired on the automobile of Prime Minister Michael Manley during the election campaign eventually won by Labor party leader Edward Seaga. One of the terrorists, Donald Webb, 25, was hospitalized under police custody.

October 10, 1980 — LEBANON — A previously unknown organization admitted firing a rocket at the United States embassy during the evening because the United States was supporting Iraq against Iran. The rocket missed its target and hit the nearby American University of Beirut, damaging a professor's house and panicking dorm students. 80101001

October 12, 1980 — UNITED KINGDOM — A bomb exploded at the Turkish Airlines office near Piccadilly Circus in London, causing no injuries. About 30 minutes later, another bomb exploded at the Swiss Center, a restaurant and shopping complex a half-mile away in London's crowded West End theater district, shattering windows but causing no damage. The Armenian Secret Army for the Liberation of Armenia and the Organization of October Third claimed credit, respectively. 80101201–02

October 12, 1980 — FRANCE — The October Third Organization, an Armenian terrorist group, bombed the Swiss Tourist Office in central Paris, causing no injuries. 80101203

October 13, 1980 — ITALY — Police announced the arrest of Front Line leader Michele Viscardi, 24, and Maria Teresa Conti, 23, believed to have been involved in three murders, in the southern resort city of Sorrento. Viscardi had taken the reins from Corrado Alunni, who was arrested in September 1978 for complicity in the Red Brigades' kidnapping of former premier Aldo Moro.

October 13, 1980 — TURKEY — Turkish Airlines flight TK-890, a B-727 flying 155 people, including 135 Turks, 6 Iranians, and 7 crewmen from Munich to Istanbul and Ankara, was hijacked at 6:30 P.M. by 4 to 6 Iranians (reports conflict) who demanded that they be flown to Tehran, Iran, or Jidda, Saudi Arabia, or they would blow up the plane. The hijackers were armed with two pistols hidden inside carved-out copies of the Koran. The pilot said he couldn't fly into a war zone (Iran), and that he did not have enough fuel. The plane landed at Diyarbakir in eastern Turkey, where the hijackers released 6 children, 40 women, and 7 sick or old people. Diyarbakir governor Erdogan Sahinoglu and Gen. Kenan Evren, head of the Turkish military junta, took part in negotiating with the hijackers. The hijackers said the plane was "under the control of the Sharia" (Islamic holy law) and forced women to cover their heads Islamic style. An American passenger later reported that "they sent around a hat, asking us to contribute to help Moslem rebels in Afghanistan. We didn't have to give, they said, but in the end there was about one thousand dollars in Turkish lira in the hat." The hijackers were variously described as medical students from Istanbul University, or former journalists who had worked for rightist Moslem newspapers.

The siege ended at 5:15 A.M. the next day, when Turkish Army troops stormed the plane, firing blanks from rifles and taking careful aim with pistols. All 4 of the hijackers were wounded, and 7 hostages, including an American, an Italian, and several Turks, were shot by the hijackers. A Turkish customs official, shot in the head, later died. Those injured passengers were identified as Fatih Ozturk, Sener Arda, Murat Tiryaki, Mavlin Kazim, Andrea Katanes, hostess Melike Goker, and American citizen Fnu Shekerton. Turkish troops beat up 2 of the hijackers who were not seriously wounded and allowed male passengers to join in before the gunmen were led away. One of the hijackers reportedly died later.

The hijackers were identified by various sources as Mehmet Aglak, Yilmaz Yalciner, Hasan Guneser, Mahdi Yatsikale (also spelled Yatsikaya), Omer Yorulmaz, and Coskun Aral. On October 17, 1980, Aral, a photographer for the Paris-based SIPA press agency, who allegedly helped the hijackers, was released. On October 26, the Diyarbakir Martial Law Military Court charged Yalciner, Yorulmaz, Yatsikale, and Guneser with conspiracy to rearrange the basic social, economic, and legal system of the state in accordance with religious principles and beliefs against secularism, engaging in propaganda with this aim, hijacking an airplane at gunpoint, violating law No. 6,136, and instigating robbery, murder, and injury. 80101301

October 15, 1980 — UNITED STATES — Faisal Abdulaze Zagallai, 35, a Libyan exile critic of the Qaddafi regime and a sociology student at Colorado State University, was shot twice in his home in Fort Collins, Colorado. Three days later, the LIBYAN NEWS AGENCY said its government was responsible. On April 23, 1981, the Federal Bureau of Investigation arrested Eugene Aloys Tafoya, 47, in Truth or Consequences, New Mexico, and charged him with the shooting. Bond was set at $1 million on charges of unlawful flight. Tafoya, a former member of the United States Special Forces Green Berets, apparently had connections with American Central Intelligence Agency retirees who worked for Libya. He posed as a recruiter for Middle Eastern firms and claimed that he had been asked to give a message to the victim, firing his gun only when Zagallai pulled a pistol on him. Zagallai lost his right eye and still carries a .22 caliber bullet in his palate behind his nose. On January 5, 1982, Tafoya was sentenced to two years for misdemeanor assault and conspiracy but was acquitted of attempted first-degree murder. 80101501

October 16, 1980 — UNITED STATES — Bruce Alan Landy, 30, of Washington, D.C., announced that he was carrying a bomb 30 minutes after an Air Florida B-737 took off from Miami after beginning its flight from Freeport, Bahamas. Two unidentified passengers overpowered him. No bomb was found on the Washington-bound plane. He was charged with interfering with the duties of an Air Florida flight crew and faced 20 years in prison if convicted. 80101601

October 17, 1980 — LEBANON — A bomb exploded inside the engine compartment of a car belonging to an employee of the Polish airline LOT at Beirut International Airport, injuring the owner and another worker. 80101701

October 18, 1980 — EL SALVADOR — A bomb destroyed a utility pole 40 feet away from the Texas Instruments offices in San Salvador. 80101801

October 19, 1980 — PHILIPPINES — The April 6 Liberation Movement claimed credit for setting off a bomb inside a delegate's bag at the opening session of the American Society of Travel Agents convention in Manila. The bomb injured 20 people, including 7 Americans, and delegates from Peru, Brazil, and South Korea. The several injured Americans were identified as Frederick and Betty Cooper of Aiken, South Carolina; June C. Breen, an employee of George Washington University; Robert Fischer of Arlington Heights, Illinois; Clifford and Lola Archer of Glendale, California; and Joseph Hofrichter of Loveland, Ohio. It also injured Don Graham, a Jamaican living in New York. The bomb exploded 50 feet from Philippine president Ferdinand Marcos, United States ambassador Murphy, and Philippine tourism minister Jose Aspiras. In the wake of a campaign of bombings by the Movement, and a special threat against the convention, strict security precautions had been imposed. A confident Marcos had told the convention minutes before the blast, "By your coming here you certainly do away with all these speculations and rumors by men whose only dream is to take over power and political authority. Let them dream. They live in a world of fantasy. Let us live in our world of reality."

Marcos ordered the arrest of 30 top dissidents, including Benigno Aquino, Jr., a Harvard Fellow now waging an anti-Marcos campaign from the United States; former senator Jovito Salonga; 4 military officers; former senator Sergio Osmena, Jr.; former congressman Raul Daza, secretary of the Movement for a Free Philippines; Raul S. Manglapus, head of the United States-based Movement for a Free Philippines; Rev. Romeo Intengan, a prominent Roman Catholic priest; former provincial governor Juan Frivaldo; former constitutional convention delegates Charito Planas and Heherson Alvarez; United States citizen Steve Psinakis; former MANILA CHRONICLE publisher Eugenio Lopez, Jr.; and Sergio Osmena III. On October 31, Marcos reported that 15 people had already been arrested. That day, Doris Baffrey, 29, a Filipino married to an American, confessed to planting the bomb, believing that it was simply a big firecracker. She had been working at the Philippine Tourism office in New York and had attended the convention. 80101901

October 20, 1980 — FRANCE — A powerful black-powder time bomb was defused in the Paris Stock Exchange (Bourse). Several bomb threats were received against the Bourse that week.

October 20, 1980 — UNITED STATES — Cuban United Nations ambassador Raul Roa complained in a letter released to the press of six bomb threats against Cuba's United Nations Mission. 80102001–06

October 21, 1980 — IVORY COAST — Nati de Souza, a Togolese dissident, escaped an assassination attempt in Abidjan, but his driver was admitted to the Treichville University Hospital with bullet wounds. 80102101

October 22, 1980 — JAMAICA — Several Cuban doctors working at two local hospitals received threats to their safety. 80102201

October 24, 1980 — HONDURAS — Honduran troops arrested Santos Lino Ramirez, mine worker and founder of the Salvadoran People's Revolutionary Army (ERP), in La Esperanza.

October 25, 1980 — LEBANON — The VOICE OF PALESTINE reported that a rocket was fired at a Beirut building inhabited by a Palestinian "revolutionary official" near Corniche al-Mazra'ah, killing a guard and wounding another. 80102501

October 25, 1980 — LEBANON — According to the VOICE OF PALESTINE, at 9:00 P.M. a bomb exploded in the car of Abu al-Walid al-'Iraqi, a Palestinian "official in charge of the technical section of the unified security," seriously wounding two of his aides. 80102502

October 27, 1980 — CUBA — Among 30 Americans pardoned by Fidel Castro and allowed to return to the United States was Anthony Bryant, a former

Black Panther who was arraigned on charges of hijacking a plane to Cuba in 1969.

October 28, 1980—TURKEY—Istanbul's HURRIYET reported that Armenian terrorists had sent a Lebanese and an Italian to Belgium to assassinate Turkish diplomats and Turkish NATO officers.

October 29, 1980—PEOPLE'S REPUBLIC OF CHINA—A bomb exploded at Peking's main railway station, killing 11 and wounding 81 others, at 6:15 P.M. Police later said the incident was perpetrated by a man, 30, who had been sent to the countryside by the authorities against his wishes, and who had just quarreled with his girlfriend.

October 29, 1980—ITALY—Maltese Liberation Front frogmen attached a bomb to a Libyan gunboat anchored in Genoa. The explosion nearly sank the vessel but caused no injuries. 80102901

October 30, 1980—TURKEY—A bomb exploded at the entrance to the Turkish-American Association in Ankara, causing one thousand dollars' damage but no injuries. The bomber escaped a police chase. 80103001

October 30, 1980—POLAND—A small explosion and fire damaged the Warsaw offices of Aeroflot, hours before the Polish leadership met with Soviet leader Leonid Brezhnev over the country's future. 80103002

October 30, 1980—HONDURAS—At 6:00 P.M., several armed members of the Popular Revolutionary Command Lorenzo Zelaya fired guns from a moving automobile at the United States embassy, breaking windows but causing no injuries. The attack took place during the signing of a peace treaty between Honduras and El Salvador. 80103003

October 30, 1980—HONDURAS—A bomb set by the Popular Revolutionary Command Lorenzo Zelaya exploded in front of the Chilean embassy's garage, injuring four policemen. The group is an affiliate of the recently formed leftist Morazanist Front for the Liberation of Honduras. 80103004

October 31, 1980—IRAN—The Korean Foreign Ministry announced that its Tehran embassy had received a telephoned bomb threat. The South Koreans believed the North Koreans were responsible. 80103101

November 1980—ARGENTINA—A leftist female guerrilla was given an 11-year prison term for her part in the April 12, 1974, kidnapping by the People's Revolutionary Army of Alfred A. Laun III, chief of the United

States Information Service in Cordoba. She gave herself up after her husband was killed in 1977 by security forces.

November 4, 1980—VENEZUELA—Joaquin Echeverria, 32, Spanish president of a group formed to help Basque prisoners and exiles from Spain, and Esperanza, 29, his wife, were machine-gunned to death in their Caracas apartment. 80110401

November 4, 1980—SWITZERLAND—A bomb exploded outside the office of the Geneva city public prosecutor in the central law court building, slightly cutting a woman with flying glass. Armenian terrorists were believed responsible. Geneva police were holding two Armenians who were injured in September while building a bomb in a local hotel. 80110402

November 6, 1980—VENEZUELA—Two Venezuelan brothers claiming to be leftists hijacked an Avenza DC-9 flying 57 passengers and crew of 5 from Caracas to Puerto Ordaz and diverted it to Cuba, where they surrendered to Cuban authorities. Some passengers claimed that the hijackers, who claimed to have a bomb, were also armed with revolvers. The duo had a bottle wrapped in a handkerchief drenched with gasoline. They also threatened to ignite gasoline they had splashed on the plane's floor. No injuries were reported. The Cuban government said that under the terms of the extradition treaty it had signed with Venezuela in 1973 and renewed in 1979, it could try the hijackers if it chose not to extradite them. 80110601

November 7, 1980—TURKEY—A pipe bomb was thrown over a perimeter fence of the civil engineering building at a United States military base in Ankara, damaging the roof, heating ducts, and interior light fixtures. 80110701

November 8, 1980—INDIA—The United States and United Kingdom embassies were evacuated after each received telephoned bomb threats at 2:00 P.M. 80110801–02

November 10, 1980—LEBANON—The Front for the Liberation of Lebanon from Foreigners vowed to avenge the setting off of bombs weighing 175 and 125 pounds in a densely populated neighborhood in Christian East Beirut. Twenty persons were killed and at least 70 were wounded. Dozens of cars were destroyed. The group said, "We shall respond to the Ashrafiyeh explosions with attacks far more severe in West Beirut, where the Syrians and Palestinians exist."

November 10, 1980—ITALY—The October 3 Group, the Party of Kurdish Workers in Turkey, and the Secret Army for the Liberation of Armenia jointly claimed credit for setting bombs outside the offices of Swissair and the nearby Swiss Railroad and Tourism offices in Rome. At least seven people were injured. 80111001–02

November 10, 1980 — FRANCE — Shortly after midnight, a bomb exploded at the Turkish consulate in Strasbourg, causing no injuries. The Secret Army for the Liberation of Armenia and the Party of Kurdish Workers in Turkey jointly claimed responsibility for the blast. 80111003

November 11, 1980 — LUXEMBOURG — The Ukraine Liberation Front fire-bombed the local Aeroflot offices, causing only minor damage and no injuries. A bottle of flammable liquid had been thrown down a ventilator duct. 80111101

November 12, 1980 — URUGUAY — Orlando Castro, 21, a Uruguayan armed with a pistol, hijacked a Uruguayan Arco flight from Colonia, Uruguay, to Buenos Aires carrying 39 passengers and 3 crewmen. He released 37 passengers and demanded to be flown to Cuba, Algeria, Mexico, Libya, or Nicaragua, threatening to set off a bomb. He agreed to release the last 3 women aboard the plane — 2 passengers and a stewardess — and just keep the pilot and copilot as hostages, after the Argentine Foreign Ministry agreed to grant him safe-conduct to be delivered by a representative of the Foreign Ministry and a representative of the Nicaraguan embassy. He was then to be accompanied by 2 Nicaraguan diplomats. At 4:45 A.M. the next day, he surrendered to police in Buenos Aires after 18 hours of negotiations. One female hostage reportedly was wounded. It was later learned that his parents were divorced and that he had begun law school. 80111201

November 13, 1980 — ISRAEL — At 7:00 A.M., an Israeli Army patrol shot and killed two Palestinian guerrillas attempting to cross the Lebanese border into Israel half a mile south of the Misgav Am kibbutz.

November 13, 1980 — HONDURAS — A masked group of leftist National Coordinating Board of Solidarity with the Salvadoran People members (4 women and 6 men) seized the Red Cross offices in Tegucigalpa in what they termed a peaceful protest against government repression in El Salvador. While many employees were able to leave the building, 40, including private citizens, 2 newsmen, the director of the institution, and Jorge Munoz, the International Red Cross delegate, were trapped during the 24-hour siege when the occupiers decided to lock all doors to the building at noon. During telephonic talks with the authorities, the group demanded the creation of a clinical aid center for Salvadoran refugees in Honduras in the border towns of Camasca, Guarita, and Nueva Ocotepeque; an end to Honduran government intervention in Salvadoran affairs; and an end to

Honduran Army aid to the Salvadoran National Guard. They left the building and released their hostages the next day after being assured they would not be arrested. No injuries were reported, and witnesses claimed they saw no weapons. 80111301

November 15, 1980 — TURKEY — Two Marxist-Leninist Armed Propaganda Unit gunmen shot and killed United States Air Force sergeant William C. Herrington, 22, of Buford, Georgia, as he was backing his car out of his Adana driveway en route to his job as a security policeman at a nearby NATO base. Senior Amn. Jay M. Perry, 22, escaped unharmed. Both men were in uniform.

On June 13, 1985, an Adana military court sentenced three members of the gang to death for Herrington's death, killing two guards and a policeman in Manisa in April 1979, and killing a Turkish noncommissioned officer on November 27, 1980; for murdering four other persons; and for armed robberies. Twenty-nine received prison terms ranging from 1 month to 20 years and 10 months; 43 others were acquitted. 80111501

November 15, 1980 — SUDAN — Osman 'Ajib, self-proclaimed leader of the Eritrean Liberation Front/Popular Liberation Forces, and his aide, Osman Jibril, were shot to death by an unidentified gunman in front of their Khartoum hotel. Osman Saleh Sabbe, leader of the Eritrean Popular Liberation Forces, condemned the killing. 80111502

November 17, 1980 — PHILIPPINES — President Ferdinand Marcos requested American protection for his son, Ferdinand II (Bongbong), who reportedly was under threat of kidnap/assassination while in the United States. 80111701

November 18, 1980 — PHILIPPINES — Police detained Duane Heist, 30, of Emmaus, Pennsylvania, and Robert Rummel, 30, of Lancaster, Pennsylvania, when their plane, which they had landed for refueling at Manila International Airport, was found to have 10 Claymore mines and blasting caps that were not on the cargo list. The Malaysian embassy later confirmed that the explosives were to be delivered to the Malaysian police on consignment from Electronics Systems International of Pennsylvania. Police held them on suspicion of providing weapons to Filipino Moslem guerrillas. On December 26, President Marcos ordered them released.

November 18, 1980 — NETHERLANDS — Two firebombs exploded at the Rotterdam consulate of Cape Verde, causing some material damage but no injuries. 80111801

November 19, 1980 — ITALY — The Armenian Secret Army for the Liberation of Armenia bombed the Rome offices of Turkish Airlines, causing no injuries. 80111901

November 19, 1980 — ITALY — A bomb exploded in the Milan office of the West German Gestetner firm, breaking windows but causing no injuries. 80111902

November 20, 1980 — EL SALVADOR — An unidentified man was injured when a grenade he threw from a passing taxi at the United States embassy prematurely exploded at 5:30 P.M. 80112001

November 21, 1980 — KAMPUCHEA — The VOICE OF DEMOCRATIC KAMPUCHEA claimed that it ambushed a Vietnamese truck at Chamka Chek along Route 4, killing three Soviets and several Vietnamese soldiers.

November 21, 1980 — ANGOLA — The National Union for the Total Independence of Angola (UNITA) claimed it shot down a Soviet Antonov-26 transport plane in Cuando-Cubango Province, 155 miles east of Menongue. It captured mechanic Ivan Cherniestsky, 46, and pilot Mollaeb Kola, 38, and sent them to a "friendly country for security reasons."

On November 16, 1982, in a complicated swap involving six nations, UNITA released the 2 Soviets; South Africa released a Soviet warrant officer and the bodies of 4 other Russians, 94 Angolan soldiers, a Cuban soldier, and the body of another Cuban; Angola released 2 American mercenaries imprisoned for 7 years and a Washington-area civilian pilot, along with the bodies of 3 South Africans, all under the auspices of the Geneva-based International Committee of the Red Cross in Lusaka, Zambia. The United States mercenaries were identified as Gustavo Grillo, 33, from Jersey City, New Jersey, and Gary Acker, 27, from Sacramento, who were captured in February 1976 while fighting for the Angola National Liberation Front (FNLA) faction in the Angolan civil war. Civilian pilot Geoffrey Tyler, 32, from Seabrook, Maryland, crash-landed on a beach 21 months earlier while flying a light plane from Abidjan, Ivory Coast, to Cape Town, South Africa. South Africans identified the 3rd Russian as warrant officer Nicolai Prestretsov, who was captured in southern Angola 16 months earlier. Americans Grillo and Acker had been sentenced to 30 and 16 years, respectively, after being convicted of being mercenaries in 1976. Another American, Daniel Gearhart of Kensington, Maryland, was executed in July 1976 on a similar charge. The Soviet pilot claimed he "came here to help improve the transport system. We were offered a contract to work for one year or two years. We were flying cargo around in boxes, and passengers. We never saw what was in the boxes. . . . We could wash. We had clothes. We were well-treated," he said of his captivity. Jonas Savimbi, UNITA leader, also promised the Vatican that he would free Angolan Roman

Catholic Archbishop of Lubango, Monsignior Alexandre do Nascimentos, who was abducted in October 1982.

November 23, 1980 — GUATEMALA — The Guerrilla Army of the Poor (EGP) claimed credit for throwing three sticks of dynamite at 7:30 P.M. at the home of Argentine ambassador Ribert Tiscornia, damaging three vehicles, but causing no injuries. 80112301

November 23, 1980 — GUATEMALA — The Guerrilla Army of the Poor (EGP) claimed credit for the 7:45 P.M. bombing of the residence of Julio Gandara, honorary Uruguayan consul. No injuries were reported. 80112302

November 23, 1980 — FRANCE — Masked gunmen from the ultrarightist Basque Spanish Battalion killed 2 French citizens and wounded 10 others in a submachine-gun attack on a bar in the Basque town on Hendaye. Three members of the commando surrendered to Spanish border authorities and were released after an identity check, according to the PARIS DOMESTIC SERVICE. Quai d'Orsay officials called in the Spanish ambassador to protest, pointing to an agreement to jointly combat terrorism that had been signed the previous week. 80112303

November 25, 1980 — FRANCE — A gunman of Arab-looking appearance about 30 years old fired eight shots at the owners of the International Travel Tour Agency, which specialized in trips to Israel and Egypt. Edwin Dewek, 52, the Cairo-born Jewish owner of the agency, and his wife, Michele, 46, were killed and a woman secretary was slightly wounded. Paris police said the gun was an Italian Beretta with a silencer, which fired Czech-produced 7.65 mm bullets. The weapon, they noted, was the same as that used in an assassination attempt during the summer against former Iranian premier Shahpour Bakhtiar and in the slaying of a Syrian exile three days later. The attack came during a wave of anti-Jewish terrorist acts. 80112501

November 25, 1980 — DOMINICAN REPUBLIC — An Avianca Air Taxi on a domestic flight was diverted to Haiti by a lone hijacker who threatened to ignite a bottle of gasoline if he was not flown to Santiago, Cuba. Claiming insufficient fuel, the pilot landed at Port-au-Prince, where police arrested the hijacker. No injuries were reported. 80112502

November 25, 1980 — SWITZERLAND — The October 3 Movement, an Armenian terrorist group, bombed the main Geneva office of the Union Bank of Switzerland at 3:00 P.M., injuring two people but causing minor damage. 80112503

November 26, 1980 — UNITED KINGDOM — Ahmed Mustafa, 32, a Libyan dissident student, was believed to have been stabbed to death by a Libyan hit squad. His body was found three days after his reported disappearance in a Manchester apartment rented by a Libyan student who with an unidentified individual had visited the victim. 80112601

November 27, 1980 — TURKEY — At 5:50 A.M., four armed members of Dev Yol jumped two armed Turkish guards and entered the grounds of the NATO Rod and Gun Club, 16 miles east of Izmir. A bomb they planted exploded before it could be defused but caused no injuries. The club's membership includes primarily Turkish, British, American, and Italian NATO personnel. 80112701

November 28, 1980 — ITALY — Nicolo Amato, Italy's public prosecutor, submitted a 286-page indictment against 19 Red Brigadists, including Mario Moretti, former electronics technician and reputed terrorist mastermind, for the March 17, 1978, kidnap/murder of former premier Aldo Moro. Moretti, 34, was still at large, having twice escaped capture.

November 30, 1980 — DENMARK — Two firebombs were thrown against the Soviet embassy, causing no injuries. 80113001

December 1980 — PERU — A bomb went off at the People's Republic of China embassy, apparently set by the Sendero Luminoso (Shining Path), a breakaway from the Maoist Red Flag, which separated from the orthodox Moscow-line Peruvian Communist Party in 1964. 80129901

December 1, 1980 — HAITI — The government arrested two Cubans for plotting to blow up a factory in Port-au-Prince and found two depots of arms and munitions. 80120101

December 2, 1980 — UNITED KINGDOM — The Irish Republican Army (IRA) was believed responsible for two bombs that went off in cars outside a British Army barracks in West London. Five people were injured. Londoners feared a wave of IRA bombings linked to a hunger strike by seven IRA guerrillas jailed in Northern Ireland. 80120201 – 02

December 2, 1980 — EL SALVADOR — American nuns Ita Ford, 40, Maura Clarke, 49, both of the Maryknoll order; Ursulan Dorothy Kazel, 40; and lay worker Jean Donovan, 27, were reported missing after leaving El Salvador's international airport when their van was found burned out. The Maryknoll nuns had worked in a poor village and had received death threats from Salvadoran rightists who believed their work was "subversive."

Their bodies were exhumed from a shallow grave on December 4, 36 hours after they were reported missing. Rightists were believed responsible for shooting 3 in the head, 1 in the chest, and raping 2 of the women 30 miles from the capital city.

In protest of government handling of the investigation, the United States suspended $20 million in economic support funds (of which $5 million had already been disbursed) and $5 million in military sales credits to buy nonlethal equipment. The United States also suspended a program under which 250 Salvadoran officers were being trained at United States Army schools in Panama in techniques of dealing with guerrillas while observing human rights.

On April 29, 6 Salvadoran National Guardsmen were held as suspects in the case. The United States Federal Bureau of Investigation (FBI) said that fingerprints of Sgt. Luis Antonio Colmindres Alemen matched a print found on the van. The FBI reported that ballistics tests indicated that a shell case found at the scene matched a military-issue, West German-made G-3 rifle issued to Cpl. Jose Roberto Moreno Canjura.

On May 24, 1984, after conferring for only 55 minutes following a 19-hour trial in Zacatecoluca, near where the women's bodies were found, a 5-member Salvadoran jury found 5 former national guardsmen guilty of the murders. It marked the first time that a Salvadoran jury had convicted members of the armed forces for murdering civilians. It had been difficult to obtain a jury — of 12 persons called, only 7 came to court. The jury included 3 men: a radio technician, a driver, and an elementary school teacher; and 2 women: a secretary and a teacher. On June 19, 1984, Judge Bernardo Rauda Murcia sentenced them to 30 years in prison, the maximum permissible. The lawyer for 3 of the defendants — Jose Moreno, 28, Daniel Canales, 27, and Francisco Contreras Recincos, 36 — said he would appeal. The lawyer of Carlos Contreras Palacios, 27, the only defendant to confess, said he would not appeal. The lawyer for Luis Colindres Aleman, 28, was silent. The judge gave 25-year sentences for each of the four murders to the 4 who did not confess, and four 20-year sentences to Carlos Contreras. The judge discounted 2 years of the sentences for time already served awaiting trial and said they would be eligible for good-conduct parole after serving 20 years. The defendants were dismissed from the National Guard after being accused of the crime. Carlos Contreras retracted his confession, and the group claimed that they had been bribed — with United States money — to confess but refused to identify the patrons. Lawyers for the victims' families said they would continue to demand an investigation of alleged governmental attempts to cover up the guardsmen's role in the killings. A United States State Department report prepared by former judge Harold Tyler indicated that it was "quite possible" that Gen. Carlos Vides Casanova — head of the National Guard at the time of the killings and currently minister of defense — was aware of the cover-up. 80120203

December 2, 1980 — UNITED KINGDOM — Irish Republican demonstrators dropped stink bombs in the food department of the posh Fortnum and Mason store in London. 80120204

December 3, 1980 — UNITED STATES — Bernardine Dohrn, 38, former leader of the Weather Underground, surrendered at Chicago's Cook County Criminal Courts Building to plead innocent to aggravated battery and other charges growing out of her participation in the Days of Rage demonstrations in October 1969. Judge Fred G. Suria, Jr., freed her on $25,000 bond. She was accompanied in court by former Weatherman William Ayers, 35, with whom she had been living in hiding for the decade. Despite coming aboveground, she criticized the United States system of government and said she had gone underground "to oppose US intervention in Vietnam; to try to support the black movement for liberation and human rights and to oppose the system built on slavery, genocide and colonialism." Ayers added, "It seems to me the current establishment goal and promise of recapturing US hegemony around the world and prosperity at home can only be attempted through war." As a result of plea bargaining in which she pleaded guilty to four of the charges against her, on January 13, 1981, Dohrn was sentenced to three years probation and fined $1,500.

December 3, 1980 — BELGIUM — Irish Republican Army (IRA) gunmen fired from a speeding auto at British European Common Market commissioner Christopher Tugendhat as he left his Brussels residence to go to work. He and his wife were not injured by the two shots, and the two gunmen escaped. 80120301

December 4, 1980 — ITALY — Giuseppe Luciani, 46, fired his way into the Belgian embassy with a sawed-off shotgun, wounded Second Secretary Leopold Carrewyn, 35, and took several hostages before police fatally wounded the gunman. Police said he had lived in Belgium and had "personal problems with the administration of Belgium."

December 4, 1980 — POLAND — Andrzej Perka, 39, a Polish national armed with a fake hand grenade, hijacked a Polish airlines LOT Antonov-24 twin-engined prop plane flying 19 passengers and 5 crew members from Zielona Gora to Warsaw and diverted it to Tempelhof, West Berlin, where he requested political asylum. One passenger suffered a slight heart attack, was given medical treatment, and returned safely to Poland. Poland requested extradition of Perka. On March 10, 1981, a West Berlin court rejected Perka's claim that he was escaping secret police oppression in Poland and sentenced him to four years imprisonment for air piracy. 80120401

December 4, 1980 — GUATEMALA — The Salvadoran Taca Airline office in the capital city was set on fire during the morning. 80120402

December 4, 1980 — GUATEMALA — A dozen gunmen armed with submachine guns shot their way into the Salvadoran embassy, forced employees to watch them plant a bomb in a file cabinet, and then fled. The bomb caused extensive damage but no injuries. Francisco Alegria Mendez, 42, an embassy guard, died in the gun battle. The anticommunist Maximiliano Hernandez Martinez Front claimed it had bombed the embassy to protest "the actions of the Guatemalan Government, which is an attempt to establish another communist government in central America." Not to be outdone, two females called on behalf of, respectively, the People's Guerrilla Army and the Guatemalan Labor Party, saying that the bombing was in reprisal for the assassination of the six Salvadoran labor leaders who were buried in the cathedral. At least two women had participated in the bombing. 80120403

December 4, 1980 — INDIA — TEHRAN INTERNATIONAL SERVICE reported that Iraqi terrorists disguised as diplomats and driving the Iraqi ambassador's car attacked a group of Iranian students on their way home in New Delhi. None of the Iranians were injured, and the attackers escaped in three cars. 80120404

December 5, 1980 — USSR — An unknown gunman murdered Sultan Ibraimov, 53, premier of the Soviet Republic of Kirgiziya and his chauffeur, both of whom were sleeping in a sanitarium believed to be situated at a lakeside resort east of the republic's capital of Frunze. The spokesman for the newspaper SOVIETSKAYA Kirgiziya said the political murder was intended to be a provocation before the 26th Communist Party Congress to be held in Moscow in February. Ibraimov was a member of the Congress's organizing secretariat.

December 5, 1980 — VENEZUELA — Four armed hijackers diverted a Venezuelan Aeropostal DC-9 35 minutes out of Porlamar, Margarita, a Venezuelan island in the Caribbean, and forced it to fly to Huiguerote, a small airfield 70 miles northeast of its intended Caracas destination. The airport had been seized by accomplices of the hijackers, who stole the $1 million in cash and six hundred thousand dollars in checks and negotiable paper being transferred to Caracas by private security guards. None of the 104 passengers and 6 crew were hurt. The hijackers escaped in a waiting pickup truck. Venezuelan police reported the hijackers were arrested and the money recovered the next day. 80120501

December 9, 1980 — CUBA — The Miami office of Alpha 66, an anti-Castro Cuban exile group, claimed that in recent weeks, in Operation Maximo Gomez, it had infiltrated Cuba with three teams of saboteurs. One group allegedly killed Robert Campos Fernandez, a Cuban state security police captain in the Marianao section of Havana, who "had a very bad reputation as far as the Cuban people were concerned." The group also claimed credit for several dozen raids, including the derailment of a cargo train, the firebombing of several match factories, and other acts of arson. Three of the agents were allegedly apprehended by Cuban authorities.

December 9, 1980 — SOUTH KOREA — Arsonists tried to torch the United States Cultural Center in Kwangju, scene of antigovernment riots. On March 25, 1982, police arrested Chong Sun-chol, 27, for this attack and the March 18, 1982, firebombing of the United States Cultural Center in Pusan. 80120901

December 9, 1980 — GUATEMALA — Thirteen leftist guerrillas posing as policemen broke into a Guatemala City home and kidnapped American citizen Clifford Bevens, 55, manager of the Ginsa Tire Company, a Goodyear subsidiary. Ginsa (Gran Industria de Neumaticos, Sociedad Anomima) is 70 percent United States owned, 30 percent Guatemalan owned. The terrorists demanded a $10 million ransom from his family. The Portland, Oregon, native was killed by three bullets to the head by the guerrillas when security forces raided their hideout in Santo Domingo Xenacoj, 40 miles west of Guatemala City, on August 13, 1981. In the gun battle, police killed five guerrillas, including two females. A large number of weapons and other material were reportedly seized. 80120902

December 9, 1980 — CUBA — Fifteen armed Cubans seeking safe passage from the country took over the Vatican's Apostolic Nunciature, holding four nuns and a Cuban employee hostage. Cuban police fired tear gas to end the siege. The Cuban employee died in the gun battle, at the hands of the "antisocial elements with criminal records," according to the authorities. 80120903

December 10, 1980 — PEOPLE'S REPUBLIC OF CHINA — A man in his 30s poured gasoline over himself and attempted to set himself on fire in front of the Polish embassy. He was taken away alive by the police.

December 10, 1980 — EL SALVADOR — Forty sticks of dynamite were found hidden along a road that was to have been taken by United States ambassador William Bowdler and William Rogers, who were investigating the deaths of four American religious workers a week previously. 80121001

December 10, 1980 — TURKEY — A bomb exploded in the Izmir offices of Pan American Airlines, causing no injuries but breaking windows. 80121002

December 11, 1980 — ITALY — Police waiting outside a Milan restaurant shot and killed two Red Brigadists, identified as Roberto Serafini, 23, and Walter Pezzoli, 23. A woman claiming membership in the Walter Alasia Lucca Column confirmed their membership to the newspaper LA REPUBBLICA.

December 12, 1980 — ITALY — The Red Brigades kidnapped Giovanni d'Urso, 49, high-ranking official of the Ministry of Justice who is responsible for running security prisons that hold terrorists. In messages found in a trash can and outside a Rome nightclub, the group released a photo of the magistrate sitting in front of the group's flag, holding a list of their demands. The group called for the closure of all of Italy's maximum security prisons and the granting of official status for the "struggle committees" organized there by terrorist prisoners. On January 5, Rome rejected a Brigades proposal that the views of terrorists in two top security prisons be given an uncensored, nationwide hearing. On January 7, Renato Curcio, founder of the Red Brigades, said from prison that the kidnappers should release d'Urso because they had achieved a victory — announcement of the imminent closure of the top security jail on the Sardinian island of Asinara. On January 10, the Brigades said they would kill d'Urso in 48 hours if the news media refused to publish texts of documents from jailed guerrillas. The next day, magistrates issued an arrest warrant for Florence University professor Giovanni Senzani, 38, believed to be a middleman for the terrorists who had organized an interview with them for a newsmagazine. On January 13, IL MESSAGGERO agreed to publish the terrorists' communiques, as did the regional newspapers SECOLO XIX of Genoa and LA NAZIONE of Florence. The government also released a terminally ill Red Brigadist. The kidnappers agreed to suspend their death sentence and released d'Urso on January 15. He was discovered bound, gagged, and wearing a headset blaring music from a cassette, under blankets in the back seat of a Fiat, 250 yards from the Ministry of Justice where he worked and 250 yards from where former premier Aldo Moro's body had been found. He claimed his captors left their hideout at 4:00 A.M., drove for two hours, and changed cars twice.

December 12, 1980 — UNITED STATES — United States magistrate Roy Rutland set $100,000 bond for Steven Van Howard, 24, and David Wayne Howard, 21, on charges of interference with interstate commerce stemming from a plot in which grocery stores were told that items on their shelves had been poisoned with strychnine, and $60,000 was demanded for the disclosure of their location. Although H.E.B. store officials believed the claim was a hoax, they closed their six stores in Waco, Texas, for 3½ days and replaced 680 tons of food rather than be proven wrong.

December 15, 1980 — PERU — Between 6:00 and 6:30 A.M., dynamite was twice thrown at the Chinese embassy, causing damage but no injuries. Three other dynamite attacks took place against two bank branches and a public office in Lima. Slogans were painted on walls throughout the city, insulting Hua Guofeng and supporting Mao Zedong's widow who was being tried in Beijing. 80121501–02

December 15, 1980— LEBANON — The home of Salah Khalaf (Abu Iyad), a Palestine Liberation Organization official, was blown up at dawn in 'Abra. Three house guards were wounded. 80121503

December 15, 1980— COLOMBIA — A dozen April 19 Movement (M-19) guerrillas armed with hand grenades hijacked an Avianca B-727 flying between Bogota and Pereira with 127 people. The Liliana Hernandez de la Torre Commando Group asked for 8 hot meals for the crew, 120 cold meals, and drinks "for everyone"; navigation charts for Mexico, Central America, and the Caribbean; a "dialogue" with the governor of Magdalena Department; and the approval by congress of a general amnesty for hundreds of persons being tried on charges of rebellion. The group that night rejected an amnesty bill approved in the Chamber of Representatives that would release political prisoners after the hijackers surrendered. In a communique signed by the M-19 leaders Jaime Bateman Cayon, Carlos Toledo Plata, and Ivan Marino Ospina, the group vowed to "join our companeros in the National Liberation Army and the Workers Self-Defense Committee." It accused the government of "seeking to conceal the torture, privileges of oligarchy, the high cost of living, the 7 million illiterates, the 300 starving children daily and the permanent state of war against the people." The plane made stops in Santa Marta and Barranquilla, Colombia; Panama City, Panama (which offered asylum); Mexico City (for refueling); and Havana, where authorities took the hijackers into custody. Various numbers of passengers and crew were released at each stop, and the plane arrived at Havana with 53 passengers and 7 crew members. No injuries were reported. Colombia requested extradition of the hijackers. 80121504

December 16, 1980— UNITED KINGDOM — The October 3 Movement, an Armenian terrorist group, placed two small bombs outside the French National Tourism and Railway office in the Piccadilly section of London. Police defused the devices without injury. 80121601

December 17, 1980— TURKEY — Police captured the founder of the Turkish People's Liberation Party Front Warriors, Faruk Aydin (the Red Doctor), who was held responsible for at least 11 murders, including the slaying in Atakoy, a summer resort 15 miles west of Istanbul, of United States Army Spec. 5 Thomas Mosley on May 11, 1979.

December 18, 1980—UNITED KINGDOM—Seven prisoners who are members of the Irish Republican Army (IRA) ended the hunger strike they began on October 27 in support of the "dirty" protest by nationalist terrorists. Sean McKenna, 26, was reported comatose and near death after his 53-day ordeal. Thirty-three other prisoners who began their fast in December also ended their protest. The Ulster Defense Association similarly called off its hunger strike by six Protestant prisoners after five days.

December 18, 1980—HONDURAS—The country's most powerful banker, Paul Vinnelli, a naturalized Honduran citizen of Italian descent and president of the Chase Manhattan-owned Atlantida Bank, was abducted in downtown Tegucigalpa by four men and two women armed with submachine guns. Robert Martinez Calderon, the banker's chauffeur, was killed, and bodyguard Demetrio Cedillos was seriously injured in the gun battle with the terrorists during the daylight attack. The terrorists beat Vinnelli and forced him into a car bearing official license plates. He was released on March 2, 1981. 80121801

December 18, 1980—FRANCE—Marco Donat-Cattin, 21, leader of the Italian Front Line terrorist group and son of former Christian Democratic government minister Carlos Donat-Cattin, was arrested during the night on the Champs Elysees. Italian police had issued international arrest warrants against him for the murder of Milan's assistant state attorney, Emilio Alessandrini, in January 1979. 80121802

December 18, 1980—UNITED STATES—New York and Bridgeport police arrested five men linked to Croatian assassination and bombing plots. Two other suspects had been arrested the previous week by New York's Westchester County police, who confiscated explosives. 80121803

December 19, 1980—UNITED STATES—Cathlyn Platt Wilkerson, a former leader of the Weather Underground, surrendered to state authorities in Chicago on charges stemming from the Days of Rage demonstration in 1969.

December 19, 1980—FEDERAL REPUBLIC OF GERMANY—Shlomo Lewin, 67, a former high-ranking Israeli Army officer who served as an aide to Moshe Dayan and who was a prominent Jewish publisher and community leader and his companion, Frida Poschke, 57, widow of a former mayor, were found dead with multiple head gunshot wounds in Erlangen, in what was described as an execution-style killing. Lewin was adjutant to then Defense Minister Dayan during the 1973 Middle East war. 80121901

December 19, 1980—COSTA RICA—Police arrested seven Nicaraguans believed responsible for an attack on RADIO NOTICIAS DEL CON-TINENTE a few days before. Authorities found Galil and FAL rifles, M-16 submachine guns, M-76 machine guns, carbines, .38 caliber revolvers, grenades, dynamite, wireless communication equipment, and more than five thousand kilograms of ammunition near the Birmania Farm in Guanacaste Province. 80121902

December 20, 1980 — UNITED STATES — A Denver District Court jury acquitted Iranian student Afshin Shariati of all charges in the shooting death of Paul Moritzky, 15, and the wounding of two of his companions on November 11, 1979, a week after the seizure of the United States embassy in Tehran, when anti-Iranian protestors broke Shariati's apartment windows with baseball bats, banged on his door, and threw beer bottles at his dwelling.

December 21, 1980 — UNITED STATES — The Puerto Rican Armed Resistance set off two powerful pipe bombs at 6:00 P.M. in New York City's Penn Station, causing limited damage and no injuries. 80122101

December 21, 1980 — COLOMBIA — All 62 passengers and 6 crewmen on a Caravelle jetliner of the Aerovias del Cesar line were killed when a bomb exploded in a rear lavatory at 2:45 P.M. The plane had left the Caribbean port city of Riohacha, known for drug smuggling, and crashed between Maticas and Berebere, along the Venezuelan frontier. A threatening phone call was received minutes before the explosion.

December 23, 1980 — ISRAEL — Israel granted amnesty to Brigitte Schulz, 29, and Thomas Reuter, 28, two West Germans who were imprisoned for attempting to shoot down an El Al airliner in 1976 in Kenya. Their five-year prison terms would have ended in February.

December 23, 1980 — TURKEY — An Ankara criminal court sentenced to death four Palestinian terrorists who took over the Egyptian embassy on July 13, 1979. On October 25, 1979, the four were sentenced to death by a lower military court. Their lawyers appealed. In late May 1980, the Turkish military appeals court overturned the death sentence and ordered a retrial in a civilian court. The Ankara criminal court also sentenced a Turk to 21 years in prison for aiding the terrorists.

December 24, 1980 — GUATEMALA — Twenty members of the People's Guerrilla Army (EGP), armed with machine guns and pistols, entered the Naturista Institute in Santa Lucia, Milpas Altas, in Sacatepeques, 38 kilometers southwest of Guatemala City, and kidnapped the health clinic's American director, Long Cummings, 50. The group drove off in a pickup truck.

The kidnappers demanded $10 million ransom. He was released on January 21, 1981. 80122401

December 24, 1980—ITALY—A crude homemade bomb exploded outside the Rome offices of the British Tourist Authority, injuring one man and causing extensive damage. 80122402

December 24, 1980—PHILIPPINES—The April 6 Liberation Movement threatened to attack Japanese businesses and tourists if Japanese prime minister Zenko Suzuki went ahead with his planned three-day state visit to begin in Manila on January 8. In a letter addressed to the prime minister, which was also given to news services, the group stated:

> Mr. Prime Minister, it is well known that your government, your country's multinationals, especially Marubeni, and your compatriot tourists are some of the biggest sources of economic support to the illegitimate Marcos regime. We appeal to you to cancel your scheduled visit as a recognition that our struggle for the liberation of our country is honorable and justified. We plead with you to do so. . . . It should be obvious that Mr. Marcos cannot possibly protect all of your business interests in our country or even one of your tourists. Your disregard of our appeal will place in jeopardy the safety of every Japanese multinational and every Japanese tourist who may stay in our country after you have gone. . . . If you do not heed our warning, you will share with Mr. Marcos the responsibility for the consequences.

80122403

December 26, 1980—LEBANON—An 11-pound bomb was thrown from a car into the French embassy, causing no injuries. In a separate incident, a car belonging to the embassy was bombed. No injuries were reported. A pro-Iranian group said it would attack again if France went ahead with its sales of Mirage fighters to Iraq. 80122601–02

December 28, 1980—GUADELOUPE—A time bomb exploded inside a locker at the international airport in Pointe-a-Pitre, injuring a Chilean man waiting for an early flight and an airport employee. Police believed the bombing was to protest French president Giscard d'Estaing's visit to the Caribbean. He used the same airport several hours later. 80122801

December 28, 1980—UNITED KINGDOM—A firebomb exploded in the entry of the London offices of Libyan Arab Airlines, causing no injuries and little damage. 80122802

December 29, 1980—EL SALVADOR—During a wave of political violence, which included the deaths of seven Americans, free-lance reporter John J. Sullivan, 26, of Bogota, New Jersey, was reported on January 7, 1981, to have been missing for over a week from his Sheraton hotel room, although his luggage was still in his room. Foul play was feared. 80122901

December 29, 1980—SPAIN—The October 3 Movement set off time bombs at the Madrid offices of Trans World Airlines and Swissair, injuring seven people. The group said it was retaliating for "a scheme planned by American intelligence" against Gerald Benoit, a defense lawyer for Armenians who was assaulted in Geneva several days previously. 80122902–03

December 30, 1980—FRANCE—Jose Martin Sagardia, 29, reputedly a Basque Nation and Liberty (ETA) leader, was killed in a car-bomb explosion in Biarritz. 80123001

December 31, 1980—UNITED KINGDOM—The Irish Republican Army (IRA) was suspected of bombing a London gas storage depot. 80123101

December 31, 1980—KENYA—A powerful bomb exploded during the New Year's Eve celebrations at Nairobi's famed Norfolk Hotel, killing 16, injuring 87, and causing $3.4 million damage to a facility whose guest list has included Ernest Hemingway and Teddy Roosevelt. One American, Kenneth Moyer, was reported killed, and 8 Americans—including W. C. Quinn, his wife Donna, and their 2 children Noah, 11, and Julie, 15, all of Hudson, New Hampshire—were injured. Two Britons—aged 10 months and 4 years—were killed and 19 injured. Also injured were 2 Italians, 4 Belgians, 2 Frenchmen, an Australian, and numerous Kenyans. The casualty list would have been more extensive if the device had not been placed over a sturdy steel girder, which apparently absorbed the major force of the explosion.

The explosion apparently took place in room 7, one of the few guest rooms in that section of the hotel. NAIROBI DOMESTIC SERVICE reported that the suspected bomber and tenant was Qaddura Muhammad abd al-Hamid, a Moroccan, who registered as Murad Aksali with a Maltese passport. He had been a Fatah member and later joined the Popular Front for the Liberation of Palestine (PFLP), who sent him to Europe in 1973, where he used several aliases, including Muhammad Havi Qaddur. He escaped Kenya at 1:30 P.M., eight hours before the bomb went off, on board a Kenya Airways KQ-358 flight that terminated in Jidda, Saudi Arabia. The man had been visited in his hotel room by a woman with a German accent. Police speculated that the attack involved Palestinian and West German terrorists, who were seeking to retaliate for Kenyan aide to Israel in arresting 2 PFLP-leaning West German terrorists in 1976 who had intended to fire a missile at an El Al plane. The 2 West Germans had been released by the Israelis earlier in the week. The Norfolk Hotel is owned by a prominent African Jewish family, the Blocks, who have close ties with Israel. The Palestine Liberation Organization denied any involvement with the incident on January 2, and the PFLP disclaimed responsibility on January 8.

Kenya later ordered that all visa applications be sent to Nairobi for approval, a move that can delay trips for up to six weeks. Ironically, the major exception to this guideline was a waiver for citizens of Commonwealth countries, which includes Malta. 80123102

1980—ISRAEL—Arab terrorist attacks dropped by nearly 50 percent in Israel during the year and killed only 1 person, compared to 19 deaths in 1979. The government attributed the drop to preemptive strikes against Palestinian targets in Lebanon, inter-Arab tensions, and the work of the 87,000-member voluntary Civil Guard.

1980—ITALY—The government recorded 115 deaths due to terrorist attacks, 85 of which were accounted for by the August 2 neofascist bombing of Bologna's main railway station. Individual victims included businessmen, judges, policemen, Carabinieri servicemen and officers, politicians, journalists, and physicians.

A CHRONOLOGY OF EVENTS

1981

January 1981—SOMALIA—The Somali Salvation Front was believed responsible for six bombings within 10 days, including one in a movie theater that injured two women. The government arrested several Soviet sympathizers.

January 1981—FEDERAL REPUBLIC OF GERMANY—Hamburg police arrested Peter-Jurgen Boock in connection with the kidnap/murder of industrialist Hanns-Martin Schleyer in September 1977.

January 1981—TURKEY—Turkish police arrested several terrorists, including four leftists believed responsible for the assassination of two American servicemen in Izmir on April 12, 1979.

January 1981—BELGIUM—A bomb exploded in the Yugoslav Airlines office. 81019901

January 2, 1981—SPAIN—Basque guerrillas shot and wounded a Frenchman in the Basque coastal resort of Zarauz. 81010201

January 2, 1981—FEDERAL REPUBLIC OF GERMANY—The Black Bloc, a group set up in May 1980 to support the Red Army Faction, attacked two United States Army helicopters in Buedingen. On July 28, Frankfurt police raided a terrorist safe house and seized instructions, materials, and components for bombs, stolen air guns and air pistols, other stolen goods, and documents on cases of arson and bombings. 81010202

January 3, 1981—EL SALVADOR—Michael Hammer, 42, of Potomac, Maryland, and Mark Pearlman, 26, of Seattle, two Americans working for the American Institute for Free Labor Development, an AFL-CIO affiliate that does contract work in union organization for the Agency for International Development, were having coffee at 11:30 P.M. in the San Salvador Sheraton Hotel with Rodolfo Viera, 43, a peasant union leader and head of the agrarian reform institute, when three armed men walked calmly into the restaurant. Two of them fired automatic pistols at the trio, killing them, then left unmolested. Viera was president of the Salvadoran Institute of Agrarian Transformation and of the Salvadoran Communal Union. On April 5, police arrested prominent businessman and playboy Ricardo Sol Meza, 34. On April 15, the Federal Bureau of Investigation arrested Hans Christ, 31, a West German–Salvadoran dual national, in Miami. El Salvador requested extradition. Four other suspects were believed to have fled abroad. Sol Meza and Christ, each married to a daughter of one of El Salvador's most prominent landholding families, were believed to have strong ties with extreme rightists and may have been involved in coup plotting. Teresa Torres Lopez, 41, a hotel waitress, testified that she saw the duo before the shooting and observed them signal the two others who fired the shots. On October 22, 1981, Sol Meza was released by the Salvadoran Supreme Court for lack of evidence. Charges were dropped against the duo on January 4, 1982. Abel Campos and Rodolfo Orellana Osorio were jailed as suspects on September 14, 1982, but released for lack of evidence on September 15. The United States embassy in San Salvador said it was "dismayed and incredulous" on October 1, 1982, after hearing of the ruling that there was insufficient evidence to indict Lt. Rodolfo Isidrio Lopez Sibrian. On October 7, 1982, the American Institute for Labor Development (AIFLD) noted that Jose Dimas Valle Acevedo and Santiago Gomez Gonzalez, who had confessed to the killings, claimed that Lopez Sibrian had ordered the attack, but that Salvadoran law prevents defendants from testifying against each other in the same case. AIFLD claimed army captain Eduardo Avila and Lopez Sibrian gave the killers their two machine guns in the parking lot of the restaurant. Avila disappeared and, at the time of the AIFLD statement, had last been seen in Guatemala.

On December 20, 1983, police in Guatemala arrested army captain Eduardo Alfonso Avila, 37, whom subordinates said ordered the killing. Avila, standing outside the hotel with Lopez Sibrian, allegedly gave Valle, a subordinate, a .45 caliber automatic weapon and a khaki windbreaker to conceal it. On January 18, 1984, the Salvadoran Army high command ordered the National Police to keep Avila in jail; Police director Col. Carlos Raynaldo Lopez Nuila said Avila would remain in custody "for an undetermined period of time" for leaving the country briefly (going to Guatemala) without the high command's permission. After his detention on December 20, 1983, Captain Avila was retired from active military service and sent to Costa Rica as an attache to the Salvadoran embassy. Costa Rican authorities expelled him a few months later, claiming he had taken part in a plot. On July 3, 1985, a Salvadoran judge refused to order Avila's rearrest.

On April 29, 1983, the Fifth Penal Court acquitted Lt. Lopez Sibrian and gave prosecutors a year to produce new evidence. On May 22, 1984, an appeals court cleared Lt. Rodolfo Lopez Sibrian of all charges. Special prosecutor Reynaldo de Jesus Llane said, "We no longer have any possibility of convicting him. There could be 100 witnesses against Lopez Sibrian, but no judge can touch him anymore." Two former National Guard corporals, including his bodyguard, had claimed that Lopez Sibrian had ordered them to kill the trio. On November 18, 1984, Supreme Court magistrate Homero Sanchez Cerna confirmed that the Supreme Court had rejected an appeal by the attorney general's office to reverse the dismissal of charges against Lopez Sibrian. Sanchez Cerna dismissed the appeal on the grounds that it had been made after the one-year limit on extensions for reopening dismissed cases. President Jose Napoleon Duarte ordered Lopez Sibrian dismissed from the armed forces the next day. Lopez Sibrian is believed to be out of the country.

On February 13, 1986, a jury of two women and three men found two former National Guardsmen guilty of aggravated homicide in the slayings. The prosecution team had six lawyers, although the defense was handled solely by Luis Arevalos Diaz, who had claimed that the duo were merely following military orders. On February 28, 1986, Salvadoran Fifth District Court judge Rolando Calderon Ramos sentenced to 30 years Jose Dimas Valle and Santiago Gomez Gonzalez. Rosemaria Fortin Hueso, court clerk, said, "Each man received a sentence of 12 years for each homicide, which would be 36 years, but under Salvadoran law, 30 years is the maximum sentence possible." 81010301

January 3, 1981 — CYPRUS — Hani al-Hindi, a prominent Syrian journalist and publisher who had founded several Arab and Palestinian movements, lost an arm when a bomb exploded as he opened his car door outside his Limassol home. On May 11, 1981, after plea bargaining, an assize court sentenced to two years imprisonment Moshe Antoine Bavli, 41, an Israeli of French origin. The police withdrew the charges of conspiring to kill the victim and attempted murder. Bavli pleaded guilty to conspiring with other persons to keep watch on al-Hindi by unlawful means, circulating a false document (a Canadian passport) with intent to deceive the authorities, driving with a forged international driving license (each charge entailing a sentence of two years), illegal entry into Cyprus without a passport (entailing three months), and use of a wireless set without a permit from the Council of Ministers (entailing six months). All sentences were to run concurrently. 81010302

January 4, 1981 — FRANCE — The Guadeloupe Liberation Army bombed the Chanel fashion and perfume store in central Paris, injuring a night watchman, shredding racks of high-fashion clothing, and smashing thousands of bottles of perfume. The group demanded "the departure of French colonial forces from Guadeloupe . . . and have begun as of Jan. 1, 1981, a war of national liberation. This morning, in the heart of Paris, French prestige was struck. From now on, we will fight on the soil of the continent for national independence." 81010401

January 5, 1981 — UNITED STATES — Abdul Hamid, 25, one of the 12 Hanafis who had taken over three buildings in Washington, D.C., and seized 149 hostages in March, 1977, was freed by a District of Columbia Superior Court judge because he had been rehabilitated. He would otherwise have been ineligible for parole until 2013. Judge Nicholas S. Nunzio placed him on five years probation. United States attorney Charles Ruff filed an appeal of the release on January 9.

January 6, 1981 — UNITED STATES — Cathlyn Platt Wilkerson was sentenced to nine months in prison for her part in the Weather Underground Days of Rage demonstrations in Chicago in 1969.

January 7, 1981 — KAMPUCHEA — The VOICE OF DEMOCRATIC KAMPUCHEA claimed that it killed three Soviet advisors and a Vietnamese and destroyed a white Mercedes in front of the Kirirom theater.

January 8, 1981 — UNITED KINGDOM — A London post office sorting clerk intercepted a Scottish Socialist Republican League package bomb addressed to Prime Minister Margaret Thatcher.

January 8, 1981 — UNITED KINGDOM — An Irish Republican Army (IRA) bomb hidden in a kit bag exploded in a block of servicemen's housing at a Royal Air Force training base at Uxbridge, in the northwestern outskirts of London, injuring two civilians. 81010801

January 11, 1981 — PHILIPPINES — The April 6 Liberation Movement reportedly threatened to attack international film celebrities due to attend the January 14 Manila film festival. 81011101

January 12, 1981 — ISRAEL — Two gunmen driving a military jeep shot and killed Sheik Mohammed Abu Rabia, the only Bedouin member of Israel's Knesset, as he sat in his car near a West Jerusalem hotel. He was the first member of Israel's parliament to be assassinated in the country's history. He was elected to parliament in 1977 on his own Bedouin Rights ticket but struck a deal with other Arabs to serve alternate terms in office. He was a forceful opponent of expropriation of Arab land in the Negev Desert.

Israeli police announced on January 23 the arrest of three Arab brothers, the sons of Sheik Jaber Muadi, a Druze rival of the victim. On January 25, Seif Muadi, 23, a lieutenant in the Israeli Army and one of the brothers, admitted firing six shots at Abu Rabia, but said that neither his father nor brothers knew of his murderous intentions.

January 12, 1981 — PUERTO RICO — Members of the Marxist-Leninist group the Macheteros entered the Muniz Air National Guard base near San Juan at 1:30 A.M. and placed bombs in the air intake ducts or the wheel wells of 13 aircraft, destroying 8 A-7 Corsair and F-104 Starfighter jets and damaging 2 other planes. Damage was placed at $45 million. The bombings came on the birthday of Eugenio Maria de Hostos, a 19th-century patriot active in the struggle for independence from Spain. The anniversary is annually marred by proindependence protests against United States rule on the island.

January 12, 1981 — EL SALVADOR — Nelson Arietta, a Venezuelan free-lance journalist, was dragged from his downtown San Salvador hotel by a group of plainclothes policemen and held for allegedly "being a spokesman for the terrorists."

January 12, 1981 — EL SALVADOR — Ian Mates, 26, a South African cameraman for the UNITED PRESS INTERNATIONAL and INDEPENDENT TELEVISION NEWS of London, died of head injuries, and his two American photographer colleagues, John Hoagland, 33, and Susan Meiselas, 32, were injured when their car was hit by a directional mine in a rural area about 20 miles north of the capital, at 9:00 A.M. 81011201

January 13, 1981 — FRANCE — A hand grenade left by the Armenian Secret Army for the Liberation of Armenia exploded at 9:00 A.M. in the car of the Turkish embassy's financial advisor, Ahmet Erdeyli, when he was leaving his house to go to work. Erdeyli escaped injury. 81011301

January 14, 1981 — SWEDEN — The government announced it would deport 4 of 12 Palestinians arrested for membership in the Popular Front for the Liberation of Palestine (PFLP)–General Command, under provisions of the country's alien and terrorism statutes.

January 15, 1981 — TURKEY — Turkish authorities arrested 14 members of the leftist Eylem Birlige who confessed to strafing the Izmir residence of the United States consul general on August 2, 1977.

January 15, 1981 — ITALY — Judicial authorities arraigned 15 Red Brigadists on charges of kidnapping and slaying Christian Democratic party chairman

Aldo Moro in 1978: Prospero Gallinari, Adriana Faranda, Valerio Morucci, Mario Moretti, Enrico Triaca, Teodoro Spadaccini, Gabriella Mariani, Antonio Marini, Barbara Balzerani, Franco Bonisoli, Lauro Azzolini, Rocco Micaletto, Raffaele Fiore, Luca Nicolini, and Cristoforo Piancne. Moretti and Balzerani are still at large. The investigating judge cleared Franco Piperno, Lanfrance Pace, Toni Negri, Patrizio Peci (the "repentant terrorist"), and Front Line leader Corrado Alunni.

January 15, 1981 — UNITED STATES — Weather Underground leader Cathlyn Wilkerson began a three-year prison term for building bombs in 1970. She told New York Supreme Court Justice Harold Rothwax that "I remain committed to fighting to change our world because I believe the beauty and productivity of the human spirit cannot be contained by the few who rule with greed, selfishness, and cruelty."

January 15, 1981 — EL SALVADOR — Olivier Rebbot, 31, a French-born photographer long a resident of New York, was wounded while accompanying a government patrol fighting guerrillas about one hundred miles east of the capital in the town of San Francisco Gotera. He died on February 9 from his wounds. 81011501

January 16, 1981 — UNITED KINGDOM — Three gunmen used sledgehammers to smash their way into a cottage near Coalisland, west of Belfast, and fired seven shots into the chest, hip, and leg of Bernadette Devlin McAliskey, 33, the prominent Roman Catholic civil rights champion and former member of Parliament, as she was getting two of her three children ready for school. Her husband, Michael, was listed in serious condition with three bullet wounds. Minutes later, police arrested three Protestants who were indicted on January 21 for attempted murder.

January 16, 1981 — YEMEN — Unidentified gunmen killed Bahrain's local administration minister Mohamed Khamis. 81011601

January 16, 1981 — LEBANON — Self-professed supporters of the Shi'ite Imam Musa as-Sadr fired four rockets at the Libyan People's Bureau (embassy) before midnight, causing no injuries. Only one of the rockets hit the building, causing some damage and breaking windows. 81011602

January 19, 1981 — SPAIN — Basque Nation and Liberty (ETA) was believed responsible for placing explosives onto a barred window of the San Sebastian offices of Iberduero, a firm building a nuclear power plant in Bilbao. The blast caused extensive damage but no injuries.

January 19, 1981 — LEBANON — Palestinian guerrillas were believed responsible for shooting and killing three Senegalese soldiers serving with the United Nations Interim Force in Lebanon in an observation post near the village of Barish, eight miles east of the port city of Tyre. 81011901

January 19, 1981 — COLOMBIA — Four masked and armed men and 1 woman, all apparently members of a dissident faction of the April 19 Movement (M-19), kidnapped Bible translator Chester Allen Bitterman, 28, of Lancaster, Pennsylvania. The group broke into a Bogota home of the Summer Institute of Linguistics, gathered 15 Americans and 1 Colombian woman present in the living room and tied them up. The victims were questioned, and the terrorists searched the house, looking for the Institute's Colombian director, Alvaro Wheeler. The group stole the house's radio/teletype and a car. They claimed the institute was a Central Intelligence Agency front and demanded it leave the country or Bitterman would be killed. The institute is a subsidiary of Wycliffe Bible Translators, which specializes in translating the Bible for remote peoples. The government, and Wycliffe, refused to negotiate, although apparently a monetary ransom — rejected by the terrorists — was offered. On January 27, the M-19 demanded the publication of a communique by several European, Latin American, and United States newspapers (including the NEW YORK TIMES and WASHINGTON POST) by February 19. The United States embassy and Wycliffe rejected the demand, although EL BOGOTANO published half of the group's 21-page manifesto and a letter Bitterman wrote to his wife. The group set its deadline back 15 days after the publication, still calling for the expulsion of American Institute employees.

The circumstances of the kidnapping brought to light a split within the M-19. On February 15, 3 reporters — Jorge Matiz, Jose Maria Romero, and Gustavo Castro Caicedo — announced that the mainstream of the M-19 had kidnapped them to claim that it was not involved in the Bitterman case. Everth Bustamante, chief of the National Coordinating Board of the Rank and File of the April 19 Movement, said that Carlos Vidales Rivera, Jorge Sanchez Rojas, and he were not involved in the incident and blamed the Central Intelligence Agency for the kidnapping. Jaime Bateman Cayo, M-19 leader, also denied involvement. On February 22, Talion, a Colombian ultrarightist group, vowed to kill a high-ranking member of the Communist party if Bitterman was killed.

On March 7 at 4:30 A.M., following anonymous calls to police and the press, Bitterman's body was found shot and draped in the M-19's black and red flag inside a hijacked minibus. He was propped up next to his driver, who was bound and gagged. Propaganda pamphlets of the M-19 were left alongside the body.

On March 8, military security was increased around the headquarters of the Summer Institute after it received threats from the Revolutionary Armed Forces of Colombia (FARC) and an M-19 faction that blamed the

Central Intelligence Agency for the murder of Bitterman.

On March 10, the government announced it had arrested 100 people, including Alfredo Torres, an evangelical pastor who had served as an intermediary between the M-19 and the institute. On March 22, police announced the arrest of Ruben Narvaez, a schoolteacher from the Arauca region of the border with Venezuela. On June 12, secret police arrested Oscar Eduardo Fonseca Alba, who claimed his name was Raul Martinez Sanchez. He had a bullet wound in one leg. 81011902

January 20, 1981 — IRAN — A few minutes after the inauguration of United States president Ronald Reagan, the United States hostages were flown out of Tehran, ending a 444-day ordeal.

January 20, 1981 — DENMARK — The Israeli manager of the Copenhagen office of El Al was beaten and seriously injured during the night by individuals who painted swastikas on the wall of the office. 81012001

January 21, 1981 — NORTHERN IRELAND — Irish Republican Army (IRA) terrorists bombed the border castle of Sir Norman Stronge, Protestant speaker of the regional parliament for 24 years. Two bodies found on the scene were believed to be Stronge, 86, and his son, James, 48. Police rushing to the scene were fired on by snipers for 20 minutes. Preceding the bombing, at least 10 heavily armed men in combat uniform had stolen two cars. Two of the gunmen held the owners of the cars hostage while the other 8 shot the Stronges, then set off the bombs. Police believed the attack was in retaliation for the attempted murder of Bernadette Devlin McAliskey a few days earlier. On July 31, 1984, Irish Supreme Court justice Tom O'Higgins extradited to the United Kingdom Seamus Shannon, 26.

January 23, 1981 — UNITED STATES — During the afternoon, a pipe bomb went off in the Manhattan New York State Supreme Court Building, rupturing water pipes, breaking windows, but causing no injuries. Although a Puerto Rican terrorist group claimed credit, a preblast warning had been received by UNITED PRESS INTERNATIONAL from the Croatian Freedom Fighters. 81012301

January 25, 1981 — UNITED STATES — While 20 inmates of New York's Metropolitan Correctional Center barricaded the 11th floor and held a guard hostage on the rooftop recreational area, a man and a woman hijacked a helicopter from a downtown landing pad in a jailbreak attempt of a convicted narcotics smuggler. The duo forced the pilot at gunpoint to land on the wire-cage roof of the detention center but were unable to cut through the quarter-inch wire. The prisoners held police off for three hours before surrendering with no injuries. The hijackers flew off to a heliport on the

Hudson River, where they escaped in a waiting car driven by a second woman. The car was found abandoned. Shawn Becker, 29, surrendered on February 9 for her role in trying to free her boyfriend, convicted killer/ drug dealer Robert Wyler. 81012501

January 26, 1981 — EL SALVADOR — A fire destroyed a United States-owned Hardee's fast-food restaurant in the capital but caused no injuries. The chain had been the target of several attacks in recent months. 81012601

January 26, 1981 — UNITED STATES — The Jewish Defense League claimed credit for bombing the Bank Melli Iran in San Francisco, breaking 7 of its windows and causing minor structural damage, and breaking 42 of the windows of the Union Bank across the street but causing no injuries. The caller said the bombing was to protest "the brutal persecution of Iranian Jewry" and demanded the release of "50,000 hostages" he said were being held in Iran. 81012602

January 26, 1981 — UNITED KINGDOM — Three Irish Republican Army (IRA) bombs went off on the tracks of the rail link between Belfast and Dublin, while bombs placed in cars and buildings exploded in six Northern Irish towns, injuring 12 people and damaging 30 shops. 81012603

January 27, 1981 — ITALY — Bombs set by the October 3 faction of the Armenian Liberation Army severely damaged the Milan offices of Swissair and the Swiss tourist office and injured two Italian women. 81012701–02

January 28, 1981 — KAMPUCHEA — The VOICE OF DEMOCRATIC KAMPUCHEA claimed that its guerrillas ambushed a Vietnamese jeep on Route 6, north of Phum Koul, Pralay commune, Stoung District, Kompong Thom Province, killing six people, including a Vietnamese three-star colonel commander, two one-star colonels and a white-shirted, caucasian foreigner.

January 28, 1981 — UNITED STATES — United States secretary of state Alexander M. Haig, Jr., declared that "international terrorism will take the place of human rights" as the key concern of American foreign policy.

January 28, 1981 — UNITED KINGDOM — Claiming that the British authorities had reneged on a deal, about four hundred Irish Republican Army (IRA) prisoners resumed the "dirty protest" by smearing their cells with human excrement and threatening a new hunger strike at the Maze Prison to gain political prisoner status with rights under the Geneva conventions.

January 29, 1981 — SPAIN — Basque Nation and Liberty (ETA) kidnapped

Jose Maria Ryan, the chief engineer who worked at Spain's Lemoniz nuclear power station near Bilbao. The group demanded that the plant, which was two-thirds completed and due to open in early 1982, be dismantled by February 6. The bullet-riddled body of Ryan was found in a ditch on February 6. Iberduero, the Spanish firm building the station, announced on February 10 that it was stopping all work indefinitely. The killing came a day after King Juan Carlos successfully ended his first visit as monarch to the Basque region. Tens of thousands of Basques staged strikes and demonstrations against the ETA's violence.

January 29, 1981 — EL SALVADOR — A powerful bomb exploded at 5:30 P.M. in a car parked in front of the Nicaraguan embassy, destroying a low wall in the main entrance and damaging furniture but causing no injuries. 81012901

January 30, 1981 — MOZAMBIQUE — South African Defense Forces (SADF) military commandos blew up the suburban headquarters of the African National Congress, the principal black nationalist group of South African exiles, killing 7 people, including a Portuguese worker, near Maputo. Mozambique claimed 13 were dead, including several South Africans. The SADF announced that 30 black nationalists and 2 white commandos died. The SADF said it had proof that the group was intending to launch terrorist raids into South Africa from the Matola office. The South Africans used mortars, rockets, and automatic weapons in the attack.

January 30, 1981 — FRANCE — A bomb heavily damaged the historic Palais de Justice in Paris but caused no injuries. The Corsican National Liberation Front and the Guadeloupe Liberation Army claimed credit. 81013001

January 31, 1981 — PERU — Ayacucho police announced the capture of 23 terrorists headed by foreign-national Chinese. 81013101

February 1981 — JORDAN — Security forces intercepted a dozen Syrian commandos led by a Syrian Army colonel who were sent to assassinate Jordanian prime minister Mudar Badran, Jordan's former security chief who was suspected by the Syrians of having sympathies for the anti-Syrian Moslem Brotherhood.

February 1981 — BELGIUM — A firebomb exploded in the Yugoslav tourist bureau. 81029901

February 1, 1981 — PERU — Argentine Hector Matiani (Hector Hugo Malvano), died when sticks of dynamite he had activated exploded, destroying a flagpole in Cusco's main plaza. It was unclear whether he had planted the dynamite or had inadvertently activated it. Police arrested, but later released, three Argentines: Hector Pereira, 29, Enrique Paracohaki, 29, and an unidentified woman; and three Chileans: Silvia Jimenez Izquierdo, 19, Maria Dolores Bicanchi Torres, 21, and Carmen Razuri Cobarrubias, 21. 81020101

February 2, 1981 — FEDERAL REPUBLIC OF GERMANY— Explosives experts dismantled pickle jars filled with an explosive connected to failed 60-minute fuses that were found on the seats of two United States Army observation helicopters at Armstrong Barracks airfield near Buedingen. 81020201

February 2, 1981 — EL SALVADOR— A group of young rebels firebombed the Esso Standard Oil compound, a subsidiary of the New York-based Exxon Corporation, outside San Salvador, leaving two people dead and damaging one of the buildings used to load trucks. 81020202

February 3, 1981 — FRANCE— Two mail bombs postmarked from Spain exploded in the homes of two Romanian exiles, writer Paul Goma and former interior minister Nicolas Penescu, who was seriously wounded in the face, hand, and torso. A bomb specialist was slightly injured while dismantling the bomb sent to Goma. Several observers believed Romanian intelligence agents were responsible. 81020301–02

February 3, 1981 — ZIMBABWE— Two armed black men killed a British missionary couple at the Seventh Day Adventist mission school near Inyazura, about 125 miles east of Salisbury. Donald Lale died after being beaten with a garden hoe and his wife, Anne, was bludgeoned with a stool and shot to death. The killers said the attack was in retaliation for "what the whites did in Maputo," an apparent reference to the South African Defense Forces (SADF) attack on the African National Congress (ANC) in Mozambique a few days earlier. 81020303

February 4, 1981 — EGYPT—AGENCE FRANCE-PRESSE in Paris reported that Egyptian authorities uncovered a plot by the Japanese Red Army and other terrorist groups to attack Cairo's international airport. 81020401

February 4, 1981 — UNITED STATES— A bomb was defused minutes before it was set to go off at the Swiss consulate in Los Angeles. A warning phone call was sent by an Armenian terrorist group called "Operation 3" (possibly a garble of the October 3 Movement). 81020402

February 5, 1981 — FRANCE— Bombs set by the October 3 Movement, an Armenian terrorist group, exploded at the Paris offices of Air France and

Trans World Airlines. AGENCE FRANCE-PRESSE was the target of a bomb threat. 81020501–03

February 5, 1981 — UNITED STATES — Manuel Morales Torres attempted to hijack a New York-San Juan flight to Cuba, saying he had a bomb. The pilot landed in San Juan, and Morales said he would thereupon surrender to the Cuban police. Puerto Rican police found no bomb. 81020504

February 6, 1981 — LEBANON — The Iraqi diplomatic pouch was stolen by gunmen who halted an Iraqi embassy car on its way from Beirut International Airport. 81020601

February 6, 1981 — VATICAN CITY — A bomb consisting of a pound of gunpowder exploded at the Taiwanese embassy to the Vatican, causing heavy damage, but no injuries. The bombers apparently mistook it for the Chinese embassy to Italy, since they were demanding the release of Chiang Ching, Mao Zedong's widow. 81020602

February 6, 1981 — COLOMBIA — Two submachine-gun-wielding young men hijacked an Aviance B-727 and forced the pilot to land at Cucuta Airport, where they released all 60 passengers. They threatened to kill, one at a time, the pilot, copilot, navigator, and 2 stewardesses if 300 soldiers who had surrounded the plane did not withdraw and permit the plane to fly to Mexico or Panama. After a 10-hour siege, the duo left aircraft KH-1717 at 10:25 P.M. and surrendered to police. 81020603

February 6, 1981 — LEBANON — Twenty gunmen attacked the residence of Jordanian charge Hisham Muheisen, 42, at 1:30 A.M., and conducted a two-hour gun battle with guards before kidnapping Muheisen and his maid, apparently mistaking her for his wife. One assailant died when one of the terrorists' cars caught fire. A passing motorist died, as did Lebanese guard Pvt. 'Abd as-Salam al-Qaralih al-Bararshah, and several people were injured. The identity of the kidnappers remains in question. A leaflet was found crediting the attack to the leftist Arab National Organization and the Pan-Arab Leftists–Vanguards of Revolutionary Violence. Another group, the Eagles of the Revolution (Nusur ath-Thawrah), charged that Jordan was allied with "imperialism and Zionism" and accused it of spreading lies about Syria. The group demanded the return of two Syrian pilots who defected to Amman last year, who it claimed were members of the anti-Syrian Moslem Brotherhood. It later demanded the return of seven defectors in Jordan and Iraq. The Syrian-run SYRIAN-ARAB NEWS AGENCY (SANA) ran an Eagles denial of involvement, however. Yet another Eagles spokesman said negotiations should be conducted through the Yemen embassy, and that the Palestine Liberation Organization, which had denounced the kidnapping and offered to search for the kidnappers and the victim, should stay out of the incident. Various deadlines for Muheisen's release were set and ignored. One call from the Eagles said he was taken to Damascus for treatment of "physical and psychological disorders," but another caller from the Eagles said Muheisen was being held in the Lebanese town of Laboue, 50 miles northwest of Beirut. Still another report had him in a Palestinian organization's office in the Shatila refugee camp. RADIO MONTE CARLO indicated that he was released on April 14 by the National Confrontation Front. 81020604

February 7, 1981 — KUWAIT — Three or four people driving an American car shot and killed Iraqi national Dr. Jasim Hammadi al-Mashhadani, an Iraqi dissident leader, as he was coming out of the Syrian Air Lines office in Kuwait. His Syrian "service" (a quasi-diplomatic designation) passport number 6250 identified him as 'Abd as-Salam Sam'an, born in 1945. The attack came at 8:50 P.M. on Fahd as-Salim Street. Referring to Dr. Hammadi, the Arab Revolution Vanguards said that its Group of Martyr Salah al-Bitar had executed a Syrian intelligence man who had taken part in killing al-Bitar. 81020701

February 7, 1981 — IRELAND — Seven masked Irish Republican Army (IRA) men armed with rifles and pistols boarded a pilot launch, took over the *Nelly M,* a British coal ship moored off the Donegal coast, forced the crewmen into a life raft, and exploded bombs that left the vessel partially submerged. No injuries were reported. The terrorists said that other British ships entering Irish waters would be similarly attacked. 81020702–03

February 7, 1981 — FRANCE — A letter bomb mailed from Madrid was detonated safely by police in the courtyard of the Romanian embassy. It was similar to those received four days earlier by two Romanian dissident exiles. 81020704

February 9, 1981 — AUSTRALIA — The country's longest criminal trial in history ended in Sydney when 6 Croatian immigrants were found guilty of terrorism charges. The trial ran for 10 months and involved testimony from 112 witnesses. The accused were identified as Maksim Bebic, 29, Jekoslav Brajkovic, 30, Anton Zvirotec, 31, Ilija Kokotovic, 32, his brother Joseph, 27, and Mile Nekic, 32. The terrorists had planned to explode bombs to disrupt Sydney's water supply, bomb various travel agencies, bomb a local theater during a performance of Croatian singers and dancers visiting Australia, and bomb properties occupied by Yugoslavia. On February 17, Mr. Justice Maxwell sentenced them to 15 years each for conspiring to make bombs, and 5½ years for possessing explosives with intent to cause injury and damage. One of the terrorists was sentenced to 3 years for stealing explosives. The sentences, to be served concurrently, were to date from the men's arrest 2 years earlier.

February 9, 1981 — GREECE — An Autonomous Resistance (Avtonomi Andistasi) bomb exploded shortly before midnight at the entrance to a Nestle milk store owned by I. Dhritsas, at 17 Arkadhia Street, Peristeri, causing some damage. 81020901

February 11, 1981 — UNITED STATES — Ten members of the Puerto Rican Armed Forces for National Liberation (FALN) were found guilty in Chicago by a federal jury on all counts of seditious conspiracy, armed robbery, interstate transportation of stolen vehicles, and violations of weapons laws. The defendants had bombed and planned to bomb 28 buildings in Chicago on 13 occasions from 1975 to 1979. On February 18, federal Judge Thomas R. McMillen sentenced them to prison terms ranging from 55 to 90 years. The defendants said that they did not recognize the court's jurisdiction and said the judge was a "puppet" of the United States government.

February 11, 1981 — GUATEMALA — Leon Don Richardson, an Australian businessman representing the Hong Kong firm Magii Industrial Company, was forced into a car by four men as he entered a factory in Guatemala City. Three other heavily armed individuals were in the car waiting. No ransom demands appear to have been made, and he was released on May 20 and returned to his Hong Kong home. 81021101

February 12, 1981 — CORSICA — The Corsican National Liberation Front was believed responsible for setting off 37 bombs around the island — at the Ijaccio Courthouse and outside shops, banks, and the home of Corsica's chief treasurer — hours after the State Security Court in Paris passed jail sentences on a group of Corsican extremists.

February 12, 1981 — DOMINICA — Several Rastafarians set on fire the Giraudel house of an American couple, then took them hostage after a gunfight with police. The wife was released the following morning, but they held her husband, demanding release of three comrades sentenced to hang. 81021201

February 13, 1981 — FRANCE — The National Front for the Liberation of Corsica set off bombs in the Italian tourist office, under a railway car at the Gare de Lyon rail station and another in a parking garage at Orly airport, causing no injuries. 81021301–03

February 13, 1981 — CUBA — Four women, 19 men, and 6 children, all Cubans demanding asylum, armed with submachine guns, hand grenades, pistols, and knives, took over the Ecuadoran embassy. Some of the group beat a Cuban security guard with an iron pipe and stole his weapons during the takeover. They seized as hostages Ambassador Jorge Perez Concha, Ecuadoran diplomats Guillermo Bassante and Francisco Proano, and Cuban secretary Mercedes Vazquez. The Cuban government said it would not grant safe conduct out of Cuba but would also not storm the building without the Ecuadoran government's permission. The group released Bassante the next day. Havana said that three of the attackers had been accused of common crimes. Four days later, they released the remaining hostages and turned over their weapons to the ambassador but did not leave the embassy. Cuban authorities stormed the building (without firing a shot) on February 2 and arrested the attackers, including their leader, Romulo Delgado. The Ecuadoran government claimed it had agreed to let the dissident Cubans stay in the embassy under its care. In protest, Ecuador recalled its ambassador from Cuba. 81021304

February 16, 1981 — UNITED KINGDOM — John Christopher Bradley, 42, an Irish Republican Army (IRA) member, after pleading guilty to murdering West German consul Thomas Niedermeyer in 1973, was sentenced to 20 years in jail.

February 16, 1981 — PAKISTAN — A few minutes before the Pope arrived in Karachi to celebrate Mass for one hundred thousand at Pakistan's national stadium, a grenade-like device exploded in the hand of a Pakistani man who had made his way near a reviewing stand reserved for VIPs. Three other persons, including a policeman, were injured, and the perpetrator was killed. At least one of the injured was a Christian. 81021601

February 16, 1981 — FRANCE — Two rockets hit the embassy of South Yemen during the early morning, blowing a hole in the wall, damaging furniture, but causing no injuries. The rockets were fired from timed launchers from an apartment building wall behind the embassy. "Remember Copernic" was written on a note near the rocket tubes, apparently in reference to the October 3, 1980, bombing of the Rue Copernic synagogue in which 4 died and 14 were injured. 81021602

February 18, 1981 — USSR — The Soviets released Jozef Mendelevich, 30, last of a group of a dozen Jews who were arrested for planning to hijack a plane out of the Soviet Union in 1970. He spent 11 years in detention camps and was finally permitted to emigrate to Israel after years of Western pressure.

February 18, 1981 — MEXICO — About 30 peasants took over the Indian embassy in the posh residential district of Polanco, taking hostage Indian ambassador Kam Tekar, 5 Indian diplomats, and 4 Mexican employees. Half an hour later, 40 peasants seized 19 hostages, including the ambassador, in the Guatemalan embassy. The members of the Isthmian Labor, Peasant, and Student Coalition (COCEI) and residents of Juchitan demanded an end to government repression in Oaxaca state and called for the release of one of their leaders, former army major Leopoldo Degibes. Two hours after the Guatemalan embassy was seized, 150 Mexican police removed the 40 protesters, via Guatemalan ambassador Jorge Palmieri's wishes. Soon afterward, 100 police officers evicted the protestors at the Indian embassy. No injuries were reported. 81021801–02

February 19, 1981 — LEBANON — Gunmen fired on the limousine of 78-year-old Patriarch Maximos the Fifth Hakim, head of the Melchite Catholic Christian community, near the Al Mataam restaurant 2 kilometers west of the resort city of Bhamdoun (22 kilometers east of Beirut) on the main Beirut-Damascus Highway. The patriarch received minor wounds in the face. His attackers apparently escaped in a Mercedes or Audi-10.

February 19, 1981 — GUATEMALA — Unidentified individuals fired from their car at a police patrol in front of the United States embassy. Shots were exchanged, but no injuries were reported. 81021901

February 19, 1981 — SYRIA — The Arab Revolution Vanguards Organization told the VOICE OF LEBANON that it had kidnapped two Soviet experts. They claimed they had executed one of the experts, (first name unknown) Zakharov, who was working in telecommunications in Hamah Governorate, at 4:00 A.M. The group called for the International Red Cross to secure the release of detainees in Syria, including Salah Jadid, a former Syrian chief of staff, before the Vanguards felt it necessary to resort to torture, executions, and assassinations. 81021902

February 19, 1981 — IRAQ — The Unified Kurdistan Socialist Party, in a statement in Beirut, claimed credit for kidnapping four Indian construction workers, a Briton, an Egyptian, and three Lebanese in Iraq's rugged northeast province of Suleimaniyah the previous month. The party joined seven other Iraqi opposition groups the previous November in launching a united front sponsored by Damascus. 81021903

February 20, 1981 — ITALY — German-speaking Tyrol separatists, who want the region returned to Austria, bombed two pylons in the Alto Adige region of northern Italy, cutting electricity supplies to several towns and villages.

February 20, 1981 — SPAIN — Separate groups of armed Basque Nation and Liberty/ Political-Military (ETA/PM) gunmen kidnapped Uruguayan consul Gabriel Biurrun, 49, from his home in Pamplona; Austrian consul Herman Diez de la Sel, 45, from his Bilbao home; and Antonio Amparo Fernandez, 47, a Spanish national handling El Salvadoran consular interests, from his Bilbao home. The group hoped to focus world attention on the death of an ETA suspect in police custody the previous week. They attacked the San Sebastian residence of the Portuguese consul but found that he was not at home. They also claimed to have attacked the San Sebastian home of the West German consul. Several policemen retired in protest after the death in detention of ETA suspect Jose Arrequi, and widespread strikes and demonstrations were conducted, reversing a trend of antiextremist public feeling. About 30 foreign consuls left the Basque region after the kidnappings. The United Nations Human Rights Commission condemned the kidnappings. The ETA/PM demanded that the media publicize reports on alleged torture and maltreatment of detainees. After an abortive military coup, the ETA/PM offered a truce to the government and released the 3 consuls on February 28. 81022001–05

February 21, 1981 — LEBANON — After police asked a group they believed appeared suspicious to stop their car in front of the French embassy, they were fired upon. No casualties were reported in the gun battle. 81022101

February 21, 1981 — HONDURAS — The Martyrs of La Talanquera bombed the United States Standard Fruit Company-owned Polymer Plastics Company offices, wounding watchman Gabriel Diaz, who kicked the suspicious package that contained the time bomb. A second bomb was found later that night but defused. The group demanded justice for Isletas, an associative peasant enterprise involved in growing and marketing bananas in Colon Department on the Atlantic coast. 81022102

February 21, 1981 — FEDERAL REPUBLIC OF GERMANY — A 22-pound bomb exploded at 8:45 P.M. in the Czechoslovakian section of the Munich offices of RADIO FREE EUROPE and RADIO LIBERTY, causing $2 million damage and injuring eight people, including a West German switchboard operator, three Czech staffers, and four passersby or nearby residents. Police intially apprehended two persons for questioning and on March 10 arrested a 30-year-old Czech driving an automobile that had been observed near the scene. The Commando of Croatian Revolutionaries in Europe sent a letter written in Croatian claiming credit. The Armed Secret Organization–Execution Group sent a similar letter written in Polish. MOSCOW DOMESTIC SERVICE suggested that neo-Nazis, the American intelligence services, or the Red Army were responsible. It claimed that the recently detained terrorist (first name unknown) Borg, apparently a Red Army Faction member, told the authorities about a bomb that was being prepared for detonation at the annual ball at American headquarters in Heidelberg. 81022103

February 23, 1981 — UNITED STATES — Jerome S. Brower, 61, of Pomona, California, was sentenced by United States District Court judge John H. Pratt to four months for conspiring with two former Central Intelligence Agency employees (Edwin P. Wilson and Frank E. Terpil) to supply weapons and training to a school for terrorists in Libya. A federal grand jury was reportedly also investigating information that the former president of a California-based explosives firm helped ship 40,000 pounds of highly powerful plastic explosives to Libya in the fall of 1977.

February 24, 1981 — NICARAGUA — The brother of Salvadoran consul Norman Francisco Chavez Zamora reported that Chavez had been kidnapped from his Esteli home by three heavily armed individuals who released him a few hours later. The Salvadoran Foreign Ministry said that Chavez had actually been arrested by members of the local security service.

February 24, 1981 — ITALY — Two Libyans fired pistols and submachine guns on passengers arriving in the international arrival area of Rome's Fiumicino Airport. The passengers had just arrived on a Kuwait Airlines flight from Algiers. Five passengers were wounded, including an Algerian, three Libyans, and Oljabi Farzat, a Lebanese. Police returned the fire, wounding one of the terrorists and capturing both. Mohammed Sidki Siad Dous (Mohammed Stoki Dosh) was found in an airport rest room and said that he was "a guerrilla of the Libyan revolution" assigned to kill "Dr. Garief," whose name did not appear on the flight manifest. The local Libyan People's Bureau denied involvement.

On November 22, 1983, Italy's Assizes Court gave 15-year sentences to Mohammed Sidki Siad Dous and Mohammed El Mesdawi. The two said that they had believed that two Lebanese arriving on the flight included Youssef el Mgherief (Dr. Garief), a leading opponent of the Libyan regime. The duo claimed that they had acted on their own, not under Libyan official orders.

On October 7, 1986, Italy quietly freed the duo and Jussef Uhida, who was serving 26 years for the 1980 murder of Gialil Abdul Aref, a Libyan businessman and Qaddafi opponent. A Red Cross plane flew the Libyans to Tripoli and returned with four Italians who had been held in Libya for the past 6 years. The swap was negotiated by Foreign Minister Giulio Andreotti. Edoardo Seliciato, a contractor, and worker Enzo Castelli were serving life sentences handed down by a Libyan military court on charges of plotting against the government following a 1980 uprising in Tobruk, where they worked. Mauro Piccin and Massimo Caporali were serving 10-year sentences for drug possession. 81022401

February 25, 1981 — ISRAEL — Security forces announced that during the previous few weeks they had arrested about 60 Arabs belonging to the Family of Jihad, which has ties to the Moslem Brotherhood, and charged them with conspiracy to conduct terrorist operations with Fatah. Several of the suspects were arraigned in Ramle's military court.

February 27, 1981 — LEBANON — Gunmen from the 'Ali Nasir Group fired submachine guns from their car at the auto generally used by the Iraqi ambassador, killing Iraqi embassy accountant Muhammad 'Ali Khudayr and driver Kamil 'Abbasi and injuring Hatim 'Azzam, a pedestrian. The Iraqi embassy reported, "'Ali Nasir was one of those who called for the release of Imam Musa as-Sadr and his two companions." It added that he was killed in Beirut by unidentified persons. The two Iraqis were on their way to work when the attack commenced at 1:45 P.M. 81022701

February 27, 1981 — LEBANON — At 11:00 P.M., individuals in a speeding car threw a grenade at the home of the Egyptian ambassador, damaging cars but causing no injuries. 81022702

February 27, 1981 — FRANCE — A hijacked helicopter landed in the middle of the soccer field of the high-security Fleury Mergois prison and freed Gerard Dupre, 33, France's most wanted criminal, and fellow inmate Daniel Beaumont, 34, both of whom were serving sentences for armed robbery. Two men had rented the helicopter at the suburban Issy-les-Moulineaux heliport, ostensibly to fly to Orleans, but put a gun to the head of the pilot, Claude Fourcade, 48, when aloft. They claimed his wife and daughter were being held by accomplices, which was later determined to be untrue. The escape, which took 30 seconds, was the first in France via helicopter. The ultramodern prison has no watchtowers and no bars on its windows. The helicopter landed 10 minutes later on a second soccer field at Jules Noel stadium near southern Paris, where 30 schoolchildren watched them enter a green Renault, driven by a fifth man. On March 6, police captured Dupre, Andre Prebet, who aided him during the escape, and an unidentified woman who had hidden Dupre. Dupre and Prebet were wounded in a gunfight with police on a crowded street. A police officer was shot in the leg. 81022703

February 28, 1981 — AUSTRALIA — Sydney police arrested Hans-Peter Knoll, a Baader-Meinhof Gang member, wanted for 10 years by the West Germans for a bomb attack on a British yacht club, which killed a man; the attempted murder of a police officer; three bank robberies; two arsons; and an attempt to release two jailed women. 81022801

February 28, 1981 — EGYPT — Cairo media reported that police had foiled a plan by Masayushi Sasha, an alleged member of the Japanese Red Army, to hijack an Egyptian passenger plane for the Libyans. 81022802

March 1981 — UNITED STATES — Irish Republican Army sympathizers were suspected in the pipe-bomb murder of Philip Testa, reputed Philadelphia crime boss suspected of the December murder of John McCullogh, head of a local roofers union and IRA supporter with close ties to local organized crime.

March 1981 — COLOMBIA — The government announced that individuals who had seized the Dominican embassy on February 27, 1980, had returned from Cuba. The authorities claimed they had killed 19 guerrillas and captured 74 others, including the leader of the embassy takeover.

March 1981 — KUWAIT — A bomb exploded at the Ariana Shipping Company, killing one person. On August 15, the State Security Court sentenced several Jordanians to life imprisonment for the attack on the Iranian office. Four of them were sentenced in absentia, having fled the country after planting five bombs in June. Five others were released for lack of evidence, while two more were sentenced to two and seven years, respectively. 81039901

March 1, 1981 — UNITED ARAB EMIRATES — A hand grenade exploded before midnight in a Dubayy restaurant owned by a Syrian, wounding three Syrians, including the owner and a doctor. Police arrested five Syrians, including the person suspected of throwing the grenade. 81030101

March 2, 1981 — UNITED KINGDOM — More than four hundred Irish Republican Army (IRA) prisoners ended a three-day "dirty protest," which focused public attention on the hunger strike of Bobby Sands, who hoped to obtain political status for IRA prisoners rather than being treated as common criminals.

March 2, 1981 — SPAIN — The Spanish-Catalan Battalion claimed to have kidnapped Spanish soccer star Enrique Quini Castro, the Barcelona club's center-forward and the league's leading scorer, because he played for a "separatist" soccer team.

March 2, 1981 — WEST BERLIN — A homemade bomb containing six pounds of explosives was discovered in a pipe at a Kraftwerk Union factory, builder of atomic power plants. Police refused to speculate on whether the failed attack was connected with antinuclear demonstrations the previous weekend.

March 2, 1981 — FEDERAL REPUBLIC OF GERMANY— Two firebombs exploded on canvases covering generators for two United States Army trailers at the motor pool compound at Frankfurt/Main, causing five hundred dollars' damage but no injuries. The attackers had apparently entered the area through a damaged wire fence. 81030201

March 2, 1981 — PAKISTAN — Three armed individuals claiming membership in the anti–Zia Al Zulfiqar organization hijacked a Pakistan International Airlines B-720 flying from Karachi to Peshawar with 145 passengers, many of them diplomats, and 3 crewmen, diverting it to Kabul, Afghanistan. The hijackers claimed to be followers of former Pakistani prime minister Zulfiqar Ali Bhutto, who was executed by the current government. The lead hijacker, Mohammed Alam Gir (Salamulla Tippu, Mohammed Salamollah; also spelled 'Alamgir), denied that his group had links to the defunct Pakistan People's Party (PPP), despite government allegations. The hijackers were armed with a grenade and light weapons when they took over PK-326 at 4:00 P.M.

The hijackers claimed that some of their group's members were responsible for the explosion that took place during Pope John Paul II's visit to Pakistan in February. They also claimed credit for the January 5 explosion in the high court building.

Pakistan sent a negotiating team to Kabul, which included its civil aviation director, airline customer services chief M. Nawaz Tiwana and Pakistani charge in Kabul Rao Ali Bahadar. The team later complained that Kabul refused them direct contact with the hijackers.

Although the runway bristled with Soviet troops and helicopter gunships from the Russian occupation army, the terrorists set a deadline of noon, March 11, for the release of 92 (later reduced to 45) political prisoners held in Pakistani jails, including Alam Gir's father and brother. Pakistan offered to release 48 on the original list, but not 44 other "hardened" criminals. Most of those on the hijackers' list were arrested during recent student unrest in Pakistan and were PPP members. They also demanded that the media broadcast that the hijackers were not affiliated with the PPP, and that Pakistani radio not broadcast anything "that hurt their prestige." The government agreed to those demands.

Among the hostages were World Bank official Geoffrey Balkind and several Americans, including Frederick W. Hubbell, 30, a Des Moines, Iowa, attorney, and his wife, Charlotte, 31, who were on a round-the-world vacation; Deborah Leighton Weisner of Auburn, Maine, and her fiance, Mian Manzoor Ahmad, a deputy sheriff in Androscoggin County, Maine; Richard Clymore of California; and Muzaffar Quereshi, a naturalized American working for Manufacturers Hanover Trust in New York City.

On March 4, the terrorists released 27 hostages, mostly women, children, and a sick man. However, Afghanistan refused landing permission to a Pakistani plane sent to transport the freed hostages out of the country.

Libya claimed that on March 6, a secretary in the Libyan People's Bureau in Kabul offered himself as a substitute hostage, but that the hijackers rejected the suggestion. The terrorists on that day shot Tariq Rahim, second secretary of the Pakistani embassy in Iran and the son of a general, and threw his body onto the tarmac after a deadline expired. Rahim later died in the hospital. Most reports indicated Alam Gir fired the murder weapon.

On March 7, the terrorists released Charlotte Hubbell and Deborah Weisner. Pakistan's defense secretary, Maj. Gen. Rahim Khan, also head of Pakistan International Airlines, said Pakistan authorized the Afghans to launch a rescue mission and offered to send its own antiterror squad to help. Khan said the hijackers were acting on the orders of Murtaza Bhutto, 25, the late prime minister's son and now dissident leader, who had "embraced" Afghan officials at the airport and introduced the hijackers. The next day, Pakistan instituted a crackdown against domestic dissidents, arresting 120 PPP members, including Bhutto's widow Nusrat.

The next day, after releasing the hostages, the terrorists threatened to blow up the plane and extended their deadline. Diplomats freed were from Libya, Iran, Bangladesh, Indonesia, Turkey, Iraq (Ambassador Fathi Husayn al'-Ali), and the Palestine Liberation Organization (Ahmadul Farah).

The terrorists on March 9 asked Iran for overflight privileges and flew on to Damascus, where the plane landed at 1:15 A.M. They released the flight attendant, Farzana Sharif, 22. Pakistan's ambassador to Syria, Sarfaraz Khan, together with Syrian security officials, negotiated with the terrorists.

On March 11, Pakistan released Alam Gir's brother and father and flew them to Damascus, where they were to join the negotiating team.

On March 12, Pakistan reportedly agreed to pay $50,000 ransom and release 55 (later decreased to 54, when one could not be located) prisoners to asylum in Libya, after the hijackers set a deadline of 11:00 A.M. before they would kill 3 American hostages they claimed worked for the Central Intelligence Agency.

According to the Rand Corporation, "Diplomats believed they wanted the money simply to cover their expenses and those of the former convicts once they arrived in Libya. . . . The leader of the hijackers also asked that a few members of the hijackers' families be allowed to stay behind in Pakistan to sell any family houses or land, with a promise from the Islamabad government that they would be allowed to leave Pakistan freely once their holdings had been liquidated. Once again, the Pakistanis agreed."

On March 13, Qaddafi initially agreed to grant safe haven, but when the plane refueled in Aleppo, Syria, he changed his mind, saying his country did not know enough about the case. The prisoners' plane flew on to Athens, where it was permitted temporary landing privileges to refuel for onward passage to Syria, which agreed to grant safe haven. Of the 54 prisoners who were released, 7 were held for the Liaquatbagh shooting incident; 21 were charged with subversion, arms smuggling, arson, and looting; 5 with murder; 2 with espionage and conspiracy against the state; 8 with spreading chaos and suspicion among the armed forces; 9 with publishing subversive materials; 2 with engaging in unspecified illegal activities.

All passengers were released at 11:30 P.M. on March 14. The terrorists thereupon surrendered peacefully to Syrian authorities, who whisked them away in three military vehicles.

The United States Department of State announced that the real Lawrence Clifton Mangum, one of the alleged American hostages, was found living safely in Brooklyn, and the person who had his alleged passport was of indeterminate nationality. He later was found to be escaped Canadian convict Lawrence G. Lome, who had faked the passport. Richard Clymore (Craig Richards), 24, was under indictment on federal drug smuggling charges, including transportation of hashish oil and heroin.

On March 16, the State Department said the Soviet Union had failed to use its influence to halt the hijacking in Kabul and may have helped it along. The hijackers had arrived in Kabul "with pistols; they left with machine guns."

On March 17, Pakistan's Federal Investigation Agency filed hijacking charges against Alam Gir and Nassir (also spelled Nasir) Jamal. The Karachi city magistrate charged Alam Gir with absconding from his trial for involvement in kidnapping and threatening to kill Sikander Hayat. The next day, Karachi said Alam Gir had trained in Kabul for four months.

On March 21, Pakistani president Zia ul-Haq had arrested five hundred civilian politicians in his crackdown, which he claimed was justified by the hijacking.

On March 23, Syria turned down Zia's extradition request, stating that the two countries had no extradition treaty.

On April 6, KARACHI DOMESTIC SERVICE claimed that one of the released prisoners, Munir Ahmed Balach, a former lieutenant commander of the Pakistan Navy, had spied for an Eastern European country. He had expressed reservations about being flown to Syria.

April 19, Murtaza Bhutto said the hijackers were members of his group, but that he had no foreknowledge of the hijacking. Alam Gir and Bhutto said the People's Liberation Army was the previous name of the Al Zulfiqar organization.

In late April, the hijackers and 25 of the political prisoners who had gone to Syria returned to Kabul via New Delhi, carrying Syrian passports issued in sequence.

On April 30, the Pakistani government offered a $20,000 reward for the arrest of Alam Gir, and $10,000 each for Nassir Jamal and Arshad Ali.

On May 1, the Federal Intelligence Agency of Pakistan announced that it had arrested a guard at the airport who had supplied the hijackers with their original arms. Three others were also arrested.

On May 18, Pakistan requested extradition from Kabul.

On May 24, 2 more accomplices were arrested in Pakistan.

On June 13, a close associate of Alam Gir was arrested near the Pakistan-Afghanistan border.

On July 7, the Dutch government rejected a United Nations High Commissioner for Refugees request to accept 10 of the political prisoners who had been released.

On July 10, 1984, Kabul's BAKHTAR news service reported the arrest and execution of Alam Gir, son of Eslamollah, leader of the hijackers. The service reported that

> on 15 March 1983, a murder took place in Kabul city. The security forces following the murder case arrested the murderer. During the investigation it was discovered that the murderer was the above-mentioned 'Alamgir, who had hijacked the plane, and the victim was a man named Parwez from the Shinwari tribe. The murderer 'Alamgir confessed that he had illegally entered Afghanistan via Pakistan and was armed at the time of entry.
>
> After the completion of the investigation concerning the hijacking and taking of hostages, the murder of one of the plane's passengers, illegal entry into the DRA [Democratic Republic of Afghanistan], and murder, his file was sent to an authorized court for judicial assessment. As a result of the judicial finding based on substantial criminal documents and the confession of the 'Alamgir as a . . . and a criminal, 'Alamgir was sentenced to death in accordance with Paragraph 2, Articles 515 and 395 of the Penal Code, and for the crimes of hijacking an airplane and taking hostages, shooting one of the plane's passengers which resulted in his death, illegal reentry into Afghanistan, and committing the murder of another person, Parwez Shinwari, while in the DRA.
>
> The death sentence has been carried out in accordance with Article 58 of the basic principles of the Democratic Republic of Afghanistan.

81030202

March 4, 1981 — FRANCE — Two Secret Armenian Army gunmen fired automatic weapons at midday in Paris, killing Turkish labor attache Resat Jorali and Islamic religious counselor Terceli Ari. 81030401

March 4, 1981 — EL SALVADOR — At 11:00 A.M., four men driving in a gray truck fired five 7.62 mm rifle shots at the United States embassy, breaking a window but causing no injuries. Acting United States ambassador Frederic L. Chapin said that attack had "all the hallmarks" of the rightist terrorism directed by Salvadoran ex-major Roberto D'Aubuisson. 81030402

March 4, 1981 — UGANDA — United Nations officials were threatened with kidnapping and death if they did not stop aid to President Milton Obote's government. The United Nations Development Program's offices were temporarily closed. 81030403

March 5, 1981 — LEBANON — The United Southern Front set off a booby-trapped bomb at 7:30 P.M. in a Palestine Liberation Organization jeep parked opposite the Arab League in the At-Tariq al-Jadidah, injuring seven people. Several cars were damaged.

March 5, 1981 — LEBANON — Baghdad's IRAQI NEWS AGENCY (INA) claimed that anti-Arab gangs and Zionist organs were responsible for the assassination of Ahmad Qasim Zughayb, a member of the health committee of the Ba'th Party Regional Command in Lebanon, who died while driving his car to his office in Burj Abu Haydar in western Beirut. INA said he was born in Yunin, Ba'labakk, in 1951, joined the Ba'th Party in 1973, and graduated with a bachelor's degree in accounting and management in 1978. 81030501

March 5, 1981 — LEBANON — Three gunmen in a speeding car in Moslem-inhabited west Beirut fired silenced weapons during the night, killing Mohammed Salih Hoseyni, 28, president of the Iranian Student Association. His predecessor was killed in Beirut the previous year. Iran accused Iraq of the attack. 81030502

March 5, 1981 — LEBANON — According to the Rand Corporation, "The ambassador-elect to Syria, an Iranian from the Iranian Embassy, was killed in Beirut. Two men in a vehicle overtook his car and shot him." 81030503

March 5, 1981 — UNITED STATES — A man who smuggled a gun through Los Angeles International Airport security in a ski boot took over a Continental Airlines B-727 at 9:30 A.M. Although 86 persons were on board, 80 of them immediately escaped. No shots or injuries were reported. Four hostages were released at 1:15 P.M., and the last passenger was released three hours later. Flight attendant Barbara Sorenson, 35, managed to escape through a rear door at 8:15 P.M. The man ended his standoff and dropped his $3 million ransom demand. On August 10, 1981, Victor Malasaukas, 44, an unemployed aerospace engineer, was sentenced to life in prison. The judge ordered him to undergo a 90-day evaluation, after which the sentence would be reviewed. 81030504

March 6, 1981 — LEBANON — In apparent retaliation for the assassination of Mohammed Salih the previous day, armed men opened fire during the night on an Iraqi embassy car carrying an embassy official. Fire broke out in the car, but the official and his driver escaped. 81030601

March 7, 1981 — ISRAEL — During the night, two cars belonging to the United States consulate in Jerusalem were set on fire, resulting in extensive damage to the cars but no casualties. 81030701–02

March 10, 1981 — UNITED STATES — The Arlington law firm of Lewis, Wilson, Lewis and Jones filed lawsuits on behalf of 29 Israeli civilians killed in a Palestinian terrorist raid in Israel and 65 persons wounded in the attack. The suit in United States District Court sought almost $1.5 billion damages from the Libyan government, the Palestine Liberation Organization, the Palestine Information Office, the National Association of Arab Americans, and the Palestine Congress of North America. The suits alleged that planning for the raid and procurement of money and weapons for the attack occurred in the United States.

March 10, 1981 — UNITED STATES — Lester Perry, who hijacked a Trans World Airlines plane to Havana in July 1969 and was freed in 1980, was arrested under an alias in South Bend, Indiana, for car theft. United States authorities thought he was still in Cuba.

March 10, 1981 — LEBANON — A sniper fired a single shot at United States ambassador to Lebanon John Gunther Dean's convoy, striking a tire of an escort car, as Dean headed from Christian east Beirut to Moslem west Beirut. Leftists claimed rightists were responsible. 81031001

March 12, 1981 — IRAN — Iranian police reported that Armenian terrorists killed two officers in a gun battle involving a car chase near the Soviet embassy. The terrorists were arrested after the shoot-out and found to be in possession of literature of the Marxist-Leninist popular fedayeen organization. 81031201

March 12, 1981 — COSTA RICA — During the morning, a member of the Costa Rican Civil Guard discovered and defused a grenade left in front of the residence of Javier Chamorro Mora, Nicaragua's ambassador. 81031202

March 12, 1981 — EL SALVADOR — Guerrillas operating during the morning in Chalatenango Department stopped and set afire a truck with Honduran plates, which was transporting bananas from San Pedro Sula to El Salvador, near La Palma. 81031203

March 13, 1981 — FEDERAL REPUBLIC OF GERMANY — A night watchman for the Frankfurt America House found a bomb, made from a medium-size fire extinguisher, placed against a door leading to an interior court yard. It was deactivated without incident that morning. 81031301

March 15, 1981 — UNITED STATES — Shortly after takeoff from Seattle, an emotionally disturbed passenger on Delta Airlines flight 268 threatened a flight attendant with a small tear-gas spray canister. A married couple faced down the passenger with their own illegal canister. The disturbed passenger was sent to a mental health clinic, while the Federal Bureau of Investigation considered pressing charges against the couple. 81031501

March 16, 1981 — FEDERAL REPUBLIC OF GERMANY — A Chicago-bound Lufthansa DC-10 carrying 210 passengers returned to Frankfurt after a three-page bomb threat letter was found in a bag in the airport, along with an automatic siren apparatus, which caught the attention of police. 81031601

March 16, 1981 — IRAN — Iranian Air Force colonel Javit Hussein defected to Turkey and requested political asylum after hijacking a C-47 four-engine cargo plane and forcing the pilot and crew of 10 to fly to Van, a largely Kurdish-populated city 55 miles west of the Iranian border. The hijacker was accompanied by his wife and son during the 2:00 P.M. flight. 81031602

March 17, 1981 — EL SALVADOR — Unidentified men fired automatic rifles from the back of a small pickup truck at the United States embassy a half hour after United States congressman Clarence D. Long ended a news conference there. Although 10 shots hit the building, no one was injured. 81031701

March 17, 1981 — COSTA RICA — The Carlos Aguero Echeverria Command fired a bazooka at a van carrying United States Marine guards to the United States embassy in San Jose. The van was destroyed in the subsequent explosion. The attack injured three Marines and two Costa Ricans: Sgt. Stephen Garcia, 23, of New York City; Sgt. John E. Roberts, 22, of Robbinsdale, Minnesota; Cpl. Jerome Walters, 21, of Queens, New York; driver Emilio Camacho; and pedestrian Vesalio Gomez Acuna, 35. The pedestrian said that two young men on a rise near the road had told him to "get out of the way; something is going to happen." The Command, which was named after a Costa Rican who fought with a band of Nicaraguan guerrillas that ousted President Anastasio Somoza in July 1979, said it was protesting United States intervention in El Salvador. Police later found a red Volkswagen, license plate 59953, which was used by the attackers. They arrested, but soon released, one man for questioning. In mid-April, they arrested four men who fired at a patrol. Initially identifying themselves as Nicaraguan citizens, the men later announced that they were Costa Rican members of the People's Vanguard organization: Javier Sanchez Valverde, Freddy Rivera Lizano, Mario Guillen Garcia, and Miguel Regueira Ederman. On April 29, police announced that Sanchez Valverde and Guillen Garcia had confessed to the first attack. 81031702

March 17, 1981 — COSTA RICA — A few minutes after an attack on a van carrying United States Marine guards, at 8:14 A.M. the Carlos Aguero Echeverria Command bombed the Honduran embassy, causing damage but no injuries. The group said it was protesting complicity by Honduras and Costa Rica in the fighting between the left and right in El Salvador. Two people were immediately arrested. 81031703

March 17, 1981 — FEDERAL REPUBLIC OF GERMANY — Three gunmen broke into an Aachen apartment with the forced help of a neighbor and killed Binan al-Attar, the wife of former Moslem Brotherhood leader Issam Attar, exiled Syrian director of a local Islamic center. British reporter Robert Moss claimed that the chief of Libya's "Green Brigades," Said Qadaf ad-Dam, and Brig. Gen. Ali Haydar, head of the special commando units of Syrian intelligence, had met in London a few weeks previously to plan such attacks against exiled opposition leaders. 81031704

March 20, 1981 — EGYPT — In Beirut, the Misr al-'Urubah (Egypt of Arabism) claimed that at 11:35 P.M. it had killed Shamir Rabin, director of the Israeli Galilee Tours Company, and another Israeli as they left the Holiday Inn near Cairo's pyramids. 81032001

March 21, 1981 — COSTA RICA — Police claimed that Argentines Carlos Villalba and Raul Cuestas, journalism professors at the national university, were Montonero leaders currently in Mexico.

March 22, 1981 — LEBANON — At 3:15 A.M., gunmen fired automatic weapons from a Mercedes at the United States embassy, causing no damage or injuries. Lebanese guards fired back but could not prevent the escape. 81032201

March 23, 1981 — EL SALVADOR — Two youths standing 60 meters away in an open field in front of the French embassy fired two bazooka shells at the Nicaraguan embassy at 3:50 P.M., causing some damage but no casualties. 81032301

March 23, 1981 — WEST BERLIN — Local police deactivated a bomb discovered outside the 10th-floor offices of Honeywell in the British sector of Berlin. 81032302

March 24, 1981—IRELAND— Three gunmen fired shots into the legs of a British Leyland executive who was addressing local businessmen at Trinity College in Dublin. 81032401

March 24, 1981—COSTA RICA—The Argentine embassy received a telephoned bomb threat. 81032402

March 25, 1981—EL SALVADOR—At least 10 gunmen firing from two directions rocketed and machine-gunned the United States embassy, causing substantial damage but no injuries. A United States Marine guard fired one shot, and a nearby contingent of Salvadoran security forces also returned the fire of the Popular Liberation Front. The terrorists said they were protesting United States "intervention against the struggle of the Salvadoran people." The operation was nicknamed "Monsignor Romero, Until Victory Always." The press later reported that at least one person was arrested, and two people traveling in a bus were wounded in the gunfire. 81032501

March 26, 1981—FRANCE—IRAQI NEWS AGENCY in Baghdad claimed that 20 Syrian terrorists arrived in Paris, London, and Bonn to assassinate Syrian dissidents. It said their deployment coincided with the arrival in London of Maj. Muhammed Khayr Salih, who is in charge of implementation of foreign operations for Syrian intelligence. It also claimed that $10 million had been transferred to a Syrian bank branch in Europe to finance the campaign, and that a Syrian diplomat, Michel Kassuhah, recently arrived in Paris "entrusted with tasks unrelated to diplomacy."

March 26, 1981—EL SALVADOR—A Datsun exploded, due either to a bomb or a grenade, near the Metrosur shopping center in the capital city, killing three persons and wounding several others, including an American newsman. 81032601

March 27, 1981—LEBANON—Gunmen fired at the United States embassy from a passing car at 10:15 P.M. 81032701

March 27, 1981—GREECE—The Autonomous Resistance Organization, acting "in solidarity with the Polish workers," set four bombs against Soviet and Bulgarian diplomatic vehicles in Athens. Two cars were damaged in the explosions, but no injuries were reported. Two of the bombs were defused. 81032702–05

March 27, 1981 — HONDURAS — At 9:30 A.M., a woman and four men armed with pistols and machine guns and claiming to be members of the Honduran leftist group Cinchonero National Liberation Front, Operation 26 March, Lempira Commando Group, took over a Honduran Air Services (SAHSA) B-727-200 flying 87 passengers and 6 crewmen from Tegucigalpa to New Orleans with a stopover in San Pedro Sula and forced pilot Capt. Jorge Torres to land in Managua. They set a 24-hour deadline for acceptance of their demands, then released 20 women, 6 children, and 4 men, among them Belizean health minister Assad Shoman and Mayra Navarro, a Honduran Channel 3 newswoman. They also released a few Americans, including Flavia Olbond of New Orleans and her son and daughter; Sister Sheila Chitik, a missionary; and an unidentified man, leaving 6 Americans still on board. The hostages included passengers from Colombia, the United Kingdom, Guatemala, Costa Rica, West Germany, and France, plus Jonathan Russell, the presidential press secretary, and 7 newsmen.

The group threatened to blow up the plane if the government did not "end the persecution of the people's leaders and the Catholic Church in Santa Rosa de Copan"; publish a manifesto in Honduran newspapers; observe neutrality in the Salvadoran civil war; dismantle camps in southern Honduras used by Nicaraguan exiles fighting to overthrow the leftist government; guarantee security for 35 Honduran leftist leaders; and release Facundo Guardado (Salvadoran leftist labor leader and member of the Revolutionary Democratic Front of El Salvador, who was arrested on January 18), Alvaro Alfaro Orellan, Alfredo Burgos, Reyes Tovar Menjivar, Jose Ricardo Castellon, Rosa Elena Castellon, Martha Castellon, Antonio Chicas Rosa, Luis Ricardo Ramirez, Carlos Manuel Lobo, Vilma Rodriguez, Augusto Cana Martinez, and Jose Fernando Aguilar Rivera (all Salvadorans), plus Rafael Angel Mendez (a Costa Rican). The government, which refused to send representatives to Managua to negotiate, claimed that only 8 of those listed were imprisoned, and 4 of them were deported. Two rightist groups threatened all Honduran "communists" if the passengers were injured. Honduras, however, announced that it would deport to Panama those being held for illegal arms trafficking. Commander Raul (Commander Carlos) then ordered the pilot to fly to Panama, where the plane landed safely at 7:45 P.M on March 28.

Nicaragua's vice minister of the interior, Commander of the Revolution Luis Carrion Cruz, had acted as mediator. Panama's ambassador to Nicaragua, Baltazar Aizpurua, also negotiated and accompanied the plane to Panama, where the hijackers released their remaining hostages and surrendered to authorities. The hijackers, who had purchased tickets using the names Maria Nivense, Raul Nivense, Marcial Rosales, and Roberto Gonzales, requested political asylum in Cuba. The Honduran government faced a difficult extradition issue, as it did not know the correct names of the hijackers. It was later noted that the group's name, Cinchonero, was the name given to a Honduran peasant leader, Serapio Romero, who led uprisings in the early 1900s. 81032706

March 28, 1981 — INDONESIA — Five hijackers armed with handguns, grenades, and explosives took over Garuda Airlines flight GA-206, a DC-9 flying 47 passengers and 9 crewmen from Palembang to Medan, and forced Capt. Herman Rante to fly to Penang, Malaysia, where they released 1 hostage, a 75-year-old Indonesian woman. They refueled and flew to Bangkok, where they demanded the release of 20 people jailed in Indonesia, threatening to blow up the plane. They set several deadlines, which passed without incident, but at one stage panicked when they noticed a copilot giving hand signals to ground crew and shot him in the head. On March 31, Robert Wainwright, 27, of Cromford, Derbyshire, United Kingdom, jumped from an emergency door and escaped. The hijackers shot an American who attempted the same move, identified as Karl Schneider, a Milchem Company oil supplier from Lubbock, Texas. President Suharto agreed to release the 20, but the hijackers upped the ante to 80. They demanded a DC-10 to fly them to Sri Lanka. The plane was offered, but the Sri Lankan ambassador informed the hijackers of her government's refusal to accept them. The hijackers then demanded the release of 4 more prisoners held in Surabaya, Medan, and Jogjakarta. Negotiations were initially conducted by Indonesian ambassador Lt. Gen. Yoga Sugama, the head of the Central Intelligence Department, 5 other officials, 1 pilot, and 18 commandos. The exasperated team gave the hijackers a list of 92 prisoners and told them to pick 80. The hijackers chose 27 names and delegated selection of the remaining 53 to a prisoner identified as Salmal. They also demanded $1.5 million, "punishment of Indonesian Vice President Adam Malik for taking kickbacks from a US aircraft company," and "expulsion of all Jew officials and Israeli militarists from Indonesia."

Believing that the hijackers had become increasingly irrational, on March 31 at 2:40 A.M., 20 Indonesian soldiers stormed the plane, killing 4 of the 5 hijackers and capturing Imron bin Mohammad Zein, believed to be a member of Komando Jihad, an Islamic fundamentalist group involved in a March 11 attack on a police station in Bandung, West Java. One of the Indonesian commandos was wounded in the abdomen. Reports of the death of a 4-year-old boy were denied by officials. Among the freed Americans were Ralph Donald Hunt, 28, a Louisiana engineer, and Thomas Heischman of Carmel, California. Passengers also included 2 Japanese and a Dutchman. Police later claimed the hijackers were members of the Indonesian Islamic Revolution Board. 81032801

March 29, 1981 — BELGIUM — One of two Molotov cocktails exploded in the Yugoslav Air Transport Office in Brussels, causing extensive damage but no injuries. The Fides Besa Bes (an Albanian group) claimed credit, saying that it was supported by the Albanian Autonomist Movement of Kosovo. 81032901

March 29, 1981 — FEDERAL REPUBLIC OF GERMANY — A group called In the Heart of the Beast bombed the United States Army intelligence building in Giessen near Frankfurt, causing $50,000 damage but no injuries. 81032902

March 30, 1981 — UNITED STATES — John W. Hinckley, Jr., wounded United States president Ronald Reagan in an assassination attempt designed to impress actress Jodie Foster. While most observers believed the attacker to be insane, columnist Jack Anderson on December 16 suggested that he had contacts with the Islamic Guerrilla Army, an Iranian terrorist group.

March 30, 1981 — FEDERAL REPUBLIC OF GERMANY — The Red Army Faction threw three firebombs into the United States Army personnel office, 5th Corps, in Frankfurt. Only one of the devices exploded, and no injuries were reported. The attackers yelled, "Death to US imperialism." 81033001

March 31, 1981 — EL SALVADOR — A bomb destroyed the offices of the New York-based Citibank in an 18-story building in the capital city. Windows in the Camino Real Hotel across the street were broken and three people driving past the building were injured by flying glass. 81033101

March 31, 1981 — HONG KONG — After Shell Oil Company received a demand for one hundred thousand dollars, a bomb exploded at their Hong Kong headquarters, injuring one man. 81033102

March 31, 1981 — UNITED STATES — Following receipt of threats that Libyan "hit squads" were in the United States to assassinate Jeane J. Kirkpatrick, the United States ambassador to the United Nations, a 24-hour guard was placed on her. Federal Bureau of Investigation surveillance indicated Libyan contact with black nationalist leaders. 81033103

April 1981 — UNITED STATES — The Red Guerrilla Resistance bombed the United States Navy Yard officer's club to protest Operation Ocean Venture 84, which they claimed was a practice invasion of Central America and the Caribbean. No injuries were reported.

On January 15, 1985, four current and former members of the John Brown AntiKlan Committee expressed sympathy with those who claimed credit but said they were not involved and thus would refuse to answer questions from a federal grand jury. The group's written statement said, "We recognize these bombings as a legitimate form of resistance to US militarism. We have and will continue to publicly state our support for them, together with other militant actions—demonstrations, civil disobedience, draft resistance." The foursome were identified as Steven Burke, 25, of Washington; and Julie Nalibov, 24, Christine Rico, 24, and Sandra Gayle Roland, 25, of New York. The four appeared before Chief United States District Judge Aubrey E. Robinson, Jr., to ask that their subpoenas be quashed and that federal law enforcement officials be forced to disclose any wiretapping against the group. The four faced possible civil or criminal contempt charges and jail terms if they refused to cooperate. They were also wanted for questioning in three bombings by the Armed Resistance Unit: in April 1983 at the War College at Fort McNair, in August 1983 at a computer complex at the Washington Navy Yard, and at the United States Capitol in November 1983 to protest United States military action in Grenada.

April 1981 — UNITED KINGDOM — Sanoussi Latiwish, 18, a Libyan student apparently in contact with the exiled opposition, was found murdered in a field outside Cambridge. Although British police did not believe the killing was political, Yousouf Lamgarief, a former ambassador to India, suggested a Libyan hit team was responsible. The student's father, an army chief of staff under the deposed monarchy who kept his job under Qaddafi for a time, died in an Athens hotel in January . 81049901

April 1, 1981 — EL SALVADOR — The Popular Liberation Forces fired a Chinese-made RPG-2 (a rocket-propelled grenade) at the United States embassy. One shell hit a nearby credit union building and a second landed in a vacant lot. Six rifle shots were also fired, breaking a window. No injuries were reported. The group said it was retaliating for United States support of the ruling junta and was commemorating the anniversary of the group's founding. 81040101

April 2, 1981 — LEBANON — IRAQI NEWS AGENCY in Baghdad blamed Sh'ubist gangs for killing an embassy employee, 'Abbadi Manjal Husayn, and injuring his colleague, Shamsi Muhammad Hamzah, by firing on them from a car. 81040201

April 2, 1981 — DENMARK — Gunmen from the Commandos of Retribution for the Armenian Genocide fired six shots into Cavit Demir, the Turkish embassy's labor advisor, as he was going to take the elevator to his apartment. He collapsed at his apartment door and was taken to the hospital during the evening. He was released from the hospital in Copenhagen on April 21. 81040202

April 3, 1981 — MOZAMBIQUE — The National Resistance Movement sabotaged a power line at the Cabora Bassa hydroelectric dam, which supplies

10 percent of South Africa's electrical power. Maputo authorities have claimed that South Africa supports the guerrillas. 81040301

April 4, 1981 — ITALY — Police arrested Mario Moretti, 35, believed to be the mastermind of the Aldo Moro kidnap/murder, Genoese literature professor Enrico Fenzi, and a man and a woman believed to be minor Red Brigadists.

April 4, 1981 — GREECE — Four firebombs set by the Revolutionary Left destroyed cars belonging to United States military personnel in four residential areas of Athens but caused no injuries. Two other bombs were defused. 81040401–06

April 6, 1981 — GUATEMALA — A bomb exploded in the garden of the British consul's residence in Guatemala City, causing little damage and no injuries. 81040601

April 6, 1981 — EL SALVADOR — Gunmen fired heavy-caliber weapons at the United States embassy, then fled in a stolen vehicle. Embassy guards pursued the attackers. The ensuing shoot-out on the road resulted in damage to both vehicles and the wounding of a terrorist. 81040602

April 6, 1981 — TURKEY — Gunmen fired at a car with four United States military experts in Istanbul but caused no injuries. 81040603

April 6, 1981 — EGYPT — Authorities arrested five Palestinians, and later three more, believed associated with a Popular Front for the Liberation of Palestine–Popular Democratic Front for the Liberation of Palestine (PFLP-PDFLP) conspiracy to bomb public places. The wife of the main defendant, Khalil 'Abd al-Fadhil, confessed that she had hidden quantities of explosive powder. 81040604

April 6, 1981 — PERU — Two gunmen failed to kidnap the 18-year-old daughter of Venezuelan ambassador Ildegar Perez Segnini a block from the embassy. Passersby surrounded the kidnap vehicle and prevented the kidnappers from forcing her in. The duo managed to escape. 81040605

April 7, 1981 — TURKEY — An Istanbul newspaper claimed that Armenian terrorists were smuggling narcotics.

April 7, 1981 — INDONESIA — Security around the Thai embassy was increased amid suspicions that the terrorist group that had hijacked an Indonesian plane on March 28 was planning an attack on the embassy.

April 8, 1981 — UGANDA — The Uganda Freedom Movement claimed credit for throwing a grenade that caused minor damage to the Indian embassy. Two pedestrians were injured by flying glass. The group said it believed India was planning to supply arms to President Milton Obote's government. 81040801

April 9, 1981 — NORTHERN IRELAND — Bobby Sands, 27, a convicted Irish Republican Army terrorist who later died from a hunger strike in Maze Prison, won a special election for a vacant Parliament seat, beating a prominent moderate Protestant, Harry West, 67, former leader of the Ulster Unionist Party.

April 10, 1981 — UNITED STATES — Rafael Fredsivindo Pellerano Albantosa, 89, a Cuban refugee, grabbed a flight attendant, spread a flammable liquid, and started a small fire during a hijack attempt on Eastern flight 17 en route from New York to Miami. He was overpowered by a passenger and an airline employee, tied up, but died minutes later. Although a witness said he swallowed a small pill, an autopsy "revealed small bruises indicating compression of the chest and neck which appeared to be related to the events surrounding his apprehension and the ensuing scuffle." 81041001

April 10, 1981 — UGANDA — The Uganda Freedom Movement exploded a grenade in a Kampala store owned by an Indian, injuring two people. 81041002

April 10, 1981 — TOGO — A bomb exploded in the French Cultural Center in Lome, causing extensive damage, shattering windows in nearby buildings. A second bomb exploded in a vehicle parked in front of a French social club, damaging several vehicles. A wheel was thrown from one of the cars into a house, just missing the occupants. No injuries were reported. 81041003–04

April 11, 1981 — UNITED STATES — In the early afternoon, a shot was fired into the lobby of the Soviet consulate in San Francisco, causing no injuries. 81041101

April 12, 1981 — FEDERAL REPUBLIC OF GERMANY — A cable was placed over the rail electrification wiring of a United States military train on the Bremen-Hanover line, damaging the engine and delaying the train three hours. Leaflets nearby declared support for the Red Army Faction and hunger strikers in German prisons. No injuries were reported. 81041201

April 12, 1981 — WEST BERLIN — An explosive device consisting of a fire extinguisher containing five kilograms of explosive was found hidden in a tote bag at the back of the American Memorial Library in the United States sector. 81041202

April 13, 1981 — PARAGUAY — A lone gunman armed with a silenced pistol entered the offices of the Ecuadoran embassy at 11:30 A.M., stole G 50,000 and $100 from Ambassador Jorge Ramos Romero, and escaped. Witnesses said he had long, honey-blond hair, an Argentine accent, khaki-colored trousers, and a sports shirt. 81041301

April 15, 1981 — AFGHANISTAN — Afghan authorities arrested two men and a woman they claimed were attempting to smuggle two bombs and four revolvers onto a Bakhtar Ariana Afghan Airlines B-727 scheduled to fly from Qandahar to Kabul, hoping to divert it to Quetta. The Afghans claimed that the attack had been planned in the Peshawar home of Burhanuddin Rabbani, and that the hijackers received their training, arms, and 4,000 kaldar (Af 18,000) to cover expenses while in the area. They then infiltrated from Paktia, arrived in Kabul, and were taken to Qandahar by a guide who was also arrested. The Afghan government claimed that the hijackers Sayyed Habibullah, Salehah, and Akbar belonged to the Islamic Society of Afghanistan and were backed by the United States, Pakistan, China, Egypt, and "reactionary petrodollar countries."

April 15, 1981 — GREECE — Three of six bombs placed under vehicles by the October-80 group exploded shortly before midnight, destroying a foreign-registered car owned by a Saudi Arabian prince, a small truck, and a pharmaceutical company's minibus. 81041501

April 16, 1981 — FEDERAL REPUBLIC OF GERMANY — Police defused a bomb made from a fire extinguisher and eight pounds of explosives found hanging by a six-foot rope from the roof of the Weisbaden United States Army Community Center. A note in German contained anti–United States statements and proclaimed solidarity with hunger-striking terrorists in West German jails. Earlier that day, Sigurd Debus, 38, one of about two dozen jailed terrorists on a hunger strike in German prisons, died in Hamburg after refusing food since February 11. He had been sentenced to 12 years in jail for robbery and attempted bomb attacks. While he was supporting demands by the Red Army Faction and the June 2 Movement for improved prison conditions, he had joined neither group. Moreover, he had a radio and television in his cell, and was not in solitary confinement, and thus had the conditions demanded by the others. The hunger strike was called off after his death. 81041601

April 16, 1981 — CORSICA — At 5:17 P.M., a bomb exploded minutes after

French president Giscard d'Estaing's plane landed at Campo Dell'Oro Airport, injuring eight people, including four Swiss tourists, one of whom died later in a Marseilles hospital, and four Corsican women, two of whom were airport employees. Extensive damage was reported. The Pasquale Paoli unit of the Corsican Guerrillas and Partisans, who claimed to be "ex-fighters of the Corsican National Front (1940–45)," claimed credit. The dead Swiss was later identified as Peter Hitz, 19. 81041602

April 18, 1981 — GUATEMALA — Gunmen fired at the Japanese embassy, damaging a window and a wall, during the morning. 81041801

April 19, 1981 — PHILIPPINES — Three grenades exploded during Easter Sunday Mass at the San Pedro Cathedral in Davao City, killing 13 and wounding 177. Thirty minutes after the blast occurred, two grenades were thrown by men aboard a jeep against curious onlookers. Several bystanders were also hit in the cross fire in an ensuing shoot-out. Police arrested New People's Army members Conceshu Napon and Nathaniel Alpolita and later picked up Rashti Dipas, 29, Em Alba, 26, and Renaldo Guzman, 18. The two former suspects fingered one another as the culprit. Authorities later reported that Graham Jones, a Protestant missionary from New Zealand, was injured in the attack. On April 30, the police said the grenades were supplied by the Moro National Liberation Front. 81041901

April 20, 1981 — INDIA — Cables in the tail section of Air India's B-707 Makalu, scheduled to fly Prime Minister Indira Gandhi, were found to be frayed, a result of sabotage. On June 11, a Bombay judge dismissed charges against five men, including a trio with Air India's engineering department and a dismissed airline technician, when Suresh Pandurang Inamdar, a defendant in a related case, claimed he had been beaten into a false confession. On June 6, police had produced Inamdar, who had confessed to cutting the cables.

April 21, 1981 — ABU DHABI — A bomb exploded in a suitcase inside a service elevator in the Hyatt Regency Hotel, killing two Sri Lankans and injuring a third. 81042101

April 21, 1981 — COLOMBIA — AGENCE FRANCE-PRESSE in Paris reported that the Colombian M-19 planned to hijack an Ecuatoriana de Aviacion flight between Cali and Quito in reprisal for Ecuador's extradition of 48 M-19 guerrillas to Colombia. The group was to ask for a large ransom and demand that the Ecuadoran government admit it had denied asylum. Police denied knowledge of such a plan. 81042102

April 22, 1981 — IRAN — A bomb planted in a minibus a mile from the

Tehran home of Ayatollah Khomeini exploded, killing a motorist and a motorcyclist and injuring 10 people.

April 23, 1981 — COLOMBIA — The M-19 threatened to kill United States ambassador Thomas Boyatt if he did not leave the country within 15 days. He and his family left for the United States on April 29 on State Department business. 81042301

April 24, 1981 — GREECE — The Revolutionary People's Army claimed credit for a bomb that exploded in the early morning at a Siemens (a West German firm) electrical appliance shop in Athens, breaking windows. Two other bombs planted outside the German-owned AEG electric products store were defused. No injuries were reported. The group said it was protesting the recent hunger strike death of West German anarchist Sigurd Debus. 81042401–02

April 24, 1981 — UNITED STATES — Alberto Sarmiento, 70, a Cuban-born Republican mayoral candidate, was shot to death in the driveway of his Miami home in Little Havana. He had pledged to "clean out the banditos" in City Hall. 81042403

April 24, 1981 — EL SALVADOR — Colonel Eduardo Mora Alfaro, coordinator of the Organization of American States (OAS) military observers on the Honduran-Salvadoran border, claimed that an OAS helicopter was fired on by a machine gun as it was patrolling Salvadoran territory in Morazan Department. 81042404

April 25, 1981 — PERU — Police arrested Nikolay Malenko, a Russian, and two Peruvians for carrying dynamite and participating in terrorist attacks. 81042501

April 26, 1981 — FRANCE — Pessah (Passover), a Jewish anti-Nazi group, fired two shots during the night at a Paris bookshop specializing in right-wing books. Pessah said it was retaliating for the profanation of the graves in Bagneux cemetery of 80 Jews who died in Nazi concentration camps. The right-wing New French Nazi Front had scrawled its initials on the tombstones and written "Nuremburg will soon be revenged," "Yes to a pure Europe," and "Death to Israel."

April 26, 1981 — EL SALVADOR — A United States Maryknoll priest disappeared after leaving the Camino Real Hotel to buy medicine. He had served as an interpreter for a CBS NEWS crew covering violence. 81042601

April 27, 1981 — UNITED STATES — At 2:31 A.M., the Imperial Iranian Patriotic Organization (IIPO) firebombed the Market Place, a Washington, D.C., store owned by Khomeini supporter Bahram Nahidian, causing one thousand dollars' damage. An IIPO caller said that Nahidian was involved in the July 22, 1980, killing of anti-Khomeini activist Ali Tabatabai. 81042701

April 29, 1981 — SPAIN — The Armed Revolutionary Groups set off two small bombs at the Madrid suburban home of the director of the Italian Tour Agency. Twenty minutes later, they bombed the agency's office in downtown Madrid. No injuries were reported. 81042901–02

April 30, 1981 — EL SALVADOR — During a guerrilla attack on the Lempa Hydroelectric Company's Auguas Calientes substation at 2:00 P.M., news-man George Thurlow of the CALIFORNIA DAILY DEMOCRAT and photographer Joaquin Romero Zuniga of the ASSOCIATED PRESS were injured, and their local interpreter, Jorge Gilberto Moran, was killed. 81043001

April 30, 1981 — PORTUGAL — Three masked men armed with automatic weapons burst into the Oporto office of British Airways and forced two employees into rest rooms. They left pamphlets, Irish Republican Army flags, and pictures of Bobby Sands, who later died of a hunger strike in a British prison. They also left a box that they claimed contained a bomb (it was filled with stones). No injuries were reported. 81043002

April 30, 1981 — GUATEMALA — The January 31 Popular Front bombed an oil storage tank at the Chevron oil products depot in the capital, blowing a large hole in the tank and starting a fire that led to the loss of five hundred thousand dollars of gasoline. The attack came at a guard shift change, when the bombers were able to cut through two chain link fences. 81043003

May 1981 — ITALY — On April 27, 1986, Jack Anderson reported that the United States consulate in Milan cabled that "Italy's military intelligence service . . . turned up evidence at the end of May [1981] that Libya and Palestinians have supplied weapons . . . to Italian terrorists." According to Anderson, police found that terrorist leader Oreste Scalzone was "thought to have received funds from the Libyans to establish a radio station and 'cultural centers' in the Rome/Naples vicinity."

May 1, 1981 — ETHIOPIA — The VOICE OF THE BROAD MASSES OF ERITREA claimed that the Russian advisers' residence had been bombed. 81050101

May 1, 1981 — AUSTRIA — Heinz Nittel, 50, president of the Austrian-Israeli

Friendship League, a leading Socialist Party official, and head of the Vienna Traffic Department, was shot in the head three times and died while getting into his car at home. His assassin, dressed in a green NATO military jacket and using a Makarov pistol, fled the scene, using several taxis in his escape. The driver of Nittel's yellow Mercedes was unharmed and described the attacker to police. Nittel had recently received several threatening anonymous letters. Abu Nidal's Al Asifah organization claimed credit for the attack and later threatened to kill Yasir Arafat and Chancellor Bruno Kreisky.

Austrian police arrested two Arabs on August 29, after they attacked a synagogue, killing 2 and injuring 20. Husham Mohammed Rajih, 21, an Iraqi, confessed to the murder. He had lived in Austria since December 1978 and was a student at Vienna's technical university. He had once met with Dr. Ghazi Husayn, the expelled former Palestine Liberation Organization representative to Austria, but did not connect him to the murder. Police also suspected the other terrorist, Hasan Marwan (Ali Yusuf), of being involved in the attack. On October 28, police arrested Bahij Younis (also spelled Bahi Yuniz), 28, a Jordanian, who was in possession of submachine guns, other small firearms, several hand grenades, and several passports. They believed he was the mastermind behind several Palestinian terrorist attacks. On January 21, 1982, a Palestinian was sentenced to life for Nittel's murder and the August 29 attack. On October 22, 1982, Bahij Mohammed Younis was sentenced to life for Nittel's murder. 81050102

May 2, 1981 — IRELAND — Claiming to have a bomb, Laurence James Downey, an Australian defrocked Trappist monk, hijacked an Aer Lingus B-737 on its Dublin-to-London flight and diverted it to France's Le Touquet airport. Four hours later, he released 5 women and 6 children, leaving 97 passengers and 5 crew on board. He demanded refueling and passage to Tehran. France refused the refueling, and Iran said it would not allow the jet to land. He also demanded publication of a manifesto (which Irish editors agreed to) calling for the publication of the "Third Secret of Fatima" a message given by the Virgin Mary to three children in Portugal during apparitions in 1917, which was subsequently given to the Pope by one of the children. He claimed he was a monk from 1950 to 1955, when he punched a superior in the nose and was expelled from the Tre Fotnane monastery in Rome. He was now married and the father of 5 children. He doused himself with gasoline and threatened to self-immolate. Four hours later, antiterrorist police stormed the plane, and overpowered the hijacker without firing a shot. No injuries were reported. The Vatican refused comment. 81050201

May 2, 1981 — BOLIVIA — Armed members of the extreme rightist Bolivian Socialist Falange, led by Carlos Valverde Barberry, at 4:30 P.M. took over the United States Occidental Oil plant in Tita, 125 kilometers from La Paz, and took 52 hostages, including United States mechanic Leonard Davis. The group set a deadline of 4:30 P.M. May 4 for the abdication of junta leader Gen. Luis Garcia Meza and transfer of power to a civil-military group. The government said its forces reclaimed the compound on May 5, capturing paramilitary troops from Argentina, Peru, Germany, and other countries, who had been financed by drug traffickers. They found grenades, M-1 rifles, sawed-off shotguns, and uniforms. The only injury came to a member of the 8th Army Division, Col. Gary Prado Salmon, who was wounded in both sides of the chest and in the spinal column when a soldier accidentally squeezed the trigger of his machine gun. Among the 120 attackers were Carlos Valverde Bravo (the leader's son), Sergio Flores, German Antelo, Jose Nunez, Jose Ortiz, and Julio Costas. 81050202

May 4, 1981 — SPAIN — The October 1 Group of the Armed Revolution (GRAPO) shot in the head and killed Gen. Andres Gonzalez de Suso, 62, as he left his home in the Salamanca district of Madrid on his way to army headquarters. The general was a close associate of the reformist deputy prime minister responsible for security affairs, Gen. Manuel Gutierrez Mellado, who had resigned from the cabinet shortly after an abortive rightist coup attempt on February 23. Police intercepted his two attackers, and in the ensuing gun battle, a policeman was killed, three bystanders were wounded, and one GRAPO member was injured and arrested. His accomplice escaped into a subway. In an apparently coordinated Barcelona attack, two men shot and killed two Civil Guards having breakfast in a bar.

May 5, 1981 — UNITED KINGDOM — Bobby Sands, a jailed Irish Republican Army militant, died at 1:17 A.M. in the Maze Prison on the 66th day of a hunger strike to gain political prisoner status, which grants rights not given to common criminals. The death touched off rioting in west Belfast. Sands had spent a third of his life in prison, having joined the IRA as an unemployed teenager. He was arrested in 1972 in a series of robberies for the IRA and served four years in prison. A year later, he was convicted of gun possession. On April 9, while on his hunger strike, he was elected to a British Parliament seat from an Ulster constituency.

May 5, 1981 — UNITED KINGDOM — A London postal employee intercepted a letter bomb addressed to Prince Charles.

May 5, 1981 — EL SALVADOR — Leftist guerrillas fired machine guns at an Organization of American States (OAS) military observer helicopter flying in the areas of Torola and Perquin, Morazan Department, near the Honduran border. 81050501

May 5, 1981—PORTUGAL—The April 25 Popular Forces bombed the Royal British Club in Lisbon, causing minor damage and no injuries. 81050502

May 6, 1981—GUATEMALA—William NcNew, director of the local office of the Western Geophysical Petroleum Company, was released by his (apparently leftist guerrilla) kidnappers on a farm two hundred kilometers north of Guatemala City after payment of a $250,000 ransom. 81050601

May 6, 1981—UNITED KINGDOM—A padded package with a hoax bomb device was sent to Queen Elizabeth II, while death threats were made against Prince Charles and Lady Diana Spencer. On June 1, police arrested Ronald Zen, 42, an American "self-employed artist" living illegally in Britain, when he tried to reenter Britain from France. 81050602–03

May 9, 1981—FRANCE—Pessah (Passover) fired shots during the night at the Syrian Airlines office in central Paris, causing no casualties. The group said it was retaliating for "Syrian persecutions in which Jews are victims, and the massacre of Christians in Libya." On May 13, police arrested Albert Nacache, 22, Alain Baruk, 20, and an unnamed minor, after a witness's report of a license plate led to the apprehension of the trio. 81050901

May 10, 1981—COSTA RICA—James Douglas Borland, 51, an American, was kidnapped from his Escazu home by an unidentified man. 81051001

May 11, 1981—FRANCE—The Jacques Mesrine Organization, named after France's former public enemy number one who was killed by police in 1979, bombed a 150-MPH express train on its Paris to Lyon run, injuring three people. It claimed it had also planted bombs on two other Lyon-Paris trains.

May 11, 1981—FEDERAL REPUBLIC OF GERMANY—The Red Army Faction (RAF) shot in the stomach and killed Heinz Karry, controversial economics minister of the southwestern state of Hesse, in his bed in suburban Frankfurt at 5:00 A.M. Karry, national treasurer of the Free Democratic party and a former Nazi labor camp prisoner, was an outspoken supporter of plans to extend Frankfurt Airport and build a nuclear fuel reprocessing plant. On May 19, the RAF threatened to follow the attack with bombings in Frankfurt and London airports. 81051101

May 12, 1981—UNITED KINGDOM—Francis Hughes, 25, jailed Irish Republican Army (IRA) gunman, died during the evening of the 59th day of his hunger strike in Maze Prison. Violent rioting erupted in Belfast and Londonderry, and two thousand people threw rocks and bottles at the

British embassy in Ireland. Hughes was serving a life term for killing a British soldier and participating in several other attacks on security forces by an IRA unit he led in the mid-1970s.

May 13, 1981 — KAMPUCHEA — The VOICE OF DEMOCRATIC KAMPU-CHEA claimed that its forces ambushed a Vietnamese truck convoy near the town of Kompong Speu, killing five, including a Soviet adviser, a Vietnamese provincial governor, and a deputy governor, wounding seven, and destroying two trucks.

May 13, 1981 — UNITED STATES — The Soviet news agency TASS reported that three incendiary devices were discovered near the country house of the Soviet mission to the United Nations in a New York suburb. 81051301

May 13, 1981 — VATICAN CITY — Mehmet Ali Agca, 24, an escaped rightist Turkish terrorist, fired five shots from a Browning 9 mm pistol at Pope John Paul II as the pontiff was being driven around in Saint Peter's Square in front of 10,000 worshippers. The attacker hit the pope three times and wounded 2 tourists: Ann Odre, 58, of Buffalo, New York, and Rose Hall, 21, of Jamaica. Agca was charged on May 14 with the 5:17 P.M. attempted assassination of the pope, who recovered fom his wounds. The terrorist had previously threatened the pope during his visit to Turkey in November 1979. He claimed he wanted to assassinate the "king of England" but gave up that plan when he discovered that the "king" is a female. He also planned to murder United Nations secretary-general Kurt Waldheim and Simone Veil, president of the European Parliament. He claimed friendship with George Habash, but the Popular Front for the Liberation of Palestine (PFLP) denied any contact with him. He was also affiliated with the Gray Wolves, a rightist organization associated with the Nationalist Action Party.

Agca had escaped from Turkey after being imprisoned for the murder of prominent journalist Abdi Ipekci. His sources of support and his whereabouts are shrouded in mystery. He claimed to have received $10,000 during his odyssey. He claimed to have received his gun in Bulgaria and was seen on a bus going from Sofia to Belgrade, Yugoslavia, in the fall of 1980. He entered Italy on April 9 with a false passport for Faruk Azgun (also spelled Uzgun), and enrolled at the University of Perugia. He then lived in the right-wing underground of West Germany among the Turkish worker population. He reentered Italy from Majorca, Spain, on May 9, using the same passport.

On July 19, 1981, Turkey asked for Agca's extradition. On July 22, after a three-day trial and a one-day hunger strike, Agca was sentenced to life imprisonment in Rome.

According to the Italian press, the publicity-conscious Agca soon began to talk about his suspected sources of support and tied Bulgarian intelligence to the case. On December 8, 1982, Italian newspapers claimed that Agca had confessed that Bulgarian intelligence had ordered him to kill the pope. He claimed that he escaped into Bulgaria with the help of Oral Celik, a Turkish terrorist with ties to the Bulgarians. In Sofia he was aided by another Turk, Bekir Celenk, whom Italian police have linked to arms and drug smuggling. Celenk introduced Agca to Sergei (also spelled Sergey) Ivanov Antonov, a Rome station chief for Balkan Airlines; Teodorov (also spelled Todor, Teodor) Ayvazov (also spelled Aivazov), a cashier for the Bulgarian embassy in Rome; and Jelio (also spelled Zelio, Zhelyo) Kolev Vassiliev (also spelled Vasilev, Vasiley), former secretary to Bulgaria's military attache in Rome. Celenk and the Bulgarians allegedly offered Agca DM 3 million ($1.25 million) to kill the pope. After several months in Sofia, Agca laid a false trail in Western Europe, then entered Italy in May 1981 and met in Milan with another Turkish terrorist, Omer Bagci, who gave Agca the assassination pistol. In Rome, Agca was given instructions by Ayvazov and Antonov, who accompanied him to Saint Peter's Square on May 11 and 12 to scout a clear firing line. On the day of the shooting, Antonov and Ayvazov drove Agca in a blue Alfa Romeo to Saint Peter's Square, where they all took positions. The Bulgarians carried pistols; Ayvazov also had a grenade. Agca was captured with a paper bearing the phone numbers of the Bulgarian embassy and consulate, Balkan Airlines, and Ayvazov's residence.

On December 9, 1982, Italian magistrates confiscated records of the Bulgarian national airline. Examining magistrate Ferdinando Imposimato ordered the confiscation after left-wing unionist Luigi Scricciolo, who was jailed on charges of spying and terrorism, claimed to have had active contact with four Bulgarian officials. Scricciolo was held in connection with the Dozier kidnapping of December 17, 1981, which two Red Brigadists said had been aided by the Bulgarians. Also on December 9, Bulgaria detained Bekir Celenk.

On November 2, 1982, police in Kriftel, outside Frankfurt, West Germany, arrested Musar (also spelled Musa) Serdar Celebi, 30, on an international arrest warrant in connection with the papal case. He was the founder of an extreme right-wing group, the Turkish Federation, which Ankara officials believe is a cover for the terrorist Gray Wolves group. He was extradited to Italy on January 14, 1983.

A few days after the attack on the pope, police in Solothurn, Switzerland, arrested Omer Bagci, a Turk, who provided a 9 mm gun to Agca. His appeal against extradition to Italy was rejected by the Swiss Supreme Court on October 13, 1982. Police believed a second gunman, Mehemet Sener, 25, was with Agca during the shooting. In March 1983, Switzerland released Sener from jail, to the irritation of the Turkish government.

Oral Celik allegedly helped Agca escape from the jail where he was serving time for the murder of journalist Ipekci. Agca turned up in 1980 in Bulgaria traveling on a fake Indian passport issued in the name of Joginder Singh. On May 11, 1983, the West German television network ZDF claimed that Oral Celik could be seen in photographs taken in Saint Peter's during the assassination attempt. Celik was charged with complicity in the attack on November 27, 1982.

Bekir Celenk, a Turkish smuggler, was charged by Judge Ilario Martella with complicity on November 27, 1982. Turkey requested Celenk's extradition from Bulgaria on December 13 and 23, 1982, and January 19, 1983, claiming he was wanted for smuggling and currency irregularities.

On November 25, 1982, Rome police arrested Sergei Ivanov Antonov, 35, a tall man with short, dark curly hair, glasses, and a moustache, for involvement in the case. He was suspected of providing a hideout to Agca, which the Bulgarian government vehemently denied. A photograph published in early December 1982 showed a man who bore a strong resemblance to Antonov close to the pope at the time of the shooting, but other investigators claimed the man was an American tourist.

Italy issued an arrest warrant for Vassiliev on December 4, 1982, but he had returned to Bulgaria six months previously. Ayvazov was transferred back to Sofia when the Italians asked that his diplomatic immunity be lifted.

On December 7, 1982, the Italian press noted that Abuzer Ugurlu, a major Turkish criminal involved in smuggling for the Bulgarians, served as a link between Agca and the Bulgarians. Omer Mersan, who allegedly provided Agca with a pilfered passport and spoke with him repeatedly on the telephone, once shortly before the assassination attempt, was linked with the now-jailed Ugurlu.

On December 15, 1982, two Italian newspapers claimed Agca was also directed by the Bulgarians to kill Lech Walesa, head of Poland's Solidarnosc Free Trade Union Movement, during his visit to Rome on January 14–19, 1981. Luigi Scricciolo had organized the trip. Agca stayed in the Isa Hotel on January 19 under the name of Faruk Azgun, the name found on the false passport he was carrying when captured in Saint Peter's Square.

On December 20, 1982, Italian defense minister Lelio Lagorio called the attempted assassination an "act of war" and claimed it may have been a "precautionary and alternative solution to the invasion of Poland." Lagorio noted that Italian counterespionage detected a sudden increase in coded messages between Sofia and Italy at the time of the papal shooting and during the Dozier kidnapping. Lagorio concluded that "this was interpreted as a result of inactive Bulgarian agents in Italy being activated."

On March 13, 1983, the WASHINGTON POST reported several gaps in Agca's testimony that cast doubt on the Bulgarian connection theory. Agca described Antonov's apartment, claiming that he met there with the three Bulgarians whose mug shots he had picked out. But Agca mentioned having seen a folding wooden door in Antonov's apartment that was actually present in other apartments in the building but not in Antonov's. Bulgarian lawyers produced hotel bills indicating that Antonov's wife Rossitska was already in Yugoslavia en route to Bulgaria when Agca said that she was present in the apartment during one of the Turk's meetings there. The Antonovs' daughter, Ani, whom Agca claimed was present, was not in Rome during that school year but in Sofia.

On February 28, 1983, an Istanbul military court said it would try Agca in default for the papal assassination attempt. A criminal court had earlier declined jurisdiction. On March 16, 1983, the Istanbul military prosecutor questioned Yavuz Caylan, convicted accomplice of Agca in the Ipekci murder, in connection with the papal shooting. Caylan had received 10 years at Canakkale prison for driving Agca to the scene of the February 1979 shooting of Ipekci.

On March 16, 1983, Adnan Agca, Mehmet Ali's younger brother, was arrested in Malatya, Turkey, after "walking towards President Kenan Evren in a hostile manner." He was freed after paying a Lt 1500 ($7.50) fine for disturbing public order by shouting, "Damn Armenians, long live Islamic Turkey," while Evren was addressing a crowd.

On June 22, 1983, the Turkish Anti-Christian Liberation Front kidnapped Emanuela Orlandi, 15, daughter of a Vatican employee, demanding Agca's release by July 20. On June 13, 1985, Agca claimed that the Italian Masonic Lodge, known as Propaganda 2, or P-2, was behind the kidnapping, and that he was convinced she was still alive.

On November 24, 1983, Agca was charged with slandering Antonov by naming him as part of a conspiracy to murder Lech Walesa in 1981.

On March 12, 1984, Omer Mersan, a Turk, surrendered to Italian authorities after being extradited from West Germany. He was wanted in Italy for false testimony in Agca's first trial. He was accused of providing a fake passport for Agca, which he used before arriving in Italy.

On June 18, 1984, Antonov was permitted house arrest to receive medical treatment for anorexia nervosa and circulatory and heart problems. He had previously been permitted house arrest on December 21, 1983.

On December 18, 1984, Turkey announced the beginning of a military trial of 7 individuals who helped Agca flee the country in June 1980, then reenter and leave in August of that year.

Agca's later charges of Bulgarian involvement in the assassination attempt sparked a new trial in Italy. State Prosecutor Antonio Albano filed a 77-page report on June 8, 1984, saying that the Bulgarian secret service hired Agca. In October 1984, Judge Ilario Martella delivered a 1243-page indictment against 5 Turks and 3 Bulgarians.

During the "Trial of the Century," which began on May 27, 1985, Agca often strained his credibility by contradicting his testimony, admitting lying, and at the start of proceedings, announcing, "I am Jesus Christ. In the name of the omnipotent God, I announce the end of the world. The world will be destroyed."

Agca claimed that the KGB was involved in the assassination attempt. On June 6, 1985, Agca claimed that he had been trained as a terrorist by Bulgarian and Czechoslovak instructors in Latakia, Syria. "In this camp there were also western terrorists, French, Italians, Germans and Spanish. The camp was under the control of the Syrian secret service." On June 7, 1985, he refused to testify against the accused Bulgarians, saying that he had received death threats from Soviet Bloc security services. On June 12, 1985, Agca claimed that the order to kill the pope came from the Soviet embassy in Sofia in July 1980 by a Soviet diplomat named Milenkov or Malenkov. In pretrial statements, Agca once mentioned meeting a Soviet official of the same name in Iran but later said he had been lying. Agca also said that he was ordered to kill Tunisian president Habib Bourguiba and visiting Maltese prime minister Dom Mintoff in Tunis in 1980. According to AGENCE FRANCE-PRESSE, "Agca told the court . . . that he obeyed Vasilev and went to Tunis where he was met by a Syrian whom he did not name. The 2 men then inspected the spot where a car with the 2 leaders would drive past on December 10, 1980. Agca decided it was 'possible' to detonate a bomb by remote control, but left for Palermo, Sicily, because Tunisian police 'had suspicions.' Agca yesterday claimed that a Soviet diplomat in Sofia handed over 3 million marks for the pontiff's assassination. In his evidence today, Agca charged that the 'Soviets wanted an attack against RADIO FREE EUROPE in Munich, and this was carried out in the autumn of 1980.'"

In late May 1985, Dutch police arrested a young Turk, carrying a false passport for Aslan Samet during the pope's visit, for possession of a 9 mm Browning, which was among the pistols purchased by Agca. It was later determined that Samet was not Oral Celik.

On June 18, 1985, Agca admitted to "inventing" testimony but promised that he was now telling the truth. He denied allegations that he had been pressured by the Italian Mafia into implicating the Soviets in the plot. Giovanni Pandico, who turned state's evidence in a Naples trial of Camorra gangsters, had claimed that the Neapolitan Mafia was acting on behalf of an Italian secret service general now being tried for abuse of office.

On June 19, 1985, Agca claimed that Francesco Pazienza served as his link with the Italian secret service, who offered him freedom if he cooperated with authorities. Pazienza was arrested in New York on March 4, 1985, and is wanted in Italy for fraud and corruption of the secret service.

On July 8, 1985, a Rome court indicated that it would ask Turkey to extradite Bekir Celenk, who had returned to Turkey the previous day after three years in Bulgaria, where authorities turned down five Italian requests for his extradition. Agca had claimed that Celenk offered him $1.2 million for the attack on behalf of the Bulgarians. Celenk was wanted in Turkey on charges of gunrunning and drug smuggling and was being tried in absentia in Rome for organizing the plot against the pope. Turkey said that it had ratified a convention that did not permit extradition of its citizens. On September 18, 1985, a Turkish martial court began the trial of Bekir Celenk on charges of smuggling drugs and arms, for which he faced a possible death penalty. Celenk died of a heart attack in a Turkish prison on October 14, 1985.

On July 17, 1985, public prosecutor Antonio Marini asked the court to attempt to secure a temporary extradition from West Germany of Yalcin Ozbey, a Turkish drug trafficker, before his jail term ended in mid-September. The court reassembled for an extraordinary three-day session during its summer break to hear testimony by Ozbey, a member of the Gray Wolves, who claimed that Agca had sought assistance from the Bulgarians but was rebuffed. Agca had claimed that Celik was with him in Saint Peter's Square during the shooting, which Ozbey contradicted. Ozbey claimed that he had learned details of the plot from Agca, Celik, and Sedat Sirri Kadem, 30, a former leftist terrorist whom Agca also claimed was with him in Saint Peter's Square. Ozbey's testimony was hurt when he was unable to describe Kadem. Abdullah Catli, held in France on drug charges, testified that Celik had been with him in Vienna on the day of the shooting. Agca also said Amer (also spelled Omer) Ay, another Gray Wolf jailed in Turkey, was with him in the Square. On July 22, 1985, Marini flew to Istanbul to interview Sedat Sirri Kadem.

On December 21, 1985, the trials' hearings ended with the cross-examination in Bulgaria of Vassiliev and Ayvazov. Bulgaria had refused Italian extradition requests. The duo had left Italy in 1982 before they could be arrested.

On March 29, 1986, having heard from over 100 witnesses, Judge Severino Santiapichi announced that the Rome jury of 2 judges and 6 lay jurors acquitted Bulgarians Sergei Antonov, Teodorov Ayvazov, and Jelio Vassiliev of charges of plotting to assassinate the pope because of insufficient evidence, following the prosecutor's recommendations of February 27. The magistrates also acquitted Turkish nationals Musar Serdar Celebi and Oral Celik. Agca, already serving a life sentence for firing the shots, was sentenced to a year in prison for illegal possession of the automatic pistol. Omer Bagci was sentenced to three years and two months for bringing the weapon into Italy but was cleared of the principal charge of conspiracy on the grounds that there was no proof that he had any knowledge of Agca's intentions. After the sentences were read, Agca clapped his hands and shouted, "The Gospel has been changed. I am Jesus Christ, I am an angel in human form." The prosecution filed an appeal regarding Antonov, blocking his departure from Italy. Lawyers for Antonov, who had been held in prison or house arrest in Italy since November 25, 1982, said they would appeal the verdict in hopes of winning full acquittal by innocence. 81051302

May 14, 1981 — ITALY — The Proletarian Internationalist Groups (GIP) bombed a Rome display room of the British Land Rover Company, protesting "the Thatcher government's policies in Northern Ireland." No injuries were reported. 81051401

May 14, 1981 — ITALY — The Florence offices of British Airways were fire-bombed, causing minor damage and no injuries. 81051402

May 15, 1981 — EGYPT — AL AHRAM reported that the State Security Investigations Department foiled two Rejectionist Front plots to bomb assembly places and assassinate prominent individuals.

May 15, 1981 — ITALY — A bomb exploded during the night at the Rome El Al office, shattering glass, damaging the door and lobby, but causing no injuries. 81051501

May 16, 1981 — UNITED STATES — A bomb exploded at 9:30 A.M. in a men's room at the Pan American World Airways terminal at John F. Kennedy International Airport, killing Alex McMillan, 19, a part-time employee, and causing extensive damage. After the explosion an anonymous caller said, "This is the Puerto Rican Armed Resistance. There are bombs in the Pan American terminal near the restaurant and main lobby, also on Flight 403 to Guatemala. You have 15 minutes to clear the terminal." No bomb was found on the B-727, but a more powerful bomb was found nine hours later in the airport. 81051601

May 16, 1981 — TURKEY — The May 15 Arab Organization for the Liberation of Palestine bombed the El Al offices in Istanbul, shattering windows but causing no injuries. 81051602

May 17, 1981 — COLOMBIA — Two Worker's Self-Defense Movement (MAO) bombs exploded at the Bogota branch of the Anglo American Bank, causing great damage but no injuries. The group was protesting the hunger strike deaths of Irish nationalists Bobby Sands and Francis Hughes. The group said it had called off an attack on British Caledonian Airways due to increased security in the area. 81051701

May 17, 1981 — UNITED KINGDOM — A Manchester-to-Toronto Canadian Pacific B-747 flying 411 passengers landed at Scotland's Prestwick airport when an anonymous bomb threat was received. No bomb was found. 81051702

May 17, 1981 — UNITED STATES — The Soviet news agency TASS claimed that an incendiary device was found on the grounds of the Soviet United Nations residence. 81051703

May 18, 1981 — GREECE — Revolutionary Solidarity firebombed a bus of the West German Grundig Electrical Company in Athens to protest capitalism and the oppression of workers. No injuries were reported. 81051801

May 18, 1981 — UNITED STATES — The Puerto Rican Armed Resistance mailed package bombs to the United States' United Nations Mission and the Honduran consulate in New York. Both devices were disarmed safely. Police reported receiving 487 reports of planted bombs in the next three days. 81051802

May 19, 1981 — FEDERAL REPUBLIC OF GERMANY — A caller claiming to represent a group fighting nuclear proliferation in South Asia claimed credit for bombing the Markdorf installation of the Hans Waelischmiller Company, causing $50,000 damage to nuclear-related equipment. The caller threatened the director with death if the company continued exporting to Pakistan.

May 19, 1981 — EL SALVADOR — Adrian Levinski, 55, of the United States, was murdered in a San Salvador hotel. The Salvadoran resident was married to Estela Menjivar, a Salvadoran who apparently was with her husband at the time of the killing.

May 19, 1981 — ABU DHABI — An Iraqi political refugee died of a bullet wound to the head. His assassin was arrested in the public square and confessed to the killing, claiming to have arrived in the country five days ago. He carried an Iraqi diplomatic passport. 81051901

May 19, 1981 — POLAND — A man claiming to have a bomb in his briefcase entered the United States embassy and demanded to be taken to Okecie Airport and then by aircraft to the United States. He was overpowered by local militia after embassy staffers left the building. 81051902

May 20, 1981 — ITALY — Four Red Brigadists posing as customs police kidnapped Giuseppe Tagliercio, an executive of Montedison, Italy's largest petrochemical group, from his downtown Venice apartment. The Porto Marghera plant had had numerous labor conflicts.

May 21, 1981 — UNITED KINGDOM — Raymond McCreesh, 24, an imprisoned Irish Republican Army (IRA) guerrilla, died at 2:11 A.M. on the 61st day of his hunger strike in Maze Prison, demanding political status for IRA prisoners, which would get the IRA prisoners separate facilities from the common criminals. He and three other IRA terrorists were captured in June 1976 after a two-hour gun battle with British paratroopers. He was sentenced in March 1977 to 14 years for attempted murder and possession of firearms. Rioting broke out in various Northern Ireland neighborhoods at the news of his death.

May 21, 1981 — UNITED STATES — A pipe bomb was found on a sanitation truck in the United Nations garage after the New York police received a tip that six bombs were planted in the United Nations basement. 81052101

May 22, 1981 — UNITED KINGDOM — Patrick O'Hara, 24, an imprisoned Irish National Liberation Army (INLA) terrorist, died during the 61st day of his hunger strike in Maze Prison. He was serving an eight-year jail term for possession of explosives.

May 22, 1981 — UNITED STATES — The Federal Bureau of Investigation arrested Leon Cordell Horton, 53, of Houston and Artis O'Dell Reed, 50, of Irving, Texas, and charged them with mailing bombs and diseased ticks to companies across the nation in a multimillion dollar extortion scheme. They were also charged with conspiring to poison food and medicinal products on retail shelves.

May 22, 1981 — ITALY — Libyan information minister Ibrahim Bishari called for a United Nations-sponsored international conference on terrorism.

May 23, 1981 — SPAIN — Eleven alleged rightists seized 200 hostages at 9:10 A.M. in Barcelona's Banco Central. They demanded the release of Lt. Col. Antonio Tejero, Maj. Gen. Luis Torres Rojas, Army colonel Ignacio San Martin, and Civil Guard captain Pedro Mas, all of whom were being held for organizing the abortive February 23 coup attempt; they also demanded a plane to fly the prisoners and the attackers to Argentina. The prisoners refused to leave, and Argentina refused to accept the band, despite a 24-hour deadline.

The terrorists released bank employee Ricardo Martinez Calafell, 32, who had been wounded in the leg, and 20 others who were suffering from shock. Two hours later, 40 hostages were released in return for food. Nine others were released later that night. Government delegate general in Catalonia Juan Rovira Tarazona and police director general Jose Luis Fernandez Dopico negotiated directly with the terrorists, who released 43 more hostages the next day.

Hundreds of police surrounding the bank rushed it at 10:15 P.M., freeing the remaining hostages. A submachine gun and 11 pistols, mostly rusting, were found. One of the terrorists, Jose Maria Cuevas, who reportedly had a record of sexual offenses, was killed in the attack, but no other casualties were reported.

Under questioning, the group's leader, Juan Jose Martinez (El Rubio, the Blond), said he had assembled common criminals and anarchists for the attack. Local leftists claimed he was a police informer in 1976–79. He said he was offered Pts 5 million in Perpignan, France, for the attack. He met Antonio Luis in March, who briefed him on May 12 in Barcelona. One of the attackers, Civil Guard captain Gil Sanchez Valiente, reportedly had fled to London after the coup. French police said three of the terrorists — Jose Martinez Gomez, 25, and two brothers, Jose and Christobal Valencuela-Barcos, 21 and 23, were wanted for six holdups in 1980 that netted three hundred thousand dollars.

On May 25, police arrested three reported accomplices in Barcelona.

May 23, 1981 — ALBANIA — Two bombs were thrown on the roof of the Yugoslav embassy at 8:00 P.M. during Youth Day, causing some damage but no injuries. Yugoslavia complained that Albanian police took 1½ hours to reach the embassy after the bombing and suggested governmental complicity. Albania suggested that the Yugoslavs planted the bombs. Belgrade charged that Hisen Trpeza, active in Kosovo during World War II, was in the area that day and had planted the bombs. 81052301

May 24, 1981 — FEDERAL REPUBLIC OF GERMANY — The tires of 35 vehicles of British military forces were slashed in two housing areas assigned to them in Hanover. No injuries were reported. Irish Republican Army (IRA) sympathizers were suspected.

May 24, 1981 — ECUADOR — A caller claiming April 19 Movement (M-19) membership said two of his group had planted a bomb on board an airplane that had crashed, killing Ecuadoran president Jaime Roldos. The M-19 later denied the claim. 81052401

May 24, 1981 — GREECE — A bomb exploded in the car of a female United States noncommissioned officer who was stationed at Ellinikon base. The explosion in Voula caused some damage. 81052402

May 24, 1981 — TURKEY — In the air over Turkey four armed Dev Sol males hijacked the *Halic,* a Turkish Airlines DC-9 flying 112 passengers and 7 crew at 7:00 A.M. from Istanbul to Bulgaria's Burgas airport. They released 8 women, 4 children, and 3 men (the total later reached 27 released hostages). They demanded five hundred thousand dollars and the release of 47 prisoners, or they would kill 5 United States Citibank officials. A Frenchman was also on board the plane. Turkish ambassador Gurun negotiated with the terrorists, who allowed the deadline to pass without incident. Two

Turks, Nurtac Korkut and Sanvar Ercan, escaped. On May 25, 2 of the terrorists left the plane to hold a news conference and were arrested by the police. Pilot Metin Ikizogu gunned the plane's engine forward, then stepped on the brakes, throwing the remaining 2 hijackers off balance. The passengers overpowered the duo, who fired their weapons randomly. The 2 hijackers were injured, as were a married Japanese couple, an Iranian student, and 2 Turkish passengers at 3:45 P.M. Explosives were later found on board the plane. The hijackers, whose extradition was requested by Turkey, were identified as Ahmed Bolkan (date of birth [DOB] January 1, 1963), Okan Bolko (DOB January 1, 1962), Aiden Jelal (DOB March 2, 1960), and Cen Gyulsai (DOB 1962). On July 6, 1983, Bulgaria extradited Ekrem Kilic (another name for one of the hijackers); the other 3 hijackers remained in Bulgaria. 81052403

May 25, 1981 — REPUBLIC OF SOUTH AFRICA — The African National Congress bombed two railways and a military recruiting office in Durban, cut a power supply line, and attacked a rural police station to protest Republic Day, which marks South Africa's break with the British Commonwealth.

May 25, 1981 — LEBANON — Three rockets fired 45 minutes after midnight hit the second and third floors of the United States embassy, slightly wounding a guard and causing some damage. 81052501

May 25, 1981 — LEBANON — A rocket destroyed a water tank at the Sudanese embassy. 81052502

May 25, 1981 — LEBANON — Two rocket-propelled grenades (RPGs) were fired at 1:00 A.M. at the Egyptian embassy, hitting the third and sixth floors and wounding Counselor Yusuf al-Hindi. 81052503

May 27, 1981 — UNITED KINGDOM — Irish Republican Army (IRA) hunger striker Brendan McLaughlin, 29, serving 12 years on firearms charges, ended his 14-day hunger strike suffering from a perforated ulcer. He became the first striker to end his fast.

May 27, 1981 — GREECE — The Greek Armed Group for the Support of the Northern Ireland Struggle bombed the fourth floor of Salonika offices of the British Council cultural organization at 3:15 A.M., shattering windows but causing no injuries. 81052701

May 28, 1981 — VENEZUELA — The Spanish news service EFE reported that Carlos the Jackal, the infamous Popular Front for the Liberation of Palestine (PFLP) terrorist, was believed in the country planning an attack on the conference of the Group of 77 (a group of less-developed countries).

May 28, 1981 — FRANCE — According to the Rand Corporation, "A bomb exploded outside the Armenian Cutural Center in Paris, killing the caretaker of an adjacent building. The attack was claimed a few days later by the Turkish Islamic Revolutionary Army. The anti-Armenian attack was unprecedented in Paris, but officials noted that it may have been in retaliation for the recent Armenian terrorist attacks against Turkish diplomats." 81052801

May 29, 1981 — UNITED KINGDOM — The national H-Block Committee (named after the Maze Prison facilities for Irish Republican Army [IRA] terrorists) reported that IRA hunger strikers would run for the Irish Republic's Parliament in the June 11 general elections. Hunger striker Kevin Lynch, 24, would run in Waterford; Kiernan Doherty, 25, in Cavan-Monaghan; Joe McDonnell, 30, in Sligo-Leitrim; and Martin Hurson, 27, in Longford-Westmeath.

May 29, 1981 — EL SALVADOR — Unknown gunmen driving by the Guatemalan embassy fired machine guns at guards but caused no casualties. 81052901

May 30, 1981 — LEBANON — The VOICE OF LEBANON claimed that Carlos the Jackal (of the Popular Front for the Liberation of Palestine) and Japanese Red Army terrorists were at a Libyan training camp planning to attack oil installations in the Gulf area.

May 30, 1981 — UNITED STATES — A federal appeals court acquitted two anti-Castro Cubans — Guillermo Novo Sampol and Alvin Ross Diaz — of charges of murder and conspiracy in connection with the 1976 assassination of former Chilean ambassador Orlando Letelier. Novo, 41, was convicted of two counts of making false declarations to a federal grand jury.

June 1981 — KUWAIT — Four Jordanians planted bombs in various parts of the country, then fled the area. They were sentenced in absentia on August 15. 81069901

June 1, 1981 — REPUBLIC OF SOUTH AFRICA — The South African Liberation Support Group firebombed three offices of the liberal Progressive Federal party in Johannesburg's northern suburbs.

June 1, 1981 — BELGIUM — Na'im Khader, 41, Palestine Liberation Organization representative in Brussels, was shot and killed by six rounds fired at 10:00 A.M. by a dark-skinned man with a thick moustache who escaped in a car bearing German license plates. The killer's raincoat and umbrella were found a few hundred meters away. 81060101

June 2, 1981 — ITALY— A Rome court sentenced Soraya Ansari, an Iranian, in absentia to 30 years for the October 1977 hijacking of a Lufthansa airliner in which the pilot was killed.

June 3, 1981 — LEBANON — An unidentified gunman fired at the car of the Iraqi embassy second secretary, hitting 'Adnan Habib Husayn in the left arm. 81060301

June 3, 1981 — SWITZERLAND — Two firebombs set by the 2 June Movement, a West German leftist group, caused $50,000 damage to the Lufthansa office and $10,000 damage to the Pestalozzianum cultural and educational institute, both in Zurich. No injuries were reported. 81060302–03

June 4, 1981 — FRANCE — Police disarmed a bomb at 9:00 A.M. set by the Turkish Islamic Revolutionary Army in front of an Armenian church in Paris. 81060401

June 5, 1981 — UNITED STATES — A valve normally locked in an open position was found shut at the Beaver Valley nuclear plant near Pittsburgh. The Nuclear Regulatory Commission (NRC) said "the chain and padlock which secured this valve in the open position were missing." With the valve shut, emergency cooling water would not have been available for high-pressure injection into the core in the event of an emergency. The NRC said it believed the motive was harassment of the utility rather than sabotage. No arrest was made and there was no suspect.

June 6, 1981 — ITALY— The Veneto Communist Cells threw a Molotov cocktail at an English tour bus in Mestre, causing no injuries. An anonymous caller demanded that the British get out of Ireland. 81060601

June 8, 1981 — UNITED KINGDOM — Announcing that a fifth prisoner, Thomas McIlwee, 23, had joined the hunger strike, the Sinn Fein said it would add one or two strikers each week, rather than merely replace each striker who starved to death, in order to increase pressure on the government.

June 8, 1981 — FRANCE — French premier Pierre Mauroy denied extradition to Spain of Basque Nation and Liberty/Military Wing (ETA/M) member Tomas Linaza Echeverria.

June 9, 1981 — SWITZERLAND — Mehmet Savas Erguz, 39, a secretary at the Turkish consulate in Geneva, was shot and killed two hundred meters from the facility by an Armenian gunman who fired three shots from a 9 mm pistol during the evening. John Kirkoryan, 23, was quickly arrested. The

Armenian Secret Army for the Liberation of Armenia claimed credit for the killing. 81060901

June 10, 1981 — LEBANON — The VOICE OF LEBANON claimed that five Syrian intelligence agents led by Captain Rustum kidnapped three Jordanians suspected of being Moslem Brotherhood members at Beirut International Airport and took them to the Cocody area.

June 10, 1981 — YUGOSLAVIA — A bomb destroyed a car belonging to the Iraqi military attache at 9:00 P.M. in front of his Belgrade office. Several other vehicles and windows were damaged, but no casualties were reported. 81061001

June 11, 1981 — LEBANON — According to the VOICE OF LEBANON, "Three gunmen kidnapped Dr. Yahiya Bakhur, doyen of Syrian engineers, and Muhammad Fayiz 'Araji of Ra's Bayrut and took them to Ar-Ramlat al-Bayda', where they were robbed of 24,000 Lebanese pounds and their car was stolen. In Al-Hamra' Street, Ahmad Hammud 'Abbush, an Iraqi national, was kidnapped. Gunmen reported to belong to an armed organization in West Beirut have kidnapped Salman Hasan and 'Isam Abu Shaqra, members of the Socialist Progressive Party."

June 11, 1981 — JAPAN — The Japanese Red Army (JRA) sent copies of their newsletter *Solidarity* to nonmembers of the group residing in Japan, along with a letter signed by group leader Fusako Shigenobu. The newsletter critiqued the JRA and sympathizers and expressed a JRA willingness to compromise with the Palestine Liberation Organization.

June 11, 1981 — FRANCE — Fifteen members of the Organization for the Liberation of Armenia occupied the Turkish Airlines office in Paris for 90 minutes, protesting attacks on Armenian churches and on a cultural center in Paris in which one person was killed.

June 13, 1981 — IRELAND — Patrick Agnew, an imprisoned Irish Republican Army (IRA) hunger striker, easily won one of the four Parliamentary seats from Lough, a county on the border with Northern Ireland. Two other IRA prisoners posted strong showings in the elections, which permit anyone on the island to run in Eire elections. Agnew, 26, was serving 16 years on a weapons conviction.

June 13, 1981 — LEBANON — A small rocket damaged the Iraqi Airways office during a night in which gunmen fired on the office's guards. No injuries were reported. 81061301

June 15, 1981 — UNITED KINGDOM — Worthing postal clerks intercepted a letter bomb addressed to Greville Janner, M.P., president of the Board of Deputies of British Jews and Labourite who was visiting Israel.

June 15, 1981 — TANZANIA — A court found six members of the South African Pan Africanist Congress (PAC) guilty of manslaughter in the 1975 killing of PAC leader David Sibeko.

June 15, 1981 — AUSTRIA — Local newspapers reported that a Syrian-supported hit squad of al Asifa was sent to Europe to assassinate Chancellor Bruno Kreisky, Yasir Arafat, Palestine Liberation Organization (PLO) European spokesman Sartawi, and PLO Vienna representative Husayn. 81061501

June 16, 1981 — GUYANA — Three hooded men kidnapped and killed Humphrey Keervelt, director of the SURINAME NEWS AGENCY, in Georgetown. Keervelt had been arrested several times in Suriname for antigovernment activity.

June 16, 1981 — TURKEY — Bunyamin Yilmaz was found guilty of providing arms to Mehmet Ali Agca, accused would-be assassin of Pope John Paul II, in his escape from Maltepe military prison (where Yilmaz was a guard) in return for a one hundred thousand lira bribe.

June 16, 1981 — ROMANIA — A Romanian airliner flying 140 passengers and 15 crewmen from Bucharest to Tel Aviv was forced to land at Turkey's Konya military airfield when a bomb threat was received over Turkey. One passenger was injured when he jumped from the plane. No bomb was found. 81061601

June 17, 1981 — FEDERAL REPUBLIC OF GERMANY — A bomb caused $130,000 damage to the NATO arms depot being constructed at Wehrendalh, 17 miles southwest of Hanover. No injuries were reported. 81061701

June 18, 1981 — SAHARA — Polisario released 48 South Korean fishermen captured off the African west coast on July 2 and August 25, 1980, to an International Committee of the Red Cross (ICRC) member in Tindouf, Algeria. Kim Yu-su had died in captivity, and the whereabouts of Yi Kang-con, 35, and Chong Sin-ung, 28, were unknown.

June 19, 1981 — SPAIN — Juan Jose Crespo, a member of the Anti-Fascist Resistance Groups of October First (GRAPO), died after a three-month hunger strike at Herrera de la Mancha Prison near Madrid.

June 19, 1981 — LEBANON — After an altercation at a United Nations Interim Force in Lebanon (UNIFIL) checkpoint near Al-Bayad, a Fatah guerrilla returned with reinforcements who fired on Fijian soldiers. One Fijian soldier was wounded in the leg and 3 Fatah members were injured. Two Fijian soldiers were kidnapped and later killed by the gang, who released a Fijian soldier held with the group along with 3 other Fijian soldiers captured in an unrelated incident. This incident brought to 13 the number of Fijians killed in UNIFIL actions, and 64 UNIFIL soldiers killed overall. 81061902

June 19–20, 1981 — UNITED STATES — The Federal Bureau of Investigation announced the discovery of a major Irish Republican Army (IRA) gunrunning ring with the arrest in Queens of George Harrison, 67, Thomas Falvey, 63, and Patrick Mullin, 43. Arrests were made after undercover agents were offered $16,000 in cash by the trio for 42 automatic rifles and handguns. The Bureau discovered a 20 mm cannon, a flamethrower, 14 machine guns, rifles, armor-piercing shells, and the Irish passport of Joe Cahill, former commander in chief of the Belfast Brigade of the IRA. In late July, the trio appeared in court to face grand jury indictments charging them with receiving and possessing firearms not registered to them, possessing firearms on which the serial numbers had been obliterated, and planning to export the arms to the IRA in Ireland. 81061901

June 21, 1981 — PANAMA — Ten masked Kuna Indians, possibly trained in Cuba, attacked an American-owned tourist hotel in Pidertupo, San Blas. National Guard sergeant Damaso Gonzalez was killed and corporals Everardo and Harmadio Smith were wounded. The Indians fired a 20-gauge shotgun at the hotel's owner, Thomas Moody, poured gasoline over him, and threw a firebomb, which did not explode. They then hanged him from a palm tree, yet again failing to kill him. They then tied down his wife, Joanne, and his daughter, threw firebombs at the installation, stole one boat, and damaged others. 81062101

June 22, 1981 — LEBANON — The VOICE OF LEBANON reported, "Clashes are now taking place between elements of the Fatah organization and the Syrian Social Nationalist Party in Ar-Ramlah al-Bayda' area in Beirut following the kidnapping of a Fatah official by the Syrian Nationalists and the ultimatum which the Fatah organization addressed to the Syrian Nationalists that unless they release the Fatah official the organization will blow up the offices of the Syrian Nationalists."

June 22, 1981 — UNITED KINGDOM — Irish National Liberation Army (INLA) member Michael James Devine, 27, serving 12 years for possessing firearms and ammunition, joined the Maze Prison hunger strike.

June 23, 1981 — UNITED KINGDOM — Two men kidnapped Reem al-Harithi, 12, daughter of former Saudi military attache Gen. Mushur al-Harithi, as she was being driven to school in London by chauffeur Susancha-Karunaratna, a Sri Lankan who was also kidnapped. The kidnappers were arrested as they were picking up a three hundred thousand dollar ransom the next day. The hostages were found in a car near the handover. 81062301

June 24, 1981 — MEXICO — The Australian embassy was evacuated after receiving a bomb threat shortly before Prime Minister Malcolm Fraser arrived in the city. 81062401

June 25, 1981 — LEBANON — The Maronite Christian Phalange Party produced two neo-Nazi members of the Karl-Heinz Hoffmann group, Walter-Ulrich Behle, 22, and Uwe Johannes Mainka, 24, who claimed they were recruited for terrorist training by Fatah leader Salah Khalaf (Abu Iyad) in Bi'r Hasan in Beirut. The duo referred to a terrorist recruiting network headquartered in Damascus and headed by Mahammad Hijaza, 'Atif Bsisu, and Amin Hindi. They claimed they entered Lebanon in October 1980, and that 20–25 Germans are in the camp, along with Japanese and Italians. They spent most of their time in vehicle maintenance and snuck out of the camp at 3:00 A.M. on June 14. They were picked up in east Beirut by the Phalange.

After initially denying the charges, the Palestine Liberation Organization produced two of its own rightist West Germans, Hans Dieter Eckner, 31, and Ulrich Bauer, 21, who claimed they had been encouraged in Germany by a Lebanese Christian to train with the Phalange militia. They arrived in early 1980 at a Phalange camp in east Beirut. They were captured by the Palestinians in January. They claimed they knew Behle and Mainka by their Arab code names. They later denied being neo-Nazi terrorists and claimed membership in Franz Josef Strauss's Bavarian-based Christian Social Union.

June 25, 1981 — IRAQ — Salih al-Yusufi, a Kurdish nationalist, was killed when a letter bomb exploded in his Baghdad home.

June 25, 1981 — UNITED STATES/CANADA — Belgrade's TANJUG reported the arrest in New York, California, Ohio, Illinois, and Canada of nine Croatian members of Otpor (Resistance), who were charged with numerous terrorist attacks.

June 25, 1981 — SUDAN — A hand grenade exploded at the main entrance to the Chadian embassy, killing two and injuring eight Chadians and destroying the entrance and several windows. A Chadian believed to have thrown the grenade was arrested, and he implicated Libya. He had been at the embassy on three consecutive days on the pretext of wanting a visa. Sudan ordered members of the Libyan People's Bureau to leave the country within 48 hours, suspended all flights between the two countries, and closed the Libyan Airlines office in Khartoum. On October 29, eight Chadians appeared before the Sudanese State Security Tribunal on charges related to the bombing. 81062501

June 26, 1981—HONDURAS—Two gunmen kidnapped Arnold McBrown, American administrator of the Adventist Hospital in Valle de Angeles, forcing him to drive to Tegucigalpa, where he was forced into an Alto de la Olla apartment. Eric Salomon Vasquez Corrales, 20, left the apartment, shot a policeman, took his weapon, then was shot to death in a gun battle with police near the apartment. Police found a rent receipt and apartment keys on his body, searched the apartment, and found a bomb and submachine gun. McBrown had been released at 5:00 A.M. by the other kidnapper, who was unnerved by his partner's absence. He demanded that McBrown deliver him L 2,400 at a park later that day but accepted a personal check. The other kidnapper has yet to be found. 81062601

June 27, 1981—LEBANON—The Lebanese Communist party and local Palestinians were believed responsible for a rocket attack against the Kuwaiti embassy. The Iranian embassy denied involvement. 81062701

June 27, 1981—UNITED STATES—A bomb exploded at 12:18 A.M. in College Park, Maryland, killing Cuo Ren Wu, 39, a visiting People's Republic of China scholar at the University of Maryland's computer science department. Four of Wu's friends were injured, and one hundred thousand dollars' damage was reported to a municipal building. 81062702

June 28, 1981—IRAN—A bomb exploded during the night at the Tehran headquarters of the Islamic Republican party, killing 70 people, including Ayatollah Mohammed Beheshti, 52, the chief justice and party leader, 4 Cabinet ministers, 8 deputy ministers, 21 members of parliament, and other party leaders. Beheshti was considered the country's second most powerful man behind Ayatollah Khomeini. Iran blamed the United States and the Mojahiddin leftist group. Behzad Nabavi, a government spokesman, dismissed the claim of the Nationalist Equity party.

TEHRAN DOMESTIC SERVICE identified the dead as including

Dr. Adibi, under secretary of science and higher education
Ayatollah Beheshti, president of the Supreme Court
Nurollah Tabataba'i Nezhad, Majlis deputy for Ardestan
Dr. Abolhamid Dialameh, deputy for Mashhad
Abbas Shahvai, under secretary at the Ministry of Commerce

Javad Assadollah Zadeh, under secretary at the Ministry of Commerce

Mohammad Khosravan, member of the Islamic Republican Party (IRP) students union

'Ali Reza Cheraghzadeh Dezfuli

An unidentified Revolutionary Guard

Gholam Hoseyn Haqani, deputy for Bandar-e 'Abbas

Hojjat ol-Eslam Tajrobi, deputy for Esfaranjan

Hasan Ejarehdar

Engineer Kalantari, minister of roads and transport

Mahdi Aminzadeh, deputy commerce minister

Seyyed Mohammad Musavi-Fard, from Qom Theological District

Hojjat ol-Eslam Emadoeedin Kariminezhad, deputy for Nowshahr

Dr. Hasan 'Abbaspur, minister of energy

Mahmud Tahririzadeh, under secretary at the Roads Ministry

Seyyed Javad Sherafat, deputy for Shushtar

'Abbas 'Ali Nateq-Nuri, deputy for Nur

Dr. Mohammad Baqer Hoseyni-Lavasani, deputy for Tehran

Engineer Gholam 'Ali Motamedi, under secretary at the Ministry of Labor

Dr. Sashem Mo'ayeri, under secretary at the Ministry of Health

'Ali Hashem Fenejani, deputy for Arak

Dorfeshan

'Ali Ahhbar Dehqan, deputy for Torbat-e Jam

'Ali Akbar Eze'i, theological professor from Esfahan

Habib Maleki

Nahavandi

Ravaqi, managing director of Iran's carpet industry

Mohammad 'Ali Heydari, deputy for Nahavand

'Ali Akbar Fallah Shushani

Dr. Shamseddin Hoseyni, deputy for Na'in

'Ali Akbar Salimi-Jahromi, secretary general of the state organization for employment and administrative affairs

Hasan Basta'i

Habibollah Mehdizadeh

Kur-Mali

Asghar Zameni, head of Hasemi-Rafsanjani's secretariat

Mohsen Mowla'i

Hadi Amini

Seyyed Hasan Hoseyn-Tabataba'i

Abdolvahad Hashemi, deputy for Sari

Mohammad Montazeri, son of Qom Friday Imam Ayatollah Montazeri and deputy for Najafabad

Mohammad Hoseyn Akbari

'Abbas Ershad

Seyfollah Abdolkarimi, deputy for Langrud

Nur Eyni
Tahbas
'Ali Mohammad Majidi
Engineer Hoseyn Akbari
Mohammad Hoseyn Danesh-Ashtiyani, deputy for Ashtajin and Tafresh
Dr. Seyyed Reza, deputy for Yazd
Javad Meleki
Javad Sarhadizadeh, managing director for urban and rural development
Seyyed Kazem Musavi
Sadeq Eslami, under secretary at the Ministry of Commerce
Mohammad Hoseyn Sadeqi, deputy for Darrus
Seyyed Mohammad Kazem Danesh, deputy for Andimeshk
Iraq Shahsavari, a Revolutionary Guard
Seyyed Fakhreddin Rahimi, deputy for Malavi in Lorestan
Qasem Sadeqi
Nasiri Lari, deputy for Lar
Habibollah Nemanpur, under secretary at the Ministry of Labor
Dr. Fayyaz-Bakhsh, minister of state and supervisor of the welfare organi-
    zation
Dr. Mahmud Qandi, minister of post, telegraph, and telephone
Shamsoddin Hoseyni Na'ini, deputy for Na'in

June 29, 1981—LEBANON—The pro-Iraqi Front for the Liberation of
Ahwaz bombed the Trans-Mediterranean Airways (TMA) office in Beirut,
causing extensive damage but no injuries. The group accused TMA of
transporting arms to Iran. 81062901

July 1981—ROMANIA—Vienna's KRONEN-ZEITUNG reported that Abu
Nidal's al-Asifah had threatened President Ceausescu for having played a
mediator's role in Egyptian-Israeli peacemaking. The news service claimed
police had foiled a terrorist attack against a large industrial complex. It also
reported Nidal undergoing medical treatment in a London hospital for
heart disease. 81079901

July 1, 1981—GUATEMALA—A Guerrilla Army of the Poor (EGP) bomb
exploded on a conveyor belt bringing a booby-trapped suitcase to an Eastern Airlines plane scheduled to fly one hundred people from Guatemala
City to Miami, killing Raul Sibalba, a baggage handler. The flight was to
have included Miss Guatemala, Euca Lobos, and Vinicio Cerezo, secretary
general of Guatemalan Christian Democracy. The EGP termed this "an act
of sabotage against Eastern Airlines in reprisal for the support this airline
gave to President Lucas Garcia's regime." 81070101

July 1, 1981—CHILE—Two time bombs destroyed the Mercedes-Benz of

Guillermo Luchetti, former Argentine consul in Punta Arenas, in Santiago, where Luchetti worked for the Argentine Foreign Ministry. The bombs were apparently placed by two well-dressed individuals who had expressed interest in buying the vehicle. 81070102

July 2, 1981 — SYRIA — The VOICE OF LEBANON claimed that the Moslem Brotherhood ambushed a Mercedes at the Euphrates Dam Road north of Aleppo, killing three Soviets who work at the dam. 81070201

July 3, 1981 — GUATEMALA — Ultrarightist gunmen shot dead the Reverend Marco Tulio Maruffo, an Italian priest, near Quirigua, 180 miles northeast of the capital, making him the ninth Catholic clergyman killed in the country in the past year. 81070301

July 4, 1981 — COSTA RICA — Civil Guards in Liberia under the command of Maj. Alexis Quiroz Elizondo captured three female Sandinista National Liberation Front (FSLN) members and a Mexican male who intended to take over the Guatemalan embassy to obtain the release of political prisoners. Two other guerrillas managed to escape. Police reported finding two M-23 machine guns and plans to threaten to kill the hostages if their demands were not met within three days. The women were identified as Sosa Matilde Mejia Alegria, Mireya Danza Moreira, and Catalina Noguera Garcia, the pregnant sister of FSLN commander Elias. The leader of the group claimed to be Jonathan Riverson Castillo of the Che Guevara Command of Guatemala, a Mexican carrying a Salvadoran passport. 81070401

July 5, 1981 — LEBANON — A bomb damaged a Trans-Mediterranean Airways B-707 at Beirut Airport during the morning. The chief of the firm's union said the bomb was planted in the incorrect belief that the firm had flown arms to Iran. 81070501

July 7, 1981 — GUATEMALA — The Guerrilla Army of the Poor (EGP) bombed the capital city offices of the United States Chamber of Commerce, located at Plazuela Espana in Zone 9, destroying windows, but causing no injuries. 81070701

July 8, 1981 — UNITED KINGDOM — Joe McDonnell, 30, an Irish Republican Army (IRA) hunger striker, died in Maze Prison on the 61st day of his fast. Rioting broke out in Belfast and Londonderry. Patrick McGeown, 25, convicted bomber, was named to replace McDonnell. McDonnell was serving a 14-year sentence for illegal arms possession after being arrested following a firebombing of a West Belfast furniture store in 1976. He was arrested and convicted with Bobby Sands, the first hunger striker to die, and replaced him in the campaign.

July 10, 1981 — UNITED STATES — Two Cuban exiles waving baby bottles filled with gasoline and holding lighted wicks forced an Eastern L-1011 flying from Chicago to Puerto Rico via Miami with 177 passengers and 13 crewmen to fly to Havana, where they were arrested, along with their wives, by Cuban police. The hijackers' four children were taken in by relatives in Cuba. No injuries were reported. Havana vowed to "rigorously" try the hijackers. 81071001

July 10, 1981 — PERU — Two powerful bombs were thrown from a fast-moving vehicle at the People's Republic of China's embassy in the early morning, causing some damage but no injuries. 81071002

July 11, 1981 — ITALY — The Extraparliamentary Group for Communism threw two small firebombs at the Trieste home of British consul Norman John Lister. The bombs hit the roof; one left a small hole, while the other fell to the ground and went out. The group said it was part of the "struggle against British and world imperialism," and Lister reported "Freedom for Ireland" had been scrawled on a wall of his home. 81071101

July 11, 1981 — CUBA — Havana arrested five Alpha 66 anti-Castro Cuban exile commandos, who carried United States-made weapons and explosives from Florida to the northern coast of Matanzas Province. They had planned to assassinate Fidel Castro on July 26. The group's Miami headquarters claimed credit. 81071102

July 13, 1981 — UNITED KINGDOM — Martin Hurson, 27, died in Maze Prison on the 45th day of his hunger strike, becoming the sixth Irish nationalist prisoner to die in the campaign. He was sentenced to 20 years in November 1977 for bombings and conspiracy to kill members of the security forces in Northern Ireland.

July 14, 1981 — LEBANON — Irish-born journalist Sean Toolan, 43, was shot and stabbed to death at 2:00 A.M. walking from the bar of the Commodore Hotel to his Beirut home. Toolan was a free-lancer associated with several British and United States newspapers, including the ATLANTA CONSTITUTION and the CHICAGO SUN TIMES, who also worked for the radio news division of ABC. 81071401

July 14, 1981 — BELGIUM — A gunman in his early 20s who had been waiting for a visa opened fire at 10:00 A.M. in the Yugoslav embassy, hitting Yugoslav economic counselor Blagoja Anakioski, 40, three times and Fran Spindler, 24, a reception clerk who gave chase, once. The individual escaped in a car. The Albanian Croat HDP claimed credit in a call to Stuttgart, West Germany. The Yugoslav press claimed that terrorists had bombed the Namir headquarters of the Association of Yugoslavs and the Yugoslav Club of citizens of Albanian nationality, Preparimi, in July. 81071402, 81079902

July 14, 1981 — CENTRAL AFRICAN REPUBLIC — The Central African National Liberation Movement (MCLN), in a statement from Lagos, Nigeria, claimed credit for setting off two bombs during the night in a crowded Bangui movie theater, killing four people, including a French citizen, and injuring one hundred. The MCLN said, "The action of July 14, 1981, the French national day, is only the first blow," and that it would conduct further attacks "until the last French soldier has left Central Africa." Francois Pehoua, president of the oppositionist Independent Group for Reflection and Action hinted that the French were behind the bombing, claiming that the French "were also the first to go unhesitatingly to the spot where bombs had been placed but did not explode." 81071403

July 16, 1981 — CHILE — The Army captured six Cubans and four Europeans who had left the Neltume guerrilla school and were attempting to cross into Argentina. Two military members were injured in the gun battle. 81071601

July 17, 1981 — UNITED STATES — The bullet-riddled body of Nabil A. Mansour, 32, a Libyan student, was found stuffed in the trunk of his car, parked in front of the Ogden, Utah, apartment of Mohamed A. Shabata, 35, a former student at Weber State College. Shabata was arrested in Chicago a few hours later, carrying a large amount of cash and tickets for onward travel to Tripoli, Libya, via London. He was convicted of second-degree murder on November 25 and was sentenced to prison on December 2 from five years to life. 81071701

July 17, 1981 — GUATEMALA — Eight members of the 31 January People's Front (FP-31) firebombed the Guatemala City offices of Honduran Air Services (SAHSA), causing $60,000 damage to the SAHSA offices and those of the Guama industrial import company, also located in the two-story building. No injuries were reported. The group was celebrating the second anniversary of the Sandinista overthrow of Nicaraguan president Somoza. 81071702

July 19, 1981 — SWITZERLAND — The Armenian June 9 Organization, an arm of the Armenian Secret Army for the Liberation of Armenia, bombed the Swiss Parliament building. 81071901

July 20, 1981 — SWITZERLAND — The Armenian June 9 Organization set off a bomb in an area that connects the Zurich-Kloten Airport entry lobby with a railway station beneath, injuring five people and causing $150,000 damage. 81072001

July 21, 1981 — LEBANON — Several passersby were injured by falling glass when a bomb went off in a pickup van parked outside the Palestine Liberation Organization administrative office in Beirut at 4:00 P.M.

July 21, 1981 — REPUBLIC OF SOUTH AFRICA — The African National Congress set off limpet mines at a power station in Camden near Ermelo, Transvaal; another power station at Arnot, 52 kilometers east of Middelburg; and an electrical transformer near Pretoria. No injuries were reported, but power was cut off to Ermelo by the 2:00 A.M. explosions.

July 21, 1981 — POLAND — A Polish airline LOT twin-engine AN-24 carrying 50 passengers and 5 crewmen from Katowice to Gdansk was diverted to Tempelhof Airport in West Berlin at 5:00 P.M. by Bernard Pientka, 21, armed with a pistol and grenade. He turned himself over to authorities, who reported no injuries. Poland demanded extradition, saying Pientka had served penalties for misdemeanors and for defying alimony warrants. On October 8, a West Berlin court sentenced him to five years in prison. 81072101

July 21, 1981 — SWITZERLAND — The Armenian June 9 Organization bombed a Lausanne department store, injuring 20 people. 81072102

July 22, 1981 — SWITZERLAND — The Armenian June 9 Organization bombed the baggage registry area in Geneva's central railway station, injuring four people. A second explosion occurred an hour later. The group threatened to continue their attacks until the Armenian detained on June 9 for the murder of a Turkish diplomat was released. 81072201

July 22, 1981 — IRAQ — Iraqi Communist party members at a roadblock detained French engineers Jim Tour and Maurice Charli and interpreter Zayya Yusuf. 81072202

July 22, 1981 — GREECE — Two Popular Front for the Liberation of Palestine (PFLP) gunmen fired silenced revolvers at Dhimitris Malandasi, 30, killing her at 11:30 A.M. in the Piraeus travel and shipping agency on the corner of Filon and Filellinon Streets. They escaped in a car with Lebanese plates driven by an accomplice. A bomb set in the office exploded soon after, killing Evyenia Angelikousi, the firm's owner, and wounding 70 others. The PFLP claimed the agency was an Israeli intelligence cover that had been used in the July 18, 1978, murder of a Palestinian commando in Glifadha: "We informed the Greek authorities about the true perpetrators of that murder, and moreover, that they wrongly had arrested two Palestinians as responsible for the murder." 81072203

July 23, 1981 — PORTUGAL — Two gunmen fired submachine guns at Carlos P. Oliveira, an executive of the United States-based Standard Electric Company, and his driver outside one of the firm's Cascais plants, injuring both of them. 81072301

July 23, 1981 — UNITED STATES — Three robbers attacked Mohamed Sahraoui, the Moroccan United Nations Mission's second secretary, in front of his New York residence, but ran from the scene when a commotion developed. Sahraoui was treated for minor head injuries. 81072302

July 24, 1981 — UNITED STATES — Oscar Lopez-Rivera, Puerto Rican Armed Forces of National Liberation (FALN) leader, was found guilty in Chicago United States District Court of seditious conspiracy, armed robbery and weapons violations, and interstate transportation of stolen vehicles, for which the 37-year-old faced a maximum penalty of 70 years in prison.

July 24, 1981 — SYRIA — Addressing the Joint Arab Defense Council in Damascus, Fatah Central Committee member Muhammad Ghunay said, "We say to the Arab regimes that we in the Palestinian revolution will not stand idly by in the face of their silence and inaction. We affirm to leaders of these regimes that if they are afraid to adopt a stand against the United States and Israel for fear for their wealth and petroleum, then we will destroy that petroleum. . . . The petroleum must be employed to serve the interests of the Arab nation. . . . The Palestinian revolution does not want statements, declarations or financial contributions, which are not enough to pay for the coffins."

July 27, 1981 — GUATEMALA — Robbers shot and killed Oklahoma Catholic Rev. Stanley Rother, 46, at midnight at his mission in Santiago Atitlan, 50 miles from Guatemala City. He had been warned he was targeted for death in January, had come to the United States briefly, but returned to Guatemala in April. Rightist terrorists were suspected. On August 4, three men were arrested and charged with murdering Rother when he attempted to prevent them from robbing the church. 81072701

July 28, 1981 — EL SALVADOR -- Presumed terrorists fired 12-gauge shotguns at American citizens Walter Johan Hale and William Menne as they were driving from the El Amatillo border post. Both were slightly wounded. 81072801

July 28, 1981 — EL SALVADOR — A bomb destroyed a bullet-proof Cherokee vehicle owned by the United States embassy, which was parked near the Sacamil Theater. 81072802

July 28, 1981 — FEDERAL REPUBLIC OF GERMANY — Emile Georgescu, a RADIO FREE EUROPE editor, was stabbed several times by a young Frenchman who was arrested, along with his French accomplice, by local Munich police. 81072803

July 29, 1981 — AUSTRIA — Schwechat Airport police arrested two Arabs carrying South Yemeni and Iraqi passports when they arrived on an Austrian Airlines flight from Damascus via Beirut. Their luggage contained a Czechoslovakian Skorpion submachine gun, 4 Soviet Kalashnikov assault rifles, 19 magazines with 525 rounds of ammunition, 6 fragmentation grenades, and 6 detonators. Police speculated that the duo worked for the Abu Nidal terrorist group and intended to assassinate either Chancellor Bruno Kreisky or Egyptian president Anwar Sadat, who was scheduled to come to Austria on August 10. The duo were met at the airport by Vienna Palestine Liberation Organization representative Ghazi Husayn. On August 3, one of the men was acquitted, while the other received a 9-month prison sentence, suspended on probation. The Justice Ministry announced that there was no evidence of intended use of the weapons, and while it was proven that the duo had participated in illegal arms transport, their culpability was not demonstrated. The two were kicked out of the country, as was the PLO representative. 81072901

July 30, 1981 — UNITED STATES — Forty anti-Qaddafi Libyan students occupied the Libyan United Nations Mission for three hours before being arrested by police. No injuries or damage were reported. A Manhattan criminal court told them to stay out of trouble for six months.

July 30, 1981 — PERU — Two bombs exploded during the early morning at the Peruvian-American Cultural Institute in Tarma, causing no injuries but closing the institute. Five suspects were detained by police. 81073001

August 1981 — LIBYA — Several threats against United States officials by the Libyans surfaced in the wake of the downing of two Libyan planes in the Mediterranean by American pilots in disputed waters. The LIBYAN NEWS AGENCY, citing an alleged Central Intelligence Agency plot to kill Qaddafi, reported that the Libyan Free Unionist Officers threatened to assassinate President Ronald Reagan. "America, despite the impossibility of implementing this crime will be responsible for the death warrant we have decided to issue in the biggest commando operation in history to strike against US interests in the world wherever they may be, and we will physically liquidate anyone who may even think of harming Qaddafi, beginning with Ronald Reagan and ending with the smallest agent inside Libya or outside."

In October, NEWSWEEK reported that Italy had deported 10 Libyans planning to assassinate United States ambassador to Italy Maxwell Rabb, 71. On October 13, Jack Anderson reported that Qaddafi, speaking on the phone with Ethiopian leader Mengistu Haile Mariam in August, had vowed to assassinate President Reagan.

August 1, 1981 — UNITED KINGDOM — Kevin Lynch, 25, an Irish National Liberation Army (INLA) terrorist serving 10 years for participating in attacks on Ulster security forces, died at 1:00 A.M. in Maze Prison on the 71st day of his hunger strike. Lynch had captained the Londonderry County's under-16 hurling team, which had won the all-Ireland championship. While on the hunger strike, he garnered more than three thousand votes in the Waterford County Irish national elections.

August 1, 1981 — UNITED KINGDOM — The family of Patrick Quinn, 29, an Irish Republican Army (IRA) man serving 14 years for an attempted attack on British soldiers in Ulster, broke his 47-day hunger strike and became the first family to obtain medical attention for one of the strikers.

August 1, 1981 — POLAND — Abu Daoud, suspected Fatah planner of the 1972 Munich Olympics massacre, was hit by five bullets fired in the early evening in the crowded Opera coffeehouse of Warsaw's Victoria Intercontinental Hotel. Two women sitting nearby were also injured. The tall, dark-skinned, slim attacker appeared to be in his mid-20s. He escaped pursuit by Abu Daoud and fled in a waiting car. The gun was found sometime later in a nearby park. Daoud had arrived in Poland on an Iraqi passport for Madhi Tarik. Israel denied Palestine Liberation Organization charges of responsibility. IRAQI NEWS AGENCY in Baghdad reported that Polish police had arrested one person, while the VOICE OF PALESTINE claimed three gunmen were involved. 81080101

August 1, 1981 — ZIMBABWE — Joe Gqabi, 52, head of the South-African African National Congress office in Salisbury, was shot to death at midnight while driving out of the front yard of his Ashdown Park home at 12:15 A.M. Police found 18 spent cartridges in the driveway, along with a silenced Beretta pistol. Police suggested two weapons were involved. South Africa denied Zimbabwean charges of responsibility. 81080102

August 2, 1981 — UNITED KINGDOM — Kieran Doherty, 25, an Irish Republican Army (IRA) terrorist, recently elected to the Irish Parliament, who was serving 22 years in Maze Prison for possession of explosives and firearms in a hijacked car, died at 7:15 P.M. on the 73rd day of his hunger strike.

August 2, 1981 — EGYPT—A bomb exploded during a wedding at the Masarrah Church in Shubra at 10:00 P.M., killing 3 and injuring 56, including Moslems and Christians. Police believed the Rejectionist Front or other foreign enemies were responsible.

August 2, 1981 — GUATEMALA—Carlos Perez Alonso, a Spanish Jesuit priest, was kidnapped in the capital city. He was later released unharmed in Mexico City on August 7. 81080201

August 3, 1981 — FEDERAL REPUBLIC OF GERMANY—More than 100 Iranian students took over the Iranian embassy in Bonn to "protest executions hostile to the Iranian People." During an eviction by the police, 10 policemen, 4 demonstrators, and 2 embassy employees were injured. Six demonstrators were arrested, but 5 were exempted from detention. The next day, the Iranian consulate in West Berlin was occupied. 81080301

August 4, 1981 — BELGIUM—A man with a pistol fatally wounded 43-year-old Yugoslav embassy clerk Stoian Djieric and wounded guard Redzo Zuko, 25, at 3:00 P.M. in a Brussels restaurant. The embassy complained that they were not informed of the incident by police until 10:00 A.M. the next day. The killer, a Yugoslav, escaped. An Albanian terrorist group was believed responsible. 81080401

August 4, 1981 — GREECE—Members of the right-wing Blue Archer group set over one hundred fires throughout the country, demanding the release of leaders of the 1967–74 military regime. One West German tourist was reported dead. The group later threatened to bomb the Greek Parliament and the capital's Hilton Hotel. 81080402–03

August 4, 1981 — CANADA—Thirty Iranian students took over the Iranian embassy, held six employees as hostages, and claimed to be demonstrating against "a reactionary regime, devoid of popular support, engaged in black terror against the Iranian people." 81080404

August 5, 1981 — BELGIUM—Belgrade's TANJUG reported that shortly after midnight, three persons threw three firebombs at the store of Yugoslav citizen Radivoje Debic on Boulevard Lemonnier, No. 85, in Brussels. 81080501

August 5, 1981 — POLAND—Franciszek Izdebski, 27, threatening to use explosive charges, failed to hijack a Polish airline LOT plane flying 49 passengers from Katowice to Gdansk and was arrested by the Citizens' Militia in Gdansk. 81080502

August 5, 1981 — GUATEMALA — The 31 January People's Front, possibly related to the Guerrilla Army of the Poor (EGP), bombed the Guatemala City offices of Pan American Airlines, destroying the building but causing no injuries. 81080503

August 6, 1981 — SWITZERLAND — Luciano Porcari, 41, sent a series of letters threatening to hijack a second plane unless he was given the $250,000 he supposedly was granted when he hijacked an Iberia Airlines plane in 1977. He had been serving a 10-year sentence for the first hijacking and had failed to return to a Zurich prison from compassionate leave. 81080601

August 7, 1981 — LEBANON — Bombs exploded in front of two French banks and the Air France office in Beirut, causing damage but no casualties. The bombers were protesting France's granting former Iranian president Bani Sadr asylum. 81080701–03

August 7, 1981 — UNITED STATES — At 8:30 A.M., 25 members of the People's Majority, an anti-Khomeini group, seized the Iranian Interests Section in Washington and held six Iranian employees hostage for an hour. Just before the group surrendered to police, one of the hostages shot a demonstrator, and two other people were hurt. The group was arrested by police. On October 23, they were put on probation after being convicted of forcible entry and ordered to complete 25 hours of community service. The gun-toting hostage was charged with assault with intent to kill while armed. He had been beaten and seriously injured after firing. Akbar Nouchedehi was also charged with carrying a pistol without a license in the wounding of Mohammed Shamirza. Abdoreza Afhami, Ahmad Aghababa, Hamid Reza Arabzadeh, Mohsen Dianatkhah, Ali Reza Khairghadam, and Asgar Momenzadeh were also charged with misdemeanor assault. It was later learned that Mahmod Kupai, 19, of Los Angeles, was trampled when the shot rang out. The group apparently were sympathizers with the Mujaheddin, a Marxist-Leninist group in Iran. 81080704

August 8, 1981 — UNITED KINGDOM — Thomas McIlwee, 23, an Irish Republican Army (IRA) terrorist, died at 11:27 in Maze Prison on the 62nd day of his hunger strike. McIlwee was serving 20 years for manslaughter for his participation in a 1976 IRA bombing attack on shops and other businesses in Ballymena in which 17 bombs went off and a woman shopkeeper was killed. His place in the strike was taken by Jackie McMullan, 25.

August 8, 1981 — HONDURAS — Salvadoran political leader Jorge Morales

Alvarado, a woman, and several children were kidnapped. Six days later, his Ecuadoran wife, Maria Garcia Osegueda, suggested that rightist terrorists were responsible. She said they had subjected her to mock executions, and had stolen money, checks, and documents from her home. 81080801

August 8, 1981 — TURKEY— A United States Air Force pickup truck carrying three Americans, including two United States Air Force airmen, and a Turk on the road outside Malatya City was fired on by two to four men with automatic weapons. No injuries were reported, but the truck was damaged. 81080802

August 9, 1981 — FEDERAL REPUBLIC OF GERMANY— The Croatian Revolutionary Cell, Bruno Busic Department, bombed the R. S. Schulz publishing house in Percha on Lake Starnberg. The group, which claims to be based in Paris, used one kilogram of Swiss Mark 2 dynamite and threatened to use two more kilograms the following week if the firm published Tito's memoirs. 81080901

August 10, 1981 — AUSTRIA— Two bombs made of gelatine-donarit exploded in a garden 30 meters from the Israeli embassy residence, injuring a woman living in the house and breaking windows. The May 15 Arab Organization for the Liberation of Palestine claimed credit. 81081001

August 10, 1981 — GREECE — The May 15 Arab Organization for the Liberation of Palestine set off two bombs at midnight outside the Israeli embassy, damaging the rear gate but causing no injuries. 81081002

August 10, 1981 — SPAIN — Twenty members of the Iranian monarchist exile group Azadegan (Freedom Seekers) using a commandeered Spanish tug seized the Tabarzin, one of the three French missile patrol boats loaded with weapons and ammunition sailing to Iran. The attack occurred at 11:00 A.M. after the ships left Cadiz harbor on the way from Cherbourg. The vessels were part of an order for a dozen initially submitted by the Shah in 1974 now being sent to Iran after France had lifted its arms embargo. The group claimed to be armed with Spanish automatic pistols purchased in Portugal and proclaimed the gunboat the seat of Iran's government-in-exile. They said the mission was planned by exiled Iranian general Bahram Aryana, 74, former chief of the Iranian armed forces, who was dismissed by the Shah a decade ago. On August 17, the group forced Casablanca harbor authorities to provide fuel, food, and water. The next day they demanded that Marseilles authorities allow them to let off 30 crewmen, while the captain and first mate remained on board. When they threatened to blow up the ship, French warships towed the ship out of Marseilles harbor. The group surrendered to French forces in Toulon on August 19. France agreed to send the boat to Iran but refused to extradite the hijackers. 81081003

August 11, 1981 — ISRAEL — Police foiled a Moslem Brotherhood plot to murder Bashir Baghruti, communist leader in Judaea and Samaria, and knife a Jew after he prayed at the Western Wall. The leader of the group, Ahmad Ikbal al-Hindi, was identified as a Pakistani resident of Sur Bahir, whose father was a janitor in the Al-Aqsa Mosque on the Temple Mount. The other suspects lived in Kafir 'Aqab in Ramallah and belonged to the Group of Holy Jihad. They had already prepared four Molotov cocktails. 81081101

August 11, 1981 — POLAND — A passenger holding a knife to another passenger attempted to hijack a Polish airline LOT flight from Katowice to Gdansk but was foiled by the Citizens' Militia. The plane landed safely at Okecie Airport in Warsaw. 81081102

August 11, 1981 — BELGIUM — Sabena flight 201, carrying 63 passengers from Brussels to Tel Aviv, landed at Limnos, Greece's Myrina Airport, after receiving a bomb threat. No bomb was found. 81081103

August 11, 1981 — DENMARK — The 9th of June Group of the Armenian Secret Army set off two bombs in front of the Swissair office in Copenhagen, breaking glass and injuring an American tourist. The group said it was retaliating for the recent arrest in Switzerland of an Armenian accused of assassinating a Turkish national. 81081104

August 11, 1981 — NORWAY — Thirty unarmed Iranian students seized the Iranian embassy and held seven hostages, including the charge, until obtaining a press conference to denounce Khomeini government "massacres." No injuries were reported. Oslo authorities held the students overnight, then returned them to Sweden where they resided. 81081105

August 12, 1981 — SRI LANKA — A bomb exploded at a Gampaha public meeting presided over by former prime minister Sirimavo Bandaranaike, injuring 19 people and badly damaging her car. One person was taken into custody for the 7:15 P.M. bombing. Mrs. Bandaranaike served as prime minister from 1960 to 1965 and from 1970 to 1977. She was expelled from Parliament in October 1980 after a special presidential commission found her guilty of abuse and misuse of power during her second term.

August 12, 1981 — ZIMBABWE — Oliver Tambo, leader of the African National Congress of South Africa, said his group would change its tactics from attacking installations to eliminating South African officials.

August 13, 1981 — ARGENTINA — Firebombs were thrown at 3:00 A.M. at the Volvo of Chilean embassy council minister Raul Schmidt in front of his home, damaging the vehicle's roof and hood. 81081301

August 13, 1981 — IRAN — The two Iranian pilots of a Bandar 'Abbas-to-Tehran F-27 carrying 12 passengers and 3 crewmen diverted the plane to Muscat, where Omani authorities refused to allow the plane to land at As-Sib International Airport. The plane landed nearby, and the passengers and navigator returned safely to Tehran. 81081302

August 13, 1981 — REPUBLIC OF SOUTH AFRICA — The African National Congress fired four Soviet-made 122 mm rockets at 11:00 P.M. from Laudium, an Indian suburb, into Voortrekkerhoogte, a military base six miles from Pretoria, injuring a black maid but causing little damage. Three men armed with AK-47 rifles seriously wounded Saheb Patel, 17, when he came upon them during the attack. A motorist and two policemen were prevented from chasing the attackers by gunfire.
    In March 1982, South African police claimed that the attack was masterminded by five white communist agents who had infiltrated South Africa. Police identified them as Belgian-born Guido Luciaan van Hecken, who fled to the Motlana Institute in Maputo, Mozambique, where he is a lecturer; Britons Nicolas Francis Henry Heath, 33, Bonnie Lou Muller, and David William Hedges, 37; and a former South African, Dr. Edward Wethli. The United Kingdom announced that it was unable to send the three Britons back to South Africa to face trial in the absence of an extradition treaty. 81081303

August 15, 1981 — JORDAN — Jordanian authorities arrested 10 Palestinians and Jordanian Army collaborators stationed in Al-'Aqabah, preventing them from firing rockets on Elat. 81081501

August 16, 1981 — KUWAIT — The Ministry of the Interior denied an AL WATAN report that four Iranians were arrested at the site of an arms cache.

August 18, 1981 — WEST BERLIN — Two one-pound bombs exploded at an outside wall of a United States Army barracks and outside a British hotel for transients near the British Army club for soldiers, causing no damage or injuries. 81081801–02

August 19, 1981 — REPUBLIC OF SOUTH AFRICA — Johannesburg judge

Charl Theron imposed the death sentence on three African National Congress (ANC) guerrillas whose actions did not involve deaths. David Moise, 25, aided others to lay mines at the SASOL complex on June 2, 1980. Bobby Tsotsobe fired a rocket and a Soviet rifle at the Booysens police station in Johannesburg on April 14, 1980; planted bombs on a Soweto railway line; and attempted to burn down a Soweto hall. Johannes Shabangu, 26, threw a hand grenade at a black policeman's home and possessed a "death list" of seven anti-ANC blacks. The trio had received military training in Angola.

August 20, 1981 — UNITED KINGDOM — Michael Devine, 27, died in Maze Prison on the 60th day of his Irish Republican Army (IRA) hunger strike one hour after polls opened for the Northern Irish Parliamentary seat in Fermanagh and South Tyrone vacated by the starvation death of Bobby Sands. The election was won by pro-IRA candidate Owen Carron, 28. Bombs went off in Belfast and Bangor, injuring 21, in protest of Devine's death. Four days later, Bernard Fox, 20, serving 12 years for possessing explosives and bombing a hotel, joined the hunger strike in replacement of Patrick Quinn, one of three prisoners who abandoned the fast.

August 20, 1981 — FRANCE — An early morning bomb set by the Armenian Movement 3 October broke the front window of the Paris office of Alitalia Airlines but caused no injuries. 81082001

August 21, 1981 — UNITED STATES — The Black Brigade bombed the Liberian embassy, causing five thousand dollars' damage but no injuries. The group was protesting the August 14 executions in Monrovia of five members of Liberia's ruling People's Redemption Council who were opposed to Liberian military leader M. Sgt. Samuel K. Doe. 81082101

August 21, 1981 — TURKS AND CAICOS — A bomb exploded on board the 73-foot *Franklin and Ian,* a boat to be used by Cubans United for an invasion of Guantanamo Bay. 81082102

August 22, 1981 — POLAND — The Polish airline LOT flight 762, an AN-24 flying 39 passengers (including 2 Americans) and 4 crewmen from Wroclaw to Warsaw, was hijacked by Jerzy Dygas (or Dygat), 25 (or 31), armed with a dummy hand grenade, who forced the pilot to land at 7:09 P.M. at West Berlin's Tempelhof Airport. He surrendered to American authorities, who turned him over to West Berlin police. No injuries were reported. Passengers Pawel Klinski, 19, and Antoni Poczatek opted to remain in the West. The hijacker claimed he was forbidden by the government from leaving the country after an abortive attempt to reach the West via third countries in 1979. He was a Solidarity messenger and had acted as a steward at demonstrations, where he had been photographed by the security police. Despite his claims of political persecution, on January 19, 1982, he was sentenced to 5½ years by a West Berlin court. 81082201

August 22, 1981 — TAIWAN — Police suggested sabotage may have been responsible for an explosion aboard a Far Eastern Air Transport, which killed 110 people, including 4 Americans and a prominent Japanese writer. 81082202

August 22, 1981 — FRANCE — The 3 October Armenian Movement bombed the Olympics Airways office in Paris in the early morning, causing minor damage and no injuries. A caller said that the timing of the bombing was to prevent injuries. 81082203

August 23, 1981 — LEBANON — A booby-trap bomb killed six Syrian soldiers and wounded nine others investigating a bombing near the Park Hotel in Shtawrah, residence of Col. Bayraq Dar, Syrian deterrent forces commander. The Syrian Liberation Army claimed responsibility.

August 23, 1981 — ECUADOR — Five men and a woman belonging to the Colombian April 19 Movement (M-19) attacked an Ecuadoran border post, killing two soldiers and seizing eight rifles, before slipping across the border. They were arrested by the Colombian Army in Colombian territory on September 3. 81082301

August 24, 1981 — SWEDEN — About 35 unarmed Iranian leftist students belonging to Peykar and Feda'iye Khalq took over the Iranian embassy residence in Lidingo, outside Stockholm, and held hostage Ambassador 'Abdol Rahim Govahi and his wife for four hours. The group demanded freedom for all Iranian political prisoners, an immediate halt to all executions, a Swedish government protest against the Iranian executions, and the dispatch of an international commission of jurists to Iran to investigate prison conditions and torture of prisoners. Police stormed the embassy at 1:00 P.M. and took the students to police headquarters for questioning. The students had taken secret documents from the ambassador's safe, broke furniture, and extensively damaged the embassy. 81082401

August 25, 1981 — BELGIUM — Twenty Iranian students supporting the exiled National Iranian Resistance Council led by former president Bani Sadr took over the Iranian embassy at 9:00 A.M. They were evicted by police 75 minutes later. 81082501

August 25, 1981 — NETHERLANDS — After six staff members barricaded the doors of the Iranian embassy, police prevented 17 members of the leftist

Iranian Peykar group from taking over the facility. The unarmed group, who had come from West Germany, were arrested. 81082502

August 26, 1981 — SWITZERLAND — In 1982, the Yugoslav DANAS newspaper reported:

> The Swiss Ministry of Justice and the police issued the following bulletin: "last night at about 2300 hours Stanko Nizic, 30, night porter at the Kindli Hotel in Zurich, was killed by a revolver bullet fired from point-blank range. The bullet struck Nizic in the forehead. The crime occurred in the early morning hours in the vicinity of the Kindli Hotel, when Stanko Nizic was returning home.
>
> "During the search of Stanko Nizic's home 2 kilograms of plastic explosive were found, a machine gun and two bazookas. The inquiry established that Stanko Nizic was one of the leaders of a very ramified network of terrorists who were smuggling arms from Switzerland into West Germany and Yugoslavia. Stanko Nizic's two closest collaborators, Bozic and Rados, who were in the Kindli Hotel just a few hours before his murder, have disappeared without a trace . . . "
>
> And on 17 December of last year, the Zurich newspaper DER BLICK carried an article: "After the cold-blooded murder of Stanko Nizic, 30, night porter in the Kindli Hotel in Zurich, following a detailed investigation in Switzerland, after a network of Croatian terrorists was broken up, the federal prosecutor's office has arrested 12 Croatian emigres and 2 Swiss accomplices, confiscating on that occasion 120 kilograms of explosives, several machine guns and hand grenades."
>
> This newspaper has learned from private sources that after Stanko Nizic's murder the police kept a close watch on his close collaborator Franjo Macukic of Zurich. Finally, on 12 December 1981 Franjo Macukic was arrested just as he was about to cross the Swiss-German border with a sizeable quantity of arms and ammunition. The report of the Swiss Ministry of Justice and the police stated on 16 December 1981: "Several emigrants have been arrested in Zurich, Basel and Solothurn. Those arrested included a Frenchman of Croatian origin and two Swiss citizens . . . "

81082601

August 26, 1981 — COLOMBIA — Four dynamite sticks exploded in a rest room of the Bi-National Center in Barranquilla, causing $40,000 damage but no injuries. 81082602

August 27, 1981 — LEBANON — The pro-Iranian Lebanese group Quwwat as-saff al-mujahid (Forces of the Struggling Line, or Mojahedin Fighters of the Ranks) fired a rocket-propelled grenade at the Saudi Embassy at 10:30

P.M., causing damage but no injuries. The group was protesting Riyadh's anti-Iran attitude in the Iran-Iraq war. 81082701

August 29, 1981 — FRANCE — At 9:30 P.M., a powerful bomb exploded in the main ground floor corridor of Paris's Hotel Intercontinental, injuring 18 people, shattering chandeliers, collapsing ceilings, burning furniture, and breaking glass partitions. Several people claimed to have seen a man leave a package in the corridor just before the blast.

August 29, 1981 — LEBANON — A 20-kilogram bomb went off at 8:02 A.M. at the Tawfiq Abu 'Assaf building in Al-Hamra' in West Beirut, damaging the Iranian television and radio offices, as well as the Turkish consulate, the Beirut-Riyadh Bank, and several local offices, killing one person and injuring two others. 81082901

August 29, 1981 — AUSTRIA — Two Arabs wearing yarmulkes fired Polish PN-63 machine pistols and lobbed grenades into Vienna's Synagogue Seitenstettengasse (which had been bombed in 1979) as worshippers were leaving a bar mitzvah at 11:30 A.M. Two people were killed and 20 injured, including 3 Austrian policemen who returned fire, wounding 1 terrorist and capturing both. The 2 dead worshippers were identified as Lotan Fried, 68, and Ulrike Kohut, 25, who died when she threw herself on top of a friend's child as a grenade went off. The wounded terrorist identified himself as Ali Yusuf, an Egyptian member of the Al Asifa (Abu Nidal) pro-Syrian terrorist group. The Palestine Liberation Organization (PLO) condemned the attack, which began when the duo were stopped by police. Police later went to the apartment of one of the terrorists at 10 Gablenzgasse in Vienna-Ottakring and arrested Muhsin al-'Ashur, 26, a Syrian student. Police received a phone call from an Arab-sounding man who threatened to bomb three movie theaters if the terrorists were not released. Searches revealed no bombs. On August 30, 6 Arabs held in the case were released, leaving only 3 others in custody. On January 21, 1982, a Vienna court sentenced Marwan Hasan (Ali Yusuf) of Jordan and Husham Mohammed Rajeh of Iraq to life imprisonment for the murder of Heinz Nittel on May 1, 1981. Hassan testified in the case against Bahij Mohammed Younis (also spelled Bahi Yuniz), a 29-year-old Palestinian, who was convicted and sentenced to life in prison for masterminding the grenade attack and for the murder of Heinz Nittel on May 1, 1981. A Vienna court passed the sentence on October 22, 1981. 81082902

August 30, 1981 — IRAN — A bomb went off at 3:00 P.M. in the Tehran office of Prime Minister Mohammed Javad Bahonar, killing him, Iranian president Mohammed Ali Rajai, an office worker, and a female passerby and wounding 9–13 others. Surviving government officials claimed the Muhajeddin e Khalq was responsible, and blamed Massoud Keshmiri, who was in charge of the prime minister's security.

August 31, 1981 — UNITED STATES — Two parcels containing six sticks of dynamite and a blasting cap, addressed to President Reagan and the DETROIT NEWS, were found in Detroit postal boxes. They were safely detonated in an island park in the Detroit river.

August 31, 1981 — UNITED KINGDOM — Hugh Carville, 25, an Irish Republican Army (IRA) bomber and former Irish football star, joined the Maze Prison hunger strike.

August 31, 1981 — GUATEMALA — Unidentified gunmen kidnapped the Guatemalan minister of public health and social assistance, Dr. Roquelino Recinos Mendez, as he was driving on a highway from the capital to Esquintla. The kidnappers demanded the freedom of four prisoners confined in Zacapa and Quezaltenango jails.

August 31, 1981 — LEBANON — A bomb damaged an empty Middle East Airlines (MEA) B-727 at Beirut International Airport, halting traffic but causing no injuries, on the third anniversary of the disappearance of Imam Musa as-Sadr. Explosives were found on an MEA jet the previous week in Tripoli, Libya. 81083101

August 31, 1981 — PERU — Sendero Luminoso (Shining Path), a Maoist group, was believed responsible for the 1:15 A.M. bombing of the United States embassy, which caused $50,000 damage. A local guard fired at a red car that sped from the scene. Ten minutes later, United States ambassador Edwin Corr's residence was bombed, damaging the swimming pool and several chairs. Later that evening, bombs went off at the Bank of America, Ford, the Coca-Cola bottling plant, and the offices of the Berkemeyer Company, a Peruvian distributor for the Carnation dairy firm. 81083102–07

August 31, 1981 — FEDERAL REPUBLIC OF GERMANY — The Sigurd Debus Command of the Red Army Faction (Baader-Meinhof Gang) set off a bomb at 7:00 A.M. outside the Ramstein headquarters of United States and NATO European Air Force operations, injuring 18 American servicemen and two West German civilians and causing extensive damage to buildings and vehicles. The injured were reported as Brig. Gen. Joseph D. Moore, assistant deputy chief-of-staff for operations, of Myrtle Beach, North Carolina; Lt. Col. Douglas R. Young, of Glendale, Arizona; Col. Philip D. Carlson; Lt. Col. Ronald H. Lynde; Sgt. Wilson R. Evans II; Lt. Col. Richard A. Myers; Capt. Marlin W. Yankee; Maj. John G. Whitcomb;

Maj. Henry Fiumara; Maj. Robert Introne; Maj. Charles V. Tookey; Lt. Robert Batterman; and West Germans Peter Hartmann and Heidi Lill. A gas container filled with explosives was found later in a nearby NATO office and disarmed. 81083108

September 1981 — UNITED STATES — Reporters suggested that explosives and electronic gear found in a storage locker in Alexandria, Virginia may have been intended to be used to assassinate President Ronald Reagan and Israeli prime minister Menachem Begin during Begin's visit to the White House. The material was found when the rental period ended. The explosives were obtained in Arizona by Harold Eugene McDowell, an international businessman who was selling communication equipment to the Palestine Liberation Organization (PLO). He was placed on probation more than a year later after he pleaded guilty to one count of conspiring to illegally possess and transport explosives across state lines. The material was placed in the locker the day before Begin arrived by Abdul-Hafiz Mohammed Nassar, a Jordanian active in Palestinian affairs. Nassar was sentenced to five years in prison after pleading guilty to the same charges. 81099901

September 1981 — ANGOLA — A mine was found along a Gulf Oil pipeline, apparently planted by the Front for the Liberation of the Enclave of Cabinda (FLEC). 81099902

September 1, 1981 — VATICAN CITY — At 10:00 A.M., 21 Iranian student members of Peykar (Moslem Protest) occupied the Iranian embassy. They surrendered peacefully three hours later.

September 1, 1981 — FEDERAL REPUBLIC OF GERMANY — Arsonists torched seven cars, five of them with United States license plates, during the night at an Air Force housing unit in Wiesbaden, destroying the cars but causing no injuries. Arsonists caused $125,000 damage to the Frankfurt conference room of the Social Democratic Party (SPD). Slogans denouncing "US imperialism" and SPD support for United States nuclear arms strategy were spray-painted at the building's entrance. 81090101–05

September 3, 1981 — REPUBLIC OF SOUTH AFRICA — At 9:00 P.M., a car carrying four gunmen drove up to the Mabopane, Bophuthatswana, police station, whereupon the attackers threw hand grenades and fired AK-47s into the station, killing two policemen and two civilians (one a three-year-old), all blacks. The African National Congress was believed responsible.

September 3, 1981 — SYRIA — An explosion in a booby-trapped car in front of Syria's Air Force Command in Damascus killed 20 and injured 50. Police shot to death the driver as he attempted to flee. The Moslem Brother-hood was believed responsible.

September 3, 1981 — UNITED STATES — After a 4:30 A.M. Jewish Defense League warning telephone call, police found two bombs taped under cars belonging to Soviet diplomats near their United Nations mission and four Molotov cocktails on a sidewalk two blocks away. A third bomb exploded under the car of a Nigerian United Nations diplomat. 81090301–04

September 4, 1981 — UNITED KINGDOM — The family of hunger striker Mat-thew Devlin, 31, of the Irish Republican Army (IRA), took him off his strike when he fell unconscious after fasting since July 15 in Maze Prison.

September 4, 1981 — LEBANON — Three gunmen driving a white BMW se-dan stopped the gray Peugeot 604 sedan of French ambassador Louis Dela-mare, 59, 200 yards from his Beirut home. When he refused to unlock his car doors, the attackers fired six shots into his head and abdomen, fatally injuring him. His chauffeur was unharmed. The Lebanese Red Brigades claimed responsibility. 'Ali Muhammad Bnat, owner of the BMW, was called in for questioning. Syria and Abu Nidal were also suspected. 81090401

September 4, 1981 — LESOTHO — A bomb exploded at the Maseru Hilton Hotel, damaging two floors and injuring five people. Another bomb ex-ploded outside the United States Cultural Center in Maseru, causing minor damage but no injuries. 81090402–03

September 5, 1981 — IRAN — Iran's prosecutor general, Ayatollah Ali Qo-dussi, died when an incendiary bomb went off in his Tehran office.

September 5, 1981 — UNITED KINGDOM — Three gasoline bombs were thrown at the ground floor windows of the United States consulate in Edinburgh, causing minor damage and no injuries. 81090501

September 5, 1981 — LEBANON — A gunman firing from a car wounded the Iraqi cultural attache in Beirut. 81090502

September 6, 1981 — UNITED KINGDOM — The mother of jailed Irish Re-publican Army (IRA) hunger striker Lawrence McKeown removed him from his 70-day fast when he became unconscious. The Irish National Liberation Army (INLA) said it would not add more prisoners to the strike.

September 6, 1981 — UNITED STATES — The Thunder of Zion faction of the Jewish Defense League (JDL) claimed credit for the 2:00 A.M. bombing of

New York City's Four Continent Book Store, which the JDL claimed was a "Soviet book store." A caller demanded the release of Soviet dissident Anatoly Shcharansky and Maria Tiemkin and Jews in the Soviet Union. UNITED PRESS INTERNATIONAL reported that a caller vowed to kill Soviet foreign minister Andrei Gromyko if they were not released in two weeks. 81090601–02

September 6, 1981 — COLOMBIA — The Workers' Autodefense Movement (MAO) bombed the Venezuelan consulate and Chilean embassy, breaking windows in the former but causing no injuries. 81090603–04

September 7, 1981 — GUATEMALA — Unidentified individuals tossed a hand grenade at the Mexican ambassador's home, causing little damage and no injuries. Police exchanged gunfire with the fleeing motorcyclists. 81090701

September 7, 1981 — LEBANON — Explosives were thrown into the Turkish embassy garden at 7:00 P.M., breaking seven windows but causing no injuries. 81090702

September 8, 1981 — HONDURAS — Twenty unarmed members of the Federation of Secondary Students took over the United Nations offices in Tegucigalpa, holding 6 employees hostage for 56 hours before the government agreed to investigate the cases of 41 alleged political prisoners and complaints of police harassment of the students. 81090801

September 10, 1981 — COLOMBIA — The Patriotic Liberation Front, acting on order of the Pedro Leon Arboleda Command of the Popular Liberation Army, threw bombs at the CARE office in Bogota and the National Police Club, injuring two people at the latter facility. 81091001

September 10, 1981 — LUXEMBOURG — The October 18 Movement threw two Molotov cocktails at the American Fletcher National Bank, causing damage but no injuries, to express solidarity with the Red Army Faction (Baader-Meinhof Gang) struggle against United States imperialism and capitalistic monopoly. The previous afternoon, a warning call was received at a local newspaper. 81091002

September 11, 1981 — UNITED STATES — Omega-7, an anti-Castro Cuban exile group, bombed the Mexican consulate in Miami at 10:13 P.M., causing $2 million damage to the Rivergate Plaza building, which houses the consulate. No injuries were reported. Simultaneously, a Spanish-language magazine was firebombed in Miami.

On February 21, 1984, Jose Ignacio Gonzalez, 41, a Miami businessman who claimed to be active in Republican party politics, pleaded guilty to having placed the time bomb in the consulate, in a trial before United States District Court judge Robert L. Carter. Gonzalez was a close associate of Eduardo Arocena, Omega-7 leader awaiting trial on charges of attempting to murder the Cuban ambassador to the United Nations in March 1980. Gerardo Necuze, 46, and Justo Rodriguez, 52, both of Miami, earlier pleaded guilty in the United States District Court in Fort Lauderdale of conspiracy in two bombings and three bomb attempts. 81091101–02

September 12, 1981 — UNITED STATES — At 1:40 A.M., an Omega-7 bomb damaged a gate, tore a metal door from the building, and broke windows at the Mexican consulate and United Nations Mission, but caused no injuries. 81091201

September 12, 1981 — ISRAEL — A grenade thrown into the midst of Italian pilgrims outside a Jerusalem souvenir shop killed 1 Italian and injured 26 Italians and 2 local Arabs. 81091202

September 12, 1981 — FEDERAL REPUBLIC OF GERMANY — Three fire-bombs, only one of which exploded (on a carpet), were thrown during the night at the Frankfurt home of the United States consul general, causing minor damage. The Red Army Faction (RAF) demanded the "grouping together of the RAF prisoners, the release of Verena Becker and Guenter Sonnenberg and the release of all interned military leftwingers." 81091203

September 13, 1981 — PERU — Police antiterrorist forces arrested five Argentines, including Carlos Sanchez Gonzalez, and a Central American citizen for illegal residence.

September 13, 1981 — UNITED KINGDOM — Gerard Hodgins, 21, an Irish Republican Army (IRA) convict, joined the Maze Prison hunger strike.

September 14, 1981 — AFGHANISTAN — The Yunus Khalis-led faction of the fundamentalist Moslem Hezb-e Eslami resistance movement, using a chauffeur as a confederate, kidnapped in broad daylight Mikhail Yevgeniy Okrimyuk, 68, a Soviet geologist directing a 50-member mission investigating the country's oil and natural gas reserves. The group demanded the release of 50 rebel prisoners. The hostage sent two letters pleading for his life to Soviet premier Nikolay Aleksandrovich Tikhonov, complaining of depression and chest pain. On April 20, 1982, the group said that a firing squad had executed him the previous month.

September 14, 1981 — GUATEMALA — John David Troyer, 28, a Mennonite missionary from Mio, Michigan, was shot in his home. 81091401

September 15, 1981 — AFGHANISTAN — KABUL DOMESTIC SERVICE denied a BBC report that rebels had fired rockets at the Soviet embassy, killing and wounding several people and causing extensive damage to the building.

September 15, 1981 — DENMARK — A bomb exploded during the night in the Turkish Airlines office in Copenhagen, injuring two people and causing extensive damage. A second bomb, found in the debris, was safely detonated by police. The Secret Armenian Army for the Liberation of Armenia claimed credit. 81091501

September 15, 1981 — FEDERAL REPUBLIC OF GERMANY— The Red Army Faction (RAF) fired two RPG-7s from a wooded area at 7:20 A.M. at the armored Mercedes of United States Army in Europe commander Gen. Frederick J. Kroesen, 58, as he, his wife Rowene, and Maj. Philip E. Bodine were being driven to the United States Army base in Heidelberg along the Neckar River from his home. The group fired small arms at the car, which sped to the hospital, where the Kroesens were treated for small cuts and released. One of the RPGs hit the car, which sustained some damage to the trunk. On October 19, police arrested Helga Roos, 27, a Frankfurt student believed involved in the attack. Police found the fingerprint of Brigitte Mohnhaput on the back of a license plate of an Audi impounded in Heidelberg. A shell fired from a Heckler-Koch .223 caliber automatic rifle was found near the car. Police also suspected that Christian Klar, 29, had driven one of the three cars used in the attack. Four hours later, an RAF confessor letter said Kroesen "is the one who orders devastation by conventional weapons and decides when and where neutron war heads will be fired. . . . He will be one of the American military men to take command — instead of Schmidt, Genscher, Strauss, Kohl, or whoever — of the FRG [Federal Republic of Germany] as soon as resistance seriously shakes the colonial status of this country. . . . The struggle in the metropolis can keep the global imperialist machine in check so that another breakthrough can be achieved with the revolutionaries in the Third World. Fighting in the metropolitan centers is the real direction of the revolution in the process of developing revolutionary resistance." The Gudrun Ensslin Commando signed the letter. 81091502

September 16, 1981 — SPAIN — Basque separatists blew up a power substation belonging to Iberduero, a company building a controversial nuclear plant at Lemoniz, cutting off electricity to most of the Pamplona area.

September 16, 1981 — IRAN — Two dynamite charges went off in the parking area for the United States interests section of the Swiss embassy at 8:50

P.M., causing slight damage. The June 9 Organization, an Armenian group, claimed credit. 81091601

September 16, 1981 — FEDERAL REPUBLIC OF GERMANY — Two 13-pound explosives packed in cylindrical fire extinguishers containing a timing device were placed on a railway line 200 yards from the United States Rhein-Main Air Base near Frankfurt. Police defused them during the morning. The Red Army Faction was suspected. 81091602

September 17, 1981 — LEBANON — The Front for the Liberation of Lebanon from Foreigners bombed a Chekka cement factory owned by former Lebanese president Suleiman Franjieh, killing 4 Palestinian guerrillas and 6 civilians and wounding 10 others. 81091701

September 17, 1981 — LEBANON — The Front for the Liberation of Lebanon from Foreigners bombed the Sidon regional headquarters of the Palestine Liberation Organization (PLO) at 9:15 A.M., 50 minutes before the Southern Area Command of the Palestinian resistance and the leftist movement were scheduled to meet. The car bomb, consisting of 200 kilograms of TNT, killed 25, including Latif al-Maysi, Khadr al-Myasi, Sahar Hammad, Samah Ramadan, and Col. Muhammad Abu al-Hadi from Fatah, injured 108, and damaged 10 buildings. 81091702

September 17, 1981 — FEDERAL REPUBLIC OF GERMANY — Terrorists attacked Dow Chemical. 81091703

September 18, 1981 — LEBANON — A car bomb set by the Front for the Liberation of Lebanon from Foreigners exploded in a narrow street in the Lebanese Shiite Moslem section of Hayy al Sullom, killing two and wounding several others. The group told AGENCE FRANCE-PRESSE, "Our organization will continue its operations until there is not a single foreigner or plotter alive on the territories of greater Lebanon."

September 18, 1981 — POLAND — Nine male and three female Polish students, aged 17 to 22, armed with a knife and broken bottles, diverted a Polish airline LOT AN-24 flying from Katowice to Warsaw with 45 passengers and 4 crewmen to Tempelhof airfield in West Berlin at 12:33 P.M. The group asked for political asylum, as did 2 Hungarians and 6 Poles, including a 4-year-old child. Poland's news agency PAP said the hijackers had threatened to kill a stewardess, and one female passenger was slightly injured. American officials initially reported that the group carried bombs made of bottles stuffed with rags and filled with gasoline. Three Swedish passengers and 1 American, Josephine Sevada of St. Cloud, Minnesota, did not return to Poland when the AN-24 left 10 hours later. 81091801

September 18, 1981 — COLOMBIA — The April 19 Movement (M-19) Group of Eight threatened to blow up the Belgian embassy if the ambassador did not leave the country. 81091802

September 20, 1981 — LEBANON — A bomb planted under a seat of a movie theater showing *The Dangerous Man,* a karate film, killed 4 and wounded 28 in Moslem West Beirut, half a mile west of the Museum Road. The Front for the Liberation of Lebanon from Foreigners said, "This operation is to prove to the PLO [Palestine Liberation Organization] that we are not an imaginary organization."

September 21, 1981 — INDIA — Police announced the arrest of two youths from the Bihar township of Hajipur, Kameshwar Prasad Singh and Ganesh Duth Singh, for participation in an Anand Marg plot to assassinate prime minister Indira Gandhi with hand grenades and small arms ammunition. A third suspect from Calcutta was being sought.

September 22, 1981 — UNITED STATES — A bomb exploded at 1:00 A.M. in the Schenectady, New York, offices of the Eastern Rugby Union, severely damaging adjacent offices, in protest of the United States tour of South Africa's Springbok national rugby team. 81092201

September 22, 1981 — COLOMBIA — A group of hooded men set afire the car of Mexican ambassador Maria Antonieta Sanchez Gavito as he was attending a conference at the national university. No injuries were reported. 81092202

September 22, 1981 — POLAND — Three Gdansk men and one woman, armed with sharp instruments, hijacked a Polish airline LOT aircraft flying from Warsaw to Koszalin at 7:40 P.M., demanding to be flown to West Berlin. Captain Jozef Filipowicz, the pilot, tricked the hijackers and returned to Warsaw's Okecie Airport, where the Citizens' Militia, using firearms, overpowered the hijackers, injuring one of them. 81092203

September 23, 1981 — CYPRUS — Mohammad Ibrahim, 26, a Lebanese-born Palestinian, threw one of his two grenades into the Shoham, Limassol, offices of the Israeli shipping firm Zim at 10:30 A.M., injuring three female and two male employees, all of them Greek Cypriot refugees. The next day, police arrested 'Abd al-Hamid Wusaym, 31, of Jordan. Limassol's district court issued orders for the eight-day detention of Muhammad Brazim Jayyusi, ('Ali Shawqi), 21, of Lebanon, and 'Abd al-Wakim, 21, of Iraq. On September 27, Larnaca airport police arrested Khalil Said Ratib. The group, apparently members of Abu Nidal's Black June organization, were captured with maps indicating other targets and their escape plans. They intended to force the government to release two Jordanians imprisoned for the assassination of Egyptian newsman Yusuf as-Siba'i. 81092301

September 23, 1981 — HONDURAS — Gunmen firing from taxi 373 injured Air Force sergeant Russell L. McFall and Army sergeant Robert L. Smith, 30, of Marshville, North Carolina, as they were driving to their military training team headquarters in the capital. The explosion coincided with a bombing of the legislative palace. The Lorenzo Zelaya People's Revolutionary Command of the Cinchoneros guerrilla group said, "This action is the expression of the Honduran people's repudiation of the use of our territory to promote counterrevolutionary aggression against the sister nations of Nicaragua and Cuba as planned through the 'hawk view' maneuvers to be staged by the Yankee army and its Honduran puppets" during October 7–9. 81092302

September 24, 1981 — UNITED KINGDOM — Irish Republican Army (IRA) hunger striker Bernard Fox gave up his fast after 32 days when told that he had a blocked tube leading to his kidneys, which required medical attention.

September 24, 1981 — FRANCE — Four Armenian Secret Army for the Liberation of Armenia (ASALA) gunmen took over the Turkish consulate in Paris at 11:15 A.M., taking 51 hostages and setting a 12-hour deadline for the release of all Armenian prisoners, 5 Turks, and 5 Kurds in Turkey. During the incident, Cemal Ozen, a Turkish security official, was killed, and Consul General Kayal Inal, 43, injured. National Education Adviser Zekai Baloglu, his assistant, Ibrahim Cankerten, Deputy Consul Hayri Erol, and about 10 students, were able to escape in the initial confusion.

The group's leader, Vasken Sicilian (also spelled Sislian), who was wounded during the shoot-out and conducted negotiations from a hospital, told his group to surrender 15 hours later as the French interior minister reportedly granted the group political asylum. The French government later said it would try the terrorists.

On September 26, Hagop Hagorian, a hooded ASALA spokesman in Beirut, told reporters that two other "suicide commando" ASALA squads would strike Turkish interests, and he accused President Francois Mitterrand of reneging on the deal. Also at the press conference, serving as translator, was Alexander Yenkomeshian, a former economist who was partially blind and missing his left hand after a bomb exploded in a Geneva hotel room in 1980 where he was with another accused ASALA guerrilla, Suzy Mahseredjian, of Canoga Park, California. (In connection with that incident, Yenkomeshian had been given a suspended sentence on extortion charges and was acquitted on an explosives charge.) The press conference was held in a building used by the Libyan-funded VOICE OF ARAB REV-

OLUTION radio station and was guarded by members of the pro-Libya Lebanese Arab Army militia. Reporters were told that future ASALA contacts would be arranged by the AL SHAGHYLA news agency, another Libyan-funded operation.

On November 27, the 4 members of the suicide commando Yeghia Kechichian, 2 of whom were wounded, and who themselves had injured 5 people in previous terrorist attacks, demanded political prisoner status by going on a hunger strike. The group were identified as Vasken Sicilian, Aram Basmadjian, Kevork Guzelian, and Hagop Chulfayan (also spelled Djulfayan).

Turkey announced that it would try the group in absentia under section 125 of the Turkish penal code: "Any person who commits a crime with the intention of transferring the whole or part of the state territory to the sovereignty of another country or for the purpose of curtailing the independence of the state or of undermining its unity or of separating part of the territory under the state administration will be liable to death punishment."

On January 31, 1984, a Paris court sentenced the three Lebanese and one Kuwaiti to seven years imprisonment, even though only one was charged with murder. On July 26, 1986, the three Lebanese (Sicilian, Chulfayan, and Guzelian) were jailed for 10 days for refusing an expulsion order to Beirut, saying that their safety was not guaranteed. Basmadjian had hanged himself in his prison cell in April 1985. 81092401

September 24, 1981 — UNITED KINGDOM — The Turkish embassy received a bomb threat. 81092402

September 24, 1981 — FRANCE — The Turkish consulate general in Lyons received a bomb threat. 81092403

September 24, 1981 — FEDERAL REPUBLIC OF GERMANY — The Turkish consulate general in Hannover received a bomb threat. 81092404

September 24, 1981 — LEBANON — A Palestinian organization defused a bomb planted in a car parked near the Turkish embassy. The VOICE OF LEBANON claimed that the Armenian Secret Army for the Liberation of Armenia (ASALA) was training in the Barr Ilyas area in western Al-Biqa' with the Workers' League (Rabitat ash-Shaghghilah) led by Deputy Zahir al-Khatib. 81092405

September 24, 1981 — IRAQ — Armed gunmen kidnapped 15 Turkish Transport International Routier truck drivers from a gas station 41 kilometers from the Habur Turkish-Iraqi border checkpoint. The group completely burned seven trucks and heavily damaged two others. One truck was able to continue on its way to Kuwait. Four of the truck drivers escaped and reported the incident to authorities. The Iraqis used helicopters to search for the truck drivers, who were released and returned to Turkey on September 28. The kidnappers were executed. 81092406

September 24, 1981 — UNITED STATES — The Ku Klux Klan was suspected of burning a cross at 11:00 P.M. on the Silver Spring, Maryland, lawn of Cameroonian cultural attache Ignatius Ndefru Nkwenti, 36. 81092407

September 25, 1981 — ITALY — A mysterious explosion toppled a building in Gioa del College, 23 miles south of the Bari Italian Air Force Base, killing United States Air Force sergeant Andrew Shenton, 34, of Baltimore and injuring Michigan United States Air Force sergeants William A. Frankowski, 24, Walter Surma, 35, Denis Johnson, 22, and Milton Crasseller, 50. The group was on a training exercise. 81092501

September 25, 1981 — UNITED STATES — An explosion and fire destroyed a home and a building housing the Evansville Rugby Club, which had tried to schedule a game with the touring South African Springbok team. 81092502

September 25, 1981 — FEDERAL REPUBLIC OF GERMANY — During the early morning, three privately owned cars were set afire in the United States Army housing area in Stuttgart, causing no injuries. 81092503–05

September 26, 1981 — UNITED KINGDOM — Jailed Irish National Liberation Army (INLA) terrorist Liam McCloskey gave up his Maze Prison hunger strike in its 55th day. He was serving a 10-year sentence for ambushing British troops, conspiring to steal military weapons, and taking part in punishment shootings.

September 26, 1981 — AFGHANISTAN — Karachi's JASARAT news service reported that at midnight, 22 Mujahidin fired 12 rockets at the Soviet embassy in Kabul, completely destroying its commercial section.

September 27, 1981 — YUGOSLAVIA — Three German-speaking Croatians armed with two pistols and a knife hijacked a Yugoslav Airlines B-737 flying from Dubrovnik to Belgrade with 101 passengers and 6 crewmen and demanded to be flown to Tel Aviv. The plane refueled at Ellikon Airport at 2:00 A.M., then landed at Larnaca at 5:41 A.M. after the Israelis refused landing privileges. All of the passengers escaped during a mock fire alarm. The hijackers surrendered to police at 8:00 A.M. and were quickly extradited to Yugoslavia. One woman and two men received slight foot injuries during the escape by the passengers, including the soccer team of Dubrovnik. On February 9, 1982, the Belgrade District Court trial of the hijackers began with Borivoje Jelic claiming to have led the hijacking after his release from a punitive-correction center and subsequent inability to find a job or passport. The other defendants were listed as Marko Krizic, Milan Prpic, Ksenija Dokmanovic, and Predrag Vidakovic. 81092701

September 28, 1981 — UNITED STATES — District of Columbia Superior Court judge Nicholas S. Nunzio re-released convicted Hanafi Moslem terrorist Abdul Hamid (Hilvan Finch) from his 36–108-year prison term for taking more than one hundred hostages at the District of Columbia B'nai B'rith headquarters in March 1977. Nunzio blamed a defense lawyer's error for Hamid's rearrest after his first release.

September 28, 1981 — LEBANON — A booby-trapped car exploded at a roadblock outside Zrariyeh, a Shiite Moslem village 10 miles north of Tyre, killing 15 persons, including 7 Syrian, Palestinian, and leftist Moslem militiamen, and wounding 40 others, including children aboard a nearby school bus. The Front for the Liberation of Lebanon from Foreigners was suspected. 81092801

September 29, 1981 — INDIA — Five members of the Dal Khalsa (a Sikh group demanding independence for Khalistan) brandishing Kirpans (Sikh holy daggers) hijacked an Air India B-737 carrying 117 passengers and crewmen from Delhi to Srinagar with a scheduled stop at Amritsar and diverted the plane to Lahore, Pakistan. The group's spokesman, Simban Singh Mukhpanch, said in a press conference in Amritsar that the hijackers wanted the release of all jailed Sikh militants, permission for them to seek political asylum abroad, and five hundred thousand dollars by 10:00 A.M. the next day. Included among the jailed militants was Sikh leader Sant (saint) Jarnail Singh Bhindranwale, 34, who was arrested September 20 in connection with the murder of a Hindu editor who opposed Sikh secessionism. While on the ground, the hijackers freed 44 women and children and a man with a sick wife. According to William Seco of Seattle, Washington, one of the hijackers cut himself on the arm with his dagger (which the Sikhs use as a hairpiece and which the Indian government permits them to wear on domestic flights for religious reasons) and told the hostages, "Now you know we mean business." Seco said, "At least one had a hand grenade while the others held travel bags at their sides with their hands inside as if they had bombs." At 7:30 A.M., Pakistani SSG commandos disguised as cleaners boarded the plane during breakfast while three of the hijackers were outside talking to government negotiators. After a 45-second scuffle, during which one hijacker was injured, the security forces overwhelmed the terrorists. The hijackers were identified as Gajedra Singh, Sardar Satnam Singh, Karan Singh, Tasbin Singh, and Rajinder Singh. On October 3, because of information gleaned from intelligence reports and statements made by the hijackers, police arrested in New Delhi a Dutch national of Indian origin, Khalid Khan, 33, one of the passengers, along with 6 extremist Sikhs. India requested extradition of the hijackers.

On April 20, 1985, trial was resumed in the special court in Lahore with all of the accused present. Defense counsels S. M. Zafar and Dr. Abdul Basit questioned jurisdiction over a case that did not occur in Pakistan. The court determined that it had jurisdiction two days later. On April 24, the accused pleaded not guilty to the charges. 81092901

September 30, 1981 — UNITED STATES — William J. Quinn, 33, a United States national suspected of being a member of the Irish Republican Army (IRA) Balcombe Street Four, which was involved in 58 bombings, shootings, and kidnappings in 1974 and 1975, was arrested in front of a south San Francisco stationery store where he had worked since his return from Ireland in 1977. He was imprisoned for a year in Ireland for IRA activities, but British authorities were unable to obtain his extradition for the 1975 slaying of an unarmed London constable. He was denied bail on October 6, and a hearing was scheduled for November 12.

October 1, 1981 — BRAZIL — A Molotov cocktail was thrown at the United States consulate general. 81100101

October 1, 1981 — LEBANON — The Front for the Liberation of Lebanon from Foreigners set off a car bomb in front of Palestine Liberation Organization (PLO) offices in west Beirut, killing 92 persons (the PLO claimed 60 initially, the VOICE OF LEBANON, 70); wounding 250; wrecking dozens of cars; badly damaging several nearby buildings; destroying the headquarters of the Communist Action Organization; damaging the offices of the PLO Foreign Information Office, FILASTIN ATH-THAWRAH magazine, the Fatah Planning Office, and the investigation department of the PLO's secret service chief; and causing a three-hour-long fire. Lebanese Phalangist radio claimed that Ahmad Jibril, commander of the Popular Front for the Liberation of Palestine—General Command, was wounded in the hundred-kilogram blast, which went off at 9:55 A.M. The VOICE OF LEBANON claimed Amin al-Hindi, Palestinian military official and personal aide to Abu Iyad (Salah Khalaf), was killed. Lebanese Communist Party leader George al-Habr was injured. The VOICE OF PALESTINE claimed Democratic Front for the Liberation of Palestine (DFLP) Central Committee member Al-Hajj Sami Muhammad Dhiyad Abu Ghawsh was killed. Spokesmen for the PLO blamed the Israelis, while other observers blamed the Syrians, the Abu Nidal group, Johnny 'Abduh and the Deuxieme Bureau of the Lebanese Army, and Bashir al-Jumayyil. 81100102

October 2, 1981 — SPAIN — Basque Nation and Liberty (ETA) frogmen were blamed for placing a bomb that ripped a 10-foot gash in the hull of the 3,370-ton *Marques de la Ensenada* Spanish Navy destroyer at 5:00 A.M. There were no casualties reported in the northern port town of Santander. The ship was one of six patrolling the Basque coast.

October 2, 1981 — LEBANON — The Front for the Liberation of Lebanon from Foreigners bombed a vacant Nabatiyeh Palestinian school, causing no injuries. Two men were arrested. 81100201

October 3, 1981 — UNITED KINGDOM — The last six convicted Irish Republican Army (IRA) hunger strikers in Maze Prison ended their fast, halting a seven-month campaign in which 10 prisoners died. James Prior, Britain's secretary for Ulster, said the government would permit prisoners to wear their own clothes at all times, increase opportunities for job training and education and for free-time association among prisoners, grant time off for good behavior, and institute more liberal mail and visitor privileges already available to conforming prisoners. Prior's package fulfilled many of the demands the strikers had made for special status.

October 3, 1981 — LEBANON — Police defused a 110-pound bomb minutes before it was set to explode at the scene of the bombing that occurred two days earlier at Palestine Liberation Organization (PLO) offices in Beirut. 81100301

October 3, 1981 — SWITZERLAND — The June 9 Organization, a branch of the Armenian Secret Army for the Liberation of Armenia, bombed the entrance of the main post office and the city courthouse in Geneva, injuring one person and shattering windows. The group is named after the date of an Armenian activist's arrest in Switzerland on charges of killing a Turkish consulate employee. The activist was to be tried in the courthouse. 81100302

October 4, 1981 — UNITED STATES — At 2:30 P.M., Washington, D.C., police detonated a package firebomb addressed to Sybrand Visagie, South Africa's top representative to the International Monetary Fund (IMF). The bomb was found on the doorstep of the Qatar embassy by a maid and gardener shortly before noon. Visagie was scheduled to return to South Africa in 10 days after two years with the IMF. 81100401

October 6, 1981 — TURKEY — Twenty-six masked members of the People's Fighters Organization (Mujahidin) took over the Iranian consulate general in Istanbul Cagloglu District at 9:45 A.M., injuring a security official and Mahmud Gergeri, an Iranian official, who were checking identity cards at the entrance. The group took the consulate employees to the basement, then trashed the building and shouted anti-Khomeini slogans. Upon leaving the building, they surrendered to police. 81100601

October 6, 1981 — UNITED STATES — Alimany Hamed Conteh, 40, former editor of a Sierra Leone opposition newspaper, who had worked as a cab-driver since coming to the United States 10 years earlier, was forced into an alley near his apartment at 1353 Langley Way in Langley Park, Maryland, at 10:48 P.M., and shot to death. Conteh was trying to organize a branch of the Sierra Leone People's Party, which opposes President Siaka Stevens's regime. 81100602

October 6, 1981 — BRAZIL — An Oriental-looking man was seen running from where a Molotov cocktail was thrown at the entrance to the British consulate in Rio de Janeiro during the evening. No personal injuries were reported, and only minor property damage was sustained. Another fire-bomb was thrown at the Danish consulate in Rio de Janeiro. 81100603–04

October 6, 1981 — EGYPT — Forty minutes past noon, Egyptian president Mohammed Anwar as-Sadat, was assassinated in a hail of automatic rifle fire and grenade explosions as he stood in review of a military parade in Nasr City celebrating Egypt's crossing of the Suez Canal in 1973. Accounts vary, but it appears that 9 others, including government officials and foreign diplomats, were killed, and 38 others injured.

While the attention of those in the reviewing stand was diverted by a spectacular air show of overflying Mirages, a Soviet truck hauling a new South Korean-manufactured field artillery piece came to a stop parallel to the stand, 15 yards away. It was later learned that the driver was not part of the assassination team but was forced to stop. Lt. Khaled Ahmed Shawki Islambouli (Second Lt. Khaled Attallah) led the four assassins off the truck, having given his assigned men a vacation and recruiting in their place two civilians with past military service and another officer on inactive reserve. The group advanced on the reviewing stand unmolested by the bodyguard squad, who ran for cover. The terrorists fired at almost point-blank range, hitting Sadat with 28 bullets. Sadat was rushed onto a helicopter, still alive, but pronounced dead at 3:00 P.M., having sustained two holes in the left side of his chest, a bullet in the neck just above the right collarbone, a wound above the right knee, a huge gash at the back of the left thigh, and a complicated fracture of the thigh. Three of the terrorists were reported killed at the scene, while three others (no explanation for this discrepancy has been offered) were captured.

The press reported that the dead included chief chamberlain Hassan Allam; Sadat's official photographer Mohamed Rashwan; an Omani battalion commander; Bishop Samuel, member of the caretaker Papal Council of the Coptic Orthodox Church; Samir Hilmi, chairman of the Central Accounts Administration; Army chief of staff Gen. 'Abd Rabb an-Nabi Hafiz; a security guard; and two unidentified persons.

The wounded included the North Korean ambassador; presidential assistant Sayyid Mar'i; Sadat's private secretary Fawzi Abdel Hafez; Belgian ambassador Claude Ruelle, 58, who sustained one bullet in the shoulder, one in the lung, and several broken ribs; Irish defense minister James Tully, who was slightly injured in the face; Egyptian defense minister Abdel Hamlim Abu Ghazala; CBS NEWS correspondent Mitchell Krauss, who was wounded by shrapnel; several other Egyptians; United States Air Force captain Christopher Ryan, 34, of Sacramento, California, stationed at the United States European Command in Stuttgart, West Germany, who was injured in the foot; Marine major Gerald R. Agenbroad, 36, of Bruneau, Idaho, of the Rapid Deployment Force Command, who was injured in the leg; Air Force lieutenant colonel Charles D. Loney, 42, of Austin, Texas, normally stationed at Air Force Headquarters in Washington, D.C., who was hit in the shoulder; and Richard McCleskey, an employee of the Raytheon Corporation. Vice President Hosni Mubarak, who succeeded Sadat and was seated next to him, was uninjured, despite plans of the assassins to mount a coup by killing the members of the administration seated at the reviewing stand. Major Gen. Mahmoud Masri, commander of the Republican Bodyguard, claimed that 12 members of his staff were wounded. He was unable to explain why the security forces turned and ran during the attack, nor how civilians were able to sneak onto the trucks with live ammunition, which was not to be issued for the parade.

The next day, 54 policemen were killed and more than 100 wounded in clashes with Moslem fundamentalists in the southern city of Asyut after the group launched coordinated attacks from 10 cars at dawn against two police stations, security headquarters, and a police unit guarding a mosque. Six militants were killed and 4 were wounded. The extremists were part of a group that had seen 1500 of their number arrested the previous month by Sadat in an antiinsurgent move against Gamaat Islamiya (Islamic Groups).

On October 17, investigators linked Lt. Col. Abu Abdel Latif Zomor, who was captured in a gun battle between police and Moslem extremists at the Giza pyramids, with the attack. His brother and 3 others were also arrested.

One of the assassins, a major, had a brother who had been arrested in the September crackdown.

The group Takfir wa Hijra (Repentant and Holy Flight) was blamed, as was Libyan leader Qaddafi and the Moslem Brotherhood. In Beirut, the exiled Egyptian opposition group known variously as the Independent Organization for the Liberation of Egypt and the Rejection Front for the Liberation of Arab Egypt, headquartered in Tripoli, Libya (and, according to Egyptian press, given $3 million by Qaddafi), claimed credit. The group is headed by Saadeddin Shazli, former Egyptian general who was chief of staff of the Egyptian Armed Forces between 1971–73, who subsequently broke with Sadat.

The assassins admitted that the ammunition had been purchased in the Upper Nile town of Deshna, 325 miles south of Cairo. One hundred rounds of ammunition had been bought by the conspirators at 15 piasters ($.18) a cartridge, and the four grenades used had cost 23 piasters ($.26) apiece.

Police later arrested 356 Moslem fanatics believed affiliated with the terrorist organization that killed Sadat.

On November 12, 1981, 24 people were indicted for the murder. Sadat's assassins were listed as Lt. Khaled Ahmed Islambouli, the commander of the artillery squad; Atta Tayem Hamida Rahim, an engineer and former reserve officer in the Egyptian Air Defense Command; Sgt. Hussein Abbas Mohammed, a member of the Home Guard; and Abdel Halim Abdel Salim Abdel Ali, stationery store owner. Abdel Salam Farag, 27, a Cairo engineer and civilian leader of the El Jihad terrorist group, was charged with "complicity and instigation" for publishing the book *Absent Duty,* of which only five hundred copies have been printed and which served as the assassins' ideological guide. A furniture dealer, 3 university students, and an 18-year-old high school student were accused of conspiracy. A blind mullah, Sheif Omar Ahmed Abdel Rahman, 43, a theology professor from Cairo's Al Azhar University, who had recently taught at Asyut, was also indicted for saying, "It is God's will," when told of the assassination plot.

On March 6, 1982, chief judge Maj. Gen. Samir Fadel Attia announced that the 3-man military court had convicted and sentenced 22 of the 24 defendants. The blind sheik was acquitted. Zomor, 35, a member of the Army's intelligence service, and his student brother, Tariq Zomor, were sentenced to life. Defendant Mohammed Salamouni read a statement in English saying, "Sadat made of himself the last pharaoh in our country. He made of himself the last shah. Sadat killed himself by his behavior here in Egypt." The defendants, at the noisy trial during which they had to be caged for their outbursts, claimed that they had been tortured while in prison.

Ignoring all clemency appeals, President Mubarak accepted the death sentences for the 4 assassins and Farag. On April 15, 1982, 2 active military officers, Lt. Khaled Ahmed Shawki Islambouli, 24, and Sgt. Hussein Abbas Mohammed, 28, were killed by a firing squad, while the 3 civilians were hanged. 81100605

October 7, 1981—LESOTHO—The Lesotho Liberation Army fired mortars and automatic weapons, apparently from South African territory, at the headquarters of the Lesotho paramilitary police in Maseru from 1:00 A.M. to 3:00 A.M. 81100701

October 7, 1981 — ITALY— A bomb exploded outside El Al's tourist information office on Rome's Via Veneto, injuring an Italian passerby and damaging furniture, a door, and windows. 81100702

October 7, 1981 — ITALY— A bomb exploded in Ostia in a public place where Soviet Jewish emigres congregate, injuring a young female Soviet Jewish refugee, her brother, and two Italians. 81100703

October 8, 1981 — ITALY— Majid Abu Sharara, the chief of the Public Relations Department of the Palestine Liberation Organization (PLO), died when a telephone-activated bomb exploded in his room in the luxury Flora Hotel on Rome's Via Veneto at 1:00 A.M. The bomb started a fire that burned the body of the moderate Fatah Central Committee member beyond recognition. Al Assifa (Black June) claimed credit. Abu Sharara was carrying a false passport for Hassah Zithouni, 47, an Algerian living in Lebanon, to attend a conference of Arab journalists. A Kuwaiti paper blamed the Central Intelligence Agency. Palestinians also suspected the Israelis. 81100801

October 9, 1981 — SYRIA— Cairo's AL-AHRAM reported that the palace between Damascus and Aleppo, where Soviet experts resided, was blown up, killing a large number of Russians. 81100901

October 9, 1981 — LEBANON— Palestinian guerrillas ambushed the vehicle of General Anoya of Nigeria, chief of staff for the United Nations peacekeeping Force in Lebanon, United Nations Interim Force in Lebanon (UNIFIL), injuring him. 81100902

October 10, 1981 — GUATEMALA— A United States embassy guard died at the hands of People's Guerrilla Army (EGP) gunmen a few minutes after a bomb exploded during the evening in front of the embassy. 81101001

October 10, 1981 — UNITED KINGDOM— An Irish Republican Army (IRA) nail bomb hidden in a laundry truck exploded outside the Chelsea army base in central London, killing Nora Field, 61, who lived nearby, and an 18-year-old male and injuring 38, including many of the 23 Irish Guards returning on an army bus from their ceremonial duty at the Tower of London, a 5-year-old boy, a 2-year-old girl, and local businessman Michael Russell. Eight of the soldiers were critically injured by the remotely detonated device. 81101002

October 13, 1981 — UNITED STATES— The United States Supreme Court refused to review a United States Court of Appeals decision that permitted the extradition to Israel of Ziad Abu Eain for the May 1979 bombing that killed 2 young boys and injured 36 civilians in Tiberias.

October 13, 1981 — EGYPT— Two parcel bombs exploded amongst luggage that had been off-loaded from an Air Malta B-737 filled with Egyptian workers who had come from Libya to Cairo International Airport, wounding one airport worker and three security men. Libya denied responsibility, although Qaddafi openly rejoiced at the previous week's assassination of Anwar Sadat. 81101301

October 14, 1981 — MALTA— A gunman opened fire on the Palestine Liberation Organization (PLO) representative to Libya, Sulayman ash-Shurafah (Abu Tariq) while in Valleta. The gunman missed, killed someone else, and was arrested by police. 81101401

October 15, 1981 — ITALY— Italian authorities discovered that Libya had sent a hit team to assassinate United States ambassador to Italy Maxwell M. Rabb, who left hastily from Milan to Washington. 81101501

October 15, 1981 — LEBANON — TEHRAN DOMESTIC SERVICE reported that a car carrying gunmen who fired machine guns equipped with silencers at a car carrying Seyyed Mohsen Musavi, the Iranian embassy's charge d'affaires, escaped onto the west Beirut grounds of the Iraqi embassy. No injuries were reported. 81101502

October 16, 1981 — UNITED KINGDOM/IRELAND— Gunmen in Armagh County near Killeen, about two hundred yards north of the Irish border, kidnapped Ben Dunne, Jr., in his mid-thirties, heir to a chain of 66 department stores, and dragged him from his limousine into Ireland. 81101601

October 17, 1981 — LEBANON— Beirut authorities released Bassam Mohammed Ferkh, a Lebanese held for three years as a suspect in the 1976 murder of United States ambassador Francis Meloy, for lack of evidence.

October 17, 1981 — UNITED KINGDOM— A bomb exploded in the Volkswagen of Lt. Gen. Steuart Pringle, 53, commander of the Royal Marines, as he was pulling away from the curb near his West Dulwich home at 11:30 A.M. His right leg was amputated below the knee. Police searched for a four- to five-man cell of the Irish Republican Army (IRA), which claimed credit. Pringle, a 35-year veteran of the Royal Marines, led a Marine commando unit on two tours of duty in Northern Ireland in the early 1970s, after having seen action in Suez and Cyprus.

October 19, 1981 — FEDERAL REPUBLIC OF GERMANY — PARIS DOMES-TIC SERVICE quoted DIE WELT as reporting that the Army for the Protection of Turkey's International Rights threatened French diplomats in Bonn the previous week unless action was taken against Armenian, particularly Armenian Secret Army for the Liberation of Armenia (ASALA), militants living in exile in France. 81101901

October 19, 1981 — FRANCE — Mate Kolic, 42, a militant Croatian nationalist exiled in France since 1958, died when his car exploded as he switched on the ignition. His wife, Branca, 41, was slightly injured. 81101902

October 20, 1981 — BELGIUM — A bomb hidden in a parked van exploded shortly after 9:00 A.M. in front of the Antwerp Diamond Club, across from a synagogue on Hoveniersstraat, killing three and injuring one hundred. Only three of the injured were Jews. Damage was extensive. The Direct Action, Section Belgium, claimed credit, but the French group denied responsibility. The Israeli embassy blamed the Palestine Liberation Organization (PLO), which denied the charge. The press later reported that Black September claimed credit, and that police were searching for an Arab who gave the name Nicola Brazzi, a Lebanese, when taking out a transit license plate of the kind issued to foreigners residing for a short while in Belgium. A caller threatened more attacks in Antwerp and Brussels in support of the Palestinians. 81102001

October 20, 1981 — UNITED STATES — Four terrorists attacked a Brink's truck outside a Rockland County, New York, bank, escaping with $1.6 million in a hail of shotgun and automatic weapons fire. Police gave chase and stopped the car at a roadblock. The terrorists fired on police, killing two (having previously killed an armed guard). Three robbers escaped, stealing cars to do so. Katherine Boudin, 38, a Weather Underground activist who had been hiding for 11 years, was captured by off-duty officer Michael Koch as she ran north on the southbound lane of a freeway. Arrested with her were Judith Clark, 31, a Weatherman who had served time for her participation in the 1969 Days of Rage in Chicago, and two males. Police also raided a New Jersey bomb factory, finding diagrams of six New York police precincts. The males were later identified as James Lester Hackford, 31, and Samuel Brown, 41, who had a lengthy criminal record that included a robbery conviction. In the initial attack, one other guard was wounded in the head, while a third was shot in the shoulder. The dead police officers were identified as Waverly "Chipper" Brown, 45, and Sgt. Edward O'Grady. Boudin and Clark were members of the May 19 Movement (named after the birthdates of Ho Chi Minh and Malcolm X) section of the Weathermen, which counseled against surfacing from the underground as the Prairie Fire faction, such as Bernadine Dohrn, Mark Rudd, and Bill Ayers, had done.

Boudin was last seen fleeing naked with Cathlyn Platt Wilkerson when a Greenwich Village bomb factory exploded in 1970, killing three.

Police also investigated the connection of the Black Liberation Army (BLA), the Puerto Rican Armed Forces of National Liberation (FALN), and the Irish Republican Army (IRA), to the attack.

After a car chase on October 23, police captured Nathaniel Burns, 36, a Black Panther. His accomplice, Mtajori Sandiata (Sam Smith), had been killed in the shoot-out, wounded by a bullet from the .38 of the dead officer O'Grady. Burns was identified as Sekou Odinga, who signed a prison registry on the day BLA leader Joanne Chesimard escaped.

On November 5, conspiracy charges were dropped against Cynthia Priscilla Boston, a black member of the separatist Republic of New Africa, although Federal Bureau of Investigation agents had identified her as one of four people who cleaned out a Mount Vernon, New York, safe house the day after the Brink's holdup. Police had also raided safe houses in Brooklyn, the Bronx, and Manhattan.

Bureau of Alcohol, Tobacco, and Firearms officers suggested a link between these groups and the bombing in September of a rugby club in Schenectady where a match with the touring South African Springboks team was scheduled. In Manhattan, Eve Rosahn, 30, was charged with rioting at Kennedy International Airport against Springboks and supplying a rented 1981 Chevrolet van, as well as her 1980 Honda, for the Brink's holdup. On November 9, she was cited for civil contempt for refusing to cooperate with a federal grand jury.

On October 30, David Gilbert, charged with murder and robbery in the Brink's holdup, was linked to the three hundred thousand dollar robbery of a Brink's truck in the Bronx in June, during which four black gunmen killed a guard and wounded another during their escape.

On November 17, 1982, William R. Johnson, 34, charged with conspiracy to commit bank robbery, was arrested by Belize authorities for narcotics possession and extradited to the United States. He was identified as having removed the contents of the Mount Vernon hideout, and his fingerprint was found in the apartment. Johnson was the common-law husband of Cynthia Boston, 34, who agreed on November 22, 1982, to surrender to federal authorities.

On November 18, 1982, a Manhattan federal grand jury indicted Sylvia Baraldini, a legal aide; Mutulu Shakur, the suspected Brink's heist mastermind; Susan Rosenberg, a fugitive; Nathaniel Burns, a reputed BLA soldier; Edward Joseph, Cecil Ferguson, and Cheri Dalton for plotting a dozen other crimes—armored-car holdups, attempted robberies, and threats to murder federal informants—including the 1979 prison escape of Joanne Chesimard.

On January 5, 1983, Bernadine Dohrn, who was sentenced on May 19, 1982, to 18 months for refusing to cooperate with the Brink's grand jury investigation, was freed by United States District judge Gerard L. Goettel.

In a federal trial that ended on September 3, 1983, Sekou Odinga and Sylvia Baraldini were convicted of conspiracy and racketeering. Cecil Ferguson and Edward L. Joseph were convicted of an accessory charge carrying up to 12½ years. Bilal Sunni-Ali and Iliana Robinson were acquitted in the Federal District Court trial in Manhattan. On March 28, 1984, Odinga was convicted of trying to murder police officers in the gun battle three days after the holdup.

On October 6, 1983, in a related state trial in Goshen, New York, 40-year-old David L. Gilbert — Kathy Boudin's husband — Judith A. Clark, 33, and Kuwasi Balagoon (Donald Weems), 36, were each sentenced to 75 years to life for robbery and murder. Judge David S. Ritter of Orange County Court said they would not be eligible for parole for 75 years. "They hold society in contempt and have no respect for human life. They anticipated resistance and went about their task armed to the teeth," said the judge. Before the judge pronounced the sentences, the trio read statements denouncing the United States as imperialist and predicting the inevitability of revolution.

On December 17, 1983, Tyrone Rison, a key witness in the Federal District Court Brink's trial, was sentenced to 12 years for a series of holdups and the murder of a guard in a June 1981 armored-car robbery.

On April 26, 1984, Kathy Boudin, 40, pleaded guilty to second-degree murder and was given a concurrent term of 12½ to 25 years for robbery. On May 3, 1984, Judge David S. Ritter sentenced her to 20 years to life in prison for her role in the robbery, to be eligible for parole in 17 years. Boudin said, "I want to express my sorrow for the deaths of Sgt. Edward O'Grady and patrolman Waverly Brown directly to the family members who are here today and continue to grieve their loss." Diane O'Grady, the widow, denounced Boudin's remorse. Bernadine Dohrn, wife of Bill Ayers, became the legal guardian of Boudin's 3-year-old daughter, Chesa.

On May 8, 1984, the Justice Department indicated that it had spent $2 million for wiretaps on Boudin and others, using 50 agents in 169 days of the investigation, which included intercepting conversations at an acupuncture clinic, an apartment, and a pay telephone. Rockland County had spent between $1.9 and $6.6 million for the Boudin case.

On June 14, 1984, Samuel Brown, 43, of Staten Island, was convicted of three counts of murder and four of robbery.

On March 17, 1985, Timothy Blunk, 27, a member of the May 19 Movement, and Susan Lisa Rosenberg, 29, of the Weather Underground, were convicted in federal court on eight charges each of unlawful possession of explosives, weapons, and counterfeit identification cards. The duo were arrested on November 29, 1984, at a Cherry Hill storage depot, where

740 pounds of dynamite, an Uzi submachine gun, an M-14 rifle, a sawed-off shotgun, and Teflon-coated "policekiller" bullets were found. They were arrested while sitting in a car after Mark DeFrancisco, a New Jersey policeman, became suspicious of their ill-fitting wigs. Rosenberg was held on $1 million bail; Blunk on five hundred thousand dollars bail. Rosenberg faced separate charges for her alleged getaway driver role in the Brink's case and the 1979 prison escape of Joanne Chesimard. Blunk was sentenced in 1982 to nine months in a New York jail for rioting and resisting arrest during an anti-apartheid demonstration against a South African rugby team at John F. Kennedy International Airport in 1981.

On May 11, 1985, the Federal Bureau of Investigation arrested Marilyn Jean Buck, 37, BLA member, in Dobbs Ferry, 37 miles from New York City. Buck had been a fugitive since she failed to return in June 1977 to a West Virginia federal prison, where she was serving a sentence on weapons charges. Buck had been indicted in the Brink's case on federal bank robbery conspiracy charges and on state charges of murder and armed robbery. Also arrested was Linda Sue Evans, 38, who was indicted in New Haven, Connecticut, in March 1985 for harboring Buck. On May 16, 1985, four deputy marshals carried Buck kicking and screaming from a federal courtroom after she refused to obey United States District Court judge John Canella's denial of permission to read a statement at her rearraignment.

On May 24, 1985, Dr. Alan Berman, 39, of New York City, was arrested with a female companion in Pennsylvania. He was ordered held without bail after authorities described him as a terrorist bent on overthrowing the government. He had allegedly treated one of the Brink's robbers for gunshot wounds.

October 21, 1981 — NICARAGUA — Nicaraguan radio accused Somozist counterrevolutionaries of killing two Cuban teachers, Pablo Rivero Cueto and Barbaro Rodriguez Hernandez, and two Nicaraguan peasants who were members of the Sandinist militia, Florentin and Jesus Castellon, in the community of Consuelo Bajo, 30 kilometers from the mining community of Ciuna in the Department of Celaya Norte.

October 22, 1981 — NICARAGUA — Nicaraguans Francisco Emilio Miranda Mungalo and Carlos Correa Lacayo hijacked a Nicaraguan Agrarian Reform Institute twin-engine Aztec crop duster, registration YMDDQ, from Los Brasiles Airport in Nicaragua to Santamaria Airport in Costa Rica, where they released their hostage, a mechanic, and requested political asylum. Mungalo told SAN JOSE'S RADIO RELOJ, "The reason I hijacked this aircraft is simply the current political situation, where communism is penetrating us in a way that is leading us to ruin and chaos. We cannot go on like that. I have been without work for the past 14 months. We have been replaced by a number of Cubans and foreigners. They have been taking our jobs away from us and have been treating us arrogantly. I am taking advantage of this occasion to request protection. I blame the Sandinist government for anything that might happen to my children. I blame it for anything that might happen to them as a result of my decision, of which they were ignorant."

Lacayo said, "We decided to carry out this operation because of the climate of uncertainty and unrest that the Nicaraguan people are currently experiencing. Our rulers have openly announced that they are Marxists-Leninists and they have created a military dictatorship in which the Nicaraguan people are viewed as second-rate citizens in the face of an avalanche of alleged internationalist Cuban engineers, who are taking away from our jobs and our own decisions to forge our own history. I think they have completely discredited it through their lack of ability, the totalitarianism which currently prevails in our country and the lack of freedom. This can be confirmed . . . newspaper LA PRENSA, the closing of many radio stations and the lack of freedom of expression." 81102201

October 23, 1981 — ITALY— The Communist Group of Proletarian Internationalism bombed the offices and reading library of the READER'S DIGEST in Rome, shattering all windows in the area and causing no injuries. 81102301

October 23, 1981 — ITALY— A bomb exploded at the Bank of America and Italy offices in Rome, damaging five nearby cars, but causing no injuries. 81102302

October 23, 1981 — ITALY— Avis Rental Car Company offices in Rome were bombed. 81102303

October 23, 1981 — VATICAN CITY— The Communist Group of Proletarian Internationalism bombed the Chilean embassy, blowing out windows but causing no injuries. 81102304

October 24, 1981 — COLOMBIA— An Aerosol DC-3, HK-388, flying from Medellin to Barranquilla, disappeared but was later found seven hundred kilometers southeast of Bogota in Caqueta. Police suggested that the April 19 Movement (M-19) had used it to ferry arms from Panama, directed by Eden Pastora. Peasants said about one hundred guerrillas had unloaded arms from the plane.

October 24, 1981 — ITALY— The American Express office in Rome was bombed, causing damage but no injuries. 81102401

October 24, 1981 — ITALY— The Communist Group of Proletarian Internationalism bombed the Guatemalan embassy and an Argentine embassy trade office, shattering windows at both locations but causing no injuries. 81102402–03

October 25, 1981 — JORDAN — Amman's AR-RA'Y reported, "Commenting on the US judiciary's decision to arrest Ziyad Abu'Ayn and hand him over to the Israeli enemy, Hamid Abu Sittah, PLO [Palestine Liberation Organization] Executive Committee member and head of the Occupied Homeland Department, has stated that if the US judiciary has decided to arrest and hand Ziyad Abu'Ayn over to the occupation authorities, then the PLO has its own revolutionary and just judiciary which considers every US citizen who has contributed to supporting the Zionist entity militarily or materially or has enlisted in the Israeli Army as having committed an unforgettable crime against the Palestinian people, who have suffered from Israeli terrorism, killing and dispersion, and thus becomes a criminal in the eyes of world jurisdiction." Abu Sittah added: "The PLO can incriminate and punish them for this. We are not threatening but explaining the consequences that will result from the US decision if Ziyad Abu'Ayn is handed over to the Zionist enemy."

October 25, 1981 — FRANCE — In late October 1986, Jack Anderson claimed that on October 25, 1981, "ASALA [Armenian Secret Army for the Liberation of Armenia] launched a series of 15 bombings in Paris to win the release of an ASALA leader, Monte Melkonian, and better treatment for four other members charged with the takeover of the Turkish consulate in Paris, in which a security guard was killed. Our sources confirm that the French cut a deal with ASALA in January 1982. The bombings stopped, Melkonian was set free and the four other ASALA prisoners were given light sentences." According to the Rand Corporation, "Some of the attacks were claimed by the mysterious Liberation Army of Canaque, but the militant separatists of New Caledonia denied responsibility. A new group called September-France also claimed credit for many of the attacks. Authorities also suspect the extreme right and Action Directe."

October 25, 1981 — UNITED STATES — The Jewish Defense League threw two firebombs, only one of which exploded, through the front window of the Egyptian tourist office in Rockefeller Center, New York City, causing extensive damage but no injuries. 81102501

October 25, 1981 — ITALY — During the early evening on a street near the Roman Coliseum, the Armenian Secret Army for the Liberation of Armenia (ASALA) fired three shots at Gokberk Ergenekon, 28, the Turkish embassy's second secretary, wounding him twice in the right shoulder and once in the left hand. In December, the Turkish government claimed that a suspect was sentenced in France to four months for carrying a false passport, but that his sentence was suspended and he was released. "Although he was not identified positively by Ergenekon, he was, together with another person, recognized by Ergenekon out of six persons shown to him. Furthermore, this person had a wound on his arm. He possessed a Beirut-Milan-Beirut plane ticket, of which he had used the Beirut-Milan part. This evidence leaves no doubt that he was indeed the person who carried out the attack against Ergenekon. Furthermore, it was known that the French police had suspicions about him. Because the crime was committed in Italy, Turkey could not demand this person's extradition. Consequently, our government made repeated and persistent representations to the Italian judicial authorities so the latter could demand the suspect's extradition from France. At the same time, our government made representations to the French authorities not to release that person pending an extradition request from the Italian authorities. The French authorities released that person before the Italian authorities could made [sic] the necessary request." 81102502

October 25, 1981 — FRANCE — The Kanaka Liberation Front claimed it planted a bomb that injured three people in Fouquet's, a fashionable restaurant in the Avenue de Champs Elysee. Observers suggested the group could be the military wing of Palika, the Kanaka (Native New Caledonian) Liberation Party. 81102503

October 26, 1981 — UNITED KINGDOM — Kenneth Howarth, 49, a policeman trying to defuse a bomb found in the basement of a Wimpy fast-food restaurant on London's Oxford Street, died when the Irish Republican Army (IRA) device went off. Two other IRA bombs were found in the Debenham's and Bourne's department stores after warning phone calls were received at 3:00 P.M. The Irish Republican Publicity Bureau in Dublin said, "Let the British people take note that the Irish children, the victims of plastic bullets fired by their soldiers, do not have the luxury of receiving warnings. In future, when we give warnings, respect them. The British people should press their government to withdraw from our country. Then there will be no bombs in London and there can be peace in Ireland." 81102601–03

October 26, 1981 — UNITED KINGDOM — A firebomb believed to have been planted by militant Welsh nationalists was defused in an army recruiting office in Pontypridd, Wales, where Prince Charles and Princess Diana were scheduled to visit.

October 27, 1981 — IRAN — PARS news agency accused counterrevolutionaries of bombing the Air France office. 81102701

October 27, 1981 — FRANCE — The Kanaka Liberation Front (the Army for the Liberation of New Caledonia), set off a 9:45 A.M. bomb in a wastebasket near an elevator in a Charles de Gaulle Airport terminal building, causing some damage. About 13 hours earlier a car in the parking lot had been destroyed by a bomb. No injuries were reported. 81102702

October 29, 1981 — FRANCE — The Kanaka Liberation Front claimed responsibility for the bombing of a central Paris cinema, injuring three people, including a pregnant woman. 81102901

October 29, 1981 — LEBANON — The VOICE OF LEBANON reported that a Palestinian named Abu Nidal died during clashes between the Popular Front for the Liberation of Palestine–General Command and the group Amal in the Burj al-Barajinah section of Beirut. 81102902

October 29, 1981 — COSTA RICA — Three male and two female Nicaraguans, claiming membership in the International Movement to Save Nicaragua from Communism (the Nicaraguan Anti-Communist Democratic Movement), armed with pistols and submachine guns, hijacked a Costa Rican airline SANSA flight 11, a Spanish-made Aviocar flying 3 crewmen and 25 passengers from Quepos to San Jose, after it had landed in San Jose. One of the hijackers fired a few rounds at reporters who tried to approach the plane. The group demanded the release from Costa Rican jails of 7 Nicaraguan prisoners and the broadcast of a communique (which was granted by RADIO RELOJ), or they would kill 1 hostage every hour. The group subsequently let 5 women and 2 children free before their two-hour deadline expired. The pilot, Franco Mora, said one gunman stayed in the cockpit through the negotiations. The group demanded to talk to the United States consul, presidential candidate Mario Echandi Jimenez, former foreign minister Gonzalo Facio Segreda, and second vice president Jose Miguel Alfaro, who received their communique. The Costa Rican Supreme Court met all night and dropped charges against the prisoners whose release was demanded. One prisoner decided to stay in the country, while the rest flew on the hijacked plane via Honduras to El Salvador, where the hijackers and prisoners were arrested on October 30 pending extradition. El Salvador reportedly agreed to extradition on November 2, but AGENCE FRANCE-PRESSE reported that the court system denied extradition on November 16 due to incorrect filing by Costa Rica of the extradition request.

The hijackers registered for the flight as Noel Blandon, Rigoberto Rosales, William Rosales, Yvonne Hunter, and Gurmelda King. Two, whose true names are Carlos Blandon Rojas and Roberto Abauza Gutierrez, had been living in Costa Rica as political exiles. The latter referred to himself as "number one" during the hijacking and had entered Costa Rica on March 7, 1980, after taking refuge in the Colombian embassy in Mana-

gua. To be extradited with them were Hugo Villagra, Jose Eliseo Gutierrez
Sampie (also spelled Guiterrez Amplie), Jose Luis Lopez Gutierrez, Luis
Humberton (also spelled Humberto) Solorzano (also given as Solorzano
Gonzales), Orlando Murillo Gonzalez, and Roger Venevides (also spelled
Benavides) Castellon, the latter for attacks against RADIO NOTICIAS
DEL CONTINENTE. The hijackers were later identified (some incorrectly)
as Wilfredo Espinoza Ramirez, Victor Ramon Huembes (also spelled
Huemberg) Jimenez, Noram (also spelled Norma) Estela Simar (also
spelled Simard) Bravo, Palacios Vega, and Yvonne (also spelled Ivonne)
Hunter Martinez, all former members of the National Guard. The 15 Sep-
tember Legion, an anti-Sandinist group, denied responsibility for the hijacking.

The passengers were identified as John Leupold of Wayland, Massa-
chusetts; John Breen and his wife, Lorraine, of Edgewater, Florida; John
L. Hans Weiz, a Swede; Emiliano Garcia; Odilio Morales; Maria Ramirez;
Victor Prendas; Garardo Munoz; Jesus Diaz; Jose Jimenez; Roberto
Murillo; Edwin Salas; Burnela Chen; Larry and John Brent; Jorge Alfaro;
Andres Chavez; Elizabeth Avilas; Mario Ezquivel; Dennis Hernandez; Ju-
lia Suen; and Philip Rossiter.

On December 5, 1981, San Jose authorities released Nicaraguans Hugo
Jose Guiterrez, Luis Humberton Solorzano, Jose Luis Lopez Gutierrez,
Roger Venevides Castellon, Orlando Murillo Gonzalez, and Jose Eliseo
Gutierrez Sampie. On December 8, 1981, the court arraigned Wilfredo
Espinoza Ramirez, 24, Victor Ramon Huembes Jimenez, 24, Rolando Wil-
liam Zepeda, 29, Yvonne Hunter Martinez, 27, and Noram Estela Simar
Bravo, 23. In his defense, Espinoza said that he had paid Costa Rican
president Carazo five hundred thousand dollars in a "discreet" motel in San
Jose for the release of the political prisoners whose release was later de-
manded. 81102903

November 1981 — SUDAN — The United States State Department reported
that "evidence of a Libyan attempt to plant explosives in the American
Embassy Club in Khartoum was uncovered. . . . Explosives had been concealed in stereo speakers and were to have been set to detonate on a Saturday evening when scores of people would have been killed, including
American and third-country diplomats and their spouses, who frequent the
club on weekends." 81119901

November 2, 1981 — FRANCE — French Navy divers disarmed a 2.2-pound
plastique bomb found below the waterline of the British Royal Navy hydro-
graphic vessel *Hecate* that had been docked in Nantes for three days. The
120 crewmen were evacuated just before dawn when a small explosive went
off on the docks. The Bobby Sands Group (named after the first Irish
Republican Army [IRA] hunger striker to die this year) said it had planted

the device to "support the political and military combat of Irish republicans for freedom and national independence." 81110201

November 3, 1981 — AUSTRIA — VIENNA DOMESTIC TELEVISION reported that Libyan leader Muammar Qaddafi planned terrorist attacks against the United States embassies in London, Paris, Rome, and Vienna.

November 3, 1981 — FRANCE — A police sergeant was killed during a holdup by a group claiming to be inspired by the Direct Action. On March 27, 1986, Bernard Blanc was arrested, and on June 10, 1986, was charged with murder and attempted murder.

November 3, 1981 — SPAIN — The Armenian Secret Army for the Liberation of Armenia (ASALA) bombed the Swissair offices in the Plaza de Espana in Madrid during the evening, slightly injuring three people, including two municipal policemen. Three individuals were arrested. 81110301

November 5, 1981 — FRANCE — The Malheur a la Police (Damn the Police) bombed a coin-operated luggage locker in the Gare de Lyon railroad station in Paris, wrecking 15 lockers and slightly injuring one person. The group also falsely claimed it had placed bombs at the Gare de L'Est and Gare d'Austevit stations. It was protesting Interior Minister Gaston Deferre's denial that the new Socialist administration wanted police to be lax about juvenile delinquency. He had urged police to keep arresting youths who steal and burn cars in factory suburbs. The Orly Group, an Armenian organization, later claimed credit. 81110501

November 6, 1981 — ITALY — Carlo Bozzo and Gianluigi Cristiani, two Red Brigades members who had turned state's evidence, told a Cagliari, Sardinia, court that Palestinian guerrillas had given them a shipment of submachine guns and hand grenades. They also told prosecutor Leonardo Bonsignore that they met with several Palestine Liberation Organization (PLO) dissidents in Mestre, near Venice.

November 6, 1981 — PHILIPPINES — Manila International Airport police arrested a Philippine-born American, Arturo Espiritu Favis, 25, of Sacramento, California, after he arrived from San Francisco with four handguns, a shotgun, three thousand bullets, two hundred capsules of heroin, one-eighth kilo of powdered heroin, and a half-pound box of marijuana leaves that was hidden inside a Campbell's Soup box. Police believed he was a Filipino dissident organization's courier. 81110601

November 6, 1981 — FEDERAL REPUBLIC OF GERMANY — No one was injured when, in the morning hours, a bomb hit an upstairs window of the

Austrian consulate general in Frankfurt and deflected back to the sidewalk, where it exploded and broke several window panes. 81110602

November 7, 1981 — FEDERAL REPUBLIC OF GERMANY — The Croatian Revolutionary Army in Germany bombed the Yugoslav Cultural Center in Stuttgart, causing $75,000 damage but no injuries. 81110701

November 7, 1981 — LEBANON — The VOICE OF LEBANON reported that three non-Lebanese gunmen attempted to kidnap Muhammad Salih al-Madani, the Saudi Arabian embassy's commercial attache, from his official car while he was passing through the Al-Hamra' district of Beirut. Failing in the attempt, they shot him in the leg during the afternoon attack, which coincided with the convocation of the Arab Followup Committee, which was seeking an end to violence in Lebanon. Abu Nidal was suspected. 81110702

November 9, 1981 — SYRIA — A booby-trapped car exploded in the courtyard of a Homs building occupied by Soviet advisers. 81110901

November 10, 1981 — HONDURAS — John R. Olson, 51, the director of the Agency for International Development, was kidnapped by two individuals with .45-caliber pistols about midnight at a gasoline station in Tegucigalpa. The duo took him to San Pedro Sula but fled as a result of a traffic accident in the Guamilito neighborhood, leaving Olson unattended in the car, from which he escaped. 81111001

November 11, 1981 — FRANCE — An Armenian carrying a false Cypriot passport for Dimitriu Giorgiu, 32, and ten thousand Swiss francs was arrested at Orly Airport as he was about to board a plane for Beirut. On November 14, top-level French political authorities ordered the release of the suspected Armenian Secret Army for the Liberation of Armenia (ASALA) militant for "reasons of expediency."

November 12, 1981 — LEBANON — The Orly Group, an Armenian organization, bombed the Air France office and French Cultural Center in Beirut to demand the release of Dimitriu Giorgiu, warning that the French had until 11:00 A.M. Sunday or "French diplomats around the world will be targets." 81111201–02

November 12, 1981 — FRANCE — A gunman about 30 with a black beard and an Arabic appearance fired a 7.65 mm pistol at Christian Chapman, 60, acting United States ambassador to France, as he was walking to his chauffeur-driven Plymouth in the quiet residential Seventh Arrondissement near the Eiffel Tower at 8:45 A.M. The gunman escaped on foot, missing

Chapman but hitting the car three times. The French Foreign Ministry said it had received threats against the United States embassy's personnel. Secretary of the Libyan diplomatic mission in Paris, Said Hafiana, rejected American suggestions of Libyan direction of the attack. The Lebanese Armed Resistance Front (LARF) claimed credit. 81111203

November 13, 1981 — UNITED KINGDOM — The Irish Republican Army (IRA) set off two bombs outside the Wimbledon, London, home of Sir Michael Havers, M.P., Attorney General, who was away with his family at the time. A policewoman was injured. 81111301

November 14, 1981 — FRANCE — The Golfech Antinuclear Army's bomb destroyed a power transformer in Agen. The group warned, "From here on we will strike at city centres."

November 14, 1981 — UNITED KINGDOM — The Irish Republican Army's (IRA's) Belfast Brigade gunmen fired seven shots and killed Rev. Robert Bradford, M.P., 40, who had demanded summary execution of all captured Catholic Irish nationalist terrorists, as he spoke with pensioners at a weekly meeting. Ken Campbell, who rushed to Bradford's aid, also died. The gunmen then ran past children who were attending a community center dance in the next room and escaped in a waiting car as Bradford's bodyguard shot at them. The IRA said Bradford was responsible for a wave of Catholic deaths, calling him "one of the key people responsible for winding up the loyalist paramilitary machine. Let the UDA [Ulster Defense Assocation] know well the cost of killing innocent nationalist people." The next day, Parliament suspended for five days M.P.s Ian Paisley, Peter Robinson, and John McQuade for disrupting a session by accusing Prime Minister Margaret Thatcher of leniency with the IRA.

November 14, 1981 — FRANCE — The Orly Group bombed an automobile parked near the Eiffel Tower to demand the release of Dimitriu Giorgiu, who was released shortly thereafter. 81111401

November 14, 1981 — FRANCE — The Orly Group threw a hand grenade at tourist boats moored in Paris during the night, damaging cars parked nearby but causing no injuries. 81111402

November 15, 1981 — UNITED STATES — Twelve shots were fired into the Glen Cove residence of Oleg Troyanovsky, the Soviet United Nations ambassador, causing no injuries. The Jewish Defense League (JDL) claimed credit, but later JDL chief Meir Kahane denied responsibility, while applauding the action. On November 25, Robert Block, 19, of Bayville, and Evan Burke, 18, of Glen Cove, were charged in Mineola, New York, with reckless endangerment and criminal mischief in a Nassau County court. 81111501

November 15, 1981 — FRANCE — The September France and Orly Group bombed the basement of MacDonald's Restaurant in Paris during the night, causing no injuries. 81111502

November 15, 1981 — LEBANON — The Orly Organization bombed the Beirut offices of Air France, Banque Libano-Francaise, and Union des Assurance de Paris, causing heavy damage but no injuries. 81111503–05

November 16, 1981 — HONDURAS — The right-wing Honduran Anti-Communist Movement set on fire a plane operated by the French volunteer agency Aviation Without Borders, which was scheduled to fly three reporters from Tegucigalpa to the refugee center of La Virtud. 81111601

November 17, 1981 — UNITED STATES — Arsonists caused $1 million damage to the former Nicaraguan embassy, which has been abandoned and partially boarded up since the 1979 overthrow of the Somoza regime. 81111701

November 18, 1981 — BRAZIL — Henry Kissinger, former United States secretary of state, was trapped in a University of Brasilia lecture hall for two hours by four hundred students who shouted anti-United States slogans, burned a United States flag, and lobbed eggs, tomatoes, and rocks at the building in protest of his trip. There were no injuries.

November 18, 1981 — COLOMBIA — The Worker's Self-Defense Movement (MAO) bombed the Bogota Hilton Hotel while an evening cocktail party was being held in honor of two Colombian government officials, injuring three policemen and a civilian. 81111801

November 18, 1981 — FRANCE — Police searched for a bomb at the Gare du Nord railway terminus after receiving a noon warning from the Orly Group. An Orly Group bomb had exploded on November 16 in a luggage locker in the nearby Gare de l'Est railway terminus, wounding two people. The Orly Group also threatened to bomb an Air France jet. The next day, Orly Airport was closed to all traffic, and the control tower cleared after terrorist threats. 81111602, 81111802–03, 81111901

November 20, 1981 — GUATEMALA — The Dominican Sisters of Grand Rapids, Michigan, reported that two of their Sisters, Jean Reimer (in the country for a year) and Helen Lavalley (working in Guatemala for 11 years), had failed to return to their home in Acatenango village with the Reverend Jose Velasquez and a seminarian after attending a church meeting in Panajachel. The Dominican Mother Superior stressed that the sisters were not engaged in political activity, instead doing religious education work and distributing food donated by Caritas. Several Americans and clerics had been kidnapped or murdered recently. 81112001

November 21, 1981 — SPAIN — Unidentified gunmen assassinated a Syrian exile member of the Moslem Brotherhood residing in Barcelona by shooting him twice in the head. Spain had refused several Syrian extradition requests. The Brotherhood claimed that a Syrian hit squad was responsible. 81112101

November 21, 1981 — UNITED STATES — The Justice Commandos of the Armenian Genocide bombed the Turkish consulate in Los Angeles, causing property damage but no injuries. 81112102

November 23, 1981 — UNITED KINGDOM — The Irish Republican Army (IRA) left an explosive device inside a toy gun on the street outside a barracks in suburban Woolwich, London. A dog sniffed it and set it off, injuring two soldiers' wives nearby. 81112301

November 24, 1981 — FRANCE — The Etienne Bandera Ukrainian group firebombed and destroyed two Soviet embassy vehicles parked in a Paris street. Police at first believed the group had called itself "The Rat Pack," but the same pronunciation is that of a 1930s Ukrainian nationalist who was put in charge of a Ukrainian force by the Nazi occupation army. He was disillusioned by the Nazis, who accused him of treason. He was deported at the end of World War II and assassinated in October 1959 in Munich. The group said it was commemorating "the rebirth of the Ukraine." 81112401–02

November 25, 1981 — FEDERAL REPUBLIC OF GERMANY — The Irish Republican Army (IRA) was believed responsible for bombing the British Army barracks in Herford, damaging the wall of an apartment building and injuring a soldier who was treated for shock. 81112501

November 25, 1981 — SEYCHELLES — An Air India B-707 flying 65 passengers and 14 crew members from Harare, Zimbabwe, to Bombay, India, touched down at Point Larue Airport in the Seychelles, where it was taken over at 10:00 P.M. by 45 mercenaries who were participating at the time in an abortive attempt to overthrow the left-leaning government of President Albert France Rene. The mercenaries, led by Irish-born former British military officer Col. Michael "Mad Mike" Hoare, at first demanded to go to Oman or Switzerland but settled for South Africa. The plane flew to Johannesburg but was forced to land in Durban, where negotiations lasted for 6 hours until the mercenaries surrendered to authorities, with no injuries reported to the hostages. Le Mouvement Pour la Resistance claimed credit for the coup attempt from London.

The mercenaries had arrived in Seychelles from South Africa by driving into Swaziland, posing as hard-drinking vacationing rugby players. They took a Royal Air Swazi Fokker F-28 flight to Seychelles, which landed at 5:30 P.M. While South African Johan Fritz's comrades proceeded through the customs lines, he mistakenly went into the "to declare" line. A customs inspector found an automatic weapon in a hidden compartment of the suitcase Fritz was carrying. The rest of the mercenaries pulled out their grenades, rocket launchers, and submachine guns, and took 100 hostages in the airport. Hoare and 13 other mercenaries got into two cars and drove toward a Seychelles military barracks. While on the way, they fired on a Tanzanian military camp, killing one Tanzanian soldier. The Tanzanians fired back, forcing the cars to return to the airport. Hoare telephoned the pilot of the Royal Swazi plane, who refused to fly the attackers out of the country. During the 20-hour gun battle, in which North Koreans reportedly aided the Seychellois, the Royal Swazi jet was hit by two rocket-propelled grenades fired by the Seychelles People's Defense Force. Fritz was killed in the shooting, and 2 other mercenaries were wounded. One Seychellois military officer died in the shooting. The mercenaries, who had seized the control tower, apparently talked Air India pilot Umesh Saxena into landing. The mercenaries reportedly were quite polite to the passengers on board the plane and were credited by many of them with saving their lives.

Hoare, 62, a former Congo mercenary, said that he recruited the team for deposed Seychelles president Robert Mancham. In his testimony in May 1982, Hoare said South African National Intelligence Service (NIS) agent Martin Dolinchek introduced him to the chief of the NIS, Alec van Wyk, and his deputy, N. J. Claassen, to discuss the coup plans. The South African cabinet turned down the mercenaries' proposal for South African assistance, but Hoare claimed Prime Minister P. W. Botha approved military intelligence assistance. Hoare claimed he received Russian-made weapons and other aid from two South African military intelligence brigadiers. The South African courts rejected any implication of government foreknowledge or approval of the coup. Various reports indicated Seychellois exiles or an Arab businessman bankrolled the operation. Hoare recruited 3 colleagues from the Five Commando of his famous Wild Geese of the Congo wars: Tullio Moneta, Peter Duffy, and Jeremiah Puren. About half of the mercenaries were South Africans, many either active or reserve members of the South African police or defense forces. One of the mercenaries, Richard Stannard, had recently been decorated for bravery in action. At least 1 mercenary was a former member of a special South African commando force. An American, Barry Francis Gribbon, 26, of Miami (one of the wounded), was a United States Army veteran of Vietnam who had also served in the Rhodesian civil war. The group included former members of the Rhodesian Selous Scouts, the Rhodesian Light Infantry, and the Special Service Battalion.

The South Africans initially charged only 5 of the captured mercenaries with kidnapping, rather than hijacking: Hoare; Peter S. Duffy, 40, a Briton; Charles Glen Coatley, 27, a Zimbabwean; Tullio Moneta, 42, a South African born in Yugoslavia of Italian parents; and Kenneth H. Dalgliesh, 32, a former British intelligence agent, all of whom were released on bail December 1. The other mercenaries were released unconditionally. President Rene demanded their return to the Seychelles as a sign of good faith that the South Africans had no official part in the coup attempt. After Western pressure, which included the possibility of invoking the Bonn declaration of boycotting commercial flights to countries aiding hijackers, the South African government rearrested all 45 mercenaries for hijacking on January 5, 1982. On July 26, Hoare was found guilty on three charges, as was South African free-lance press photographer Peter Duffy. Hoare's second in command, Moneta, and 5 others were found guilty of the single charge of jeopardizing the Air India plane and passengers. Charles Dukes, 25, the American Vietnam veteran, was acquitted of hijacking, although he had done most of the fighting in the Seychelles. Severely wounded, he was drugged with morphine before being put on the plane and spent most of the flight unconscious. On July 29, 1982, Hoare was sentenced to 20 years, with 20 years suspended. Seven others received 1 to 5 years. The remaining 34, including Gribbon, called by Judge Neville James "basically decent people who have fallen for the lure of easy money, adventure and comradeship," received 5 years, all but 6 months suspended. On August 5, 1982, the South African Supreme Court blocked Hoare's appeal.

The Seychelles news agency initially said that 10 South African mercenaries were captured on the island, while several others were still hiding out in the hills. President Rene suspected foreknowledge of Kenyan minister of constitutional and home affairs Charles Njonjo. The Seychellois claimed South African Susan Ingles, 48, handled the money locally for the operation in the Seychelles. On June 21, 1982, 4 of the group of 3 South Africans, 2 Zimbabweans, and a Briton pleaded guilty to charges of high treason and waging war against the Seychelles. On July 5, 1982, death sentences were passed on Aubrey Brooks, 28, from Zimbabwe; Roger England, 27, from Zimbabwe; Bernard Carey, 39, the Briton; and Jeremiah Puren, 57, from South Africa, all of whom had pleaded guilty. Martin Dolincheck, 42, the NIS agent, received 20 years. On July 7, the Seychelles High Court jailed South African Robert Sims for 10 years for arms smuggling.

On November 27, 1982, South Africa released 34 of the 42 mercenaries.

On July 22, 1983, Seychelles president France Albert Rene pardoned 6 foreign mercenaries, including 4 who had been sentenced to death. The released mercenaries were reunited with their families at South Africa's Jan Smuts Airport on July 23. The 2 Britons were given permission to stay in the country for only 14 days. Jerry Puren said that big business interests, and not the South African government, had supported the coup attempt that was carried out by supporters of former president Robert Mancham.

According to the JOHANNESBURG SUNDAY TIMES, "In the middle of their detention another abortive coup—this time involving Seychellois—took place. The mercenaries were offered a fleeting apparition of freedom by the rebels—if they agreed to help topple Rene. The mercenaries refused. Partly in consideration of that action President Albert Rene announced on Friday the pardon and release of the men."

November 27, 1981—ITALY—Four bombs exploded in Merano a few days before the German-speaking South Tyrol People's Party was scheduled to hold its annual congress. A fifth bomb went off at nearby Bressanone near the Austrian border. No casualties and only minor damage were reported.

November 29, 1981—KAMPUCHEA—The VOICE OF DEMOCRATIC KAMPUCHEA claimed that its guerrillas had ambushed a Vietnamese vehicle moving from Kompong Som port to Phnom Penh along route 4 near 0 Chamnar village, destroying the vehicle and killing one Vietnamese and four Soviets.

November 29, 1981—SYRIA—At 11:30 A.M., a Damascus security officer noticed an individual suspiciously leaving a car near a military recruiting center. When the individual pulled a gun after being ordered to stop, the security guard shot him dead. Minutes later, the booby-trapped car exploded, killing 90 and wounding 135 others, mostly civilians, and demolishing 3 five-story buildings while badly damaging about 10 others. The Front for the Liberation of Lebanon from Foreigners took credit, but the government blamed the Moslem Brotherhood. "We do not exclude the possibility that the crime committed by the Moslem brothers in Damascus . . . is a prelude to the arrival of US envoy Philip Habib . . . and part of a campaign to put pressure on Syria to promote capitulationist solutions which Washington and its allies are struggling to impose on the Arabs." 81112901

December 1981—UNITED STATES—The WASHINGTON POST reported that the Immigration and Naturalization Service had been given intelligence from "a host of sophisticated intelligence-collection capabilities" warning against the entry of two Libyan-sponsored hit teams targeting President Reagan and other high government officials. The first group was reportedly led by Popular Front for the Liberation of Palestine (PFLP) Venezuelan terrorist Carlos, and included three Syrians and three Libyans. The second team comprised two Iranians, a Palestinian, a Lebanese, and an East German. The names of some of the individuals were given as Ahmat Abass, Ali Chafic, Luitz Schewesman, Ahmed Jooma, and El Haya. Some reports had the teams in Mexico or Canada. 81129901

December 1, 1981 — EL SALVADOR — A United States embassy military advisor was unhurt when gunmen opened fire from a passing vehicle as he was driving to work. Several guerrilla groups claimed credit for the machine gun attack in San Salvador. 81120101

December 3, 1981 — FRANCE — Two Socialist members of the Chamber of Deputies received envelopes containing bullets and threatening letters; others received intimidating letters.

December 4, 1981 — FEDERAL REPUBLIC OF GERMANY — The Dusseldorf Court sentenced Baader-Meinhof Gang member Stefan Wisniewski, 28, to life imprisonment for the 1977 murder of industrialist Hanns-Martin Schleyer and his four bodyguards. Wisniewski was arrested on May 11, 1978.

December 4, 1981 — LEBANON — Ten massive time bombs were defused by Lebanese police before they could explode. Eight of them were close to a roadblock of the Syrian peacekeeping force or near the Kuwaiti embassy. They were connected to 150 rocket-propelled grenades, and, according to security officials, would have destroyed "everything within a radius of one mile and probably parts of the airport." Another bomb, containing 47 sticks of dynamite, was dismantled on Hamra Street, Beirut's busiest shopping district, before it was set to go off at 8:00 A.M. Another bomb was discovered outside the Lebanese Evangelical School for Girls. 81120401

December 5, 1981 — NORWAY — A voice analysis of a tape-recorded phone call indicated an Arab had told police that a North Sea oil rig would be blown up. Police alerted all oil rigs on the Norwegian and British continental shelf. Police discounted a London report of Palestine Liberation Organization (PLO) involvement. 81120501

December 5, 1981 — UNITED STATES — A flight engineer subdued a man attempting to hijack Trans World Airlines Flight 534 on the ground at Cleveland's Hopkins Airport. Passengers were transferred to another plane, which took off to New York. Federal Bureau of Investigation spokesman said the man, who was taken into custody, "was not a ticketed passenger. He bolted onto the plane and claimed (incorrectly) he had a bomb." 81120502

December 6, 1981 — AFGHANISTAN — Four rifle-toting men dressed in traditional Afghan garb ordered two Afghan employees of the United States embassy to drive their United States embassy carryall south. The duo were held overnight, interrogated, given a "thank you" note and a "receipt" for the vehicle, then released unharmed the next morning.

December 7, 1981 — VENEZUELA — About a dozen hooded men carrying hand grenades and automatic weapons hijacked three Venezuelan airliners, taking a circuitous 10,000-mile trip to Havana. Claiming membership in the previously unknown Ramon Emeterio Betances (a 19th-century Puerto Rican leader) Puerto Rico Independence Commandos, the three hijacking leaders referred to themselves only as commanders 9, 10, and 11 and claimed that there were at least 10 hijackers on each plane. They expressed support for several Latin leftist causes and wore Spanish arm bands that said El Salvador Will Win.

The hijackings began with the seizure of an Aeropostal DC-9 that had left Caracas for Barcelona, Venezuela. Another Aeropostal DC-9 was hijacked from Puerto Ordaz, on its way to Guyana City. It landed in Aruba, where 21 passengers were permitted to disembark. The third plane, an Avensa B-727-200 on its way from Caracas to San Antonio, Venezuela, joined the other planes at Ernesto Cortizo Airport in Barranquilla, Colombia. The planes, which carried 262 passengers among them, landed between 6:30 and 8:32 A.M.

The hijackers, deeming their act the Manuel Rojas Luzardo International Solidarity Operation, demanded refueling, food, medicine, and maps showing air routes to all Central American countries. Although they permitted 77 passengers, mostly women and children, to deplane, they threatened to set off explosives if their demands for directions to the Latin cities were not met. The group also demanded $10 million: $5 million in $100 bills of different series, and $5 million in 50s, 20s, and 10s of different series. They also called for the publication of their proclamation in the main newspapers of Venezuela, El Salvador, Guatemala, and Honduras, and the reading of their text on Venezuelan radio and television every 30 minutes. In addition, they demanded the release of Venezuelan political prisoners being held at the San Carlos barracks in Caracas, in La Pica Prison in Monagas State, in Modelo Jail of Caracas, and in El Dorado Prison in Bolivar State. Among others, they demanded the release of Ivan Padilla, Carlos Lang Pedrovich, Miguel Radas, Rafael Pina, Luis Soto, Ruben Gomez, Carlos Mesto, Jose Luis Dominguez, Humberto Sanchez, Antonio Arias, Pedro Moreno, Franklin Navas Chinchilla, and Ignacio Pacheco.

After 10 hours of negotiations, two of the planes flew to Tegucigalpa, Honduras, where the hijackers requested the presence of the Venezuelan ambassador and papal nuncio. One of the planes had touched down at El

Salvador's international airport for 10 minutes before going to Honduras. The third plane flew to Guatemala City. All three then proceeded to Panama, then to Havana, where the remaining 83 passengers and 19 crewmen were released. Havana authorities said the hijackers would appear before "pertinent courts." None of the hostages were injured, and they returned to Maiquetia Airport in Venezuela on December 9.

The Faribundo Marti National Liberation Organization (FMLN) denied responsibility for the hijacking. On April 9, 1982, Venezuelan police arrested Gabriel Puerta Aponte, Red Flag leader, who claimed his organization was not involved. "I believe (the hijacking) was organized by a Caribbean tropical power. The person who was responsible was a Venezuelan who works for the Cuban secret police." 81120701–03

December 7, 1981 — SWITZERLAND — Three Lebanese Moslem gunmen hijacked a Libyan B-727 flying 44 passengers and crew to Tripoli from Zurich and diverted it to Beirut, where they demanded that Libya announce the whereabouts of Imam Musa as-Sadr, who was last seen alive in Libya in 1978. The Kuwaiti news service KUNA said the hijackers left the plane when it landed in Beirut and were joined by two others. They were, according to KUNA, then replaced by 10 Shiite militiamen deployed by the Amal. "Amal militiamen," KUNA claimed, "stormed the airport's control tower, the power station, and removed fire brigade water tankers from the runways to facilitate the landing." Shouting, "Death to Qaddafi, the imperialist agent," the hijackers claimed they had shot and wounded 1 hostage and would kill the rest if their demands were not met. Beirut airport officials claimed they had heard two shots ring out on board the plane. After refueling, the plane flew to Athens, where a pregnant woman and 2 children were released. The plane flew to Rome, then back to Beirut. Amal militiamen took hostage 30 passengers deplaning from a flight from London and held them while the plane again refueled. The hijackers next landed in Tehran at 6:30 P.M., where Iranian officials pledged to mediate the hijackers' demands for information. On December 8, the plane again landed in Beirut, at 7:30 P.M. The hijackers demanded the presence of Lebanese premier Shafiq al-Wazzan but settled for Gen. al-Haj, head of the internal security forces, who negotiated indirectly. On December 9, the passengers were released unharmed. The hijackers surrendered to Nabih Berri, head of the Shi'a Amal Movement, and Syrian colonel Muhammad Ghanim, intelligence chief of the Syrian peacekeeping troops, at 0:20 A.M. Per agreement with the hijackers, the passengers and plane left for Larnaca, Cyprus. 81120704

December 7, 1981 — LEBANON — Two gunmen walked into the Beirut office of former Arab Liberation Front chief Abd al-Wahhab al-Kayyali, shot him dead, then escaped in a waiting car at 10:00 A.M. The VOICE OF

PALESTINE accused "criminal Zionist agents" of having assassinated the 42-year-old owner of the Institute for Arab Studies and director of the Third World Center in London. Kayyali was felled by 11 bullets. He had been living in London for three years with his American wife and their two young daughters. 81120705

December 7, 1981 — FEDERAL REPUBLIC OF GERMANY — A bomb was thrown through the window of a United States Army unit commander's office near Kassel, injuring two soldiers. Only the detonator of the fire extinguisher packed with explosives exploded. 81120706

December 8, 1981 — JAPAN — A guard at the United States consulate in Kobe challenged a man holding two lit torches and wood at the door. The individual tossed the torches into a puddle of kerosene, then escaped over the consulate fence. The guard quickly extinguished the fire. 81120801

December 8, 1981 — LEBANON — A bomb hidden in a fruit cart killed one man and injured four others when it exploded near the Beirut residence of French ambassador March-Henry, who had been in town only a week. His predecessor was killed in September. 81120802

December 9, 1981 — SUDAN — Khartoum's SUNA news service reported that Libya had instigated threats against Sudanese diplomatic missions in Bonn, Washington, and Kuwait. 81120901–03

December 10, 1981 — LEBANON — The Armenian Secret Army for the Liberation of Armenia (ASALA) threatened to "attack all French institutions if the government does not respect its undertaking and grant political asylum" to four ASALA members who took over the Turkish embassy in September. The group's press conference included Dimitriu Giorgiu, who was released from French custody earlier in the week after being arrested in November at Orly Airport while carrying a false passport. The ASALA denounced "collusion between Turkish fascism, Zionism, the French pseudo-socialist Government, and American imperialism." 81121001

December 12, 1981 — UNITED STATES — The United States extradited to Israel 21-year-old Ziad Abu Eain, who was accused of the May 14, 1979, bombing of a Tiberias marketplace in which 2 were killed and 36 injured.

December 12, 1981 — MEXICO — Police believe a bomb was responsible for an explosion that ripped through an Aeronica B-727 at 12:40 P.M. on the ground at Mexico City's Benito Juarez Airport, wounding pilot Capt. Agustin Roman, stewardess Matilde Sitoya, and two Aeromexico workers, Miguel Soto and Jaime Gutierrez. 81121201

December 12, 1981 — GUATEMALA — The Guerrilla Army of the Poor (EGP) shot and killed Maximiliano Sosa Zecena, local bodyguard for United States ambassador Frederic Chapin, in an ambush on the highway to Escuintla during the afternoon. Sosa's brother and a companion shot and killed two of the guerrillas, who were found inside an automobile some yards from the scene. 81121202

December 13, 1981 — UNITED KINGDOM — A bomb apparently being transported in a Datsun exploded in London's Connaught Square, killing two of the Iranian terrorists and seriously wounding a third, who were trapped inside the car. The owner of the car acknowledged lending it to a friend, Kolosh Foladi, 19. 81121301

December 13, 1981 — GREECE — A bomb was thrown by the Autonomous Resistance from a car at the Soviet Trade Mission in Athens, causing only minor damage. 81121302

December 14, 1981 — TURKEY — Abu Firas (Fadl Shrur), Palestine Liberation Organization (PLO) representative in Ankara, said,

> Palestinians in the United States are living under continuous threat and the danger of being turned over to Israel. . . . A student named Ziyad Abu 'Ayn who was studying in the United States was turned over to Israel by the US administration. . . . The incident is not the problem of only one student. We believe that no power in the world can halt the Palestinian people. We will protect our citizens' rights wherever they are. . . . The retaliation against the United States will be determined and carried out in the most appropriate place and at a most appropriate time. The only guilty party in the handing over of the Palestinian student is the US administration and it will bear the consequences. We know there are US interests in the Middle East and we will strike a blow to these interests. . . . This crime will lead to more crimes and Reagan and the US administration will be responsible for them.

December 14, 1981 — PERU — A stick of dynamite was thrown at the Sheraton-Lima Hotel, damaging the building and adjacent sidewalk but causing no injuries. 81121401

December 15, 1981 — LEBANON — A man driving an explosives-laden car crashed into the building housing the Iraqi embassy, setting off two noon explosions that toppled the five-story building, killing 61, including the Iraqi press attache, Haress Taqa, and injuring over 100, including Khaled Gheidan, chief of the Iraqi News Agency. Guards shot and killed the man before the explosion but were too late to prevent the car's momentum from finishing the job. Scores of people were buried in the rubble. Iraqi ambassador Abdel Razzal Mohammed Lafta was in a nearby building and escaped unharmed. The blast was claimed by the Army for the Liberation of Kurdistan as well as by the Iraqi Liberation Army–General Command; Iraq blamed Syrian and Iranian intelligence agents. Local news services claimed that two days before the explosion, 4 persons reconnoitered the embassy from a black Buick, a station wagon, and another vehicle. The group was led by Col. Al-Jabali, according to the VOICE OF LEBANON. The station also claimed that five charges, each containing 20 kilograms of explosives, were involved.

On July 26, 1985, AGENCE FRANCE-PRESSE in Paris reported that

A Lebanese military prosecutor has called for the death penalty against two Lebanese, a Palestinian and an Egyptian accused of involvement in suicide bomb attacks against the US and Iraqi embassies here in which 112 people died, legal sources said today. The 4 men were identified by the sources as Husayn Salim Harb, 40, and Mahmud Musa al-Daraki, 42, both Lebanese, an Egyptian, Sami Mahmud al-Haji, 47, and a Palestinian, Muhammad Nayif al-Zadah, whose age was not known.

They were accused of abetting the April 18, 1983, attack on the US Embassy in Beirut, in which a bomb-laden truck crashed into the building and exploded, killing 64 people and injuring 123. The attack was claimed by the Islamic Jihad, a Moslem fundamentalist group that has been linked with Iran.

Husayn Salih Harb and Sami Mahmud al-Haji are also accused of involvement in another bomb attack, on December 15, 1981, against the Iraqi Embassy. . . .

Legal sources said that the charges had been filed by the prosecutor, known in the Lebanese system as an examining magistrate, with a military tribunal but a date had yet to be set for the trial.

81121501

December 17, 1981 — UNITED STATES — Secret Service agents disarmed a six-by-nine-inch manila envelope containing a letter bomb mailed to President Ronald Reagan from San Juan, Puerto Rico, at 1:30 P.M., in the White House mail room. 81121703

December 17, 1981 — MOZAMBIQUE — Anticommunist National Resistance Movement guerrillas kidnapped Briton John Burlison, director of the Chitengo Wildlife School, and Chilean math teacher Moises Carril, along with 20 local employees, from the Gorongosa animal preserve, 115 miles west of the port of Beira. Carril was released on November 14, 1982, in Mushokwana. 81121701

December 17, 1981 — ITALY — Members of the Red Brigades (RB) posing as plumbers kidnapped Brig. Gen. James Lee Dozier, 50, from his home at 5:30 P.M. Dozier was senior United States officer at NATO southern Europe ground forces base in Verona, Italy, and deputy chief of staff for logistics and administration. One of the kidnappers hit Dozier over the head with a pistol butt, then threw him into a trunk, which the kidnappers dragged to a waiting van, a rented blue Fiat. They tied the hands and feet of his wife, Judith, 47, with chains and covered her mouth and eyes with adhesive tape. The group searched the apartment for guns and documents. Police later said the group of 4 in the house were aided by 4 others who were in contact by radio. One of the attackers was a woman.

President Ronald Reagan called the kidnappers "cowardly bums. . . . They aren't heroes, or they don't have a cause that justifies what they're doing."

On December 18, a Red Brigades caller said the kidnapping was organized by the Venetian Column, and that branches from Milan, Naples, and Rome had participated in the kidnapping of the "hangman." This was the first Red Brigades operation against a military officer and against a foreigner.

On December 19, a 6-page mimeographed document was found in a Rome garbage pail after an anonymous phone call was placed. The document described United States military personnel as an "occupation army" and called for war against NATO and "the American military Machine" in "communique no. 1." The Red Brigades would go on to praise the West German Red Army Faction and the Irish Republican Army. The RBs called for closer ties to "other European revolutionary forces" and for solidarity with French political prisoners. The group said only an "anti-imperialist civil war can wipe out war. War against imperialist war is an essential passage for the transition to communism."

On December 20, 6 United States Department of Defense antiterrorist specialists joined Italian forces in the nationwide manhunt for Dozier.

On December 22, a caller speaking perfect Arabic told the Italian ANSA news agency in Beirut that "the Red Brigades of the Baader-Meinhof claim responsibility for the death sentence and execution of the American General, James Dozier, found guilty by a people's tribunal. The corpse of the American pig is in a country village and the police will find it after 8 p.m." In Bonn the Italian news agency ANSA received a nearly incomprehensible telex message in English addressed to "China Cooper and Dr. Trimble car of the audio-optical division Washington," and signed "condolences for and from another victim, James Lee Dozier." Police attributed the message to cranks.

On December 24, police arrested Pasqua Aurora Betti, 34, a former schoolmistress believed to command the RB's Milan cell, along with another suspect in the case.

On December 27, the Red Brigades left a photo of Dozier, a communique saying his trial had begun, and a 188-page "strategic resolution" in a gift-wrapped package tied with a yellow ribbon, in a trash can.

On January 2, 1982, a group describing themselves as "friends" of Dozier offered L 2 billion ($1.67 million) for information leading to his release. They vowed not to give the money to the RBs. The United States and Italy reiterated that they would not negotiate with the kidnappers, although no demands for his release had been made.

On January 3, police said the RBs may have failed to kidnap Gen. Wilson C. Cooney, vice commander of the 5th Allied Tactical Air Force base at Vicenza, about 28 miles northeast of Verona, where Dozier was kidnapped. A description of the man who rented the Dozier kidnap van was similar to that of a man seen trying to enter Cooney's Vicenza home under false pretenses about 2 weeks before the Dozier kidnapping.

Also on January 3, Red Brigades blasted open a five-foot hole in a wall of the Rovigo women's prison, killing a passerby, carpenter Angelo Furlan, and injuring 6 others, while freeing Sussana Ronconi, 28 (who was arrested 13 months earlier), Marina Premoli, Federica Meroni, and Loredana Biancamano. After the blast, the attackers passed weapons to their confreres inside the wall. Three of 4 men exchanged submachine-gun fire with police guards before all escaped in several autos.

On January 4, police arrested Stefano Petrella and Ennio di Rocco after a gunfight and chase near the Spanish Steps. Police believed they were preparing the kidnapping of Cesare Romiti, managing director of Fiat. Defense lawyers said a week later that the duo, who had provided information about RB hideouts, had been beaten and tortured for 5 days.

On January 7, anonymous callers said the RBs had killed Dozier, and his body would be found in a farmhouse near Pescara, in central Italy. Meanwhile, the RBs left a 7-page statement describing Dozier's "interrogation" in Padua and Rome.

On January 9, police arrested alleged RB political mastermind Giovanni Senzani, 40, in an east Rome tenement building, along with Franca Musi, accused of being a courier. Police made three other dawn raids on Rome hideouts, arresting 9 others and finding French and Soviet arms, including ground-to-air missiles, bazookas, and rocket-propelled grenades. Senzani, a former Florence University criminology professor, headed the Rome and Naples cells of the RBs. He had been an adviser to the Justice Ministry, where Judge Giovanni d'Urso was a top official. He vanished shortly after the kidnapping of d'Urso, who was later released unharmed. Investigators believed the reason Senzani and his group were betrayed by the northern RB "militarists" was the capture of di Rocco and Petrella.

On January 12, police said documents seized in weekend raids showed the RBs planned to attack the national headquarters of the governing Christian Democrats in Rome. The same day, police arrested Prof.

Fernando Iannetti, 42, lecturer in moral philosophy at the University of Salerno and friend of Senzani, in his Formia apartment. Police believed Ianetti's apartment, the "cold hideout," was to be used for the kidnapping of Romiti.

On January 25, the RBs released their fifth communique and a Polaroid snapshot of a now heavily bearded Dozier to indicate that he was still alive. The 6-page communique said, "Negotiate? Whatever for? The proletariat has nothing to negotiate with the bourgeoisie."

On January 28, a 10-member special police rescue squad stormed a second-floor apartment of the nine-story Via Piedmonte 2 building in Padua and freed Dozier after a 42-day ordeal. One terrorist, Giovanni Ciucci, 32, was holding a pistol to Dozier's head. A member of the Special Agents for Security Operations of the Interior Ministry felled Ciucci with a blow to the head, and the remaining 2 men and 2 women gave up. No shot was fired in the 90-second rescue mission. Dozier was found blindfolded, bound, his ears stuffed with wax, lying in a tent set up in the living room. The other kidnappers were identified as Antonio Savasta, 27, and his girlfriend, Emilia Libera, 21, who were both sentenced the next day to 30 years for their role in a 1980 shoot-out in Sardinia. With them were Emanuela Frascella (also spelled Frasella), 21, and Cesare Leonardo (also spelled Di Leonardo, di Lenardo), 22. The apartment had been under surveillance for 3 days by 80 plainclothes agents before the 11:36 A.M. raid, which followed a tip-off. The raid, the first time that Italian police have succeeded in locating and freeing an RB prisoner, netted 5 pistols, 15 submachine guns, 7 hand grenades, 6 packets of plastic explosive, ammunition, $16,000 in lira, several typewriters, a mimeo machine, false identity cards, and file cards with information about prominent Veneto persons. The apartment had been rented by a Padua lung specialist for Frascella, who had done the shopping for the group. Police had been told to expect 8 terrorists.

Savasta, Dozier's inquisitor, reportedly smuggled guns from Lebanon in 1979. Dozier said the group was rather amateurish and used poor English. They did not try to extract military secrets from him. His biggest confrontation with them was over the kind and volume of music to which he was forced to listen. Savasta turned state's evidence, being one of several "repentant" terrorists to profit from a new law for "turned" terrorists that led to the arrests of 200 terrorist suspects.

On January 29, Italian police discovered eight new hideouts and arrested 23 more RBs.

On January 30, ANSA said Ciucci had spent time in Libya at a paramilitary training camp.

Most Italian newspapers said a leftist extremist drug addict was among 40 arrested on January 22–23 in Verona. One of those arrested, Luigi Damoli, was released then picked up later when weapons were found in a search of his apartment. Damoli gave police the name of Paolo Galati, 22, a heroin addict and extremist with 2 brothers, one a suspected drug dealer and another, Michele, who was jailed for Red Brigades activities. Galati allegedly provided the Padua apartment address after a confrontation with Stefano Petrella. According to ANSA, police also got Galati's name from Massimiliano Corsi, RB member arrested on January 10 for participating in the shooting and attempted kidnapping of Rome's deputy police chief, Nicola Simone, a few days earlier.

On March 25, 1982, a Verona court sentenced 17 RBs for the kidnapping. Lo Bianco, Balzarani (also spelled Balzerani), Catabiani, Antonini, Novelli, Remo Pancelli, 36, all in hiding and all members of the RB's strategic leadership, received 26 years. Vanzi, in hiding, received 26½ years. Antonio Savasta received 16½ years. Emilia Libera received 14 years. Emanuela Frascella received 13½ years; Giovanni Ciucci, 14 years. Repentant defendant Leonardo received 27 years; repentant Armando Lanza 12 years, 2 months. Roberta Zanca, the RB nurse, received 12 years. Alberto Biatola received 17½ years. Ruggero Violinia received 2 years and 2 months after aiding in dismantling the Venetian Column, under Article 4 of the so-called Cossiga Law.

On May 24, a Dozier kidnapper sentenced in absentia was killed during a shoot-out with Pisa police.

On May 29, police shot and captured Marcello Capuano, sentenced in absentia to 26½ years, after a running gun battle in which a bystander was seriously wounded.

On December 21, 1982, the appeal of 16 RBs sentenced for the kidnapping began in Venice as police investigated the claims of Antonio Savasta, repentant RB, that Bulgarian intelligence had proposed liaising with the RBs over the kidnapping. Luigi Scricciolo, recently arrested, was allegedly involved as a unionist contact. Police reported having arrested 1,357 terrorists since the end of the Dozier kidnapping.

On July 15, 1983, Rome's ANSA news service reported that

> Four members of the Italian police's crack anti-terrorist squad were found guilty here [in Padua] today of torturing a member of the Red Brigades captured when the unit released US General James Lee Dozier from a RB hideout in January last year. Di Lenardo was found with other RB members in the flat where the urban guerrilla group held the high-ranking NATO official after kidnapping him in Verona, the city where NATO command for Southeast Europe is located.
>
> The four—Danilo Amore, Giancarlo Aralla, Carmelo di Janni, and Fabio Laurenzi—received light sentences ranging from a year to 14 months plus a ban from public office and damages of about $60.
>
> The RB member, Cesare di Lenardo, was burned with cigarettes, beaten and had electrodes applied to his genitals. He also said he had been put through a fake execution in a field near Padua.
>
> The public prosecutor had called for an "exemplary" sentence to

strengthen confidence in the law, earning praise from President Sandro Pertini, who said yesterday that Italy had fought terrorism with "ordinary law and democracy."

On October 14, 1985, AGENCE FRANCE-PRESSE in Paris reported that a Verona court sentenced 5 RB members to 26 years in prison: "A leading figure of the Red Brigades, Barbara Balzarani, who was arrested a few months ago and has been sentenced to life in prison on several other charges of terrorist attacks, was among the five. After the verdict was read, Balzarani shouted, 'The Red Brigades are not finished, they exist and have international connections.' The five . . . had already faced trial in 1982. They were sentenced to 27 years in jail but an appeals court had found that the case contained irregularities, and the sentence was repealed." 81121702

December 18, 1981 — ZIMBABWE — A bomb placed in a top-floor boardroom exploded in the headquarters of Zimbabwe's ruling ZANU party in Harare, killing 6 persons in the next-door bakery and wounding between 120 and 150, including a woman, Senator Sunny Takawira.

December 19–20, 1981 — LEBANON — A time bomb hidden in a pickup truck exploded in a Beirut residential neighborhood, killing 5 policemen and 6 pedestrians. The next day, 2 persons died when a bomb exploded in their Mercedes as it was turning a corner in an area where several Palestinian and Lebanese leftist groups have offices. The blasts brought to 211 the number of persons killed in a spate of bombings in Lebanon since September 17.

December 20, 1981 — FRANCE — The Paris offices of Botrans, a Polish freight company, were badly damaged in an attack claimed by the far-right Carles Martel Group and later by the Bakunin Gdansk Paris Group. 81122001

December 20, 1981 — GUATEMALA — The Roque Dalton Command, a Salvadoran group, firebombed the Salvadoran consulate. 81122002

December 20, 1981 — FEDERAL REPUBLIC OF GERMANY — Police were uncertain whether the blast in Schwabach that blew up the car of a member of Britain's Rhine Army who worked with explosives and killed its driver was accidental or intentional. 81122003

December 20, 1981 — LEBANON — The Armenian Secret Army for the Liberation of Armenia (ASALA) from Beirut said it would attack Swiss interests and representatives if the Swiss did not reconsider the murder conviction of an ASALA member within a week. 81122004

December 23, 1981 — FRANCE — Direct Action set off four bombs before dawn in Paris, damaging a Rolls-Royce showroom, two stores, and a restaurant. 81122301

December 26, 1981 — FEDERAL REPUBLIC OF GERMANY — Police dismantled a bomb consisting of a tin can containing explosives and a fuse, which had been found at the Soviet ambassador's home in Bad Godesberg. A caller said his group was protesting and marking the second anniversary of the Soviet invasion of Afghanistan. Ambassador Vladimir Semyonev was spending the holidays in Moscow. 81122601

December 29, 1981 — SPAIN — Two men abducted Dr. Julio Iglesias Puga, 66, father of famed Spanish singer Julio Iglesias, outside a Madrid travel agency. They demanded $2 million on January 7 from the doctor's attorney in Madrid, Fernando Bernaldez. The money was to be in cash, half in Spanish pesetas and half in dollars. The singer drained his Miami account of $1 million and flew it to Madrid, where the rest of the money was waiting. On January 17, 150 Spanish antiterrorist police freed the hostage from a house in Trasmoz and arrested 4 members of the political-military branch of the Basque separatist ETA (Basque Nation and Liberty). Police initially thought the kidnappers were Latin Americans. Nine other ETA members connected with the kidnapping were arrested the previous week.

December 29, 1981 — PHILIPPINES — Tomas Manotoc, 33, a professional basketball coach, top amateur golfer, and purported son-in-law of Philippine president Ferdinand Marcos, was kidnapped outside his parents' home while driving home from a restaurant after dining with Maria Imelda Imee Marcos, 26, the President's daughter. The two had been secretly married in Arlington, Virginia, on December 4. He was estranged from his first wife, Aurora Pijuan, by whom he had two children. He had arranged for Swiss and Vatican annulments of his first marriage the previous month, since divorce is not recognized in the predominantly Catholic Philippines; but he had obtained a Dominican Republic divorce. Some sources speculated that the Marcos family, displeased by the marriage, had arranged the kidnapping. Manotoc was the nephew of two anti-Marcos exiles who lived in Washington: Raul Manglapus, head of the Movement for a Free Philippines, and ex–newspaper publisher Eugenio Lopez. On January 2, the family of Manotoc received one of two ransom notes demanding, "1. Amnesty for our group; 2. Release [Communist leaders] Jose Maria Sison, Commander Dante [a nom de guerre for Barnabe Buscayno], Fidel Agcaoli and Saturnino Ocampo; 3. Prepare 20 million pesos [$2.5 million]. Wait for my next letter. Happy New Year. Tom." Family sources discounted the notes, but when Manotoc was freed, he indicated that he had written the notes, and several which had not been received, while handcuffed by leftist guerrillas.

On February 8, Manotoc was freed when the Special Military Intelligence Group stormed a guerrilla hideout in the mountains 55 miles east of Manila. One New People's Army guerrilla was killed in the raid. Manotoc said he was held in two locations during the six weeks.

The ASSOCIATED PRESS in Manila was phoned by a female member of the National Democratic Front, which speaks for dissidents. She denied oppositionists were involved and said the family had been "victimized by the Marcos regime's whimsical and arrogant use of power."

December 30, 1981 — PERU — Six Molotov cocktails were thrown through the second-floor windows of the Fiat offices in Lima, causing $30,000 damage but no injuries. 81123001

1981 — COLOMBIA — On March 29, 1983, Colombian Army troops in Florencia reported the capture of three guerrilla commanders, including Gonzalo Osorio (Lt. Raul), an M-19 (April 19 Movement) leader in El Caqueta who was accused of "participating in the hijacking of an Aeropesca aircraft in 1981, which was carrying a shipment of arms for the rebels in Colombia from someplace in Central America."

The military forces in Morelia announced the capture of Juan Ballen Garzon and Roberto Bolanos Moyano (Albert), two leaders of the Finance Committee of the Tenth Front of the Revolutionary Armed Forces of Colombia (FARC), which is active in El Caqueta in the southern part of the country near the Amazon region.

1981 — LIBERIA — Liberian president Samuel K. Doe claimed in 1983 that Libyan leader Muammar Qaddafi inspired an assassination attempt against him in 1981.

A CHRONOLOGY OF EVENTS

1982

January 1982 — ITALY — The Italian news agency ANSA in Rome reported on August 5, 1986, that two Libyans were expelled from Italy on suspicion of planning a terrorist attack against the then Italian head of state Sandro Pertini. 82019901

January 2–3, 1982 — LEBANON — Unidentified gunmen shot and killed a Ghanaian soldier attached to United Nations Interim Force in Lebanon (UNIFIL) north of Khirbet Flim. A second UNIFIL soldier was injured. That same day, an oil tanker loading 150,000 barrels of oil at the port of Tripoli was shelled. The next day, saboteurs were suspected of responsibility for an explosion that set fire to the newly reopened pipeline in northern Lebanon, which carries crude from Iraq to Tripoli. 82010201, 82010301

January 5, 1982 — SPAIN — Eight members of Basque Nation and Liberty/ Military kidnapped West German industrialist Josef Lipperheide, 76, from his Guecho bedroom. His chauffeur, kidnapped earlier in the day by two gang members, had opened the house's door. The group escaped in stolen cars with three other terrorists. The family heard the abductors say they would request a "high ransom." Three workers found Lipperheide alive near a harbor on the outskirts of Bilbao on February 4. 82010501

January 5, 1982 — GUATEMALA — Fifteen heavily armed men shot a church lectern and then kidnapped Rev. Pablo Childermans, 33, of Belgium's Missionhurst-CICM order, and Rev. Roberto Paredes, a local diocesan priest, from their Nueva Concepcion church about 80 miles southeast of Guatemala City. Officials said a Guatemalan nun, Sister Victoria de la Roca, 48, kidnapped from a church house at Esquilpapas, was "linked to the guerrillas" and suggested that other religious workers allegedly involved in similar activities leave the country. On January 7, RADIO HORIZONTE said the bodies of the two churchmen were found shot to death at kilometer 148 on the highway linking Guatemala City to Tiquisate. However, the WASH- INGTON POST reported that the duo was freed on January 8, citing a report from the Apostolic Delegate. 82010502

January 5, 1982 — ITALY— Two members of the Popular Front for the Liber- ation of Palestine were arrested at Rome's Fiumicino Airport for possessing explosives. 82010503

January 8, 1982 — COSTA RICA— On February 19, 1983, the PANAMA CITY STAR AND HERALD reported:

> Panama's Attorney General Rafael Rodriguez plans to probe an alleged kidnapping of a wealthy Iranian youth by Salvadoran guerrillas in Costa Rica a year ago and held in Panamanian territory until he managed to escape last month. Although National Guard authorities have declined official comment on the incident, newspapers in San Jose have been giving prominence to Kaveh Yazdani's captivity and subse- quent escape. The 21-year-old Yazdani was kidnapped January 8, 1982, while in a San Jose parking lot. He was moved from place to place until he was taken to a Punta Chame house, 48 miles west of Panama City, as guerrillas bargained fruitlessly with relatives for ransom. The young Iranian, whose relatives possess large holdings in Costa Rica, finally escaped Jan. 30 of this year [1983] and was returned to the neighboring country by National Guards, dispatches from San Jose said.

82010801

January 9, 1982 — TURKEY— A bomb exploded outside the El Al ticket of- fice in Istanbul, also damaging the neighboring Lufthansa office but caus- ing no injuries. 82010901

January 10, 1982 — LEBANON— Three gunmen stole the car of a Soviet diplomat in the Mar Ilyas quarter in Beirut's western sector. 82011001

January 10, 1982 — FRANCE— The Bakunin Gdansk Paris Group bombed an insurance company and two business firms identified as Esmil, a United States company; Slava, a Soviet company; and Metallex, a Polish firm, causing considerable damage but no casualties. The group said it was pro- testing "against the interments [*sic*] trials, murders of workers in Poland, organized starvation, torture, and massacre of people in Latin America and Afghanistan . . . the political and economic interests of the Moscow and Washington imperialists." 82011002–04

January 10, 1982 — FRANCE — The Ukrainian anarchist group Fils de Makhno (Sons of Makhno) set three Soviet-made Lada cars on fire in Perpignan. 82011005–07

January 11, 1982 — JORDAN — A bomb went off at 9:45 A.M. in the Cinderella grocery in Jabal Amman, wounding owner Sa'adih Salih Salamih Haddadin; Muhammad Ibrahim 'Ali ash-Shatanawi and Muhammad 'Ali ad-Darawishah from As-Sarih village; Rashid 'Atiyat Allah Rashid from At-Fatilah; 'Abdallah Muhammad 'Ali ad-Darduk from Nablus; and one of the Indian employees of the Indian embassy.

AMMAN DOMESTIC TELEVISION SERVICE reported that

1. The person who placed the explosive charge inside the grocery is 'Abdallah Muhammad 'Ali ad-Darduk from Nablus, 20 years old, who lives and works as a carpenter in Ar-Rusayfah. 2. The person who drove 'Abdallah to the scene of the incident is his uncle, Hijazi Munib Hasan ad-Darduk from Nablus who lives in Amman and works as a driver on the Amman-Damascus-Beirut route. 3. The person who delivered the explosive charge to them is Hisham Mustafa Qanbar, a Syrian from Idlib Province who works as Third Secretary in the Syrian Embassy in Amman. 4. The investigation has also revealed that Hisham Qanbar was able a few months ago to enlist Hijazi Munib Hasan ad-Darduk to the service of Syrian intelligence. The latter had once worked as a driver to the former Syrian ambassador in Amman. 5. Upon the request of Hisham Qanbar, Hijazi ad-Darduk enlisted his nephew 'Abdallah ad-Darduk to the service of Syrian intelligence. 6. Hisham Qanbar, Third Secretary of the Syrian Embassy, commissioned Hijazi ad-Darduk and his nephew 'Abdallah ad-Darduk with carrying out explosion operations in some of the groceries which sell alcoholic drinks to implicating Muslim factions in these attacks. 7. On the morning of Monday, 11 January 1982, Hijazi ad-Darduk and his nephew 'Abdallah ad-Darduk arrived at the Syrian Embassy in Amman in Hijazi ad-Darduk's car, a Plymouth with license plate No. 22922, and met Hisham Qanbar inside of the embassy's offices. Hisham had prepared an explosive charge and handed it to 'Abdallah ad-Darduk in the presence of Hijazi and gave them advice on how to time it for a period of 10 minutes. He asked them to place it at the target on which they had previously agreed, that is, the Cinderella grocery. After this, Hijazi and 'Abdallah ad-Darduk left the embassy at approximately 0930 of the same day. 8. After they arrived at the grocery, Hijazi parked his car on the opposite side of the grocery and 'Abdallah ad-Darduk, who was carrying a paper bag in which he had placed the explosive charge, left the car after having timed it in accordance with Hisham Qanbar's instructions and entered the grocery. Shortly afterwards, the explosive charge went off in his hands while the grocer was busy preparing some bottles of beer for 'Abdallah ad-Darduk. 9. Upon studying the border

records, it became clear that Hijazi Munib ad-Darduk had left the country for Syria in his car via the Ramtha borders on the morning of 11 January immediately after the incident. It also became evident that the Third Secretary at the Syrian Embassy in Amman, Hisham Qanbar, had also left the country after the incident.

82011101

January 12, 1982 — AUSTRIA — Vienna's KURIER reported it had received a tip indicating that a "bomb commando" headed by the Venezuelan terrorist Carlos (Ilich Ramirez Sanchez) of the Popular Front for the Liberation of Palestine was planning to attack the Kaprun hydroelectric plant in the Salzburg Tauren region on February 7. "The organization, financed by Libyan chief of state Al-Qadhdhfi [*sic*], has hired a Frenchman as an explosives expert, who is apparently also a trained mountaineer. He was reportedly offered a 'contingent fee' of DM 300,000." State Security Police experts suggested that the planned bombing could be connected with the trial of terrorists who attacked a Vienna synagogue. 82011201

January 12, 1982 — GUATEMALA — Four individuals threw dynamite bombs from a car at the embassies of Israel and Argentina and the consulate of Haiti. The bomb thrown at the Argentine embassy did not detonate; the other two caused only minor damage and no injuries. Israeli guards opened fire at the attackers. A caller said the group was protesting Israel's supplying arms to the Guatemalan Army. 82011202–04

January 13, 1982 — LEBANON — Gunmen kidnapped Rabah Kheroua, 37, from his Beirut home, then shot him in the head and dumped his body along Ad-Dakkash Street in Haraft Hurayk in a southern Beirut slum. Kheroua served as Algerian charge and chief adviser to Ambassador Mustafa Hishmawi. 82011301

January 14, 1982 — ITALY — The Italian news service ANSA and the Milan daily LA NOTTE were phoned by the Nuclei Armati Comunista, who claimed they had placed two gasoline bombs in the United States consulate office. One bomb was found in a seventh-floor stairwell. A sign nearby said Get NATO out of Italy: Break the Italian Link in the Imperialist Chain. 82011401

January 15, 1982 — FEDERAL REPUBLIC OF GERMANY — A bomb exploded in the Mifgash-Israel Restaurant in West Berlin, injuring 25 people and killing a 14-month-old baby girl. News agencies received calls claiming credit for the People's League of Free Palestine (a Dutch group) and the Arab May 15 Organization for the Liberation of Palestine. Police arrested, but later released, 6 Arabs believed to be members of the Popular Front for the Liberation of Palestine. The restaurant was owned by Israeli citizens Dany Mezger and Naftali Schoenberg, who said they had not received any threats since opening the restaurant in 1968. Mayor Richard von Weizsaecker noted that the bombing took place six days before the 40th anniversary of the Berlin meeting at which Nazis agreed on the "Final Solution." The previous week, police raided the homes of 12 teenagers and confiscated Nazi propaganda and 26 detonators. 82011501

January 16, 1982 — INDIA — Unidentified men shouting slogans hurled five homemade bombs through the gate and over the walls of the United States consulate in Calcutta. Three of the bombs exploded, damaging only a window shutter and causing no injuries. Police disposed of the other two bombs. 82011601

January 17, 1982 — ISRAEL — A bomb exploded near the rear entrance of the Lufthansa office in Tel Aviv, causing minor damage and no injuries. 82011701

January 17, 1982 — FEDERAL REPUBLIC OF GERMANY — Gunmen ambushed and killed three Yugoslavs in Untergruppenbach, 40 miles north of Stuttgart, as they were riding in their BMW 316. Driver Bardhosh Gervalla, 30, and passengers Zeka Kadai, 28, and the driver's brother, Jusuf Gervalla, 36, supported Albanian nationalist demands for the Yugoslav province of Kosovo to secede and join Albania. Before he died in the hospital, Jusuf Gervalla blamed Yugoslav secret police for the 10:00 P.M. attack on the Red Front members. Jusuf and Zeka had been reporters for RADIO-TV PRISTINA and RILINDJE. Zeka had arrived in Switzerland the day before. Zagreb DANS claimed they had been armed but apparently knew their attackers. 82011702

January 18, 1982 — FRANCE — A man with a pistol fired a single bullet into the head of Lt. Col. Charles R. Ray, 43, United States assistant military attache, as he was walking to his car at 9:00 A.M. in civilian clothes on the Boulevard Emile Augier in the 16th arrondissement near the Bois de Boulogne. The short man with long, dark hair, shabbily dressed, fled on foot. An eyewitness said he appeared to be an Arab. In Beirut, the Lebanese Armed Revolutionary Faction (LARF) claimed credit. Other reports list this group as the Movement of Arab Revolutionary Brigades. The lone shell casing found on the ground near the assassination was the same brand as the six 7.65 mm shells found after the November 12, 1981, assassination attempt against United States charge Christian Chapman. The Lebanese Armed Revolutionary Faction had also claimed credit for that attack. The same gun was used later in the April 3, 1982, slaying in Paris of Israeli embassy attache Yacov Barsimantov by a woman firing a Czech CZ 7.65 mm pistol for the Lebanese Armed Revolutionary Brigades (the same group as LARF).

On October 1984, Lyons police arrested a Lebanese man, Georges Ibrahim Abdallah, in connection with the case. On July 2, 1985, a Paris court issued homicide charges against Abdallah, considered one of the leaders of the LARF, after a Czech pistol found in his Paris hideout was determined to be the weapon that killed Lieutenant Colonel Ray and Yacov Barsimantov. Abdallah was sentenced to four years in prison in July 1986 for associating with a banned group, using false documents, and possessing arms and explosives. The United States embassy complained that the sentence was too light.

The Committee of Solidarity with Arab and Middle Eastern Political Prisoners conducted a series of bombings in Paris in September 1986, demanding the release of Abdallah. On November 19, 1986, Abdallah was indicted in Paris for a failed assassination attempt against the United States consul general in Strasbourg, Robert Onan Homme, on March 26, 1984.

On January 28, 1987, Abdallah was ordered to stand trial before a seven-magistrate Court of Assizes for the attacks on Ray, Barsimantov, and Homme. Italian authorities suggested that they might request extradition for Abdallah's role in the 1984 assassination in Rome of Gen. Leamon Hunt, the United States head of the multinational Sinai observation force. 82011801

January 19, 1982 — FRANCE — The Pacifist and Ecologist Committee fired five Soviet-made rocket-propelled grenade (RPG-7) antitank rockets, from a hill six hundred yards away across the Rhone River, at the Creys-Malville 1,200-megawatt fast-breeder nuclear reactor, scoring four direct hits on the plant's concrete outer shell. There was no danger of radioactive leaks because the reactor, still under construction and due to join the French nuclear grid in 1983, was unloaded, and there were no radioactive materials at the site.

January 19, 1982 — LEBANON — Shells fired at the car in which he was riding wounded 'Abd al-Fattah Ghanim, member of the Political Bureau and secretary general of the Palestine Liberation Organization (PLO) Central Committee, and member of the Palestine National Council and of the PLO Central Council, as he was entering the Burj al-Barajinah Camp in Beirut in the evening. The bullets entered his back and his right lung and chest. 82011901

January 20, 1982 — ITALY — The Groups of Internationalist Communists bombed the Rome office of the Italian Chamber of Commerce for the

United States (a private organization), causing extensive damage but no injuries. 82012001

January 21, 1982 — CANADA/UNITED STATES — United States police arrested two individuals with Irish Republican Army (IRA) ties trying to enter the United States illegally from Canada. British M.P. Owen Carron, who succeeded Bobby Sands, the IRA terrorist who died of a prison hunger strike, was stopped at the Whirlpool Bridge at Niagara Falls and charged with conspiracy to smuggle (himself) and giving false information to immigration officers. Elsewhere, Danny Morrison, IRA director of public relations, was arrested 20 miles away at the Peace Bridge in Buffalo, New York. Two Canadians were charged with aiding the duo. Carron claimed he had landed immigrant status in Canada, while Morrison presented immigration officers with a Canadian citizenship certificate that did not belong to him. The duo were trying to get to a New York City IRA fund-raising dinner. The United States consulate in Belfast had denied the duo visas.

January 21, 1982 — HONDURAS — The Juan Rayo Guerrilla Group bombed the Coca-Cola subsidiary in San Pedro Sula, causing extensive damage but no injuries. The group threatened a sabotage campaign if Col. Gustavo Alvarez Martinez, who it claimed repressed labor movements, was made chief of the armed forces. 82012101

January 22, 1982 — ITALY — An incendiary device went off at the Commission for Cultural Exchange between Italy and the United States (an affiliate of the Fulbright program) in Rome, causing minor damage but no casualties. The Bank of Iran on the same floor was also firebombed. 82012201–02

January 23, 1982 — SWITZERLAND — A self-exiled Romanian was seriously injured when a bomb exploded under his car as he was backing out of a Geneva hotel parking lot. 82012301

January 26, 1982 — FEDERAL REPUBLIC OF GERMANY — During the afternoon, gunmen fired four shots at United States Army's 5th Corps soldiers' quarters in Frankfurt, causing slight damage but no injuries. 82012601

January 27, 1982 — FEDERAL REPUBLIC OF GERMANY — A bomb went off at the Yugoslav Cultural Office in Dortmund, causing $22,000 damage but no injuries. 82012701

January 27, 1982 — COLOMBIA — Six men and a woman, claiming April 19 Movement (M-19) membership, hijacked a Colombia Aerotal B-727 flying

128 people from Bogota to Pereira at 1:09 P.M. and forced it to return to Bogota's International Airport. The plane stayed on the ground for three hours with its engines running. When it flew on to Cali, the aircraft was damaged when it hit an Army truck and two jeeps that were parked on the runway. The hijackers, claiming to have grenades and explosives, released 44 women, children, and elderly people at Palmaseca Airport. They threatened to blow up the plane if another plane was not provided. Carlos Ardila, a Colombian textile magnate and millionaire, provided his executive jet to the hijackers, who freed the remaining passengers and 6 crewmen, and flew on to San Andres, a Colombian island. The leader of the hijackers, Commander Tres, was identified as Fernando Gonzalez. He and the woman, Commander Una, Luz Carmine Garzon, 23, from Pereira, demanded the presence of a journalist; a member of the government-created Peace Commission, Cali's auxiliary bishop Msgr. Juan Francisco Sarasty; and Enrique de Lamatta, International Red Cross president who was visiting Colombia. The group was told that all Colombian airports and Tocumen airport in Panama were closed to them. After refueling, the group flew to Havana, where they requested political asylum. Although shooting had been heard on board the plane, none of the passengers appeared to have been hurt. Colombia requested extradition on February 4. Two Americans were on the hijacked plane: John Archolecas, of Deerfield Beach, Florida, and Abraham Rozental, a naturalized American citizen believed to be from Miami. 82012702

January 28, 1982 — UNITED STATES — At 9:45 A.M., two young men walked up to the car of Turkish consul general Kemal Arikan, 54, as he was waiting at a stoplight in west Los Angeles and, firing 14 shots, shot him to death. As his assailants fled into the residential area behind Wilshire Boulevard, Arikan's car drifted across the street, hitting the red Volkswagen Rabbit of a Korean student at the University of California–Los Angeles, Kwang Lim Kim, 29. The pistols were found in bushes beside a house two blocks from the scene. Police said there had been several threats against Turkish officials in recent weeks, and Arikan had been warned. The Justice Commandos of the Armenian Genocide claimed credit. Hours after the shooting, police took into custody four persons, including Armenian immigrant Harry M. Sassounian, 19, who pleaded innocent to murder charges on February 1. Police were also searching for a Lebanese-Armenian immigrant, Krikor (KoKo) Saliba, 21. The trial of Harout Sassounian, Harry's brother, for the 1980 firebombing of Arikan's residence ended in a mistrial in May 1982 because of publicity about Armenian assassinations.

After deliberating from November 28, 1983, to early 1984, a four-man, eight-woman jury found Armenian immigrant Hampig Sassounian, 20, of Pasadena, guilty of first-degree murder. Their deliberations were twice interrupted so that the defense could call prison inmates to dispute testimony by other inmates who claimed that the accused had admitted the crime in jailhouse conversations. Superior Court sentenced Sassounian to life without possibility of parole on June 16, 1984. 82012801

January 30, 1982 — AUSTRIA/LEBANON — The General Command of Al-'Asifah Forces–The Revolutionary Council, headed by Abu Nidal, distributed a statement in Beirut warning Austrian chancellor Bruno Kreisky that he and his government were "fully responsible for the safety of our colleagues, for preserving their lives and for providing all humanitarian conditions for them as prisoners of war. We consider the sentences passed against them null and void and warn that carrying out those sentences will make the Austrian Government liable to face several problems." The Austrian government was counseled to declare "total neutrality with regard to the Arab-Zionist conflict and to stop interfering in the affairs of our Palestinian people." The press speculated that the group was referring to two Arabs who were being held for the attack on a Jewish synagogue in Vienna in August.

January 31, 1982 — LEBANON — A bomb exploded in the parking lot of the Moroccan embassy, causing minimal damage and no injuries. 82013101

February 1982 — PAKISTAN — A shoulder-fired missile was launched at President Zia's airplane as it taxied on the Rawalpindi Airport runway for a flight to Lahore.

February 1, 1982 — COLOMBIA — In an interview with EL ESPECTADOR, Leandro Barozzi, an Italian citizen suspected of being a member of the Red Brigades, said that he was only a friend of Antonio Negri and would present himself to the police to deny charges that he shared membership with Negri in that group. Italy had requested the extradition of the 38-year-old professor of engineering at the University of El Valle. On January 15, 1983, he received a visa to remain in Colombia after the Supreme Court determined that the extradition request was improper and the crimes were political.

February 2, 1982 — UNITED STATES — A homesick Cuban who had entered the United States in the May 1980 Mariel boat lift, Sergio Ortega Rojas, 20, fortified himself with a cocktail, then told the crew of Air Florida's flight 710, a B-737 flying from Miami at 2:40 P.M. for Key West, that he had a gasoline-filled bottle, hijacking the plane to Havana's Jose Marti International Airport. The 72 passengers and 5 crew members continued on to Key West after the Cubans took Ortega into custody. There were no injuries reported. Air Florida reported that the hijacker did not meet the Federal Aviation Administration profile of potential hijackers. 82020201

February 3, 1982—THAILAND—Three Americans, a West German, an Australian, and an Israeli living in Norway were taken hostage by guerrillas during a tourist trip to Chiang Mai and were held for three days in Burma. The hostages were released following the release of some villagers detained two weeks earlier. 82020301

February 4, 1982—AUSTRIA—A pipe bomb went off during the night at the Vienna apartment of chief rabbi Akiba Eisenberg, causing minor damage and no injuries.

February 4, 1982—ITALY—Police announced that in a mountain region near Treviso the Red Brigades had cached weapons—including three surface-to-air missiles, three antitank rockets, and a large assortment of machine guns—obtained from the Popular Front for the Liberation of Palestine (PFLP).

February 6, 1982—UNITED STATES—Immigration authorities arrested two Northern Ireland residents and three Canadians trying to slip into the United States at Niagara Falls to buy some arms for the Irish Republican Army (IRA). Authorities confiscated an apparent shopping list of weapons and $8,000 to $10,000 in Irish and United States currency. Two of the suspects were charged with attempted illegal entry and making false statements. The other three were charged with alien smuggling. The United States attorney said he would not prosecute on criminal charges. 82020601

February 8, 1982—IRAN—Unidentified gunmen fired on the armored limousine of West German ambassador Jens Petersen, who escaped with only minor scratches from flying glass. Meanwhile, security forces raided a northern Tehran house and killed 13 leading members of the Mujaheddin e Khalq, including public enemy number one Mussa Kheyyabani, his wife, and Ashrai Rabii, wife of Massoud Rajavi, Paris-exiled leader of the group. 82020801

February 8, 1982—GUATEMALA—Ten young men and women carrying handguns burst into a closed Hardee's restaurant in Guatemala City, forced the employees to leave, then poured gasoline inside the building. The resulting fire exploded propane cooking tanks, destroying the facility but causing no injuries. 82020802

February 9, 1982—FEDERAL REPUBLIC OF GERMANY—A letter bomb went off in an office reception area in the Marienhof Hotel in Bad Toelz, south of Munich, injuring Kay Mierendorff, 36, and his wife, Antje. Mierendorff lost several fingers and suffered a severe stomach wound. He had helped smuggle more than one thousand persons out of East Germany in specially rebuilt cars in recent years. The office and reception area were destroyed in the blast.

February 11, 1982 — FRANCE — The Bkounine-Gdansk-Paris-Guatemala-Salvador group bombed the Paris headquarters of the Colombian steel firm Acerias Paz del Rio, the United States appliance firm Bendix, the Chilean airline office, a firm importing Argentine meat, and an electrical appliance shop selling United States products, causing slight damage and no injuries. 82021101–05

February 12, 1982 — POLAND — Claiming that his Polish airline LOT 38-seater had been hijacked on its Warsaw-to-Wroclaw run, a Polish pilot originally identified as Czeslaw K., 32, landed at the United States Air Force base at Tempelhof in West Berlin. The pilot requested political asylum, claiming he did not like the martial law government, and that he was about to lose his job. He was granted asylum, as was his wife, his two daughters aged 2 and 3, his cousin, his cousin's wife, their 14-month-old daughter, the copilot, and a 19-year-old passenger. A Polish crew flew the other 14 passengers back to Poland. A United States Army spokesman said, "It's a good legal question whether it's a hijack or not." Hamburg's GERMAN PRESS ASSOCIATION (DPA) on July 19 reported that the pilot and copilot had been acquitted of the Berlin hijacking. 82021201

February 13, 1982 — GUATEMALA — Four hooded gunmen fired submachine guns from their speeding car, killing United States Christian Brothers Winona Brother James Arnold Miller, 37, of Custer, Wisconsin, outside his mission, the Colegio La Salle school in Huehuetenango, a provincial capital 130 miles northwest of Guatemala City, as he was repairing a window. Miller had just returned from complaining to the authorities about the detention by soldiers of a student at the school. Miller had been in Guatemala for two years, having previously served in Nicaragua, which he asked to leave because "he was not in agreement with what the Sandinistas were doing," according to a colleague. 82021301

February 16, 1982 — FRANCE — Police arrested Bruno Breguet, 34, of Switzerland, and West German Magdalena Kaupp (also spelled Kopp), 34, after a gun battle that began in a Champs Elysees underground parking lot when watchmen challenged them as robbery suspects. Breguet twice tried unsuccessfully to fire his 9 mm Herstall automatic pistol at pursuing French policemen. He had served 7 years of a 1970 Israeli 15-year sentence for possession of explosives. The duo was charged with attempted homicide, death threats, falsified identity papers, and illegal possession of the pistol, 4.4 pounds of explosives, and two small bottles of cooking gas. Their Peugeot 504 had fake license plates. They were carrying two thousand dollars in cash. West German police believed Kaupp belonged to a terrorist group and was a friend of Johannes Weinrich, a member of the Baader-Meinhof Gang. On March 1, Popular Front for the Liberation of Palestine (PFLP) terrorist Carlos demanded that the French release his friends. 82021601

February 16, 1982 — UNITED STATES — Jesus Villa Munoz, 41, of Hialeah, Florida, attempted to hijack to Cuba an Air Florida B-737 being loaded at Miami International Airport. As he approached the boarding gate, agent Bob Dundas alerted the crew that the passenger appeared suspicious. Agent Oscar Guzman ran into the passageway and slammed the airplane door. When Guzman and Dundas attempted to search the passenger, Villa pulled out a .25 caliber automatic handgun he had smuggled past the security guards and fired two shots. Villa exchanged shots with responding policemen before he was captured with no injuries to anyone. Villa was charged with attempted first-degree murder, attempted air piracy, and use of a firearm to commit a felony. 82021602

February 17, 1982 — FRANCE — Following a week that saw 26 bomb and gun attacks in Corsica, the National Liberation Front of Corsica set off 19 bombs in post offices, tax offices, and banks in Paris and Versailles, causing some damage but no casualties.

February 18, 1982 — SYRIA — A man claiming to be a newspaper dealer picking up copies of AL BAATH ended his conversation with guards by gunning his car's engine and crashing into the Syrian Information Ministry in Damascus, heavily damaging the building in the resultant explosion, killing the driver and wounding 40 people. The Syrian government blamed the blast on a Moslem Brotherhood terrorist who it claimed doubled as an agent for Israel and the Central Intelligence Agency. The blast coincided with the 17th day of Syrian Army efforts to end a fundamentalist revolt in Hamah, 120 miles to the north. Three groups in Beirut, Paris, and New York claimed credit. The Moslem Brotherhood's Combatant Avant-Garde, outlawed in 1980, said it was headed by a former Syrian Army officer, 'Adnan al-'Uklah, 31, and was fundamentalist in nature. The Islamic Revolutionary Command said it was a mainstream Moslem Brotherhood group.

February 18, 1982 — LEBANON — Gunmen fired automatic weapons during the morning in front of the car of Thomas Anderson, vice president and managing director of the United States oil firm Caltex; his Lebanese colleague, the general manager of the United States-owned Mediterranean Refinery Company; and their driver as they were driving to work south of Sidon. The three men were kidnapped. The kidnappers, believed to be disgruntled job applicants and oil workers, demanded raises and job improvements. They released unharmed the three hostages six hours later, in the early afternoon. 82021801

February 18, 1982 — COLOMBIA — The National Liberation Army (ELN) machine-gunned and bombed the Honduran consulate in Bucaramanga around midnight, destroying the front of the building and the private car of the consul, who, along with his wife and two others who were in the building, escaped unharmed. 82021802

February 19, 1982 — UNITED STATES — The Jewish Defense League claimed credit for setting off two bombs outside the Washington, D.C., offices of Aeroflot, causing three thousand dollars' damage, at 12:50 A.M. 82021901

February 19, 1982 — UNITED STATES — Two bombs exploded at 11:00 P.M. at the offices of Trans Cuba and REPUBLICA MAGAZINE in Miami. The Federal Bureau of Investigation believed Omega-7 was responsible. No structural damage was reported. 82021902–03

February 21, 1982 — UNITED STATES — According to the Federal Bureau of Investigation (FBI), "At approximately 10:45 P.M., two sophisticated bombs exploded at the Administration Building, UPR [University of Puerto Rico], Rio Piedras, Puerto Rico. The two devices consisted of a propane tank, a five-by-two-inch pipe bomb, external packages of high explosives, a clock timing mechanism, and an electric blasting cap. The communique claiming credit for this incident reportedly urged students to form semiclandestine groups to fight against American imperialism." No injuries were reported. The FBI believed the Antonia Martinez Student Commandos responsible. The FBI indicated that the group is composed of anti-United States university students and is named for Antonia Martinez, a student at the University of Puerto Rico who was killed during a UPR riot on March 4, 1970, while standing on the porch of a boarding house near the campus. Martinez, 19, was struck in the head by a bullet. Among radical students she is considered to be a martyr.

February 21, 1982 — COSTA RICA — Terrorists used a hand grenade to blow open the front door of the San Jose apartment of an anti-Sandinista Nicaraguan, injuring a Canadian neighbor woman. The intended victim was not at home, but the group shot two other people, including the intended victim's son. 82022101

February 21, 1982 — UNITED STATES — Omega-7 claimed credit for firing a submachine gun at the windows of the Hispania Freight Company in Miami, which handles shipments to Cuba; firing at the company's Hialeah offices; and setting the third failed firebomb in three days at the Padron

Cigars factory in Miami. None of the incidents involved injuries. 82022102–04

February 23, 1982 — LEBANON — Two cars laden with bombs exploded in a Beirut seafront area, killing 7 and wounding 60. The Front for the Liberation of Lebanon from Foreigners claimed credit, as did the previously unknown Organization of Holy Struggle, which said it was beginning a war against Syria. The latter group said the bombs had been aimed at Syrian intelligence and occupation "in reply to the extermination to which our families in beloved Tripoli were subjected."

February 23, 1982 — IRELAND — Twelve masked Irish Republican Army (IRA) gunmen carried explosives and automatic weapons into the 1,200-ton *St. Bedan,* a British coal-carrying vessel in the Lough Foyle sea inlet between Ireland and Northern Ireland. The group set the 10-member crew adrift, planted bombs in the engine room, and escaped in another boat before the explosion sank the vessel. The *St. Bedan's* crew told police the attackers threatened to fire rockets at any other British ships sailing into Irish waters. 82022301

February 24, 1982 — LEBANON — A dozen Shiites carrying AK-47s and led by Hamzah, who had hijacked a Libyan plane on December 7, 1981, drove a black Mercedes onto the airfield at Beirut International Airport and forced 105 passengers back onto a Kuwaiti Airlines B-707, which had just arrived from Tripoli, Libya, with a delegation of Lebanese leftist leaders including the Communist party chief, George Hawi. The Imam Musa as-Sadr Brigades demanded that Lebanon break diplomatic relations with Libya because of the disappearance in 1978 of Sadr. While 4 hijackers stayed in the plane and the other 8 ringed it, the group threatened to blow up the plane if Lebanon did not grant it fuel for a trip to Tehran. Iran closed its airspace, and the fuel was not granted. Negotiations were carried out with the leftist Lebanese National Movement and the government, led by tourism minister Marwan Hamadeh. A caller from the Sons of the South Movement claimed that this was part of an integrated plan. During the negotiations, the group fired their weapons three times, hitting the airport control tower and injuring 2 people. Unknown attackers fired three rockets onto the runway from outside the airport, causing no injuries. The group then permitted Ja'farite Mufti Shaykh 'Abd al-Amir Qabalan; Brig. Gen. Nur ad-Din, commander of Syrian forces at the airport; and Amal council member Al-Haj 'Ali 'Ammar to enter the plane. The group agreed to release their 105 hostages in return for a promise that the issue of Sadr would be raised in the United Nations, International Court of Justice, and the Arab League. The group exited the plane with 2 Lebanese and 6 Libyan hostages, whom they agreed to release at 1:30 A.M. in return for safe conduct to a Syrian Army border post, ending the nine-hour hijacking. The 49 passengers bound for Kuwait stayed on board. The gunmen reportedly escaped by fading into crowds at the blacked-out airport. One source indicated this was Hamzah's seventh hijacking. 82022401

February 24, 1982 — CANADA — Canadian Mounties issued warrants for South Korean-born Canadian citizen Choe Chung-hwa (James Choi), 31, and Nathan Israel Klegerman, 52, of Toronto, both of whom fled Canada after word leaked of their North Korean-backed plot to assassinate South Korean president Chon Tu-hwan. Choe allegedly paid three Canadian men $68,000 to kill Chon, probably during his expected visit to Ottawa. Toronto police had raided several homes a fortnight earlier and had seized the funds. Charged with conspiracy to kill Chon were Charles Stephen Yanover, 36, and Alexander Michael Gerol, 33, of Toronto, along with Choe. The former two were also charged with conspiracy to defraud and, with Klegerman, of illegal possession of funds in connection with the crime. The investigation, which lasted six months, led Canadian police to the Caribbean and involved police in the United States, France, West Germany, Austria, Belgium, the Netherlands, Martinique, and South Korea. A Toronto attorney was the original tipster in the case. Klegerman, Yanover, and Gerol reportedly had connections with a criminal organization engaged in narcotics trafficking, arms smuggling, and contract killings. Choe Chung-hwa was the son of former South Korean ambassador to Malaysia Choe Hong-hui, 64, former president of the International Tae Kwon Do Federation who had made frequent trips to North Korea. Choe Chung-hwa, the former Korean Army general and Canada-based dissident, had a brother living in North Korea and met with North Korean president Kim Il-song during a September 1980 visit to the country. On March 4, 1982, South Korean police announced they were investigating a Korean-born Canadian citizen, Mun Chi-sik, 34, an owner of a Toronto grocery store, who was arrested in Seoul in September. Mun, a Seoul college dropout, reportedly bombed a Toronto restaurant in January 1980 to obtain insurance money.

On February 17, 1984, Charles Yanover of Toronto and Alexander Gerol admitted in a county court trial that they had plotted to kill Chon. They were tried for defrauding the North Koreans who hired them, and they pleaded guilty to the charge. Choe's absence led to dismissal of the murder charge. The duo claimed that they tried to get the Canadian police to pay them $1.5 million for details about the plot. The men indicated that the attack was to take place while Chon golfed with Philippine president Ferdinand Marcos at the Philippine resort of Puerto Azul. Seoul's YONHAP news service reported, "A contract was tendered by the North

Koreans and signed in Austria by Yanover. In Macao, at a meeting they attended in bulletproof vests, Yanover and Gerol were given suitcases containing $400,000 in U.S. $100 bills. They went to Puerto Azul and extensively photographed the golf course from land and by water. Even as they negotiated with the impatient North Koreans in exotic locales around the world, Yanover contacted embassies in South Korea and Canada, according to Yanover's lawyer Irwin Koziebrocki. It was Yanover who tipped off the South Korean Government in time to have Chon's golfing trip cancelled, Koziebrockie said." Yanover was sentenced to two years for his part in the case. Gerol received one year. Of the money paid by the North Koreans, $21,000 was to be recovered by Canadian authorities via court order.

Yanover was already serving a nine-year term for bombing a Toronto disco. Gerol was serving a six-year term for the same crime. Earlier in the week, Yanover was sentenced to six months for his part in a failed attempt in 1981 to overthrow the government of Dominica.

Canadian officials issued a warrant for the arrest of Choe, who was last seen in June 1982 by Austrian police. They indicated that Choe was driven into Czechoslovakia from Vienna by North Koreans in a car bearing diplomatic license plates. 82022402

February 26, 1982 — TANZANIA — Five youths in their 20s claiming to be members of the previously unknown leftist Revolutionary Youth Movement of Tanzania hijacked a Tanzanian Airways B-737 flying 99 passengers from Mwanza to Dar es Salaam. The hijackers, accompanied by their families, were carrying automatic weapons and various explosives and forced the pilot to land at Nairobi, Kenya. While on the ground for 6½ hours, the group demanded the resignation of Tanzanian president Julius Nyerere. They released six passengers but threatened to kill the copilot. Kenyan foreign minister Robert Ouko, who was negotiating with the hijackers, replied, "Don't do that. You are going to need him." The hijackers' claim to Ouko that they had killed 2 passengers turned out to be false.

The plane flew on to Jidda, Saudi Arabia, which initially refused landing clearance but relented when the pilot said he was low on fuel. After landing at 3 A.M. and refueling, the plane took off at 6:30 A.M. The copilot was injured by either a gunshot or a knife before the plane landed in Athens, where the hijackers released a Belgian and a Somali. Twenty-four hours after the hijacking started, the plane landed at Stansted Airport in the United Kingdom, where they negotiated for 24 hours. They released a pregnant woman and child but warned police not to storm the plane, claiming they had placed bombs at the doors. Explosives were later found wired to the aircraft doors and placed in a toilet. After dark, two military helicopters landed out of sight of the plane. Four vans of police antiterrorist officers wearing ski masks entered the airport. A British police negotiator promised to publish a list of the hijackers' demands, but at one point, the lead hijacker said, "We are going to blow the plane. We are going to die now. Bring one hundred coffins now." They demanded to talk to Tanzanian high commissioner to London Amon James Nsekela, who agreed to talk. On February 28, the hijackers sent a boy and girl, both aged 10, apparently relatives of the hijackers, out of the plane with their weapons. They surrendered shortly thereafter. None of the other 76 passengers and 6 crewmen were injured, although 4 were treated for shock.

On September 17, 1982, a London court found the hijackers guilty and sentenced the leader to eight years in jail. The other four hijackers were to serve three to six years. 82022601

February 27, 1982 — LEBANON — A car bomb exploded near a military checkpoint in west Beirut, destroying a small warehouse and killing 8 persons and injuring 20 others. The Front for the Liberation of Lebanon from Foreigners claimed credit for the anti-Syrian attack.

February 28, 1982 — UNITED STATES — The Federal Bureau of Investigation reported "a bomb exploded at the American Stock Exchange at 86 Trinity Place, New York City. An improvised explosive device was placed on a window sill causing damage to windows on the street level. No witnesses were reported and no evidence was recovered." There were no injuries. The FBI believed the Puerto Rican Armed Forces of National Liberation (FALN) was responsible. 82022801

February 28, 1982 — UNITED STATES — The Federal Bureau of Investigation reported that "a bomb exploded at the Merrill Lynch Office, 1 Liberty Plaza, New York City. An improvised device had been placed at the Cortland Street entrance. Extensive damage was caused to glass in the building. No physical evidence was recovered." No injuries were reported. The Puerto Rican Armed Forces of National Liberation (FALN) was believed responsible. 82022802

February 28, 1982 — UNITED STATES — The Federal Bureau of Investigation reported that "a bomb exploded at the Chase Manhattan Bank, 1 Chase Manhattan Plaza, New York City. The device was placed between a pillar and a window on Nassau Street, causing extensive glass damage to the Plaza entrance level and the mezzanine level. A witness observed gray smoke and a strong odor of cordite, but did not see the perpetrator." No injuries were reported. The Puerto Rican Armed Forces of National Liberation (FALN) was believed responsible. 82022803

February 28, 1982 — UNITED STATES — The Federal Bureau of Investigation reported that "a bomb exploded at the New York Stock Exchange, 18 Broad Street, New York City. An improvised explosive device was placed next to a door on the north side of the building causing damage to a metal security door, glass doors and windows, and 2 windows in adjacent buildings. Parts of a timing device were recovered. The ASSOCIATED PRESS in New York City received a call from a male with a Spanish accent who stated that a communique from the Puerto Rican Armed Forces of National Liberation (FALN) had been left in a telephone booth at 91st and Riverside Drive, claiming FALN responsibility for these incidents." No injuries were reported. 82022804

March 1, 1982 — NETHERLANDS — The French embassy received a letter from Carlos, the famed Popular Front for the Liberation of Palestine (PFLP) terrorist, threatening unspecified action against the French government and interior minister Gaston Defferre if Bruno Breguet and Magdalena Kaupp (also spelled Kopp), arrested on February 16, were not released within a month. The letter, marked with two thumbprints of Carlos, said, "You have arrested two members of my organization although they had no special orders to carry out an attack on French territory. I give you a month to release them. Otherwise I will personally attack the French government and more especially Interior Minister Gaston Defferre." French ambassador Jean Jurgensen was provided a bullet-proof limousine. The letter demanded that the duo be "flown to a destination of their choice." Carlos had not been heard from since his December 1975 attack on the Organization of Petroleum Exporting Countries in Vienna, Austria. 82030101

March 1, 1982 — FEDERAL REPUBLIC OF GERMANY — Stuttgart police arrested three Syrians suspected of planning to attack Syrian Moslem Brotherhood supporters. Syrian commando groups in the Middle East threatened reprisals if the trio was not released. The West German school and two German-run institutes in Beirut were closed for security reasons in late March. Ambassador Horst Schmidt Dornedden returned to Bonn to report on the situation. On March 25, the Stuttgart prosecutor said there was insufficient evidence to prosecute the trio, except on minor charges, and arranged for them to be deported on March 25. 82030102

March 1, 1982 — UNITED STATES — Threatening to light a bottle filled with an unidentified liquid, Guillermo Lazaro Major-Diza, 23, attempted to hijack United Airlines flight 674, a B-727 carrying 92 passengers and 9 crewmen from Chicago to Miami. The pilot flew south to the Florida Keys to confuse the would-be hijacker, who was yelling, "Cuba, Cuba, Cuba," then circled back to Miami International Airport. The passengers went along with the hoax, said passenger Nita Johannson of Denmark. "We all yelled 'Cuba' to make him think he was in Cuba." Passenger John Celestin of Chicago wrestled Lazaro to the ground. The hijacker was tied up by the crew and taken into custody by the police at 9:00 P.M. Lazaro had claimed that he wanted to attend a wedding, then that his mother had died the previous day. He was arraigned before a federal magistrate, who ordered a psychiatric evaluation. Lazaro had spent a year in a Cuban mental hospital and had been arrested several times since entering the United States in the 1980 Mariel boat lift. He was charged with air piracy and utilizing a weapon in the commission of a felony. 82030103

March 1, 1982 — UNITED STATES — Puerto Rican Armed Forces of National Liberation (FALN) bombed the New York and American Stock Exchanges, the New York headquarters of Merrill Lynch, and the Chase Manhattan Bank at midnight, causing extensive damage but no injuries. The blasts came on the 28th anniversary of the Puerto Rican nationalist attack on the House of Representatives in which five congressmen were wounded by gunfire. Since 1974, the FALN had claimed credit for 120 bombings in New York City, Washington, D.C., and Chicago. 82030104–07

March 1, 1982 — SPAIN — Nabil 'Aranki Hawwad, 35, an Arab Liberation Front member studying pharmaceutical sciences, was shot twice in the neck by an Arabic-looking man who killed him in broad daylight in front of Hawwad's Madrid home. The Haifa-born Palestinian had lived in Spain since 1972 with his Spanish wife and two children. He had used an Iraqi passport on his recent return from Beirut. The Palestine Liberation Organization (PLO) had said before April 25, when Israel turned the Sinai Peninsula over to Egypt, "Several European governments informed the PLO that Israel would commit terrorist acts, particularly in Europe, against Palestinian figures." 82030108

March 1, 1982 — EL SALVADOR — Two American reporters were injured when one of them tripped a mine by hitting a thin fishing line stretched across a path east of Suchitoto. Ross Baughman, founder of the photography agency Visions in New York, suffered a shattered knee and James Nachtwey of NEWSWEEK was hit by shrapnel. NEWSWEEK reporter Richard Sandza and WASHINGTON POST reporter Joanne Omang were uninjured, having stayed in their pickup truck. Salvadoran Army soldiers rescued the injured reporters with a helicopter airlift. Leftist guerrillas were believed responsible. 82030109

March 2, 1982 — LEBANON — A car bomb exploded near a Syrian Army checkpoint in Tripoli, injuring 20.

March 3, 1982 — BELGIUM — A gunman fired a submachine gun inside a Yugoslav emigre club in Brussels, killing two Yugoslav guest workers and wounding three others. The assassin, who had been previously introduced at the club as a Belgian, escaped after the 5:00 P.M. attack. 82030301

March 6, 1982 — LEBANON — A car containing 90 pounds of explosives blew up in the middle of the main road on the west Beirut seafront, near the Iranian and Algerian embassies and the former Iraqi embassy, killing 2 and injuring 12. 82030601

March 10, 1982 — PHILIPPINES — Pablo Sola, mayor of Kabangkalan, was killed in an ambush led by a Filipino priest, Vicente Dangan, according to a prosecutor on Negros island. The attack came a few months after the bodies of 7 farmers were dug up on the plantation of Sola, who was charged with the murders. On February 26, 1983, 3 Roman Catholic priests, including Rev. Brian Gore of Australia and Rev. Niall O'Brien of Ireland, and 14 other persons were charged with the murder. 82031001

March 10, 1982 — ITALY — Police arrested 20 Red Brigades (RB) members planning a missile attack on the United States military base at Camp Darby, a few miles from Pisa. The Tirrenia safe house was raided after Giovanni Ciucci, an imprisoned RB member who had kidnapped United States general Dozier, tipped off police.

The previous evening, Naples police had arrested Mauro Acanfora, a professor and friend of RB ideologue Giovanni Senzani, who, together with Antonio Chiocchi and Vittorio Bolognesi, headed the RB's Naples section and was responsible for the $1.15 million kidnapping the previous year of Christian Democrat city official Ciro Cirili. 82031002

March 14, 1982 — UNITED KINGDOM — A 10-pound bomb exploded at 9:00 A.M. at the Pentonville, North London, offices of the South African African National Congress, causing extensive damage. The next day, South African minister of law and order, Louis le Grange, denied charges that South Africa was responsible. Lieutenant Gen. Johann Coetzee, head of the South African security police, said that five white agents of the South African Communist party infiltrated South Africa from the United Kingdom to organize the ANC rocket attack last August on the Voortrekkerhoogte army base near Pretoria. He identified the group as Britons Nicholas Francis Henry Heath, Bonnie Lou Muller, and David William; Belgian-born Guido Lucian van Hecken; and former South African citizen Dr. Edward Wertlee. 82031401

March 14, 1982 — FRANCE — A young man threw a bottle of gasoline through the ground-floor window of the United States consulate in Bordeaux, causing five hundred dollars' damage. The youth escaped on foot into a nearby amusement park. 82031402

March 15, 1982 — GREECE — Two bombs went off during the night at the Athens branch offices of the United States Citibank, damaging a parked car but causing no injuries. Leaflets nearby were signed by AOI, Solidarity with the El Salvador People, and the 4 August National Organization. Later, the Revolutionary Greek Battalions claimed credit from Kavala, Xanthi, and Yannina, saying it was trying to free the military officers who imposed a military dictatorship in Greece in 1967. 82031501

March 15, 1982—COSTA RICA—Agents of the Organization of Judicial Investigation arrested nine Latins—three Salvadorans, two Nicaraguans, a Chilean, an Argentine, a Costa Rican, and an unidentified individual—and charged them with running guns to Salvadoran guerrillas from Costa Rica through Nicaragua and Honduras. Police found 10 cars with secret compartments used to transport arms, M-16 and FAL automatic rifles, a grenade launcher, a small rocket launcher, shotguns, five hundred uniforms, and radio transmitting and receiving equipment. Police also confiscated false passports and driver's licenses from Ecuador, Costa Rica, and Sweden, and rubber stamps from 30 countries. The United States embassy said two days later that four of those captured in the San Jose safe house were planning to kidnap an unidentified American diplomat. The four were seen "staked out in strategic locations near the diplomatic mission watching the movements of officials," said a United States spokesman. 82031502

March 15, 1982—LEBANON—Five kilograms of TNT exploded during the early evening outside the Beirut French Cultural Institute, injuring a dozen students and teachers inside. No French diplomats were harmed. 82031503

March 15, 1982—LEBANON—The VOICE OF LEBANON reported that the second secretary of the British embassy, Muhammad al-Miqdad, was kidnapped by armed men in western Beirut as he was going to work. The family was told that the group wanted a $150,000 ransom, which was not paid. The Lebanese-born diplomat was released the next day in the Barbir quarter of west Beirut, near the Museum Passage, which links the Christian and Moslem sectors of the city. 82031504

March 16, 1982—LEBANON—A morning explosion near the former Egyptian embassy building in Ramlat al-Bayda' killed 1 person and wounded 12 others, damaging the north Yemeni embassy. 82031601

March 16, 1982—LEBANON—The Algerian embassy received several threats during the previous few days. The Saudi ambassador had been out of Beirut for three months, and the Kuwaiti ambassador and his staff had departed for their country a few days earlier. 82031602

March 17, 1982—EL SALVADOR—Four Dutch journalists—Jacobus Andries Koos Koster, Jans Ter Lan, Johannes Joop Willemsen, and Jan

Quiper — were shot to death in a cross fire between a military patrol and a guerrilla band the journalists were hoping to interview in Chalatenango Province north of the capital city. A 5th foreigner, described as either a journalist or a mercenary, was also killed in the 40-minute firefight in which 3 guerrillas also perished. Friends of the journalists suggested that the treasury police had surveilled the journalists at the Hotel Alameda, which served as a contact point between journalists and guerrillas. The 4, and others staying at the hotel, had received numerous death threats in person and by telephone during the previous week. The killings brought to 7 the number of foreign newsmen killed in El Salvador in a year. Two others, including American John Sullivan, were still missing.

The latest killings took place after the El Salvador Anticommunist Alliance issued a death list threatening the lives of 33 foreign and Salvadoran journalists, as well as Howard Lane, the United States embassy's public affairs officer. On the list were representatives from the WASHINGTON POST, NEW YORK TIMES, MIAMI HERALD, VOICE OF AMERICA, NEWSWEEK, NBC, UNITED PRESS INTERNATIONAL, and ASSOCIATED PRESS, among others. The list included WASHINGTON POST foreign editor Karen DeYoung and the POST's Central American correspondent Chris Dickey (erroneously listed as Christ Dickinson); Alma Guillermoprieto, of the WASHINGTON POST and MANCHESTER GUARDIAN, and NEW YORK TIMES correspondents Alan Riding and Raymond Bonner. 82031701–02

March 18, 1982 — WEST BERLIN — A bomb exploded at the Amerika House in the British sector, during the evening, causing $4,200 damage but no injuries. 82031801

March 18, 1982 — SOUTH KOREA — Two females entered the Pusan branch of the United States International Communications Agency carrying two plastic bags containing gasoline. When a Korean janitor questioned them, a male accomplice and the women spread the gasoline over the carpet and ignited it. One Korean student died and three others were injured in the ensuing inferno. Leaflets found nearby said, "We demand that the United States stop making this country a subject state and withdraw from this land" and end relations with the "fascist" government of President Chun Doo Hwan. This was the first attack on a United States mission since South Korea's founding in 1945.

Seoul police instituted a massive crackdown, arresting 5,739 people and offering a reward of $28,000 for information leading to the arrest of Jung Soon Chun, suspected leader of the arsonists. Of those arrested, 3,877 were tried and fined or given short prison sentences, 1,633 were released with a warning, and 199 were released pending the completion of investigations. Jung, 27, a college dropout, had gone into hiding on December 9, 1980, when he led an abortive plot to set fire to the United States information office in Kwangju. He was arrested in late March, but National Police reported he had no connection with the Pusan incident. He was, however, booked for the Kwangju incident. On April 1, police in Wonju City arrested Mun Pu-Sik, 25, suspected mastermind of the operation and his female companion, Kim Un-suk, 25. On April 8, Wonju police arrested Catholic diocesan priest Choe Ki-shik, 39, who allegedly hid the arsonists, and Kim Hyon-chang, 32, another arsonist leader. Police also reported the arrest of Kim Hwa-ok, 22, and Pak Chong-mi, 23, of South Cholla Province. Prosecutors indicted Kim Pong-chin, 37, head of a branch temple of the Won Buddhist Church in Yongsan, and Chong's relative, Chong Chong-hyo, 31, manager of Tonam-dong branch of the Hanil Bank, for offering Chong a hiding place.

On August 11, 1982, defense lawyers vowed to appeal death sentences handed down against 2 activists. Two women were sentenced to life imprisonment and 12 other persons received 15-year terms. Two Roman Catholic laymen received suspended sentences. Sixteen of the defendants appealed their sentences. Kim Myong-hui, 27, and Kang Myong-kun, 22, claimed that they and Kim Hyon-chang, one of the other defendants, attended classes on leftist ideology held at a Christian training camp in 1981. On March 8, 1983, the Supreme Court dropped the appeals and upheld the appeals court's verdicts. Mun Pu-sik, a dropout of a seminary, and Kim Hyon-chang were again sentenced to death. Also upheld were the 10-year prison terms for three coeds — Kim Un-suk; Choe In-sun, 21; and Kim Chi-hi, 23 — as well as 2 others. Other prison terms ranged from 1 to 7 years. Members of the group were first indicted for arson on April 29 and convicted by a Pusan district court on August 11, 1982. President Chun Doo Hwan commuted the death sentences to life in prison on March 15. 82031802

March 18, 1982 — SOMALIA — A time bomb exploded inside the North Yemeni embassy, causing minor damage and no injuries. 82031803

March 19, 1982 — GREECE — Bombs destroyed two cars, belonging to United States military personnel, carrying United States military license plates, in Thessalonika, but caused no injuries. 82031901

March 19, 1982 — GREECE — Arsonists were believed responsible for a fire at an American school in Athens. No injuries were reported. 82031902

March 20, 1982 — PERU — A false bomb threat was made against a Colombian Avianca jet carrying 150 passengers. The previous day, the Lima offices of the Peru-Helvetica company were bombed. 82032001 82031903

March 20, 1982 — CONGO — The Congolese Armed Patriotic Group claimed credit for bombing a Brazzaville movie theater in the Poto-Poto suburb, killing 9 and injuring several others. The group claimed the attack killed 15 and called for an explanation of the March 19, 1977, assassination of former head of state Marien Ngouabi and the imprisonment of Gen. Joachim Yhombi-Opango, the president overthrown in February 1979 for "high treason."

On August 17, 1986, Paris AGENCE FRANCE-PRESSE in Paris reported that

> The Congolese Revolutionary Court sentenced to death Claude-Ernest Ndalla in the trial of persons accused of having planted 2 bombs in 1982 in Brazzaville leaving 9 dead and 92 wounded. The verdict of the court broadcast live by the Congolese radio and TV monitered in Kinshasa is not subject to appeal. Jean-Pierre Thystere-Tchicaya, former #2 man of the regime, and Colonel Blaise Nzaladanda of the Peoples National Army, have been given 5-year suspended sentences. Frenchman Jean Bouissou, 61, accused of having devised and prepared an explosive device, has been sentenced to 10 years of hard labor along with his compatriot Michel Le Cornec who has been tried in absentia. The accused Kembissila, Gaspard Kivouna, and the Peoples Army officer Cadet Daniel Biampandou, have been sentenced to 20 years of hard labor along with 2 other aliens tried in absentia, CAR [Central Africa Republic] national Robert Keouane and Zairian Ndolo.

82032002

March 20, 1982 — GUATEMALA — Gunmen from the Guerrilla Army of the Poor stormed onto the farm of J. Pitts Jarvis, 63, of Swan Lake, Arkansas, who had lived in San Christobal Verapuaz, 33 miles north of the capital city, for eight years. The group demanded money and guns, ordered his wife, Marguerite, to flee, then dragged him outside and killed him in a blaze of gunfire. The guerrillas set fire to the Jarvis farmhouse but, during their escape, were fired on by a passing Army helicopter. An Army spokesman did not know if the guerrillas sustained casualties or were able to flee when additional Army units were called in. 82032003

March 22, 1982 — LEBANON — Three gunmen fired from a car on Al-Hazimiyah-Al-Jamhur Road in the east Beirut suburb of Hazmiy, killing Ali Hajem Sultan, the Iraqi embassy's third secretary, who was driving home to west Beirut at 3:00 P.M. from the embassy premises in Al-Hazimiyah. 82032201

March 22, 1982 — UNITED STATES — The Cambridge Central Square office of Orhan Gunduz, the honorary Turkish consul in Cambridge, Massachusetts, and Topkapi Imports, his import/export store, were bombed by the Justice Commandos for the Armenian Genocide, causing extensive structural damage but no injuries, only five hundred yards from police headquarters, at 7:55 P.M. 82032202

March 22, 1982 — WEST BERLIN — Two Ethiopians were injured at the Hotel Domus in West Berlin–Wilmersdorf when a bomb they were working on exploded. A second bomb was found in a hollowed-out book. Extensive structural damage was reported to the building and its neighbor, and cars below were damaged. The duo may have intended to kill a West Berlin church official who criticized the Ethiopian government. 82032203

March 24, 1982 — LEBANON — Saboteurs bombed the pipeline carrying Iraqi crude oil to Lebanon, halting pumping for 10 hours while firefighters battled the blaze just inside Lebanese territory. 82032401

March 25, 1982 — ISRAEL — An Israeli soldier was killed in Gaza when a grenade was thrown at him by a Palestinian youth. The Democratic Front for the Liberation of Palestine initially took credit, then said the general Palestine Liberation Organization (PLO) command under Yasir Arafat was responsible. Hours later, Mahmoud Labadi, PLO spokesman, reversed the earlier PLO statement and said the group was not responsible. The PLO did, however, hail an uprising on the West Bank: "The PLO executive committee, as it assumes its responsibilities in action on various levels in these dangerous and delicate circumstances, took a number of decisions and measures to assure broad support for the uprising of the masses and the indefinite strike and achievement of the broadest Arab and world support for this struggle."

March 25, 1982 — INDIA — Between 40 and 50 people firebombed the United States consulate in Bombay, damaging the consulate and 11 cars, including that of the consul general. No American injuries were reported, but Indian guards killed one of the protestors when they fired at the demonstrators. Police arrested 30 people, including Digambar Dhingre (Bandu Shingre), leader of the Free India Army (Free India Party, Indian Independent Forces, Azad Hind Sena), and charged them with attempted murder, trespass, rioting, and arson. The group said the United States was attempting to attack India via its arms sales to Pakistan. 82032501

March 26, 1982 — LEBANON — Five kilograms of dynamite exploded at 1:30 A.M. in a Burj Hammud movie theater in a section of northeast Beirut controlled by Bashir al-Jumayyil's United Christian Militia, killing 2 people, including 1 person who carried an Egyptian identity card, and wounding 20 others, including Joseph Damuri Sami al-Khiz, Tony Jirjis, who lost a leg, Hasasn Darwish, Jean 'Arnut, Egyptian citizen Hisham 'Abd al-'Aziz, and another Egyptian. The Front for the Removal of Foreigners from Lebanon said it would continue these attacks until April 28, after the Israelis withdraw from the Sinai. 82032601

March 26, 1982 — ECUADOR — Demonstrators threw five Molotov cocktails at the United States consulate office and staff apartment building in Guayaquil. Only two devices ignited, causing minor damage to the building and three cars. The devices were made of kerosene and lubricating oil rather than gasoline. 82032602

March 27, 1982 — COLOMBIA — The April 19 Movement (M-19), supporting the Faribundo Marti National Liberation Front (FMLN) in opposing the Salvadoran elections, threw a grenade and a dynamite bomb over the wall surrounding the Salvadoran embassy, damaging windows, furniture, and a door. A guard exchanged fire with the bombers and captured a wounded female terrorist. A wounded man escaped with his companions on foot. 82032701

March 27, 1982 — EL SALVADOR — Michel Setboun, a French photographer working for TIME magazine, was shot in the side when his car was riddled in a cross fire between guerrillas and soldiers guarding a military tanker truck convoy near San Vincente, 60 kilometers from San Salvador. Setboun managed to walk to a hospital. 82032702

March 28, 1982 — ITALY — Israel asked European governments to close Palestine Liberation Organization (PLO) offices after what it termed violations of its cease fire with the PLO, including a bombing of Jewish-owned stores in Rome. Bombers also attempted to attack the Rome branch of El Al Airlines. 82032801

March 29, 1982 — FRANCE — The Spanish Basque Battalion bombed the Paris-Toulouse Capitole express train, killing five and wounding 28. The group said it would "attack in France every time that the military wing of the Basque Nation and Liberty [ETA] carried one out in Spain." Friends of Carlos also claimed credit. Carlos had threatened to attack French interests if his incarcerated friends Magdalena Kaupp (also spelled Kopp) and Bruno Breguet were not released before April 15. 82032901

March 29, 1982 — COLOMBIA — The United States consul found four sticks of dynamite leaning against the wall of his Cali home. The fuse had gone out a half-inch from the primer. 82032902

March 30, 1982—SOUTH KOREA—KOREAN CENTRAL NEWS AGENCY (KCNA) in Pyongyang reported that a fire broke out at the Walker Hill resort of the United States Army near Seoul during the morning. Two persons were burned.

March 31, 1982—FRANCE—Three gunmen fired a Sten machine gun at a police hut outside the Israeli consulate in Paris, then drove off. No injuries were reported. The Lebanese Armed Revolutionary Faction claimed credit. On April 8, police raided a garage in an outer district of Paris and found an arms cache, including the Sten gun, belonging to the leftist Direct Action group. On April 9, they arrested two members of Direct Action who were opening the garage. 82033101

March 31, 1982—GUATEMALA—The Guerrilla Army of the Poor fired an RPG-2 rocket and several submachine gun rounds from a truck at the United States embassy, causing some damage but no injuries. 82033102

April 1982—AFGHANISTAN—Rebels reportedly poisoned the Kabul water supply of the Soviet housing complex.

April 1, 1982—POLAND—Two Polish Army pilots, Jerry Jan Czerwinski, 29, and Andrzej Malek, 31, ended their paratroop training at Krakow at 11:00 A.M. by forcing mechanic Boleslaw Wronner, 35, to aid them in taking the plane to the West. The plane landed in Poland to pick up the pilots' wives, their four children, aged 1, 3, and 4, and civilian Krzystof Wasiliewski, 29, who wished to join his wife who had earlier left for the West. Flying across Czechoslovakia and Poland at treetop level to avoid radar detection, the AN-2 biplane landed at 1:47 P.M. at Vienna's Schwechat Airport with tree branches embedded in its wings. The pilots, requesting political asylum, were arrested and taken to Vienna Landesgericht Prison; the others were taken to Traiskirchen refugee camp. Wronner returned to Poland. Facing maximum sentences of 10 years, on July 20 the duo were sentenced to 1 year. Malek had claimed that he was being coerced into joining the Communist party. 82040101

April 1–2, 1982—GREECE—The Revolutionary Popular Struggle, protesting United States policy and military bases in Greece, set off a time bomb in front of the United States ambassador's residence at 2:00 A.M., breaking windows, damaging the garden wall, but causing no injuries. The People's Revolutionary Combat Group also claimed credit. Another bomb was found after midnight the next evening but was safely detonated by police away from the residence of Ambassador Stearns. A third parcel bomb was found in an outside water pipe of the United States embassy. 82040102 82040201–02

April 3, 1982 — CYPRUS — Nicosia's O AGON reported that several Arabs were declared personae non gratae and deported after the police received information that plans were afoot to murder an Iraqi merchant and to attack the Israeli embassy. The next day, the Palestine Liberation Organization (PLO) said, "Those who carry out such activities have no relation with the PLO, and they are enemies not only of the Cypriot but also of the Palestine people."

April 3, 1982 — FRANCE — A short, stocky, dark woman wearing an overcoat and beret to hide her hair stepped out from behind an ornate column in the lobby of 17 Avenue Ferdinand Buisson in Paris's 16th arrondissement and fired five shots from a Czech 7.65 mm pistol, hitting Yacov Barsimantov, 43, second secretary in charge of political affairs at the Israeli embassy, twice in the head as his wife and 8-year-old daughter watched in horror from the doorway of their apartment. His 17-year-old son chased her into a nearby subway station but was forced to retreat when she turned the pistol on him. The woman, in her 20s, reportedly used the same pistol as that used to assassinate United States military attache James Charles Ray in January. The Lebanese Armed Revolutionary Brigades claimed credit, as did the Movement of Arab Revolutionary Brigades, the Revolutionary Lebanese Forces, and the Lebanese Armed Revolutionary Factions (LARF) (al-fas'il ath-thawriya al-musallahah al-Lubnaniyah), the latter in "retaliation for the massacre committed by the US and Israeli forces against the Lebanese people." Sa'id Sayil, Fatah Central Committee member and joint forces central operations chief, said the diplomat was killed by Israeli intelligence to create an excuse for aggression against the Palestine Liberation Organization (PLO). Many quarters in Israel declared the attack a violation of the cease-fire in Lebanon and called for reprisals.

On October 1984, Lyons police arrested a Lebanese man in connection with the case. On July 2, 1985, a Paris court issued homicide charges against Georges Ibrahim Abdallah, considered one of the leaders of the LARF, after a Czech pistol found in his Paris hideout was determined to be the weapon that killed both Lt. Col. Ray and Barsimantov. Abdallah was sentenced to four years in prison in July 1986 for associating with a banned group, using false documents, and possessing arms and explosives. The Committee of Solidarity with Arab and Middle Eastern Political Prisoners conducted a series of bombings in Paris in September 1986, demanding the release of Abdallah. On November 19, 1986, Abdallah was indicted in Paris for a failed assassination attempt against the United States consul general in Strasbourg, Robert Onan Homme, on March 26, 1984. 82040301

April 5, 1982 — UNITED STATES — According to the Federal Bureau of Investigation, "At approximately 1:50 A.M., a fire was set at the Tripoli Restaurant, 162 Atlantic Avenue, Brooklyn, New York. The restaurant was located on the ground floor of a four-story apartment building. One person died and the 7 injured were admitted to hospitals. In claiming credit, a spokesman for the Jewish Defense League stated, 'This should serve notice that Jewish blood is not cheap.'"

April 5, 1982 — UNITED STATES — A middle-aged, Spanish-speaking man and two youths who called him "Father" doused a stewardess with gasoline and hijacked the Delta Airlines flight 591 flying 93 passengers and 7 crewmen from Chicago to Miami, diverting it to Cuba. One of the hijackers told a passenger he did not like the United States. Havana authorities arrested the trio. No one was injured. 82040501

April 5, 1982 — HONDURAS — Gunmen fired .38 caliber weapons and submachine guns at the United States embassy and Agency for International Development building in Tegucigalpa at 5:00 A.M., then escaped in their speeding white taxi. Minor damage and no injuries were reported. 82040502

April 6, 1982 — ARGENTINA — During the Falklands crisis, a bomb partially destroyed the home of British naval attache Captain Mitchell, whose family had received a warning. No casualties were reported. The Swiss embassy, British protective power after the United Kingdom and Argentina broke diplomatic relations, refused to give details. An earlier bombing attack against British interests damaged a school in the Buenos Aires suburb of San Andres. 82040601–02

April 7, 1982 — SYRIA — The VOICE OF LEBANON reported that two Soviet experts and two other individuals were killed in an armed ambush in the Euphrates Dam area in Aleppo. 82040701

April 7, 1982 — ISRAEL — A hand grenade thrown at tourists in a cave under the Greek Orthodox church at Jacob's Well in Nablus wounded Vellonia Kaptizia, a Greek nun in her mid-50s, and an Arab. Israeli Army chief of staff, Lt. Gen. Raphael Eitan, said this was another violation of the cease-fire. "There is no difference if the guerrillas throw a grenade in Gaza or fire a mortar shell at an Israeli settlement on the Lebanese border." Police defused a time bomb near the entrance to Nablus at Joseph's Tomb, a site holy to Jews and the Samaritan sect. 82040702

April 7, 1982 — WEST BERLIN — A fire extinguisher filled with five kilograms of explosives exploded in front of the American Memorial Library in Berlin-Kreuzberg, causing minor structural damage and broken windows, but no injuries. 82040703

April 8, 1982 — CANADA — One or more gunmen from the Armenian Secret Army for the Liberation of Armenia shot in the shoulder and leg Kemalettin Kani Gungor, 50, the Turkish embassy's commercial counselor, as he was entering his station wagon in his apartment's garage to go to work. 82040801

April 11, 1982 — ISRAEL — At 9:00 A.M., Alan Harry Goodman, 38, a Jewish immigrant from Baltimore, wearing an Israeli Army uniform, burst into the Dome of the Rock Mosque in Jerusalem and fired his M-16 assault rifle at random, killing 2 and wounding at least 9 persons. At least 30 others were wounded in 3 hours of rioting by Palestinians in protest of the attack.

Goodman, who immigrated to Israel two years previously, was initially stopped by an Israeli and an Arab policeman, both of whom he shot and wounded. He then ran toward the Mosque, shooting and killing Arab guards Haj Saleh Yamen, 70, and Jihad Ibrahim Azzizi, 20. The Israeli news agency ITIM said some victims of the attack were American tourists. He was captured 30 minutes after his ammunition ran out by 4 Israeli border policemen and the police commissioner of Jerusalem, Yeshoshua Capi. Thirty persons were wounded by gunfire, some fired by Israeli security forces and border police who tried to contain the rioting. Dozens more were injured when hit by stones.

Although Jewish Defense League (JDL) literature was found in Goodman's room, no link to the organization was found, and the JDL formally denied responsibility for the attack. However, Rabbi Meir Kahane, JDL leader, said that the JDL would provide a lawyer. On September 8, 1982, Goodman's trial began. He pleaded insanity, and psychiatrists said he lived in a fantasy world. The court rejected the insanity defense.

Arab nations strongly condemned the attack, and said this proved that Israel could not be counted upon to safeguard non-Jewish holy sites.

On April 7, 1983, Goodman was sentenced to life plus 40 years.

April 12, 1982 — LEBANON — In retaliation for Goodman's actions, the Al Aqsa Group fired several rocket-propelled grenades at the United States embassy in the early morning, causing minor damage and no injuries. 82041201

April 12, 1982 — ITALY — Three carloads of Red Brigades fired heavy shotgun pellets at Carabinieri police guarding the building where the trial of 63 Red Brigades members was to begin on April 14. The group lobbed two hand grenades to deter pursuit. The 63 defendants were to be charged in the kidnap/murder of Aldo Moro in 1978.

April 13, 1982 — SPAIN — At 30 minutes past midnight, a bomb exploded at the Madrid offices of Alia, the Jordanian airline, damaging that office and the neighboring one of LAN, the Chilean airline. A caller warned that another explosion was imminent. A second bomb damaged the Madrid offices of Egypt Tours. No injuries were reported. 82041301–02

April 14, 1982 — SWITZERLAND — Twenty unarmed members of the Iranian Marxist group Peykar took over the Iranian consulate in Geneva, holding eight people. They released two women applying for visas almost immediately but held six officials for two hours while ransacking the offices. They surrendered peacefully to police. No injuries were reported. 82041401

April 15, 1982 — ITALY— Turin police arrested Loredana Biancamano, 25, a Front Line guerrilla who had escaped from Rovigo women's jail on January 3 in a sensational escape with three other terrorists. Police found large quantities of weapons and publications in the Front Line hideout where Biancamano was staying.

April 15, 1982 — LEBANON — Dinner guests found the bodies of French consulate employee Guy Cavallo and his wife Caroline. News services suggested that a silencer had been used in the assassinations. French ambassador Paul-Marc Henry suggested that Carlos, the famed Venezuelan Popular Front for the Liberation of Palestine (PFLP) terrorist, was involved, noting his threat against French interests if two of his comrades, a Swiss man and a West German woman, were not released from a French prison by April 15. 82041501

April 15, 1982 — JAPAN — Police arrested Makoto Maemura, a member of the rightist Asia Corps, after he threw a smoke bomb into the Tokyo theater that Mrs. Francoise Mitterrand, the French president's wife, had just left after a concert. No damage or injuries were reported. 82041502

April 17, 1982 — LEBANON — BEIRUT DOMESTIC SERVICE reported that snipers slightly wounded Frederick Charlhoff, assistant military attache at the United States embassy, in the shoulder as he was crossing from the eastern to the western part of the capital across the port area at 4:00 P.M. 82041701

April 17, 1982 — NETHERLANDS — A caretaker found a bundle of newspapers and magazines containing a plastic substance, wire, batteries, and an alarm clock at the Kuwait consulate in The Hague. Police safely disarmed the device. A local newspaper claimed it had received an anonymous letter that referred to the date of April 28, 1981. 82041702

April 19, 1982 — AUSTRIA — Shortly after midnight, a bomb exploded at the Air France office in Vienna, causing no injuries and little damage. Two suspicious men were seen shortly before the attack on Kaertnerstrasse. Later, a bomb was thrown into the garden of the French embassy on Schwarzenbergplatz. VIENNA DOMESTIC SERVICE reported the damages ran into the millions of shillings, but no injuries were reported. The Islamic Revolutionary Guard, whose existence the Interior Minister doubted, claimed credit. 82041901–02

April 21, 1982 — HONDURAS — Six people in a blue pickup truck threw bombs at 7:00 P.M. at the embassies of Argentina, Peru, and Chile, causing no injuries but some damage, including damage to the car of Dr. Jose Oqueli, who was attending a party at the Chilean embassy. The Lorenzo Zelaya Revolutionary People's Command claimed credit. 82042101–03

April 21, 1982 — AUSTRIA — A 30-year-old man attacked a policeman guarding the French military attache's office in Vienna, seriously injuring him. The afternoon attacker escaped. 82042104

April 22, 1982 — FRANCE — Undaunted by protesters who exploded a teargas bomb inside the courtroom, a Paris court sentenced German-born Magdelena Kaupp (also spelled Kopp), 34, to four years in jail and a Fr 10,000 fine ($1,600) and colleague Bruno Breguet, 31, Swiss-born, to five years in jail, a Fr 10,000 fine, and a five-year prohibition from entering France. The prosecutors had asked for only two- and three-year sentences, respectively. Venezuelan-born Popular Front for the Liberation of Palestine (PFLP) terrorist Carlos had threatened French interests if the duo was not released before April 15 from the firearms possession charges.

April 22, 1982 — FRANCE — Friends of Carlos made 81 telephoned and written bomb threats against the Paris-Marseille train run. Police did not connect these threats with the discovery of 47 sticks of dynamite and 40 detonators at the Central Paris Station, which serves southeast France. 82042201–02

April 22, 1982 — FRANCE — An Opel registered in Vienna, Austria, exploded at 7:00 A.M. outside the Rue Marbeuf Paris office of the Lebanese paper AL-WATAN AL-ARABI, killing a 30-year-old woman and injuring 62 others. Journalists at the paper had previously received threats for publishing investigations into the killing of the French ambassador in Beirut. The government declared Maj. Hassan Ali, Syrian military attache, and cultural attache Mika Kassouha personae non gratae and recalled the French ambassador from Damascus for consultations. The car that exploded in front of the pro-Iraqi newspaper had been rented in Yugoslavia (other reports said Switzerland) with false papers. Syria retaliated for the expulsions by ordering two French diplomats out of Syria within 48 hours and recalling its ambassador. LE MONDE reported that French counterespionage had been on alert for two weeks because of information on "Syrian hit squads." FRANCE SOIR also noted that Carlos had made threats against French interests in retaliation for the trial of two of his friends. 82042203

April 24, 1982 – LEBANON – A bomb exploded at 7:30 P.M. at the As-Sana'i (Beirut) offices of AGENCE FRANCE-PRESSE, causing material damage. 82042401

April 24, 1982 – FEDERAL REPUBLIC OF GERMANY – Roughly 150 pro-Khomeini demonstrators attacked the international student dormitory in Mainz, beating and stabbing anti-Khomeini students. One German woman died of stab wounds. German police arrested 86 attackers. Many suggested that Tehran and the Iranian embassy in Bonn were responsible. 82042402

April 26, 1982 – GREECE – The Popular Revolutionary Struggle (ELA) bombed two International Business Machines (IBM) facilities in Athens at 4:00 A.M., causing $16,077 damage to the IBM technical services facility, shattering glass in nearby buildings and a small hotel, and damaging the IBM corporate office, but causing no injuries. 82042601–02

April 26, 1982 – GREECE – Four sticks of dynamite and a failed timing device left three days earlier by People's Struggle (Laikos Agonas) were found near a wing of classrooms at the American College of Greece in Athens. 82042603

April 27, 1982 – SPAIN – A man and a woman fired three shots through the windshield of the car of Hassan Dayoub, Syrian cultural attache in Madrid. He returned the fire, but the duo escaped. No injuries were reported. 82042701

April 27, 1982 – GREECE – The Revolutionary People's Struggle planted a firebomb that went off after midnight in the car of United States embassy secretary Walerka Stanislas, who had parked the car in a private garage in an apartment building at 15 Fokilidhis Street in the Kolonaki district of Athens. No injuries were reported. 82042702

April 28, 1982 – HONDURAS – Four pistol-wielding members of the

Lorenzo Zelaya Popular Revolutionary Forces hijacked a Honduran four-engine turboprop Dash 7 flying 48 passengers, including 13 Americans, from La Ceiba on a domestic flight. The plane landed at Tegucigalpa airport, where the group released 13 women, 1 child, and 1 man. The group demanded $1 million and the release of 86 political prisoners held by Honduras, but these demands were later scaled down in the face of Honduran refusal to negotiate. The government claimed it was not holding 52 of the prisoners, and the hijackers dropped their ransom demands from $1 million to $250,000, then $150,000, and then $100,000. The hijackers threatened to set off the 60 sticks of dynamite they had wired to the plane but claimed they would first shoot United States Standard Fruit Company executive Greg Barcom.

On May 1, NBC news correspondent Brian Ross led 7 passengers and 3 crewmen to freedom by diving from the emergency exit, racing across the darkened one hundred-yard wide landing strip, and smashing through a glass window of the airport terminal. The other 9 followed close behind. Ross suffered a severed nerve in his hand and facial bruises. Shortly after sunrise, an 8th American escaped. The group had permitted papal delegate Andres Cordero Lanza d'Mondezemolo, who served as mediator, aboard the plane. They also allowed pilot Dario Zelaya to be visited by his children on board the plane. After the escape, during which some of the passengers were injured, the hijackers released the remaining 15 hostages and asked for a plane to fly them to Cuba. While a government-owned Tan Airlines plane blocked the runway while police made sure that the dynamite was neutralized, the rest of the hostages deplaned. Havana authorities took the 4 hijackers into custody upon arrival. Robert Corbett and Heroldo Martinez, NBC cameramen, had been scheduled to fly on the plane with their colleague when the plane was hijacked. Zelaya, after whom the group was named, was a student killed in 1976 when police opened fire on a demonstration he was leading. 82042801

April 28, 1982 — UNITED STATES — The Jewish Defense League set off a small pipe bomb in front of the New York City Lufthansa office, breaking glass but injuring no one, at 2:00 A.M. 82042802

April 28, 1982 — UNITED STATES — The Iraqi United Nations Mission was bombed in the early morning, causing no damage or injuries. The Jewish Defense League (JDL) was suspected. 82042803

April 29, 1982 — ITALY — Imprisoned Red Brigades terrorist Antonio Savasta claimed that the Red Brigades promised to conduct "military operations" against Israeli embassies and Zionist targets in Europe in exchange for large quantities of Palestine Liberation Organization (PLO) arms. Savasta claimed that two large batches of arms were received by Mario Moretti of the Red Brigades' Rome column. According to the Italian news service ANSA in Rome, "The first arms shipment was loaded onto a pleasure craft and transported from Cyprus to northern Italy, where the weapons were immediately distributed among the organization's various columns, he said. The second was brought across the Franco-Italian border on foot by Moretti and other brigadists. They carried rifles, machine guns, Kalashnikovs, and calibre-nine Browning handguns. . . . The contacts with the PLO were broken off, both because Moretti and his cohorts were arrested and because the BR [Brigate Rosse] proved incapable of pulling off actions against targets on a multinational level." The PLO denied Savasta's charges.

April 30, 1982 — GREECE — At 2:30 A.M., a bomb shattered windowpanes at the American Express Bank at 17 Tsimiski Street in Thessalonika. No injuries were reported. 82043001

April 30, 1982 — GUATEMALA — The January 31 Popular Front (FP-31) fire-bombed one of two McDonald's franchise restaurants in Guatemala City to commemorate the burning of the Spanish embassy in January 1980. 82043002

April 30, 1982 — POLAND — Eight men overpowered security guards, injuring 2 guards, in hijacking a Polish airline LOT Antonov 24 twin-engine prop flying 60 passengers and crew on a domestic flight from Wroclaw to Warsaw and diverting it to the Tempelhof United States Military Airbase in West Berlin. The hijackers requested political asylum, as did 28 other passengers who remained in West Berlin. Sixteen passengers, including 6 security men, who asked to return to Poland, were taken to East Germany, then flew back home to Poland. On October 28, 1982, the 16th Criminal Bench of the Berlin Regional Court sentenced 7 hijackers to terms of 3 to 4 years for endangering air traffic. The court rejected the pleas of the 7 — including 5 members of the banned Solidarity labor union — that they were refugees rather than terrorists. However, the hijackers were permitted to remain in the West with their 16 family members — 4 wives, a fiancee, and 11 children — who landed with them. 82043003

May 1982 — HONG KONG — Chong Shing-Keung of Hong Kong was found guilty of staging a bombing plot against the Shell Oil Company. He had hoped that homing pigeons would deliver Shell's extortion payments.

May 1982 — ARGENTINA — The United States embassy received a bomb threat during a period of mounting anti–United States feeling as a result of United States support to the United Kingdom during the Falklands/ Malvinas war. 82059901

May 1982 — SUDAN — A Chadian court sentenced two Chadians to death and four others to prison terms for bombing the Chadian embassy in Khartoum in an attempt to kill opposition leader Hissene Habre. 82059902

May 1982 — LEBANON — Two Syrian workers were slightly injured when a car bomb exploded outside a mosque facing the villa of the Grand Mufti Sheikh Hassan Khaled. 82059903

May 1, 1982 — UNITED STATES — The Nuclear Regulatory Commission (NRC) reported that instrument valves at the Salem atomic power station in southern New Jersey were "apparently deliberately mispositioned" in a way that knocked out the steam generator feed-water pump, forcing the operator to reduce power immediately to keep the reactor from going into an emergency shutdown. The NRC said, "The licensee (plant owner) concluded that this deliberate act could have been the result of a labor dispute."

May 2, 1982 — IRAQ — Kurdish rebels kidnapped Renaldo Franceschi, 40, a United States employee of Atco of Calgary, Alberta, Canada, while he was working on a hospital construction project in northern Iraq. He was able to send his wife, Millie, two letters in June and July, which stressed that he was well treated. He was freed on October 3, 1982, with the help of the Iranian government and was flown home via Switzerland. 82050201

May 2, 1982 — LAOS — A hand grenade exploded at the Soviet cultural center in Vientiane during the afternoon, wounding several persons and damaging part of the three-story building. The attack followed the closing of the Third National Congress of the People's Revolutionary Party. Two young Laotians were arrested. Anticommunist guerrillas were believed responsible. 82050202

May 3, 1982 — FEDERAL REPUBLIC OF GERMANY — A bomb exploded in 4:00 A.M. in front of the Yugoslav library in Stuttgart, causing considerable damage but no injuries. The nearby Yugoslav Cultural Information Center was bombed a year earlier. 82050301

May 4, 1982 — LEBANON — A bomb exploded in the Shihin township building of Munif 'Uwaydat, killing one man, injuring three others, and destroying the offices of Syrian intelligence and the village municipality. Local residents said it was "common knowledge" that the intelligence service was located there.

May 4, 1982 — LEBANON — A bomb went off at 7:00 P.M. in the Hasan Center Building, damaging the offices of the Islamic printing and publishing house and shattering the doors of the American Life Insurance Company, the windows of Yasin's cafeteria, and the stores of Mabsut and Zayft. 82050401

May 4, 1982 — UNITED STATES — A member of the Justice Commandos of the Armenian Genocide, wearing a jogging suit and sunglasses, fired a .38 and a 9 mm handgun nine times through the windshield of Orhan R. Gunduz, the honorary Turkish consul, in Somerville, 10 miles from Boston, killing him as he was driving his car. The jogging suit and pistols were found nearby. The consul's store had been bombed in March 1982. The 6:50 P.M. shooting took place near Union Square. 82050402

May 6, 1982 — EGYPT — The Al Aqsa Organization told an ATHENS RIZOSPASTIS reporter in Nicosia that its military tribunal had tried Egyptian president Husni Mubarak on April 26 in Cairo and had condemned him to death. The statement, signed by General Omar and colonels Muhammad and Tuhami, said, "Taking into consideration Husni Mubarak's treacherous actions and the serious crimes committed by him, the military tribunal of the Al Aqsa Organization condemns Mubarak to death by shooting. The verdict is final and will be executed by commandoes of the organization." The group claimed it had condemned Anwar Sadat to death on October 28, 1978, and had executed him on October 6, 1981. 82050601

May 9, 1982 — IRAN — A car containing 40 pounds of TNT exploded at 7:30 A.M. in front of the four-story Syrian embassy, destroying the building, damaging a number of parked cars and nearby buildings, and injuring 16 passersby, including several children. No Syrian embassy employees were injured. Syrian ambassador Ibrahim Ahmed Yunis blamed Iraq and "elements of imperialism and Israel." 82050901

May 10, 1982 — NICARAGUA — Francisco Lopez and Camilo Marti, two Nicaraguans carrying pistols and grenades, hijacked an Aeronica C-046 flying 50 passengers from Bluefield to Managua and diverted it to Limn, Costa Rica, where they released all of the passengers. They held the crew, however, while requesting political asylum. Once their safety was guaranteed, they surrendered to police. No injuries were reported. Nicaragua requested extradition. 82051001

May 10, 1982 — LEBANON — A rocket was fired from a bridge 50 meters away from an apartment building housing two French embassy employees and their families but did not cause any casualties. The rocket was diverted by a second-floor balcony. It went through a window and a door and stopped in a hallway. 82051002

May 11, 1982 — SPAIN — Ninety technicians of the Iberduero Company, which was constructing the Lemoniz nuclear power plant near Bilbao in the Basque region, went on strike to protest "unbearable family, personal, and professional conditions" after Basque National and Liberty (ETA) terrorists killed technical director Angel Pascual Mugica the previous week.

May 11, 1982 — DOMINICAN REPUBLIC — The police bomb squad removed a French-made hand grenade found in a street near the entrance of the United States Agency for International Development (USAID) building across from the United States embassy in Santo Domingo. 82051101

May 11, 1982 — ARGENTINA — During the Falklands/Malvinas war, unidentified men kidnapped NEW YORK METROMEDIA CHANNEL FIVE television journalist Christopher Jones and two members of his crew. Jones was left naked on a street corner after being driven around for two hours during the night. The crew members, abducted separately, were released after their equipment was stolen. 82051102

May 12, 1982 — PORTUGAL — Juan Fernandez Krohn, 32, a dissident Spanish priest shouting, "Down with the Pope, down with Vatican Two," was stopped six yards from Pope John Paul II in the shrine of Our Lady of Fatima. A security guard was slashed while disarming the priest of his 15-inch dagger at 11:00 P.M. Krohn was charged with attempted homicide and ordered held for trial. Although Krohn claimed he had been ordained a priest by traditionalist Archbishop Marcel Lefebvre, his Swiss headquarters said Krohn "has not been a member of our religious community for the past two years," as a result of doctrinal quarrels. On May 1, 1983, a Vila Nova de Ourem court sentenced him to 6½ years for attempted murder, 7 months and a $180 fine for disrupting the courtroom, and expulsion from Portugal.

May 12, 1982 — ARGENTINA — During the Falklands/Malvinas war, unidentified gunmen, described by one of their victims as "not unofficial," kidnapped three THAMES TELEVISION crewmen (Julian Manyon, a reporter; sound man Trevor Hunter, 38; and cameraman Edward Adcock, 41, all of London) at 2:00 P.M. as they left the foreign ministry, where they were seeking an interview with Argentine foreign minister Nicanor Costa Mendez. A blue Ford Falcon cut off their car on a one-way street. THAMES producer Norman Fenton immediately jumped out of the car and watched the kidnapping from a nearby park. A .45 caliber pistol was placed against Manyon's head when he tried to resist being placed into the Falcon. Hugo de Lucca, the driver of the THAMES vehicle, was released by the kidnappers after being forced to drive 30 miles outside Buenos Aires. Manyon said that the crew were left "practically naked" in the middle of some farmland, where they flagged down passing motorists who took them to a telephone. He had been struck several times and thought he would be killed. Fenton said the kidnappers were from military security forces. Manyon said, "They had official equipment, they drove an official car and they were on an official mission for a particular interest group in this country." 82051201

May 12, 1982 — LEBANON — A bomb exploded at the Iraqi Airways office in the Ar-Rawshah area of western Beirut. 82051202

May 12, 1982 — GUATEMALA — Thirteen peasants, including several women dressed in western-region Indian costume, carrying two guns and nine Molotov cocktails, took over the Brazilian embassy, holding nine embassy staffers hostage, including Ambassador Antonio Carlos de Aheu e Silvan and Secretary Ronaldo Vera. The group, members of the Committee for Peasant Unity (CUC), unfurled a flag of the January 31 Popular Front (formed after a group of Indian peasants occupied the Spanish embassy on January 31, 1980). The group demanded a press conference to denounce the ruling military junta. On May 13, the group freed their hostages in return for guarantees of safe passage out of the country. Guatemala City's CAENA DE EMISORAS UNIDAS news service reported, "General Efrain Rios Montt, president of the ruling military junta . . . spoke personally with the CUC group and gave each activist an undetermined amount of money in Mexican pesos." The group was then bused to the airport and on May 14 flown on an Air Force DC-6 to Merida, Yucatan State, Mexico, where they were granted political asylum. In addition to the CUC members, three members of the Brazilian delegation and Antonio Chocano Batres, chief of protocol at the Guatemalan foreign ministry, flew with the peasants at their request. No injuries were reported. 82051203

May 13, 1982 — ARGENTINA — Two American banks were bombed. 82051301-02

May 15, 1982 — UNITED STATES — A federal jury sitting in Manhattan convicted six Croatian members of OTPOR for 2 murders, 4 unsuccessful murder plots, more than 50 acts of extortion against their countrymen, 3 cases of arson, 4 arson plots, and interstate transportation of explosives. Four other defendants in the three-month trial were acquitted. United States District Court judge Constance Banker Motley had the six held on bail ranging from three hundred thousand dollars to $1 million and set sentencing for June 30.

May 16, 1982 — PUERTO RICO — Unidentified gunmen fired from a passing car in front of the San Juan Yacht Club near the city's Condado district, killing Darryl T. Philips, 22, of Dublin, Georgia, and injuring Larry Skowronski, Jr., 22, of Dire, Pennsylvania; Randell L. Keyte of Adrian, Michigan; and Anthony L. Phaneuf of Ashville, Maine. The sailors were in civilian clothes, returning to the *Pensacola,* their amphibious assault vessel docked in San Juan during the Ocean Venture 1982 military maneuvers in the Caribbean. The Group for the Liberation of Vieques and the Boricuan People's Army/Macheteros claimed credit. 82051601

May 17, 1982 — UNITED STATES — At 1:15 A.M., the ALMACEN EL ESPANOL in Union City, New Jersey, was firebombed. An Omega-7 caller stated, "This is only the beginning, there will be more incidents." Minor damage to the store front was reported. 82051701

May 19, 1982 — COLOMBIA — Copilot Jairo Aranguren was wounded when he wrestled with Jose Orlando Rebellon Castano, who pulled a knife and attempted to hijack to Cuba a Taxi Aereo del Guaviare flying out of Llanos Orientales airport. "I want you to fly to Cuba, where I intend to stay. There are several bombs in the aircraft, which will explode whenever I deem it necessary," the hijacker said. Some of the 50 passengers then jumped Rebellon and turned him over to authorities at Villavicencio airport. No bombs were found. 82051901

May 19, 1982 — BOLIVIA — A bomb exploded after midnight at the United States consulate in Santa Cruz, damaging the consulate and other buildings but causing no injuries. The United States ambassador had left hours before. 82051902

May 19, 1982 — INDIA — Madras police arrested Pravakaran (Karatikalan) and Shiv Kumar (Raghavan), who were attacking two fellow Sri Lankans in the busy market area. The duo admitted to being members of the Sri Lankan extremist group Liberation Tigers (possibly identical with the Tamil Liberation Tigers). 82051903

May 21, 1982 — SOUTH KOREA — The clandestine VOICE OF THE REVOLUTIONARY PARTY FOR REUNIFICATION claimed that an individual phoned the hotel that housed United States presidential envoys to the centennial of the establishment of United States–Korean diplomatic relations and said he was a member of an Anti–United States Suicide Action Squad. He warned, "I oppose the events marking the centennial. You should return to the United States immediately. If you reject our demand, we will blow up the hotel. Yankee go home." 82052101

May 21, 1982 — GREECE — At 1:20 A.M., terrorists set off one of three propane cylinders they had planted at the United States Ellinikon airbase next to the airport. The air conditioning system was damaged when a hole was blown in the wall of the base's dairy plant. No injuries were reported. 82052102

May 22, 1982 — NICARAGUA — Three men and a woman, led by Odoniel Ortega, a leader of the Confederation for Unity of Trade Unions (CUS), hijacked the blue and white helicopter of Rodolfo Reeder Escobar from Chinandega Department and forced it to fly to Choluteca, Honduras. The Nicaraguan foreign ministry noted that the foursome were not members of the Sandinist People's Army as had been previously reported, and that Ortega had been jailed three times for trying to artificially bankrupt a business. Nicaragua requested extradition. 82052201

May 24, 1982 — LEBANON — The Moslem Holy Warriors and the Free Nasserite Revolutionaries both claimed credit for remotely detonating a car bomb inside the French embassy compound, which killed 12 and injured 25. The bomb killed a French paratrooper, part of a guard brought to the embassy recently in the wake of several attacks on French interests; Anna Cosmides, the French employee whose car was bombed; three Lebanese employees (a plumber and two messengers) of the embassy; a secretary; and several passersby or people who had come to the embassy on business. Only slight damage was reported to the embassy, but offices and shops nearby were damaged. The Liberal Nasserite Organization later claimed credit for the blast. The Al-Jihad al-Muqaddas (Holy War) organization said it was responsible "for all explosions which have already taken place, or will take place, to avenge the murder of its people in Tripoli [northern Lebanon] and in southern Beirut . . . it will attack leaders of the [leftist] Lebanese National Movement." The Front for the Liberation of Lebanon from Foreigners had claimed credit for three blasts three days ago that had killed 4 and wounded 15 others in Beirut. One of those explosions was near the United States embassy. 82052401

May 25, 1982 — FEDERAL REPUBLIC OF GERMANY — Belgrade TANJUG press service reported that bombs exploded in the Ausburg and Buttelheim Yugoslav clubs, causing no casualties and minor damage. TANJUG suggested that "a group of the anti-Yugoslav fascist and terrorist underground" was responsible. 82052501–02

May 27, 1982 — MOROCCO — A 35-year-old male Moslem fundamentalist seized a Royal Air Maroc airliner from its Casablanca-bound flight from the Mideast with one hundred passengers and landed at Tunis, where he surrendered. He handed the pilot a list of demands to be transmitted to the Moroccan government: prohibition of sale or consumption of alcoholic drinks throughout the country; a harsh crackdown against "dissolute morals;" strict application of Koranic principles and laws; and restriction of Casablanca radio broadcasts to dissemination of Islamic teachings and religious sermons. 82052701

May 27, 1982 — IRAQ — Kurdish rebels were believed responsible for kidnapping eight employees of the Yugoslavian firm Djuro Djakovic at the Tasluchi cement plant under construction. 82052702

May 28, 1982 — FRANCE — Direct Action gunmen fired three shots from their car at the Bank of America offices in central Paris, damaging glass entrance doors but causing no injuries. 82052801

May 28, 1982 — ITALY — The Rome offices of Pan American World Airways, the READER'S DIGEST, and the Italian subsidiary of the United States Intercontinental Insurance Company were bombed, causing some damage to the buildings and parked cars. 82052802–04

May 29, 1982 — ZIMBABWE — An Argentine got into an argument with two members of the British military training team in Harare and shot one of them in the head. The soldiers were identified as S. Sgt. Anthony Lancaster (who was grazed by the bullet) and Sgt. Keith Lamb. Argentine businessman Orlando Mendez was accused of opening fire from his car outside a nightclub, charged with attempted murder, and released until June 14 on $560 bail. He was ordered to surrender his passport.

May 30, 1982 — UNITED STATES — Three Armenians were detained for placing a bomb at the Air Canada freight terminal at Los Angeles International Airport. According to a Federal Bureau of Investigation surveillance team, the trio drove from Van Nuys at 1:45 A.M. to the airport, where one placed a package against the wall of the Air Canada cargo entry area. The bomb squad of the Los Angeles Police Department defused the bomb 15 minutes before it was set to explode. Police believed the bomb was placed in retaliation for the arrest of Armenians in Canada two weeks earlier. On June 6, 1982, police at Orly Airport, Paris, arrested Vicken Tscharkhutian, 29, of Iraq, for complicity in this incident and a Swiss bank bombing. On August 18, 1982, the Paris Appeals Court recommended against extradition of the Armenian Secret Army for the Liberation of Armenia (ASALA) member. 82053001

June 1982 — FRANCE — Prime Minister Pierre Mauroy reportedly called for antiterrorist forces to bring back Popular Front for the Liberation of Palestine (PFLP) terrorist Carlos dead rather than alive.

June 1982 — UNITED STATES — Harout Sassounian, an Armenian, was convicted of firebombing the home of Turkish consul general Kemal Arikan, who was later shot and killed by Sassounian's brother, Hampig.

June 1982 — PAKISTAN AND AUSTRALIA — The Turkish intelligence service reportedly foiled Armenian terrorist plots to assassinate Turkish diplomats in Karachi and Sydney. 82069901–02

June 1982 — POLAND — Police prevented the hijacking of a flight from Katowice to Warsaw, which would have been diverted to West Berlin, by some men from Sosnowiec. 82069903

June 1982 — FRANCE — Two bombs exploded outside Israeli-owned Paris cafes. 82069904–05

June 1982 — EGYPT — The United States embassy received a bomb threat. 82069906

June 1982 — FRANCE — A bomb outside the American Express office in central Paris was defused. 82069907

June 1982 — FEDERAL REPUBLIC OF GERMANY — A West German neo-Nazi shot and killed two black Americans and an Egyptian at a Nuremberg disco frequented by United States soldiers. 82069908

June 1982 — MOZAMBIQUE — Members of the Mozambique National Resistance Movement kidnapped an Italian priest, Giuseppe Alessandro. 82069909

June 1982 — MOZAMBIQUE — A 30-year-old Portuguese technician who worked at a Mozambique sawmill was shot dead at his doorstep. His wife claimed his killers were white South Africans who had blackened their faces for the Mozambique National Resistance Movement attack. Soon afterwards, 50 Swedes abandoned their jobs and fled into Zimbabwe. 82069910

June 1, 1982 — FEDERAL REPUBLIC OF GERMANY — Between 12:30 and 3:00 A.M., the Revolutionary Cells bombed three officers' clubs at United States military bases in Hanau, Gelnhausen, and Bamberg, shattering windows and, in Gelnhausen's empty officers' club, seriously damaging the club's interior. Another bomb went off at the headquarters building of the United States 5th Army Corps in Frankfurt, destroying 40 windows. In Duesseldorf, bombs went off at the International Business Machines Corporation and Control Data Corporation, causing extensive damage to the lobbies. No injuries, but $150,000 total damage, were reported. A bomb was safely defused at a West Berlin ARMED FORCES RADIO transmission tower. The Revolutionary Cells tied their bombings to the visit of President Ronald Reagan to West Germany and his meeting with NATO leaders on June 10 in Bonn. "We are not waiting until Reagan comes. As a start for a hopefully very loud, eventful and unforgettable reception, we have today attacked some of the nests of the US military in the Federal Republic of Germany." 82060101–07

June 1, 1982—ITALY—A bomb caused a fire that destroyed the suburban Rome building of the Ford Car and Truck Company and several tractors and cars. No injuries were reported. 82060108

June 2, 1982—CANADA—Judge Paul Martineau of the Superior Court of Quebec released Italian physicist Francesco Pieperno because of a total "lack of evidence" that he was in collusion with the Italian Red Brigades.

June 2, 1982—FEDERAL REPUBLIC OF GERMANY—The German International Telephone and Telegraph offices in Hanover were bombed, causing extensive damage but no injuries. 82060201

June 2, 1982—GREECE—At 4:00 A.M., the Popular Revolutionary Struggle (ELA) bombed two American Honeywell Corporation offices in Athens (one was on the third floor and one on the fifth floor at 46 Singros Avenue), causing damage to windows. At the same time, the ELA firebombed three cars: the car on Mikhalakopoulos Street belonged to a United States serviceman, the one at the corner of Libya and Krataios streets belonged to the Yugoslav embassy, and the one on Gazia Street belonged to the Bulgarian embassy. No injuries were reported in any of the incidents. 82060202–06

June 3, 1982—ITALY—The American Express office in a Rome suburb was bombed, shattering windows and damaging a newsstand. Two Molotov cocktails were thrown against a Ford dealership in Rome, but no damage was reported. A bomb shattered windows at a Carrier Company warehouse and damaged five cars. No injuries were reported in any of the incidents. 82060301–03

June 3, 1982—FEDERAL REPUBLIC OF GERMANY—The Revolutionary Cells firebombed the German-American Institute in Teubingen, causing little damage. 82060304

June 3, 1982—FRANCE—The VOICE OF LEBANON reported that French authorities prevented an assassination attempt against French president Mitterrand by a group led by Yusuf at-Tabbal. 82060305

June 4, 1982—INDIA—A gunman fired from a car and killed Mustafa M. al-Marzook, first secretary of the Kuwaiti embassy, as he stood near his car outside his home in Geentanjali, a south Delhi suburb. A laundry man alerted the police, who searched for a man who escaped in an Indian car. 82060401

June 4, 1982—FRANCE—Direct Action bombed the American School in St. Cloud outside Paris, causing $25,000 damage but no injuries. 82060402

June 4, 1982—ITALY—A bomb exploded at the General Motors dealership in Ostia. 82060403

June 4, 1982—SWAZILAND—A bomb exploded in the car of Petros Nyawose, deputy chief representative of the South African African National Congress (ANC) in Manzini, killing him and his wife, Jabu. Several people were injured. Nyawose left South Africa in the 1970s after working with the ANC and the South African Congress of Trade Unionists. 82060404

June 4, 1982—UNITED KINGDOM—An Arabic man pulled a Polish-made WZ-3 9 mm submachine gun out of a bag and fired at Israeli ambassador Shlomo Argov, 52, as the ambassador was leaving a party at 11:00 P.M. at London's exclusive Dorchester Hotel. The party was being held for the diplomatic community by the De La Rue Company, a British-based currency printing and security systems firm. A single bullet passed completely through Argov's head as he walked to his car. Argov was paralyzed in all four limbs and will have impaired vision for life.

Argov's London policeman bodyguard pursued the attacker and winged him in the neck before arresting him. Police also arrested two more Arabs in what was believed to be the getaway car; a fourth Arab was arrested later. Two of the terrorists were students, including the injured assassin, and were from Jordan; one terrorist was from Syria; and the fourth, a merchant, was reported to be from Iraq. Police suggested that the four, only one of whom held a passport (which may have been falsified), were Palestinians living in those countries. Police seized a 9 mm submachine gun believed to be the would-be assassination weapon, two Beretta handguns, a large amount of ammunition, and hand grenades. Prime Minister Thatcher reported that a "hit list" containing the name of a Palestine Liberation Organization (PLO) official in London, who presumably was to be killed, was found on one of the suspects.

Nabil Ramlawi, the PLO representative in London, denied that his organization was involved in the shooting. "The Israeli Ambassador is a victim of a determined campaign now being waged in European capitals to discredit the PLO and to undermine the understanding and friendship which exists between the Palestinians and the [European Common Market] governments." Al Asifa (Black June), led by Abu Nidal, later claimed credit for the attack. The attackers reportedly admitted under interrogation that they were Black June members. On December 6, 1982, the Israeli newspaper HA'ARETZ noted that "the three had been in contact with the military attache office at the Iraqi Embassy in London. It seems that the weapons used in the assassination attempt were supplied by the Iraqi military attache."

Israel considered this an unacceptable breach of the cease-fire in Lebanon, and its jets bombed suspected PLO hideouts in Lebanon. On June 6, Israeli military forces invaded Lebanon and forced the PLO guerrilla units north into their Beirut stronghold, where the PLO held out for 79 days. The PLO were finally persuaded to disperse their forces to various Mediterranean countries.

On January 26, 1983, the two Jordanian students and the Iraqi merchant pleaded not guilty to charges of shooting the ambassador. The trio were identified as Ahmad Ghassan Said, Marwa Al Banna, and Novoff Nagib Meflehel Rosan. On March 5, Said, 23; Banna, 20, of Jordan; and Rosan, 36, from Iraq, were convicted in London's Central Criminal Court. Said, who fired the shots, received a 30-year sentence. Banna, the driver of the getaway car, also received 30 years. Rosan received 35 years because, in the view of the judge, he was "older and deserved more substantial punishment." Police indicated that the trio arrived in the United Kingdom in 1980 or 1981 and took language courses while preparing "for acts of assassination or sabotage." The prosecutor claimed that "they spent considerable time collecting information about Jewish interests and personalities in London, including top secret details of security at the Israeli Embassy." Police found hit lists of prominent British Jews and Jewish institutions, including kindergartens and synagogues. Police later said that Rosan was a colonel in the Iraqi intelligence service, as well as the deputy commander of Abu Nidal's special operations section. 82060405

June 5, 1982—FRANCE—The Air Zimbabwe B-707 carrying Zimbabwean prime minister Robert Mugabe, his wife Sally, and the Zimbabwean ministers of finance, manpower, industry, foreign affairs, and agriculture was forced to land at Orly Airport after Gatwick received a bomb threat against the Harare-bound plane. The Mugabes and more than 150 other passengers safely evacuated the plane, and no bomb was found. Mugabe had left Harare on May 17 for a tour of the United Kingdom, Italy, Belgium, West Germany, France, Greece, and the Netherlands. 82060501

June 5, 1982—FRANCE—The Benchella Column, possibly linked with Direct Action, bombed the International Monetary Fund and World Bank in Paris, causing moderate damage and no injuries. 82060502

June 7, 1982 — PORTUGAL — A member of the Justice Commandos for the Armenian Genocide, wearing a track suit and a white stocking mask, assassinated Erkut Akbay, a Turkish embassy attache, outside his Linda-a-Velha home in the Lisbon suburbs. His wife was critically wounded. The killer threw a Belgian-made gun under Akbay's car before escaping on foot. Mrs. Nadide Akbay died from brain injuries on January 10, 1983. 82060701

June 7, 1982 — ROME — Ten members of the Communist Anti-Imperialist Movement threw two Molotov cocktails through the smashed showroom window of the General Motors-owned Opel dealership in Rome, causing minor damage. 82060702

June 7, 1982 — LEBANON — At 2:00 P.M., a rocket fired from the direction of 'Ayn al-Muraysah hit the sixth floor of the United States embassy, causing material damage, but no injuries. 82060703

June 8, 1982 — FEDERAL REPUBLIC OF GERMANY — The Revolutionary Cells mailed packages resembling parcel bombs to nine United States–owned firms throughout the country from Hagen/Westfalen. The padded envelopes contained a cardboard lining with an alarm clock, a flat battery, and a cigarillo packet filled with a plasticinelike substance, which was inflammable but not explosive. A sticker said, "In the next war no one will be innocent. Stop the madness. We wish mister president and his friends a hot reception." (President Ronald Reagan was visiting the country.) The firms that received the parcels included Dow Chemical; Dupont and Morgan Bank in Duesseldorf; International Business Machines in Muenster; Rank Xerox and Coca-Cola in Essen; and Opel, GRAETZ RADIO, and an oil firm in Bochum. 82060801–09

June 8, 1982 — SWITZERLAND — The Revolutionary Cells bombed the Israeli and United States consulates in Zurich, causing $50,000 damage to the United States facility and slightly less damage to the Israeli consulate. No injuries were reported. 82060810–11

June 9, 1982 — POLAND — Janusz Telarczyk, a sanitarian pilot, hijacked his Morava survey plane from Szczecin to Sturup Airport outside Malmo, Sweden, where he and his wife, his two children, and a friend requested asylum. The plane was assigned to control the Polish coastal fishing sphere on the Baltic. Marian Deminicki, a senior inspector of maritime fishing who was also on the plane, asked to return to Poland. 82060901

June 11, 1982 — AUSTRIA — The Vienna home of Simon Wiesenthal, 73, founder and head of the Jewish Documentation Center, which had ferreted out nearly one thousand Nazi war criminals, including Adolf Eichmann, was bombed during the night, causing severe damage but no injuries. Police had warned Wiesenthal to take precautions, but he said threats did not worry him. Wiesenthal, a World War II concentration camp survivor who had twice been placed before firing squads, once told an interviewer, "My entire family is gone. What can they do to me now?" 82061101

June 14, 1982 — SPAIN — The Autonomous Anti-Capitalist Commandos, possibly with Basque Nation and Liberty (ETA)/Military Wing ties, fire-bombed two empty buses in Torremolinos that had been used to transport Scottish soccer fans to the World Cup being played in Spain. 82061401

June 16, 1982 — KENYA — Several shots were fired at a safari bus carrying Americans in Nairobi. One shot hit the bus, but no injuries were reported. 82061601

June 16, 1982 — FEDERAL REPUBLIC OF GERMANY — An incendiary device was found in a cable shaft of the Sperry Univac building in West Berlin after the German press agency received a telephone call regarding an attack on the firm. The attack was "in solidarity with the Palestine people . . . against imperialist war." 82061602

June 16, 1982 — BRAZIL — A bomb was found by Capt. Henzo Battagliarin on the Liberian supertanker *Hercules*. Its 28 crewmen abandoned ship and Capt. Juliano Galo, a spokesman for the Rio de Janeiro naval base, said the ship was ordered to leave port for the high seas until the bomb was removed or defused. 82061603

June 16, 1982 — ARGENTINA — No bomb was found after the United States embassy received a bomb threat. 82061604

June 17, 1982 — EL SALVADOR — Rebels shot down the helicopter of deputy defense minister Col. Francisco Adolfo Castillo as he was flying at 5:00 P.M. over the village of Azacualpa, a few kilometers north of San Fernando in Morazan Department. His death was initially reported to the rebels' clandestine RADIO VENCEREMOS by guerrilla commander Claudio Armijo (Francisco), but later Castillo's voice was heard over the rebel radio. Military sources denied that the guerrillas were holding Castillo.

June 17, 1982 — LEBANON — The Israeli Defense Ministry claimed it had captured Armenian and Turkish terrorists at Palestinian camps in southern Lebanon. Elomo Benu, director of the Turkish desk of the Israeli Foreign Ministry, said, "The organic ties between PLO [Palestine Liberation Organization] and the Secret Army for the Liberation of Armenia (ASALA) are being coordinated by one of the officials of the Soviet Embassy in Beirut with whose name and reputation we are quite familiar. Despite the fact that the aims of the PLO differ from those of ASALA, members of ASALA manage to receive training in terrorism at the PLO camps through the mediation of the Soviet Embassy. We have concrete proof of this."

June 17, 1982 — ISRAEL — A three-judge panel convicted Ziad Abu-Eian, 23, of El Bireh, of murder and sabotage in the May 14, 1979, explosion in Tiberias that killed 2 Israeli teenagers and wounded 36 others. He was sentenced to life imprisonment and given 45 days to appeal. Reportedly working for Al Fatah, Abu-Eian was extradited to Israel in 1981 after losing a lengthy battle against extradition in the United States.

June 17, 1982 — ITALY — Nazeyk (also spelled Nazih) Matar, 32, a Lebanese medical student, journalist, and Palestine Liberation Organization (PLO) sympathizer, died in Rome when four gunmen fired at him from a car outside his home shortly after midnight. The Jewish Armed Resistance of the Jewish Defense League told the New York ASSOCIATED PRESS office it was responsible. 82061701

June 17, 1982 — ITALY — Just a few hours after he visited the scene of the attack on Nazeyk (also spelled Nazih) Matar, a Lebanese student killed by a terrorist attack, Hussein (also spelled Husayn) Kamal (also given as Kamal Hussein), 33, Jordanian medical student and deputy of the Palestine Liberation Organization (PLO) office in Rome died when a shrapnel time bomb exploded as he backed his car out of his garage at 7:00 A.M. Again the Jewish Armed Resistance of the Jewish Defense League told the New York ASSOCIATED PRESS office it was responsible. A female passerby was hurt in the bombing. The PLO charged that Israeli terrorists were responsible. Suheil Natur, spokesman for the Democratic Front for the Liberation of Palestine, said, "Israel is profiting from our situation in Lebanon to kill our comrades throughout the world. The names of Hussein Kamal and Nazeyk Matar join those of so many Palestinians assassinated by the Zionist agents, but their death will not halt our march towards the revolution." 82061702

June 18, 1982 — ITALY — Police at Rome's Fiumicino Airport arrested Christa Margot Frohlich, believed to be a member of the West German Red Army Faction, after customs authorities found she was carrying a false-bottomed suitcase filled with 3½ kilos of T-4 explosives, 2 electric detonators, and a timing mechanism. She also had falsified Austrian and West German passports, an authentic West German identity card, $3,500 in several currencies, and train schedules for the Rome-Paris line. 82061801

June 18, 1982 — TURKEY— Two armed men and two women forced a night watchman to open the doors of the Pan American Airlines offices in Ankara, which they then firebombed. The foursome escaped in a Mercedes, having caused extensive damage but no injuries in their protest of the Israeli invasion of Lebanon. 82061802

June 19, 1982 — ITALY— Bombs caused minor damage and no injuries at the Rome offices of the American Express firm, the Italian-Israeli Chamber of Commerce, and the Hebrew Immigrant Aid Society. 82061901–02

June 24, 1982 — ZIMBABWE — At 3:30 A.M. gunmen suspected of being army deserters fired an RPG-7 rocket launcher and small arms at the guards in front of the homes of Prime Minister Robert Mugabe and National Supplies Minister Enos Nkala. The arms and truck the group used in the two-hour attack were stolen from the nearby King George VI barracks. Guards returned the fire, killing one of the attackers, a black man, near Nkala's home. Others may have been injured in the fighting in the Borrowdale suburb. Some press members speculated that the attackers were "dissidents," the Zimbabwean code word for former members of Joshua Nkomo's anti-Mugabe Zimbabwe African Peoples Union (ZAPU) guerrilla group. On June 30, the minister of home affairs, Herbert Ushewokunze, announced the arrest of three officers, five enlisted men, and several civilians in connection with the attacks.

June 24, 1982 — INDIA— About 50 people protesting the invasion of Lebanon sacked the United States International Communication Agency (USICA) library in Calcutta, causing $50,000 damage. They dragged one watchman two blocks before he was released and injured two others. 82062401

June 27, 1982 — LEBANON — Gunmen driving a Peugeot fired a rocket-propelled grenade and automatic weapons at the United States embassy, missing the building but wounding two passersby. 82062701

June 28, 1982 — EL SALVADOR— Guerrillas captured six journalists on a road north of the capital. Listed as missing were Julian Harrison, a British cameraman for UNITED PRESS INTERNATIONAL TELEVISION NEWS, Salvadorans Victor Tobar, Pedro Garcia, Rafael Magana, and Carlos Rosas, television crew for the local NBC NEWS affiliate; and freelancer Eduardo Vazquez Becker. Their car and van were found at noon near Palacios in Cuscatlan Province, parked near a bus still smoldering after a guerrilla attack. The group was reported alive and well a day later by armed forces in Suchitoto, 30 miles north of the capital. 82062801

June 30, 1982 — INDIA — Wearing dynamite sticks around his neck, Sepala Ekanayaka, 33, a Sri Lankan, hijacked Alitalia Flight 1790, a B-747 flying from Rome to Tokyo via New Delhi, Bangkok, and Hong Kong with 261 people. Upon landing in Bangkok, he released 138 passengers but threatened to blow up the plane if he was not given $3 million and if his estranged Italian wife and 4-year-old son were not brought to him from Italy. Two hostages escaped, and 4 more were released shortly thereafter. He released the remaining hostages 32 hours later, when he was given $300,000 and was reunited with his wife and son. Thai antihijack commandos had been perched near the jet. An Air Lanka plane brought him to Colombo, where he emerged carrying $297,700 and was cheered by the crowd. He and his family stayed at the luxury Intercontinental Hotel in Galle, 72 miles from Colombo, where he bought a shirt with the slogan, I Am a Genius. Follow Me. After he deposited $280,000 in a bank, he was arrested on July 3 and charged with extortion. Before his arrest, he said, "If the government attempts any action against me, my wife, my child, or my friends, I have the means to deal with such a threat. I will safeguard my interests either by good or by bad means." 82063001

July 1982 — TURKEY — On February 24, 1983, the Ankara ANATOLIA news service reported that "the Martial Law Court of Istanbul acquitted and released from custody Thursday the 3 Palestinian guerrillas accused of perpetrating attacks against the Israeli consulate and its personnel. The Palestinians, Sukur Mohamed Ibrahim, Abdulfettah Jalhan and Izettin Rida Masrojeh were on trial for 'conspiring to commit a felony' facing prison terms of 10 years each. They were captured at Istanbul's Yesilkoy airport last July. The three thanked the judges shouting 'shukran' ('Thank you' in Arabic)."

July 1982 — VATICAN CITY — A Frenchwoman carrying a fake gun and a New Zealander carrying a knife were arrested shortly before Pope John Paul II's weekly audience in St. Peter's Square.

July 1982 — PHILIPPINES — President Ferdinand Marcos blamed Moslem terrorists for the attack by gunmen on the Philippine minister of state for foreign affairs outside his home. Emmanuel Palaez was shot and wounded, while his driver died.

July 1982 — FRANCE — Armenian terrorists and the rightist French Revolutionary Brigades were blamed for setting off four bombs in a 24-hour period. One of the bombs was intended to kill a top adviser to President Francois Mitterrand. 82079901–04

July 1982 — NETHERLANDS — DE TELEGRAAF and ALGEMEEN DAGBLAD reported that a group of Moluccan terrorists who had been recently arrested for shooting at police had plotted to kidnap Queen Beatrix and Prime Minister Andries van Agt. 82079905

July 1982 — COSTA RICA — A bomb destroyed the San Jose offices of Honduran Air Services (SAHSA) but caused no injuries. 82079906

July 1982 — MOZAMBIQUE — Members of the National Resistance Movement kidnapped six Bulgarian road technicians in the northern central province of Zambezia. 82079907

July 1982 — HAITI — The WASHINGTON POST reported on March 20, 1983, that

> The [Federal Bureau of Investigation] has been involved in efforts to combat the subversion since Haitian exiles attempted last July to land a commando team from a light plane that flew from Miami to a mountain road near Bonaives, north of Port-au-Prince. The five-man group, armed with US-made submachine guns bought in Miami, intended to assassinate the president at his nearby farm, US and Haitian authorities later said. But the efforts flopped and the group flew back to the US after wounding one American tourist. In what US diplomatic sources qualified as a gesture to Haiti, a Haitian exile was arrested in Miami Jan. 12 and charged with violating the Arms Export Control Act and the Neutrality Act in connection with the July raid. He was identified as Joel Deeb, son of a former mayor of Port-au-Prince who was an adviser to the current president's father. Sixteen persons, mostly businessmen of originally Middle Eastern families, were arrested here shortly after the raid. They were interrogated and released after about two weeks, diplomatic sources reported. Deeb is of Lebanese extraction.

82079908

July 1982 — SPAIN — Jack Anderson reported in the April 9, 1986, WASHINGTON POST that the United States embassy in Madrid had learned of a Libyan plot to assassinate King Fahd of Saudi Arabia. Quoting from what he purported to be an embassy cable, Anderson wrote, "The group which would carry out the murder had access, through a US agency intimately connected with the [Central Intelligence Agency], to the Saudi royal family's security measures." 82079909

July 4, 1982 — KUWAIT — The State Security Court sentenced three Palestinians to prison terms, fines, and deportation for smuggling one hundred kilograms of explosives — the most ever confiscated in Kuwait — for "an act of sabotage in the country." Ahmad 'Attiyah Ahmad 'Abdallah was sentenced to 15 years imprisonment for "abusing the hospitality of Kuwait." Sa'id Yusuf 'Abd al-Fattah received 10 years for harboring the explosives in his house. His wife, Jihad al-Fattah, was fined three hundred Kuwaiti dinars for possessing the explosives without a license. The court ignored their plea that the explosives were to be used only in Israel, suggesting that they should have been shifted directly from Iraq, where they originated, to occupied territory. Most of the explosives were reportedly manufactured in Eastern Bloc countries.

July 4, 1982 — UNITED STATES — At 5:45 P.M. a pipe bomb exploded at the offices of Frlan Travel, Astoria, New York. The offices and four nearby cars were damaged. The Federal Bureau of Investigation believed the Croatian Freedom Fighters (CFF) were responsible. The Bureau said the CFF is a generic name used by the Croatian National Resistance, an international anti-Yugoslav organization committed to the establishment of Croatia. The name is used to claim responsibility for terrorist attacks. 82070401

July 4, 1982 — UNITED STATES — At 8:30 A.M., the bomb squad of the New York Police Department discovered a pipe bomb scheduled to detonate at 9:20 A.M. in front of the Yugoslav Airlines office in New York City. Police defused the bomb, believed by the Federal Bureau of Investigation to have been placed by the Croatian Freedom Fighters. 82070402

July 5, 1982 — QATAR — The clandestine VOICE OF PALESTINE reported: "A brother Palestinian living in Doha, Qatar, this morning rammed the US Embassy building with his car, which was full of rubber tires and incendiary material. He set fire to the car, which exploded, setting fire to the embassy's entrance. This action is to protest the US stand, which supports the Israeli enemy in invading Lebanon, and to seek revenge for the operations of annihilation to which the Lebanese and Palestinian peoples are being subjected — operations being carried out by US arms of devastation and destruction." 82070501

July 5, 1982 — UNITED STATES — Two small pipe bombs exploded at 9:15 A.M. at the Lebanese and French consulates, breaking windows but causing no injuries. Earlier in the day, bombs made from fireworks broke four shop windows and damaged three telephone booths in lower Manhattan. The Jewish Defense League (JDL) was suspected. 82070502–03

July 6, 1982 — ITALY — The Italian news service ANSA reported that Interior Minister Virginio Rognoni told the Chamber of Deputies that "since 1969,

13,000 attacks [by terrorists] were carried out, claiming 315 lives and injuring 1,075. Since 1974, 11 magistrates and 72 policemen have been killed by terrorists. Since December 17, 1981, the day Dozier was kidnapped, more than 400 leftist suspects and 58 rightist suspects have been arrested."

July 7, 1982 — LEBANON — Turkey's Istanbul GUNES news service reported:

> It has been disclosed that militants belonging to 40 terrorist organizations from various countries received training in the past 5 years in the PLO [Palestine Liberation Organization] camps in Lebanon. It has been stated that among the foreign terrorists trained in these camps, Turkish terrorists top the list. According to information, the following are some of the organizations trained in the PLO camps:
>
> Turkish: Dev-Sol (Revolutionary Left); Dev-Yol (Revolutionary Way); TKP-ML (Turkish Communist Party-Marxist-Leninist); TKIP (Turkish Communist Workers Party); Acilciler (The Swift Ones); Halkin Devrimci Conculeri (People's Revolutionary Pioneers); Dev-Savas (Revolutionary Fight); MLSPB (Marxist-Leninist Armed Propaganda Union [or Unit]); Devrimci Halk Birligi (Revolutionary Turkish People's Union); Turkiye Devrimci Kommunist Partisi (Turkish Revolutionary Communist Party); Apocular (Followers of the Abdyllah Ocal Group).
>
> European: Red Brigades; ETA [Basque Nation and Liberty]; IRA [Irish Republican Army]; RAF (German Red Army Faction); the Italian Marxist-Leninist Vanguard Organization; the Corsican Separatists; the Swiss Anarchists Union.
>
> United States, Asian and Africans: The Secret Army for the Liberation of Armenia (ASALA); the Japanese Red Army; the National Liberation Front of El Salvador; the Nicaraguan Sandinista guerrillas; the Argentine Montoneros guerrillas; the Peronist Revolutionary Movement; the American Indian Movement; Sri Lanka guerrillas; the Ku Klux Klan; the Dhofar Front guerrillas.
>
> The WSG, known as the War Sports Groups, representing the neo-Nazis, is also reported to have received training in the PLO camps. It is reported that these militants, who have embarked on various acts of militancy against foreign workers in Germany, particularly against Turkish workers, are among those trained in the PLO camps. In the past few months, two Turkish workers were killed by members of this organization.

July 7, 1982 — LEBANON — Iranian radio blamed lax Lebanese security for the kidnapping by Phalangists of Seyyed Mohsen Musavi, the second-ranking official of the Iranian embassy, and his three companions as they were on their way from Damascus to Beirut. The kidnapping occurred at a border checkpoint. 82070701

July 7, 1982 — FRANCE — Orly police arrested an Iranian carrying two kilograms of explosives. Police reported he planned to assassinate former Iranian president Abol Hassan Bani-Sadr, who was living in exile in France. 82070702

July 15, 1982 — FRANCE — The Corsican National Liberation Front was believed responsible for setting off several bombs during the night at an empty Swedish tourist coach near Ajaccio, Corsica; at a German-owned hotel at Ile Rousse on the west coast; at a newly built casino in Calvi; and at restaurants in Ajaccio, causing heavy damage but no injuries. 82071501–02

July 16, 1982 — THAILAND — An antitank 72 mm mortar shell just missed hitting a convoy of Prime Minister Gen. Prem Tinsulanon in the artillery center compound, Narai Maharat camp, in Lop Buri Province. The shell exploded on a nearby hill, causing no damage or injuries. The Bangkok MATICHON news service reported on August 25 the "arrest of Master Sgt. Somchai Koetphon of Lop Buri Military District. Somchai, who is a relative of Supreme Commander General Saiyut Koetphon, was later released because of lack of evidence. . . . On 5 August Colonel Auai Kutsuwan led a number of soldiers to arrest four noncommissioned officers of the Lop Buri Military District's service company: Master Sgt. Surasak Kusonsuk, a unit commander; Master Sgt. Chaiwat, or Chaiwai, Rotsamoe; Sgt. Sutchai Ma-Im; and Sgt. Thongchua Nonloet. On 7 August, Private Wichai Saengdet was arrested on the same charge. . . . Eyewitnesses confirmed that they saw M. Sgt. Chaiwat Rotsamoe and Sgt. Sutchai Ma-Im running away from the site where the investigating officers found three mortars, one of which had been fired. The other two mortars were loaded, but the shell in one of them was a dud. The five accused are now being detained at the first military circle's prison. They denied the charge. It has been reported that Colonel Khemchat Nitisiri, deputy chief of staff of the Lop Buri Military District, who is suspected of being implicated in the incident, has gone on leave until 19 August. The investigating officers could find no evidence against him."

On October 28, M. Sgt. Prawet Phumphuang and Prem Thanomwong were arrested in Loei Province. On December 21, 1982, army sources indicated that Phumphuang claimed the mastermind of the plot was Maj. Phairat Phophruksawong, who had fled to Malaysia and then to Burma.

July 19, 1982 — LEBANON — Two gunmen kidnapped David Dodge, 60, acting president of the American University of Beirut, founded by his missionary grandfather in 1866, on campus. When Dodge resisted, the duo hit him on the head with a pistol butt and shoved him into the back of a red

Renault station wagon. One of the men shouted, "Amal," an Arabic word for "hope," which is the name of the Shiite Moslem militia. Dodge was also kidnapped during the 1975–76 Lebanese civil war. On August 3, Lebanese security sources reported that Dodge was still alive, but unconscious, and probably in the custody of a pro-Iranian Amal group. Several government officials theorized that Dodge was being held in the Iranian embassy to obtain the release of the Iranian charge d'affaires and two high-ranking Iranian military officers who were abducted in early July.

On July 21, 1983, a United States military plane brought a freed Dodge back to the United States from Frankfurt, West Germany, where he went from his release in Iran. Dodge had been spirited out of Lebanon shortly after his capture. A White House announcement praised the "humanitarian efforts" of Syrian president Hafez Assad and his brother, security chief Rifaat Assad, in the case. United States sources said no ransom had been paid nor other deals made to obtain Dodge's release. 82071901

July 20, 1982 — FRANCE — Police suspected a pro-Palestinian group was responsible for exploding three bombs in front of an Israeli bank and the Paris office of a company that imports Israeli electronic components. Leaflets with the slogan Palestine Will Live and the Paul Eluard poem "Liberty" were found at the bank. No injuries were reported. 82072001–02

July 20, 1982 — FRANCE — The Orly Group, a faction of the Armenian Secret Army for the Liberation of Armenia, set off a bomb in a metal trash can in the Place St. Michel, about four hundred yards from Notre Dame, injuring 16 people, including several foreign tourists who were crowded into a Paris cafe terrace. 82072003

July 20, 1982 — UNITED KINGDOM — Nine soldiers died and 49 other persons were injured when the Irish Republican Army (IRA)–Provisional Wing set off two bombs in London where ceremonial military units were performing for tourists. At 11:00 A.M., a bomb went off as a detachment of scarlet-coated troopers from Queen Elizabeth's Household Cavalry rode through Hyde Park on their way to the changing of the guard ceremony at the Horse Guards military parade ground in Whitehall. A remote control device was apparently the trigger for the explosion of a pale blue car that set off a rain of four- to six-inch nails inside a plastic bomb. Two soldiers of the Household Cavalry were killed, and 4 soldiers and 17 civilians injured. Eight horses died on the spot. At 1:00 P.M., a bomb exploded under a Regent's Park bandstand where the Royal Green Jackets band was playing. Six army bandsmen died, and 24 soldiers and 4 civilians were injured. A 9th soldier later died of his wounds. An IRA statement released in Dublin invoked the recent British victory over Argentina in the Falkland Islands and declared, "The Irish people have sovereign and national rights which no task or occupational force can put down. . . . Now it is our turn to properly invoke Article 51 of the UN statute and properly quote all Thatcher's fine phrases on the right to self-determination of a people." Police believed the bombs may have been an answer to the conviction in Ireland the previous week of Gerard Tuite of the IRA, who was charged under a 1976 Irish law aimed at prosecuting terrorist offenses committed in the United Kingdom. Five other IRA members were arrested in Ireland during the weekend for a major arms discovery in Donegal County, on the western border with Ulster. 82072004–05

July 21, 1982 — NETHERLANDS — Kemalettin Demirel, the Turkish consul general in Rotterdam, escaped injury when four gunmen fired on his car while he was being driven to work in the morning. Dutch policemen wounded and captured one of the Armenian terrorists, but the other three escaped in their car. A news agency in Beirut was phoned by the previously unknown Armenian Red Army, which claimed responsibility. 82072101

July 21, 1982 — LEBANON — The Italian news service ANSA in Rome reported that Israeli forces in Lebanon captured two Italian Red Brigadists from Bolzano and Milan who had killed an unarmed Israeli officer. The Israeli MA'ARIV daily wrote that several Red Brigadists were captured near Sidon. Beirut's Phalangist Radio had reported on January 13 that 620 Brigadists, 153 West German Red Army Faction members, and 8,000 other foreign terrorists were in Palestinian camps in Lebanon. 82072102

July 23, 1982 — UNITED STATES — Two men shouting "Cuba" splashed gasoline on Michael Monroe, 36, a Key West charter boat captain and hijacked a Marco Islands Airways twin-engined Martin 404 prop plane taking commuters from Miami to Key West. The men diverted the plane to Havana, where they were taken into custody. The plane finally arrived in Key West at 2:06 A.M. with its other seven passengers. No one was hurt, although the hijackers held a lighter just a few feet from Monroe. 82072301

July 23, 1982 — FRANCE — Three men threw a bomb from their car into the car of the assistant director of the Palestine Liberation Organization (PLO) Paris office, Fadl ad-Dani, 37, who was getting ready to drive to work. Dani was killed immediately in the 8:30 A.M. attack. The Jewish Armed Resistance, a splinter group of the Jewish Defense League, called a Paris radio station to claim credit. Later, Abu Nidal, a group of Palestinian dissidents named after their leader, also claimed credit, saying ad-Dani was a traitor executed "to avenge the January 1980 murder in Paris of a Lebanese national who fought for the Palestinian cause, Yusuf Mubarak." The VOICE OF PALESTINE, blaming the Israelis, who denied the charge, said, "This abominable crime comes a few days after the assassination of struggler Muhammad 'Isa al-Qaddumi, chairman of the Palestinian student union branch in Turkey, and strugglers Nazih [also spelled Nazeyk] Matar and Husayn [also spelled Hussein] Kamal [Kamal Hussein] in Italy." 82072302

July 23, 1982 — ZIMBABWE — Bandits believed to be dissident members of Joshua Nkomo's Zimbabwe African People's Union (ZAPU) opposition party and former members of his guerrilla group kidnapped 6 foreign tourists — 2 Americans, 2 Britons, and 2 Australians — in the Bulawayo area. The tourists were in a converted truck on the last part of a cross-Africa tour when rebels halted them at a roadblock between Victoria Falls and South Africa. The driver and 3 women were released. Due to harsh tactics of the security services in searching for the 12 dissidents, local cattlemen provided the kidnappers with food, shelter, clothing, and cover from the authorities. On July 29, Prime Minister Mugabe, rejecting the dissidents' demand for the release of ex-guerrilla leaders Dumiso Dabengwa and Lookout Masuku, approved of their being charged with treason in court along with 5 of their ZAPU followers. The kidnappers threatened to kill their hostages if the 2 men were not released. Mugabe replied, "We shall never ever allow a gang of criminal bandits and the party which sponsors their criminality to usurp sovereignty over the people. Accordingly, I shall be invoking extremely harsh and short-shrift measures to administer shock treatment to these harmful pests and their deceitful mentors. The bandits are operating on instructions from a number of ZAPU leaders. These men are ZAPU. The weapons are from ZAPU. . . . ZAPU alone has created the bandits and ZAPU alone must unmake them." Joshua Nkomo, ZAPU leader, publicly appealed for the release of the hostages. During the fifth day of the search, soldiers found a cache of army camouflage uniforms, believed used by the kidnappers, and civilian clothes, which may have been those of the hostages. On August 1, a motorist claimed to have found 3 decomposed bodies of what may have been 3 of the hostages. On August 11, Zimbabwean security forces reported that they may have killed 4 of the original 12 kidnappers in a gun battle. By the end of the year, clues were drying up, and the hostages had not been found.

The hostages were identified as Kevin Ellis, 24, and Brett Baldwin, 23, both United States citizens; Britishers James Greenwell, 18, and Martyn Hodgson, 33; and Australians Tony Balzelj, 25, and William Butler, 31. Their parents offered to pay the legal costs of Dabengwa and Masuku if their sons were released. On February 27, 1983, AGENCE FRANCE-PRESSE reported that the families had received two replies to their full-page ad regarding the legal fees. On March 22, 1983, Zimbabwe High Court judge Hilary Squires dismissed treason charges against 6 of the 7 defendants, effectively ruling out conspiracy charges as well. Dumiso Dabengwa still had to face charges stemming from a letter he wrote in 1980 to the then chairman of the Soviet KGB, Yuri Andropov, asking for Soviet assistance. The seven also faced lesser charges of illegal possession of weapons. A message from individuals claiming to be the kidnappers had been received on March 17, 1983, threatening the hostages' lives if the accused were not freed within the month. On April 27, 1983, Judge Squires found the defendants not guilty of treason and illegally caching arms for a coup. However, the defendants were immediately detained again by police under Zimbabwe's Emergency Powers Act, a holdover from colonial times, which permits detention without trial.

On June 12, 1983, the press reported that 5 captured dissidents indicated that the hostages had been killed within two days of their abduction.

On June 21, 1983, the Zimbabwean government claimed that it was holding 5 dissident guerrillas who had kidnapped the tourists. Although the dissidents claimed that the tourists were killed shortly after their abduction, the prisoners were unable to locate the graves. On August 19, the government claimed to have killed the kidnappers' leader on August 9, 1983, near the Lupane area of western Zimbabwe.

On July 30, 1983, 2 Zimbabwe People's Revolutionary Army (ZIPRA, ZAPU's paramilitary wing) dissidents wanted for the murder of 2 Matabeleland farmers surrendered to police and demanded a meeting between Mugabe, ZAPU leader Joshua Nkomo, and United Kingdom diplomats to arrange for the tourists' release. Gilbert Sithela Ngwenya (Eskimo Mwasi, Ntjela), leader of the group, claimed on April 3, 1984, that the 6 were still alive and being held in Zambia but refused to specify their whereabouts. He claimed the 6 had been kidnapped to force the government to return ZAPU properties and to release detained opposition leaders. The properties were confiscated in 1982 after arms caches were found on them. On November 22, 1984, High Court judge Wilson Sandura sentenced to death Gilbert Sithela Ngwenya, 42, and Austin Mphofu, 25, admitted members of a 17-member gang that had kidnapped the group. On March 8, 1985, Ngwenya claimed during a meeting with Minister of Justice Eddison Zvobgo that a message was sent to Nkomo notifying him of the death by strangulation of the tourists. He claimed that Nkomo then urged the bandits to continue the fight to topple the government. HARARE DOMESTIC SERVICE reported that villagers in Lupane "have since been arrested for their part in the murders, and all have admitted to have complicity in the burial and reburial of the bodies." On April 7, 1986, the sheriff of Zimbabwe announced the hanging of Ngwenya and Mphofu.

On December 19, 1984, Zimbabwean rebels said that the 6 tourists were still alive, according to a spokesman for the Australian embassy in Harare.

On February 28, 1985, Zimbabwean authorities were investigating reports that two jungle graves had been found with the skeletons of the tourists. Australian high commissioner Alan Edwards said a captured rebel had volunteered to show the graves where the tourists were buried after having been shot three days after their capture. Prime Minister Mugabe announced on March 7, 1985, that the bodies were positively identified. HARARE DOMESTIC SERVICE quoted Mugabe as saying,

> The dissidents killed the tourists after a government helicopter search-
> ing for the six flew past the hut in which they had been huddled. The
> tourists had cried out for help, after which the dissidents killed them.
> He said with the assistance of the villagers the people buried the tourists
> in three shallow graves. The dissidents also forced the villagers to drive
> some cattle over the graves to obliterate any sign that might have ex-
> posed them to the security forces. Comrade Mugabe said some of the
> villagers who participated in the bloody act have since been arrested.
> . . . Sixteen of the team of 22 dissidents have either been arrested or
> killed in contact with security forces.

82072303

July 24, 1982 — FRANCE — Armenian terrorists bombed a Left Bank cafe in Paris, slightly injuring two women. 82072401

July 24, 1982 — POLAND — Members of the Citizens' Militia prevented the hijacking of a Polish airline LOT plane which was to depart at 5:55 P.M. from Wroclaw to Warsaw. The militia detained nine men and two women, who had hoped to fly to West Germany. 82072402

July 24, 1982 — THAILAND — Channel 9 Director Suwan Mettayanuwat re-ceived a threatening letter from the Popular Front for the Liberation of Palestine (PFLP), demanding that the station stop referring to the PFLP as "bandits." The letter was mailed from P.O. Box 997, Jidda, Saudi Arabia, on July 10, and was signed by George Habash, the PFLP chieftain. The letter's English was generally unintelligible but said, in part, "We knew from Thais in Saudi Arabia, you called us bandit, you talk about Palestin-ions [sic] against Israeli anywhere in the world. . . . We are Popular Front for the Liberation of Palestine. We fight for our right in Palestine land. If you see the movie Rider [sic] of the Lost Ark on that movie showed Pales-tine land not Israel. . . . We fight against Israel not Thailand, not your organization. We love Thais, we don't want to hurt you. Why do you hurt us? . . . Remember we used to occupied Israel Embassy in Bangkok, after than we knew that day is your prince's birthday. . . . This is a last request letter. Hopefully, your next broadcast about us." The incident the PFLP was referring to was the December 28, 1982, takeover of the Israeli embassy by Black September on the investiture, not the birthday, of Crown Prince Vajiralongkorn. 82072403

July 25, 1982 — PEOPLE'S REPUBLIC OF CHINA — Five men in their 20s hijacked a (CAAC) Civil Aviation Administration of China Soviet-built Il-yushin 18 turboprop Flight 2505 flying from Xian to Shanghai at 9:59 A.M. and demanded to be flown to Taiwan. Several of the passengers and crew jumped the hijackers, who exploded a grenade. Reports differ as to whether all or any of the hijackers were killed or wounded in the explosion, which bore a three-foot square hole through the plane, or whether any of the 72 passengers, including 19 Americans and 10 Japanese, were wounded. The plane landed at Shanghai. RADIO PEKING on August 19 reported that the 5 hijackers were executed, and that the 8 crew members and 13 passengers received citations and monetary rewards for foiling the hijacking. Tokyo's NHK Television Network reported "a rumor since the end of last year that an abortive hijacking incident took place in Guangzhou in the southern part of China. It was also near the end of last year that airport security was suddenly tightened in China. Moreover, a CAAC passenger plane crashed in Guilin in April of this year killing all of the 110 crewmembers and passengers aboard. A Chinese antiestablishment group issued a statement claiming responsibility for the Guilin incident and suggesting that the plane was bombed." 82072501

July 25, 1982 — PERU — Bombs exploded at the United States embassy and at the local distributors of Coca-Cola and of Alfa Romeo cars in Lima, causing light damage but no injuries. 82072502–04

July 26, 1982 — FRANCE — Interior Minister Gaston Defferre denied reports that he had agreed not to arrest any non-French Armenian militants. The LIBERATION newspaper reported an interview in Beirut with the Armenian Secret Army for the Liberation of Armenia (ASALA) Orly Group leader Mihran Mihranian who claimed that such an agreement had been broken in December with the arrest of an Armenian-American. The group responded with two bomb attacks on Left Bank cafes that injured 17 people on July 20 and 24.

July 26, 1982 — FEDERAL REPUBLIC OF GERMANY — West German press services noted that police had found a suspected Red Army Faction (RAF) vehicle parked in a visitors' car park at a rehabilitation center in Meisenheim in Rhineland-Palatinate. The floor of the luggage compartment contained a forged Austrian plastic identity card for Henning Beer, 23, who was suspected of carrying out the RAF attacks on the United States Ramstein Airbase and on United States general Frederick Kroesen in Heidelberg along with RAF leaders Christian Klar and Brigitte Mohnhaupt.

July 27, 1982 — EL SALVADOR — Patricia Cuellar, 24, a United States citizen, was abducted from her luxury home in San Salvador. The next day, her father, Mauricio Cuellar, manager of the Salvadoran Industry Association, was kidnapped from his San Salvador home. 82072701

July 31, 1982 — LEBANON — Hagop Hagopian, a spokesman for the Armenian Secret Army for the Liberation of Armenia, and his bodyguard died from injuries suffered in an Israeli bombing of the group's Beirut headquarters the previous day.

July 31, 1982 — FRANCE — A suspected Armenian terrorist believed responsible for two Latin Quarter explosions the previous week died in his Paris apartment when one of his bombs exploded prematurely. 82073101

July 31, 1982 — FEDERAL REPUBLIC OF GERMANY — A bomb exploded at 3:00 P.M. inside a suitcase in the passenger terminal of El Al Airlines at Munich Riem airport, injuring two police guards, an El Al security officer, and four civilians. Extensive damage was reported. 82073102

August 1982 — ZIMBABWE — Two mineworkers were shot dead 15 miles north of Bulawayo.

August 1, 1982 — KENYA — Kenya Air Force senior sergeant Pankras Oteyo Okumu and senior private Hezekiah Ochuka, seeing that the coup attempt they had participated in had failed to overthrow Kenyan president Daniel arap Moi, hijacked an air force plane and flew it to Tanzania, where they were granted political asylum. Kenya's protests and request for extradition were rejected by Tanzania's chief magistrate, Goodwill Korosso, who said that Kenyan Air Force pilots, Maj. Nick le Leshani and Maj. William Marende, had not been kidnapped by the hijackers but had willingly flown to Tanzania to escape the loyalist army attack on the air force coup plotters. 82080101

August 1, 1982 — EL SALVADOR — Unidentified gunmen shot and killed Bernard Dewerchin, a Belgian architect overseeing construction of a hospital in Santiago Texacuangos, six miles southeast of the capital. The hospital project was for the San Salvador archdiocese of acting archbishop Arturo Rivera y Damas. 82080102

August 1, 1982 — IRAQ — Abu Hilal crashed his car, filled with 250 kilograms (about 550 pounds) of TNT, into the information section of the Iraqi Ministry of Planning in Baghdad, killing himself and 19 others and wounding 138, including the Greek ambassador and 2 of his employees. Among the dead were 5 of the ministry's police guards and 5 women employees. The Iraqi Mujahedeen Movement, whose members follow the Iraqi Shiite leader, Ayatollah Mohammad Baqer al-Hakim, who lives in Iran, claimed credit. 82080103

August 3, 1982 — FEDERAL REPUBLIC OF GERMANY— A time bomb set off fires from several cans of gasoline, causing $16,000 damage to two United States Army jeeps and an army truck outside the Schwaebisch-Gmuend barracks of the United States 56th Field Artillery Brigade. A second bomb failed to explode. No injuries were reported. 82080301

August 4, 1982 — FEDERAL REPUBLIC OF GERMANY— Police learned of a threat two weeks previously to poison the Blankenese district of Hamburg's water system if an extortionist was not paid eight hundred thousand dollars. Police found out about the plot after the water authority, which did not report the demands to avoid alarming the public, made an unsuccessful attempt to hand over the money. The water authority claimed that measures had been taken to react quickly if supply cuts became necessary.

August 4, 1982 — INDIA— A police inspector and passengers overpowered a bearded young Sikh who had hijacked an Indian Airlines jetliner with 135 people on board. The group jumped the Sikh, who was armed only with a rubber ball, while the plane was on the ground at Amritsar, India. He had demanded three hundred thousand dollars and the release of various militants of his Hindu sect. Lahore, Pakistan, airport authorities had refused landing clearance. 82080401

August 5, 1982 — HONDURAS— Three bombs were set off at the Tegucigalpa offices of International Business Machines, Air Florida, and a local business, injuring 10 people. The Lorenzo Zelaya Revolutionary Front said it was protesting United States "intervention" in Central America and claimed that 38 United States pilots and crewmen were shuttling 1,000 Honduran troops to a new army base near the Nicaraguan border. Several suspects were interrogated by police. 82080501–02

August 5, 1982 — FEDERAL REPUBLIC OF GERMANY— Incendiary devices destroyed two American vehicles. Other devices were defused at United States military bases near Stuttgart. Letters expressing pro–Palestine Liberation Organization (PLO) sentiments were found near the sites of the blasts. 82080503–05

August 7, 1982 — TURKEY— Three members of the Martyr Kharmian Hayrik Suicide Squad of the Armenian Secret Army for the Liberation of Armenia fired submachine guns and set off a bomb in a crowded international flight terminal passenger lounge at Ankara's Esemboga Airport as passengers waited to pass through customs for a Dutch flight. One terrorist took a bomb out of a black attache case and hurled it at the passengers, while the others strafed them with submachine gun fire, yelling, "More than a million of us died; what does it matter if 25 of you die?" Police returned the fire and wounded one of the terrorists, Levan Ekmekjian (also spelled Levon Ekmekgian), 25, who carried a French passport. Two other attackers ran into the nearby cafeteria and held 20 persons hostage for two hours. When a police officer entered the cafeteria to accept a proffered message, one of the terrorists panicked and set off a bomb. Security forces then rushed the cafeteria, killing 1 terrorist and wounding Bekir Sitki Sancar, a Turkish terrorist. The group had entered Turkey through Syria. The Armenian Secret Army for the Liberation of Armenia (ASALA) told news agencies in Beirut that the group was protesting "the Turkish fascist occupation of our land" and warned of suicide attacks in the United States, Canada, France, United Kingdom, Switzerland, and Sweden unless 85 prisoners held in those countries were freed in seven days. Among the dead was American citizen Jean Bosworth, 50, shot in the back, of Falmouth, Massachusetts. Her husband, D. F. Bosworth, was wounded in the attack. Also killed was a West German, Herbert Osanowski, 53, and 3 Turkish policemen in the three hours of fighting. Approximately 72 people were wounded in the attack, which killed at least 9.

On March 20, 1983, AGENCE FRANCE-PRESSE reported from Ankara that

> Levon Ekmekgian, the militant Armenian executed in January after killing 9 people in an attack on Ankara airport, claimed that Armenian liberation leaders had set up in the Greek sector of Cyprus, well informed sources here said. Mr. Ekmekgian reportedly made the claim in a "confession" to members of the Turkish Political Police who interrogated him in prison. He reportedly said that leaders of the ASALA aimed at "tearing away" parts of Turkey to create an independent state with Armenians from the Soviet Union. He also said they planned to assassinate more Turkish diplomats in foreign countries, the sources said. The organization has already claimed responsibility for killing numerous Turkish diplomats, mainly in West European capitals. During his trial, Ekmekgian reportedly sent letters to Turkish authorities protesting ASALA actions. He also denounced his former comrades in a press conference organized by authorities at Mamak Prison. At a press conference Friday, Turkish Foreign Minister Ilter Turkmen repeated charges that the Greek part of Cyprus had "welcomed Armenian terrorist leaders," and added that "recent discoveries would give weight to our suspicions."

82080701

August 8, 1982 — VENEZUELA — Luis Posada Carriles, an anti-Castro Cuban, and Hernan Ricardo, a Venezuelan, wearing military uniforms, escaped from San Carlos Prison in central Caracas and fled to the Chilean embassy, where they requested political asylum. A military court had ruled in 1980 that there was not sufficient evidence to hold the duo (as well as the leader of the anti-Castro group, Orlando Bosch, and Freddy Lugo) on charges of planting a bomb in a Cubana Airlines plane, which exploded off the coast of Barbardos in October 1976, killing all 73 on board. The two men were not released, however, pending Supreme Court ratification of the verdict. A Chilean embassy spokeswoman said the men were transferred to Ambassador Carlos de Costa Nora's residence in the Valle Arriba area of the capital. Twenty National Guard troops ringed the residence. The two returned to their cells on August 11 when Chile turned down their asylum request but announced that their "security and physical integrity" was assured. 82080801

August 9, 1982 — FRANCE — Two slightly built gunmen in their 20s with dark hair walked into Jo Goldenberg's Restaurant on Rue des Rosiers in the heart of the heavily Jewish Marais Quarter and fired Polish-made WZ-63 machine pistols at the staff and customers. They backed out of the restaurant, still firing, then opened up on a group of people in front of a nearby synagogue, setting off a grenade. They escaped into a waiting white car by walking slowly toward it and firing at anyone who watched from nearby windows. Direct Action claimed credit but later denied responsibility. The Palestine Liberation Organization (PLO) also denied responsibility. Abu Nidal's Black June organization was suspected by Austrian police, who reported that the weapons used were similar to those used in the August 29, 1981, attack in Vienna and the shooting of Israeli ambassador Shlomo Argov in London on June 4. On August 16, a gardener at Paris's Bois de Boulogne found one of the guns in a clump of bushes near a busy intersection in the forest park.

Two Americans and 4 French citizens were killed and another 22 people were wounded. United States citizen Grace Cutler, 66, was killed. She had been traveling with Eva Shure, 65, a Chicago resident who was seriously wounded. Also killed was Ann Van Zanten, 31, of Evanston, Illinois, who was curator of the archaeological collection at the Chicago Historical Society. Her husband David, 38, an art history professor at Northwestern University, suffered minor shrapnel wounds. One of Goldenberg's Moroccan employees was killed outside the restaurant and another was wounded trying to shield a child. In the confusion, Marko Goldenberg, the restaurant owner's son, fired a shotgun and seriously wounded a plainclothes policeman, whom he took to be a terrorist. Several of the wounded had their legs amputated. One hour before the attack, Goldenberg received a call from someone who said, "Palestine will win." On August 17, President Francois Mitterrand appointed Joseph Francesci to a cabinet-level post to coordinate the country's antiterrorism actions at home and abroad. The next day, the government invoked a 1936 law against private militias to formally dissolve Direct Action, whom police said might have helped a radical Palestinian group in the attack. About 20 Direct Action members had been taken in for questioning.

On February 20, 1983, the WASHINGTON POST reported from Bonn that "West Germany said that it has asked for the extradition of two suspected neo-Nazi terrorists held by Britain, one of whom French police want to question about the attack on a Jewish restaurant in Paris last summer. Two West Germans identified as Walter Kexel and Ulrich Tillman were arrested by British police Friday in the coastal town of Poole, 115 miles southwest of London. In Paris, a French police spokesman said officials would fly to London today to question Kexel about the attack by machine-gun wielding terrorists on the Goldenberg restaurant in Paris' Jewish quarter." 82080901

August 10, 1982 — FRANCE — Thirty-six hours after the Goldenberg restaurant attack, Direct Action bombed the Banque de Gestion Privee in the early morning near the Champs Elysee, severely injuring a woman walking her dog. The bank had been the Jewish-owned Banque Meyer before the socialist government nationalized private banks earlier in the year.

August 11, 1982 — AFGHANISTAN — During a midnight one-hour raid, Afghan rebels wounded two Afghan soldiers guarding the Soviet embassy and captured two others.

August 11, 1982 — FRANCE — A van pulled up to the Iraqi embassy on the Rue de General Appert in Paris's exclusive 16th District and exploded at 6:00 P.M., injuring at least six people and setting fire to a parked bus and several other vehicles. Tehran's IRANIAN REVOLUTIONARY NEWS AGENCY (IRNA) news service reported that the Iraqi Islamic Amal Organization claimed credit, saying it was retaliating for "Iraq's severe treatment of its political prisoners and . . . warning . . . France to discontinue its arms sales to Iraq." The group said it supported the Islamic revolution of Iran. Tehran's INTERNATIONAL SERVICE news group said that the Group of the Martyr Talid Shahim al-'Alubi, under the command of the Special Operations Section of the Islamic Action Organization, claimed that, in the name of Sadat's assassin, Khalid al-Islambuli, the "organization warns the treacherous Egyptian regime and the other reactionary regimes against supporting the infidel Ba'thist regime." The same group claimed credit for a bombing in Thailand on December 2, 1982. 82081101

August 11, 1982 — GUATEMALA — Unidentified individuals threw a package of dynamite at the Israeli embassy, then sped off in their pickup truck. The dynamite exploded one thousand feet from the embassy, damaging five cars and breaking one of the embassy's windows but causing no injuries. Guards fired on the attackers, apparently wounding one terrorist. Elsewhere in the city during the night, dynamite was thrown at a synagogue but did not explode. Police suggested the communist-led Guatemalan Labor Party (GLP) was responsible. Leaflets condemning Israel's bombing raids on Beirut were found near the synagogue. Interior minister Col. Ricardo Mendez Ruiz had paid for the publication of a GLP statement condemning Israeli support for the military government in compliance with a demand by rebels holding his kidnapped son. The statement appeared in the newspapers of seven Latin American nations, San Francisco, Los Angeles, and Miami. 82081102

August 11, 1982—JAPAN—An explosive device went off under the passenger seat of Toro Ozawa, 16, who was flying on a Pan American World Airways B-747 with 284 others from Tokyo to Honolulu. The blast killed him, wounded 16 others, and blew a 12" × 36" hole in the passenger cabin's floor. 82081103

August 12, 1982—FEDERAL REPUBLIC OF GERMANY—A small bomb damaged a car in the United States military housing area in Frankfurt but caused no injuries. 82081201

August 14, 1982—FRANCE—Terrorists firebombed a small working class district synagogue belonging to the Beth Roch Pinah sect in Paris, causing serious damage but no injuries. The group believes in Jesus as the Messiah but adheres to strict orthodox Jewish teachings. Police found a cardboard box with sheets of paper bearing Nazi swastikas and Star of David symbols underneath a parked car.

August 15, 1982—PORTUGAL—The Zionist Action Group bombed the Air France and Lufthansa offices in Lisbon, causing heavy damage but no casualties, to protest French and West German policies toward Israel. 82081501–02

August 17, 1982—MOZAMBIQUE—Ruth First, 59, director of research at Maputo's Eduardo Mondlane University and wife of exiled African National Congress and South African Communist party leader Joe Slovo, was killed when she opened a parcel bomb sent to her office from Europe. The bomb caused extensive damage and injured Dr. Bridget O'Laughlin, a United States lecturer at the University's Center for African Studies; South African social scientist Paulo Jordan; and Aquino de Braganca, university rector and close adviser to Mozambiquan president Samora Machel. Mozambique security services claimed the South African government was responsible and suggested that the bomb was intended to explode during the previous week's United Nations Conference on Social Science, which featured many prominent South African exiles. Coincidentally, Mondlane, a Mozambiquan independence leader, was killed in exile in Tanzania when he opened a parcel bomb. 82081701

August 19, 1982 — ITALY—Led by an experienced 24-year-old female terrorist, a dozen Red Brigadists raided a lightly guarded Italian Air Force barracks in southern Rome, bound and gagged its sentries, and stole 14 submachine guns and 3 pistols.

August 19, 1982 — LEBANON—A Palestine Liberation Organization (PLO) source claimed that Japanese Red Army (Nihon Sekigun) members would leave Beirut with their Palestinian protectors in the wake of the Israeli invasion of Lebanon. The source said, "They are not terrorists but are members of the PLO who fought against Israel," and that they would not be abandoned.

August 19, 1982 — EL SALVADOR—Guerrillas ambushed an army patrol 38 miles east of San Salvador near San Vicente, killing 1 soldier and injuring 6 soldiers and a British cameraman, Julian Harrison, 32, who was working for UNITED PRESS INTERNATIONAL TELEVISION NEWS and who sustained injuries in his left arm and his chest. 82081901

August 19, 1982 — FEDERAL REPUBLIC OF GERMANY—A bomb set by the Baader-Meinhof Gang malfunctioned at United States Army European headquarters in Heidelberg. The bomb was set at the airfield's radar antenna. 82081902

August 19, 1982 — FRANCE—Direct Action, which had been banned the previous day by the Mitterrand government, bombed the right-wing weekly MINUTE, claiming it was a "fascist and racist sheet" that supported Israel's war against Palestinians in Lebanon. Police also reported a fire that began in a pile of telephone directories stacked outside a Jewish-owned bakery in suburban Creteil. Another bomb exploded in an Arab-owned bar, and in Corsica several bombings against Arab interests were reported. In Toulouse, a bomb, causing considerable damage but no casualties, exploded during the night outside the offices of a construction firm that was working on the site of the Golfech nuclear power plant. Police arrested a dozen Direct Action members in a dawn operation, but group leader Jean-Marc Rouillan was still being sought. 82081903–04

August 20, 1982 — INDIA—Waving a pistol and holding a grenade, Museebad Singh, a member of India's Sikh religious minority, hijacked an Air India B-737 flying 63 passengers and 6 crewmen from Bombay to New Delhi. Singh hijacked the plane after it took off from Jodhpur, demanding that it fly to Lahore, Pakistan. Circling for 1½ hours over Lahore, the plane finally landed at Amritsar, India, after Pakistani authorities repeatedly denied landing permission. The hijacker permitted Parveen Sathe, an ailing woman, and her infant daughter, Madhri, to leave the plane. He demanded $85,000 in West German marks, direct negotiations in Amritsar with Prime Minister Indira Gandhi, the installation of a radio transmitter at the Golden Temple, the holiest of Sikh shrines, and the release of various imprisoned Sikh militants. When the cockpit crew turned off the plane's air conditioning, the passengers panicked, injuring an air hostess in the melee. Leaning out of the plane's window, the frightened hijacker fired three shots, whereupon Indian police shot and killed him. The remaining passengers were freed unharmed. 82082001

August 20, 1982 — PUERTO RICO — The Federal Bureau of Investigation reported that

> An improvised explosive device detonated on a side street of the Fortaleza (Governor's mansion) section of Old San Juan. The device consisted of a small (3-inches-long and ½-inch- diameter) galvanized pipe and nipple filled with an unknown low explosive filler and fused by a match. No injuries or damages resulted. The incident was claimed jointly by the Armed Forces of National Liberation (FALN) and two newly emerged groups, the Guerrilla Column 29 September and the Boricuan Anti-Imperialist Commandos. The motive for the bombing was the failure of the local news media to publish terrorist communiques and for the practice of censoring news articles related to the struggle for independence and socialism by clandestine groups in Puerto Rico.

August 20, 1982 — AUSTRIA — Several men discovered an iron pipe filled with chlorate of potash and sugar, which had a defective black-powder fuse, on the former premises of the banned rightist radical association Babenberg in Vienna Neubau Ward on 38 Siebensterngasse. Vienna had been the scene of several anti-Semitic attacks by bombers.

August 21, 1982 — FRANCE — A bomb exploded under the car of United States embassy commercial counselor Roderick Grant, 55, a week before he was set to end his five-year tour, killing French policeman Bernard Le Dreau, 46, a bomb disposal expert; injuring Le Dreau's colleague, who lost both arms and legs; and injuring a neighborhood policeman. The bomb, which went off at 10:30 A.M. — half an hour after Grant left for work — was found near the Eiffel Tower, on the Avenue de la Bourdonais in the seventh district of Paris, in front of the home of the Spanish delegate to United Nations Educational, Scientific and Cultural Organization (UNESCO). An individual claiming to be Jean-Marc Rouillan, leader of Direct Action, claimed credit, but the group later denied responsibility. The Lebanese

Armed Revolutionary Factions also later claimed credit. 82082101

August 22, 1982 — AUSTRIA — At 6:00 A.M., a policeman discovered an unexploded bomb on the first floor of the United States Chamber of Commerce in Vienna-Alsergrund, 9 Tuerkenstrasse. It consisted of an aluminum lunch box stuffed with chlorate of potash and sugar. The words *US imperialism — no good. Bang (bumsti)* were found on the walls of the building. Vienna's KURIER reported,

> A few days ago state police received through international channels confidential information about plans being made to attack certain embassies. Security authorities subsequently abruptly intensified protective measures. At that time, however, US missions were not considered to be in danger. Police are only slowly advancing in their investigations of the suspects in the black-powder attacks in Vienna and Salzburg. Ekkehard Weil, 33, . . . is still doggedly keeping silent and his Salzburg companion, 23-year-old Attila Bajtsy, is evidently taking pleasure in playing the role of terrorist: He had received his training in a [Palestine Liberation Organization] camp, he told companions shortly before his arrest.

82082201

August 22–23, 1982 — HONDURAS — Police reported that the Lorenzo Zelaya Command had sent a communique indicating that it would bomb ESSO offices in Tegucigalpa, the Bank of America, the United States embassy, the National Children's Guardianship, and Rio Lindo textiles. Police were placed on alert, and the story was given to the media. 82082202–04

August 23, 1982 — GUATEMALA — Unknown individuals broke into private homes in Solola Department, west of Guatemala City, to kidnap two Guatemalan employees of the United States Agency for International Development (AID), Jose Rocael Flores and Rafael Quintanilla. Rocael was chief of the AID program to provide drinking water to the country's western highlands; Quintanilla was his employee. 82082301

August 23, 1982 — KUWAIT — A Palestinian carrying a Jordanian passport fired three shots into Mohammed Ibrahim al-Jowaid, the United Arab Emirates charge d'affaires in Kuwait, seriously injuring him. 82082302

August 23, 1982 — UNITED STATES — A metal tube packed with a quarter-pound of TNT but not rigged to explode was found at 7:15 P.M. in the driveway of the Yugoslav embassy. 82082303

August 25, 1982 — UNITED STATES — A book-sized bomb was found under a seat on board a Pan Am flight from Miami. Police noted its apparent similarity to a bomb that exploded under a seat on a Pan Am jet from Japan earlier in the month.

August 25, 1982 — HUNGARY — The Polish airline LOT flight 10116 from Budapest to Warsaw was hijacked by two Polish men carrying explosives who forced the plane to land in Munich at 8:30 P.M. None of the 63 passengers or 8 crew were injured. On February 14, 1983, the Munich Regional Court sentenced Ryszard Paszkowski, 27, and Franciszek Sarzynski. 82082501

August 26, 1982 — INDIA — An unknown gunman fired three shots through the car of the United Arab Emirates consul general in Bombay, Ibrahim Jawad, but caused no injuries. Police were still investigating the assassination of a Kuwaiti diplomat in his garage the previous month by the Arab Revolutionary Brigades Organization. 82082601

August 27, 1982 — CANADA — Colonel Atilla Altikat, 45, the Turkish military attache, was killed in Ottawa by a dozen 9 mm bullets fired into his car while it was stopped at a red light. The assassin was an Armenian terrorist who emerged from a car sitting behind Altikat's. A man found in the vicinity was arrested but later released. Canadian police were searching for other suspects in the first diplomatic assassination in Canadian history. New York State police also were alerted. 82082701

August 28, 1982 — HONDURAS — The Lorenzo Zelaya Commando of the Revolutionary People's Front of Honduras bombed the United States-owned Rosario Resources Corporation, a mine firm in San Pedro Sula three hundred kilometers from the capital. The bombing, which caused serious damage, took place during Honduran congressional consideration of exempting the firm from paying taxes. The firm had threatened to dismiss its one thousand employees due to operating losses. 82082801

August 28, 1982 — FRANCE — Paris police arrested three Irish National Liberation Army members identified as Michael Plunkett, 31, Stefan King, 36, and Mary Reid, 29, all born in Ireland, who were fabricating a bomb for use in a strike against the British military attache in The Hague. Documents found at the scene tied the three to terrorist activity in West Germany and Switzerland as well. Other explosives were found in the suburban apartment and were believed to be used for attacks within France. 82082802

August 29, 1982 — UNITED STATES — Several Saudi students working in Ottumwa, Iowa, were beaten with clubs. One of the group was hospitalized. Two of the Saudis on September 2 were shot at as they were riding in their car. The Saudis left the Indian Hills Community College, where 149 of them were learning language skills for two Saudi companies that had contracted with the Northrop Technical Institute of Hawthorne, California. Mayor Jerry Parker lamented the terrorism, saying, "Less than a dozen people were able to remove about $2 million in [future] income to Ottumwa." 82082901, 82090201

September 1982 — ANGOLA — The National Union for the Total Independence of Angola (UNITA) kidnapped three Brazilian agronomists, Alberto Pimenta, Alvaro da Cunha, and Romel Costa, who were working on the development of new farming techniques in a plantation 285 kilometers south of Luanda. Although treated well, they were forced to march for 44 days to UNITA headquarters. On June 20, 1983, safely in Brazil, they reported that UNITA chief Jonas Savimbi planned to free the remaining hostages — 64 Czechs, 20 Portuguese, and 1 German. 82099901

September 2, 1982 — UNITED STATES — At 9:30 P.M., an Omega-7 bomb exploded next to the women's rest room adjoining the Venezuelan consulate in Miami, causing no injuries. 82090202

September 3, 1982 — ITALY — Unknown gunmen fired AK-47 Kalashnikov rifles into the car of Gen. Carlo Alberto Dalla Chiesa, 62, Italy's top anti-terrorist policeman, killing him while he was on his way home from work in Palermo, Sicily. He unsuccessfully tried to shield his wife, Emanuela, 32, who was driving. The two had married in July. Their bodyguard, in a following car, was also killed. Dalla Chiesa had been assigned to investigate Sicilian heroin traffic, and many believed he had made significant inroads into Mafia activity. A caller claimed credit for the Party of the Guerrilla. Police found a getaway car that had been set afire. Dalla Chiesa had led the successful search for the kidnappers of United States general James Lee Dozier. Government officials called his death "a mortal challenge launched by the Mafia against the democratic state."

September 4, 1982 — ZIMBABWE — Zimbabwean Army soldiers foiled an attempt by dissidents (a local term for ex–Zimbabwe People's Revolutionary Army guerrillas) to kidnap two Swiss tourists 70 miles northwest of Bulawayo. 82090401

September 6, 1982 — IRAN — A car bomb went off on Kayhan Avenue in Tehran, killing at least 6 and wounding 60 others. Some sources indicated that 40 were killed and 200 injured in the 11:00 A.M. blast.

September 6, 1982 — SWITZERLAND — Poles carrying automatic rifles seized the Polish embassy in Bern at 10:00 A.M. and took 13 people hostage, all of them Polish diplomats but one. Speaking in broken English and Russian, the group's leader demanded an end to Polish martial law, abolition of Polish prison camps, an end to repression by the government, and the release of political prisoners, or he threatened to set off 55 pounds of dynamite. Solidarity Union spokesmen in Brussels, Zurich, and Paris denied his claims that the group was linked with the banned union. He gave several names for his group, which he said numbered 3,000, including the Polish Insurgent Home Army, the Home Army–Front of National Liberation, the Revolutionary Patriotic Army, and the Polish Revolutionary Home Army. "Commandant Wysocki" claimed that his group was planning a terrorist offensive in Western Europe "to bring the fascist regime in Poland to an end and free the people." He claimed he was aided by 10 armed men, but police speculated he could have as few as 3 with him.

The group released a pregnant woman 14 hours into the 73-hour siege. They later extended their deadline 48 hours from the original deadline of 10:00 A.M. on September 8 and released 3 women at 1:30 A.M. Three more hostages — 2 women and a Zurich University student visiting the embassy — were released shortly after. However, the group also found that the Polish military attache, Zygmunt Dobruszewski, a colonel, was hiding elsewhere in the embassy. The attache unsuccessfully attempted suicide by swallowing pills, according to the terrorists. The same day, a Polish diplomat, Jozef Matusiak, who was hiding in another location in the embassy escaped down a ladder from a second-floor window during the evening.

The group wavered in its demands and on September 8 permitted Joseph Boschenski, 80, a Polish emigre, Dominican priest, and former professor of philosophy at Fribourg University, to enter the embassy for negotiations. The group asked for safe passage out of the country with several sensitive documents they found in the embassy, along with SFr 3 million ($1.43 million). The Swiss government refused all demands. The group asked for food for the hostages, saying that they had brought their own. The Swiss rejected a Polish request to send a "special group" to aid in obtaining the hostages' release. They similarly rejected offers of aid by other, unnamed, countries.

On September 9, members of the Swiss police "Star" squad of antiterrorist experts burst into the embassy and rescued the remaining 5 hostages in 12 minutes without firing a shot. The raid began after the explosion of a remote-controlled stun bomb that police had concealed in a food basket brought into the embassy at 10:42 A.M. No injuries were reported in the raid.

The leader of the group, Florian Kruszyk, 42, had a colorful career. He had claimed that he was a descendant of Piotr Wysocki, a Polish national hero who led a rebellion of Polish cadets against Russian occupiers in 1930. He then claimed he was a former Polish Army officer who resigned after martial law was declared in December. He said that he and his friends had escaped from the country and made their way to Switzerland. Police revealed that he had been a member of Polish intelligence in 1962–65, and that he had been convicted of spying in Vienna in 1968. He had lived in Wysocko, Poland, before leaving the country. He was arrested in Vienna again in 1969, this time for robbing a jewelry store and holding hostage, with the help of 3 other gunmen, the family that owned it. He served a 9-year sentence for the robbery. He then moved to Holland, where he married a Dutch woman, thereby gaining a residency permit. While there, he had made threats against the Polish embassy in The Hague.

On September 30, Poland requested extradition of Florian Kruszyk, Krsysztof (also spelled Krzystof) Wasilewski, Miroslaw Plewinski, and Marek Michalski, who the government said had taken over the embassy. Poland also requested extradition from West Germany of Tadesz Workiewicz, who it claimed had cooperated in the preparation for the attack but had stayed in Munich during its implementation. Switzerland turned down the extradition request. Tough antiterrorist laws came into effect in Switzerland the next day.

The group's trial for the 73-hour drama began on October 3, 1983. On October 10, 1983, Florian Kruszyk received 6 years in prison and 15 years banishment from Switzerland. Marek Michalski and Miroslaw Plewinski received 2½ years in prison and 5 years banishment. Krsysztof Wasilweski received 3 years imprisonment and 5 years banishment. 82090601

September 8, 1982 — UNITED STATES — The Federal Bureau of Investigation reported that at 2:00 A.M.

> an individual was apprehended by the Chicago Police Department as he fled from the front of the Roxy Record and Book Company. The police had noticed his car parked in front of the bookstore. As he pulled away, a small explosion occurred. After he was arrested, the individual claimed he had perpetrated the bombing. The bomb, consisting of a bottle filled with black powder and capped with cloth, had been taped to the front window of the store. The bomb did not explode completely as was intended and only a flash took place. Damage was minimal. A communique left at the scene stated that Omega 7 was responsible and the motive was that the bookstore was selling communist literature. The communique warned that attacks on communist businesses would continue.

82090801

September 9, 1982 — BULGARIA — Armenian terrorists ambushed and killed Bora Suelkan, 45, administrative attache for the Turkish consulate general, in front of his home in Burgas. Written in English on a cloth at the scene was, "We shot dead the Turkish diplomat: Combat Units of Justice Against Armenian Genocide." 82090901

September 9, 1982 — UNITED KINGDOM — London police arrested two Armenians planning an attack on the Turkish embassy. 82090902

September 13, 1982 — FRANCE — Dissident Romanian writer Virgil Tanase, who had resurfaced on August 31 after hiding with the help of French intelligence from a Romanian assassination squad, said that President Francois Mitterrand was on the hit list of Romanian president Nicolae Ceausescu.

September 13, 1982 — GREECE — Having left the Turkish embassy to observe anti-Turkish demonstrations at Athens University, air attache Lt. Col. Osman Boyalar was wounded when attacked by the demonstrators. The senior military attache, Col. Tuzuner, dressed in civilian clothes, was also attacked when he tried to rescue his colleague. 82091301

September 14, 1982 — LEBANON — A 77-pound TNT bomb exploded at 4:00 P.M. in the Phalangist party office in east Beirut, killing President-elect Bashir Gemayel, 34, and at least 8 others, and injuring at least 50 people. The VOICE OF LEBANON claimed that the bomb was placed on the roof of the building and consisted of 300 kilograms of explosives. The explosion also killed John Nazir, head of the Phalangist party, Fu'ad Abu Najm, Sasin Karam, Michel Thalj, Elie Najjar and his wife, John Asmar, Pierre Fadil, and Shakir 'Amr. RADIO FREE LEBANON claimed 27 were killed and 37 injured. Amin Gemayel, the slain president-elect's brother, was elected to serve in his stead. Various rumors indicated that the bomb was set off either by a crude alarm clock device or by a Japanese-made, sophisticated remote detonator more than two miles away. Some sources indicated that the bomb consisted of 440 pounds of TNT. Habib Tanyus ash-Shartuni (also spelled Shartouni), 26, grandson of the headquarter's landlord, allegedly confessed to the bombing. The Syrian Socialist Nationalist party denied it had links with the alleged assassin. Phalangist security said it arrested 3 men working with unnamed Palestinian groups who had confessed to the attempted assassination of Gemayel in a car bomb explosion on February 23, 1980, in which Gemayel's 18-month-old daughter Maya was killed. They suggested that the individual arrested for Gemayel's murder had connections with these 3 men, an "ideological organization well known for its links abroad," and a second man who escaped after the murder. Phalange turned Habib ash-Shartuni over to the Lebanese government on April 26, 1983. Phalange believed the mastermind was NSSP official Nabil Ferlaghi (Nabil Alam), who escaped to Syria.

September 16, 1982 — UNITED STATES — Sources within Congress indicated that seven counterterrorist experts on contract to the Department of Energy used forged credentials to infiltrate the government's Savannah River nuclear weapons plant, seize hostages, and take over the control room of a large atomic reactor during a security test in 1980.

September 16, 1982 — EGYPT — Police arrested an undisclosed number of members of Jihad, a clandestine Islamic extremist group responsible for the assassination of President Anwar Sadat. The press indicated that the group had planned to storm prisons where Jihad members were being held, assassinate unidentified persons (apparently including President Hosni Mubarak), and take over the country. An alternative plan would have entailed hijacking a civilian airliner to obtain the release of the imprisoned Jihad members and their safe conduct out of Egypt. The group allegedly had the help of unspecified foreign elements.

September 16, 1982 — PAKISTAN — Kuwait's acting consul general in Karachi was wounded by glass splinters when a gunman fired three bullets into his car near the consulate before escaping. Hammad Saleh al-Jutaili recovered from his wounds. 82091601

September 16, 1982 — SPAIN — Najeeb Sayed Hashem Refai, the Kuwaiti first secretary in Madrid, was killed and his chauffeur wounded when Ibrahim Nasser, a Palestinian, fired six times into his limousine in central Madrid. Police arrested Nasser, who was carrying a silenced pistol. 82091602

September 17, 1982 — MOZAMBIQUE — Members of the National Resistance Movement kidnapped five missionaries working as teachers and medical staff at the Muvamba, Inhambane, Province facility of the Order of Consolation. The order identified the Catholics as Father Adelino do Conceicao Francisco of Portugal; Helena Cariolata, Sebastiana Pischeda, and Luisa Casiraghi of Italy; and Ana Mainhardt of Brazil. 82091701

September 17, 1982 — FRANCE — The Lebanese Armed Revolutionary Factions, with the assistance of Direct Action, set off a bomb in the saddlebags of a motorbike parked next to the car of Amos Man-El (also spelled Mandel), an official of the Israeli embassy's military purchasing mission, as he was getting into his car with his wife, Juliana, and two visiting relatives, his cousin and his cousin's wife. Two teenagers walking past the car and the Man-Els were the most seriously injured, although 40 of 500 students across the street at the Lycee Carnot were injured by flying glass. The bombing occurred on Rue Cardinet in Paris's 17th District a few blocks east of the Arc de Triomphe on the eve of Rosh Hashana.

The next day, police reported that they had arrested 2 members of

Direct Action who supplied the names of their faction and tipped police to two arms caches, where they found 150 dynamite sticks, sodium chlorate, detonators, slow-burning cord, two Sten submachine guns, a Kalashnikov assault rifle, and an M-1 carbine. Police arrested 14 members of Direct Action in an operation they claimed was not related to the bombing the previous day. However, observers noted that Direct Action had been suspected of several anti-Semitic attacks in recent months. 82091702

September 17, 1982 — HONDURAS — Twelve members of the leftist Chichoneros Popular Liberation Movement attacked the one-story building housing the Chamber of Commerce in San Pedro del Sula at 6:30 P.M., taking hostage 105 businessmen attending a convention being addressed by Honduran treasury minister Arturo Corleto and economics minister Gustavo Alfaro. Several foreigners, but no Americans, were among the hostages, who included Central Bank president Gonzalo Carias. The terrorist group was named after a 19th-century Honduran peasant leader. The terrorists demanded the release of 40 — later increased to 60 — political prisoners and individuals who had disappeared, including several Salvadoran guerrillas. Among those whose release was demanded was Alejandro Montenegro, the chief of the Salvadoran People's Revolutionary Army. He had been captured by government troops in Tegucigalpa on August 22 and was a key planner of the raid that destroyed most of the Salvadoran Air Force on the ground earlier in the year. The group called for the release of Hondurans, Salvadorans, and other Latin Americans they believed had been captured by the government. They also called for an end to the Honduran Army's alleged cooperation with the Salvadoran Army and for the "dismantling" of base camps in Honduras used by Nicaraguan rightist exiles in their fighting against the Sandinista government in Managua. Their first communique also called for the expulsion of "gringo, Israeli, Chilean, and Argentine" military advisers, the repeal of an antiterrorist law, and the withdrawal by Honduras from the newly formed anticommunist Central American Democratic Community.

The government initially took a hard line against the terrorists and offered only safe passage out of the country. The negotiating team was headed by the papal nuncio, Archbishop Andrea Cordero Lanza of Montezmolo. Negotiations were conducted inside the building, which used to house the United States consulate, by Honduran Roman Catholic bishop Jaime Brufau and Venezuelan charge d'affaires Hugo Alvarez. They managed to get the terrorists to ignore their first deadline, after which they had threatened to kill the hostages. The terrorists released 15 captives on September 18, including 6 women and 8 men (among them a young man, Cupertino Fugon). Jose Antonio Castellanos, adviser of the Chamber of Commerce and former director general of internal trade was released the same day, after he persuaded his captors that he was just another employee of the chamber. A businessman with a perforated ulcer was carried out by Honduran Red Cross volunteers. The group released 4 other hostages the next day. Three others escaped, including 2 early that morning. About 200 police and soldiers surrounded the building and were joined on September 19 by the antiterrorist Cobra rescue team. The terrorist group, according to former hostage Ramon Milla Neda, 44, a business adviser, carried automatic rifles and told their hostages that the small boxes they carried labeled Medicines were filled with dynamite.

The chief gunman identified himself only as "Uno" and claimed that his group was responsible for only two other incidents—the March 1981 hijacking of a Honduran Air Services (SAHSA) B-737 that led to the release of another Salvadoran guerrilla leader and the seizure of a Honduran radio station several months earlier.

On September 19, Honduran authorities claimed that Montenegro may already have been turned over to Salvadoran authorities under another name.

On September 21, 5,000 demonstrators rallied at the government's request to protest the guerrillas' takeover of the building.

On September 22, the terrorists released 21 more hostages and dropped all demands save for the release of the 60 prisoners.

On September 24, they released 2 more hostages.

On September 25, the incident ended when the leftists accepted safe passage out of the country. Their remaining 32 hostages rode with them to the airport in a bus and lined up as a human shield as the terrorists boarded a Panamanian plane, which the Honduran president had requested of the Panamanian president. The Panamanian National Guard took the group into custody when the plane touched down later that day. The group arrived safely in Cuba on September 28, where they were presumably given asylum.

The founder of the Chichoneros, Fidel Martinez Rodriguez, was reportedly killed by Honduran government forces in June 1981. 82091703

September 18, 1982 — ANGOLA — National Union for the Total Independence of Angola (UNITA) guerrillas handed over 15 hostages to South African Red Cross officials in southern Angola, who then flew them to Waterkloof Air Force Base near Pretoria, South Africa. The hostages included six Portuguese, three Brazilians, four Spaniards, an Argentine, and a Swiss nurse, all civilians who had been captured in battles with Angolan government forces. Father Benjamin Fernandez, a Spanish priest, was captured in 1981. Jose Domingo de Matos Botelho, one of the Portuguese, was captured by UNITA in 1979. The others were more recent victims.

September 18, 1982 — LEBANON — The Front for the Liberation of Lebanon from Foreigners claimed credit for killing nearly one thousand Palestinian refugees in Sabra and Shatila refugee camps. Survivors claimed that right-wing Phalangist militiamen and troops under the command of cashiered Lebanese Army major Saad Haddad were also involved.

September 18, 1982 — UNITED STATES — Federal Bureau of Investigation (FBI) and Bureau of Alcohol, Tobacco, and Firearms authorities in Albuquerque, New Mexico, arrested Jordanian-born Abdul-Hafiz Mohammed Nassar, 29, for hiding 95 sticks of industrial grade explosives, blasting caps, batteries, and 3 walkie-talkies in a locker in Alexandria, Virginia. On October 19, 1982, a grand jury indicted him on firearms and conspiracy charges. He was held in District of Columbia jail in lieu of $750,000 bond. He had made four trips to Beirut in the previous 19 months and may have been planning to smuggle the explosives into Lebanon. The FBI said, "The explosives seized are the essential components for the construction of an improvised explosive device which could be detonated by use of radio signals by the walkie-talkie equipment." He apparently obtained the explosives for $52,000 from unindicted coconspirators Harold Eugene McDowell and Harold Wendell Greene, the latter of whom delivered 2 cases of explosives to Nassar in September 1981 in Phoenix, Arizona. The 95 dynamite sticks were found in May 1982 in locker number 134, which Nassar had rented the previous September 8 at the Self-Storage Service Corporation, 4551 Eisenhower Avenue, Alexandria, Virginia. Officials said the explosives were enough to destroy one city block. The FBI noted that Nassar's 1979 Volvo had been ticketed on the same day he rented the locker for being parked in a tour bus space "within the immediate vicinity of the White House." Nassar entered the United States legally in 1973. 82091801

September 18, 1982 — BELGIUM — Four worshippers entering the synagogue on the Rue de la Regence in central Brussels were wounded when a gunman fired two machine-gun bursts during Rosh Hashana. A plainclothes policeman fired several shots at the man, who successfully fled on foot. The Palestine Liberation Organization (PLO) denounced the attack. Black Lebanon claimed credit, saying that it had attacked an "Israeli intelligence center" in "retaliation for the bestial massacres perpetrated by Zionist forces in Lebanon's Sabra and Shatila camps." 82091802

September 19, 1982 — FRANCE — Professor Ibrahima Kake, a Guinean exiled opponent of President Ahmed Sekou Toure, evaded a kidnap attempt by five Guineans, one armed and two allegedly carrying Guinean diplomatic passports. Paris police arrested the group but later released them after discovering their diplomatic status. The incident occurred at the end of a demonstration by the Guinean Opposition Collective against President Toure, who ended a four-day visit to France. Kake reportedly had received several death threats from Toure supporters in Paris. 82091901

September 20, 1982 — IRAN — Twenty persons were wounded and one was killed when a concussion bomb exploded at 11:00 A.M. in a Tehran bus terminal.

September 20, 1982 — AUSTRIA — Bombs went off around midnight at the Iraqi embassy and Iraqi Airlines offices, causing damage to the buildings and cars nearby but causing no injuries. 82092001–02

September 20, 1982 — UNITED STATES — The Federal Bureau of Investigation reported that at "12:40 A.M., an improvised explosive device exploded at Bankers Trust, 280 Park Avenue, [New York City]. A man with a Spanish accent who claimed to be with the Armed Forces of National Liberation (FALN) stated, 'We have just bombed a mid-town bank to protest the US support of the Israeli massacre of Palestinian people.' The explosion caused extensive damage to Bankers Trust and some glass damage to the building across the street at 300 Park Avenue." No injuries were reported. 82092003

September 21, 1982 — SPAIN — At 4:30 A.M., an individual threw a hand grenade at the Iraqi Cultural Center in Madrid, damaging the building's first three floors. 82092101

September 23, 1982 — COLOMBIA — The April 19 Movement (M-19) fired a bazooka while other gunmen in a speeding car machine-gunned the Israeli embassy residence, injuring two people, including the wife of Israeli ambassador Hayin Aharon. The group said it was acting "in solidarity with the Palestinians killed in Beirut." 82092301

September 23, 1982 — PAKISTAN — Eugene R. Clegg, 35, a teacher from Castle Rock, Washington, was ordered held until October 1 pending an investigation into charges of gunrunning and illegal possession of explosives in Islamabad. 82092302

September 24, 1982 — EGYPT — Protesting recent government arrests of the Jihad extremist organization, Osama Salah din Abdel Satar, 18, armed with two pistols and several knives, fired on a tourist bus at the Great Pyramids of Giza, wounding an Egyptian guide and two Soviet tourists. A camel driver struck him on the head, allowing police to arrest Satar. 82092401

September 25, 1982 — UNITED STATES — An unexploded Omega-7 bomb was found outside the Nicaraguan consulate in Miami, Florida. 82092501

September 25, 1982 — ALGERIA — Igor Shkouro, 32, born in Leningrad, living in Rome, and holding an Australian passport, hijacked an Alitalia B-727, flight AZ-871 from Algiers to Rome, about 20 minutes after it took off with its 101 passengers and crew. He apparently decided to hijack the plane after Algerian authorities initially refused him entry when he arrived in Algiers from Rome on an earlier flight. He released the passengers and cabin crew when the plane landed in Catania, Sicily. The cabin crew then overpowered Shkouro, who appeared to be under the influence of drugs and did not give a reason for the hijacking. He carried only a knife. 82092502

September 27, 1982 — LEBANON — Thirty gunmen, armed with automatic rifles and rocket-propelled grenades, ambushed Saad Sayel (Abu Walid), the head of the Palestinian Liberation Army's operations room, shooting him in the abdomen as he was traveling between Baalbek and Rayak behind Syrian lines. He died later in a Damascus hospital. Sayel had been an officer in the Jordanian Army until Palestinian guerrillas were ousted in 1970. He organized Palestinian defenses during the battle for Beirut earlier in 1982. Nearly 10,000 Palestinians attended his funeral. Yasir Arafat said in his eulogy, "The blood of Saad Sayel and our martyrs in Sabra and Shatila will be avenged." Sayel was given a statesman's funeral. The Palestine Liberation Organization (PLO) blamed "Zionists and their criminal agents." Others suggested that infighting among leftist Lebanese gunmen and guerrillas of the Shiite Moslem group Amal may have led to his death.

September 28, 1982 — UNITED STATES — Officials of the Gulf Oil Company petrochemical plant in Cedar Bayou, Texas, received a letter threatening to set off 10 bombs if the extortionists were not paid $10 million. The seven-page letter indicated where one of the bombs was and said 4 others were easily found. Police detonated one of the bombs harmlessly by firing a water cannon at it and found the other 4 bombs. The last 5 bombs were found when the Federal Bureau of Investigation agreed to free a suspect's wife in return for information as to their location. On October 27, five Durango, Colorado, residents stood trial in Houston before United States magistrate Calvin Botley who set two hundred thousand dollars' bail for the woman and scheduled a jury trial for December 14. On November 1, Timothy Keith Justice, 30, a Vietnam veteran and former reserve police officer from Durango pleaded guilty to 2 federal charges in return for the dropping of 12 other charges. He agreed to testify against the other defendants: Jill Renee Bird, 34; her common-law husband, John Marvin McBridge, 46; Theodore Duane McKinney, 48; and Michael Allen Worth, 34. Justice claimed he had cut a hold in the Cedar Bayou security fence on September 26 and planted the 5 bombs under chemical tanks.

September 30, 1982 — ITALY — A bomb went off at Milan's Jewish Community Center, causing light damage and no injuries, after the Center had received several bomb threats in retaliation for the massacre of Palestinian refugees in Israeli-occupied Beirut camps. The Communist Armed Group claimed credit.

September 30, 1982 — LEBANON — One United States Marine died and three others were injured when a 155 mm shell they were defusing exploded at Beirut International Airport. The slightly injured Marines were identified as Cpl. Anthony D. Moran, 21, of Macon, Georgia, and L. Cpl. George Washington, 19, of Elgin, Illinois. 82093001

October 1982 — CYPRUS — O AGON claimed "police believe that Turks, either defectors or agents, lurk behind . . . bomb explosions of automobiles in Nicosia and Limassol." 82109901–02

October 1982 — MOZAMBIQUE — The National Resistance Movement kidnapped seven Portuguese citizens: Orlando Martins, Jose Antonio de Jesus Antunes, Aloino Ferreira da Costa Pinto, Maria Amelia Pereira, Maria de Fatima Diogo e Antunes, Maria Eufemia de Concalves Pinto, and Maco Bruno Antunes. They were released on November 9, 1982, in Chipunga, Zimbabwe. The group also claimed it had shot down a Mozambique government helicopter, killing two Soviet advisers. 82109903

October 1982 — ITALY — Bombs exploded outside Rome's Islamic Center and the Syrian embassy. 82109904

October 1982 — UNITED KINGDOM — Mark Thatcher, the prime minister's son, postponed a plane trip to the United States after learning of an Irish Republican Army (IRA) assassination plot. 82109905

October 1982 — POLAND — The French embassy received two anonymous phone calls threatening to kidnap children attending the French school. 82109906

October 1, 1982 — IRAN — A bomb hidden in a truck parked at Imam Square on Naser Khosrow Avenue in Tehran exploded at 8:35 P.M., destroying a five-story hotel and three passing buses, severely damaging seven other hotels, leaving a crater 6½ feet deep and 20 feet around, killing 60 persons, and wounding 700. Iranian interior minister Nateq Nouri said "a number of suspects" had been arrested, and he blamed "US mercenaries." The Mujaheddin-e-Khlaq opposition group said in Paris that the government set off the bomb "in preparation for further repression and executions and to conceal its forces' defeat in the latest offensive in Iraq."

October 2, 1982 — GUATEMALA — Richard Kehagy, 43, a United States businessman, was kidnapped near his Guatemala City house by unidentified gunmen. His bullet-riddled body was found on October 7 in Villanueva, 18 miles outside the capital. 82100201

October 3, 1982 — LEBANON — Half a mile east of Alayh on the Beirut-Damascus highway about six miles from Beirut in Israeli-controlled territory, gunmen fired from a house at 2:30 p.m. at a bus carrying Israeli troops, killing 6 and injuring 22. The attackers used automatic weapons, a rocket-propelled grenade, and hand grenades.

October 3, 1982 — ITALY — Naples police arrested Vittorio Bolognesi, 32, leader of the Red Brigades (RB) Naples faction, along with 10 other gang members in a raid on three RB hideouts.

October 3, 1982 — PAKISTAN — United States ambassador Ronald Speiers received a letter, dated September 23, threatening that he would be shot immediately if he did not leave the country. 82100301

October 4, 1982 — IRAN — Three Iranian men and a woman hijacked an Iranian Air Force C-130 Hercules military transport carrying 79 passengers, mostly Iranian military officials and relatives, on a domestic flight and diverted it to Dubai International Airport, where they released all of the passengers, including 19 women and 26 children. Dubai authorities rejected their request to arrange political asylum in the United States, and the plane left the airport at 1:05 P.M. after refueling. It flew 20 miles north to Sharjah, another of the seven United Arab Emirates (UAE) sheikdoms, where the hijackers requested political asylum. A negotiating team led by UAE defense minister Sheik Mohammed bin Rashid rejected the request. The plane refueled and took off again. Lebanese authorities denied overflight privileges, and airport officials in Dubai and Muscat airports parked trucks and jeeps on the runways to prevent a landing. On October 5, Iranian Air Force jets entered UAE airspace and forced the plane back into Iran. The plane landed in the afternoon at Bandar Abbas, Iran, where the hijackers were arrested. 82100401

October 7, 1982 — LEBANON — RADIO FREE LEBANON reported that "eleven Baader-Meinhof terrorists, who have been wanted by Interpol for years, and 3 prominent Italian Red Brigade terrorists, who according to sources had participated in major assassination operations in Italy, have been arrested," presumably in Army sweeps of west Beirut.

October 7, 1982 — LIBYA — Speaking to a rally, Libyan leader Muammar Qaddafi threatened to assassinate exiled dissidents overseas. "The Libyan Arab people would meet their full responsibilities of liquidating escaped agents of America. . . . There shall be no mercy for the agents of America.

The escaped hirelings, enemies of the Libyan people, shall not escape from this people." He said the Libyan People's Congress, due to meet in January, "will take the final decision of implementing the liquidation." A senior ambassador suggested that two primary targets would be former Libyan ambassador to India Mohammed Youssef Lemgurief and Somalia-based Abdul Hamid Bakush, the next to last prime minister under deposed King Idris. Lemgurief was the secretary general of the National Front for the Liberation of Libya, which broadcasts anti-Qaddafi speeches from Sudan.

October 7, 1982 — SWITZERLAND — The Swiss agreed to extradite Rolf Clemens Wagner, 38, a member of the Baader-Meinhof Group, who was arrested in 1979 after an armed raid on a Zurich bank and a gun battle with police. He was sentenced to serve a life sentence in Switzerland and would return there to finish his sentence. If convicted in West Germany, he would be sent back to West Germany (if he was paroled early in Switzerland) to serve any sentence imposed for the kidnap/murder in 1977 of industrialist Hanns-Martin Schleyer.

October 8, 1982 — ISRAEL — Around midnight, arsonists set a kerosene fire to the Baptist Church of Jerusalem, about six hundred yards from the home of Prime Minister Menachem Begin in the Nahlaot quarter, causing $1 million damage in an antimissionary attack. The church had been vandalized twice since 1972. It was run by Dr. Robert Lindsey, 65, the Oklahoma-born pastor of the church, who denied the facility was engaged in illegal missionary work. In New York, a representative of a "leftwing, socialist, revolutionary arm" of the Jewish Defense League claimed credit. 82100801

October 9, 1982 — ITALY — On Simhas Torah, the ninth and final day of the Jewish harvest festival known as Sukkot, 4 gunmen threw 4 hand grenades and fired at least 30 9 mm cartridges from submachine guns at worshippers at Rome's main synagogue around noon. Stefano Tache, 2, died in a hospital. His brother Marco, 4, was reported near death, and his parents were among 33 others injured. The terrorists, 2 of whom were described as "dark-skinned," escaped on foot. Angry Jews accused Pope John Paul II and Italian president Sandro Pertini of creating a climate for the attack by having met last month with the Palestine Liberation Organization's (PLO) Yasir Arafat. A PLO spokesman condemned the attack. An anonymous caller said the PLO–Red Brigades was responsible. The Black Lebanon Organization also claimed credit, saying the synagogue was a "den of Israeli intelligence rather than a place of worship."

On November 22, 1982, border police in Kipi, Greece, arrested Abd al-Usamah al-Zumar, a Palestinian, when customs officials found 60 kilos of dynamite, detonators, and other material hidden in a Mercedes with a Bari license plate. On March 23, 1985, the Italian news service ANSA in Rome reported that Greek justice minister Georgios Alexandros Mangakis had decided to extradite him to Italy for the attack on the synagogue. 82100901

October 10, 1982 — BOLIVIA — Italian neo-Nazi Pierluigi Pagaliai, 28, was injured in the nape of the neck by a Bolivian policeman's bullet while trying to escape from his surrounded home. He was wanted for questioning in the 1980 Bologna bombing in which 85 people were killed. He was extradited to Rome, but died on November 5, 1982, after remaining in a coma for three weeks. 82101001

October 12, 1982 — FRANCE — Frederic Oriach, 29, and Christian Gauzens, 25, top members of the outlawed Direct Action leftist group, were arrested after picking up documents from a rail station baggage locker that linked them to the alleged assassins of United States and Israeli diplomats in Paris. Oriach was ordered held without bail and was indicted on charges of committing assassinations, involuntary injuries, and attacks by explosives.

October 13, 1982 — FRANCE — Police in Saint-Jean-de-Luz arrested Jesus Abrisketa Korta, 33, a leading member of the Basque Nation and Liberty (ETA), during a routine check of identity papers. Abrisketa had been sought since the April 28 discovery of a large cache of ETA weapons in a Bayonne apartment traced to him.

October 13, 1982 — EL SALVADOR — The Salvadoran government claimed that United States citizen Michael David Kline was a mercenary for leftist guerrillas and was slain by a soldier in northeastern Morazan Province. United States embassy officials reported that an autopsy showed that two shots had been fired point-blank into Kline's back from a G-3 rifle. On May 7, 1983, Subsergeant Jose Desposorio Lopez Garcia claimed that he had killed the 32-year-old after he was forcibly removed from a bus suspected of transporting guerrillas. Kline allegedly tried to grab a rifle of one of Lopez's colleague. Two other soldiers, Hector Antonio Urbina Reyes and Cristobal Garcia, also from the Armed Forces Commando Training Center in Morazan Department, were held in connection with the killing.

October 14, 1982 — GUATEMALA — Three armed gunmen, members of the Christian Group Against Repression, kidnapped Marios Rios Munoz, 20, a medical student at the national university and nephew of President Efrain Rios Montt, as he was walking in a neighborhood on the southwestern outskirts of Guatemala City. On November 22, he was rescued when government security forces staged a gun battle at the guerrillas' hideout. Two of the kidnappers were killed. Rios was uninjured.

October 14, 1982 — BULGARIA — Zbigniew Purgall, 28, a Pole, and his wife Maria, 22, hijacked a Bulgarian Tupolev 134 carrying 76 people from Burgas, Bulgaria, to Warsaw, Poland, and diverted the plane to Vienna's Schwechat International Airport at 5:33 P.M. A Bulgarian stewardess, Pauline Dimitrova, 29, received a slight knife wound on her neck in the takeover. Upon landing, the two immediately surrendered to police and requested political asylum. On November 18, Purgall was sentenced to two years imprisonment and his wife was given a one-year suspended sentence for conspiracy. 82101401

October 15, 1982 — CANADA — Direct Action bombed the Litton Systems of Canada plant in Toronto that produces the guidance system for cruise missiles. The three hundred to five hundred pounds of dynamite was cached in an orange-colored box marked Danger, Explosives beside a blue van parked in front of the plant. The bomb went off at 11:31 P.M., 13 minutes after a woman's telephone tip. Four factory workers and three policemen who were approaching the bomb were injured. The bomb caused $5 million damage. The plant had received three or four bomb threats previously and was the focus of antinuclear demonstrations.

October 20, 1982 — ITALY — A bomb exploded in front of the Lebanese embassy, injuring a passerby and seriously damaging the embassy and nearby shops. Lebanese president Amin Gemayel was due in town the next day for talks with Italian officials and Pope John Paul II. 82102001

October 20, 1982 — SEYCHELLES — Two men, Mike Asher and Simon Denouse, were blown up by their own bomb, which apparently went off before they could launch a coup against the government of President Albert France Rene. Seychelles news services claimed the plotters were London based, South African-backed Seychelles exiles who worked for Italy. Their talks reportedly were monitored in a London hotel. The Seychelles Resistance Movement claimed Asher, formerly of Durban, and Denouse were tortured. 82102002

October 23, 1982 — UNITED STATES — The Federal Bureau of Investigation announced the arrest of five members of the Justice Commandos of the Armenian Genocide (JCAG) in southern California and Boston. The luggage of a JCAG suspect was x-rayed in Boston and found to contain an armed dynamite bomb. The x-ray was prompted by an alert concerning a planned attack to be conducted against the honorary Turkish consul in Philadelphia. One individual was charged with interstate transportation of an explosive device; four other JCAG members were arrested in Los Angeles. 82102301-02

October 25, 1982 — SUDAN — Security officials discovered a milk can containing two explosive charges weighing five kilograms connected to a battery-operated timer in the residence of Libyan exiled opponents of Muammar Qaddafi. Police believed Libyan intelligence was behind the assassination attempt. 82102501

October 26, 1982 — POLAND — Gdansk farmer Jerzy Zawistowski, described by police as mentally ill, shouted that World War III was about to begin as he poured gasoline onto the lobby of the American school in a Warsaw suburb. The 162 pupils and 25 staff members were evacuated when he threatened to light the gasoline. Police wrestled him to the ground and arrested him before he could start a fire.

October 27, 1982 — UNITED STATES — William Hoffman, 25, attempted to hijack Trans World Airlines flight 72, an L-1011 flying 97 passengers to St. Louis, on the ground at Los Angeles International Airport. Rookie sheriff's deputy Dennis Robinson, 24, a passenger, persuaded him that the cabin was getting hot, had a stewardess open the service door to get air, then shoved Hoffman out the door to the ground, 30 feet below. Hoffman sustained head and pelvis injuries. No one was injured by the knife-wielding hijacker. 82102701

October 27, 1982 — LEBANON — Unknown attackers killed three Irish United Nations Interim Force in Lebanon (UNIFIL) soldiers at a checkpoint north of Tibnine. Since the inception of UNIFIL in 1978, the force had lost 86 soldiers, 16 of them Irish. An Irish soldier kidnapped on April 28, 1981, is still missing. 82102702

October 28, 1982 — ITALY — Terrorists threw Molotov cocktails at a building housing a small synagogue and Jewish community center in the Nomentana section of Rome, causing slight damage and no injuries.

November 1982 — TUNISIA — Tunisian police arrested 10 people, including 2 journalists, for trying to form a "terrorist organization with a view to creating armed unrest in Tunisia." The minister of the interior, Driss Guiga, denied rumors that 50 Palestinians had entered France using Tunisian passports.

November 1, 1982 — FEDERAL REPUBLIC OF GERMANY — A bomb went off under an automobile parked in the United States Army housing area in

Giessen, causing $40,000 damage but no injuries. This was the third attack against United States military areas in the Frankfurt area in three weeks. 82110101

November 1, 1982 — LEBANON — A booby-trapped car exploded 30 yards from a United States Marine beachhead on the coastal highway at Ouzai, south of Beirut, seriously injuring two Lebanese civilians and grazing United States lance corporal Solomon Llewellen, 19. 82110102

November 3, 1982 — FEDERAL REPUBLIC OF GERMANY — Nine members of Devrimci Sol, the Turkish Revolutionary Left, took over the Turkish consulate in Cologne in a blaze of gunfire and seized 73 hostages. The group unfurled a banner saying No to the Junta Constitution in Turkey in both German and Turkish. The group demanded that "a comprehensive political manifesto" be broadcast over radio stations but were turned down. The terrorists talked by telephone with a Turkish diplomat, after having demanded to speak to the senior diplomat in the country. The group released 60 hostages during the 16-hour negotiations. They surrendered when they were told they could request political asylum. Four other people, including Consul General Ilban Kioiman, had hidden inside the consulate during the seige. One of the hostages was a German female employee at the consulate. Two of the hostages were slightly injured. One sustained a head injury and another was in shock. The 9 terrorists were arrested. The group is one of the militant Marxist-Leninist organizations that operated in Turkey before generals seized power in Ankara in September 1980. Currently 781 Dev Sol members are on trial in Turkish martial law courts. 82110301

November 4, 1982 — SPAIN — Two youths on a motorcycle fired into the official car of two-star general, Victor Lago Roman, 63, chief of the Brunete First Armored Division — the largest and most modern in the Spanish Army — in the Moncloa area at 8:30 A.M. Roman was killed and his driver, Juan Carlos Villalba, 22, was slightly injured. Police blamed the Basque Nation and Liberty's (ETA) military wing for the attacks.

November 4, 1982 — UNITED STATES — According to the Federal Bureau of Investigation, "At approximately 9:10 P.M., two persons threw two smoke grenades down the aisle of Carnegie Hall Cinema, New York. One device ignited and several patrons extinguished the burning can by stomping on it. The theater was exhibiting Russian films. Damage was limited to two burn marks on the carpet." The Jewish Defense League (JDL) was suspected.

November 4, 1982 — AFGHANISTAN — Afghan resistance fighters blew up the Soviet oil pipeline at Dashte Kalagia, in northern Samangan Province.

Diplomatic sources were quoted as saying that Soviet workers who attempted to repair the line were killed by guerrilla-laid mines.

November 5, 1982 — ANGOLA — The National Union for the Total Independence of Angola (UNITA) kidnapped a Brazilian engineer and a Brazilian topographer from the Fazan da Longa farm near the town of Calulo, 220 kilometers southeast of Luanda. 82110501

November 5, 1982 — NETHERLANDS — Protesting what they termed "the Constitution of the American-influenced fascist junta" in Turkey, 10 members of the Dev Sol (Revolutionary Left) seized 2 hostages at the Turkish tourism office in Amsterdam at 1:30 P.M. The group held the 2 staff members for three hours, until Dutch police raided the building and arrested the group. 82110502

November 7, 1982 — AFGHANISTAN — Afghan rebels ruptured the Soviet oil pipeline near Bagram Airbase outside Kabul.

November 7, 1982 — HONDURAS — The Lorenzo Zelaya People's Revolutionary Forces set off three bombs in subsidiaries of the United States multinational Castle and Cook Company. 82110701

November 7, 1982 — USSR — Three Soviet citizens of German origin brandished knives to hijack the Aeroflot AN-24 on a Novorossiysk-to-Odessa flight with 37 passengers and a crew of 5 and forced it to fly to the Sinop NATO base in Turkey. There they requested political asylum in West Germany, where they claimed to have relatives. The pilot and 2 passengers were hospitalized for wounds they suffered attempting to subdue the hijackers. Observers ruled out their extradition to the USSR, as Turkey had yet to ratify the 1977 treaty. On December 13, the trio began their trial in Sinop's High Criminal Court for hijacking a plane, assault, and carrying arms without a permit. The 3 Soviet students, identified as brothers Boris Schmidt (also spelled Schnidi), 20, and Vitali Schmidt (also spelled Schnidi), 27, along with Arthur Scheller (also spelled Schiller), 23, said they had spent four years studying Soviet airport security. They claimed they had a choice between prison, banishment to Siberia, or hijacking. The trio was acquitted of hijacking on December 20, 1982, by a Sinop court. On the prosecutor's appeal, the Supreme Appeals Court in Ankara reversed the verdict and ordered a retrial in Zonguldak. On July 9, 1983, the new court sentenced to eight years and four months Vitali Schmidt and his brother Boris for air piracy. Arthur Scheller received a sentence of nine years and two months on an additional charge of possessing and using a weapon. 82110702

November 8, 1982 — DOMINICAN REPUBLIC — Marino Perez Rojas, 34, an exiled Dominican student, his Chilean exile wife, and their three children occupied the Peruvian embassy and took as hostage Luisa Carpio de Colado, the third secretary. Carpio told REUTERS by telephone that Perez wanted either for his government to find him work or for Peru to grant him political asylum. His wife, Mireyz Lopez, said they wanted to carry out a peaceful protest. Neither was armed. They surrendered peacefully, and Perez was arrested. Perez had been exiled from the Dominican Republic during the government of Joaquin Balaguer, who was President from 1966 to 1978. 82110801

November 9, 1982 — IRAQ — The WASHINGTON POST reported that Iraq had permitted Abu Nidal (Sabri al Banna), 43, the head of Black June, to reestablish his headquarters in Baghdad in March 1982. The POST suggested that this information would embarrass the United States government, which had moved to take Iraq off the list of nations supporting international terrorism on February 26, 1982. Nidal had been based in Damascus since being expelled from Iraq in 1978 after a rift with Saddam Hussein over Iraqi support for Yasir Arafat and the Palestine Liberation Organization (PLO). Nidal broke with Arafat in 1972 and was sentenced in absentia to death by Fatah in 1978. Nidal claimed credit for the attempted assassination of Israeli ambassador Shlomo Argov in London on June 3, which set off the Israeli invasion of Lebanon. He was also accused of plotting to assassinate Austrian chancellor Bruno Kreisky in 1981 for his encouraging the late Egyptian president Anwar Sadat to make peace with Israel.

November 9, 1982 — FRANCE — Seven Turkish opponents of the new Constitution took over the Turkish Airlines offices in Paris at 11:00 A.M. to demand the freeing of nine Dev Sol members who were arrested earlier in the week for seizing hostages at the Turkish consulate in Cologne, West Germany. 82110901

November 9, 1982 — COSTA RICA — Six members of the Salvadoran Revolutionary Party of Central American Workers (PRTC) in San Jose attempted to kidnap Japanese citizen Otaiasuk Tesuji Kosuga, president of the National Electric Corporation of Costa Rica, as he was going to work. A nearby patrol car gave chase and foiled the kidnapping, wounding two of the kidnappers. A student and Kosuga were also injured. Kosuga was erroneously reported dead in initial radio broadcasts. The group apparently intended to demand a large monetary ransom and obtain the release of Argentine citizen Esbezi, who was being held at La Reforma prison on charges of illegal association and arms trafficking. The Faribundo Marti Liberation Movement denied responsibility for the incident. Police found one of the kidnappers in Alajuelita and claimed that all of the attackers were foreigners, with methods similar to those used by terrorists from Uruguay, Argentina, and Brazil. Police also claimed that 15 people were behind the kidnapping. A woman with what police claimed was a Nicaraguan accent was among the 5 initially held. She was later identified as Sofia Lopez (Dalia Escobar Alas), who claimed she was born in San Salvador on February 17, 1962. Arrested with her was Carlos Alberto Marroquin (Antonio), who was born in San Salvador on April 20, 1950. He claimed to be a painter who served only as a courier of information and money between Salvador and Costa Rica. A third prisoner, Jose Santos Martinez Calles, 24, was wounded by gunfire. 82110902

November 9, 1982 — SPAIN — A Madrid newspaper reported that Felipe Gonzalez, future Spanish prime minister, tipped off French prime minister Pierre Mauroy that three Basque Nation and Liberty (ETA) Military terrorists were intending to assassinate the pope during his visit to Spain. Among the alleged plotters was a Frenchman and an Italian, who would conduct the attack in Loyola, where the pope's helicopter was to land. After a gunfight, French police arrested Jose Luis Ansola Larranaga and Carlos Ibarguren Aguirre, two ETA Military leaders, in St. Jean de Luz. 82110903

November 11, 1982 — FEDERAL REPUBLIC OF GERMANY — Frankfurt police arrested 2 of the most wanted members of the Baader-Meinhof Gang, Brigitte Monhaupt, 33, and Adelheid Schulz, 27, who were believed linked to the 1981 bombing of the United States Air Force European headquarters in Ramstein, which injured 20 persons. The two were arrested as they approached a weapons cache outside Frankfurt. The duo was also wanted in connection with the 1977 murder of banker Juergen Ponto and the 1977 kidnap/murder of industrialist Hanns-Martin Schleyer. Schulz was also wanted for the murder of federal prosecutor Siegfried Buback. Monhaupt was wanted for the 1981 assassination attempt against Gen. Frederick J. Kroesen, commander in chief of the United States Army in Europe.

November 11, 1982 — ITALY — Nine Red Brigadists were arrested and one was killed when he slipped on a fire escape and plunged to his death in Milan. Police arrested three terrorists in Milan and six in the Frabosa Soprana area, near Turin, in police raids on two hideouts.

November 11, 1982 — LEBANON — A huge explosion in the Israeli Army's south Lebanese headquarters in Tyre killed 75 Israeli soldiers, border guards, and security men as well as 14 Palestinian and Lebanese prisoners. Another 19 people were injured in the 7:15 A.M. explosion. Military authorities initially claimed that a man crashed an explosives-laden car into the building. The Armed Struggle Organization (Munazmat an-Nidal al-Musallah) claimed credit, and the Palestine Liberation Organization's Yasir Arafat credited the blast to Palestinian guerrillas and their leftist allies still working in the area. The Popular Front for the Liberation of Palestine denied responsibility for the blast. An Israeli commission decided that the blast was the result of a gas leak in the poorly constructed building. On April 10, 1984, a Shiite code-named Mahmoud told the WASHINGTON POST he had loaded the car that crashed into the building with dynamite. 82111101

November 13, 1982 — HONDURAS — Individuals in a car threw a homemade bomb at the Tegucigalpa office of Air Florida during the night but caused no injuries or damage. Their aim was impeded as a result of their noticing that a night watchman had spotted them. 82111301

November 13, 1982 — EL SALVADOR — Michael Cross, a United States journalist, was wounded in a cross-fire between Faribundo Marti Liberation Movement guerrillas and government forces on the Pan American Highway near the El Junquillar area. His assistant, Judith Preston, was not injured. 82111302

November 15, 1982 — FEDERAL REPUBLIC OF GERMANY — Bomb disposal experts defused a bomb hidden in the garage of an Eschborn, Frankfurt, 25-story apartment building housing many United States servicemen. A resident noticed a bag near his car containing a fire extinguisher with wires attached. 82111501

November 16, 1982 — FEDERAL REPUBLIC OF GERMANY — Friedrichsruh police arrested Baader-Meinhof terrorist Christian Klar, who was armed with a pistol. His male companion escaped. Klar's fingerprints had been discovered on a car in Bochum, 55 miles north of Bonn. Police had offered a $40,000 reward for information leading to the arrest of Klar and fellow BMG terrorist Inge Viett.

November 17, 1982 — UNITED STATES — Ex–Central Intelligence Agency (CIA) employee Edwin P. Wilson was convicted by a federal jury of seven of eight counts of attempting to smuggle handguns and an M-16 rifle to Libyan officials as part of a $20 million operation. The Alexandria jury rejected his defense that this was part of a CIA intelligence-gathering ploy. On December 20, 1982, District judge Richard L. Williams sentenced Wilson to 15 years in prison and a two hundred thousand dollar fine. One of the Smith and Wesson .357 magnums was used in the May 1980 assassination of a Libyan dissident ex-diplomat in Bonn, West Germany.

November 18, 1982 — INDIA — Two individuals riding a motorcycle threw a hand grenade during the night at the Soviet embassy's residential compound, shattering windows and damaging a door. 82111801

November 19, 1982 — SPAIN — Bilbao police defused a C-2 bomb at the Banco Hispano Americano. Another bomb had exploded in the Banco de Viscaya in this Basque area town. 82111901

November 20, 1982 — FEDERAL REPUBLIC OF GERMANY — At 9:43 P.M., the Red Army Faction phoned the SECOND GERMAN TELEVISION sports studio to demand that sports broadcaster Dieter Kuerten read a call for the release of Baader-Meinhof terrorist Christian Klar, who was captured earlier in the week in the Sachsenwald Forest near Hamburg. The studio was cleared, but no bomb went off after the 10 P.M. deadline.

November 20, 1982 — SOUTH KOREA — Kown Kyong-kong, 22, threw a beer bottle filled with flaming gasoline on the roof of the American Cultural Center in Kwangju at 11:10 P.M. Two guards immediately put out the fire. Kwon surrendered to Suwon police on November 25. 82112001

November 20, 1982 — FRANCE — The Internationalist Hooligans–Group Bakunin-Gdansk-Paris-Guatemala-El Salvador claimed credit for the nighttime bombings of the Paris offices of the South African citrus fruit firm Outspan and the French chemical company Promo-Chimie. Damage to the Outspan firm was heavy, and several other offices in the building were also damaged. The chemical firm reported only slight damage. The group condemned "the Soviet bureaucratic order" and "American imperialism." Targets have included the Soviet watch and jewel company SLAVA, a firm selling Franco-American built television sets, the Chilean Airlines offices, an importer of Argentine meat, and a firm selling Polish goods. 82112002–03

November 21, 1982 — GREECE — Police in Komotini arrested two Palestinians who were smuggling 60 kilograms of explosives, timing devices, detonators, and fuses beneath their Mercedes with a Bari license plate. The duo, identified as Abd-al Usamah az-Zumar, 22, a student living in Varese, Italy, and Mohammad Faytz, 33, an auto mechanic from Madaba, Jordan, said the explosives were not intended for use in Greece. The duo had crossed the Greek-Turkish border by posing as tourists. They were jailed pending trial for smuggling. On March 23, 1985, Rome's ANSA news service reported that Greek justice minister Georgios Alexandros Mangakis decided to extradite one of the terrorists for the attack on October 9, 1982, on Rome's synagogue in which a two-year-old died and 34 were injured. 82112101

November 22, 1982 — POLAND — A Polish militiaman, Piotr Winogrolzki 22, assigned to guard against hijackings, used his two pistols and two hand grenades to hijack a Polish airline LOT AN-24 carrying 31 passengers and 5 crew members from Wroclaw to Warsaw at 9:17 A.M. Upon landing at Tempelhof Airport in the United States sector of West Berlin, the hijacker jumped from the plane but was fired on by two other guards on board, wounding him in the right foot. He fired back at the guards but aimed his shots to avoid injury. Three other passengers requested political asylum. On April 18, 1983, the Berlin regional court sentenced Piotr Winogrolzki to five years imprisonment. 82112201

November 26, 1982 — ECUADOR — A youth left a sophisticated time bomb in a suitcase in the Israeli embassy. Victor Jimenez, a security officer, was killed while trying to remove the bomb. A fellow officer was also killed, as was a woman in a nearby apartment building who was thrown through a window by the force of the concussion. Several other injuries were reported in the 10:50 A.M. blast. Several people were arrested. The Palestine Liberation Organization (PLO) condemned the attack. A smaller bomb went off on the Jewish new year, slightly damaging the Israeli-Ecuadoran goodwill association near the Quito synagogue. 82112601–02

November 27, 1982 — POLAND — Dariusz, S., a security officer from Olsztyn, used a pistol to attempt to hijack a Hungarian Malev Tupolev-154, flight 121 on the Leningrad-Warsaw-Budapest route with 85 passengers, at 5:50 P.M. He demanded that Capt. Imre Nagy and copilot Tamas Antalik fly him to Tempelhof Airport in West Berlin. Authorities demanded that he release the women and children hostages during five hours of negotiations, but he instead released the male passengers. At 10:35 P.M., he was overpowered by flight security protection personnel in the metropolitan Warsaw command of the Citizens' Militia, with no injuries reported to the passengers. The hijacker was carried off the plane with serious head injuries. Polish authorities announced that since the beginning of 1981, 290 Poles had attempted to hijack planes to the West and another 32 had been arrested before they had a chance to put similar plans into action. The successful hijackings since the imposition of martial law went unmentioned. 82112701

November 28, 1982 — BOLIVIA — Bolivian constitutionally acting president Jaime Paz Zamora was jumped at noon as he was leaving the presidential palace by Carlos Fajardo and Argentine Mario Migola, who were both immediately arrested. A presidential spokesman said Migola was a member of the paramilitary group that Col. Luis Arce Gomez organized during his tenure as interior minister of Gen. Luis Garcia Meza's government. The government had been tipped off to an assassination attempt being planned against Paz Zamora, one of the three leaders of the Movement of the Revolutionary Left (MIR).

November 30, 1982 — UNITED KINGDOM — A package measuring 8″ × 4″ ignited while being examined by Peter Taylor, the manager of the Prime Minister's Office, slightly burning him at 10 Downing Street. A note on the package to Prime Minister Margaret Thatcher was from the Animal Rights Militia, which sent similar incendiary devices, intercepted in the mails, to Labor party leader Michael Foot, Liberal party leader David Steel, Social Democratic party leader Roy Jenkins, and Timothy Raison, the minister responsible for animal legislation. The Irish National Liberation Army also claimed credit for sending the package to the Prime Minister.

December 1982 — FEDERAL REPUBLIC OF GERMANY — Unknown individuals stole three submachine guns and one hundred rounds of ammunition from the bodyguards of Hans-Dietrich Genscher, West German foreign minister.

December 1982 — PERU — The Palestine Liberation Organization (PLO) denied responsibility for an attack on the Jewish synagogue in Lima. 82129901

December 1982 — EL SALVADOR — The Armed Forces announced that among the 120 guerrillas killed in a two-week period were five foreigners: Italian Francisco Sanchez; Nicaraguans Emanuel Amador and Rene Moralex; Cuban Pedro Rosa; and Honduran Francisco Romero. The army said the terrorists had been trained in the USSR, Cuba, and Czechoslovakia. 82129902

December 1982 — ITALY — In the April 9, 1986, edition of the WASHINGTON POST, Jack Anderson reported that the United States embassy in Rome had discovered that 15 Sardinians had been arrested by Italian authorities because they were part of a Libyan plot to separate Sardinia from Italy. Anderson indicated that an Italian political party was implicated, and, according to an embassy cable, evidence pointed to "a Libyan by the name of Geri Mehed Tabet, currently at large, with whom the separatists apparently had contact in October 1981." The Libyans were to fund the group, who would "undertake a number of ambitious acts of sabotage at airports and a NATO military base and . . . kidnap an American military officer." 82129903

December 1982 — IRAN — The Soviet news agency TASS reported that "riotous elements" attempted to force their way into the Soviet embassy during a demonstration against the invasion of Afghanistan. The Soviets claimed the Iranian government supported the demonstrators' attack. 82129904

December 1, 1982 — LEBANON — As the Mercedes of Druze leader Walid Jumblatt, 33, was passing by a car bomb, it exploded in midafternoon on Chiel Chiha Street, the extension of west Beirut's main Hamra thoroughfare. Four persons, including Jumblatt's personal bodyguard, Jamal Saab, and a Lebanese policeman, were killed, and 15 others, including Jumblatt and his wife, Gervette, were injured. At least a dozen nearby cars were damaged. Jumblatt's father, Kamal, was assassinated in March 1977, touching off a Druze massacre of hundreds of Christians. Syrians were later suspected of the killing.

December 2, 1982 — REPUBLIC OF SOUTH AFRICA — The government released from prison prominent Afrikaans poet Breyten Breytenbach, 44, who had served seven years of a nine-year sentence for attempting to recruit young Afrikaner dissidents for the African National Congress. He was the first political prisoner to be granted early release. He left the country for Paris after visiting with his parents in the eastern Cape Province for two days. Police said he would be permitted to live unrestricted in South Africa if he returned.

December 2, 1982 — THAILAND — A bomb in a briefcase left in the former Iraqi consulate by a tall, thin, mustachioed Arab wearing sunglasses exploded 3½ hours later at 4:40 P.M., killing Thailand's top bomb disposal expert, police lieutenant colonel Surat Sumanat, and injuring 6 policemen and 11 civilians. The building houses the offices of the RBM and AE Nana companies and is owned by the secretary-general of the Democrat party, Lek Nana, who serves as Iraq's honorary consul general in Bangkok. The explosion caused B 5 million worth of damage. In a phone call to Paris, the Iraqi Islamic Action Organization claimed credit, saying that 10 kilograms of TNT were packed in the Samsonite suitcase. The operation was carried out by the Mujabbar Bakr commando group, named after the chief of the bombing of the Iraqi mission in Rome two years earlier. The raid was called Uprising of Safar 20 to mark the February 5–6 Shiite uprising in several Iraqi cities against Ba'athist rule. The group also claimed credit for an attack on Iraq's embassy in Paris in August. Police were searching for 4 Pakistanis believed involved in the bombing, at least 3 of whom left the area on November 29. Mohammed Waheed, thought responsible for planting the bomb, was believed hiding in the house of a local collaborator. Waheed and Mohammad Barod Basod, Jawig Quibo, and Manlia Plod Jayed were believed to have arrived on November 27 at the Grace Hotel on Sukhumwit Soi 3. Police suggested that three motives could have been involved. Lek Nana supplied food to Iraq; the Pattani United Liberation Organization (PULO), which received financial aid from Libya and whose leader, Tunku Piror, received military training in Pakistan, may have been involved; private business rivalry may also have been involved. Iranian charge d'affaires Hushang Rahimian denied responsibility, saying his country would prefer to settle its differences with Iraq on the battlefield. 82120201

December 3, 1982 — COLOMBIA — Nine male and three female armed Palestinians burst into a Medellin synagogue, spilled red ink on the dozen elderly worshippers inside, tore Bibles into pieces, and burned the Bibles and United States and Israeli flags. 82120301

December 4, 1982 — NICARAGUA — A deserting Sandinista army officer hijacked a Cessna 180 II airplane, taking hostage the pilot and a crewman and forcing them to land in Costa Rica, where he requested asylum. He was granted territorial asylum while officials considered his case. 82120401

December 5, 1982 — SPAIN — Juan Martin Luna (also spelled Lunz), 28, the last at-large founder of the October 1 Anti-Fascist Revolutionary Group (GRAPO), fired a pistol at police when told to halt in front of a Barcelona grocery store. Police returned the fire, fatally wounding him at 9:00 A.M. No injuries to police were reported. On January 11, GRAPO said it would resume guerrilla activities, ending a two-month truce declared after Spain's Socialist party won the October parliamentary elections. Police said only 12 GRAPO members were left. Martin Luna, from Cadiz, was married with one son. A welder, he was sentenced to 37 years in jail for the murder of army captain Herdera. In December 1979 he and 4 other guerrillas had dug a tunnel under the walls of the high-security Zamora prison in northern Spain and escaped. He was the only one of the 5 not yet captured. Police said he was behind a wave of bomb attacks on public buildings in Spain in September.

December 5, 1982 — CYPRUS — A bomb exploded during the morning outside the Nicosia offices of R. A. Travelmasters, causing £200 damage. R. A. Travelmasters is a tourist bureau that represents Gulf Air. 82120501

December 6, 1982 — NORTHERN IRELAND — The South Derry Brigade of the Irish National Liberation Army set off 35 pounds of gelignite next to a main supporting pillar in the Droppin Well pub/disco in Ballykelly, 10 miles northeast of Londonderry, sending the concrete ceiling crashing down on 150 dancers, many of them off-duty British soldiers from the Shackleton Army barracks. The 11:13 P.M. blast killed 11 servicemen (mostly from the 1st Battalion, Chesire Regiment), 4 women, and a civilian male, and wounded 66 other people.

December 6, 1982 — MOZAMBIQUE — The South African-backed Mozambique National Resistance Movement claimed credit for the sabotage of a fuel depot that supplied the oil pipeline to Zimbabwe from Beira. Six foreigners, who worked at the offices of the foreign-owned shipping firm, Manica Freight Services, were arrested shortly thereafter. Dion Hamilton, a British citizen, was director of the company. A Portuguese, Benjamin Fox, was a section chief of the firm. The other four Portuguese, Joao Benedito Fernandes, Maria Odete Rodrigues, Cipriano Exartocao Monteiro, and Joaquim Martino da Silva were clerical workers. Police said radio transmitters, pistols, rifles, boxes of ammunition, grenades, and military uniforms were found in two Beira houses. On January 19, 1983, local police agreed to allow Portugal to recall a Portuguese diplomat who was wanted for questioning in the incident. 82120601

December 7, 1982 — UGANDA — Two gunmen injured two Indian employees of the Indian High Commission during the morning as the two were leaving their car. The gunmen escaped in another car. 82120701

December 7, 1982 — LEBANON — In the Al-Biqa' area, a booby-trapped car exploded at 1:15 P.M. in Barr Ilyas, on the Shtawrak-Damascus highway, injuring several people and hitting a Mercedes truck bearing a Kuwaiti license plate, killing its two Syrian drivers, Muhammad Yasin and Yasin 'Abd al-Ghani Shunumi. 82120702

December 8, 1982 — UNITED STATES — Norman Mayer, 66, a hotel maintenance man from Miami Beach, pulled a van up to the base of the Washington Monument at 9:20 A.M. and claimed that he would set off one thousand pounds of explosives if something was not done about nuclear weapons. Ten hours later, police opened up on the van as Mayer tried to drive away, killing him. No explosives were found. Nine tourists who were inside the monument at the time of the takeover escaped uninjured.

December 8, 1982 — GREECE — A bomb exploded outside the Kuwait Air offices in Athens, killing one of the alleged perpetrators and injuring the other, who confessed to the bombing. The Armenian Secret Army for the Liberation of Armenia (ASALA) phoned AGENCE FRANCE-PRESSE to say:

> Our organization declares that the bomb explosion at the Kuwait Air office early on 8 December was a premeditated attempt to murder the two young ASALA members. We have remained silent until now [December 9] in order to avoid any exacerbation in Greek-Turkish relations. However, since the police have exploited our silence, we are obliged to declare the truth. The two ASALA members are the victims of

special commandos dispatched by Evren to murder Armenian fighters. Barely 1 month ago, Turkish agents killed the Armenian fighter Novar Sialiman in the Netherlands. We will never remain silent in the face of such acts, and all those who consciously or unconsciously plot against the Armenian people will be punished in the proper way.

Police identified the living attacker as Vaheh Kontaverdian, 21, from Isfahan, Iran, who temporarily resided in Athens at 28 Renee Piau in Neos Kosmos. The terrorist claimed his dead collaborator, who was named Sako, had instigated him to throw the bomb from their motorcycle at the offices of Saudi Airlines, but that they had made a mistake. The bomb hit an electrical utility pole and exploded. 82120801

December 9, 1982 — LESOTHO — Approximately 100 South African commandos attacked 12 locations in Maseru, killing 42 people. The attack was designed to eliminate the African National Congress (ANC) terrorist presence. Local residents claimed the South Africans were armed with bazookas, machine guns, grenades, and incendiary devices. Several civilians were killed. Cecilia Sehlakaba, 28, who had gone to her window to see what the noise was about, was killed by a bullet to the chest. A young girl died in a house that formerly belonged to the ANC. Attacks were also made in the precincts of Thamaes and Qoalen, on the outskirts of Maseru. One house was the scene of eight deaths. South Africa was roundly condemned, and Lesotho claimed most of those killed were refugees, not terrorists. Lesotho police later said 30 ANC members and 12 Lesotho citizens, including 5 women and 2 children, were killed. Among the ANC members killed were Zola Ngini, 48, the ANC's chief representative in Lesotho; Adolph Mpongosohe, trained in Angola; Limpho Sekamane, wife of an ANC official; and Jackson Tayo, an explosives expert who had done time in Robben Island prison. Sekamane was believed to have been secretary of the ANC women's section in Lesotho.

Pretoria's military intelligence claimed that it had fought a two-hour battle with Lesotho paramilitary police, and that 4 South African Defense Force (SADF) commandos were wounded. The ANC, claimed SADF, was planning terrorist attacks during the holiday season and "a number of well-trained terrorists moved from other southern African states to Lesotho during the past month to execute these plans." The attack began at 1:00 A.M. and lasted five hours. A local ANC resident claimed that the SADF was led to the locations by informers with dated information, which led to the deaths of many non-ANC individuals. Among this group was Sally Ralebitso, 21, daughter of a former Lesotho cabinet minister and ambassador to Mozambique. She lived in 28 Koena Flats, whose previous tenant was Chris Hani, a top ANC member, who had left Lesotho several months ago. Another individual known as Gini jumped through a window above

Sally's apartment, injured his leg as he hit the ground, and was shot dead on the spot. Mathabatha Sexwale and his wife Buni, 2 ANC members who had lived several years in Maseru, escaped after engaging in a brief fire-fight. Their house was destroyed.

December 9, 1982 — MOZAMBIQUE — The Mozambique National Resistance Movement (RENAMO) sabotaged the Munhava oil tank farm near Beira, destroying the British Petroleum part of the complex and damaging the facilities belonging to Caltex and Mobil. Mozambique blamed South Africa for the attack. Forty tanks were destroyed, but no injuries were reported. The raiders apparently aimed at fuel scheduled to be pumped to Zimbabwe, which recently had sent troops to Mozambique to guard the pipeline. On February 22, 1983, the Maputo radio station reported that a Beira court had sentenced to death five Mozambicans for the attack. They were identi-fied as Auguto Andicen, Jorge Lebombo, Evid Alredo, Joao Dias, and Dileep Nekit. The latter was alleged to be "the leader of a group of 200 terrorists and had killed 45 people." Finlay Dean Hamilton, the British director of a shipping firm in Beira, was sentenced to 20 years. The court found that he had prior knowledge of the attack, which resulted in the destruction of $12 million worth of fuel. According to the radio, "Hamilton had warned his friends to stock up with petrol because there would soon be a shortage. He himself had planned to leave for South Africa in his private plane on the day of the attack. Hamilton was also convicted of concealing at his Beira home four pistols, three grenades, and 200 rounds of ammunition." The court acquitted seven Portuguese citizens for the attack but convicted two other Portuguese. Benjamin Fox received 8 years, and Joao Fernandes received 4 years. Antonio Fonseca, a Portu-guese who was acquitted, had been accused of spreading anti-Mozambique propaganda and insulting government leaders. Another Portuguese who was released was Elsino Costa Pinto, who had been kidnapped by RE-NAMO in 1982. Nine Mozambicans were acquitted. Fifteen received jail terms of between 6 and 15 years. A Zimbabwean was acquitted. 82120901

December 10, 1982 — SWAZILAND — A bomb, apparently planted at 3:00 A.M., went off an hour later at the Fairview residential area of Manzini, causing extensive damage. The house was leased by a Mozambican, Mr. Corriea, who was not in it at the time. The house belonged to Mr. Dlamini, the owner of a shop at Lomahasha border post. 82121001

December 14, 1982 — ITALY — A Potenze court sentenced Red Brigades members Raffaele Fenio and Vincenzo de Stefano to life imprisonment for killing state prosecutor Nicola Giacumbi on March 16, 1980, in Salerno.

December 14, 1982 — GUATEMALA — Armed members of the Pedro Diaz

Command of the IXIM Revolutionary Movement of the People kidnapped Dr. Xiomara Suazo Estrada, 33, an x-ray physician and Guatemalan daughter of Honduran president Roberto Suazo Cordova, as she was on her way to work at Guatemala City's San Juan de Dios hospital. The group established a deadline of December 17 for the publication by 14 Central American and Mexican newspapers of a 12-page statement. The group demanded that the Honduran ambassador to Guatemala broadcast a statement that the group's demand had been fulfilled. On December 15, Honduran and Guatemalan officials, although saying that they would not negotiate with the kidnappers, agreed to permit the newspapers to run the statement. The group's communique, which ran in Guatemalan newspapers on December 22, said in part that United States "imperialism took the necessity to reinstall the civilian facade and placed the civilian Roberto Suazo Cordova to fool the Honduran people, assigning him the role of buffoon in plans of intervention, invasion, and aggression." Suazo became Honduras' first civilian president in 10 years when he was installed the previous November in United States–backed elections. On December 23, Dr. Suazo was released unharmed. The group had previously kidnapped Public Health Minister Dr. Roquelino Recinos Mendez. 82121401

December 14, 1982 — FEDERAL REPUBLIC OF GERMANY — An explosives-packed fire extinguisher blew up against the car of Sp.5c Ricky Seius near a United States military camp at Butzbach, about 25 miles north of Frankfurt. According to the 5th United States Army Corps, Seius was admitted to a hospital with severe cuts and burns. His car was destroyed.

According to Hesse criminal police, a second bomb did not go off because the United States Army driver had noticed a hard object under his seat. He got out and saw the explosives-packed fire extinguisher, which also had a pressure switch, under his seat. 82121402

December 15, 1982 — FEDERAL REPUBLIC OF GERMANY — An explosives-packed fire extinguisher exploded in the car of Capt. Howard Bromberg, 29, as he started his Mercedes at the United States Army base at Darmstadt, about 20 miles south of Frankfurt. He was admitted to a United States military hospital with burns on his legs. The car was completely destroyed by fire.

On March 15, 1985, the state protection branch of the Frankfurt higher regional court sentenced five right-wing terrorists for attempted murder, membership in a terrorist organization, explosives offences, grievous bodily harm, and bank robbery in connection with the December 14–15 incidents. According to the German press agency DPA in Hamburg, "Walter Kexel, 23, was sentenced to 14 years, Helge Blasche, 42, Hans Peter Fraas, 24, and Dieter Sporleder, 24, received 10, 8½, and 7 years, respectively. Ulrich Tillmann, 22, who at the time of the crimes was still under age, was sentenced to 5 years' juvenile detention. Kexel manufactured the bombs with primitive methods and placed them under the driving seats of the 2 vehicles, where they exploded. A third attack in Frankfurt failed because Fraas had second thoughts and did not connect the fuse." 82121501

December 16, 1982 — UNITED STATES — A bomb exploded at 3:00 P.M. after one hundred people were evacuated from an Elmont, New York, building that housed the South African Railways Procurement Office. No injuries were reported. An anonymous phone caller had sent a warning from the United Freedom Fighters/United Freedom Federation. 82121601

December 16, 1982 — UNITED STATES — A powerful bomb exploded at 7:40 P.M. at a Westchester County, New York, International Business Machines office in Harrison, causing no injuries. The bomb went off four hours after a bomb had exploded at a South African transport office on Long Island. International Business Machines has extensive operations in South Africa. The IBM office, one of 27 facilities in the county, was a sales and service branch where 500 persons usually work. Only about 30 — all of whom were evacuated — were in the building when a telephoned warning was received a few minutes before the blast from the United Freedom Fighters/United Freedom Federation. 82121602

December 18, 1982 — SWAZILAND — A high-ranking officer with the Umbutfo Swaziland Defense Force said that a contingent of his men and two armed members of the South African African National Congress fired at each other at the Lomahasha border post before the ANC members escaped back into Mozambique. 82121801

December 19, 1982 — REPUBLIC OF SOUTH AFRICA — The African National Congress (ANC) set off four bombs at the Koeberg nuclear power plant, which was scheduled to go on line in six months. The station was under construction 17 miles north of Cape Town. Officials announced that commissioning of the $1.85 billion plant would be delayed for at least nine months. A Paris official of Framatone, a French firm involved in the plant, said one of the station's two nuclear reactors was damaged. One of the reactors was loaded with nuclear material but was not operating. No injuries were reported. The ANC in Dar es Salaam, Tanzania, said the attack was a salute to "all our fallen heroes and imprisoned comrades, including those buried in Maseru [Lesotho] this afternoon. The beginning of the end of the apartheid system that has caused so much immeasurable suffering to our black people, the people of Namibia, Lesotho, Mozambique, Angola and other neighboring states, has begun."

December 19, 1982 — IRAN — Tehran's Foreign Ministry denied responsibility for the bombing of the IRAQI NEWS AGENCY.

December 19, 1982 — EL SALVADOR — Salvadoran newsman and cameraman Jose Luis Diaz and his wife Fidela Nunez, who worked for a Canadian television group and a Dutch network, were taken into custody for questioning as suspected guerrillas. Early reports had said the duo was kidnapped. They were released after several hours of questioning. 82121901

December 20, 1982 — COLOMBIA — Maria Antonia Garces de Lloreda, director of the Fine Arts Institute of Valle del Cauca Province and sister-in-law of Colombia foreign minister Rodrigo Lloreda, was kidnapped from a Cali medical center by two armed men who forced her into a white automobile. She was married to Alvaro Jose Lloreda, director-manager of the Cali newspaper EL PAIS. She was released on July 5, 1983, during the night.

December 20, 1982 — UNITED STATES — Ricardo Morales, 43, an anti-Castro Cuban exile, was shot dead from behind with a .32 caliber pistol fired by a patron at the Cherries bar in Key Biscayne, Florida. "Monkey" Morales had claimed that he helped plan and carry out the 1976 bombing of a Cubana airliner in which 73 persons died near Barbados. He claimed that while an officer of DISIP, the Venezuelan intelligence service, he had helped provide the C-4 explosive used. He also was a friend of former Central Intelligence Agency case officer Edwin P. Wilson. He said he had built and planted bombs for anti-Castro activists in Miami, while working as a Federal Bureau of Investigation informer. He claimed he had worked for the CIA in 1963–64 in the Congo and had tailed Carlos the terrorist and CIA turncoat Philip Agee while working for DISIP. 82122001

December 20, 1982 — UNITED STATES — Assistant United States Attorney James P. Walsh, Jr., filed documents in a Los Angeles court that indicated that former sports car maker John Z. De Lorean received help from the Irish Republican Army to finance his cocaine-trafficking scheme. De Lorean's firm had been based in a Belfast neighborhood until it was closed by the British government the previous fall for lack of funds. The building was firebombed in 1981. On December 27, 1982, Kathleen Montague of the Irish Northern Aid Committee read a letter from the IRA denying "any dealings with the gangster John De Lorean." The group said the Belfast factory "was part and parcel of a British government counter-insurgency project aimed at undermining our base in west Belfast, through bribes of jobs and prosperity."

December 21, 1982 — SWAZILAND — Members of the African National Congress of South Africa attacked members of the Umbutfo Swaziland Defense Force before escaping into Mozambique. 82122101

December 21, 1982 — UNITED STATES — According to the Federal Bureau of Investigation (FBI), "At approximately 1:42 A.M., the NEW YORK POST received a telephone call from an anonymous male caller who stated a bomb had been placed under a car with diplomatic license plates at the corner of 66th Street and 2nd Avenue, New York City. Members of the [New York City Police Department] NYPD recovered a pipe bomb underneath the right rear of a red Renault and rendered it safe. Due to the nature of the call, it was determined that the perpetrators thought they were placing the bomb under a Soviet diplomat's car. The car was parked 1½ blocks from the Soviet Mission to the [United Nations]." The FBI believed the United Jewish Underground was responsible. The Bureau indicated that the UJU is a group of extremists that has proclaimed violence as its only means to accomplish its objectives. An extension of the Jewish Defense League, many members of the group consider themselves protectors of "Jewish rights" and are avid supporters of the State of Israel. 82122102

December 22, 1982 — MOZAMBIQUE — The Mozambique National Resistance Movement (RENAMO) kidnapped two French nationals working on a high-voltage electric line project in Morrumbala, Zambezia Province, for the French company CGE-Alsthom. A third Frenchman was wounded but managed to escape. On January 3, 1983, the RENAMO said, "One of the men captured is seriously wounded in the arm. The wound was sustained from a shot fired by our weapons during the ambush. He is being looked after by our medical personnel. However, we cannot guarantee his survival. If he dies it will not be due to mistreatment but because of sanitary limitations." On January 30, 1983, Robert Soumillion and George Ferret were released near the Malawian police post at Caia. Construction by the French-Italian consortium on the electricity network had been delayed while the French government negotiated through the Red Cross for the release of the two men. 82122201

December 22, 1982 — UNITED STATES — Twelve masked, club-wielding Libyan students took over the Libyan student aid office at 6805 Poplar Place, McLean, Virginia, at 8 A.M. The group claimed the People's Committee for Students of Libyan Arab Jamahariya actually housed the headquarters of antiexile terrorist operations. The "People of Omar" demanded that WJLA-TV reporter Jim Clarke come to the scene. They initially tied up 3 Libyan male employees — Mohammad Sasi, 52, Mohammed Ayeb, 48, and Leu Barrope — but freed them after five minutes. July Holt and Andrea Barnett, 2 female employees, were released immediately. A police Special Weapons and Tactics team broke the building's glass front door nine hours after the takeover but successfully negotiated a peaceful surrender. No injuries were reported. Fairfax County General District Court judge Conrad Waters refused to reveal the names of the perpetrators but arraigned them on three counts of abduction. The group feared that publication of their names would threaten their lives and those of their family and friends. On December 19, 1982, Libyan leader Muammar Qaddafi had said in a nationwide broadcast that "the revolution has destroyed those inside the country and now it must pursue the rest abroad."

The decision to keep private the names of the accused followed a 1981 decision by a New York judge who agreed to keep secret the names of 40 Libyans who had occupied the Libyan United Nations Mission. Four of those in the McLean incident had been involved in the New York case. Bond for them was set at $30,000. The bond for the other 8 was set at $15,000. Eight of the 12 were undergraduates, 2 were graduate students, and 2 were unemployed.

Richard C. Shadyac, the lawyer for the plaintiff, said the group had caused $250,000 worth of damage in their search for documents that proved their case against Qaddafi.

On December 30, 1982, Fairfax County released the names of the accused after General District Court judge Frank B. Perry ruled that Virginia law requires disclosure. The group was identified as Mohammad R. Elaneizi, Otoman A. Mohamad, and Qusine E. Muftah of Milwaukee; Salah H. Elbakkoush; Muftas S. Gorgum; Tariq M. Elgassier of Los Gatos, California; Nagib A. Awad of Florida; Jamal M. Buzayan of Davis, California; Fathi M. Faituri of Florida; and Shaib M. Mahmod-Agily and Ali M. Mansour of Hattiesburg, Mississippi.

The Libyan student aid group sued the defendants for $12 million in Fairfax Circuit Court. On February 7, 1983, the students countersued for $15 million.

Each of the students pled guilty on January to unlawful assembly, assaulting 2 office employees, and destroying private property. County prosecutors dropped felony charges of abduction.

On March 4, Judge Barnard F. Jennings sentenced the 12 to one year in jail.

On September 9, 1983, a Fairfax County judge released 10 of the 12 protesters after they presented proof to the court that they were enrolled for the fall term at accredited United States colleges. 82122202

December 22, 1982 — DOMINICAN REPUBLIC — Santo Domingo police arrested Hilertaut Dominique, who was trying to smuggle 8 machine guns, 8 Uzi machine pistols, 4 M-16 rifles, 11 pistols, and communications equipment disguised as Christmas presents from Miami. Police claim Dominique had traveled to Libya, the German Democratic Republic, Angola, Cuba, and Nicaragua and that he carried one Venezuelan and two Haitian forged passports. Police claimed the lawyer and journalist had participated in the unsuccessful assassination attempt against Haitian president for life Jean Claude Duvalier. He was alleged to be connected with Dominican extremists and Haitian exiles living in Santo Domingo. 82122203

December 23, 1982 — AUSTRALIA — Bombs exploded at the Israeli consulate, injuring two, and at a Jewish club in Sydney. The Organization for the

Liberation of Lebanon from Foreigners claimed credit. Israel accused the Palestine Liberation Organization (PLO), who denied involvement. 82122301–02

December 24, 1982 — AFGHANISTAN — SAUDI PRESS AGENCY in Riyadh quoted travelers who claimed that Afghan mujahidin fired rockets at the Soviet embassy, causing extensive damage.

December 25, 1982 — GREECE — The Secret Armenian Army for the Liberation of Armenia (ASALA) told the Greek media that "all Turkish institutions and offices throughout the world are henceforth considered military targets of the Armenian Liberation Army. This includes airline offices, ships, business concerns, cultural centers and hundreds of other establishments. We warn citizens to stay clear of such places which we consider as enemy targets." The group claimed that Turkish secret agents murdered one of its members near the Beirut harbor and seriously wounded another. 82122501

December 26, 1982 — FRANCE — The Internationalist Hooligans (the Bakunin-Gdansk-Paris-Guatemala-Salvador Group) bombed a small Paris-based firm owned by Belgian industrialist Baron Edouard Empain, victim of a sensational 63-day kidnapping in 1978. Earlier targets included a branch of the Rothschild bank and firms trading with the Eastern Bloc. 82122601

December 27, 1982 — PHILIPPINES — After an unsuccessful extortion attempt, the Moro National Liberation Front bombed the interisland ship *M. V. Lady Ruth,* docked at Pagadian Harbor, killing 6 and wounding 70. The group also bombed a public market in Pagadian City, killing a nine-year-old girl selling vegetables and injuring 20 other people.

December 27, 1982 — FEDERAL REPUBLIC OF GERMANY — A Yugoslav tourist office and a Yugoslav grocery store in central Stuttgart were bombed, causing $8,000 damage but no injuries. 82122701–02

December 28, 1982 — UNITED STATES — Alexander Raffio, an associate of jailed ex–Central Intelligence Agency employee Edwin P. Wilson, told the TODAY SHOW that Wilson tried to ship explosives to the Palestine Liberation Organization (PLO). Wilson had been sentenced to 15 years in prison the previous week for smuggling arms to Libya. He faced three other trials for arms deals with Libya, including illegally exporting 20 tons of explosives. Raffio claimed that Wilson diverted three 5-gallon drums of explosives to Rotterdam for the PLO from a 1979 shipment that was destined for Libya.

December 29, 1982 — SPAIN — Two Basque terrorists fired submachine guns in the train station in Irun on the French border, killing two Customs Office guards, aged 22 and 40.

December 30, 1982 — ITALY — The Italian Communist party announced to the Italian news service ANSA that its report on terrorism in Italy in 1982 showed a 46.7 percent decrease in the number of terrorist incidents. "There were 39 murders compared to last year's 24. Three persons were wounded in ambushes compared to last year's 9. . . . There were no political kidnappings this year compared to 6 last year. There were 30 robberies for 'self-financing' or to buy arms and cars, compared to 19 last year. The most worrying data was that relative to homicides. Only the year 1980 was worse due to the bomb attack on the Bologna train station."

December 30, 1982 — NICARAGUA — Twelve Nicaraguan peasants were kidnapped in Las Rampas by counterrevolutionaries who took them across the Honduran border.

December 30, 1982 — UNITED STATES — Michael James Will, 30, an unemployed commercial pilot from Colorado Springs, tried to hijack to the state of Washington a United Airlines plane en route from Ontario, California, to Pittsburg, California, by claiming that a concealed hair dryer was a bomb. The crew convinced him that the plane did not have enough fuel. Will was charged with endangering the lives of others and terrorist threats and was held on two hundred thousand dollars bond. 82123001

December 31, 1982 — ZIMBABWE — Suspected Zimbabwe People's Revolutionary Army (ZIPRA) dissidents kidnapped Benjie Williams, 74, a well-known farmer in Matabeleland, and his grandson David Biland, 22, from Williams's farm 60 miles north of Bulawayo. The captors forced their hostages to write a note indicating that the group demanded the return of Zimbabwe African People's Union (ZAPU) property confiscated by the government following coup-plotting charges. On January 2, 1983, Williams's beheaded body was found. There was no word on the fate of Biland.

December 31, 1982 — GERMAN DEMOCRATIC REPUBLIC — The West German magazine STERN claimed that Paul Essling, 41, a heating engineer, tried to kill German Democratic Republic head of state Erich Honecker as the Communist party leader was driving in a motorcade through Klosterfelde, north of East Berlin. Essling tried to penetrate the convoy to get behind Honecker's car but was forced off the road by security guards. He jumped out of his car and opened fire, severely wounding one guard, then shooting himself in the head. The East German ADN news service denied the assassination attempt but gave details of a "traffic incident" confirming the report, claiming Essling was under the influence of alcohol and had refused to halt after being ordered to do so. STERN claimed that the 1:00 P.M. attack took place because Essling had seen "how members of government and party officials lived in luxury."

December 31, 1982 — UNITED STATES — The Fuerzas Armadas Liberation Nacional (FALN) set off four bombs in Manhattan that injured three policemen, including one whose leg was amputated. One blast at 9:25 P.M. damaged the Brooklyn Federal courthouse; the other blasts occurred in lower Manhattan. A fifth bomb, made of four sticks of dynamite, a blasting cap, a nine-volt battery, and a pocket watch, was deactivated in lower Manhattan.

Officer Rocco Pascarella, 33, lost his leg while investigating a suspicious package at the north entrance of the Manhattan police headquarters. Five minutes later, a bomb caused extensive property damage outside the United States District Court in Brooklyn. While police were removing two more packages in St. Andrew's Plaza, one of the bombs exploded, injuring two bomb squad detectives: Salvatore Pastorella, 42, and Anthony Senft, 36. Local Chinese residents claimed that a man with a package had warned them away from the scene shortly before one of the bombs exploded. 82123101–05

December 31, 1982 — ZIMBABWE — Suspected Zimbabwe People's Revolutionary Army (ZIPRA) dissidents killed six people, including Frenchman Phillipe Boiron, 42, who had been working on a farm northwest of Bulawayo since 1979. The group consisted of five whites, including two children, and a black security guard who were traveling in a car between Nyamandhlovu and Bulawayo. The dead were identified as farmer David Walters, his sons Michael and Sean, aged 2 and 4, his brother-in-law John Hearn, 45, their friend Boiron, and security Tamba Ndebele.

A CHRONOLOGY OF EVENTS

1983

January 1983 — AUSTRALIA — Two extortionists fired a homemade missile through a Canberra bomber on exhibition at Brisbane Airport, then demanded $1 million for not shooting down a Trans Australian Airlines passenger plane flying in and out of Brisbane. The demands were made in a series of five extortion notes. Police delivered the money through a circuitous route, but the money was never picked up. Federal minister for administrative services Kevin Newman took charge of one of the largest manhunts ever conducted in the state of Queensland.

January 1983 — PEOPLE'S REPUBLIC OF CHINA — A hijacker, after ordering the Civil Aviation Administration of China (CAAC) pilot of a domestic flight to divert the plane to Taiwan, fatally shot the pilot. An ax-wielding navigator then killed the hijacker. 83019901

January 1983 — IRELAND — Four gunmen abducted Shergar, 5, a $13 million racehorse, from the Aga Khan's stud farm in County Kildare. A $3 million ransom was demanded by individuals who may have belonged to the Irish Republican Army (IRA). On May 24, police in Belfast said, "We're convinced he's dead. We believe he was stolen by a paramilitary group who put the horse down when no money was forthcoming." Shergar was the winner of the 1981 English and Irish Derby classics. 83019902

January 1, 1983 — PHILIPPINES — A man escaped after throwing a fragmentation grenade into a New Year's crowd in Rizal Park in Manila at 1:00 A.M., injuring 42 people watching tribal dances.

January 1, 1983 — HAITI — The Miami-based Hector Riode Group was believed responsible for setting off a bomb in a car two blocks from the

351

presidential palace in Port-au-Prince, killing the driver, Allen C. Mills, a Miami man, along with three Haitians, and wounding nine others. Mills was suspected of having set the bomb, which went off prematurely. Haitian authorities claimed to be searching for two "US mercenaries." 83010101

January 1, 1983 — NICARAGUA — Forty ex-members of the National Guard kidnapped 67 peasants, most of them children, and forced them to march at gunpoint 5 miles into Honduras from their homes in Siuse, 130 miles north of Managua.

January 1, 1983 — TURKEY — Interpol and Italian police informed the Istanbul HURRIYET newspaper that the Armenian Secret Army for the Liberation of Armenia (ASALA) was sending "Death Calling Cards" written in German, French, Italian, and English to Turkish diplomats in Switzerland, France, and Italy. The telex messages were assassination threats. 83010102–04

January 3, 1983 — AFGHANISTAN — Mujahiddin resistance fighters kidnapped in broad daylight 16 Soviet advisers working as technicians in a flour mill in the market area of Mazar-i-Sharif, northern Afghanistan. The group initially wanted to attack a Soviet armored vehicle but settled for the advisers' minibus when it showed up first. Soviet and Afghan authorities arrested several women to determine the whereabouts of their husbands and sons, who were believed to be responsible for the attack. On January 25, a house-to-house search was made in the city, but the hostages were not found.

Two groups claimed responsibility for the seizure of the 16, who included two women. Dr. Azim Nasri, spokesman for the Jami'at-e Eslami, said on January 11 that the Soviets would be taken to Peshawar, Pakistan, unless they were detained "in a secret location." As of January 17, the group's leader, Burhanuddin Rabbani, had made no decision about possible ransom demands.

Rafiullah Al-Muazin, spokesman for the Harakat-e Enqelabe Islami, said that his group wanted the release of resistance fighters jailed in Kabul. The group's leader, Qari Nehman, met with members of a search team, who came back empty-handed.

AGENCE FRANCE-PRESSE believed that Comdr. Zibih-Ullahi was responsible for the attack.

Unconfirmed reports indicated that one or two of the hostages died of heart attacks. Other reports indicated that one of the Soviet men was shot while trying to escape, or was shot because he was unable to maintain the group's pace because of wounds suffered in the initial attack. One of the hostages allegedly told the captors, "If you kill us, it is not important. But if you release us, we will shoot down Babrak Karmal," the president of Afghanistan.

January 3–4, 1983 — ZIMBABWE — Security forces reported the recovery of a pistol and letter bomb in the Beitbridge area. The items were abandoned in a local hotel by a South Africa-bound tourist. Police also reported that telephone lines between Harare and South Africa were blown up, and the main power lines from Lake Kariba to the eastern border town of Mutare were sabotaged.

January 4, 1983 — UNITED STATES — Douglas M. Schlacter, 39, was sentenced to six months in prison and three years probation and fined ten thousand dollars for helping former Central Intelligence Agency operative Edwin P. Wilson ship explosives to Libya. Schlacter returned voluntarily to the United States from his home in Burundi in November 1981 to plead guilty to two of the charges of conspiracy to export munitions and exporting munitions without a license.

January 5, 1983 — LEBANON — Two Israeli soldiers were killed when their military truck hit a mine placed at the side of the road between the Al-Hadath police station and the St. George Hospital in Beirut.

January 5, 1983 — FRANCE — The Corsican Revolutionary Brigade broke through a roof of a Justice Ministry building in Bastia, Corsica, to steal arms; shot and wounded a policeman guarding the Vazzio power station on the outskirts of Ajaccio, Corsica's capital; and attacked a police headquarters and an electrical store in Peri. Using a 1936 law regarding armed groups, the French government banned the Corsican National Liberation Front, which it held responsible for the growing separatist terror campaign. Robert Broussard was named the chief of Corsica's new police and gendarmerie organization.

January 5, 1983 — USSR — According to Ankara's ANATOLIA news service, "The public prosecutor of Sinop has appealed against the decision of a local criminal court which had acquitted three Soviet citizens of German origin who had hijacked a Soviet airliner to the Black Sea port while on a domestic flight. Prosecutor Unal Canpolat said he had made his appeal a week ago, and the case was now before the Court of Cassation in Ankara. The three hijackers had wounded a crew member and a passenger while forcing the aircraft to land at Sinop."

January 5, 1983 — GREECE — Two Arab youths attacked an official of the Syrian embassy as he was putting two mail sacks into his car at Ellinikon

Airport. One of the youths was arrested by a policeman while the second youth grabbed one of the sacks and escaped in a nearby Fiat Mirafiore. 83010501

January 5, 1983 — MOZAMBIQUE — The National Resistance Movement blew a hole in the Beira-to-Mutare, Zimbabwe, oil pipeline at Maforga, the halfway point of the pipeline in Mozambique. This section of the pipeline was guarded by Zimbabwean troops. 83010502

January 6, 1983 — TURKEY — According to Ankara's ANATOLIA news service,

> Repatriate hijacker Haci Ozdemir, who gave himself up at the Turkish Embassy in Vienna last summer after 10 years abroad, appeared before an Istanbul martial law court Thursday to face trial for hijacking a Turkish airliner with 71 passengers abroad to Sofia back in December 1972, along with three accomplices. The four had been tried by a Bulgarian court and sentenced to 2½ years in prison. At Thursday's hearing, the military prosecutor charged the defendant with hijacking for the purpose of obtaining a release from prison of Ziya Yilmaz, Yusuf Kupeli and other members of the terrorist organization known as People's Liberation Party/Front 'THKP/C.' He was also guilty of attempting to kill the pilot. . . . The prosecutor asked that charges against Ozdemir as a suspected spy working for Bulgaria be transmitted to General Staff headquarters. Ozdemir, who is now 33, said his years in Bulgaria had given him time to think things over, and he had given himself up in Vienna because he was repentant.

January 7, 1983 — UNITED STATES — Korean Airlines flight 007 was diverted to Tokyo when company officials received a letter saying one of the passengers was carrying a bomb. No bomb was found. Wing Ming Kwok, a Canadian resident, was charged with "disrupting flight operations." KAL-007 was shot down by the Soviet Air Force over the Soviet Union on August 31, 1983, when it veered off course from Alaska to South Korea. 83010701

January 8, 1983 — ISRAEL — The Palestine Liberation Organization (PLO) and Black June claimed credit for throwing a hand grenade at a civilian bus in Tel Aviv in which 12 were injured. The previous day, gunmen had ambushed an Israeli military bus south of Beirut, injuring 21 Israeli soldiers.

January 11, 1983 — LEBANON — The VOICE OF LEBANON claimed that "during the night gunmen assassinated Lebanese diplomat 'Ali as-Sulayman in his house in Ar-Rumaylah near Sidon. The deceased was from the Al-Biqa' township of Bidnayil."

January 11, 1983 — GUATEMALA — Army authorities announced the arrest of Michael Glenn Ernest, 26, of North Dakota or Denver, Colorado, and Maria Monteverde Ascanio, 27, of La Grotava, Spain, on charges of leading two guerrilla raids the previous week against farms between the towns of Patulul and San Lucas Toliman, Solola Department, in western Guatemala, and for the January 6 killing of Enrique de Leon, administrator of a sugar plantation. Local peasants allegedly identified the two as leaders of the raids. The duo were freed on February 8, 1983, for lack of evidence. 83011101

January 12, 1983 — SOUTH KOREA — The Japanese embassy received a telephone call in which the life of Prime Minister Yasuhiro Nakasone was threatened. The prime minister was scheduled to spend two days in South Korea. 83011201

January 12, 1983 — MALAYSIA — Several gunshots were fired through the windowpanes of the Soviet embassy building in the morning. Police found an SLR gun and several bullets on the building's lawn. The gun was similar to one stolen from a guard at the Penang governor's residence on December 30. The International Moslem Brotherhood Organization claimed credit a few days later in Penang, telling a local newspaper that the Soviet ambassador should "get out of Afghanistan or next time we will kill the ambassador or any of the embassy employees." The caller spoke fluent English with a local accent. Police believed that four men fired between 8 and 12 shots from the self-loading rifle where Ambassador Dr. B. T. Koulik was incorrectly believed to be staying. The spokesman for the Brotherhood said his name was Abdullah Omar Mokhtar, and that his group had links in Thailand, India, and Pakistan. The group would ensure that innocent people did not get hurt in the Brotherhood's future attacks. "If the Russians continue with their barbaric acts and murder innocent people in Afghanistan, they should not deserve any pity." 83011202

January 15, 1983 — ITALY — Milan police arrested Sergio Segio, a wanted terrorist.

January 15, 1983 — AFGHANISTAN — Afghan rebels handed over a 19-year-old Soviet soldier to the Red Cross in Peshawar, Pakistan, the 8th to be freed in an agreement by which Soviet prisoners of war would be held at a Red Cross facility in Switzerland for two years before being returned home.

Meanwhile, the AFGHAN ISLAMIC PRESS reported that mujahiddin fired 20 mortar rounds at the Soviet-built Mikro-Reyan housing complex in Kabul, killing 8 Soviet advisers and wounding 10 others.

January 18, 1983 — MEXICO — There were conflicting reports that three gunmen fired automatic weapons from a moving car at the residence of Israeli ambassador Yisra'el Gur-Ayre. Other reports indicated that police guarding the embassy noted three suspicious individuals in the vicinity at 9 P.M. When the police gave chase, the group tried to run them over in their car. The police opened fire, but the trio escaped. A third report indicated that the incident involved only an air rifle being shot at a lamppost. 83011801

January 20, 1983 — COLOMBIA — The secret police arrested a man who was apparently pointing a revolver from the second floor of a nearby building as Colombian president Belisario Betancur was leaving government offices in Cali. The individual worked for a private security firm.

January 20, 1983 — SYRIA — Four Palestinian gunmen hijacked an Al Yemda B-707 flying 44 passengers and 10 crew from Damascus to Aden and diverted it to Djibouti. During the three hours of negotiations with ground authorities, the pilot and copilot escaped. A gun battle broke out in which two of the passengers were wounded, but the hijackers were captured. On January 22, the interior minister of Djibouti, Youssouf Ali Chirdon, said that Djibouti would keep the promise it made to the hijackers during the negotiations and would permit them to depart the country safely and give them "documents entitling them to travel to the country of their choice." 83012001

January 20, 1983 — UNITED STATES — Glenn K. Tripp, 20, of Arlington, Washington, attempted to divert to Afghanistan Northwest Orient Airlines flight 608, a B-727-200 carrying 41 people from Seattle to Portland. The crew managed to separate Tripp, who claimed he held a bomb in a shoe box, from the passengers by luring him into the otherwise-empty first-class area. Tripp had permitted about half of the 35 passengers to leave the craft, and as they were leaving, Federal Bureau of Investigation officers crept on board through a cockpit window. After 2½ hours of negotiations, the hijacker was shot and killed with a .38 caliber revolver as the rest of the passengers slid down an emergency exit chute. The shoe box contained no bomb. Tripp had been convicted of attempting to hijack a plane at the Seattle-Tacoma airport in 1980 and was on 20 years' probation. 83012002

January 20, 1983 — FRANCE — The extreme leftist Bukunin-Gdansk-Paris-Guatemala-Salvador Group, also known as the Internationalist Hooligans, conducted its 15th attack in Paris in two years when it set off a bomb in the early morning that damaged the lower floors of a 14-story building containing military publications offices. One person was slightly injured by flying glass. In the group's Communique Number 8, they said, "A dangerous bureau of armed propaganda maintaining very close links with the international arms dealers (private or state) to destroy humanity for the profit of capital has been discovered today by the Internationalist Hooligans." The group referred to the "'socialist' management of this criminal organization," which "has only strengthened its privileges as well as its banning of newspapers in barracks, also the colonial occupation of New Caledonia, Corsica, Guiana. . . . Let us paralyse by every means the murderous acts of the big dumb one [the army]." 83012003

January 20, 1983 — IRAQ — Turkish truck driver Hamit Ahmet Calikhan of Gaziantep was shot in the chest and killed and Cumba Bogaz Altinbas, another driver, was kidnapped by 15 masked gunmen near the town of Zakhu, Iraq. Police later reported that Turkish truck driver Hasan Ocak had been killed on January 16 during a shoot-out between outlaws and Iraqi border guards. 83012004 83011601

January 21, 1983 — UGANDA — Armed gunmen attacked a bus at Kalule village north of Kampala, killing 30 people.

January 22, 1983 — UNITED STATES — Officials in Abbeville and Delcambre, Louisiana, flushed the public water systems after receiving threats that cyanide had been dumped into the water. More than 13,000 homes were without water. Water had been cut off in the southern Louisiana town of St. Gabriel the previous week for similar reasons. Chlorine was added to the water to neutralize any cyanide.

January 22, 1983 — FRANCE — Two Armenians threw two hand grenades into the Paris Turkish Airlines offices, wrecking the office and injuring three people. One of the suspects, who was carrying a pistol, was captured. The Armenian Secret Army for the Liberation of Armenia claimed credit. 83012201

January 22, 1983 — FRANCE — Workers at Orly International Airport discovered a bomb hidden inside a paper-wrapped box near the Turkish Airlines counter. Police defused the two-pound device outside. The Secret Armenian Army for the Liberation of Armenia claimed credit. The caller said the operation commemorated the "heroic defense of Shebin Karahissar," an eastern Turkish city, during "the genocide of 1915." 83012202

January 23, 1983 — MALAYSIA — An Aeroflot plane was diverted to Kuala Lumpur airport after an anonymous caller said a bomb was on board. Police said that, after landing in Kuala Lumpur, a "mystery" passenger among the 30 people on board left a suitcase and vanished from Subang International Airport tarmac minutes after police ordered a search. 83012301

January 23, 1983 — SUDAN — DAMASCUS DOMESTIC SERVICE reported, "Sudan's ruler Ja'far Numayri was the target of an assassination attempt when he came under attack by students during his visit to the Rumbek preparatory school in southern Sudan. An aide, who is a ranking military officer, was wounded during the attempt."

January 25, 1983 — INDIA — Officials in Imphal, Manipur, offered a Re 50 ($55) reward for information regarding Triple X members who threatened to hijack domestic aircraft unless "corrupt officials and ministers" in the state administration were not removed by January 26, India's Republic Day anniversary. The group had earlier circulated a pamphlet threatening to kidnap airline officials if air services there were not stopped.

January 25, 1983 — POLAND — Two Poles, aged 24 and 26, diverted their Soviet YAK-12A to Tempelhof United States military airfield at 12:58 GMT, where they requested political asylum. The flight mechanic on board the plane, Bogdan S., 31, claimed they were members of an aviation club scheduled to fly from Lodz to Poznan, and that he knew nothing of the planned diversion. 83012501

January 25, 1983 — UNITED KINGDOM — Two letter bombs in white 6″ × 4″ envelopes were sent to the Aeroflot office in Piccadilly and a Soviet travel agency, Intourist, on Regents Street. A secretary opened the Aeroflot letter bomb, which failed to go off. The Intourist letter bomb was left unopened until police arrived. The letters both contained incendiary devices. A greeting card, but no message, was found in the first letter bomb. 83012502–03

January 26, 1983 — HAITI — The antigovernment Miami-based Hector Riode Brigade sent a letter dated January 21 to the apostolic nunciature in Port-au-Prince that threatened, "We will not hesitate one moment in jeopardizing the security of Pope John Paul II during his visit to Haiti [on 20 March 1983] should the high pontiff shirk his duty as head of the Catholic Church and place himself at the services of the Duvalier family now ruling Haiti." Hector Riode was killed in an armed clash with the police in 1963. The group said the pope "should not enter into a pact with the devil," who, in their eyes, was President Jean Claude Duvalier. 83012601

January 26, 1983 — COLOMBIA — The Colombian Army reported that in the past few days it had freed three hostages, including two pilots identified as Eduardo Alvarez and Peruvian citizen Edgar Blanco, and four planes seized by the Revolutionary Armed Forces of Colombia. At least 15 other people had recently been kidnapped by the FARC. 83012602

January 27, 1983 — LESOTHO — The Lesotho Liberation Army was believed responsible for setting off three bombs in Maseru before the two-day conference of the Southern African Development Coordinating Conference was to begin.

January 27, 1983 — ITALY — Milan police arrested Diego Forastieri, 33, a leader of the Front Line group. Forastieri had escaped from prison, where he was serving a 24-year sentence, in October 1980. He is accused of involvement in four murders, armed robbery, and other crimes.

January 28, 1983 — LEBANON — A car bomb containing 331 pounds of explosives was set off in front of the three-story building in Shtawrah that housed the offices and arms dump of the Palestine Liberation Organization, killing 30 people and wounding 20 others. The Front for the Liberation of Lebanon from Foreigners claimed credit, as did the previously unknown Lebanese Cedar Force to Free Lebanon from Lebanese Terrorists. 83012801

January 29, 1983 — COLOMBIA — Armed guerrillas kidnapped Liberal representative Nubia Correa de Luna, wife of Trino Luna Moron, former Magdalena Department governor, while she was going to her ranch in Playitas Corregimiento in the San Martin de Loba Municipality. A million-peso ransom was paid for her release to the Army of National Liberation. She was freed in the southern part of Magdalena Department on March 27.

January 29, 1983 — UNITED STATES — The Revolutionary Fighting Group bombed the Federal Bureau of Investigation offices on Staten Island, New York, causing no injuries.

January 29, 1983 — UNITED STATES — Three Latin gunmen broke into the Miami home of the widow of a slain Nicaraguan general and gunned down Reimar Perez-Vega, her eight-year-old son, when he pleaded, "Don't hurt my mommy." The child's mother, Mary Louise Perez-Vega, 42, a self-employed tour and shopping guide, suffered superficial wounds but tricked the gunmen by pretending she was dead. The attack occurred early Saturday morning in the family's bedroom. General Reinaldo Perez-Vega was kidnapped and murdered in Nicaragua in 1978. 83012901

January 30, 1983 — LEBANON — One of two motorcyclists threw a grenade at a French Marine troop truck as it traveled through a predominantly Moslem section of west Beirut. Pascal Garby of Paris was wounded, as was a Lebanese road crewman who was working nearby. The assailants escaped in the heavy traffic. 83013001

January 30, 1983 — LEBANON — Terrorists wearing civilian clothes fired two rocket-propelled grenades at an Israeli patrol in Beirut, killing Pvt. David Barda and wounding three others. The Lebanese Front for National Resistance claimed credit. 83013002

February 1983 — SWITZERLAND — The Swiss on April 29 asked Libyan charge Mohammed Abdelmalek to leave the country because he had supplied arms to two convicted Swiss terrorists. The two handguns found on the Swiss men, who were tried in Zurich in February, came from the Libyan embassy via the United Kingdom. The duo were found guilty of supplying explosives to West German terrorists. 83029901

February 1983 — COSTA RICA — Panama City's LA PRENSA claimed that a Salvadoran guerrilla group kidnapped Kaveh Yazdani, an Iranian, in Costa Rica and brought him into Panama. He was moved several times until he escaped in Punta Chame. The news service believed that another kidnap victim who was held with Yazdani was murdered. 83029902

February 1983 — TUNISIA — The VOICE OF LEBANON claimed that Yasir Arafat's security squad apprehended four armed Palestinians carrying forged passports in Tunis. The group was sent by a rejectionist Palestinian, aided by Arab intelligence services, with orders to assassinate Arafat. 83029903

February 1983 — LEBANON — The WASHINGTON POST reported that at least 6 Palestinian men were abducted from their homes in Sidon and murdered within two weeks. Four others were abducted and wounded. At least 45 Palestinians reported that their cars had been stolen, and others claimed that their homes and stores were burglarized or bombed. 83029904

February 1983 — SYRIA — The VOICE OF LEBANON reported that two Soviet advisers were assassinated on the Euphrates Dam road. 83029905

February 1983 — LESOTHO — Bombs damaged the Caltex fuel depot in Maseru. The Lesotho Liberation Army was thought responsible. 83029906

February 1983 — SPAIN — A grenade rocket was fired at the United States embassy in Madrid. The rocket missed the embassy and blew up a car parked in front. On July 24, 1984, Spanish police arrested four Iranians suspected of carrying out the rocket attack. The Iranians were alleged to be members of the extremist group, Martyrs of the Islamic Revolution. Seye

Jabbar Hosseini was among the Iranians arrested. 83029907

February 2, 1983 — GUATEMALA — The Supreme Court, claiming that military "tribunals of special jurisdiction had violated guarantees and human rights," suspended the executions of three Guatemalans and one Honduran sentenced to be shot at dawn for terrorist activity.

February 2, 1983 — ITALY — Police in Rho, near Milan, arrested Mustafa Savak (Mustafa Savas), 48, a Turk, on charges of plotting to murder Pope John Paul II during a scheduled visit to Milan in May. An unnamed Italian being held on drug charges told police that Savak had offered to hire him to shoot the pope. When arrested, Savak was carrying two passports, one of which gave his date of birth as 1945. He arrived in Italy two months earlier, driving a car with West German plates. More recently he had been seen driving a Renault with Rome plates. 83020201

February 2, 1983 — LEBANON — A gunman fired at and wounded two unarmed French soldiers who were jogging in the Beirut coastal area. 83020202

February 2, 1983 — EL SALVADOR — Special Forces S. Sgt. Jay T. Stanley, 26, of Towson, Maryland, became the first United States military adviser to be injured in the Salvadoran insurgency when a 7.62 mm bullet hit his upper left leg while he was flying in a UH-1H helicopter 10 miles from the city of Berlin, which had recently been taken by leftist guerrillas. A door gunner was also wounded in the 9:00 A.M. attack near a strategic bridge on the Pan American Highway. 83020203

February 3, 1983 — UGANDA — Antigovernment guerrillas killed one hundred people in an ambush of a bus on the main highway north of Kampala, near Kakarenge village in the Luwero District.

February 3, 1983 — MOZAMBIQUE — Maputo's radio reported that "five foreign residents of . . . Beira are to be tried in connection with acts of sabotage. The five are Finlay Dion Hamilton, a British citizen, and Benjamin Fox, Jaos Fernandes, Alcino da Costa Pinto, and Antonio da Cunha Fonseca, all Portuguese. The five are suspected of belonging to a network of agents and collaborators of the South African-sponsored Quizumba bandits who carry out terrorist actions and sabotage in Mozambique." 83020301

February 5, 1983 — LEBANON — The Front for the Liberation of Lebanon from Foreigners set off a remote-controlled bomb consisting of 130 pounds of high explosive (equivalent to more than 300 pounds of TNT) at 2:00 P.M.

at the Palestine Research Center in Beirut, killing 18 people and injuring 109. The bomb hurled a car off the street into the entrance of the temporary embassy of Libya and shook buildings throughout the central Hamra shopping district in west Beirut. Shafiq Hout, the Palestine Liberation Organization's (PLO) diplomatic chief in Lebanon, described the explosion as a "cold-blooded Israeli crime," while the ultraright VOICE OF FREE LEBANON, a radio station founded by the Lebanese Forces of Christian Militia, blamed Syria. Hanneh Yiyris, wife of the center's director, was killed; her husband Sabri was not seriously injured. The dead included three Lebanese Army soldiers posted outside the center, a concierge, a telephone operator, and three people trapped in an elevator. Seventeen plainclothesmen were wounded. The VOICE OF THE PLO in Baghdad later reported that Hanni Shahin and Sana' 'Awdah were also killed. 83020501

February 5, 1983 — LEBANON — JERUSALEM DOMESTIC SERVICE reported that the car of Israeli Knesset member Amal Nasir ad-Din was fired on near 'Alayh. The car was destroyed, but ad-Din was uninjured. Ad-Din later said that he had been caught in shelling between Druze and Christians while visiting the village of Baysur, but that he was not targeted. 83020502

February 9, 1983 — GUATEMALA — Anthropologist and linguist Patricio Ortiz Maldonando disappeared along with his assistant, Abdel Ortiz Jacinto, his pilot Obispo Santos, and his slightly crippled mother, Catarina Ortiz de Jacinto, 53, as they were traveling near the town of San Ildefonso Ixtahuacan in Huehuetenango Province. Ortiz was an employee of Interamerica, which received $1.4 million from the United States Agency for International Development to develop bilingual education for Indian children. Authorities initially refused to discuss the case with his worried colleagues. On March 4, the Defense Ministry said it had picked up (kidnapped) Ortiz and his companions at a checkpoint but they had escaped to, perhaps, the mountains or Mexico. On March 8, the Defense Ministry said the foursome were killed "while trying to escape" and fell into a stream from a bridge. The ministry said Ortiz "moved about especially on weekends from the capital city to Huehuetenango Department with the purpose of imparting military training to a group of subversives who operate in that region." An independent investigation showed that the group was picked up one mile outside San Ildefonso by an army group commanded by Lt. Jorge Echeverria, who drove them to an army detachment near the town of La Democracia. The group was not seen again. The Guatemalan Army said the commander was remanded to a military court to "determine the responsibilities for this incident."

February 9, 1983 — LEBANON — The VOICE OF LEBANON reported that the Popular Front for the Liberation of Palestine (PFLP) kidnapped Sister

Therese, a sibling of Bishop Joseph Iskandar, the Maronite Bishop of Zahlah, as she was traveling between Sa'd Nayil and Ksarah. 83020901

February 10, 1983 — PEOPLE'S REPUBLIC OF CHINA — TAIPEI RADIO reported, "A passenger plane flying from Antung to Shenyang in northeastern part of China was hijacked by two young men last April. Explosives carried by one of the youths went off and killed all passengers aboard the plane. Another incident happened in Fukien Province. A plane from Nanchang City, Kiangsi Province, to Foochow City, Fukien Province, also exploded mid-air above Chienning County with no one aboard found alive. . . . There were a total of 12 plane hijacking cases on the mainland during last year."

February 10, 1983 — ISRAEL — A hand grenade planted beneath a van owned by a leader of Israel's Peace Now movement exploded while a Peace Now demonstration outside of Prime Minister Menachem Begin's office was breaking up. Those at the demonstration demanded the resignation of Defense Minister Ariel Sharon; the demonstration coincided with an Israeli cabinet's 16-to-1 vote to accept the report of the inquiry commission into the Beirut Camp Massacre. The grenade killed one person and injured nine, including the son of Interior Minister Yosef Burg. Dead was Emil Grinsweig, a member of the Peace Now Movement. On January 20, 1984, a 28-year-old man, Yonah Aburushmi, was arrested for planting the grenade. He was apparently motivated by personal reasons stemming from the deaths of relatives during the 1973 Middle East War and the 1982 war in Lebanon. Also arrested was David Shemtov, who supplied the grenade.

February 11, 1983 — INDIA — A bomb hurled at the American embassy caused damage to a portion of the embassy. There were no injuries or claims of responsibility. 83021101

February 13, 1983 — ALGERIA — An assassination attempt on Palestinian leader Yasir Arafat was foiled while Arafat was in Algeria to attend the Palestinian National Council meeting. An undisclosed Arab country was believed responsible. Presumably, this country had intended to assassinate Arafat and Salah Khalaf (Abu Iyad) and to disrupt the National Council. The assassination attempt was uncovered when three people arrived at the Algerian airport on February 13, 1983, carrying arms. They had come on an Italian plane from Rome. Algeria had implemented tight security measures throughout the National Council meeting. 83021301

February 14, 1983 — EL SALVADOR — Three journalists were captured by guerrillas in the Guazapa Hill area. The captured included Michael Luhan, from America, and Jens Rydstrom and Tom Thulin, from Sweden. On

March 5, 1983, Luhan was released, suffering from weight loss and insect bites. The Swedish journalists were released on March 14, 1983. 83021401

February 15, 1983 — FRANCE — An agent of France's foreign intelligence service, DGSE, Alpine division, Lt. Col. Bernard Nut, was murdered on a mountain road near Nice. Reports suggested that Nut might have been murdered because he knew too much about Soviet Bloc espionage operations in Southern France and Italy. Nut was also involved in the Italian investigation of the "Bulgarian connection," associated with the attempted assassination of Pope John Paul II in 1981. Nut's intelligence activities were connected to the later (April 5, 1983) expulsion of 47 Soviet diplomats, journalists, and other residents suspected of espionage activity. The motive for the murder remains a mystery.

February 15, 1983 — UNITED STATES/MEXICO — An Iranian with a submachine gun, Hossein Shyrh Olya, hijacked a United States commuter plane with 20 people aboard and demanded to be flown to Cuba. The plane was hijacked in Killeen, Texas, and forced to land in Nuevo Laredo, where the hijacker eventually turned himself into the Federal Security Directorate. After five hours of negotiations in Nuevo Laredo, he surrendered upon being promised safe conduct out of the country. No one was injured in the hijacking. The hijacker was later flown to Mexico City and indicted there on March 4, 1983, for hijacking and hostage-taking. The United States had requested extradition. 83021501

February 17, 1983 — SCOTLAND/UNITED KINGDOM — A letter bomb exploded into flames in Glasgow's city hall, just prior to Princess Diana's first official visit to Scotland. The Scottish National Liberation Army, who protested the princess's visit, claimed responsibility. No one was injured.

February 17, 1983 — LIBYA — The Libyan People's General Congress issued threats against Libyans living abroad who were "enemies of the people and the revolution." Amnesty International said that a similar call in 1980 preceded the assassination of 11 Libyans and the attempted assassination of 4 others.

February 17, 1983 — TURKEY — Four Palestinian terrorists — Merban Seban, Mustafa Besheshi, Husayn Sulayman Abdullah, Muhammad Abu Zarat — were found guilty and again sentenced to death for their part in the July 13, 1979, raid on the Egyptian embassy in Ankara that resulted in the death of two security guards. Omer Faruk Erdem was also sentenced to 21 years in prison for assisting the attackers. Four others were sentenced to prison terms ranging from 1 to 5 years for their part in the assault. The terrorists had been tried twice before — at the Ankara Martial Law Command's First

Military Court and at the Ankara First High Criminal Court—but both times their sentences had been annulled.

February 17, 1983 — UNITED STATES — At 11:10 P.M. a pipe bomb blew out a window of the Aeroflot offices, located at 16th and L streets NW, in Washington D.C. It was the fourth bombing in six years at these offices, used for foreign-travel reservations. Damages were light and no one was injured. A caller identifying himself as a member of the Jewish Defense League claimed responsibility. The anti-Castro group Omega-7 also claimed responsibility. No arrests were made in connection with this or with the previous bombings. 83021701

February 18, 1983 — REPUBLIC OF SOUTH AFRICA — At 10:35 A.M. a bomb exploded at a government building. The bomb wounded 76 blacks, waiting to apply for work and housing permits. Eighteen people sustained serious injuries. The police blamed the incident on the African National Congress, which made no comment.

February 18, 1983 — CZECHOSLOVAKIA — A hijack attempt of a TU-134 aircraft with 34 passengers was foiled by national security corps members who were aboard the plane. The plane was scheduled to fly from Poprad to Bratislava, and then Prague. The attempted takeover occurred when Marian Pesko, a Czechoslovak, violently attacked an air hostess and tried to enter the cockpit, while claiming to have explosives. Pesko was injured when he failed to surrender to the national security guards. He later died of his injuries; no one else was injured. 83021801

February 19, 1983 — SPAIN — In the Basque region of Llodio, the police disbanded an armed group with ties to the Basque Fatherland and Liberty (ETA) terrorist organization. Jesus Maria Gomez, Angel Ibarrola, Jesus Maria Guaresti, and Juan Manuel Garcia Alartia were arrested and charged with having engaged in two bombings and seven planned executions of so-called "informers." The police operation also netted an arms cache including five guns, four hand grenades, five kilograms of Goma-2 explosives, detonators, and ammunition.

February 19, 1983 — COLOMBIA — Fifty-nine soldiers and 104 civilians were arrested in Bogota for alleged ties to the Death to Kidnappers paramilitary group, thought responsible for at least three hundred assassinations of guerrillas and other leftists in the previous two years. The 59 military personnel included high officials of the National Police.

February 19, 1983 — PAKISTAN — Four French offices in Karachi and one in Lahore sustained damage from bombs during the evening. The five bombs exploded within 25 minutes of one another and hit the French consulate general, the Air France booking office, the Air France cargo office, the Alliance Francaise Cultural Center, and the home of the honorary French consul in Lahore. No one was injured. On February 20, 1983, the Pakistan police arrested 10 Iranian students on suspicion and held them for 24 hours. Authorities thought that the bombing was designed to protest the French sale of arms to Iraq, which was at war with Iran. On February 21, 1983, an Iraqi dissident group, the Iraqi Mujahidin in Beirut claimed responsibility in a phone call to the Lebanese daily AL-NAHAR. The group threatened to continue to hit French targets worldwide unless French support of Iraq in its war against Iran ended. 83021901–05

February 20, 1983 — LIBYA — A Boeing 727 of the Libyan Arab Airlines was hijacked during an internal flight and flown to Valletta's Luqa International Airport in Malta. The plane carried 159 passengers and 6 crew members. The 2 hijackers demanded airplane fuel and food and medicine for the people aboard the plane while parked in Malta. The hijackers threatened to blow up the plane if these demands were not met. After nearly two days, the hijackers released a stewardess and promised to release all their hostages in Morocco if the airplane was refueled. This request was not granted. Negotiations between the hijackers and the prime minister and three cabinet ministers of the Maltese government continued for a total of three days before the hijacking ended peacefully with the hijackers' surrender. The hijackers had struck an agreement with the Maltese prime minister, Dom Mintoff, who promised that they would not be sent back to Libya and would, instead, be flown to a country granting them asylum. No one was injured by the hijackers, who were dissident Libyan Army officers. 83022001

February 21, 1983 — SPAIN — Three masked men overcame a guard and set fire to warehouses of the French-owned Michelin tire company in Oyarzun, Spain. Estimates of damages were set at $8 million. The Autonomous Anticapitalist Commandos (CAA), a splinter group from the Basque Nation and Liberty separatist movement claimed responsibility. No one was injured and no motive was given. The fire coincided with labor unrest at the plant. 83022101

February 21, 1983 — AFGHANISTAN — Mujahadeen groups marked the third anniversary of a major anti-Soviet demonstration with a series of rocket and bomb attacks that left at least 25 progovernment soldiers and civilians dead. The attacks were in and around the capital city of Kabul. Targets included the Darul Aman Palace, the Soviet embassy, and the Soviet military headquarters in the Taj-Beg Palace. On February 22, three explosions hit the Microrayon quarter where housing for Soviet officials and Afghan partisans were located. Other targets included the offices of the Bank of Afghanistan, a bus with six government employees aboard, and several Russian houses and vehicles. 83022102

February 23, 1983 — GREECE — The Autonomous Resistance, an extreme left-wing group, claimed responsibility for an explosion near a restaurant where Soviet prime minister Nikolay Tikhonov and a Soviet delegation were dining with Greek officials. The phone caller indicated that the explosion was to demonstrate solidarity with Polish political prisoners. The Greek police ruled out a bomb and attributed the explosion to a car backfiring. 83022301

February 24, 1983 — ISRAEL — Five bedouins were killed when their two vehicles set off two antivehicle land mines planted along a road commonly traveled by the bedouins. Israeli authorities believed that terrorists from Egypt placed the mines in the Negev after crossing the border, and that the aim of the attack was to strike at green patrol inspectors and the nature reserve authority. 83022401

February 24, 1983 — FRANCE — Pedro Aztorkitza Ikazurriaga, the alleged leader of the Basque Nation and Liberty political-military organization, was captured in a sweep of southwestern France, where Spanish Basque militants were known to reside. Four other men and three women were also detained.

February 24, 1983 — PERU — Four United States and four Israeli technicians of the Agricultural Research Institute in Lima, Peru, were released by striking employees. The eight had been held hostage for an undisclosed amount of time by strikers from the Agriculture Ministry. The technicians were unharmed. 83022402

February 25, 1983 — EL SALVADOR — The mutilated body of a free-lance journalist, John J. Sullivan, was returned to the United States for identification. Sullivan had been missing for over two years. His body had been exhumed 12 miles south of San Salvador in July.

February 28, 1983 — FRANCE — The Armenian Secret Army for the Liberation of Armenia claimed responsibility for the bombing of a Turkish travel agency located in central Paris. The bomb killed a woman employee, slightly wounded four others, and severely damaged the building. The anonymous caller, who claimed responsibility 20 minutes after the blast, threatened further attacks against Turkish buildings in Paris. 83022801

February 28, 1983 — LUXEMBOURG — A bomb was discovered outside the home of Erkut Onalp, the Turkish embassy's charge d'affaires. A Luxembourg Army bomb disposal expert exploded the bomb away from the residence without injury. The bomb was believed planted by the Armenian Secret Army for the Liberation of Armenia. 83022802

February 28, 1983 — FRANCE — Threats were mailed to the owner of the Paris building that housed the offices of the Czech magazine SVEDECTVI. Pavel Tigrid, the magazine's editor, brought complaints against persons unknown. Other threats were later sent to residents of the building. French police believed Czechoslovak authorities to be behind the threats. 83022803

February 28, 1983 — ITALY — Roman magistrates sent judicial warnings to three Bulgarians (Teodorov Ayvazov, Jelio Kolev Vassiliev, and Ivan Dontchev), a second Italian trade unionist (Salvator Scordo), and an unnamed Italian state employee in connection with an alleged plot to bomb Lech Walesa's car during his January 1981 visit to Rome. The first Unione Italiana del Lavoro official warned was Luigi Scricciolo, who was already detained in jail for alleged espionage activity with the Bulgarian secret services. Sergei Ivanov Antonov and Mehmet Ali Agca were also warned by the magistrate. Antonov, a Bulgarian, and Agca, a Turk, were serving jail sentences for the shooting of the pope. The bomb was never planted in Walesa's car. 81019902

March 1983 — IRAQ — The Iraqi Airlines office was bombed using a booby-trapped briefcase. On May 6, 1983, an Iranian intelligence agent, Muhammad 'Abd' Ali 'Abbas Fidalah confessed to the bombing in an interview carried by Baghdad television. 83039901

March 1983 — AFGHANISTAN — Moslem rebels fighting the Soviet-backed Afghan government were suspected of killing a Soviet journalist, A. A. Kaverznez, in Kabul. 83039902

March 1983 — UNITED STATES — Six people were murdered and two wounded in a remote Alaskan community in connection with a one-man plot by Louis Hastings to destroy the trans-Alaska pipeline. Hastings was sentenced to 634 years in prison after pleading no contest to the murder charges. Hastings murdered the McCarthy, Alaska, residents when they gathered to meet the weekly mail plane. Apparently, Hastings intended to hijack the plane and use it in his attempt to sabotage the pipeline. An intended victim escaped the mass murder in a small plane and managed to forewarn the mail plane and state troopers. 83039903

March 1983 — UNITED KINGDOM — The trial of Iranian businessmen Benham Nodjaumi and Dogan Arif began. The two were charged with the kidnapping of six Iranians in London and in Belgium.

March 2, 1983 — POLAND — The pilot of a Polish airline LOT flight from Warsaw to Sofia carrying 78 passengers claimed the plane had mechanical failures, turned toward Vienna, and made an emergency landing of the Ilyushin 18 plane at Vienna's Schwechat Airport. The pilot, the flight mechanic, their wives, and two children on board requested political asylum in Vienna, thus raising questions about whether the diversion had been planned. The other passengers and crew continued their flight to Bulgaria on another plane. No injuries were reported. 83030201

March 2, 1983 — EL SALVADOR — Jorge Enrique Zapporoli, an American, was released on March 3, 1983, after all charges that he belonged to a guerrilla organization, the Popular Liberation Front, were dropped. Zapporoli had been arrested on March 2 along with four other Salvadorans when handguns and a shortwave radio were found in a car in which they were riding.

March 3, 1983 — UGANDA — Bandit leaders warned diplomats and representatives of international organizations to leave Uganda or risk injury from "accidents." The Ministry of Internal Affairs discredited the bandits' abilities to disrupt the government and labeled the bandits' threats as a desperate attempt.

March 3, 1983 — GUATEMALA — Six convicted kidnappers and terrorists, five Guatemalans and one Honduran, were executed by a firing squad. The executions, denounced by Pope John Paul II, came just three days before his visit to Guatemala. The executed were Carlos Subyuc, Pedro Tepet, Mario A. Gonzalez, Hector H. Morales Lopez, Sergio R. Marroquin, and his brother Walter V. Marroquin.

March 3, 1983 — UNITED KINGDOM — Three unidentified, masked persons attacked a Turkish radio and television correspondent, Ovul Tezisler, in his London office. Tezisler sustained head injuries from the baseball bats used in the attack. 83030301

March 4, 1983 — EL SALVADOR — A guerrilla suspect told of a plot to kill Pope John Paul II during the pope's stay in El Salvador. The suspect alleged that 18 sharpshooters had entered the country intending to assassinate the pope. The allegations were never substantiated. 83030401

March 4, 1983 — HONDURAS — A bomb caused minor damage to the Guatemalan consulate in the eastern outskirts of Tegucigalpa. Witnesses claimed that the bomb was thrown at the consulate from a speeding car, later identified as a stolen vehicle. The Lorenzo Zelaya People's Revolutionary Forces claimed responsibility and indicated that the attack was in protest of the March 3, 1983, Guatemalan execution of Honduran Mario Antonio Gonzalez. 83030402

March 5, 1983 — IRAQ — An explosion at the Air France office in Baghdad seriously wounded the office director and slightly wounded several employees. Some office equipment was also destroyed. Agents from the Iranian and Syrian regimes were suspected by Iraqi authorities. 83030501

March 6, 1983 — IRAQ — An explosive charge at the Kuwait Airways office in Baghdad was defused without incident. 83030601

March 6, 1983 — NAMIBIA — Between 6 to 10 SWAPO guerrillas attacked a farm in northern Namibia. No casualties were reported.

March 7, 1983 — BULGARIA — An attempted hijacking by four Bulgarians of a Balkan Bulgarian flight from Sofia to Varna ended in the death of one hijacker and the arrest of the other three. The hijacking was stopped by security guards on board as the hijackers attempted forcibly to divert the plane from its intended route. No other injuries were reported. 83030701

March 7, 1983 — COLOMBIA — Kenneth Stanley Bishop, an American executive of the Texas Petroleum Company in Colombia, was kidnapped north of Bogota while he was enroute to work. Both his driver and bodyguard were killed during the abduction. The People's Revolutionary Organization (ORP) claimed responsibility. Bishop was released April 14, 1983, after payment of an undisclosed amount of ransom demanded from Bishop's relatives and the Texas Petroleum Company. On August 21, 1983, the Colombian secret police captured and charged Ivan Dario Murcia Reyes, Guillermo Rojas Franno, and Zolanda Umana, a woman, in the kidnapping. They were also charged with the July 23, 1982, murder and kidnapping of Gloria Lara de Echeverri, a Liberal political leader. 83030702

March 7, 1983 — HONDURAS — The Lorenzo Zelaya Popular Forces (FPR), a leftist guerrilla group, accused Argentine colonel Oswaldo Riveiro of plotting to assassinate Pope John Paul II during his March 8 visit to Tegucigalpa.

March 8, 1983 — FRANCE — Two unidentified men were killed in their car by a bomb, which they had apparently intended to leave in front of a Marseilles synagogue. The car had slowed while passing the synagogue, but continued on when police guards were spotted. The blast occurred within one hundred yards of the synagogue. It was later disclosed that the car had been stolen. Two parked cars were damaged and neighborhood windows were shattered by the blast.

March 8, 1983 — INDIA — An explosion in an underground shopping center in New Delhi injured seven people, one seriously, and damaged five shops. A second bomb was discovered and defused by police. The militant All Sikh Students Federation claimed responsibility. The bombings were in support of autonomy for the Punjab, a predominantly Sikh state. No arrests were made.

March 8, 1983 — COLOMBIA — The Grupo organization issued communiques in Cali, Colombia, that threatened to attack thieves, muggers, kidnappers, and other criminals.

March 8, 1983 — FEDERAL REPUBLIC OF GERMANY — The Philippine embassy in Bonn sustained damage after an explosion and fire. The building was unoccupied during the early morning blast, which also damaged nearby houses. No injuries were reported. 83030801

March 9, 1983 — YUGOSLAVIA — The Turkish ambassador to Belgrade, Galip Balkar, and his driver were seriously injured during an armed attack by two members of the Justice Commandos of the Armenian Genocide. The attack occurred in downtown Belgrade when the ambassador's car was stopped at a traffic light. Balkar later died from his wounds. One passerby was killed and two were wounded when Yugoslavian agents near the scene attempted to arrest the two attackers. The agents managed to wound and capture Haroutioun Levonian, one of the two assailants. The other attacker, Raffi Elbakian, escaped but was captured eight hours later. On March 9, 1984, the two attackers, Lebanese citizens of Armenian extraction, were found guilty and sentenced to 20 years each. On June 4, 1987, Turkey demanded to know why Levonian had been released from prison that year. Yugoslavian authorities responded that Levonian was half-paralyzed and suffering from ailments that could not be treated in Yugoslavia. Elbakian remains in prison. 83030901

March 9, 1983 — FRANCE — Following the conviction of three Arabs accused in the June 6, 1982, attempted assassination of the Israeli ambassador to Britain, a caller threatened the British judges involved in the trial. An alleged representative of the Abu Nidal Palestinian group telephoned the threat to the AGENCE FRANCE-PRESSE office in Paris. 83030902

March 10, 1983 — LEBANON — An assassination attempt was made against Palestine Liberation Organization office director, Tawfiq as-Safadi. A barrage of bullets was aimed at the director's car when he was returning home in Beirut. No one was injured. 83031001

March 10, 1983 — JORDAN — The government of Jordan issued strong protests after an armed Jewish group attempted to storm the Al-Aqsa Mosque and the holy Dome of the Rock. The attack was labeled by Jordan as a serious terrorist operation in the holy city of Jerusalem.

March 12, 1983 — ANGOLA — In an armed battle at Alto Catumbela industrial complex, the National Union for the Total Independence of Angola (UNITA) kidnapped 66 Czechoslovaks and 20 Portuguese, who provided technical assistance to the hydroelectric and paper mill complex. The battle lasted three hours and involved up to 1,000 UNITA troops. Casualties included 30 government soldiers and 1 UNITA guerrilla. After the battle, the 86 captured civilians, which included 21 Czechoslovak children, were forced to march over eight hundred miles to the UNITA camp. During the march, the hostages were divided into three groups. The first group of 8 arrived at the UNITA camp on May 1; the second group of 30 arrived on May 12; and the remainder arrived some time later. Early reports that 3 children died in the forced march proved to be unfounded; however, one Czechoslovak adult did die due to exhaustion. Jonas Savimbi, UNITA guerrilla leader, offered to exchange the hostages for 7 British mercenaries held in Angola since 1975. Savimbi also demanded the release of 30 jailed UNITA leaders. The kidnappers warned government forces that any attempt to free the hostages would result in their death.

On March 25, shortly after the South African government refused to help, the Czechoslovak government solicited the aid of the Federal Republic of Germany in obtaining the hostages' freedom. As the kidnapping dragged on, the Czechoslovak government also asked Switzerland, Austria, the United Nations, and the International Red Cross for assistance. Promises made by UNITA on April 29, 1983, to release some hostages were not immediately carried out. The first group of 45 Czechoslovaks (21 of whom were children) and 10 Portuguese were freed on June 30, 1983. The remaining 10 Portuguese were released on September 28, 1983, along with 25 other Portuguese hostages taken in other kidnappings. On June 19, 1984, the last 20 Czechoslovaks were released after nearly 15 months of captivity. What, if anything, was traded for these hostages is not known. The final release did, however, require the Czech deputy foreign minister, Stanislav Svoboda, to visit UNITA's headquarters in Jamba, southern Angola. 83031201

March 12, 1983 — ANGOLA — The National Union for the Total Independence of Angola (UNITA) captured Cuban lieutenant Adofo Esteves during an operation in the Huambo region.

March 13, 1983 — GREECE — Unknown persons raided a military airfield, located on the Greek island of Khios. The raid resulted in some damage to fuel installations and to the runway. Before fleeing, the attackers exchanged fire with security forces. No injuries were reported. The incident resulted in the appointment of Brig. Gen. Ioannis Tangas to replace Brig. Gen. Kurupios as the military commander of the island.

March 14, 1983 — SAUDI ARABIA — A bomb hoax forced a Saudi airliner with 167 passengers of various nationalities and 15 crew on board to make an emergency landing at the Cairo airport. A hostess had found a note that read, "The bomb will explode." The note was in German and had been written on a roll of toilet paper, found in the plane's water closet. A 7½-hour search by explosives experts found nothing. 83031401

March 15, 1983 — UNITED KINGDOM — One American serviceman sustained minor burns when a letter bomb exploded in the United States Naval Intelligence Building in North Audley Street, Mayfair, London. A second incendiary letter bomb was sent to Prime Minister Margaret Thatcher but was intercepted during a routine mail screening. Three separate groups were suspected of the bombings: the Argentine 2 April group, the Scottish National Liberation Army, and a group of Ukrainian anarchists known as the Mahkno Anarchist Army, all of whom claimed responsibility. Scotland Yard linked the bombs to the Ukrainian anarchists, who were also suspected of sending letter bombs in January to the United States and Soviet embassies in London, the London offices of Aeroflot, the SOVIET WEEKLY, and the Russian Intourist. 83031501–02

March 15–16, 1983 — LEBANON — A patrol of the Italian contingent of the multinational peacekeeping forces was attacked by gunmen. The attack left five Italians wounded (two seriously) and two jeeps destroyed. The incident occurred at 10:15 P.M. near the Burj al-Barajinah crossroads. A second attack was reported on March 16. In total, the two attacks left eight Italians wounded and one killed. 83031503, 83031601

March 16, 1983 — UNITED KINGDOM — A letter bomb was sent to Prime Minister Margaret Thatcher and was defused without injuries by police at a postal sorting office. A 14-year-old London boy pleaded guilty on December 17, 1983. He sought attention with his action.

March 16, 1983 — LEBANON — Five United States Marines were wounded in Beirut by a hand grenade thrown at the 12-man patrol stationed near the Beirut airport. This was the first attack on the United States peacekeeping forces. In an anonymous telephone call, the Islamic Jihad (Islamic Holy War) claimed responsibility and protested "the American occupation army." On April 23, 1983, Nazmi Sakka was arrested on suspicion for the hand grenade attack. He was a member of a Syrian-backed guerrilla organization. 83031602

March 16, 1983 — HAITI — A bomb exploded at the offices of the Haitian state-run newspaper LE NOUVEAU MONDE in Port-au-Prince. No casualties were reported at the offices, which were near the United States embassy.

March 16, 1983 — ZIMBABWE — Dyre Smith, a white, United Kingdom-born farmer was kidnapped in southwestern Zimbabwe. A message left at the scene warned that six foreign captives (kidnapped on July 23, 1982) and the farmer would be killed unless two imprisoned guerrilla leaders on trial for treason were released. The kidnappers were thought to be supporters of self-exiled opposition leader Joshua Nkomo. The note was signed "Comrade Cuba from the Soviet Union." Automatic rifles (AK-47) were used in the abduction, which also left a farm employee injured. 83031603

March 16, 1983 — JAPAN — The Kansai Regional Revolutionary Army claimed responsibility for a gasoline time bomb planted in an ammunition dump at Sasebo United States Naval Base. The bomb was discovered after an anonymous caller alerted the base. This bomb attempt was thought linked to protests planned to mark the arrival of the nuclear-powered aircraft carrier *Enterprise* during the following week. 83031604

March 16, 1983 — CYPRUS — In a smuggling incident, nine kilograms of heroin was seized from Panayiotis Theodosiou at the Larnaka Airport. Interpol, who was carrying out the investigation, believed that heroin smuggling in the Greek Cypriot sector of Cyprus was financing activities of the Armenian Secret Army for the Liberation of Armenia (ASALA). Interpol also suspected that Nikos Sampson, who was engaged in terrorist acts aimed at annexing Cyprus to Greece, was involved with the heroin smuggling ring.

March 17, 1983 — LEBANON — Three persons were arrested in southern Lebanon after having attacked some Netherlands United Nations peacekeeping soldiers. One soldier was stabbed. 83031701

March 17, 1983 — LEBANON — Italian soldiers in the United Nations peacekeeping forces exchanged gunfire with unknown assailants. Lebanese security sources attributed the incidents to nervous peacekeeping forces who fired at a minibus, wounding two of the three occupants. An Italian officer claimed that the minibus occupants fired first and then fled. One Italian was slightly wounded. 83031702

March 17, 1983 — COMOROS — After crash-landing a Cessna 310 at Moroni Airport, six airmen from Tanzania requested political asylum in the Comoros Republic. The Comoros government did not want to grant asylum and informed the Tanzanian government of the incident. Comoros awaited further information from Tanzania.

March 18, 1983 — ZIMBABWE — Four whites were murdered by armed men, said to be loyal to self-exiled opposition leader Joshua Nkomo. The dead included an elderly farm couple and their two grandchildren. During the previous year, 40 whites had been killed by dissidents.

March 18, 1983 — LEBANON — Two Franciscan nuns, Jacqueline Hawwa and Amirah Qaddum, and another woman, Samirah Hanna Hayruz, were reported to have been kidnapped by Fatah lieutenant Yasin Khmais 'Ayyad in the vicinity of Al-Biqa township.

March 18, 1983 — LEBANON — Two grenades were hurled at French soldiers by a lone assailant in a car. No casualties were reported in the incident, which included bursts of gunfire aimed at the soldiers. Only one of the two grenades exploded. 83031801

March 18, 1983 — FRANCE — A Saudi airliner enroute from Paris to Jeddah made an emergency landing at Rome's Fiumicino Airport after the pilot was informed of a bomb threat. No bomb was found on the plane which carried 250 passengers and 18 crew. While exiting through emergency escape chutes, one passenger suffered a broken foot. 83031802

March 18, 1983 — UGANDA — An armed attack by antigovernment guerrillas in Uganda left three persons dead on a Kenya-bound passenger train. 83031803

March 18, 1983 — GUATEMALA — A twin-engine Piper plane with several people on board was thought to be hijacked on a flight from Guatemala City to Flores. The plane was believed to have landed in Honduras. No demands were issued, and the exact fate of the National Transport Enterprise airplane remains a mystery. Honduran authorities claimed to have no knowledge of the incident. 83031804

March 19, 1983 — HAITI — In a bombing at the Toyota sales office in Port-au-Prince, one person was killed and damage was heavy. Motive and perpetrator remain unknown.

March 19, 1983 — LEBANON — Explosives left at the Libyan embassy in Beirut were deactivated without incident. 83031901

March 21, 1983 — ISRAEL — In the village of Arrabah (near Jenin) in the

Israeli-occupied West Bank, over 300 Palestinian schoolgirls were hospitalized after complaining of symptoms stemming from an alleged Israeli attempt to poison them with a gaslike substance. Similar incidents followed over the next few days in the West Bank, affecting about 900 people in total. The Israelis denied the charges. Independent investigations by the World Health Organization, the Atlanta-based Center for Disease Control, and Israeli doctors never produced hard evidence of poisoning. The Israelis thought the incidents stemmed from mass hysteria. About 40 students were later arrested by security forces, who accused the students of fabricating the poisonings.

March 21, 1983 — POLAND — Twelve Poles in a single-engine biplane, which had taken off from Rzutown, Poland, made an emergency landing near Kristianstad, Sweden, and then asked for political asylum. The plane had been stolen from an agrotechnical service enterprise by two employees who were accompanied by their families on the flight.

March 21, 1983 — FRANCE — A car bomb failed to explode in an attempt to murder Jean-Marc "Ara" Toranian, a leader of the National Armenian Movement, which has some links to the terrorist organization, the Armenian Secret Army for the Liberation of Armenia. No one was hurt in the incident. 83032101

March 22, 1983 — TURKEY — Turkish intelligence sources and the Turkish Foreign Ministry issued warnings regarding proclamations of the Justice Commandos (ESAK) and the Armenian Secret Army for the Liberation of Armenia (ASALA) to make April the "11 month of revenge." Turkish sources provided governments in Greece and France with names of suspected Armenian militants.

March 24, 1983 — ARGENTINA — Two bombs were discovered and deactivated in British schools in the northern part of Buenos Aires. The two schools were Saint John's School in Martinez Neighborhood and Saint Patrick's School in the neighborhood of Acassuso. The bombs were discovered after an anonymous telephone warning. In the previous week, an anonymous caller had threatened the British schools if the British did not stop their activities in Argentina before the end of the month. This warning was said to represent the 2 April Group and Captain Giacchino Command. 83032401–02

March 26, 1983 — PERU — Two bombs exploded at the headquarters of the Peruvian-United States Cultural Institute in Cuzco and caused some damage to the institute. No injuries or claims of responsibility were reported. 83032601

March 26, 1983 — FEDERAL REPUBLIC OF GERMANY — An unidentified arsonist broke into a British Army camp supply center in Bielefeld and set fire to two military trucks before being arrested. 83032602

March 26, 1983 — CYPRUS — A bomb was discovered under the car of Mrs. Maria Khatzikleanthous, a sister of the late Archbishop Makarios. A bomb disposal expert was injured when a booby-trap device ignited the bomb. Police speculated that the bomb had been intended for the publishers of a Libyan magazine, the AL-MAWQIF AL-'ARABI, with overseas circulation. The magazine's publishers and Mrs. Khatzikleanthous lived in the same building in Nicosia and had cars of the same make and color. Unnamed Arab factions were suspected. 83032603

March 27, 1983 — INDIA — No casualties were reported following a large bomb blast in the compound of a high official of the Assam state government.

March 24, 28, 1983 — VENEZUELA — The Mexican embassy in Caracas was peacefully occupied on March 28, 1983, by four women and three men of the Venezuelan Committee of Solidarity with Revolutionary Political Prisoners. An earlier occupation by the group involved the Spanish consulate in Valencia on March 24. Before that, the group had occupied the Swedish embassy in Caracas. The purpose of all three occupations was to demonstrate for better prison conditions for more than three hundred political prisoners and to demand quicker trials.

March 28, 1983 — ZIMBABWE — Dr. Attati Mpakati, the national chairman of the Malawi Socialist League, was assassinated while in Harare. He had been shot in the head. The slain chairman resided in Mozambique. The Malawi Socialist League accused the government of the murder, but the accusations were denied. 83032801

March 28, 1983 — AUSTRIA — Chancellor Bruno Kreisky of Austria was apparently the target of an assassination plot involving the Abu Nidal group. The chancellor made the disclosure on April 11, 1983, after the assassination of 'Isam as-Sartawi, an Arab moderate, in Portugal. Abu Nidal was also suspected of Sartawi's murder. No details concerning the plot on the chancellor's life were given. 83032802

March 29, 1983 — CYPRUS — A bomb similar to the one discovered under a car on March 26 was found and disarmed. The bomb had been placed in a bag on the grounds of the Libyan Cultural Center in Nicosia. Unnamed Arab terrorists were suspected. 83032901

March 29, 1983 — ARGENTINA — Bomb threats were received by the British Hurlingham Golf Club in northeast Buenos Aires. Members of the 2 April Command phoned in the threats, which stemmed from the group's support of Argentinean claims to the Falkland Islands. A bomb attack between the first and fifth of April was indicated by the caller. 83032902

March 31, 1983 — FEDERAL REPUBLIC OF GERMANY — A member of the Armenian Secret Army for the Liberation of Armenia (ASALA) made a threatening phone call to the central office of the TERCUMAN newspaper in Frankfurt. The caller said, "If your writers write against our Armenian cause again, we will bomb your bureau and kill your staff." 83033101

March 31, 1983 — BRAZIL — Lionel David Samuels, Guyana's ambassador to Brazil, was found dead in his Brasilia residence. He had been shot in the head. The police did not release information as to whether the ambassador had been murdered or had committed suicide. Neighbors had heard the shots. 83033102

April 1983 — UNITED STATES — In New York State, 2 men held 16 people hostage for eight hours before giving themselves up. One of the men was identified as Lawrence Gladstone, who had once been convicted of gunrunning for the Irish Republican Army.

April 1983 — NIGERIA — Jack Anderson and Joseph Spear reported in an April 15, 1986, column an alleged April 1983 plot by Qaddafi to overthrow the Nigerian government. According to the columnists, the American ambassador in Lagos filed a detailed report in Washington alleging that Qaddafi personally approved the plan and that $40 million had been earmarked. In the same column, Qaddafi was tied to a foiled attempt to assassinate a Libyan opposition leader in Cairo in November 1984. The hit squad had been captured before the assassination could be carried out.

April 1983 — LEBANON — Colonel Qassem Siblini was wounded in an assassination attempt near Sidon. Six members of the Popular Front for the Liberation of Palestine (PFLP) were arrested for the machine-gun and rocket attack. On August 20, 1983, a Lebanese military court sentenced two of the men to death. Two were given prison sentences and two were acquitted.

April 1, 1983 — SPAIN — Diego Prado, a direct descendant of Christopher Columbus, was kidnapped by four Basque Nation and Liberty terrorists. The government offered a $147,000 reward.

April 3, 1983 — ZIMBABWE — Dissidents loyal to Joshua Nkomo attacked a ranch owned by a white Zimbabwe senator, Paul Savage. The attack left Savage, his daughter Colleen, and a British visitor, Sandra Bennett, dead from gunshot wounds. Senator Savage's wife, Betty, was critically wounded but survived the attack. Twenty dissidents were believed to have taken part in the raid. One of the attackers died from shots inflicted accidentally by the other attackers. In later weeks, the government captured three of the attackers and continued its search for others. One of the captured dissidents confessed to having taken part in the raid. In October 1984, Phineas Ndlovu was hanged for the three murders. 83040301

April 4, 1983 — ALGERIA — About 100 Algerians working at an oil prospecting site held 13 foreign technicians hostage for a week in order to press their demands for higher salaries and improved working conditions. The hostages included 2 Britons, 10 West Germans, and 1 Yugoslav, who worked at the West German geophysical prospecting firm located six hundred miles south of Algiers. The situation was resolved when local authorities in Hassi Messaoud finally intervened. 83040401

April 5, 1983 — BOLIVIA — A French citizen, Jacques LeClerc, was held on charges of drug trafficking and leading a paramilitary, neo-Nazi group known as The Bridegrooms of Death.

April 6, 1983 — IRAN — An Iranian Air Force C-130 was hijacked and flown to Dhahran, Saudi Arabia. When the plane returned to Tehran, one passenger was reported missing. 83040601

April 6, 1983 — NICARAGUA — In Managua, Melida Anaya Montes (Comdr. Ana Maria) was assassinated and one of her aides wounded by members of her own Salvadoran rebel group, the Popular Liberation Forces (FPL). Rogelio A. Bazzaglio Recinos, a member of the central command of the FPL, was suspected of having plotted the assassination that took place in Montes's home in the early morning hours. Six Salvadoran FPL members were later arrested for the crime: Rogelio Recinos, Walter Ernesto Diaz, Andres Vasquez Molina, Julio A. Soto Arellano, Alejandro Romero Romero, and Maria Argota Hernandez. Incriminating evidence, including the murder weapon and blood-stained clothing, were found in their possession. When the leader and founder of the FPL, Salvador Cayetano Carpio, learned on April 12 that one of his trusted comrades killed his second in command, Carpio committed suicide. 83040602

April 7, 1983 — COLOMBIA — Catherine Wood Kirby, a United States citizen, was kidnapped and held for ransom by the leftist Revolutionary Armed Forces of Colombia (FARC), a pro-Soviet group. On or about August 15, 1983, Kirby was released unharmed after a large ransom had been paid by her family. Reportedly, her nephew negotiated with FARC for his aunt's release. Ten to 12 men are believed to have taken Kirby and her foreman from her farm in southeastern Colombia. The fate of the foreman is not known. 83040701

April 8-9, 1983 — FRANCE — On the evening of April 8, 1983, Witold Bialoboki, a Pole, fired a .22 caliber rifle at least 13 times at the Soviet consulate in Marseilles. He was apprehended the next evening for firing at the facade of the Aeroflot office in Marseilles following a car chase by police. He was charged with property damage and arrested for the two confessed shootings, which left no one injured. His motive was not disclosed. 83040801, 83040901

April 9, 1983 — CORSICA — Ten bombs exploded and caused damage to property owned by French people who had come from the mainland to settle on this Mediterranean island. Nine of the 10 bombings occurred in the island's capital of Ajaccio and were viewed as a challenge to Pierre Broussard, who had been appointed by President Francois Mitterrand to curb mounting terrorism. No injuries were reported.

April 9, 1983 — LEBANON — The Islamic Jihad claimed responsibility for shots fired at French peacekeeping forces. No one was injured. 83040902

April 10, 1983 — COLOMBIA — Four hundred members of the Revolutionary Armed Forces of Colombia indicated that they were prepared to lay down their arms and accept an amnesty offer made by the government in November 1982. They said they were willing to act if the government was sincere.

April 10, 1983 — PORTUGAL — A key figure in the Palestine Liberation Organization (PLO), 'Isam as-Sartawi, was assassinated while serving as the PLO representative at the Socialist International Conference held in Albufeira. The murder occurred in the Montechoro Hotel, the scene of the conference. Sartawi's secretary was also wounded during the attack. The PLO was quick to blame Israeli agents, despite repeated claims of responsibility by Abu Nidal, a rival Palestinian group headed by Sabri Khalil al-Banna. Sartawi, a moderate, had been openly critical of the extremist Abu Nidal group, which also claimed responsibility for the assassination attempt against the Israeli ambassador to England. The attempt on Ambassador Shlomo Argov in London provoked the Israelis to attack Palestinian targets throughout Lebanon, causing widespread losses for the PLO.

A previously unknown group, the Antiterrorist Iberian Command, also claimed responsibility for the assassination of the PLO leader, but the claim was not credible. Mohammed Hussein Rashid (Youssef Awad), an Arab radical, was later arrested for Sartawi's murder after confessing. In order to gain Rashid's freedom, the Abu Nidal group threatened Portuguese interests and citizens worldwide. The Portuguese authorities took precautionary security measures but did not give in to the threats. On January 11, 1984, Rashid was acquitted of the murder charge and sentenced to three years for using a forged passport. During the trial, he had claimed that his confession was meant to draw attention away from the true killers. In all likelihood, the Abu Nidal group was responsible, but the exact number and identity of the people involved has never been determined. In June 1984, the Supreme Court overturned the lower court's acquittal. On May 10, 1985, a second trial again acquitted Rashid of murder and sentenced him to three years for using a false passport. Some have speculated that the secretary, Anwar Abu 'Isah (who had been shot in the thigh during the attack), was involved in the plot. He had joined the PLO only a year prior to the shooting. 83041001

April 11, 1983 — EGYPT— The Egyptian National Security Organization disclosed that the Greek-Cypriot administration had issued 225 unused and sealed passports to the Armenian Secret Army for the Liberation of Armenia (ASALA). At least two bombings have been linked to these passports. One bombing, perpetrated by Winter Cherkovisian, involved the consulate general in Los Angeles; the second bombing, perpetrated by Dimitru Gregoriou, involved a Jewish synagogue in Paris.

April 12, 1983 — HONG KONG — Wang Teh-heui, a real estate tycoon, was kidnapped and held for ransom. After an $11 million ransom was cabled to a Taipei bank account, Wang was released unharmed about 10 days after his abduction. Three men and a woman were arrested on April 27 in connection with the kidnapping. Only half of the ransom was recovered, and no political motives for the abduction were disclosed. This was Wang's second kidnapping; the first had occurred in the 1960s when he was freed after the payment of a multimillion-dollar ransom.

April 12, 1983 — CAMEROON — An assassination attempt by seven Chadian FAN terrorists was foiled when their intended targets (Ibrahim Jean and Captain Masangar) were not at home. Neighbors alerted the police. The seven assassins, who were armed with guns and grenades, were arrested without injuries. The attack occurred in the northern city of Kousseri. 83041201

April 12, 1983 — LEBANON — Several vehicles and the monument of Jamal 'Abd an-Nasir were damaged by a bomb. A second explosive device was found and defused. The second bomb had been left in front of AGENCE FRANCE-PRESSE offices in the Najjar building in As-Sanayi'. 83041202

April 12, 1983 — ITALY — An arson attack at a NATO hangar in Vicenza caused an estimated seven hundred thousand dollars' damage. An unnamed, self-styled Communist terrorist group claimed responsibility. 83041203

April 13, 1983 — GREECE — In Athens a rental car packed with explosives blew up near the Saudi embassy. The powerful blast damaged two Saudi Arabian embassy cars that were passing by at the time. Jaffar Ghazi, a Saudi diplomat, his driver, and two women were slightly injured in the bombing, which also damaged parked cars in the vicinity. Responsibility was claimed by the People's Revolutionary Solidarity, which accuses Saudi Arabia of ties with Zionists' interests. Bruno Rivera, an Italian, was charged with the bombing; he had rented the car. 83041301

April 14, 1983 — LEBANON — One Israeli soldier was killed and two wounded in an armed attack against an Israeli transport vehicle. The attack occurred near Tyre. The Lebanese National Resistance Front claimed responsibility.

April 14, 1983 — COLOMBIA — The April 19 Movement (M-19) took credit for a large bomb blast in the Honduran embassy in Bogota. Consul Felipe Paredes (the charge d'affaires) and his secretary were severely injured. A trade bank in the same building also sustained damages. 83041401

April 15, 1983 — ICELAND — A bomb explosion outside the United States embassy in Reykjavik caused minor damage and no injuries. Because the elections were a week away, authorities speculated that the bomb was meant to oppose the United States base at Keflavik. 83041501

April 15, 1983 — TURKEY — A Turkish airliner was hijacked after leaving Istanbul by a lone man, Mahmut Kalkan, and made to fly to Ellinikon Airport near Athens. The hijacker approached the cockpit shortly after the plane was airborne, and an argument ensued with an attendant. When the captain left the cockpit to investigate, Kalkan held a knife to his neck and threatened to blow up the plane if he was attacked. The hijacker also had what looked like a bomb but was actually a can of putty. The incident ended at Ellinikon Airport when Greek security forces stormed the plane, after the hijacker had released the 106 passengers (6 of whom were Americans) and 3 of the 7 crew members. No casualties were reported in either the hijacking or the rescue effort. The Boeing 727 returned the next day to Izmir, Turkey, the plane's original destination. Kalkan apparently wanted to go to Australia or Iceland. He said that his actions were motivated to gain freedom from the Turkish regime. Greek law forbade the extradition request of Turkey, because Kalkan's actions were politically motivated.

Kalkan claimed to be a member of Dev Sol, a leftist extremist group in Turkey, but under interrogation claimed not to belong to any group. On February 5, 1984, Kalkan was sentenced by an Athens court to 13 years and 5 months imprisonment for hijacking. Haydar Hayirli, a security guard who had conducted the preboarding search of Kalkan, was arrested under order of martial law. 83041502

April 17, 1983 — LEBANON — A grenade explosion near the Shatila traffic circle in Beirut injured a French soldier. 83041701

April 17, 1983 — LEBANON — An American soldier escaped injury when fired upon by an unidentified assailant. The attack occurred within 15 minutes of the grenade incident near the Shatila traffic circle in Beirut. 83041702

April 17, 1983 — REPUBLIC OF SOUTH AFRICA — Orlando Cristina, second in command of the rebel Mozambique National Resistance (RENAMO), was shot while asleep in a farmhouse near Pretoria and died from the wound two days later. Cristina is credited with forming the Pretoria-backed RENAMO. No arrests were made. 83041703

April 18, 1983 — LEBANON — A United States embassy car, stolen in southern Lebanon, broke through a security barrier in front of the United States embassy in Beirut. An unidentified man then abandoned the vehicle just before it blew up, causing the collapse of the central section of the seven-story embassy building. Sixty-four people, including the fleeing terrorist, 17 Americans, 32 local embassy staffers, and 14 visa applicants and passersby, were killed in the blast, and another 88 people were wounded. The top Mideast expert from the Central Intelligence Agency, Robert Ames, and the deputy director of the Agency for International Development, William McIntyre, were among the dead, which also included members of the United States Defense Department and the United States State Department. Even though Iran dissociated itself from the bomb attack, the Iranian-based Islamic Jihad (Moslem Holy War) claimed responsibility. The booby-trapped car was filled with 330 pounds of Hexogene, equivalent to 1,320 pounds of TNT. Many of the injured were in the section of the embassy devoted to visa applications. Other Americans killed in the blast were Phyllis Faraci, Deborah Hixon, Kenneth Haas, James Lewis, Frank Johnston, William Sheil, Thomas R. Blacka, Terry Gilden, Monique Lewis, S. Sgt. Ben Maxwell, Cpl. Robert McMaugh, S. Sgt. Mark Salazar, Janet Stevens, M. Sgt. Richard Twine, and Albert Votaw.

On July 26, 1985, 4 Lebanese extremists were charged with the crime by a Lebanese military magistrate. The four were identified as Hussein Saleh Harb and Mahmoud Moussa Dairaki, both Lebanese; Mohammed

Nayef Jadaa, a Palestinian; and Sami Mahmoud Hujji, an Egyptian. Harb and Hujji were also charged with the 1981 bombing of the Iraqi embassy in Beirut where 48 had been killed. By May 1986, Saleh Harb had been freed on two hundred thousand pounds bail, after having apparently been captured and held for some time. In November 1986, the military court magistrate called for the death sentence for 6 extremists accused of the United States embassy bombing, including the 4 just named, all of whom were on the run. At least 8 others were suspected of having aided the accused in the bombing. 83041801

April 18, 1983 — NICARAGUA — A pilot, Ricardo Espinoza Castro, stole a single-seater plane used for agricultural spraying and landed it at the San Jose airport in Costa Rica, where he requested political asylum. His request was granted.

April 19, 1983 — ISRAEL — A bomb threat was phoned into the United States embassy in Tel Aviv. No bomb was ever discovered. 83041901

April 20, 1983 — ETHIOPIA — The Tigre People's Liberation Front (TPLF) kidnapped 12 people in an attack staged at Korem in Welo province. The 12 included 8 Europeans, 2 Ethiopians, 1 American (Rev. Gregory Flynn), and 1 Indian, all of whom were connected with various relief efforts. Although the hostages were held for seven weeks, the guerrillas freed them unharmed. The group apparently seized the hostages to publicize the plight of the drought-stricken Tigreans; they charged that the Tigreans and their hunger are ignored by the Ethiopian government. 83042001.

April 20, 1983 — GUATEMALA — The Guatemalan government announced that it had uncovered a plot to assassinate President Efrain Rios Montt, some other government officials, and some (unidentified) political leaders. Ricardo Garcia, a Nicaraguan, and two unnamed Hondurans were sought in the plot. The identity and approximate location of the so-called hire killers were supposedly known by the government. No arrests were reported. 83042002

April 20, 1983 — TURKEY — Sener Yigit was executed for the murders of the wife and daughter of the Austrian envoy to Turkey. The murders were committed four years earlier and may have been sexually motivated.

April 21, 1983 — REPUBLIC OF SOUTH AFRICA — One man was slightly injured in a bomb explosion at the old Supreme Court building in Pietermaritzburg. The building sustained damages.

April 21, 1983 — ARGENTINA — The 2 April Commando Group telephoned death threats to two British journalists — James Burns and Theodore Oliver — living in Buenos Aires. Other nonspecific threats were directed at the Anglo-Dutch Shell Petroleum Company and British schools. Announcement of the threats was made by the Swiss embassy, who received the call. The threats were issued in retaliation for a recent British decision to bar relatives of fallen Argentine soldiers from visiting grave sites on the Falkland Islands. 83042101

April 21, 1983 — ARGENTINA — In a phone call to the BUENOS AIRES HERALD, the Argentine Anticommunist Alliance told the editor, James Nielson, that he had "48 hours to get out of the country." The newspaper is owned primarily by American interests. 83042102

April 21, 1983 — IRAQ — An unknown number of Iraqi citizens were killed and injured in two separate car bombing incidents in Baghdad. One bomb was near the radio-television building, and the other was near the Air Force Administrative Center. In a statement, a Tehran-based Iraqi opposition group — Martyr Sadr Brigade — claimed responsibility. 83042103–04

April 23, 1983 — UNITED STATES — Shortly after 8:00 P.M., a Molotov cocktail was thrown through a window at the Justice Department offices near Ninth Street and Pennsylvania Avenue NW. The resulting fire was quickly extinguished and caused minor damage to the environmental crimes unit office.

April 23, 1983 — MEXICO — A Guatemalan refugee, Manuel Robledo, was abducted by three men thought to be Guatemalan soldiers in civilian clothes. Later, Robledo's bullet-ridden body was found a few yards from the Guatemalan border. Robledo was the refugees' representative at the Hamaca Camp.

April 23, 1983 — LEBANON — A raid on the Palestine Research Center by the Lebanese Army yielded a machine gun, five pistols, and two detonators. The center is run by the Palestine Liberation Organization in west Beirut.

April 24, 1983 — REPUBLIC OF SOUTH AFRICA — In Durban, a radioactive device was stolen from a pickup truck. The unnamed device was found on April 28. A male suspect had been arrested.

April 24, 1983 — GRENADA — A sniper wounded the daughter of the Venezuelan charge d'affaires in St. Georges. As Romulo Nucete, his wife, and his daughter were on the steps of their suburban home, a shot struck the girl in the leg. She recovered after an operation removed the bullet. 83042401

April 25, 1983 — FRANCE — In an interview, the Abu Nidal group indicated its plans to continue its attacks on "Zionist enemies and Palestinian traitors." Assurances were also given that the group would not attack French or Italian interests.

April 25, 1983 — FALKLAND ISLANDS — British technicians deactivated a booby-trapped device placed between two jeeps belonging to a British agriculture expert. After a thorough search of other vehicles in the area, no other bombs were located. The bomb was thought to protest the British refusal to permit the Argentine ship *Lago Lacar* to dock in the Falklands. On board were 50 relatives of slain Argentine soldiers. 83042501

April 26, 1983 — UNITED STATES — At the entrance of the National War College building, a small bomb exploded causing about one hundred thousand dollars' damage. The War College is located at Fort McNair in southwestern Washington, D.C. Just prior to the 10:00 P.M. blast, the Pentagon's main switchboard received three calls and the Washington, D.C., offices of the UNITED PRESS INTERNATIONAL received one call warning of the bomb. The tape-recorded call also mentioned United States imperialism and American bases and Guatemala. No one was hurt in the blast.

April 26, 1983 — TAIWAN — The Taiwan-based CENTRAL DAILY NEWS urged the United States to deport terrorists of the "Taiwan independence movement," a movement connected to numerous bombings in Taiwan.

April 26, 1983 — ECUADOR — The Honduran embassy in Quito was the scene of an occupation by Ecuadoran students and left-wing politicians, who demanded that Ecuador recognize the El Salvadoran leftist rebels. The 27 protesters took 3 Honduran diplomats hostage. After 14 hours of negotiations, the hostages (2 women and a man) were released unharmed. The Ruminahui Front claimed responsibility for the incident and demanded that Ecuador support peace proposals for Central America, remove its ambassadors from Honduras, and declare the El Salvadoran Democratic Revolutionary Front a "belligerent force." A journalist, a nun, and the former foreign minister, Julio Prado, negotiated a peaceful end to the hostage incident. Once the police agreed to leave the embassy vicinity, the 3-person mediating commission entered the embassy and carried on discussions, which eventually ended the standoff. In return for the hostages, the occupiers were allowed to leave. The political demands were not part of the final agreement. 83042601

April 28, 1983 — ARGENTINA — In a phone call to NOTICIAS ARGENTINAS news agency, the 2 April group claimed that Chileans in a spy ring were acting on behalf of British interests. The male caller indicated that they had already identified one of the "spies"—a woman named Lidia Evans.

April 28, 1983—LEBANON— In an early morning incident, United States Marines fired at a car that crashed through a barbed wire checkpoint near the British embassy, which had been providing space to American embassy workers since the April 18 bombing of the United States embassy. No injuries were reported.

April 28, 1983—COLOMBIA—Jaime Bateman Cayon, the leader of the April 19 Movement (M-19), died in an airplane accident that occurred in northwest Colombia, near the Panama border. Apparently, the plane crash was due to a mechanical failure during bad weather. The guerrilla leader and his companions were enroute to a meeting in Apartado with leaders of the Maoist People's Liberation Army (EPL) in an effort to unite Colombian guerrillas. Ivan Marino Ospina was named as Cayon's successor to lead the M-19 group.

April 28, 1983—FRANCE—After a two-year truce in mainland France, the Corsican National Liberation Front (CNLF) planted 20 bombs in Paris, Marseilles, and Aix-en-Provence. Fifteen exploded, causing no injuries but heavy damage to banks, railway stations, and public buildings. The police arrested 22 people in France and Corsica in connection with the bombings. Among those arrested, Jean-Klaude Gladieux admitted organizing CNLF terrorist acts in the Paris region. Four other arrested CNLF members admitted a hand in the bombings. The arrests also led to the detention of 3 men implicated in dealing forged currency. Information gained in the arrests enabled the French police to uncover two CNLF arms caches. In total, 8 CNLF members were charged with terrorist and forgery activities. The arrests were a severe blow to the CNLF separatists. 83042801–20

April 30, 1983—ARGENTINA—Raul Clemente Yaguer, a major figure in the Montonero guerrilla organization, was killed in a shoot-out with security forces in Cordoba.

May 1983—IRAN—Nic A. Fougner, the Norwegian ambassador to Iran, was fired upon while driving in Tehran. The assassination attempt occurred just after Fougner had cleared a checkpoint. The bullets, which entered the driver's window, narrowly missed the ambassador, who was slightly injured by glass from the shattered window. 83059901

May 1, 1983—JAMAICA—Yvon DeSulme, a Haitian exile and general manager of Thermo Plastics in Kingston, was the target of an assassin, who failed in his attempt when DeSulme was not at his home. A maid at De-

Sulme's house alerted police, who killed the assassin in a shoot-out. Papers on the dead man linked him to an unnamed Haitian diplomat in Kingston for whom Jamaican authorities were attempting to get a waiver of diplomatic immunity. The identity of the dead gunman was not revealed. 83050101

May 1, 1983 — PUERTO RICO — A Capitol Airlines DC-8 with 202 passengers and 10 crew was diverted to Havana, Cuba, by a single hijacker, Rigoberto Gonzalez Sanchez. Flight 236 from San Juan, Puerto Rico, was bound for Miami when Sanchez demanded to be flown to Havana. He claimed to be armed. Sanchez was on parole at the time of the hijacking. Four years prior to this incident, Sanchez, a Cuban, had been convicted of an attempted hijacking in the United States. Sanchez gave himself up without a struggle to Cuban authorities. No injuries were reported. 83050102

May 1, 1983 — LEBANON — Two Chinese-made Katyusha rockets landed and exploded within one hundred yards of the United States ambassador's house in Beirut. The attack came while United States secretary of state George Schultz was spending the night at the ambassador's residence. Schultz was in Beirut to negotiate the withdrawal of United States peacekeeping forces. There was no way of knowing whether the rockets represented a deliberate assassination attempt. No one was injured.

May 3, 1983 — POLAND — The Warsaw headquarters of Polish primate Jozef Cardinal Glemp's Committee for Aiding Victims of Repression was the scene of vandalism by club-carrying hooligans. The attack resulted in property damage and the beating of several people at the headquarters. Four youths, abducted by the gang, were beaten and abandoned just outside Warsaw.

May 3, 1983 — PERU — Renata Hehr, a West German citizen, was arrested in Arequipa and accused of terrorist activities, including the bombing of the Peruvian–United States Cultural Institute in Arequipa. At the time of her arrest, she had 39 sticks of dynamite, 83 fuses, 2 revolvers, and subversive materials. Hehr was charged with terrorist activities committed in 1978, 1980, and 1983 while she was a member of the Shining Path terrorist group, headed by Alberto Segura. Hehr maintained that Segura forced her to commit the terrorist attacks — some 25 acts in Peru. The attacks were directed at stores, banks, power line towers, electricity stations and radio stations, in the cities of Cusco, Puno, and Arequipa. On November 7, 1986, Hehr was sentenced to a 12-year prison term to end on April 30, 1995. Hehr's first attorney, Vasquez Huayca, disappeared under mysterious circumstances. Martha Huatay, head of the Peruvian Democratic Lawyers Association, charged that government forces abducted Huayca in the corridors of the court building. Nothing has been heard from Huayca since his disappearance.

May 3, 1983 — ITALY— Socialist party official Gino Giugni was shot in the shoulder and legs while leaving his university office in Rome. The Combatant Communist Party, a militant wing of the Red Brigades, claimed responsibility for the assassination attempt. The incident fueled speculation that the Red Brigades had regrouped in order to carry out another terrorist campaign. This was the second attack by Red Brigade elements since imprisoned leaders of the group asked their comrades for a halt of the armed struggle. The attack on Giugni came several days after the government announced the arrest of three alleged members of the Red Brigades. Giugni, a Rome University law professor, recovered from his injuries.

May 4, 1983 — UNITED STATES— The Nuclear Regulatory Commission (NRC) warned atomic power plants of a growing number of "insider" sabotage incidents by disgruntled employees. The NRC cited incidents in which control wires were cut, metal chips were dumped into the reactor's coolant pumps, and valves were tampered with. Although no serious accident has resulted thus far from sabotage, the NRC warned of possible disaster. Two potentially dangerous incidents were cited: (1) On May 1, 1982, instrument valves were "deliberately mispositioned," thereby shutting off the steam generator feedwater pump. (2) On June 5, 1981, a valve was locked in the wrong position, thus shutting off an emergency cooling system. The second incident occurred at the Beaver Valley plant near Pittsburgh; the location of the May 1, 1982, incident was not revealed. Labor disputes were suspected to have caused these incidents.

May 4, 1983 — LEBANON— Two separate bombing incidents wounded nine Israeli soldiers. Six were injured in the outskirts of Beirut near where United States secretary of state George Schultz was meeting with Lebanon negotiators on Israeli troop withdrawals. The second attack involved a land mine in the Chouf Mountains east of Beirut.

May 4, 1983 — ITALY— Ludovica Rangoni Machiavelli, a model, was freed after her family paid a one hundred thousand dollar ransom to her kidnappers. She had been a captive in a tent for three months. The original demand of $1 million was reduced when her father could not raise the money.

May 4, 1983 — MEXICO— The United States embassy in Mexico City was evacuated in response to an 8:30 A.M. anonymous phone call to the embassy warning of a high-powered bomb. No bomb was found. 83050401

May 5, 1983 — LEBANON— Colonel James Mead, the commander of the

United States Marine contingent, narrowly escaped injury when his helicopter was hit by three .50 caliber rounds while he was on a reconnaissance mission in the Israeli-held mountains near Beirut. 83050501

May 5, 1983 – PEOPLE'S REPUBLIC OF CHINA – A Civil Aviation Administration of China (CAAC) jetliner was hijacked during a domestic flight from Shenyang to Shanghai. Flight 296, a British-built Trident with 105 people aboard, including 8 crew, had taken off from Shenyang airport at 10:49 A.M. Just prior to the hijacking, navigator Wang Peifu reported suspicious activity in row 6 to the plane's pilot, Wang Yixuan, and to an attendant. About 40 minutes into the flight, 6 passengers from the sixth row rushed the cockpit with drawn pistols. Several shots were fired by the hijackers, 5 men and 1 woman, whose leader was Zhuo Changren. Upon hearing the shots, the pilot ordered the radio operator, Wang Yongchang, to report the hijacking to the ground. The pilot's intention to land at Qingdao Airport was foiled when 4 hijackers forcibly entered the cockpit. In the ensuing melee, Wang Yongchang was seriously injured from a gunshot wound in the leg. The navigator was also shot in the leg. The 2 injured crew members had tried to fight the hijackers off with axes. After the hijackers had gained control of the cockpit, they forced 2 crew members at gunpoint to carry the injured men to the rear of the plane.

While holding pistols to the heads of the pilot and copilot, the hijackers shouted, "To the east! To the east! Seoul, Seoul!" The hijackers instructed the pilot to drop to a lower altitude and to change course for South Korea. Pilot Wang Yixuan tried repeatedly to outwit the hijackers by secretly changing his heading back to China, but his actions were discovered each time. The pilot's actions agitated Zhuo, who shouted abuses and grabbed at the controls, thereby causing the plane to fly erratically. At times, the plane was a mere 600 meters above sea level.

The pilot and copilot were closely watched by the hijackers as they flew southward for almost 1½ hours before spotting South Korean Air Force fighters near the demilitarized zone (DMZ). By waving the plane's wings to the right and left, the pilot signaled his request for permission to land. The plane was almost out of fuel due, in part, to the numerous changes of course. The South Korean fighters then escorted the jetliner to the nearest landing strip, Camp Page, an American military airbase, 30 miles south of the DMZ near Chunchon. Under adverse winds, the pilot landed the plane safely on the short airstrip that was not suited for handling large airliners. After landing at Chunchon, the hijackers held the pilot and copilot hostage in the cockpit. The passengers were also held on board for almost 8 hours before being freed. During this interval, crew members destroyed sensitive documents on the plane to keep them from falling into the hands of the South Korean government. The hijackers finally freed their prisoners and gave themselves up to South Korean security forces, requesting political asylum in Taiwan.

At 10:00 P.M., pilot Wang Yixuan met with South Korean authorities and asked that the United States embassy and the Japanese embassy be contacted. With 3 Japanese aboard, Wang Yixuan thought it advisable to alert the Japanese embassy. The other passengers were all Chinese. The pilot demanded that no contact be made with Taiwan; he also asked the South Korean government to ensure the safety of the passengers, crew, and airliner. Finally, the pilot asked that international civil aviation conventions be followed in handling the aftermath of the hijacking.

Flight 296 represented the first successful hijacking of a Chinese airliner to a foreign country. The incident is also noteworthy because it forced the South Korean and Chinese authorities to make their first official contact in over 30 years. On May 7, Chinese aviation director Sheh Tu arrived with a delegation to negotiate the return of the passengers, crew, and hijackers. After three days of talks, South Korea agreed to return the plane, passengers, and crew. On May 10, the Chinese passengers and all but one crew member flew to Shanghai on board the plane that had brought Sheh Tu's delegation; the Trident plane, the 6 hijackers, and injured crew member Wang Yongchang remained in South Korea, the latter to be allowed to return to China once his wounds had healed sufficiently. The 3 Japanese had flown on to Japan days before.

South Korean maintenance men repaired the Trident's landing gear, damaged in the emergency landing at Chunchon. On May 18, the Trident returned to China, carrying the injured radio operator and remaining members of the Chinese delegation.

China's request to extradite the hijackers was denied by the South Korean government, which instead put the 6 on trial. China, of course, raised protests regarding South Korea's refusal to extradite. The 6 mainland Chinese defendants were Zhuo Changren, a supply official of the Liaoning Provincial Government; Wang Yen-da, an environmental agency official; An Chien-wei, a security official at the Shenyang Institute of Physical Culture; Chiang Hung-chun, another security official at the Shenyang school; Wu Yuan-fei, a procurement official at the Kwantung Provincial foreign trade office; and Kao Tung-ping, Zhuo's lover. Charges of violating Korean aviation safety law, illegal possession of firearms, and violating immigration law were leveled against the defendants on June 2.

On July 18, 1983, the first trial began at Seoul Criminal District Court and ended in a guilty verdict for the 6 defendants. Zhuo received a six year sentence; Wang and Chiang received five year sentences each; and the remaining 3 received four year sentences. The defendants appealed their sentences to a higher court on December 6, 1983, but the higher court upheld the sentences. On May 22, 1984, a final appeal was made to the Supreme

Court but once again the higher court upheld the sentences. The hijackers' sentences were commuted to time served on August 13, 1984, at which time the hijackers were banished from South Korea. Their request for asylum in Taiwan was honored. On August 14, 1984, the hijackers arrived in Taiwan to a hero's welcome. 83050502

May 6, 1983 — UNITED STATES — Argentina requested the extradition of Michael V. Townley on charges that he helped assassinate Gen. Carlos Prats and his wife in a car bombing on September 30, 1974, in Buenos Aires. Townley, an Iowa-born ex-member of the Chilean security organization, was serving time for the confessed 1976 car bombing and murder of Chilean ambassador Orlando Letelier and his research aide in Washington, D.C. Townley's pending release from jail was blocked by the extradition request; he had served 62 months of a 10-year sentence for the murder of Letelier. Townley had been given a lenient sentence owing to a plea bargain arrangement whereby he agreed to testify against other suspects in the murder of Letelier. The timing of the Argentine extradition request was linked to a United States request of Argentina to extradite Bolivian ex-interior minister Arce Gomez on cocaine trafficking charges. On July 25, 1983, a federal magistrate denied Argentina's extradition request. A witness protection program helped relocate Townley in an undisclosed location.

May 6, 1983 — PORTUGAL — The Abu Nidal group threatened to attack Portuguese targets and interests if the confessed assassin of 'Isam as-Sartawi was not freed. Security measures were increased in Portugal and at its diplomatic installations abroad. 83050601

May 7, 1983 — LEBANON — The *Fairfax County,* a United States Navy support ship, was fired upon while off the coast of Beirut. No injuries or damage resulted from the five rounds of artillery that landed within five hundred yards of the ship. The ship was in Beirut waters to assist the United States peacekeeping forces. 83050701

May 8, 1983 — NICARAGUA — A small, twin-engine, two-seater Cherokee was hijacked and made to fly to Llano Grande airport in Liberia, Costa Rica, near the Nicaraguan border. The hijacking of the Salas air taxi plane began at the Sandino Airport in Managua when an Interior Ministry official, Miguel Bolano, who had contracted the plane on an internal flight, diverted it to Costa Rica. Upon landing, both the pilot and Bolano were arrested on air piracy charges. Bolano asked for political asylum; the pilot said that he was forced to fly to Costa Rica. 83050801

May 9, 1983 — SENEGAL — The Niger embassy in Dakar was the scene of a peaceful occupation by one hundred Niger students, protesting police intervention during a recent strike by Niger university students in Niamey. The sit-in was also to protest the previous month's closing of an agronomy college following a dispute. In released statements, the students drew attention to the "unbearable conditions" of President Seyni Kountche's regime.

May 9, 1983 — COLOMBIA — United States businessman Elias Alexander Dower, one of the primary shareholders of Pat Primo Clothes Factory, was kidnapped in Bogota and held for ransom by criminals. After 15 days, he was released unharmed after the payment of a $578,000 ransom. 83050901

May 9, 1983 — JORDAN — Within minutes of one another, two small incendiary devices exploded in the main offices of the American Life Insurance Company and at the Amideast Educational Center. Both targets were in Amman and represented United States interests. A little-known group, the Jordanian Revolutionary and Military Committee (Mouab), claimed responsibility. In a letter to AGENCE FRANCE-PRESSE in Athens, Mouab protested "U.S. plots and the imperialist schemes of Schultz," who had recently worked out an agreement on foreign-troop withdrawals from Lebanon. The targets sustained minor damage with no personal injuries. 83050902–03

May 9, 1983 — SYRIA — Yasir Arafat, Khalil al-Wazir (an aide to Arafat), and Fatah member Salah Khalaf were threatened by the Abu Nidal group, which accused the three of kidnapping and killing five of its members the previous Saturday in Al-Biqa'. 83050904

May 10, 1983 — BRAZIL — Orlando Gaetano, a former member of the Revolutionary Action Movement, was arrested at the request of Interpol, who had been asked by the Italian embassy to take action. Gaetano was apprehended in Foz do Iguacu, Parana State, where he was staying after having entered Brazil from Paraguay. He faced a 15-year prison sentence in Italy for several terrorist attacks that occurred in Europe during 1979. In December 1983, the Supreme Court approved Italy's extradition request.

May 10, 1983 — LIBYA — 'Abd al-Qadir Musa al-Khatib, a Palestinian, was arrested and held for allegedly planning to kill Col. Muammar Qaddafi. The Libyan government claimed that he was a Central Intelligence Agency recruit who had confessed to the alleged United States–Fatah plot to assassinate the Libyan leader. Fatah called the Libyan allegations "ridiculous."

May 11, 1983 — BOLIVIA — Just after midnight, Attorney General Hernando H. Siles's home was the scene of a bomb attack that caused some damage but no injuries. General condemnation of the attack was expressed.

May 11, 1983 — SOUTH KOREA — Chon Tu-hwan was shot at in a failed assassination attempt while he inspected the Myolgong-83 exercise near the demilitarized zone (DMZ). The Voice of the Revolutionary Party for Reunification in Korea claimed that another officer had taken part in the assassination attempt. This was not the first attempt on Tu-hwan's life.

May 12, 1983 — PUERTO RICO — A Capitol Air DC-8 with 248 people on board was hijacked by a lone black female with a 12-gauge flare gun. The mostly plastic gun had escaped detection by metal detectors. Flight 236 was on a regularly scheduled flight from San Juan, Puerto Rico, to Chicago, with an intermediate stop in Miami. About 30 minutes into the flight (8:30 P.M. EDT), the hijacker threatened the chief stewardess with the flare gun and demanded to be flown to Cuba. The plane landed at Jose Marti International Airport in Havana at 9:06 P.M., where the hijacker gave herself up to Cuban authorities. After 3½ hours, the plane took off for Miami. The same flight had been hijacked to Cuba on May 1 by a lone man. 83051201

May 13, 1983 — CHILE — A bomb, planted in a crowded area of Valparaiso, exploded causing damage to property and injury to 10 people. Two people, including a police officer, received serious injuries from the bomb, which consisted of ammonia gelatin, iron, and tar. Across the street, investigative officers were meeting in the civil police building at the time of the explosion.

May 13, 1983 — ITALY — Five Italians and a Lebanese, Isaac Salmassi, were arrested on drug and arms trafficking charges. Those arrested included a Milanese engineer, the director of a transport business at Genoa, and Renato Gamba, an arms manufacturer in Brescia, northern Italy. The smuggling operation involved trucks that allegedly left Czechoslovakia or Bulgaria with vegetables or bathroom equipment that were unloaded and replaced with arms in Varna, before traveling on to Lebanon with papers issued for the original cargo by the Italian customs.

May 13, 1983 — BOLIVIA — Four British subjects, Brian Vivett, Arthur Ross, Colin Brown, and Neil Howie, were taken hostage in Magdalena and held by local residents led by Ricardo Cuellar to protest the termination of air service to this remote region. The hostages were freed unharmed when President Siles Zuazo ordered Lloyd Aereo Boliviano (LAB) and the Military Air Transport Enterprise (TAM) to resume air service to Magdalena after it had been cut off for almost a year.

May 14, 1983 — ITALY — An Eros pornographic movie house in Milan was torched by a neo-Nazi Italian group, Ludwig. Evidence found at the scene supported the group's claim of responsibility for the fire, which left six dead. Ludwig is also suspected of an arson attack on a Munich disco the previous month, which injured seven. The group also claimed responsibility for ritualistic murders of prostitutes, drug addicts, two friars, and a homosexual in northern Italy.

May 14, 1983 — ARGENTINA — Osvaldo Cambiasso, a Peronist party activist, and Eduardo Pereira Rossi were killed in an alleged shoot-out with police along the Pan American Highway in Buenos Aires. Rossi had ties to the Montonero guerrillas, loyal to the late president Juan Peron. Human rights groups claimed that the shoot-out was a fabrication and that the two victims had been abducted from a bar in downtown Rossario by army members dressed in civilian clothes. The Argentine authorities denied the allegations. Rossi had recently acquired Italian citizenship. 83051401

May 14, 1983 — SPAIN — In Valladolid, Spanish police arrested Jose Carlos Bravo del Amo, Jose Carlos Ramos Mateos, Juan Alberto Rodriguez Martin, and Jose Maria Martinez Ferreira, suspected members of 28 October National Armed Syndicalist Group, an ultraright-wing group, formed to protest the Socialist party's electoral triumph. At least two murders have been attributed to the group.

May 16, 1983 — IRAN — A hijacking of an Iranian Air Force B-3 plane ended when Mohammad Hasan, the Iranian hijacker, parachuted over Oman's capital after the Omani authorities refused to grant permission for the plane to land. Hasan was jailed, and the pilot returned the plane to Iran. 83051601

May 17, 1983 — ITALY — In a Rome post office, a robbery attempt by three suspected members of the Red Brigades became a barricade and hostage incident when police surrounded the facility. One robber, Carol Caravaglio, was captured and another managed to flee. The third robber, Francescu Donati, held two postal employees hostage for almost five hours as Italian antiterrorist police, the Digos, carried on negotiations. Donati surrendered after allowing Rome prosecutor Domenico Sica into the post office for negotiations. No one was injured.

May 17, 1983 — LEBANON — In Syrian-controlled Al-Biqa', a student was wounded by gunfire when he tried to hang a picture of President Shaykh Amin al-Jumayyil. An Iranian gunman was suspected of the shooting. 83051701

May 17, 1983 — GREECE — In Athens, two bombs exploded destroying a Syrian embassy car and causing property damage. The first bomb blew up near the Syrian embassy and had been placed in an embassy car; the second bomb exploded just 150 meters from the embassy and caused minor damage. No one was injured in the two blasts, claimed by the hitherto unknown organization, Group for Martyred 'Isam as-Sartawi. (Sartawi, a Palestine Liberation Organization leader, had been assassinated in Portugal on April 10, 1983.) The Army for Iran's National Liberation also claimed responsibility in a phone call. 83051702–03

May 17, 1983 – SOUTH KOREA – In Seoul, United States ambassador Walker received a threatening phone message from an anonymous caller who said, "Take measures to have those involved in the arson at the U.S. Cultural Center in Pusan immediately released. We give you seven days of leeway. If you do not comply with our demand, we will kidnap you and all of your family and will blow up the residence, too." 83051704

May 18, 1983 – ITALY – Adalberto de Witt, a member of the Rome underworld, was arrested in a field in Rome as he was preparing 10.5 ounces of uranium 238 for shipment in three lead containers to the Middle East. The weapons-grade uranium was recovered at the time of the arrest. The intended destination of the shipment was not identified.

May 19, 1983 – HONDURAS – According to Honduran officials, Misael Brenes, Nicaraguan consul to Choluteca, was requesting political asylum in Honduras. In Managua, Nicaraguan authorities charged that Brenes had been kidnapped by right-wing guerrillas.

May 19, 1983 – UNITED STATES – Eastern's flight 24, bound from Miami to New York La Guardia Airport with 125 passengers and 7 crew members, was hijacked to Cuba by a man claiming to have a bomb. Cuban authorities arrested the lone hijacker; the Boeing 727 returned to Miami after a short delay in Havana. An NBC reporter was a passenger on the plane. 83051901

May 20, 1983 – REPUBLIC OF SOUTH AFRICA – At 4:30 P.M., a large car bomb exploded outside the Nedbank Plaza Building on Church Street, leaving 19 dead and 215 wounded, some seriously. The dead included 7 Defense Force staff and 2 white women; the injured included 78 military personnel, many of whom were blacks. Two of the 8 blacks killed in the blast were later believed to have placed the bomb outside the Air Force headquarters in Pretoria during the rush hour. In an official statement, the Pretoria government laid the blame on the African National Congress (ANC), which, in a statement by Oliver Tambo, denied responsibility for the blast. Apparently, the 2 black ANC members had placed the bomb in the parked car's engine and had intended to detonate it by remote control. When it exploded prematurely, the 2 were killed and the engine was hurled some 165 feet through the air. In a later statement issued in Dar es Salaam, Tanzania, the ANC claimed responsibility for the explosion that Tambo had previously denied. The Pretoria government threatened reprisals to ANC bases in Mozambique. On May 23, the South African Air Force bombed suspected ANC hideouts near Maputo, the capital of Mozambique. The raid left at least 6 dead, including 2 children, and 40 wounded. In a conflicting statement, South Africa claimed that 64 people had been killed, including 41 ANC guerrillas, and 44 had been wounded. Between 5 to 10 jet fighters were thought to have taken part in the raid.

May 20, 1983 — SPAIN — Two Chilean consulates were peacefully occupied by people protesting the current Chilean military regime. In San Sebastian, 12 people occupied the Chilean consulate for an hour; in Zaragoza, 7 people occupied the Chilean consulate for an undisclosed amount of time. In Barcelona, about 30 people attempted a third occupation of a Chilean consulate but gave up when they encountered locked doors. No one was injured in the three incidents, in which banners attributing criminal acts to the Chilean government were displayed.

May 20, 1983 — ITALY— In Milan, an evening bomb explosion destroyed the rostrum from which Pope John Paul II was scheduled the next day to celebrate Mass. A Molotov cocktail was linked to the blast, which caused no injuries.

May 21, 1983 — FEDERAL REPUBLIC OF GERMANY— No injuries were reported in a bomb blast near the review stand for the annual military parade of United States, French, and British troops. The explosion occurred hours before the intended review of troops.

May 22, 1983 — UPPER VOLTA— Student unrest destroyed French embassy cars during an attack on the embassy meant to protest French interference in Upper Volta. No injuries were reported in the incident in Ouagadougou, the country's capital. 83052201

May 22, 1983 — CORSICA— One person, thought to be responsible, was injured in Corte during a series of blasts that caused property damage to shops and houses. In total, 20 explosions were reported in the island's northern region, 7 of which occurred in Ajaccio. At least 6 other bombings were reported in the southern reaches of the island. Leaflets of the Corsican National Liberation Front claimed responsibility for that group.

May 23, 1983 — LEBANON — Salah Khalaf (Abu Iyad) escaped uninjured from a planned assassination by gunmen in two cars, who waited for Khalaf to pass a crossroad near a scheduled meeting between Khalaf and leftists. The plot against the Fatah official was uncovered some 30 minutes before the scheduled rendezvous. 83052301

May 24, 1983 — HONDURAS — In Santa Rosa de Copan, Honduran security forces killed three Guatemalan guerrillas in an ambush.

May 24, 1983 — BELGIUM — The Armenian Secret Army for the Liberation of Armenia (ASALA) claimed responsibility for two bombs in central Brussels. One bomb destroyed a Turkish tourism office; another bomb destroyed a travel agency dealing with Turkish customers. No injuries were reported. 83052401–02

May 25, 1983 — INDIA — A hijacking alert was issued to security personnel at India's international airports. Intelligence reports warned of possible hijackings by pro-Khalistan Sikh extremists and members of the Al Zulfikar movement of Pakistan.

May 25, 1983 — EL SALVADOR — The Popular Liberation Forces (FPL) claimed responsibility for the assassination of Navy lieutenant commander Albert A. Schaufelberger, the deputy commander of United States military advisers in El Salvador. Schaufelberger was shot three times in the head by four assassins in a passing minibus, while the United States commander waited in his own car for a friend at the Central American University in San Salvador. Schaufelberger had recently granted interviews to television networks and others. Pedro D. Alvarado Rivera, an engineering student and a member of the FPL, allegedly confessed to the murder on September 1, 1983, while in Salvadoran Treasury Police custody. After reviewing evidence and polygraph exams, the United States government concluded that Rivera's confession was forced and that he was innocent of the murder. The Clara Elizabeth Ramirez Front (CERF), a dissident faction of the Farabundo Marti Popular Liberation Forces (FMLN), is now thought responsible for the murder. 83052501

May 26, 1983 — MEXICO — Mexican judicial police and Interpol uncovered a plot to attack the interparliamentary meeting between United States and Mexican legislators scheduled to be held in Puebla at the beginning of June. A raid against a safe house in Puebla led to the capture of Puerto Rican Guillermo "William" Morales, who had been wanted for eight years by the United States Federal Bureau of Investigation. A second raid in Cholula left Puerto Rican Adelaido Villafranco Contreras dead. Another Puerto Rican, who was Morales's common-law wife, was killed in the Interpol raid that also uncovered a large cache of weapons, dynamite, and propaganda. Two police officers were wounded in the raids. The United States government filed papers for the extradition of Morales; he was wanted for numerous Armed Front for National Liberation (FALN) bombings. 83052601

May 26, 1983 — REPUBLIC OF SOUTH AFRICA — In the center of Bloemfontein, a car bomb destroyed nearby vehicles and damaged buildings. No casualties were reported.

May 26, 1983 — SPAIN — Guns, ammunition, and explosives were confiscated in raids in Guipuzcoa Province, in which 21 presumed members of the Basque Nation and Liberty's (ETA) military wing were arrested. In Viscaya Province, the police reported yesterday the arrest of 8 other alleged members of the ETA.

May 27, 1983 — USSR — A 30-year-old Antonov-2 monoplane was flown to Gotland from Soviet Latvia. The civilian pilot asked for political asylum.

May 27, 1983 — UNITED STATES — The Federal Aviation Administration announced that, following three recent hijackings, armed air marshals had begun traveling on flights to and from southern Florida. Security in Florida's airports was also tightened.

May 28, 1983 — ISRAEL — Five Arab teenagers were arrested after police uncovered a plot to poison the water in a Jewish village, Lotem, in Galilee.

May 28, 1983 — FRANCE — Le Club de l'Abbaye, a gathering place for right-wing extremists in Paris, was the scene of a bomb explosion that injured two passersby. The restaurant sustained extensive damage. Damage was also reported to apartments and a school in the vicinity. No one claimed responsibility.

May 28, 1983 — PERU — The Shining Path guerrillas were believed responsible for a score of bombings in Lima. The bombings included 10 Lima electric towers, targets near the United States embassy, and other capital targets. No one was injured. At the Bayer chemical plant, the bomb started a fire that caused an estimated $30 million in damages. The government claimed to have arrested between 11 and 14 members of the Shining Path rebel group in connection with the Bayer bombing. Among those arrested were Jorge Cruz, the alleged leader of the Shining Path. Only the bomb at the Bayer plant caused extensive damage.

May 29, 1983 — FRANCE, FRENCH GUIANA, MARTINIQUE, GUADELOUPE — The Caribbean Revolutionary Alliance (ARC) claimed responsibility for a dozen bombs that exploded in French territories in South America and the Caribbean. One person, believed to have been planting a bomb at the time, died in Cayenne, French Guiana. Bombs in Guadeloupe and Martinique damaged police headquarters, courts, government buildings, and the Air France office. In Paris two bombs, planted outside an employment office for French overseas territories, caused no injuries; a third bomb, near the employment office, injured three persons. The ARC did not claim responsibility for the Paris bombings. 83052901–03

May 30, 1983 — LEBANON — Muhammad 'Ali 'Abbas Salih, an Iranian Revolutionary Guard, was arrested by Lebanese security forces on charges of subversion.

May 31, 1983 — FRANCE — Six members of the left-wing extremist group Action Directe shot at policemen, who had stopped the members on a Paris street for a routine identity check. Two policemen were killed and one was wounded. Regis Schleicher (the alleged leader of Action Directe), Claude Halfen, and Nicolas Halfen were later arrested for the murders. On December 8, 1986, the trial for the three was stopped because jurors, intimidated by death threats, failed to show up for the trial. It was believed that a new trial would not begin for several months.

June 1983 — LESOTHO — The military post at Qachas Nek was fired on from South Africa. The Lesotho Liberation Army was believed responsible. 83069901

June 2, 1983 — UNITED STATES — The prison sentence of Abdul Hamid, who was convicted in the 1977 takeover of the B'nai B'rith headquarters in Washington, was upheld for the second time by the Washington, D.C., Court of Appeals panel. The 1977 seizure involved the holding of over 120 hostages for 39 hours.

June 5, 1983 — CENTRAL AFRICAN REPUBLIC — Andre Feissona, an accused terrorist, admitted in his trial that he had taken part in a bomb attack in Bangui on July 14, 1982. Feissona also claimed that he had been recruited by Iddi Lala, the leader of the Central African National Liberation Movement (MCLN). According to Feissona, he had been trained by the MCLN while in Libya.

June 5, 1983 — LEBANON — Libyan charge d'affaires 'Abd al-Qadir Ghuqah was wounded in an attempted assassination at the Napoleon Hotel on al-Hamara street in Beirut. A gunman, later identified as Khalid 'Uthman 'Alwan, approached Ghuqah after he had entered his hotel and shot him seven times. The assassination attempt occurred at 11:45 P.M. The Liberation of Lebanon from Foreigners and the Islamic Jihad Organization claimed responsibility. Alwan, a member of the Syrian Social Nationalist party, confessed to the assassination attempt after being arrested. Wasif

As'ad al-Hilu was arrested on charges that he instigated the crime. Arrest warrants were also issued in absentia against Muhammad Qasim Ba'labakki and Syrian brigadier general Muhammad al-Hallal. Ghuqah recovered from the attack.

On February 6, 1984, Alwan escaped from prison and joined the Al-Murabitun in At-Tariq al-Jadidah. On September 3, 1984, the socialists who had kidnapped Alwan from the Al-Murabitun executed him after a court martial and returned his corpse to west Beirut. 83060501

June 7, 1983 — SPAIN — Ibrahim Amin, a prominent Palestine Liberation Organization member, was seriously wounded by an assassin's bullet. A companion with Amin was also shot in the Barcelona attack and later died. There were no leads on the assassin. 83060701

June 7, 1983 — UNITED STATES — Jurgen Albert Draeger, a West German embassy aide, was found dead in his bed at his Bethesda home. He had been shot in the chest. The death was under investigation.

June 8, 1983 — LEBANON — An Israeli patrol was the apparent target of a car bomb at the Galerie Semaan intersection in Beirut. The bomb was detonated at 10:50 A.M. as the patrol was passing by. Two Israeli soldiers were killed, two were wounded, and five Lebanese civilians were wounded.

June 9, 1983 — AFGHANISTAN — Several Soviets were kidnapped by an Afghan resistance fighter in Qandahar. The abduction coincided with a visit by the Soviet-backed ruler, Babrak Karmal. Resistance fighting in Kabul and elsewhere in Afghanistan was at a marked increase. No other details on the kidnappings or the fate of the hostages were disclosed.

June 9, 1983 — IRAN — The two-man crew of an Iranian helicopter asked permission to fly to another country, after diverting and then landing the helicopter in Bahrain.

June 9, 1983 — IRAN — The British embassy in Tehran sustained heavy damage from a fire, ignited by an explosion. 83060901

June 9, 1983 — ITALY — Two Italian terrorists, Anna Laura Braghetti and Maria Pia Cavallo, were each sentenced in Rome to an additional 17 years in jail for holding a prison guard hostage for eight hours. Braghetti, a member of the Red Brigades, was serving a life sentence for the kidnapping and killing of Premier Aldo Moro in 1978. Cavallo, a member of the Front Line Group, was serving a 19-year sentence for her participation in armed attacks.

June 9, 1983 — REPUBLIC OF SOUTH AFRICA — Thelle Mogoerane, Jerry Mosololi, and Marcus Motaung were hanged for the murder of four policemen stemming from armed attacks against police stations between 1979 and 1981. In addition, the death sentences of Antony Tsotosobe, Johannes Shabangu and David Moise were commuted to life imprisonment by state president Marais Viljoen. All six men were members of the African National Congress.

June 10, 1983 — LEBANON — A guerrilla ambush, seven miles northeast of Tyre, killed three Israeli soldiers and wounded one soldier. The Lebanese National Resistance Front claimed responsibility for the attack that Israel blamed on the Palestinians. The Front also claimed to have captured one Israeli soldier, but the Israeli Army denied the kidnapping. The murdered soldiers brought Israel's death toll in Lebanon to 495 since the June 6, 1982, invasion.

June 10, 1983 — LEBANON — In the eastern city of Baalbek, a bomb killed Mahmoud Ibrahim and his wife in their home. Ibrahim, a Lebanese, was working for the Palestinian guerrilla faction that supports Arafat's ouster. 83061001

June 11, 1983 — LEBANON — An Israeli military convoy escaped injuries when a bomb exploded near the first Israeli Army checkpoint south of Beirut. Six Lebanese civilians waiting to clear the checkpoint were injured in the bomb blast. Attacks against Israeli troops escalated during Israel's stalemate with Syria and the Palestine Liberation Organization over troop withdrawals from Lebanon.

June 11, 1983 — KUWAIT — Arafat disclosed that the Palestinian Liberation Organization (PLO) had executed five men suspected of assassination attempts on Salah Khalaf, second in command to Arafat, and Khalil Wazir.

June 11, 1983 — BELGIUM — In Brussels, a man with a machine gun entered the Brazilian embassy and fled after a scuffle with an employee. No injuries were reported. 83061101

June 12, 1983 — IRAN — An Iranian helicopter made an emergency landing at Bahrain Airport. As in the June incident, the pilot requested permission to fly to another country. Regarding both incidents, Iranian prime minister Mir-Hoseyn Musavi commented, "It is said that these fugitives are the same people who feared to be questioned in connection with the case of spying Tudeh Party. In any case, the fleeing of a few people can have no connection with our country's high-flying pilots or mar the memory of their heroic victories in the mind of our great nation."

June 13, 1983 — UNITED STATES — Allen P. Ellis, a guard at the Oak Ridge National Laboratory in Tennessee, suffered gunshot wounds during a mock terrorist attack on the nuclear reactor. Live ammunition was apparently mixed in with blanks for the simulated barricade-and-hostage-taking defense exercise. Ellis was recovering from bullet-fragment wounds to his hand, arm, and side.

June 13, 1983 — PERU — In Cuzco, Shining Path guerrillas blew up three electrical towers, leaving the city in darkness for two hours. Sticks of dynamite were also hurled by guerrillas at the United States–Peruvian Cultural Center and at a hotel in coordinated attacks that caused minor damage and no injuries. Ironically, the attacks came within hours of a statement by President Fernando Belaunde Terry that vowed, "We are going to show them that they are not weakening us." 83061301

June 14, 1983 — TAIWAN — Terrorism was suspected in an explosion on a Taiwan Passenger Bus Company vehicle enroute from Tainan to Kaohsiung. The blast injured 18 passengers, 8 of whom were listed in serious condition. Officials suspected "Communist bandits and spies."

June 14, 1983 — UNITED STATES — An Eastern Airlines Airbus-300 enroute from Miami to New York was hijacked to Havana by Nelson Betancourt, a United States resident of Cuban origin. Betancourt was arrested by Cuban authorities after the plane landed in Havana. Apparently, the hijacker wanted to get his ailing mother out of Cuba. The plane returned the next day with its 84 remaining passengers and 11 crew. 83061401

June 15, 1983 — JAPAN — An Osaka-based left-wing newsletter, JINMIN SHIMBUN, carried an announcement of a recruitment drive by the Japanese Red Army, which had lost a number of members during Israel's invasion of Lebanon.

June 15, 1983 — ANGOLA — Joana Presley, a Swedish missionary worker, was shot twice in the leg by mercenaries thought to be from South Africa. The ambush occurred along the Capuna-Caluquembe road while Presley was escorting six patients to the hospital. 83061501

June 16, 1983 — LEBANON — No injuries were reported in two bomb blasts at the Beirut building that housed the offices of REUTERS, CBS TELEVISION, and the Jordanian news agency PETRA. 83061601

June 16, 1983 — TURKEY — Three terrorists planted a bomb in a trash can in a narrow alley of the four-thousand-shop Grand Bazaar in Istanbul. Moments after the first bomb exploded, one of the terrorists pulled out an automatic weapon and fired at the shoppers. The gunman was killed when a second bomb that he was carrying exploded prematurely during a gun battle with security forces. The other 2 terrorists escaped. In total, 3 persons (including 1 terrorist) were killed and 21 persons were injured in the attack. In an anonymous phone call to AGENCE FRANCE-PRESSE, the Armenian Secret Army for the Liberation of Armenia (ASALA) claimed responsibility and threatened further attacks. The phone call specifically warned tourists to stay clear of Turkey during the summer. The Turkish government suspected terrorist leaders of separatist and subversive Marxist organizations living outside of Turkey but stopped short of accusing the ASALA. Further investigations by Turkish security forces revealed that at least 2 terrorists involved in the incident entered Turkey covertly through its southern border. Moreover, Turkish security personnel suspected Syria and sympathizers in Turkey of having aided the terrorists, whose bombs were of Soviet make and whose automatic weapon was manufactured in Beretta, Italy. 83061602

June 16, 1983 — VENEZUELA — A crude bomb was found and deactivated shortly before the arrival of Mrs. Betty Urdaneta de Herrera Campins, wife of the Venezuelan president, at a fashion show held in an elegant disco nightclub. An anonymous phone call warned of the bomb.

June 16, 1983 — LEBANON — Masked men in a speeding car opened fire at a beach crowd in Tripoli. The attack killed 18 and left 20 injured. Beirut radio blamed the attack on Sunni Moslems who were believed to be avenging the recent shooting of a comrade. 'Alawite sources in Tripoli claimed responsibility for the attack, which was meant to avenge the deaths of an 'Alawite official and two members, all of whom had been killed in recent clashes in Tripoli. 83061603

June 18, 1983 — IRAQ — The Iraq-Turkey oil pipeline was sabotaged. 83061801

June 19, 1983 — SYRIA — At a Palestinian camp outside Damascus, Lt. Col. Ezzedin Sherif (Abu Ziad) and his son were injured in an assassination attempt by gunmen from mutinous factions within the Palestine Liberation Organization. Sherif, a top military aide to Yasir Arafat, was wounded in the legs and one arm. Neither of the victims was in serious condition. 83061901

June 20, 1983 — LEBANON — Seven Syrian soldiers were killed when guerrillas detonated a roadside bomb as their two jeeps were passing. The unidentified guerrillas opened fire at the jeeps after they exploded into flames.

Two colonels were among the dead. The attack occurred 40 miles north of Beirut, near the Christian town of Anfah.

June 21, 1983 — LEBANON — In a failed assassination attempt, gunmen in a green Range Rover pursued Arafat while enroute to Tripoli on the Homs-al-Qa'-Tripoli Road. The gunmen exchanged fire with Arafat's security guards and then drove away. No one was injured. The 'Alawite Syrian intelligence service is known to use green Range Rovers in Syria. 83062101

June 21, 1983 — PERU — Justice of the peace Pablo Cardenas, Yacan's lieutenant governor Isidoro Cardenas, Paucar's school director Eladio Lavado, and three peasants were killed during armed attacks in Cerro de Pasco by Shining Path guerrillas. Later that day, police engaged the terrorists and killed two. In the engagement, the police managed to seize arms, explosives, subversive propaganda, and a stolen vehicle from the terrorists before they fled.

June 22, 1983 — PERU — Raul Cordova Rojas was apprehended by a Peruvian security guard when he tried to plant a bomb at United States ambassador Frank Ortiz's residence in Lima. The terrorist was discovered as he approached the residence with three sticks of dynamite and a detonator. 83062201

June 22, 1983 — CYPRUS — Palestinian fighters, in transit from Tunis to Lebanon, had their 14 Kalashnikovs confiscated by Larnaca Airport customs. The Palestinians had arrived on a Cyprus Airways flight from Athens when their weapons were taken. The Palestinians had declared the weapons in customs.

June 22, 1983 — TURKEY — The Turkish government notified the Syrian government that some Turkish terrorists, including Abdullah Ocalan (leader of Apocular), had fled to Syria. In response to the diplomatic representations, Syria assured Turkey that there were no Turkish terrorists there.

June 22, 1983 — ITALY — Emanuella Orlandi, 15-year-old daughter of a Vatican messenger, was kidnapped after attending a music lesson in central Rome. The Anti-Christian Turkish Liberation Front (TACTLF), a previously unknown group, claimed responsibility for the abduction and demanded the release of Mehmet Ali Agca, the man convicted of the 1981 attempted assassination of Pope John Paul II. On July 18, 1983, a phone call to the Italian news agency ANSA threatened that Emanuella would be killed on July 20 if Agca was not released from jail. A young woman's voice recorded by ANSA in the phone conversation could not be confirmed to be that of Emanuella. Emanuella's father, Ercole Orlandi, and Pope John Paul II appealed repeatedly to the kidnappers to release the girl. On July 23, 1983, phone calls to ANSA and to the newspaper IL MESSAGGERO again demanded the release of Agca. On August 4, 1983, a new death threat was issued: If Agca was not released by October 30, then Emanuella would be killed. In response to the kidnapper's demand, a direct telephone line was set up with the Vatican's cardinal secretary of state Augustino Casaroli to arrange the "prisoner's swap." On September 5, 1983, the supposed kidnapper issued a message stating that "the adversary operation of Vatican citizen Emanuella Orlandi was closed in all aspects." Thus the case remained for almost a year. The identity of the caller remained a mystery. Moreover, no hard evidence was ever provided that the proclaimed kidnapper really had Emanuella or that she was still alive. Police efforts turned up nothing in spite of a large-scale detention of over two hundred people on July 27, 1983, for questioning.

On August 21, 1984, TACTLF issued the following demands for the release of Emanuella: the signing of an extradition treaty between the Holy See and Italy; the Pope's urging that a prisoner exchange take place; the transferring of Agca from an Italian prison to the Vatican territory; and the signing by the Vatican and Costa Rica of an extradition order for Agca. On November 22, 1984, TACTLF again demanded the release of Agca in return for Emanuella. On neither occasion did the kidnapper provide evidence that they had Emanuella or that she was alive. 83062202

June 23, 1983 — PERU — A leader of the Shining Path, Antedoro Quispe Camayo (Comrade Ante), was arrested at the San Martin Plaza in Lima. When arrested, Camayo was carrying a plan of downtown Lima, allegedly marked with intended targets for bombings. On the same day, the police arrested another leader of the Shining Path group: Similiano Chavez Yanac (Comrade Jorge) was apprehended in Huaraz. In a police operation in Curahuasi, two unidentified foreigners, thought to be Danes, were detained on charges that they had links to the Shining Path group. These four arrests coincided with hundreds of arrests carried out in Lima and throughout Peru by police. In the evening, dynamite sticks were hurled against the Rimac municipal office located behind the government palace in Lima. No casualties were reported, but the municipal office and its files sustained serious damage. Another bomb caused significant damage to the municipality of the Comas district; personal injury was averted when people attending a meeting at the municipality departed shortly before the blast. Another bomb exploded in Campo de Marte in Jesus Maria neighborhood of Lima; a fourth bomb was deactivated at the entrance of the Labor Ministry. Authorities suspect the Shining Path group of the bombings.

June 23, 1983 — URUGUAY — Eight suspected members of the Union of Young Communists were prosecuted by Uruguayan military courts for subversive activities that included the preparation and distribution of so-called subversive propaganda. Those arrested include Francesca Vaselli, Virginia Nichoelson, Javier Martincorenan, Danilo de Marco, Marcelo Munoz Fernandez (an Argentinean), Beatriz Lando, Gisella Marsiglia, and Mabel Araujo.

June 23, 1983 — GREECE — Mahdi Su'du Hasan and 'Arif Ahmad Raja, two Lebanese, hijacked a Romanian airliner chartered by the Libyan Arab Airways. The Boeing 707 with 23 passengers and 11 crew on board had departed Athens at noon for Tripoli, Libya, when the hijackers pulled out pistols and demanded to be flown to Beirut. The plane landed at the Ciampino Airport in Rome for refueling before flying to Beirut. Once reaching Beirut airspace, the plane requested permission to land, but Lebanese authorities refused. The plane then asked Cyprus for permission to land, but the request was again denied. Only Syria offered to allow the plane to land, but the terrorists refused the offer. At twenty minutes past midnight, the plane finally landed at the Larnaca Airport in Cyprus when officials there acted on humanitarian motives because the plane was nearly out of fuel. The plane was parked at a remote part of the runway, where security guards surrounded it. The hijackers demanded that the plane be refueled so that they could fly to Tehran in the morning. Because Iranian officials also refused the terrorists' request to land on Iranian territory, the plane remained parked in Cyprus. Negotiations between the hijackers and the Cypriot government ended when the hijackers agreed to surrender their guns to the pilot and to give themselves up unconditionally. The hijacking ended at 10:00 A.M., approximately 22 hours after it had started. A time bomb left on board was deactivated by security forces minutes before it was set to explode. The 21 passengers included 13 Egyptians, 4 Libyans, 3 Thais, and 1 Sudanese, all of whom were released uninjured. The demands of the hijackers were never made clear during the incident. It was later learned that the terrorists were members of a Shiite Moslem militia group who wanted an independent investigation to look into the 1978 disappearance in Libya of Musa as-Sadr, the group's spiritual leader. On August 2, 1983, the hijackers were sentenced to seven years in jail after having pleaded guilty in a Nicosia court. 83062301

June 24, 1983 — CUBA — Cuba agreed to publicize its stiff jail sentences for hijackings in the hopes of stemming the recent rise in such incidents. Sources disclosed that the list of sentences would indicate that hijackers served an average of 3 years in jail for first offenses committed in 1980. Second offenders received sentences of 12 to 20 years. Cuban authorities stated that hijackers could be sentenced to 20 years in jail in the future.

June 24, 1983 — SUDAN — Fifteen guerrillas of the Liberation Front for Southern Sudan raided a Presbyterian mission at Boma, about 18 miles from the Ethiopian border. In total, 11 Westerners were taken hostage, including John Haspels, his wife, 3 children, and Ron Pontier, all of whom were Americans. The secessionist rebels also captured a Dutchman, William Nort, a West German, Aloi Pscheidt, a Canadian, Martin Overdun, and an Englishman, Conrad Aveling. The kidnappers demanded a $95,000 ransom, food, medical supplies, clothing (150 shirts, 150 pairs of shoes, and 150 pairs of trousers), and extensive publicity for their cause in local and international media outlets. On June 27, the captors released Haspels's wife, his 3 children, Aveling, and one other. The 6 were allowed to leave on one of the two planes captured from the mission. In the ensuing days, the guerrillas repeatedly allowed deadlines to pass without carrying out their threat to kill the 5 remaining hostages. Negotiations between the guerrillas and the Sudanese government were carried on by radio.

On July 5, Haspels and his fellow captives received a coded radio transmission from the missionary headquarters that led them to believe that a rescue attempt was imminent. To assist the rescuers, Haspels put phenobarbital into a stew, which he then shared with the guerrillas. When the drug had taken effect, the 5 hostages escaped into the bush but were recaptured after several hours. The real rescue did not come until July 8 when the Sudanese army in helicopters swooped down on the guerrillas. In the ensuing melee, 18 guerrillas were killed and a number were wounded; the Sudanese army lost 1 man; and the 5 hostages were freed unharmed. The Sudanese government claimed that 2 members of the guerrilla raiding party had been trained by Cuban forces in Libya. The government's communique also indicated that there was irrefutable evidence that the guerrillas received support from Libya. The Liberation Front for Southern Sudan seeks to liberate the black and Christian population of the south from domination by the mostly Arab Moslem population of the north. Before President Jaafar Nimeri granted greater autonomy to the south in 1972, the north and south waged a bloody civil war. The kidnapping was motivated by a deteriorating relationship between the northern and southern factions. 83062401

June 24, 1983 — GREECE — The Front for the Liberation of Northern Ipiros (MAVI) claimed responsibility for a bomb planted in the Albanian ambassador's car parked in front of the Albanian embassy in Athens. When the bomb exploded, no one was injured. Two embassy cars were destroyed and windows in the vicinity were shattered. A leaflet sent by MAVI indicated that the bombing was "an act against the tyrannical Albanian regime." On June 26, the Albanian government sent a strongly worded protest to the charge d'affaires ad interim of the Greek embassy in Tirana. The protest requested the Greek government to take strong measures to end anti-Albanian activities in Greece, which jeopardized the relationship between the two countries. In addition, the Albanian communication demanded that the terrorists be punished and that better protection be given to Albanian interests in the future. Compensation for material damages was also demanded. 83062402

June 24, 1983 — MEXICO — An Aeromexico airliner on a Mexico City–Merida–Miami flight was hijacked by a professional parachutist. The Mexican hijacker was eventually subdued and arrested by personnel from the Federal Directorate of Security. All the passengers were released unharmed after the plane landed safely in Merida. Only a stewardess suffered minor injuries. Further details on the hijacker were not released by the authorities. 83062403

June 24, 1983 — SYRIA — Ten Palestinians loyal to Arafat were killed or wounded when their convoy was ambushed on the Damascus-Homs road by unidentified attackers. The attack came hours after Arafat returned to Damascus. A Palestinian official with the convoy blamed the Syrian police for allowing the attack to occur. 83062404

June 25, 1983 — CUBA — Cuban authorities announced that hijackers would now face from 12- to 20-year sentences, instead of the average 3-year sentences enforced since 1980.

June 26, 1983 — CHAD — A Canadian Roman Catholic priest and four young companions were killed by antigovernment guerrillas. 83062601

June 27, 1983 — EL SALVADOR — The People's Liberation Forces (FPL), a Marxist guerrilla group, launched a rocket-grenade and rifle-fire attack against the United States embassy in San Salvador. The RPG-2 rocket attack came during the night. No one was injured and no damage to the embassy was reported. 83062701

June 28, 1983 — ITALY — Professor Toni Negri, on trial for terrorist activities, was elected to parliament on the Radical party ticket. Negri was the leader and ideologue for the April Seventh group, an autonomy movement. Negri could invoke parliamentary privilege to keep from serving any sentence that he might receive.

June 28, 1983 — ISRAEL — A small bomb exploded in a supermarket in Jerusalem and slightly injured two women shoppers. Ten people were detained on suspicion.

June 29, 1983 — GUATEMALA — Marta Elena Rios de Rivas, the sister of President Efrain Rios Montt, was kidnapped by four men armed with pistols and submachine guns as she entered a drugstore. The kidnapping occurred at 12:10 P.M. in Guatemala City on the same day that President Montt had earlier announced a "state of alarm" and restrictions on civil liberties. At the time of the abduction, Marta Rios, a schoolteacher, was five months pregnant and on medication. The kidnappers forced her to get into a vehicle and threatened another schoolteacher who had accompanied her. Marta Rios's disappearance led to a door-to-door manhunt for the kidnappers. The government repeatedly indicated that they would not negotiate with terrorists. On September 8, 1983, firemen found a body they mistakenly believed to be hers in a well located in San Cristobal City, a suburb of Guatemala City. In return for her release, the kidnappers later demanded publication of a declaration in newspapers throughout Central America, the United States, Mexico, Venezuela, Panama, and Colombia. On October 24, the WASHINGTON POST published a paid advertisement from the Rebel Armed Forces (FAR) as one of the conditions for the release of Marta and Celeste Aida Mejia de Velasco, sister of then Guatemalan leader Gen. Oscar Humberto Mejia Victores. Celeste Mejia had been kidnapped by the same group on September 10, 1983. The manifesto published in the WASHINGTON POST and elsewhere accused the government of murdering 243 since Rios Montt was deposed in a coup on August 8. On October 26, the leftists released both of the women. 83062901

June 29/July 3, 1983 — UNITED STATES — On June 29, four members of the Armed Front for National Liberation (FALN) were arrested in Chicago. The investigation that led to their arrest also led to the discovery of arms caches in Chicago on July 3. Authorities believed that the arms and explosives were to have been used on July 4 to attack military sites and Illinois prisons holding FALN members. The two raids by federal, state, and local officials resulted in the discovery of dynamite, bombs, guns, ammunition, and other weapons of terrorism.

June 29, 1983 — COSTA RICA — Two members of the Democratic Revolutionary Alliance (ARDE), Rodrigo Alfonso Cuadra Clachar and Mario Gutierrez Serrano, died from a powerful bomb that shattered nearby windows in San Jose and wounded a passerby, Panfilo Chavarria Fallas. That morning, Cuadra and Gutierrez had entered a blue Fiat with Nicaraguan plates that had been parked in a downtown lot for 52 hours. The blast occurred at 8:20 A.M. as the car was pulling away from the parking lot. Evidence suggests that the bomb was in a briefcase carried by Cuadra and that it went off accidentally. The two men were on their way to a meeting with the anti-Sandinista ARDE. The Costa Rican national bureau of investigations speculated that the bomb was intended to assassinate top leaders in the ARDE. If such was the case, then Cuadra was a spy for the Nicaraguan government who had infiltrated ARDE for the purpose of assassinating its leadership. Reports indicated that the ARDE members whom Cuadra was to meet were already suspicious that he was a Sandinista agent. First reports identified the second dead man as Francisco Luis Martinez, the car's owner, but the identity was later changed to that of Gutierrez. 83062902

June 30, 1983 — PERU — On June 30, three Danish citizens were arrested for alleged links with the Shining Path terrorist group. On July 5, the three, who included Viveca Turcson and Peterson Binarwa, were turned over to the Danish embassy in Lima.

July 1, 1983 — CHAD — Mark Frohardt, an American working as a technician for a Belgium-based volunteer group, was captured by rebels in northern Chad. The abduction took place in Faya-Largeau and coincided with a rebel takeover of the city. The rebels claimed that Frohardt was a Central Intelligence Agency operative, whose cover was the "Doctors without Borders" relief group. 83070101

July 2, 1983 — GREECE — In Athens, a court sentenced in absentia 21 Palestinian university students to eight-months imprisonment for their participation in a November 18, 1977, armed occupation of the Egyptian embassy in Athens to protest Sadat's visit to Israel.

July 2, 1983 — UNITED STATES — Omar Merida and Angel Martinez, two Mariel refugees, hijacked Pan Am's flight 378, enroute from Miami to Orlando. The Pan American Airlines *Disney World Special* took off at 11:00 A.M. and was diverted about 20 minutes into the flight when the 2 hijackers waved a plastic bottle of gasoline and a cigarette lighter and threatened to start a fire on the Boeing 727 jetliner with 55 passengers and 6 crew members on board unless the plane was flown to Cuba. The plane landed in Havana at 12:04 P.M. Cuban authorities arrested the hijackers, and the plane was allowed to return at 3:31 P.M. This was the second hijacking since the Federal Aviation Administration announced on May 27, 1983, that it would put federal marshals on board planes scheduled for southern Florida flights. A Federal Bureau of Investigation spokesman said that no marshals were believed to have been on the flight. 83070201

July 2, 1983 — UNITED STATES — Four men, Charles O'Reilly, Paul O'Reilly, Steven O'Reilly, and Ray Laskas, were arrested by federal agents after the four had made remarks about hijacking the United Airlines plane to Cuba and had burned money. The men were arrested in Omaha, Nebraska, when the Chicago-bound plane made a scheduled refueling stop. The reports did not indicate that the four men, enroute to a wedding of the O'Reillys' sister, had any real intention of hijacking the plane.

July 4, 1983 — ISRAEL — A Soviet-made rocket was fired by Palestinian guerrillas inside Jordan at an Israeli town, Bet Shean. No one was injured in the first rocket attack from Jordan in over two years. 83070401

July 4, 1983 — UNITED STATES — Four alleged members of the Armed Front for National Liberation (FALN) plotted to bomb an army reserve center and a Marine training center on this date. In a raid at the end of June, the four had been arrested. Their arrest led to the discovery of arms and explosives, believed intended for the July 4 attack. A United States District Court judge in Chicago found the four — Edwin Cortes, Alejandrina Torres, Alberto Rodriguez, and Jose Luis Rodriguez — guilty of conspiracy. Sentencing was set for October 4, 1985. Three of the defendants were sentenced to 35 years for seditious conspiracy. A fourth defendant received a suspended sentence and five years probation. 83070402–03

July 5, 1983 — JAPAN — The Senki faction of Kyosando, an ultraleft-wing group, claimed responsibility for five bomb attacks in and around Tokyo to protest the planned visits of the United States battleship *New Jersey* and the United States nuclear-powered aircraft carrier *Carl Vinson*. Molotov cocktails and time ignition devices were used against United States military bases in Yokota and Yokosuka. A pipeline facility for the new Tokyo International Airport was also a target. There were no reports of injuries or damage. 83070501–02

July 5, 1983 — USSR — Two men attempted to hijack a flight from Moscow to Tallin. One of the hijackers told a stewardess that there was a bomb aboard and that his accomplice was prepared to detonate it unless the plane was flown to London or Oslo. The hijackers agreed to a refueling stop in what they believed was Kotka, Finland, but was actually Leningrad. Once the deception was discovered while on the ground, one hijacker shouted to the other, who was holding two wires attached to the alleged bomb, to blow up the plane. It was then that security guards, who had entered the plane, shot the man holding the bomb. The injured hijacker died, while the other was arrested. No one else was hurt. 83070503

July 6, 1983 — COLOMBIA — The pro-Castro National Liberation Army (ELN) claimed responsibility for three dynamite explosions that caused no injuries. One explosion occurred in the Salvadoran consulate in Medellin and resulted in considerable property damage. The other two bombs were directed at a police post and at the Criminological Studies Department, both of which are in the suburb of Aranjuez. An anonymous caller warned a Medellin radio station of the three attacks. The caller threatened future attacks on the Chilean consulate in Medellin and on police stations in a terrorist campaign called Free Central America Operation. 83070601

July 6, 1983 — IRAN — Six Iranians, armed with machine guns and explosives, hijacked an Islamic Republic of Iran airliner with 372 passengers and 18 crew on board. The Boeing 747 was seized while airborne, enroute from Shiraz to Tehran on an internal flight. At 8:30 P.M., the plane was allowed to land at Kuwait International Airport, where it was parked at the end of a runway and then surrounded by Kuwaiti security personnel. The hijackers, who included 2 deserters from the Iranian Army, initially demanded food and fuel for the release of 60 hostages. Negotiations continued between Kuwaiti officials and the hijackers. The Iranian ambassador in Kuwait, 'Ali Shams Ardakani, joined the negotiators at the airport. After four hours, a deal was struck in which the hijackers released 186 passengers (women, children, and the elderly) in exchange for fuel to fly to Paris. At 2:00 A.M. on July 7, the plane took off with 204 men on board. The plane landed at Orly Airport at 7:40 A.M. and was immediately surrounded by French security forces (GIGN). In response to the hijackers' threat to blow up the plane, the security forces agreed to the demand to pull back. Shortly thereafter, the hijackers released 6 additional hostages, who included the copilot and 5 passengers, suffering from acute shock. Negotiations were carried on by radio between the 6 hijackers and Massoud Rajavi, the Paris-based exiled leader of the Iranian opposition group, Mojahedin-e Khalq. The hijackers claimed to be members of this group. Moreover, they claimed to have hijacked the plane as a protest against the Iranian government. After two hours of negotiations, the hijackers finally released the remaining hostages and gave themselves up. The government of Iran demanded their extradition. In a strongly worded statement, Iran's speaker of the parliament Hojjat ol-Eslam Akbar Hashemi-Rafsanjani blamed the United States, Kuwait, France, Saudi Arabia, Iraq, and others for the hijacking. The French government announced that they planned to put the hijackers on trial and later would consider granting them political asylum. No one was injured in the hijacking, which lasted over 14 hours. 83070602

July 7, 1983 — CYPRUS — British troops were placed on alert after receiving reports of a possible attack on the British radar installation at Troodos.

July 7, 1983 — LEBANON — Prime Minister Shafiq al-Wazzan escaped injury in an apparent assassination attempt. The prime minister's motorcade had passed by a Honda Civic station wagon, parked near the residence of Deputy Fu'ad Lahhud. A minute later, as the motorcade entered the government house gate some one hundred meters away, the Honda Civic exploded and burst into flames. Only about 5 kilograms of the 70 kilograms of explosives had detonated. Nevertheless, several vehicles were destroyed and windows in the vicinity were broken. No injuries were reported. Authorities speculated that several casualties would have resulted had the entire explosive charge detonated.

July 7, 1983 — UNITED STATES — Robert Patrick Richter, an American in his early 20s, hijacked Air Florida flight 8, enroute from Miami to Tampa with 42 passengers and 5 crew members on board. Once airborne, Richter handed a note to a stewardess, which read: "This is a hijacking. I have an explosive device. Take the plane to Habana [sic] Cuba now! Liberty or death. Power to the revolution." Throughout the remainder of the flight to Havana, Richter sat silently holding a gym bag containing a cylinder with wires running to a push-button device. The alleged bomb was a hoax. Upon landing in Havana at 8:41 A.M., Richter was arrested by Cuban security forces. The plane was allowed to return to Miami at 10:05 A.M. carrying 41 passengers and 5 crew, none of whom were harmed. Cuba had announced on July 6 that hijackers would face jail sentences of up to 40 years. 83070701

July 7, 1983 — JAPAN — At 6:30 A.M., seven hundred police officers from Tokyo and elsewhere searched 58 homes in Chiba prefecture. The search was directed at the residences of suspected members of Chukaku-ha (Middle Core Faction), which claimed responsibility for the June 7, 1983, arson attack on a construction company involved in the Narita Airport pipeline project. The search supposedly uncovered incriminating evidence.

July 7, 1983 — COLOMBIA — Four armed members of the National Liberation Army (ELN) occupied the AGENCE FRANCE-PRESSE office in Bogota. The occupiers included three men and a woman, who painted signs on the walls alluding to the Manuel Vasquez Castano command. Manuel was a founder of the ELN. No injuries or arrests were reported in the short-lived occupation. 83070702

July 7, 1983 — COLOMBIA — A bomb left at the Chilean consulate in Medellin was deactivated. The Peoples Liberation Army (EPL) claimed responsibility for the attack, which they linked to Operation Free Central America. Another bomb exploded at a gas station. 83070703

July 8, 1983 — UNITED STATES — Clelia Eleanor Quinones, wife of former Salvadoran ambassador Roberto Quinones Meza, was kidnapped by three men at 4:50 P.M. outside her Miami suburb home. She was bound and then driven to an apartment at 2327 15th Street NW in Washington, D.C., where she was held for $1.5 million ransom. Once he was contacted by the kidnappers, her husband alerted the Federal Bureau of Investigation (FBI), which placed a wiretap on the Quinones's phones. On July 10, the abductors made a call from a Miami pay phone to the Quinones's residence. Federal Bureau of Investigation agents, who traced the call, managed to get to the pay phone in time to spot the caller, Juan Caceres. Caceres's phone calls eventually led agents to a phone booth outside the Pitts Hotel at 1451

Belmont Street NW in Washington, D.C. On July 14, the FBI freed
Quinones and arrested two kidnappers. The arrest came at 10:00 P.M. after
the kidnappers had taken Quinones to the phone booth outside the Pitts
Hotel so that she could contact her husband to prove that she was still alive.
No one was injured in the rescue.

In total, eight people were arrested following further investigations,
including Guatemalans Juan Caceres and his wife, Dora Ileana Caceres,
Jennifer Brown, Mack Lewis Carr, Robert Anthony Gerald, Clifford Bibbs,
and Craig Blas. Dora Caceres held diplomatic rank of third secretary to the
Guatemalan mission to the Organization of American States. When the
Guatemalan government learned of the crime, it waived her diplomatic
immunity. The other five arrested in Washington, D.C., were nearby residents who had formed an agreement with the Cacereses to participate in the
kidnapping. The kidnapped woman was held in Jennifer Brown's apartment. In Miami, Guillermo Salvador Lacayo, a Salvadoran, was charged
with helping to abduct Quinones. Charges leveled against Lacayo's sister,
Margarita Guadalupe Lacayo, were later dropped. On December 2, 1983,
Lacayo, the alleged ringleader, was sentenced to two life terms. The Washington residents pleaded guilty and cooperated with the investigation. Craig
Blas, a 16-year-old, received a sentence of no more than 6 years in a youth-
ful offender facility. Mack Lewis Carr was sentenced to a maximum of 4
years; Clifford Bibbs was sentenced to 15 years; and Jennifer Brown was
sentenced to 2½ years. Only Juan Caceres, Dora Caceres, and Guillermo
Salvador Lacayo pleaded not guilty. 83070801

July 10, 1983 — IRAN — Irac Ghazali, an Iranian pilot seeking political asylum in the United States, flew an F-5 jet fighter from Tabriz into Turkish
airspace. The plane landed at Van in eastern Turkey and returned to Iran
after an Iranian pilot had been flown to Van. Ghazali remained in the
custody of Turkish authorities, pending the United States response to his
asylum request.

July 11, 1983 — COLOMBIA — Eight students — two women and six men —
from the medical school at the Free University of Cali occupied peacefully
the Panamanian embassy, located north of Bogota. The students wanted
their internships at the Rafael Uribe Hospital reinstated. Reports indicated
that the students had also requested political asylum in Panama. After four
hours of negotiations, carried on between the students and embassy officials, police, and security officers, the students left for an undisclosed destination. The negotiated agreement was not revealed. 83071101

July 11, 1983 — CORSICA — Ten explosions were reported at police buildings
and property owned by French mainlanders. No one claimed responsibility
for the blasts, which caused property damage but no injuries. This was the

first bombing campaign since the disappearance on June 17, 1983, of Guy Orsini, who headed the Corsican National Liberation Front.

July 11, 1983 — PERU — The Shining Path guerrillas were thought responsible for an armed attack against the women's branch of the ruling Popular Action Party. Two people were killed and 30 wounded in the machine-gun and dynamite assault on the party's main headquarters. On the same day, 15 bombings without injuries were reported in Lima. On July 12, the government mobilized 15,000 people to wage war against the leftist terrorists responsible. Over 500 people were reported to have been detained for questioning.

July 13, 1983 — UNITED KINGDOM — By a margin of 116 votes, the British parliament defeated a motion to restore hanging in terrorist cases. The vote coincided with a day of violence in Ulster that left six persons dead. Four militiamen, members of the Protestant Ulster Defense Regiment, died when their vehicle hit a five-hundred-pound land mine, and two Catholics, suspected of informing, were murdered in Armagh. The Irish Republican Army claimed responsibility for the land mine and is suspected in the murder of the Catholics.

July 13, 1983 — EL SALVADOR — New security procedures were ordered by the United States embassy following death threats issued against Americans working in El Salvador. The threats came from the Popular Liberation Forces, which had claimed responsibility for the May 25 assassination of Navy lieutenant commander Albert Schaufelberger. Embassy military and civil personnel were advised not to jog in public places, frequent nightclubs, or allow themselves to be photographed. 83071301

July 13, 1983 — JORDAN — 'Aziz 'Umar ash-Shunayb, a Libyan envoy to Jordan, defected and revealed a plan of Qaddafi's to assassinate King Hussein. According to the envoy, surface-to-air (SAM) missiles were to be placed near the airports at Amman and Aqaba and were to be fired at Hussein's plane after takeoff. An unnamed second Arab country was to help in the plot but later refused to take part. 83071302

July 14, 1983 — BELGIUM — Dursun Aksoy, an administrative attache in the Turkish embassy in Brussels, was shot twice in the head as he sat in his car before departing for work. In fleeing the scene, the gunman, Husnu Gol, dropped the .22 caliber revolver used to kill the diplomat. On July 22, Gol was arrested in the Netherlands. He was later extradited to Belgium to face trial. Three groups had claimed responsibility for the assassination, including the Armenian Secret Army for the Liberation of Armenia (ASALA), the Justice Commando of Armenian Genocide, and the Armenian Revolutionary Army. 83071401

July 15, 1983 — PEOPLE'S REPUBLIC OF CHINA — Hu Guichao, the ringleader of a gang trading in women and children, received the death penalty. Another member of the gang, Xiao Tangquan, was sentenced to life imprisonment. Of the remaining 63 people arrested on November 25, 1982, 30 individuals were given sentences ranging from 2½ years to 20 years; 22 were released after receiving a moral lecture; 6 were sent to a reeducation program; and 5 were still being tried. The kidnapping ring abducted women from Sichuan and Shaanxi provinces and shipped them through the railway center at Anyang. Customers included bachelors in need of a wife.

July 15, 1983 — FRANCE — In Toulouse, offices of two companies working on the construction of the Golfech nuclear reactor sustained heavy damage from bombs. Responsibility for the bombings was claimed by an antinuclear group.

July 15, 1983 — SYRIA — Sabri al-Banna, leader of the Abu Nidal group, set up an information office on a side street near the diplomatic missions in Damascus. The opening of the office indicated the first attempt by the Abu Nidal group, founded in 1973, to begin public relations. Informed intelligence sources in Damascus believed that Abu Nidal had three other offices in Damascus and maintained a training camp in the Syrian-controlled Bekaa Valley in Lebanon. Abu Nidal's open attacks against Arafat followed dissension and mutiny in Arafat's Palestine Liberation Organization.

July 15, 1983 — ITALY — Toni Negri, an Italian terrorist suspect, took his seat in the Italian parliament amid protests stemming from his parliamentary immunity. He was elected on the Radical party ticket by voters who were outraged by his four-year imprisonment while the government prepared its case against him. His election put a stop to his pending trial on terrorist charges, which included robbery, murder of a policeman, and involvement in the kidnapping and accidental death of Milanese heir Carlo Saronio.

July 15, 1983 — FRANCE — A bomb placed among bags in the main hall of Orly Airport's south terminal exploded, killing 8 and wounding 53, some seriously. The one-pound bomb attached to a gas bottle was within four meters of the Turkish Airlines counter, the apparent target of the attack. Those killed included Anthony Peter Schultze, an American, Jean-Claude Blanchard, a Frenchman, and Halit Milmoz, a Turk. The wounded included 38 Turks, 11 French citizens, 2 Yugoslavs, 1 Swede, and 1 Algerian. An anonymous caller representing the Armenian Secret Army for the Liberation of Armenia (ASALA) claimed responsibility for the bomb in phone calls to the Athens and Paris offices of the AGENCE FRANCE-PRESSE.

On July 18, the French police detained 51 people suspected of ties to Armenian militant circles. The raids also uncovered automatic guns, detonators, and a kilo of explosives. Varadjian Garbidjan, a Syrian, was among those arrested. Garbidjan was believed to head the military wing of the ASALA in France. Of those arrested, 20 persons were deported to Turkey and 11, including Garbidjan, were held for trial on terrorist activities. Shortly after his arrest, Garbidjan admitted planting the bomb at Orly Airport but could not accurately describe where the bomb had been placed. On July 29, Garbidjan renounced his confession before a judge in Paris and claimed that his confession was motivated to protect those arrested. The Turkish government asked that the 11 charged be extradited to Turkey.

On October 8, the French police arrested another 7 persons thought responsible for the bombing: Six Armenian suspects were arrested in Paris, and Nayir Souner, believed to have made the bomb, was arrested in Marseilles. On December 21, 1983, 5 of the Armenians arrested were found guilty of activities connected with the Orly Airport bombing. 83071501

July 17, 1983 — UNITED STATES — Delta flight 722, enroute from Miami to Tampa with 107 aboard, was hijacked to Cuba. The hijacking occurred shortly after takeoff when one hijacker seized a stewardess and held a knife to her throat. Another hijacker ignited an aerosol spray to indicate a threat of fire if the plane was not diverted. About an hour later, the plane landed in Havana where seven people were arrested by Cuban authorities. Those arrested included a teenage boy and a 12-year-old girl who had accompanied the hijackers. The plane flew to Tampa 3½ hours later. No one was injured. 83071701

July 18, 1983 — JORDAN — 'Aziz 'Umar ash-Shunayb, a Libyan envoy who defected to Jordan on July 13, claimed today that Imam Musa as-Sadr, head of the Lebanese Shiite Moslem community, was assassinated in 1978 with two aides while guests of the Tripoli government. Ash-Shunayb accused Qaddafi of the killings. In Beirut, Nabih Birri, leader of the Lebanese Shiite movement, denied the charges and stated that as-Sadr was still alive. Neither as-Sadr nor his two aides had been seen since their disappearance in Tripoli in 1978.

July 19, 1983 — PANAMA — In a phone call to the United States embassy, the Vanguard Panamanian Liberation Movement (MVLP) indicated that it considered the United States an ally in its struggle. The MVLP had claimed responsibility for a recent bombing campaign in Panama City.

July 19, 1983 — UNITED STATES — The second United States commercial airliner in two days was hijacked to Cuba. The L-1011, enroute from New York to Miami, was just 40 miles from Miami when it was hijacked. 83071901

July 20, 1983 – UNITED STATES – A study by David E. Kaplan of the Center for Investigative Reporting listed 37 accidents involving reactors of nuclear-powered naval ships in the past 30 years. The Kaplan study refuted the Navy's claim that "there has never been an accident involving a naval reactor, or any release of radioactivity which has had a significant effect on individuals or the environment." The Navy issued a detailed statement disputing the Kaplan study. The sinking of the nuclear submarine *Thresher* with 129 crewmen was the worst accident cited in the study. The *Thresher* sank east of Boston on April 10, 1963.

July 20, 1983 – ITALY – Mario Tuti, Luciano Franci, and Piero Malentacchi were found innocent of involvement in a 1974 train bombing that killed 12 and injured 48. The 20-month trial of the 3 right-wing extremists ended on grounds of insufficient evidence. This was the second such trial of suspects in the bombing that ended in acquittal.

July 20, 1983 – LEBANON – A lone man parked an explosive-packed car in Beirut's seaside resort complex and fled on foot after shooting two guards to death. The ensuing blast caused a conflagration to the main building of the complex. At least 16 people were injured in the parking lot and in the building.

July 21, 1983 – IRAN – A caller claiming to represent the Armenian Secret Army for the Liberation of Armenia (ASALA) threatened French interests throughout the world unless the 11 people charged in the July 15 bombing of Orly Airport were released unconditionally. The phone call was received by AGENCE FRANCE-PRESSE offices in Tehran. 83072101

July 21, 1983 – IRAN – No one was injured when two grenades were thrown at the French embassy's trade office in Tehran. In another incident without injuries, an explosion damaged the Tehran offices of Air France. The Armenian Secret Army for the Liberation of Armenia (ASALA) claimed responsibility for both attacks in a phone call to the AGENCE FRANCE-PRESSE and threatened further actions if those arrested in connection with the July 15 bombing of Orly Airport were not released. 83072102–04

July 21, 1983 – UNITED STATES – Northwest Orient flight 714, enroute from Tampa to Miami with 90 passengers and 7 crew, was the scene of a foiled hijacking. Rodolfo Bueno Cruz, an ex-political prisoner from Cuba, seized a stewardess and threatened her with a knife that was overlooked in a body and baggage search prior to boarding. In response to the hijacker's demand, the plane was diverted to Cuba. Within 60 miles of Havana, 2 passengers jumped Cruz and, aided by a punch from the stewardess, wrestled him to the ground. Once the hijacker was securely bound by seat belts, the plane changed course for Miami. Federal Bureau of Investigation agents arrested Cruz upon landing. He was charged with air piracy, which carried a maximum sentence of life imprisonment. 83072105

July 22, 1983 — ST. LUCIA— Prime Minister John Compton accused the left-wing opposition Progressive Labour Party (PLP) of having recruited 18 St. Lucian men and women to be trained as terrorists in camps in Libya. Compton accused Qaddafi of having financed the operation in order to eventually make St. Lucia a satellite. The PLP denounced the accusations.

July 22, 1983 — UNITED STATES— Eduardo Arocena, alleged leader of the anti-Castro terrorist group Omega-7, was apprehended in the Little Havana district of Miami. He was wanted on charges of interstate transportation of explosives connected with the failed attempt to assassinate Raul Roa-Kouri, the Cuban ambassador to the United Nations. The assassination was foiled when the bomb, attached to Roa's car, fell off before the assassins could detonate it. New York sanitation workers later found the device. Omega-7 had claimed responsibility for more than 30 bombings involving diplomatic offices and newspapers in the New York and Miami area. Federal agents seized 30 guns and materials to make bombs when arresting Arocena in Miami. On December 29, 1983, Arocena was indicted on 14 bombing or attempted bombing charges. Other indictments were pending.

July 22, 1983 — UNITED STATES— Four Provisional Irish Republican Army supporters— Gabriel Megahey, Colum Meehan, Eamon Meehan, and Andrew Duggan— were sentenced to two- to seven-year prison terms for plotting to smuggle guns, explosives, and surface-to-air missiles from New York to the IRA in Northern Ireland. All the contraband acquired by the men was seized in May 1982 before its planned shipment. The men had never managed to obtain missiles or explosives.

July 22, 1983 — PANAMA— National Guard members deactivated a small explosive device left in a trash can at a classroom of the Pan-American Institute in Panama City. Anonymous threats were also phoned to the National Cash Register Company and to a furniture store, Ana de la Americana, but the threats proved to be a hoax. 83072201–02

July 22, 1983 — CHILE— In Santiago, the Honduran embassy sustained minor damage when unknown persons fired at the building. 83072203

July 23, 1983 — LEBANON — The MIDDLE EAST TELEVISION mobile van, owned and operated by the CHRISTIAN BROADCASTING NETWORK, was destroyed by a large car bomb planted in a Pontiac parked beside the van. Nearby vehicles were also destroyed. No one was injured.

July 24, 1983 — UNITED STATES — A Southwest Airlines Boeing 737, enroute from Phoenix to Albuquerque, returned to Phoenix minutes after takeoff when a bomb threat was phoned into the airline. No bomb was found.

July 24, 1983 — IRAN — A crude bomb, hurled at the French embassy trade office in north Tehran, caused minor damage and no injuries. The same office had suffered a similar attack on July 21. Incidents directed at French interests had been threatened by the Armenian Secret Army for the Liberation of Armenia (ASALA), following the arrest of ASALA members in connection with the July 15 bombing of Orly Airport. 83072401

July 27, 1983 — ISRAEL — Three masked gunmen fired Kalashnikov submachine guns at students milling about a courtyard at the Hebron Islamic College. The assailants also threw a grenade in the attack that killed 3, including 2 teachers, and wounded 30. Later, Israeli Defense Forces killed an Arab girl in a rock-throwing demonstration, sparked by the murders earlier in the day. Menachem Livni, 40, Shaul Nir, 33, and Uzi Sharabaf, 35, were arrested for the gun and grenade attack and sentenced to life imprisonment. On March 27, 1987, President Chaim Herzog commuted the sentences to 24 years each.

July 27, 1983 — UNITED STATES — Eight men — Abbott Van Backer, Alan G. Harvey, Robert B. Krejcik, William Moravcik, Oldrich Pastorek, Honza Klugar, Mirek Zavadil, and Dennis Mach — were charged by federal authorities in Manhattan for conspiring to sell $2 billion of sophisticated weapons to Iran and $15 million of machine guns to the Irish Republican Army (IRA). The charges came after an eight-month investigation by the Bureau of Alcohol, Tobacco and Firearms, whose agents posed as representatives of Iran and the IRA. The masterminds of the conspiracy included Backer, Harvey, and Krejcik. The other five defendants were believed to be independent middlemen, engaged in weapons transactions between the manufacturer and the buyer. At the time of the arrests, authorities seized over one hundred machine guns intended for shipment to the IRA.

July 27, 1983 — LEBANON — At 10:15 P.M., a car bomb exploded outside the Fatah offices in Tripoli. An unknown number of persons were killed and injured.

July 27, 1983 – IRAN – A twin-engine Aero Commander with three Iranians aboard made an emergency landing at Bahrain International Airport. After refueling, the plane took off for an undisclosed destination.

July 27, 1983 – UNITED STATES – Antonio Jarquin, the Nicaraguan ambassador to the United States, stated in an interview with BARRICADA that, "In fact, our efforts stress a policy of moderation, of attaining understanding by all possible means, but we find ourselves in an atmosphere of hostility. The threats made by telephone, the bomb threats to all our personnel, keep us in a virtually constant state of tension." The allegations of threats were not substantiated. Further details of the alleged threats were never disclosed.

July 27, 1983 – FRANCE – In a Paris suburb, a bomb caused substantial damage to the Armenian Center. No one was injured.

July 27, 1983 – PORTUGAL – At 10:30 A.M., two cars filled with weapons and explosives drove up to the Turkish embassy on the outskirts of Lisbon. Five armed men left the cars and approached the embassy building. Security guards began to fire on the assailants, killing one of them. One security guard was wounded in the legs during this exchange of gunfire. The remaining four terrorists ran down the driveway and entered the nearby residence of the charge d'affaires, Mustafa Michcioglu, whose wife and son were taken hostage. In a bid to free the hostages, a policeman entered an upper-story window, and he also was seized. In a typewritten message left earlier that day in a REUTERS news agency mail box, the terrorists, who identified themselves as members of the Armenian Revolutionary Army (ARA), stated, "We have decided to blow up this building and remain under the collapse. This is not suicide nor an expression of insanity, but rather our sacrifice to the altar of freedom." "This building" was apparently a reference to the embassy. At noon, approximately an hour after the seige began, the gunmen set off a large bomb and a series of smaller explosions, which started a fire on the upper floor. The residence had already been surrounded by 170 members of the Portuguese special police force GOES (Group for Special Operations). Not until 1:40 P.M. did the GOES forces storm the building, where they found the charred bodies of the four terrorists and the policeman on the upper floor. Cahide Michcioglu, the charge d'affaires' wife, had been seriously injured in the blast and died later in the hospital. Michcioglu's son had been shot in the leg and had escaped shortly after the blast by leaping off a first-floor balcony of the burning building.

The terrorists were later identified as Strak Onnik Ajamian, Ara Hovsel Karvikian, Sarkis Abrahamian, Simon Khacher Yahniyon, and Vatch Navar Tagihitan, whose ages ranged between 19 and 21 years. Authorities believed that the five had entered through Lisbon Airport as tourists bearing Lebanese passports, one of which had expired in March 1983. One of the two cars, a Ford Escort, had been spotted at the embassy the day before by security guards. When challenged by the guards, the two men in the Escort claimed that they had come to apply for visas but left in haste when they could not produce their passports.

The seige of the ambassador's residence induced Portuguese authorities to reevaluate their security measures around foreign embassies. The use of GOES forces in the incident marked the first time that the British-trained commandos had been deployed.

On August 13, the Commando for the Defense of Western Civilization (CODECO) sent pictures of an alleged sixth attacker to the AGENCE FRANCE-PRESSE office in Hong Kong. The CODECO letter identified ARA member Jhosepian as the sixth terrorist. The allegations were never confirmed. 83072701

July 28, 1983 — TURKEY— In an interview on British television, Turkish foreign minister Ilter Turkmen denied reports that Turkish secret police were engaged in action against Armenian terrorists in Western Europe. Turkmen called on other countries to cooperate in stemming the campaign currently waged by Armenian terrorists against Turks.

July 29, 1983 — UNITED STATES— Three explosions at Hotel Rajneesh in downtown Portland, Oregon, injured two, including the suspected terrorist. Stephen P. Paster, who was charged with first-degree arson, was seriously injured with burns to his hands, arms, face, and torso. A policeman suffered minor injuries from smoke inhalation. The incident was related to growing hostility against guru Bhagwan Shree Rajneesh and his followers who had purchased large landholdings in Oregon.

July 29, 1983 — IRAN— Threats to blow up the French embassy in Tehran were made to the AGENCE FRANCE-PRESSE by an anonymous caller from the Orly Group. 83072901

July 30, 1983 — FRANCE— An anonymous caller from the Armenian Secret Army for the Liberation of Armenia (ASALA) telephoned the Orly Airport at 9:30 A.M. to claim that a bomb had been planted on an Air-Inter domestic flight that had departed at 9:15 A.M. Because two Air-Inter flights had departed then, both flights were ordered to make emergency landings. A Caravelle flight to Rennes with 110 people landed at its original destination; an Airbus flight to Toulon with 314 people landed at Lyons. No bombs were found. 83073001

July 30, 1983 — PORTUGAL— An anonymous caller to AGENCE FRANCE-

PRESSE threatened to kill a person close to Portuguese prime minister Mario Soares in retaliation for the deaths of five members of the Armenian Revolutionary Army (ARA) during their July 27 assault on the Turkish embassy in Lisbon. The caller said that he spoke for the ARA, which held the prime minister responsible for the police attack that led to the five deaths. 83073002

July 30–31, 1983 — FRANCE — Clashes between the Tamils and the Sinhalese, two Sri Lanka ethnic groups, left two Tamils dead in Paris. One Tamil was pushed to his death from a window on July 30, and the other was stabbed to death in a Paris underground station on July 31.

August 1983 — EL SALVADOR — Carroll Ishee, an American fighting on the side of leftist guerrillas, was killed by gunfire from a government helicopter. Ishee was a member of the Democratic Revolutionary Front, the rebel's political wing.

August 1983 — INDIA — Sukhbir Singh Khalsa and Baljit Singh Rana, two Sikh activists arrested later in February 1984, admitted to carrying out a grenade attack against the Soviet embassy in New Dehli. The attack resulted in minor damage and no injuries. 83089901

August 2, 1983 — POLAND — Crewmen overpowered Slawomir K. when he tried at knifepoint to commandeer a hydrofoil enroute from Szczecin to Swinoujscie. The hijacker wanted to divert the craft to Sweden. Slawomir was arrested.

August 2, 1983 — LEBANON — A group of United States Marines, out on a jog, were shot at by unidentified gunmen. No one was injured in the incident that occurred at the perimeter of their encampment near Beirut International Airport. 83080201

August 2, 1983 — UNITED STATES — Alfredo Ayala, a Cuban national, attempted to hijack Pan American Airlines flight 925, a Boeing 727, enroute from Miami to Houston with 121 passengers and 7 crew on board. Twenty minutes into the flight a struggle between a flight attendant and Ayala ensued when Ayala tried to force his way into the cockpit. Spicer Lung and his son, with an assist from Ralph Symons, acted quickly to subdue the would-be hijacker and bound him with belts to a seat for the flight's duration. Mr. Lung, who had been recently laid off by Pan American, was the real hero in thwarting the hijacking. When questioned about his bravery, Mr. Lung answered, "I didn't want to go to Cuba. I just had to do something to stop him. I wasn't sure whether he was armed, but I'm not scared of a weapon." Ralph Symons, a Miami trial lawyer, said, "I figured, I may go but I'm not going without a struggle." Symons disclosed that the 3 passengers dealt harshly with the hijacker, who "was happy to get to the FBI." Ayala was taken into custody by 5 marshals once the plane landed two hours later in Houston. He was charged with air piracy and interference with a flight crew; both are felony charges. No weapon was found on the hijacker. Pan American announced that Mr. Lung would be found another job with the airline. 83080202

August 3, 1983 — ETHIOPIA — The Tigrean People's Liberation Front (TPLF) kidnapped 10 Swiss nationals at Jari, 280 miles north of Addis Ababa. Six of those abducted worked at an orphanage set up by Terre Des Hommes, a humanitarian organization. The other 4 were relatives of the 6. On August 28, the 10 hostages were released unharmed near Makele, the capital of Tigre province. 83080301

August 4, 1983 — LESOTHO — At 12:40 P.M., a car parked in downtown Maseru on a vacant building site on Constitution Road exploded with great force minutes after Lesotho's prime minister, Chief Leabua Jonathan, had driven past on his way to lunch. The blast caused damage to windows in the vicinity, but no one was injured in the apparent assassination attempt. The car had a Republic of South Africa license plate from the Orange Free State. In a statement issued the next day, the South African government rejected claims by Lesotho that South Africa was responsible. 83080401

August 4, 1983 — PUERTO RICO — Capitol Air flight 236, enroute from San Juan to Miami with 248 passengers and 10 crew, was hijacked to Cuba for the third time in 1983. At 7:05 P.M., shortly after takeoff, a Spanish-speaking passenger splashed gasoline in the rear of the passenger compartment after sending a note to the cockpit demanding to be flown to Havana. The DC-8 was diverted and landed safely in Havana at 8:42 P.M. The hijacker, who was also armed with a handgun, gave himself up without a struggle to Cuban authorities. Reports indicated that the hijacker was a Cuban who had 6 children in Cuba. After the hijacking, the Federal Aviation Administration (FAA) announced that more rigorous security screening procedures had been installed at both the San Juan and Miami airports. The FAA noted that since 1961 there had been 116 successful hijackings of United States planes and 110 unsuccessful hijackings. 83080402

August 5, 1983 — PEOPLE'S REPUBLIC OF CHINA — The trial of Peng Zwei, Xu Limin, and Xu Zhiping opened in the Wuhan Intermediate People's Court. On March 12, 1983, the three were arrested when their attempt to hijack a ship, enroute from Wuhan to Qingdao, failed.

August 5, 1983 — LEBANON — A massive car bomb outside the Al-Baqqar

Mosque in Tripoli killed 19 and injured 38. The blast occurred at 1:00 P.M. just as worshippers were leaving the mosque following Friday services. The mosque is located in a pro-Syrian neighborhood in the Ash-Sha'rani quarter of Al-Qubbah. No one claimed responsibility. In a statement, the leader of the fundamentalist Islamic Unity Party accused "agents" of the Lebanese government and the Christian Phalangist Party, headed by the father of Lebanese president Amin Gemayel. Government investigations suggested that a local organization with "external ties" carried out the bombing in retaliation for the recent murders of Rajab Su'ayfan and 'Abd al-Qadir.

In Beirut, a powerful blast toppled a five-story residential building in Ain Rummaneh, killing one and injuring nine in this Christian neighborhood. No one claimed responsibility.

These two bombings came as President Ronald Reagan's new Middle East envoy, Robert C. McFarlane, indicated that he would soon be meeting with Syrian officials in Damascus in the hopes of ending the bloodshed in Lebanon. Syria was unwilling to withdraw its Lebanese troops unless Israel unconditionally withdrew its troops.

August 5, 1983 — THAILAND — After receiving unconfirmed reports that two Armenian terrorists had entered its borders, the Thai government increased security outside the Turkish embassy in Bangkok.

August 6, 1983 — REPUBLIC OF SOUTH AFRICA — A synagogue, the Temple of Israel on the corner of Claim and Paul Nel streets in Hillbrow, Johannesburg, sustained extensive damage from a bomb. The blast came at 5:57 A.M. on the same morning when Marais Viljoen, the state president, was to attend a ceremony marking the 50th anniversary of progressive Judaism at the temple. Security police suspected that the bomb was meant to assassinate Viljoen and other dignitaries. The African National Congress (ANC) was suspected when limpet mine remnants were discovered in the debris. In previous bombings, the ANC had used limpet mines. From London, an ANC spokesman denied any responsibility.

August 7, 1983 — IRELAND — The Irish Police Antiterrorist Special Task Force foiled an attempt to kidnap Galen Weston, president of George Weston, a Toronto-based food conglomerate. After receiving a tip, the task force sent its men to Weston's Wicklow estate. In the early morning, seven gunmen approached the residence and engaged the forces in gunfire, which seriously wounded four of the attackers. No police were injured and no group claimed responsibility for the attempted kidnapping.

August 7, 1983 — LEBANON — A car packed with 220 pounds of dynamite exploded at noon outside the fruit and vegetable market in Baalbek, a Shiite Moslem town located in the Bekaa Valley some 35 miles east of

Beirut. The blast killed 35, injured 125, and caused extensive damage to nearby vehicles and buildings. The Front for the Liberation of Lebanon from Foreigners claimed responsibility in a letter. Although the group has taken credit for previous bombings, no firm evidence has ever proven the group's existence. Two Syrian soldiers were among the dead, who were mostly Lebanese.

August 7, 1983 — IRAN — In a phone call to AGENCE FRANCE-PRESSE, the Orly Group claimed responsibility for two bombs that exploded in offices in the French embassy used by Egyptian interests. The offices and a car parked outside were damaged, but no one was injured. This was the third incident in three weeks to French diplomatic buildings. 83080701

August 7, 1983 — FEDERAL REPUBLIC OF GERMANY — A bomb caused $75,000 damage to a United States officer's club near Hahn Air Force Base in the Rhine-Hunsrueck district. No one was injured in the blast, later claimed by Venceremos Beginning of Autumn. In a letter sent to the HUNSRUECK-FORUM newspaper, the self-proclaimed perpetrators stated that "38 years after Hiroshima we have attacked the officer's club at Hahn U.S. Air Force Base." 83080702

August 9, 1983 — FRANCE — The Air Algerie offices in Marseilles sustained extensive damage from a bomb, claimed by the Charles Martel group. No one was injured. 83080901

August 10/15, 1983 — ANGOLA — On August 10, the National Union for the Total Independence of Angola (UNITA) hit an Antonov aircraft in the Cangamba region in Moxico Province during a government offensive against rebel positions. The damaged plane landed safely. On August 15, UNITA claimed to have killed 11 government soldiers and a Portuguese priest during an assault on a military and civilian convoy on the road connecting Lubango and Bengul. The group indicated that it released two other Portuguese nationals and destroyed seven military vehicles. The claims were made in a letter sent to the Lisbon offices of AGENCE FRANCE-PRESSE on August 23. 83081501

August 10, 1983 — LEBANON — Druze militiamen abducted three Lebanese cabinet ministers who had traveled to the Druze stronghold in the mountains to mediate between the Druze and the government. On the next day, the three were released unharmed from Al-Mukhtarah Palace after complex negotiations involving an Israeli general, the Druze, and the Lebanese government. The government agreed to Druze demands to give Moslem interests a greater role in the affairs of state. The three ministers were Pierre al-Khuri, 'Adnan Muruwwah, and 'Adil Hamiyah. Walid Jumblatt, leader of the Druze, is believed to have ordered the detention and the subsequent release.

August 10, 1983 — IRAN — In Tehran, a bomb attached to an embassy staff member's car exploded on the French embassy grounds, causing considerable damage but no injuries. An Armenian terrorist group claimed responsibility in a phone call to AGENCE FRANCE-PRESSE. 83081001

August 10, 1983 — LEBANON — The Progressive Socialists shelled the Beirut International Airport, its vicinity, and the Khaldah-Al-Awza'i road. Two Lebanese, a woman and a 4-year-old girl, died and eight others, including a United States Marine, were injured in the early morning incident. Over 20 shells were reportedly fired. 83081002

August 11, 1983 — LEBANON — In Beirut, the Air France offices in the Nadiyah Salmon building escaped damage when only the detonator connected to a 1-kilogram bomb exploded. No one claimed responsibility. 83081101

August 12, 1983 — ARGENTINA — The United States rock group Kiss canceled a planned tour after threats were issued by several right-wing groups to bomb the Buenos Aires football stadium where Kiss was scheduled to perform. The extremists objected to the group's image of sex, drugs, and rock and roll.

August 12, 1983 — UNITED STATES — In Surf, California, a sheriff's deputy and highway patrol officers arrested a man brandishing a knife, who tried unsuccessfully to hijack an Amtrak passenger train enroute from Los Angeles to Sacramento. No one was injured.

August 12, 1983 — FRANCE — A bomb destroyed a statue of Pontius Pilate near the Lourdes basilica where Pope John Paul II was scheduled to appear later that week. In a telephone call to a news agency, a man claimed responsibility on behalf of Stop the Priests, an unknown group protesting the commercialization of Lourdes. On August 15, the Toulouse police arrested two men who tried to set fire to Saint Etienne Cathedral. Under questioning, the two confessed to the Lourdes bombing. Authorities also suspected them of arson at the Toulouse offices of LA CROIX DU MIDI, a Roman Catholic newspaper.

August 13, 1983 — UNITED KINGDOM — In Belfast, Christopher Black provided evidence that sent 22 former Irish Republican Army (IRA) colleagues to jail. Black and 30 other informers — 19 Catholics and 11 Protestants — had led to the arrest of almost 300 suspects from the Marxist Irish National

Liberation Army (the IRA provisional wing) and the Protestant Ulster Volunteer Force. A police officer said about Black that the IRA "will be going flat out to find him and there's no doubt in anybody's mind what they'll do if they ever catch up with him." British authorities provided Black, his wife, and four children with new identities in another country.

August 13, 1983 — SWEDEN — In a telephone call to a Stockholm newspaper, an alleged defector from the Armenian Secret Army for the Liberation of Armenia (ASALA) threatened to abduct King Carl XVI Gustaf, Anita Gradin (the Minister without Portfolio), and Carola Haeggkvist (a popular singer). The caller was believed linked to the July 15 bombing at Orly Airport. Police later arrested a Turk and questioned him about the threat. 83081301

August 14, 1983 — FRANCE — An arms cargo, intended for the Irish Republican Army, was seized and an Irishman and two Frenchmen were arrested. The shipment included 28 pistols, 12,000 cartridges, 100 rifle magazines, 2 hand grenades, 22 pounds of explosives, 200 detonators, and 500 yards of detonating wire. 83081401

August 15, 1983 — COLOMBIA — Martin Stendal, an American rancher living in the jurisdiction of San Martin municipality, was kidnapped by members of the Army of National Liberation (ELN) and held for a five hundred thousand dollar ransom. Stendal was abducted when he disembarked from a light plane that he had been piloting. In early January 1984, Stendal was released in good health after his family had paid an unknown ransom. 83081502

August 15, 1983 — FRANCE — Yahya Nasir 'Ali, chauffeur to the charge d'affaires of the South Yemen embassy, was killed when his car burst into flames near the Bois de Boulogne on the outskirts of Paris. No one claimed responsibility. 83081503

August 16, 1983 — FEDERAL REPUBLIC OF GERMANY — The Bonn daily, DIE WELT, disclosed that a Yugoslavian secret service agent gave himself up to the Bavarian police. The agent alleged that he had participated in the plotting of several assassinations of Croat exiles in the Federal Republic of Germany, France, and Switzerland. Authorities hoped that the agent's disclosures would shed light on a number of murders of exiled Croats.

August 16, 1983 — UNITED STATES — Carlos Martinez, a 34-year-old unemployed Spanish national, took four hostages, including Consul General Joaquin Munoz del Castillo, at the Spanish consulate in Los Angeles. For 10 hours, Martinez held the hostages at gunpoint while negotiating with the police. Martinez demanded that three of his family members be given tickets to Puerto Rico. The incident ended without bloodshed, when Martinez released the hostages and gave himself up. No political motive was involved in the barricade event.

August 16, 1983 — PHILIPPINES — The government disclosed today the alleged disappearance of nine pro-Shah Iranian students over the last eight months. Blame has been placed on so-called "death squads" loyal to the current Iranian government. Relatives of the missing students concur that they had not been seen or heard from since their abduction. 83081601–09

August 16, 1983 — IRAN — At 1:15 P.M., a grenade was thrown through the front entrance of the Japanese embassy in Tehran. The blast broke windows but resulted in no injuries. During the prior week, Japanese foreign minister Shintaro Abe visited Iran and may have requested that Iran end its hostilities with Iraq. 83081610

August 17, 1983 — UNITED STATES — Edwin P. Wilson, an ex–Central Intelligence Agency agent, was indicted by a federal grand jury in New York for bribing two fellow inmates to murder his wife and other witnesses scheduled to testify against him. Wilson was serving a 32-year sentence for smuggling arms and explosives to Libya.

August 17, 1983 — IRAN — In a phone call to AGENCE FRANCE-PRESSE, the Orly Group claimed responsibility for firing six shots at Air France representative Jean Claude Eluard while Eluard was driving in Tehran. The victim was grazed in the leg by a shot from two unidentified gunmen. 83081701

August 18, 1983 — UNITED KINGDOM — The police arrested two men believed involved in the kidnapping of Harry Kirkpatrick's wife, stepfather, and stepsister. Kirkpatrick had become an informer against his Irish Republican Army colleagues. Earlier that day, the police released six members of the Irish National Liberation Army, apprehended when a police raid freed Kirkpatrick's stepfather, Richard Hill, and Hill's daughter from a Donegal farmhouse. Kirkpatrick's wife remained in IRA hands under a death threat if her husband testified.

August 18, 1983 — UNITED STATES — Delta Airlines flight 784, enroute from Miami to Tampa with 74 passengers and 7 crew, was hijacked to Cuba by a man carrying a flammable liquid. At 9:47 P.M. the flight departed Miami, and at 10:58 P.M. it landed in Havana. The hijacker was arrested by Cuban authorities. 83081801

August 18, 1983 — UNITED STATES — In a taped phone message to the Navy Yard, the FMLM, a splinter group of the Armed Front for National Liberation (FALN), claimed responsibility for a small bomb that caused a thousand dollars worth of damage to a building housing a Washington Navy Yard computer operation. The blast occurred at 12:04 A.M. and resulted in no injuries. Taped messages received by the WASHINGTON POST and UNITED PRESS INTERNATIONAL indicated that FALN claimed responsibility. 83081802

August 19, 1983 — UNITED STATES — A pipe bomb caused minor damage to an office building at 4801 Massachusetts Avenue NW in Washington, D.C. No one claimed responsibility.

August 19, 1983 — LEBANON — At 2:25 P.M., a car bomb exploded outside Al-Bitar Hospital in Tripoli. The blast destroyed part of the hospital and caused a large, but undisclosed, number of casualties.

August 19, 1983 — USSR — A man was severely beaten by Soviet guards and then arrested after he had driven his car into the British embassy compound in Moscow. A homemade bomb was later discovered in the man's car. 83081901

August 20, 1983 — PHILIPPINES — Benigno Aquino, Jr., leader of the opposition party, was assassinated when he was descending the stairs of the China Airlines plane that had brought him back to the Philippines after a three-year, self-imposed exile in the United States. Rolando Galman, who was in the vicinity of the assassination, was killed by security forces. In the subsequent weeks, the government labeled Galman a "notorious gunman for hire" and tried to blame Aquino's assassination on communist rebels. On August 23, President Ferdinand Marcos appointed a five-judge fact-finding commission, headed by Chief Justice Enrique Fernando. From its inception, the first commission was accused by critics as being favorable toward the government.

On September 4, Galman's girlfriend — Anna Oliva — and his sister were abducted from a nightclub. They were never seen again. Galman had been with them the night before the assassination.

On October 9, the first commission resigned amid growing reports that it was biased. A second commission, headed by Corazon Agrava, was appointed by Marcos on October 22. Agrava had been a former justice of the Court of Appeals. On September 18, 1984, the new commission issued its findings, which implicated Gen. Fabian C. Ver, armed forces chief, and 25 others in a conspiracy to assassinate Aquino. On November 5, 1984, murder conspiracy charges were filed against General Ver, Gen. Luther Custodio, Gen. Prospero Olivas, Capt. Felipo Valerio, Sgt. Claro Lat, Sgt. Arnulfo de Mesa, Filomendo Miranda, Armando de la Cruz, Constable Regelio Moreno, Constable Mario Lozaga, and others. Moreno and Lozaga were two members of the Philippine Constabulary Metropolitan Command (Metrocom) who had been on either side of Aquino when he was escorted down the stairs at the time of the assassination. General Prospero Olivas was the person in charge of the police investigation.

During the trial, an eyewitness, Rebecca Quijano, known as the "crying lady" said that she saw one of the Metrocom escorts, identified as Regelio Moreno, put a gun to the back of Aquino's head and kill him. A recording made by news crews at the time indicated that the escorts were saying, "I'll do it. Let me do it. Shoot him." In an important ruling on June 14, 1985, much of the testimony against the defendants was barred by the Supreme Court. On December 2, 1985, all of the defendants were acquitted of the charges.

On September 16, 1986, 21 of the original defendants, including Rogelio Moreno and Mario Lozaga, were arrested and a retrial was set for March 1987. General Ver and Capt. Felipo Valerio, however, had already left the country for Hawaii with Marcos.

August 20, 1983 — GREECE — Ma'mun Muraysh, a close aide to the deputy chief commander of Palestinian Liberation Organization (PLO) forces, was assassinated by two young men on a red Motorcross motorcycle at a traffic light in Athens. At 10:13 A.M., the attack occurred at the intersection of Posidhonos Street and Alimos Street. The driver, 'Ali Mustafa Hassan, and Muraysh's four-year-old son were also injured, though not seriously. Muraysh and his family had been living in Athens during the previous year and a half. All those injured held Moroccan passports. In a telephone call to a French news agency in Tunis, the Movement for Rebuilding Fatah, a rival PLO group, claimed responsibility. A PLO spokesman, however, accused Israeli agents; the Israeli government denied any responsibility. 83082001

August 21, 1983 — MOZAMBIQUE — In a dawn raid, the South African-backed Mozambican National Resistance (RENAMO) captured 24 Soviet technicians and 4 Mozambicans working at the Morrua tantalite mine in central Zamberzia Province. Two Soviets, Victor Voronov and Misakir Zaidinov, and two militiamen were killed during the RENAMO attack. Tantalite is considered a "strategic metal" and is used in nuclear reactors, aircraft, and missiles. On September 8, RENAMO offered to exchange the 24 Soviet hostages for the Soviet fighter pilot who shot down the South Korean passenger jetliner. On September 16, RENAMO released two Soviet hostages in Erururume. In a statement on December 8, Soviet authorities announced that Mozambican government troops freed 6 additional Soviet hostages abducted in raids on October 27 in Mureremba and December 1 in Mongoe. The communique also indicated that 2 Soviets died in captivity and that 14 remained prisoners. On January 25, 1984, 12 Soviets were released on the border with Malawi. The release followed negotiations between RENAMO, the USSR, and an unnamed neutral intermediary. In a communique, the South African government also claimed credit for the release. Malawian authorities picked up the 12 Soviets and flew them to Maputo. Two Soviets, Yuriy Gravilov and Viktor Estamin, remained in RENAMO hands as "security" against enemy attack. On September 17, 1985, the Mozambican Foreign Ministry issued a statement saying that the 2 remaining Soviet hostages were dead. Documents captured by Mozambican forces in a raid of the RENAMO headquarters at Serra da Gorongosa confirmed the 2 deaths. RENAMO, however, claimed that the 2 were still alive. The fate of the 4 Mozambican hostages is unknown. 83082101

August 22, 1983 — COLOMBIA — Corinne Hues, a United States sculptress, was kidnapped in Bogota. 83082201

August 23, 1983 — IRAN — The Export-Import Bank of the United States received $419.5 million from the Khomeini government in a settlement of debts owed by the prerevolutionary government of Shah Mohammad Reza Pahlavi. As of August 23, 1983, the Khomeini government had repaid $895.9 million of the $1.418 billion owed to United States banks. The latter figure was agreed upon in the January 1981 deal for the release of 52 American hostages held in Tehran.

August 23, 1983 — EL SALVADOR — Government troops fired on a vehicle occupied by four foreign technicians when it failed to stop for a roadblock on the Pan American Highway at Quebrada Seca, about 40 miles east of San Salvador. Vittorio Andretto, an Italian, was killed, while Claude Bernard Levanchy, a Swiss, was wounded in the leg. On May 25 in the same area, Faribundo Marti National Liberation Forces (FMLN) terrorists tortured and then murdered 42 soldiers.

August 23, 1983 — PERU — In an effort to curb terrorism, Interior Minister Luis Percovich announced that all foreigners, including tourists, were being investigated to ascertain the purpose of their visit and the nature of their activities while in Peru. The Shining Path terrorists have recruited foreigners into their organization.

August 23, 1983 — MOZAMBIQUE — Dion van Rensburg, a South African, was captured with a time bomb shortly after he had entered Mozambique on his way to Maputo. 83082301

August 25, 1983 — LEBANON — At 4:45 P.M., a bomb exploded on the third floor of the east Beirut building where the Air France offices were located. Three Lebanese — Janin Misrobian, George Fayiz Faraj, and Antoine Rizq — were slightly injured. The elevator and ground floor of the building in Al-Ashrafiyah also sustained damage. 83082501

August 25, 1983 — LEBANON — In the Al-Musaytibah area of west Beirut, a French ammunition truck exploded, killing two French peacekeeping soldiers and wounding seven others. Although some reports suggested that a bomb had been planted under the truck, the bulk of the evidence indicated that the explosion had been an accident started by a fire near the truck's crates.

August 25, 1983 — WEST BERLIN — On the Kurfurstendamm shopping mall, the French consulate building sustained major damage from a bomb explosion that killed 1 and injured 23. Portions of the front facade and upper stories collapsed as a result of the 11:20 A.M. blast. An anonymous call to the West Berlin office of AGENCE FRANCE-PRESSE indicated that the Armenian Secret Army for the Liberation of Armenia was responsible. Since Armenian terrorists had been arrested in France following the July 15, 1983, bombing of Orly Airport, French targets have come under attack. In a letter sent to the West German embassy in Saudi Arabia, Carlos also claimed responsibility. The letter bore the fingerprint of Ilich Ramirez Sanchez, the famed terrorist known as Carlos. 83082502

August 26, 1983 — KUWAIT — An alleged plot by the Iranian foreign ministry to bomb the United States embassy in Kuwait was disclosed by CBS NEWS, citing United States government sources. Security was believed to have been increased around the embassy when United States intelligence officials told the Kuwaiti authorities about the plot. No bombing was attempted. 83082601

August 27, 1983 — SYRIA — A large bomb exploded outside the Syrian Intelligence Center in Damascus, killing 8 and wounding 24. Most of the casualties included members of the intelligence department. No one claimed responsibility.

August 27, 1983 — AUSTRIA — Air France flight 781, enroute from Vienna to Paris with 106 passengers and 8 crew, was hijacked by 4 Arabs armed with grenades and submachine guns. The Boeing 727 was taken over after it had been airborne for one hour. The plane stopped for refueling in Geneva where the hijackers released 37 hostages after negotiations with a senior Geneva judge. After leaving Switzerland, the hijackers requested permission to land in Sofia, Bulgaria, but the request was denied. Hence, the plane headed for Athens where it was again denied permission to land. A request to land in Libya was also turned down. The plane, now low on fuel, was granted landing rights in Catania, Sicily, where it remained for several hours during tense negotiations. The hijackers repeatedly threatened to kill the hostages if the plane was not refueled. Finally, a deal was struck—55 additional hostages were set free and the plane was refueled. Early on the morning of the 28th, the plane landed in Damascus. A sick stewardess was released, which then left 17 remaining hostages including 7 crew and 10 passengers. Of the remaining passengers, 2 were Americans, 1 was British, 1 was Swedish, and 6 were French. In Damascus, the plane was refueled and the hijackers indicated that they would fly to Iran next. The Iranian government threatened to shoot down the plane if it entered Iranian airspace. Heedless of the warnings, the plane flew to Tehran and landed at Mehrabad Airport at 9:50 A.M. on the 28th. The Iranian deputy foreign minister Hossein Sheikholeslam condemned the hijacking as an "inhuman act." Permission to land had been granted by Iran owing to humanitarian considerations.

Once on the ground, the hijackers issued their demands, which included freeing Lebanese captives held in French jails and ending French military support to Iraq, Lebanon, and Chad within 48 hours. The hijackers also asked that their demands be made to the French people through the mass media. They threatened to blow up the plane if their demands were not met. Negotiations between Iranian officials and the hijackers continued for the next 2½ days. Jean Perrian, the French charge d'affaires to Iran, was also involved in the talks. The deadline to blow up the plane was extended three times. By August 30, the hijackers had also set deadlines to kill some of the hostages, but these deadlines were allowed to pass uneventfully several times. On August 30, they released a French couple who needed medical attention. At 1:45 P.M., the hijackers made one of the hostages leave the plane and walk onto the tarmac with hands held high. A hijacker then fired at the hostage but purposely missed. With the one hostage in their sights, the hijackers left the plane and cleared away obstacles around its wheels; they then reboarded the plane with the hostage.

The hijackers' demands for fuel and food were finally met after they had abducted an interpreter sent to the plane to help with the negotiations. On two occasions, the plane appeared to be getting ready to take off, but it never left Tehran. At 1:30 P.M. on August 31, the hijackers gave themselves up and asked for political asylum after reading a statement to the press. Thus ended the four-day odyssey of flight 781.

The fate of the hijackers remains a mystery. Moreover, their nationality remains unknown. They traveled on Tunisian passports that were thought to be forged. During the incident they first claimed to be Lebanese and later claimed to be Iraqi. They said that they were members of the Islamic Liberation Movement, a previously unknown group. 83082701

August 27, 1983 — UNITED STATES — In Washington, D.C., the Philippine embassy at 1617 Massachusetts Avenue NW was the scene of a firebombing by three unidentified youths. The building sustained two thousand dollars' damage to the chancery's front door and lobby. The bombing came two hours after a man with a Philippine accent phoned the embassy and said, "Why are you not practicing democracy in the Philippines? We'll get even." 83082702

August 28, 1983 — FRANCE — Direct Action claimed responsibility for two early-morning bombings on the Left Bank of the Seine River. Minor damage resulted at the Defense Ministry and the Socialist Party headquarters. In a statement sent to a French news organization, Direct Action demanded the immediate withdrawal of French troops from Chad.

August 28, 1983 — LEBANON — A joint United States Marine–Lebanese Army outpost came under fire by Shiite militiamen. The 90-minute battle marked the first time that the United States Marines fired their weapons in a hostile action in Lebanon. No marines were injured. 83082801

August 29, 1983 — PAKISTAN — At 5:45 P.M., a pedestrian threw a grenade into a crowd of progovernment demonstrators who had gathered outside the Liaqatabad police station in Karachi. Twenty-eight people were injured, including 7 policemen.

August 29, 1983 — LEBANON — Two United States Marines — 2d Lt. Donald George Losey and S. Sgt. Alexander M. Ortega — were killed and 14 were wounded amid heavy shelling and fighting in and around Beirut International Airport. Fifteen Lebanese soldiers were killed and 76 were wounded in the shelling and fighting, attributed to the Shiite Moslem militia and the Druze militia. The two marine deaths were the first since the United States peacekeeping forces were deployed 11 months earlier. 83082901

August 29, 1983 — HONDURAS — The Cinchoneros People's Liberation Movement of Honduras claimed responsibility for three bomb explosions in three Honduran cities. One bomb damaged property owned by the Standard Fruit Company, a United States firm, in La Ceiba; a second bomb damaged a high rise under construction in San Pedro Sula; and a third damaged property of the Tela Railroad company in La Lima. In a communique, the terrorist group indicated that the bombings were meant to protest United States intervention in Central America. 83082902

August 29, 1983 — GREECE — In a statement to a news agency, the Armenian Secret Army for the Liberation of Armenia (ASALA) claimed to have executed two Turkish collaborators, Aram Vartanian and Garlem Ananian, for their part in the murder of two Armenian militants last July. There was no confirmation of the claims. 83082903

August 29, 1983 — LEBANON — The United States ambassador's residence in Al-Yarzah was shelled. 83082904

August 30, 1983 — COLOMBIA — In Barranquilla, armed men stopped a bus, removed three Americans — Gerald Burgin, Charles Krauskrap, and James McKenzie — and shot them. Only McKenzie survived. 83083001

August 30, 1983 — LEBANON — One French peacekeeping soldier was killed and two were wounded by a shell that landed near their truck in the southern suburbs of Beirut. Two French soldiers and a paramilitary policeman died in a shelling attack on the French embassy. Four others were wounded. 83083002–03

August 30, 1983 — LEBANON — British peacekeeping soldiers guarding the British embassy in Beirut came under fire. No one was injured. 83083004

August 31, 1983 — UNITED KINGDOM — In London, bombs exploded outside the Israeli-owned Leumi Bank near Oxford Circus, in the doorway of a diamond merchant's home in Holborn, and outside an American construction executive's house in Knightsbridge. Extensive damage to the bank's ground floor was reported. No one was injured. 83083101–02

September 1983 — MEXICO — Two Cuban diplomats were arrested and expelled after being caught with a bomb at a Mexico City bus depot. Two Cuban exiles with United States citizenship were also deported to the United States in connection with the incident.

September 1983 — CHILE — Hugo Norberto Ratier Noguera, a leader of the Movement of the Revolutionary Left (MIR), was killed in Santiago in a shoot-out with agents of the National Intelligence Center.

September 1–24, 1983 — CORSICA — The Corsican National Liberation Front (FNLC) carried on a bombing campaign against government buildings. In a communique to the French media, the FNLC claimed responsibility for 44 bombings on the island that caused property damage but no injuries. The FNLC also claimed responsibility for the murder of Pierre-Jean Massimi, accused of bribery by the FNLC in the mysterious disappearance of Guy Orsoni, a Corsican separatist.

September 6, 1983 — LEBANON — Corporal Pedro J. Valle and L. Cpl. Randy M. Clark, two United States Marines, were killed during a shell bombardment of the outpost near the Beirut International Airport. Two other marines were wounded. 83090601

September 6, 1983 — JAPAN — A Molotov cocktail was hurled from a speeding car at the Soviet consulate in Sapporo. The bomb was an apparent protest against the Soviet downing of a South Korean airliner. No damage or injuries resulted. 83090602

September 7, 1983 — IRAN — Two embassy employees were slightly injured from a car-bomb blast near the French embassy in Tehran. In a phone call to AGENCE FRANCE-PRESSE, the Orly Group claimed responsibility and warned others to stay clear of French interests and its diplomats. 83090701

September 7, 1983 — THAILAND — The press room at the Interior Ministry received a New Thai Leftist Front's threat against United States president Ronald Reagan, scheduled to visit on November 7–8. 83090702

September 7, 1983 — LEBANON — Two French soldiers were killed and five wounded in heavy shelling from the Syrian-backed Druze militia in the mountains surrounding Beirut. One United States Marine was wounded. 83090703

September 7, 1983 — LEBANON — In Beirut, artillery shells injured six Italian peacekeeping soldiers on the southern outskirts of the city. 83090704

September 7, 1983 — ANGOLA — The National Union for the Total Independence of Angola (UNITA) claimed to have killed 3 Soviet advisers and 17 Cuban troops during raids in central and eastern provinces. The group also claimed to have captured 27 foreigners who included mostly Portuguese, Brazilians, and Spaniards. Some of the kidnapped Portuguese were among the 35 Portuguese hostages later released on September 28, 1983. 83090705

September 8, 1983 — LEBANON — In Tripoli, a large bomb killed 5, wounded 25, and caused extensive damage to the Islamic Unification Movement building. The Movement is the most formidable of the militias vying for control of the city.

September 10, 1983 — LEBANON — Well-informed Western diplomatic sources disclosed that Turkish commandos launched a military operation against a base of the Armenian Secret Army for the Liberation of Armenia (ASALA) in Al-Biqa'. A large number of ASALA personnel were believed killed.

September 10, 1983 — GUATEMALA — Celeste Aida Mejia de Velasco, sister of Guatemalan leader Gen. Oscar Humberto Mejia Victores, was kidnapped by four armed men of the Rebel Armed Forces. She was abducted when leaving her place of work at the Guatemalan Social Security Institute General Hospital in Guatemala City. In return for her release, the kidnappers demanded publication of a declaration in newspapers throughout Central America and in the United States, Mexico, Venezuela, Panama, and Colombia. Mejia Victores reaffirmed Guatemalan policy never to negotiate with terrorists. On October 24, the WASHINGTON POST published a paid advertisement from the Rebel Armed Forces as one of the conditions for the release of Celeste and Marta Elena Rios de Rivas, sister of former Guatemalan leader, Gen. Efrain Rios Montt. Marta Rios had been kidnapped by the same group on June 29, 1983. The manifesto published in the WASHINGTON POST and elsewhere accused the government of murdering 243 people since Rios Montt was deposed in a coup on August 8. On October 26, the leftists released both of the women. 83091001

September 10–11, 1983 — KAMPUCHEA — Khmer Rouge rebels killed six and wounded seven Vietnamese occupation forces in raids near the Thai-Kampuchea border. One rebel was killed and three injured.

September 12, 1983 — LEBANON — Three United States Marines were wounded when their compound near the Beirut International Airport came under heavy shelling. 83091201

September 12, 1983 — HONDURAS — In downtown San Pedro Sula, a bomb caused extensive damage to the building that housed the offices of Costa Rican Airlines, Pan American Airlines, and the Honduran National Airlines. No one was injured. In a communique, the Cinchonero group claimed responsibility for the bomb, meant as a reprisal for the bombing of Managua's Sandino Airport, allegedly planned in Costa Rica. 83091202

September 13, 1983 — THAILAND — At 3:45 A.M., an M-26 grenade caused damage to the Bangkok offices of the Soviet airline Aeroflot, located in the International Business Machines building on Silom Street. The attack was believed motivated by the Soviet downing of Korean Airlines flight 007 with 269 persons aboard, including 8 Thais, on September 1. 83091301

September 14, 1983 — BRAZIL — Federal police officials disclosed that Luis Fergarde Lopez, an accused Argentinean terrorist, was living in Sao Paulo. Lopez was wanted in connection with attacks against opposition leaders in Argentina.

September 14, 1983 — AFGHANISTAN — In Kabul, a bomb blast killed several members of the Tudeh Party and injured others at their office. The Tudeh Party had fled Iran. 83091401

September 14, 1983 — THAILAND — Extensive damage, but no injuries, resulted from a fire, believed set by arsonists, at the International Business Machines building housing the office of Aeroflot. Just the day before, the same Aeroflot office had been bombed and then had moved elsewhere. 83091402

September 15, 1983 — BRAZIL — Two Molotov cocktails hurled at the United States consulate in Sao Paulo caused no injuries or damage. Two brothers — Paulo Jacobo Rosani and Ismael Rosani — who wanted to travel to the United States but were denied visas, admitted having thrown the bombs. In an unrelated incident in Osasco City, a bomb destroyed the car of Sebastiao Buguina, a member of the Worker's Party.

September 15, 1983 — UNITED STATES — Two unidentified Cubans were arrested at Miami International Airport when they tried to board a Tampa-bound jet. The men carried a toy handgun and containers filled with an unknown liquid. 83091501

September 17, 1983 — POLAND — A Soviet AN-2 biplane with five adults and four children flew from Jelenia Gora to the American military base at Tempelhof, West Berlin. The plane's occupants asked for political asylum in Australia, where they had relatives.

September 19, 1983 — FEDERAL REPUBLIC OF GERMANY — The Revolutionary Cells claimed responsibility for an explosion at a computer center of the MAN works in Ginsheim-Gustavsburg. Over a million dollars worth of damage resulted, but there were no injuries. In a letter to the FRANKFURTER RUNDSCHAU, the group accused MAN of being one of West Germany's largest arms producers. The group also accused the company of being a representative of multinational capital involved in destroying liberation movements in the Third World.

September 19, 1983 — LEBANON — A spokesman for the Organization of France's Friends in Lebanon claimed responsibility for two bombs at stores in Mulijian and Maximara, allegedly owned by the Armenian Secret Army for the Liberation of Armenia. 83091901

September 19, 1983 — COSTA RICA — Gregorio Jimenez Morales, a member of the Basque Fatherland and Liberty (ETA), and 11 others arrested in Costa Rica were alleged to be plotting the assassination of anti-Sandinista leaders Eden Pastora and Alfonso Robelo. According to the director general of police, Rafael del Rio, the plot was a joint effort between the ETA and Nicaragua to destabilize the Costa Rican government. On November 6, 1984, the Superior Criminal Court of Alajuela authorized the extradition to Spain of Morales after his trial in Costa Rica. 83091902

September 21, 1983 — UNITED STATES — Firmin Joseph, owner of a Haitian newspaper, was shot to death in his Brooklyn home. The TRIBUNE D'HAITI had a circulation of 20,000 throughout the United States. A month earlier, Joseph had received a death threat demanding that he stop the series *One Hundred Fifty-Seven Days in Haitian Jails.* 83092101

September 21, 1983 — MOROCCO — The Moroccan police averted an attack on Turkish athletes who had participated in the Ninth Mediterranean Games in Casablanca. Acting on information that the Armenian Secret Army for the Liberation of Armenia (ASALA) was planning to attack the athletes at the airport, the Moroccan police advised them to depart from a secure military airport. The athletes returned home safely. 83092102

September 21, 1983 — GREECE — An article in AKROPOLIS reported that the Turkish intelligence had alerted the Greek Central Intelligence about possible attacks against the Turkish embassy and its personnel by the Armenian Secret Army for the Liberation of Armenia (ASALA). 83092103

September 22, 1983 — HONDURAS — James F. Carney, a Roman Catholic priest from St. Louis, apparently died from exhaustion while escaping with rebel comrades in the jungles of Olancho during a government rebel offensive.

September 22, 1983 — SOUTH KOREA — Around 9:30 P.M., a bomb exploded in front of the American Cultural Center in Taegu. One South Korean was killed and five injured. Most of the damage was confined to the main entrance. On December 3, 1983, two North Korean infiltrators — Chon Chung-nam and Yi Sang-kyu — were captured and their boat sunk in waters off Pusan. Information provided by the infiltrators laid the blame for the bombing on North Korean agents. 83092201

September 22, 1983 — UNITED STATES — American Airlines flight 625, enroute from New York to the United States Virgin Islands with 112 people aboard, was hijacked to Cuba by an unidentified man who threatened to detonate a bomb. The Boeing 727 was diverted when it had been airborne for twenty minutes. It landed safely in Havana at 1:43 P.M. There were no reports on whether or not the bomb was a hoax. 83092202

September 22, 1983 — FRANCE — A bomb threat delayed the formal opening of the Paris-Lyon route for the French High-Speed Train. An anonymous caller, representing the Armenian Secret Army for the Liberation of Armenia (ASALA), claimed that a bomb had been planted in a tunnel along the route. A search turned up nothing and delayed the train's arrival by 27 minutes. 83092203

September 23, 1983 — PAKISTAN — The Arab Revolutionary Brigades, a little-known group, claimed responsibility for the crash of an Emirates-owned Boeing 737-200 enroute from Karachi to Abu Dhabi with 111 persons aboard. In an anonymous call to AGENCE FRANCE-PRESSE in Paris, the group's spokesman said that a bomb caused the crash near Abu Dhabi, resulting in the death of all aboard. The group claimed that an aide to one of the six emirs in the Emirates was the target of the attack; but passenger lists did not identify any prominent Emirate. 83092301

September 24, 1983 — UNITED KINGDOM — Irish authorities disclosed that three recently expelled Russian diplomats — Gennadiy Saline, Vicktor Lipasov, and his wife, Eudokia — had made contact with the Irish Republican Army in Ulster. Authorities speculated that the Russians were going to trade arms for information on British military installations in Northern Ireland.

September 24, 1983 — UNITED STATES — A box of Sparrow air-to-air missile parts, scheduled for shipment to Japan, disappeared from the Expedair International Freight Company's warehouse, located on Rockaway Boulevard near Kennedy International Airport. The box contained the missile's arming, firing, and relocking mechanism, but no explosives.

September 24, 1983 — LEBANON — In Beirut, the Spanish ambassador's residence was destroyed by shelling as a result of fighting between government forces and militiamen operating from the mountains to the east. No injuries were reported at the residence. 83092401

September 25, 1983 — PHILIPPINES — During a beauty contest in Davao, fragmentation grenades thrown near the stage killed 10, including 6 children, and injured scores of others. Although no one claimed responsibility, local police suspected communist rebels.

September 25, 1983 — NORTHERN IRELAND — In the largest jailbreak in British history, 38 Irish Republican Army guerrillas escaped Maze Prison after killing 1 guard and wounding 6 others during an armed battle at the main gate. The convicts used knives and guns smuggled into the prison to overpower the guards and steal their uniforms. One group of escapees made it through five security checkpoints in a stolen food truck. Seventeen prisoners were recaptured within hours and 2 others were apprehended three days later. A countrywide manhunt was initiated.

September 26, 1983 — SWITZERLAND — The Coordination of Anti–Atomic Power Plant Saboteurs took responsibility in a letter to the SWISS NEWS AGENCY for a bomb-damaged electrical tower near Wolflinswil.

September 27, 1983 — NORTHERN IRELAND — Authorities said that the use of informers, known as supergrasses, had been responsible for the recent decline in bombings. Officials indicated that there had been thus far 138 bombings in Northern Ireland in 1983; in the peak year of 1972 there had been 1,495. In 1983, about 48 murders were attributed to terrorist activities; in 1982, 97 murders were attributed to such activities.

September 27, 1983 — ARGENTINA — President Reynaldo Bignone signed an antiterrorism law that allowed authorities to search homes without having warrants, to open mail, to tap phones, and to detain suspects for up to two days without notifying a judge. Under the new law, suspects could also be held for ten days before being charged.

September 27, 1983 — CANADA — In Toronto, a man in a crowd of antinuclear protesters and Irish Republican Army sympathizers rushed British prime minister Margaret Thatcher as she was entering a hotel to deliver a scheduled speech. Police grabbed the assailant and arrested him. No one was injured. 83092701

September 30, 1983 — COSTA RICA — The British ambassador to Costa Rica, Peter Wayne Summerscale, accused Basque Fatherland and Liberty (ETA) members of attacking his home in San Jose in a failed attempt to abduct him. Further details were unavailable. 83093001

September 30, 1983 — FRANCE — A bomb at an international trade fair in Marseilles killed 1, injured 26 (8 seriously), and destroyed the American, Soviet, and Algerian pavilions. The Orly Group claimed responsibility in a phone call, but police authorities doubted the claim. The right-wing Charles Martel group was second to claim responsibility. In a call to AGENCE FRANCE-PRESSE, a spokesman for the Lebanese Armed Revolutionary Factions also claimed credit and threatened further incidents if French troops were not withdrawn from Lebanon. 83093002

October 1983 — EGYPT — An undisclosed number of Abu Nidal members were captured in Cairo along with arms, bombs, and plans of future attacks against United States and Israeli establishments.

October 1983 — BOLIVIA — Seven alleged terrorists were arrested in La Paz by the Army. Two of those arrested, Pablo Manuel Cepada Camillieri and Rene Patricio Lizama Lira, were Chileans.

October 1983 — JORDAN — In Zerka, a car bomb exploded near the army officers' club. On November 8, an anonymous caller to AGENCE FRANCE-PRESSE in Paris claimed that the Arab Revolutionary Brigades was responsible, a name that the Abu Nidal group sometimes uses. 83109901

October 1983 — FEDERAL REPUBLIC OF GERMANY — In a letter sent to the West German embassy in Saudi Arabia, Ilich Ramirez Sanchez (Carlos) threatened to kill Bonn interior minister Friedrich Zimmermann if authorities prosecuted Gabriele Kroecher-Tiedemann for her alleged role in the 1975 attack against the Organization of Petroleum Exporting Countries (OPEC) headquarters in Vienna. Kroecher-Tiedemann was currently serving 15 years in Switzerland for seriously wounding two customs officers. 83109902

October 1, 1983 — CYPRUS — Security measures were increased after British secret services received information that unidentified Arab commandos were planning to sabotage British bases here. 83100101

October 1, 1983 — AFGHANISTAN — In Kabul, the Soviet embassy was attacked by Afghan Mujahidin. Further details were unavailable. 83100102

October 1, 1983 — PAKISTAN — In Peshawar, three small bombs, one placed near the American consulate, exploded. No injuries were reported. 83100103

October 5, 1983 — SWEDEN — The Stockholm Stock Exchange, which also housed the Swedish Academy of Letters, was evacuated following a bomb threat meant to protest Lech Walesa's Nobel Peace Prize. No bomb was found. 83100501

October 6, 1983 — LEBANON — London's ASH-SHARQ AL-AWSAT reported an alleged Israeli plot to kidnap Yasir Arafat on the high seas when he was scheduled to depart Tripoli by boat for his headquarters in Tunis. In recent days, the Israeli Navy had been stopping ships in the Mediterranean and detaining Palestinian passengers. The alleged plot never materialized when Arafat canceled his travel plans. 83100601

October 6, 1983 — COLOMBIA — In Bogota, four members of the 19 April group (M-19) occupied the offices of AGENCE FRANCE-PRESSE. The two men and two women wanted to urge President Belisario Betancur, currently on tour in Europe, to open up a dialogue with the guerrillas. The terrorists painted slogans on the walls before leaving peacefully. 83100602

October 6–7, 1983 — COSTA RICA — Security measures were increased around suspected targets throughout San Jose following the government's official announcement that Basque Fatherland and Liberty (ETA) terrorists were operating in the country. Threatening calls had been made daily to police chiefs and other officials since the arrest of Gregorio Jimenez Morales and Jorge Chaverri, two ETA members. On October 7, ETA member Humberto Abella Lopez gave himself up to the Spanish ambassador, Gonzalo Fernandez. Following a request from Fernandez, a detachment of the Special Operations Group of the National Police was dispatched from Spain to protect its embassy and personnel.

October 7, 1983 — THAILAND — Thai intelligence agents warned security officials at the Don Muang Airport about an intended hijacking by four to five foreigners. Further details were not disclosed publicly.

October 7, 1983 — CORSICA — Within 20 minutes, 10 bombs caused extensive damage, but no injuries, to five banks, two stores, and three other targets in Bastia. An 11th bomb exploded in Corte. Authorities blamed Corsican separatists.

October 7, 1983 — GUATEMALA — In Guatemala City, Julieta Esperanza Sanchez Castillo, a supervisor at the Guatemalan Education Ministry, and Piedad Esperanza, Sanchez's 22-year-old daughter, were kidnapped by armed men. On November 11, their bodies were found along with another Guatemalan linguist, who worked for the United States Agency for International Development. The other linguist, Jose Felipe Ralac Xioloj, had been abducted with his wife, Celia, on October 18. Sanchez, Ralac, and Ralac's wife were made to look as though they had died in a fiery car crash. Witnesses said that the bodies had been placed in the car before gasoline was used to ignite it. 83100701

October 7, 1983 — FRANCE — Rashid Said Mohammed Abdullah, a Libyan wanted by Italy for the 1980 murder in Milan of Azzedin Laheri, was arrested in Paris. On October 28, he was released when Italy had not provided extradition papers.

October 7, 1983 — SPAIN — In Madrid, a French school received a bomb threat from an anonymous caller. Threats against other French schools in Spain were mentioned in the call. No bomb was discovered. 83100702

October 8, 1983 — COLOMBIA — Retired frigate lieutenant Lisardo Marquez Perez, a member of the Red Flag group, was arrested for his alleged participation in an attack on Cutufi on the Venezualan-Colombian border, where one national guardsman was killed and eight others injured in September.

October 8, 1983 — SPAIN — In Madrid, EL PAIS reported a two-hour meeting between Colombian president Belisario Betancur and two 19 April leaders — Ivan Marino Ospina and Alvaro Fayad — in a private home. Details of the meeting were sketchy but presumably involved possible reconciliation between the government and 19 April.

October 9, 1983 — GUATEMALA — Pedro Julio Garcia, 60, the editor of PRENSA LIBRE, was kidnapped from his home by guerrillas who demanded a ransom and the publication of a political tract of the Guatemalan Labor (Communist) party in newspapers in Guatemala, the United States, El Salvador, Honduras, Nicaragua, Costa Rica, and Panama. On October 13, three Guatemala City newspapers ran the tract. PRENSA LIBRE also paid the WASHINGTON POST and other foreign newspapers to publish it as a paid advertisement. The Guatemalan government called PRENSA LIBRE's action "a violation of the law" and threatened prosecution. In the published tract, criticism was leveled against the Reagan administration for current tensions in Guatemala. Garcia was released unharmed on October 24, 1983. 83100901

October 9, 1983 — LEBANON — Two United States Marines were slightly wounded and a United States helicopter was hit by small arms fire near Beirut International Airport during clashes between Shiite Moslem militia and the Lebanese Army. 83100902

October 9, 1983 — BURMA — At 10:23 A.M., a bomb exploded in the ceiling of the Martyr's Mausoleum in Rangoon and resulted in the death of 17 South Koreans, including 4 cabinet ministers, and 4 Burmese journalists. Forty-six people were wounded, including 14 high-ranking South Korean government officials and 32 Burmese, 2 of whom were cabinet ministers. The claymore-type fragmentation bomb, packed with lead pellets and attached to an incendiary device, was designed to kill as many as possible. The bomb was undoubtedly intended for South Korean president Chun Doo Hwan, who escaped injury by a mere three minutes when his motorcade was delayed by traffic.

Just before the blast, the South Korean and Burmese dignitaries had lined up inside the wooden pavilion to honor the 9 Burmese heroes assassinated in 1947 during that nation's fight for independence. Lee Kai Chul, South Korea's ambassador to Burma, arrived and began shaking hands. A trumpeter then rehearsed a requiem dirge scheduled for the wreath-laying ceremony by President Chun. In hearing the dirge, the 3 terrorists, positioned some five hundred meters away near the Shwedagon Pagoda, mistook Lee for Chun and set off the blast by remote control. A cloud of smoke and dust engulfed those beneath the pavilion as the ceiling collapsed and thousands of deadly pellets rained down. A second ceiling bomb failed to detonate. If it had, the loss of life would have been even greater.

The 4 dead cabinet ministers included foreign minister Lee Bum Suk, deputy prime minister and economic planning board minister Suh Suk Joon, energy and resources minister Suh Sang Chul, and commerce minister Kim Dong Whie. Ambassador Lee Kai Chul, presidential secretary Hahm Pyong Choon, and deputy finance minister Lee Ki Uk were also killed along with other deputy ministers and journalists. The wounded included Gen. Lee Ki Paik, chairman of the South Korean joint chiefs of staff; Than Maung, Burmese deputy minister for culture; and Aung Kyaw, Burmese minister for information and culture.

On hearing the explosion, the president's motorcade turned from the cemetery and headed back to the guest house. The president then made arrangements for an immediate departure for Seoul. Prime Minister Kim Sang Hyup, who had remained in South Korea, notified India, Sri Lanka, Australia, New Zealand, and Brunei that the remainder of the president's tour was postponed. An emergency cabinet meeting was then held in Seoul. Following the meeting, the armed forces and the police were put on alert. On October 10, President Chun returned to South Korea to rebuild his government.

The 3 terrorists were apprehended in 3 separate incidents. On October 9 at 9:45 P.M., Maj. Zim Mo was spotted swimming in the Nyaungdon Creek, east of Rangoon, in an apparent attempt to steal a small boat. When police summoned him to come ashore, he refused. As the police tried to remove him from the water, Zim set off a grenade that seriously injured himself and slightly injured three police. On October 11, villagers from Thakutpin in Kyauktan township alerted authorities to 2 suspicious foreigners. While the 2 suspects were searched by the police, they panicked. One terrorist, Capt. Kim Chi Oh, was shot dead, and the other, Capt. Kang Min Chul, escaped. When Kang was cornered the next day, he set off a grenade that killed 3 Burmese police and blew off his arm. Both of the captured men carried commando survival kits and had lead pellets and a remote control device in their possession identical to those recovered at the mausoleum.

Prior to the trial on November 17, Kang had confessed that the 3 had been sent to Burma under orders from Gen. Kang Chung Su, a commander of a division of North Korean commandos, to assassinate President Chun. On September 17, the three arrived by sea on the North Korean freighter, the *Tong Gon,* which remained in Rangoon harbor until September 21 when it sailed for Sri Lanka, the next leg of President Chun's trip. North

Korean embassy staff hid the terrorists at the West Rangoon house of Chon Chang Hui, a counselor at the embassy. From Chon's residence, the terrorists prepared for the bombing.

On October 7, the terrorists left Chon's house and went to the mausoleum. While Zim stood watch, Kim and Kang climbed the roof and planted the two bombs, each of which were connected to incendiary devices. For the next two days, the terrorists hid in nearby bushes, awaiting the time of the assassination. According to Kang's statement, Zim detonated the bomb. On December 12, Zim and Kang were found guilty of murder and sentenced to be hanged.

On November 14, Burma broke off diplomatic relations with North Korea. South Korean officials speculated that Kim Jong Il, son of North Korean president Kim Il Sung, was behind the planned assassination in a ploy to increase his authority so as to ensure that he would succeed his father. 83100903

October 11, 1983 — INDIA — Hundreds of Tibetan refugees clashed with police in New Delhi when the refugees were denied access to the Chinese embassy, where they intended to protest the planned execution of 18 Tibetan political dissidents in Lhasa. Nine refugees were injured. 83101101

October 11, 1983 — TURKEY — Haji Yuzdenir, who with three others hijacked a Turkish Airlines flight to Sofia on October 22, 1972, was sentenced to 20 years by an Istanbul martial law court. Yuzdenir had been given political asylum in Bulgaria following the hijacking. After 10 years as a fugitive, he gave himself up to the Turkish embassy in Vienna in July 1982. The pilot and one passenger had been wounded during the hijacking.

October 12, 1983 — TURKEY — The Armenian Secret Army for the Liberation of Armenia (ASALA) was split when some members formed an opposition group, the Revolutionary Movement. The splinter group protested the ASALA's bloody terrorist acts, including the bombing at Orly Airport on July 15, 1983.

October 13, 1983 — JORDAN — In Amman, two hand grenades were thrown at a police post nearby the queen mother's palace. The Arab Revolutionary Brigades took credit for the attack. 83101301

October 14, 1983 — COLOMBIA — In Medellin, police deactivated a bomb planted in a window of the Venezuelan consulate. Other bombs were left throughout Las Flores. Police suspected a guerrilla group. 83101401

October 14, 1983 — MALAWI/MOZAMBIQUE — A goods train traveling between Malawi and Beira, Mozambique, was derailed by the Mozambique

National Resistance Movement (RENAMO). Dozens of people, using the train as an alternative to suspended passenger service, were murdered in the armed attack that followed the derailment. 83101402

October 14, 1983 — LEBANON — One United States Marine, Sgt. Allen H. Soifert, was killed and another wounded by Shiite Moslem sniper fire directed at the marine compound near the Beirut International Airport. Prior to the attack, the marine positions came under a rocket-propelled grenade attack. 83101403

October 15, 1983 — UNITED STATES — A People's Express Boeing 737 with 101 passengers and 5 crew was hijacked by an unidentified man falsely claiming to have a gun. Shortly after it had departed Buffalo, New York, for a flight to Newark, a man took a flight attendant hostage, demanded the fares that had been collected from the passengers, and then diverted the plane to Atlantic City. Once in Atlantic City, the hijacker released all of the passengers and crew with the exception of one attendant. He offered a hostage substitution for another airline employee. When the second hostage came forward, the hijacker surrendered to federal agents and police. No one was injured. 83101501

October 16, 1983 — MALAYSIA — Airports were placed on alert to watch for a terrorist squad consisting of Algerians, Italians, and South Yemenis, who were thought to be planning a hijacking.

October 16, 1983 — LEBANON — One United States Marine was killed and three wounded, two of them seriously, from small-arms and grenade fire directed at marine positions near the Beirut International Airport. Shiite Moslem militia was believed responsible. 83101601

October 17, 1983 — MUSTIQUE — The LONDON SUNDAY TIMES disclosed an alleged plot by the Argentine Navy to assassinate Prince Andrew while he was vacationing on this Caribbean Island. No plot was carried out.

October 18, 1983 — FEDERAL REPUBLIC OF GERMANY — Guenther Maria Rausch, a suspected member of the Red Army Faction (RAF), gave himself up to a West German embassy in a neighboring country.

October 18, 1983 — LEBANON — One Italian soldier was injured in cross fire between the Lebanese Army and guerrillas in Beirut.

October 18, 1983 — GUATEMALA — The extended Thanksgiving vacation by United States ambassador Frederic L. Chapin was regarded as indication of increased United States displeasure over attacks against persons working for United States-funded government programs to educate Guatemalan Indians. United States officials suspected that death squads, consisting of members of the Guatemalan Army, were responsible for incidents that included the kidnapping and murder of Jose Felipe Ralac Xiloj, a program linguist at Inter-America Research Associates, a Virginia-based company under contract to the United States Agency for International Development. Ralac was kidnapped on October 18; he and his wife were found dead on November 11 under suspicious circumstances. 83101801

October 18, 1983 — BURMA — Jacques Bossu, 26, and his wife Martine, 24, were kidnapped by Karen guerrillas during a raid on a cement factory of the French-owned Five-Cail-Babcock firm. Twelve Burmese civilians were also taken hostage during the incident in Myaing Galay, located about 90 miles east of Rangoon near the Thai border. On November 2, the guerrillas released the Burmese hostages unharmed but continued to hold the French engineer and his wife. In return for the couple, the guerrillas demanded an end to French economic and technical assistance to Burma. The Karen rebels, an Adventist Christian and anticommunist group, had been fighting for their autonomy from the Rangoon government since 1948. During the couple's captivity, Gen. Bo Mya, the Karen strongman, threatened to put the couple on trial for "collaborating with the enemy of the Karen people." In early November, negotiations began between the International Committee of the Red Cross (ICRC) and Karen leaders, Bo Mya and Saw Than Aung, to obtain the couple's release. On November 23, the Karen leaders delivered three demands in a letter to the ICRC: (1) Paris recognition of the Karen National Union (KNU), (2) reduction of French aid to the Rangoon government, and (3) French aid to the KNU if French assistance to Rangoon was not stopped. If these demands were not met, then the KNU would put the couple on trial on December 2. On humanitarian grounds, the guerrillas released the couple unharmed after 38 days of captivity, even though the rebels' demands had not been met. 83101802

October 18, 1983 — HONDURAS — In Tegucigalpa, a bomb exploded in the parking lot of the United States embassy. No damage or injuries resulted. 83101802

October 19, 1983 — LEBANON — At 4:30 p.m., a blue Mercedes exploded in front of the Kuwaiti embassy in Beirut while a United States Marine patrol was passing. Two marines and a Kuwaiti security guard were slightly injured in the blast that damaged a marine jeep and truck. 83101901

October 20, 1983 — UNITED STATES — Edwin P. Wilson, an ex–Central Intelligence Agency agent, was convicted of the attempted murder of a business associate and five government witnesses who had testified against him for selling explosives to Libya.

October 20, 1983 — PERU — Papers found in a Shining Path hideout in Huancavelica indicated that Alberto Kouking, an Italian ANSA news agency journalist, was targeted for kidnapping. 83102001

October 20, 1983 — LEBANON — At 3:45 P.M., a bomb planted near the Fu'ad Shihab Bridge in Lebanon exploded and wounded a French soldier in a passing patrol. 83102002

October 21, 1983 — MEXICO — Terrorists worldwide gathered in Mexico City for a conference to discuss ways to increase their campaigns against Western targets, especially those of the United States.

October 21, 1983 — INDIA — In Punjab, Sikh extremists were thought responsible for a train derailment that killed 16 and injured 112.

October 23, 1983 — LEBANON — A yellow Mercedes truck, packed with two thousand pounds of a plastic explosive equivalent to six tons of TNT, drove through a barbed-wire perimeter fence and then passed a sandbag sentry post before coming to rest in the lobby of the Battalion Landing Team building, housing some of the United States Marines at Beirut International Airport. The ensuing blast created a crater 30 feet deep and 120 feet across and caused the four-story building to collapse instantly into a smoldering rubble. Windows over a half-mile away were shattered by the explosion. The 6:20 A.M. blast killed 241 American servicemen and injured over 80. Marine sentries were unable to fire on the truck because their weapons were kept unloaded on orders. A heavy iron gate placed between the barbed-wire fence and the ill-fated building had apparently been left open, allowing easy access for the suicide bomber.

About 20 seconds after the blast, a second suicide bomber drove his car into the eight-story apartment building housing 110 French Paratroopers. When the bomb detonated, the building folded, one floor upon the other, killing 58 soldiers and injuring at least 15 others. The second blast was two miles to the north of the airport in the Ramel el-Baida district in central Beirut.

In a phone call to AGENCE FRANCE-PRESSE (AFP) offices in Beirut and Paris, Islamic Holy War, or Islamic Jihad, claimed responsibility for both blasts. The caller issued the following statement: "We are the soldiers of God and we crave death. Violence will remain our only path if they [foreign forces] do not leave. We are ready to turn Lebanon into another Vietnam. We are not Iranians or Syrians, or Palestinians. We are

Lebanese Moslems who follow the dicta of the Koran." Islamic Jihad is closely linked to the Hezbollah, the Party of God, whose leader is the radical Shiite Moslem, Mohammed Hussein Fadlallah. Fadlallah's headquarters were in Baalbek, Lebanon. Hussayn Musawi, Fadlallah's strongman, heads the Islamic Amal faction, which is associated with the Hezbollah. The Islamic Amal has ties to Iran's Ayatollah Khomeini. Newspaper reports linked the Islamic Amal, Fadlallah, and Musawi to the two blasts.

In an anonymous call to AFP, the suicide bombers were identified as Abu Mazin, 26, and Abu Sijan, 24. In another call to AFP, the Free Islamic Revolution Movement (also known as the Islamic Revolutionary Movement) claimed responsibility for the bombings. The linkage between Hezbollah, Islamic Jihad, Islamic Amal, and the Free Islamic Revolution Movement is difficult to disentangle. 83102301–02

October 24, 1983 — UNITED STATES — Tania Zelensky, wife of an Iranian, was shot to death in the convenience store in Pittsfield, Vermont, owned by the couple. The murder may have been motivated as a violent reaction to the October 23 bombing of the United States Marines barracks in Beirut. William Harvey pleaded innocent after being charged.

October 25, 1983 — INDIA — Mohammad Ali Kourme, the Jordanian ambassador to India, was shot at least six times by a lone gunman with an automatic gun. The incident occurred in New Delhi as the ambassador was walking to his home for lunch. The assailant escaped in a taxi. In a phone call to AGENCE FRANCE-PRESSE in Paris, an Arab Revolutionary Brigades spokesman claimed responsibility. Kourme recovered from the serious wounds he sustained. 83102501

October 25, 1983 — JAMAICA — In Kingston, the New York Mission received a bomb threat and was evacuated. 83102502

October 26, 1983 — GREECE — A government spokesman confirmed the ELEVTHEROTIPIA report of an alert for a terrorist attack.

October 26, 1983 — ITALY — Taysir Alaedin Toukan, Jordan's ambassador to Italy, and Mohammed Hidar Baud, his Egyptian driver, were seriously wounded in Rome. At 1:40 P.M., two men in a car pulled beside the ambassador's car and opened fire with pistols. Toukan was hit seven times but recovered. In a phone call to the ITALIAN NEWS AGENCY, a caller claimed that the gunmen belonged to the Syrian Struggle Front. The Arab Revolutionary Brigades claimed responsibility in a call to AGENCE FRANCE-PRESSE in Paris. The Abu Nidal Group also claimed responsibility in a separate statement. Both Toukan and Baud recovered from their wounds. 83102601

October 26, 1983 — BOLIVIA — The Peruvian embassy in La Paz sustained serious damage from a dynamite blast. 83102602

October 27, 1983 — SYRIA — The Armenian Secret Army for the Liberation of Armenia (ASALA) moved its headquarters to Tehran following the Syrian government's insistence that it leave. The ASALA first moved its headquarters to Syria from Beirut after the Israeli attack on Lebanon. Reports indicated that Dr. Halatyan, a member of the Majlis in Iran, would head the ASALA, which was reorganizing under the name Armed Propaganda Union for the Liberation of Turkish Armenia. The capture of Nayir Souner and other ASALA members believed involved in the Orly Airport bombing had weakened the leadership of the ASALA.

October 27, 1983 — UNITED STATES — The Federal Aviation Administration cautioned airlines and security personnel to be particularly attentive to screening and other security procedures following the October 25 invasion of Grenada. A hijacking to Cuba could pose additional problems in light of Cuba's involvement in Grenada.

October 28, 1983 — REPUBLIC OF SOUTH AFRICA — Thembinkosi Paulson Ngcobo, believed to be an African National Congress guerrilla, was arrested carrying a powerful bomb outside a hall where South African prime minister P. W. Botha was giving a speech. No one was injured. On March 15, 1984, Ngcobo was sentenced to 20 years.

October 28, 1983 — MALAYSIA — The director general of the Department of Civil Aviation, Dr. Abdul Kuddus, announced that Interpol had informed him that an American mercenary, aged 65, had entered Malaysia from Thailand with the intention of hiding out until President Ronald Reagan visited Seoul on November 12. The unidentified mercenary had indicated plans to assassinate Reagan in South Korea. 83102801

October 29, 1983 — CHILE — A bomb planted near the director's office caused damage, but no injuries, at the United States Chilean Cultural Center in Valparaiso. 83102901

October 29, 1983 — LEBANON — Two United States Marines were slightly injured from a rocket-propelled grenade fired on their position at the Lebanese University. 83102902

October 29, 1983 — LEBANON — An Armenian was arrested after throwing a hand grenade at the Turkish embassy in B'abda. No casualties resulted from the 10:00 A.M. attack. 83102903

October 30, 1983 — FEDERAL REPUBLIC OF GERMANY — At 4:00 A.M., slight damage resulted from a bomb blast in front of the Turkish consulate general in Stuttgart. The Brigades for the Liberation of the Turkish People, a previously unknown group, claimed responsibility in the attack aimed at impeding elections in Turkey. 83103001

Fall 1983 — SPAIN — A bungled terrorist attack against a Saudi aircraft at Madrid's Barajas International Airport was suspected when a rocket launcher was found by security guards near the main runway. Four Iranians, including Seye Jabbar Hosseini, were thought responsible and were arrested on July 24, 1984. 83999901

Fall 1983 — ITALY — Ciro Rozzato, an Italian Red Brigades member, was killed during an armed attack on a French bank executed by Direct Action. The presence of Rozzato in the Direct Action terrorist squad fueled speculation on a merger between French and Italian terrorists. 83999902

November 1983 — COLOMBIA — The Black Liberation Force, a previously unknown group, took credit for a bomb attack on an army bus in southern Bogota as a protest for an alleged racist incident involving the army's failure to promote a black. No one was injured.

November 1, 1983 — MARTINIQUE — In Fort-de-France, an explosion caused slight damage to a building housing the American consulate and the Chase Manhattan Bank. No one took credit for the attack. 83110101

November 2, 1983 — SWITZERLAND — Acting on information that three bombs were planted in the Inter-Continental Hotel in Geneva, Swiss authorities searched for the bombs but failed to find them.

November 2, 1983 — COLOMBIA — Luis Suarez, the alleged head of Death to Kidnappers (MAS), was assassinated in his La Dorada home by several armed men. The MAS group was created by drug traffickers to protect themselves against kidnappings and extortion.

November 3, 1983 — SPAIN — Prime Minister Felipe Gonzalez announced stricter measures to combat terrorism, including amended policies on prison terms, court procedures, prison conditions, and international cooperation. He reiterated the country's no-negotiation policy and criticized France for providing asylum to terrorists on its territory.

November 4, 1983 — LEBANON — Twenty-nine Israeli paramilitary border police and 32 Arab prisoners died when a Chevrolet pickup truck, loaded with 1,200 pounds of explosives, blew up beside an Israeli compound near Tyre in occupied territory. Sentries failed to impede the attack when they shot the driver.

November 5, 1983 — GUATEMALA — Four gunmen in two passing cars fired at the Guatemala City home of United States ambassador Frederick Chapin. Security guards returned the fire, but apparently no one was injured in the attack, claimed by the Rebel Armed Forces (FAR) as a response to the United States invasion of Grenada. The Guatemalan Labor Party (PGI) also took credit for the attack in a call to the news media. 83110501

November 5, 1983 — BELGIUM — In a phone call to the BRUSSELS DOMESTIC SERVICE, the Basque Fatherland and Liberty (ETA) threatened attacks against Belgium unless three ETA members arrested recently were released within three days. 83110502

November 7, 1983 — INDIA — In Assam, 14 persons were killed and 60 injured in a bomb blast at a Gauhate railway station.

November 7, 1983 — UNITED STATES — Kathy Boudin, a Weather Underground member, was scheduled to stand trial in Goshen, New York, on 13 counts of robbery and 3 counts of murder connected with the 1981 holdup of a Brink's armored car.

November 7, 1983 — COLOMBIA — A guerrilla group calling itself the Shining Path Group kidnapped a wealthy miner, Luis Carlos Hernandez, in Oro, located in northwestern Colombia. About 20 men also attacked Puerto Claves and looted stores. The relationship between this guerrilla group and a group bearing the same name in Peru is unknown.

November 7, 1983 — COLOMBIA — The Popular Liberation Army (ELP) issued death threats against local judges. The ELP criticized the Betancur administration and its recent offer of amnesty to all guerrilla groups.

November 7, 1983 — LEBANON — A booby-trapped French jeep, parked near the Iranian embassy in Beirut, was disarmed without mishap. 83110701

November 7, 1983 — FEDERAL REPUBLIC OF GERMANY — About 40 Palestinian supporters of Yasir Arafat occupied the Arab League office in Bonn to protest "against the war of destruction against the PLO [Palestine Liberation Organization] and Fatah supported by the mutineers and pro-

Syrian troops." The PLO, Arafat's organization, had come under increasing pressures from rival factions. 83110702

November 7, 1983 — GREECE — Two security guards — Muhammad Karim Shadid and Ahmad 'Uqlah — at the Jordanian embassy in Athens were seriously wounded by a gunman. Shadid later died from the attack, claimed by the Arab Revolutionary Brigades in a call to AGENCE FRANCE-PRESSE in Paris. 83110703

November 7, 1983 — AUSTRIA — Seven men and one woman occupied and vandalized the Iran Air office in Vienna as a protest against mass murder, war, and political imprisonment by the Khomeini government. All but the woman were arrested. 83110704

November 7, 1983 — UNITED STATES — A bomb blast to the United States Capitol caused about three hundred thousand dollars in damages. The bomb was placed in the Mansfield Room, across the hall from the Republican cloakroom and diagonally across from the minority leader's office. The blast damaged the Republican cloakroom, nearby walls, and artwork. No one was injured in the 11:00 P.M. explosion. In a taped message to the WASHINGTON POST, the Armed Resistance Unit claimed responsibility in support of "all nations' struggle" against United States military aggression in Grenada, Lebanon, El Salvador, and Nicaragua. Investigations by the Federal Bureau of Investigation were disclosed in a closed session of the subcommittee on security and terrorism in March 1984. An FBI spokesman indicated that the Armed Resistance Unit was not suspected as the perpetrator. On June 1, files seized in a Baltimore apartment linked members of the United Freedom Front (UFF) to the bombing.

November 7, 1983 — PERU — Jose Antonio Onrubia, an executive of the Bank of Credit of Peru and a Spaniard, was kidnapped in the Miraflores section of Lima. Onrubia's driver was murdered during the kidnapping. On April 7, Onrubia was released in good health. 83110706

November 8, 1983 — PORTUGAL — The Portuguese government increased its security around French firms and interests after receiving intelligence reports that an anti-French Iranian commando squad had been sent there. The Iranian Islamic regime had been highly critical of France since its October delivery of five Super Etendard jets to Iraq.

November 8, 1983 — JAPAN — Incendiary devices caused minor damage to a Ground Self-Defense Force outpost on the outskirts of Osaka. The Middle Core Faction, an extreme left-wing group, took credit for the devices as a protest to the upcoming visit of President Ronald Reagan.

November 8, 1983 — CYPRUS — In a phone call to the Libyan magazine AL-MAWQIF AL-'ARABI, a Greek-speaking person threatened to blow up their offices located in Nicosia. 83110801

November 8, 1983 — GUATEMALA — Herminio Edelfo Ramos Perez, a linguist working for the United States Agency for International Development, was kidnapped from his Los Corrales home by seven men armed with submachine guns. Perez was the fourth linguist at the United States–funded project kidnapped this year; the other three were later found murdered. 83110802

November 9, 1983 — LEBANON — A new terrorist group, the Black October Organization, was formed to carry out a number of assassinations.

November 9, 1983 — GUATEMALA — In Guatemala City, security police deactivated a powerful bomb minutes before it was timed to explode at the crowded Interfair.

November 9, 1983 — NETHERLANDS — Alfred Heineken, 60, and his chauffeur, Ab Doderer, were kidnapped by three armed men as the two were leaving the Heineken Breweries in Amsterdam. Heineken had just hosted a reception for police responsible for foiling an extortion plot against the breweries. The masked kidnappers forced Heineken and Doderer into an orange van and took off at a high speed. Heineken is believed to be the wealthiest person in the Netherlands with assets estimated at $500 million.

On November 11, Dutch newspapers reported that an $8.1 million ransom was demanded. To prove that the two were still alive, the kidnappers sent a picture of Heineken and Doderer holding a newspaper dated after the kidnapping. As negotiations dragged on, the kidnappers demanded a news blackout. A ransom of over $10 million was stuffed into six suitcases and left for kidnappers at a designated location on November 28, but the two were not released. On November 30 at 5:00 A.M., police raided an Amsterdam warehouse and found Heineken and Doderer behind a false wall. The two were handcuffed and tethered by long chains to the walls of concrete cells. Both men were in surprisingly good health after their 21-day ordeal. Authorities had been watching the warehouse since November 16 after receiving an anonymous tip. Fearing injury to the captives, the police had waited to act until sure that Heineken was in the warehouse. The delivery of two Chinese take-out meals provided the proof. After the raid, the police arrested 26 Dutch citizens, most of whom were relatives of one another. Twenty were released after questioning due to lack of evidence. Cornelis Van Hout and William Holleeder, suspected of the abduction, were arrested in Paris on February 29 and later extradited to the Netherlands. Over $8 million of the ransom was discovered at various locations throughout the country. In a news conference in early December, Heineken described his captivity in the damp, unheated cell, during which he was given little food and water and was forbidden to speak.

November 9, 1983 — UNITED STATES — In New York, Edwin P. Wilson, a former agent of the Central Intelligence Agency, was fined $75,000 and sentenced to 25 years for attempting to kill two prosecutors, five government witnesses, and two business associates in connection with Wilson's trial on illegal arms deals with Libya. Wilson allegedly tried to pay fellow inmates to assassinate the nine people. At the time, Wilson was serving a 15-year prison term for the November 17, 1982, arms-sales conviction. The alleged hit list included Jerome S. Brower, an explosives dealer; Reginald Slocombe, a business associate; Edward Coughlin, Wilson's ex-financial manager; John Heath, a former army weapons expert recruited by Wilson to train Libyan terrorists; Ernest Keiser, who helped lure Wilson out of Libya; Raphael Quintero, an associate of Wilson; Frances Heydt, another associate; E. Lawrence Barsella, a United States prosecutor; and Carol Bruce, another United States prosecutor. Wilson also faced charges that he offered $1 million to have dissident Libyans murdered; the trial on these charges ended in acquittal. On February 18, 1983, Wilson was convicted of smuggling explosives to Libya, a charge unconnected with his arms-sales conviction.

November 9, 10, 12, 1983 — JORDAN — In Amman, three bombs were found and deactivated without injury. The bombs included a 12.5-pound bomb left near the Saudi Arabian Airlines office, a 25-pound bomb placed in a vacant lot near the Chinese embassy, and a 25-pound bomb planted in the Third Circle in Jabal Amman. 83110901, 83111001, 83111201

November 11, 1983 — LEBANON — Security sources disclosed that the Husayn Musawi group was preparing an armored personnel carrier, seized from the Lebanese Army, for an attack against United States or French interests.

November 11, 1983 — FEDERAL REPUBLIC OF GERMANY— In Stuttgart, members of the Red Front, an anti-Yugoslav Albanian extremist group, disrupted a performance by a folk ensemble from Yugoslavia. Red Front members smashed tables and assaulted members of the Yugoslav general consulate staff, who attended the performance. Fifteen Yugoslavs sustained injuries. The perpetrators were arrested. 83111101

November 12, 1983 — IRAN — No one was injured in a bomb blast to a building in Tehran that housed some 150 Italian technicians working on the power plant being constructed at Bandar Abbas. The Aref Boluki Dynamite Group, an anti-Khomeini organization, took credit for the blast in leaflets left at the scene. 83111202

November 13, 1983 — ANGOLA — The National Union for the Total Independence of Angola (UNITA) kidnapped 17 Europeans, including 5 British and 12 Portuguese, in raids against government positions in Kazombo and Kavungu. 83111301

November 14, 1983 — GUADELOUPE — In Basse-Terre, a car bomb in the parking lot of the prefecture exploded as people were coming to work. Twenty were injured, 10 seriously. Five other bombs, believed placed by individuals who wanted independence from France, damaged several cars and an airplane in Pointe-a-Pitre. The studios of RADIO CARAIBE INTERNATIONALE were also destroyed. The Caribbean Revolutionary Alliance claimed responsibility.

November 14, 1983 — BOLIVIA — Michael Wurche, the general manager of Lufthansa Airlines, was kidnapped by unidentified assailants in downtown La Paz. 83111401

November 15, 1983 — JORDAN — Three members of the Abu Nidal group were arrested after arriving from Syria. Documents on their person indicated intended acts to blow up the Jordanian intelligence headquarters and British, French, and United States airline offices. Other seized documents included plans to assassinate various foreign ambassadors.

November 15, 1983 — SPAIN — Demonstrations outside the United States embassy in Madrid left several people injured, one seriously, when police moved in. Thirteen demonstrators, who were protesting United States policy in Central America, were arrested.

November 15, 1983 — GREECE — United States Naval captain George Tsantes, 53, was assassinated at 7:30 A.M. by two youths on a motor scooter while Tsantes's car was stopped at Kifisia Avenue in Athens for a traffic light. Tsantes was hit by four .45 caliber shots in the chest and head. Nikolaos Veloutsos, Tsantes's chauffeur, was also killed in the attack. The November 17 Movement, a group named for the violent demonstrations in 1973 that led to the overthrow of the junta in 1974, claimed responsibility for the attack. Two days later, Athens police announced that the murder weapon had been linked to the 1975 assassination of Central Intelligence Agency station chief, Richard Welch. In a newspaper message published in ELEVTHEROTIPIA, the terrorist organization claimed that it killed the captain to express its dissatisfaction with the ruling Greek Socialist government. On May 22, 1984, authorities arrested Fuad Kourad, a Jordanian, for the murder. 83111501

November 15, 1983 — GREECE — The parked car of Orbie Sullivan, United States chief sergeant at the Ellinikon base, was the target of two Molotov cocktails. The resulting fire caused minor damage. 83111502

November 15, 1983 — SPAIN — In Bilboa, two explosions caused minor damage to the Bank of America on the Arrequivar Square and to Rank Xerox on Mazarredo Avenue. No one was injured in the midnight blasts. 83111503–04

November 15, 1983 — SUDAN — In two separate attacks, the Sudanese People's Liberation Army kidnapped 11 technicians working on the building site of the Jonglei Canal in southern Sudan. Those kidnapped included 7 French, 2 British, and 2 Pakistani citizens. In a signed leaflet, the Sudanese government was given 48 hours to stop construction of the canal. The terrorists also demanded that France recognize the rebels and end its aid to Sudan. On November 17, government forces freed the 2 British hostages who worked for the Chevron Oil Company. The rebels had threatened to kill the hostages by 8:00 P.M. on November 17 if their demands had not been fulfilled. On November 18, government forces managed to free the remaining hostages in an attack against a rebel camp. The British citizens had been held for 40 hours; the other hostages had been held for approximately 72 hours. All escaped unharmed. 83111505–06

November 16, 1983 — LEBANON — An alleged operation against the United States Marine forces in Beirut was foiled by authorities. Further information was not disclosed.

November 16, 1983 — AUSTRIA — Mrs. Stefan Svrudlev and her 13-year-old son were believed kidnapped sometime after they left Munich by train for Vienna. Stefan Svrudlev, a former Bulgarian secret service officer, had testified in connection with the assassination attempt against the Pope. Stefan had alerted authorities to the disappearance of his wife and son. 83111601

November 17, 1983 — LEBANON — A caller claiming membership in the Islamic Jihad Organization threatened to blow up the American University in Beirut if the Americans did not withdraw from Beirut. 83111701

November 18, 1983 — FRANCE — Fourteen French planes from the aircraft carrier *Clemenceau* carried out a reprisal raid against Islamic Amal targets in the Bekaa Valley. These raids were coordinated with those of Israel. Both countries were retaliating against suicide truck-bombing attacks in Lebanon. French sources put the death toll at 50; however, Iranian radio said that 3 Revolutionary Guards were killed. Husayn Musawi's home was destroyed in the raid. Musawi heads the Islamic Amal, which is believed responsible for the October 23 bomb attacks in Beirut that killed 58 French paratroopers and 241 United States Marines.

November 18, 1983 — JAPAN — Two men, Yi Chong-sik and Hidekichi Yonesato, fired 10 revolver shots in the Tokyo office of the pro-Pyongyang General Association of Korean Residents in Japan. Chong-sik, a South Korean, and Hidekichi, a Japanese, staged the attack to protest the October 9 bomb explosion in Rangoon, blamed on the North Korean government. No one was injured in the Tokyo attack. Both gunmen were later arrested. 83111801

November 18, 1983 — USSR — Aeroflot flight 6833, enroute from Tbilisi to Leningrad with an intermediate stop in Batumi, was the scene of an attempted hijacking by 5 men and 3 women, traveling in a wedding party with prominent Georgians. Shortly after takeoff, Guia Tibidze approached the cockpit to demand that the plane be flown to Turkey. One of the pilots shot and killed Tibidze, and then locked the bulletproof door of the cockpit. Rather than concede to the hijackers' demands, the pilot circled Tbilisi and later landed. David Mikhaberidze, another hijacker, committed suicide upon learning that the plane had returned to Tbilisi. For eight hours, the plane and its 59 passengers waited on the tarmac under a terrorist threat to blow up the plane. The incident ended when antiterrorist commandos stormed the plane in an operation that killed 3 crew, 4 passengers, and a hijacker. The pilot, copilot, and a flight attendant were among the dead. In August, Teymiraz Chikhladze, German Kobakhidze, and Dakha and Paata Iverieli, were sentenced to 14 years, and Anna Varsimashvili, an Aeroflot lounge attendant, was given a suspended sentence of 5 years. Varsimashvili had helped the terrorists smuggle their weapons aboard. Chikhladze was a priest; Kobakhidze was the son of a well-known movie director; and the two Iverieli brothers were doctors. This was the 14th known hijacking in the Soviet Union since 1970. Aeroflot pilots have been armed after a rash of incidents in 1973. 83111802

November 19, 1983 — ITALY — Three armed men kidnapped Anna and Giorgio Calissoni from their family's estate in Aprilia, Rome, and then held them for a L 7 billion ($4.2 million) ransom. On December 18, an anonymous call led police to a trash can containing the ear of the 16-year-old son and heir to the jewelry store fortune. The kidnappers also sent a photograph to the IL MESSAGGERO daily, which showed Anna and Giorgio chained together. In the photograph, Giorgio's right ear was missing and his face was bleeding. The Communist of the Attack, a previously unknown group, took credit for the kidnapping. After the payment of $2.5 million ransom, the mother and son were released on Christmas Eve near their family estate. On January 4, five shepherds were charged in the kidnapping.

November 20, 1983 — GUADELOUPE — In Grand-Bourg, a bomb damaged the police station. No injuries were reported.

November 20, 1983 — FRANCE — Shortly after midnight, one of two men on a motorcycle hurled a bomb into the L'Orée du Bois restaurant filled with diners. Twenty people, including children, were injured from flying glass. Only one serious injury was reported.

November 20, 1983 — NORTHERN IRELAND — The Catholic Reaction Force, a previously unknown group, attacked a Protestant church at Darkley in the county of Armagh. The Sunday attack came during services and left three dead and seven wounded. 83112001

November 21, 1983 — UNITED STATES — Republic Airlines flight 275, a DC-9 enroute from Kalamazoo, Michigan, to Chicago with 35 passengers, was the scene of a foiled hijacking by Rasul Ali Shakar, 33. The hijacker, a Detroit bus driver also known as Russell Chappelle, claimed to have a bomb in his carry-on luggage and threatened to blow up the plane if he was not allowed to talk to Democratic presidential candidate Jesse Jackson. One of the 5 crew members subdued Shakar prior to landing in Chicago, where he was arrested by federal agents. One passenger suffered a heart attack in the incident. 83112101

November 21, 1983 — COLOMBIA — At 7:00 A.M., Jacques Kergelius, son of the French consul in Monteria, was kidnapped by 20 guerrillas as he drove toward the La Ceiba Farm in Tierra Alta Municipality. The Army for National Liberation (ELN) claimed responsibility. 83112102

November 22, 1983 — AUSTRIA — Michael Kuehnen and Thomas Brehl, chairman and functionary of the Action Front of National Socialists/National Activists, were arrested on the Westautobahn near Ybbs for possession of an automatic and a gas pistol. Kuehnen founded the neo-Nazi organization in 1977.

November 22, 1983 — SWAZILAND — In an armed attack at a house in Elugaganeni in Manzini, two African National Congress (ANC) members — Sandile Njanza and Keith McFadden — were killed. A third ANC member, Cyril

Raymond, was captured by police. The ANC blamed the Pretoria government for the murders. 83112201

November 23, 1983 — COLOMBIA — Lawyer Jaime Betancur, 53-year-old brother of President Belisario Betancur, was kidnapped by the Army for National Liberation (ELN), a left-wing extremist group that rejected the president's 1983 amnesty offer to guerrilla groups to end years of warfare. According to Betancur's driver, five heavily armed men abducted the dean of the law school on the campus of Catholic University in Bogota after he had finished teaching a class. In a November 25 statement to the CARACOL network, the ELN demanded higher wages for workers, release of political prisoners, a freeze on consumer prices, and reductions in the price of public services in return for the release of Betancur. On November 30, the ELN warned in a letter to the EL BOGOTANO daily that they would kill their hostage by December 10 if their demands were not met. The death threat was withdrawn on December 1, and the kidnappers promised to release him on December 7 immediately following a national peace demonstration. The lawyer was freed unharmed as promised on December 7, following strong condemnations of the kidnapping by Fidel Castro. Leftist guerrillas are believed to still be holding 50 persons.

November 23, 1983 — LEBANON — The United States Marines were alerted to a possible car-bombing attack.

November 24, 1983 — IRAQ — ASH-SHARQ AL-AWSAT, a London-based newspaper, reported that the Abu Nidal group had closed its Baghdad headquarters after the group's members and families were deported to Syria.

November 24, 1983 — BOLIVIA — In La Paz, a 4:00 A.M. bomb blast caused extensive damage, but no injuries, to the Bolivian Parliament building.

November 24, 1983 — SPAIN — Proposed legislation aimed at curbing terrorist attacks was presented by the Socialist government to parliament. The measures included restrictions on the media, bans on political groups, and the rights of judges to detain terrorist suspects without trial for up to 2½ years.

November 24, 1983 — REPUBLIC OF SOUTH AFRICA — Carl Niehaus and Johanna Lourens, two white students, were sentenced to 15 and 4 years, respectively, for their ties to the African National Congress (ANC). Niehaus is a confessed member of the ANC, who had allegedly photographed the Johannesburg municipal gasworks in a plan to sabotage the plant. Lourens, Niehaus's fiancee, was accused of helping Niehaus and serving as a messenger.

November 24, 1983 — GERMAN DEMOCRATIC REPUBLIC — The government here issued a protest to the West Berlin Senate regarding a terrorist bombing at an East Berlin plant. 83112401

November 24, 1983 — NETHERLANDS — The Costa Rican consulate was temporarily occupied by 25 youths of the Movement of Solidarity with the Central American Peoples, who asked the Costa Rican government to end its joint military exercises with United States Marines. In addition, the youths demanded that the leaders of the Democratic Force (FDN) be expelled from Costa Rica. 83112402

November 24, 1983 — IRELAND — Don Tidey, a grocery chain executive, was kidnapped by four armed men in police uniforms as he was driving his daughter to school. After abducting Tidey, the kidnappers drove off, leaving the daughter unharmed in her father's car. On December 16, police and the army's Ranger Corps fought a gun battle in Ballinamore with the Irish Republican Army (IRA) guerrillas who had kidnapped Tidey. The executive was freed unharmed in the rescue effort that left a policeman and a soldier dead and three people wounded. The IRA was holding Tidey for a $7.5 million ransom. Two of the kidnappers were captured, but the others, including Dominic McGlinchey, managed to escape. McGlinchey is Ireland's most-wanted terrorist. 83112403

November 24, 1983 — UNITED STATES — Security was tightened around the White House and the State Department following a letter sent to the Manassas Police Department that warned of a suicide truck-bombing attack on the State Department. Police guards at the Capitol also indicated that they received an early morning call threatening a bombing there. Dump trucks filled with sand were placed near access roads to the White House, the State Department, and the Capitol. Officials said that intelligence reports supported the fears raised by the Manassas letter. The WASHINGTON POST reported on December 7 that Shiite Moslems were behind the threat. 83112404

November 26, 1983 — UGANDA — Antigovernment guerrillas disabled a Red Cross van with a rocket-propelled grenade that killed a nurse, Catherine Musoke, and the driver, Ali Ramathan. Three other Ugandan relief workers were wounded in the attack in Luwero district, north of Kampala.

November 28, 1983 — CHAD — The Organization for the Liberation of Chad from Imperialism and Fascism (OLTIF) claimed credit for an attack against the Zairian embassy in Ndjamena in which three persons were killed. Tahir Said, OLTIF leader, signed the letter sent to Lagos, in which other domestic terrorist acts against the government were attributed to the group. 83112801

November 29, 1983 — LEBANON — Sixty employees of the Middle East Airlines were kidnapped while returning home in two buses from work at the Beirut International Airport. The employees were released unharmed by the gunmen a short while later.

November 29, 1983 — ITALY — In Milan, a total of 210 alleged leftist guerrillas were on trial for over eight hundred crimes connected to a six-year guerrilla campaign in the Lombardy region during the 1970s. Earlier in the week, Marco Barbone and Paolo Morandini, confessed killers of Walter Tobagi of Italy's CORRIERE DELLA SERA newspaper, received suspended sentences after cooperating with authorities in apprehending over 50 other suspected terrorists.

November 30, 1983 — LEBANON — Beirut VOICE OF LEBANON reported the formation of the Black Autumn and Revenge group by Yasir Arafat. The group was alleged to consist of 350 Palestinians, sent to European capitals where attacks were planned against dissident Palestine Liberation Organization members and Syrian political and military officials.

November 30, 1983 — URUGUAY — Salvador Horacio Paino, alleged founder of the Triple A terrorist organization, was arrested in Montevideo. The Argentine Foreign Ministry had requested his extradition.

December 1983 — PERU — After an extended manhunt, authorities arrested in Huaraz, 250 miles north of Lima, the chief ideologue and second in command of the Maoist Shining Path guerrillas, Emilio Antonio Diaz.

December 1983 — ISRAEL — In Tel Aviv, the Egyptian embassy received numerous bomb threats. 83129901

December 1983 — KUWAIT — A Kuwaiti plane, enroute from Dubai to Karachi, was hijacked to Mehrabad Airport in Tehran. No details were available. On January 8, 1986, Iran and Kuwait agreed to resolve their differences over the return of the airliner, parked in Tehran since the incident. 83129902

December 1983 — IRAN — An Iraqi youth attempted to hijack an Islamic Republic of Iran airline, enroute from Bushehr to Shiraz. Shortly after takeoff, he went to the washroom, where he removed a gun and some explosives from his briefcase. Upon leaving the washroom, he announced to the passengers that he was hijacking the plane. As he walked to the cockpit to tell the pilot the new destination, he was jumped by a steward. The ensuing struggle sent off a small explosion that wounded a stewardess and the hijacker. On landing in Shiraz Airport, the wounded were taken to a hospital. The stewardess's wounds were minor and she was later released. No further details were available. 83129903

December 1, 1983 — LEBANON — In two separate Beirut attacks, French peacekeeping forces sustained casualties. While on patrol at 5:25 A.M., three French soldiers were wounded from three rocket-propelled grenades; at 5:50 A.M., a French soldier was fatally wounded by sniper fire. 83120101–02

December 2, 4, 1983 — IRAQ — Jean-Christophe Lefas, Robert Laurent, and Yves Moy, three French technicians working for the Thompson company near Dahuk, were kidnapped by the Kurdish Democratic Party (KDP). Two demands were made for their release: the return of 8,000 Kurdish families deported by the Iraqi regime, and the release of 57 Kurds sentenced to death by the Baghdad regime. In later communiques, the second demand was dropped. On December 4, an Italian, an Egyptian, and a Thai were kidnapped by the KDP, who also made their release contingent upon the first demand. The Austrian and French governments carried on negotiations that finally obtained the release of the three French hostages on July 23, 1984. 83120201, 83120401

December 2, 1983 — GREECE — No one claimed credit for a Molotov cocktail attack that destroyed a British embassy car parked near the center of Athens. No injuries were reported. 83120202

December 2, 1983 — PHILIPPINES — A small explosive device was removed without incident at the United States embassy in Quezon City. 83120203

December 3, 1983 — THAILAND — At noon, a hand grenade was thrown at the Israeli embassy in Bangkok. No one was injured in the attack that damaged a wall surrounding the compound. 83120301

December 4, 1983 — FRANCE — The Antiterrorist Liberation Groups (GAL), bent on revenging Basque Fatherland and Liberty (ETA) terrorist acts, kidnapped Segundo Marey, a Spaniard connected to the ETA, in southern France. Marey was later released unharmed. 83120402

December 5, 1983 — LEBANON — In Moslem west Beirut, a Fiat, packed with three hundred pounds of Hexogene, exploded in a crowded neighborhood, killing 14 and wounding 84. The blast occurred on Rawas Street during the morning rush hour and set 30 cars and nearby buildings on fire.

December 5, 1983 — FRANCE — Ara Toranian, leader of the National Armenian Movement, escaped serious injury from a bomb planted in his car. No one claimed responsibility for the blast. 83120501

December 6, 1983 — ISRAEL — At 12:50 P.M. in Jerusalem, a bomb planted under a city bus exploded killing 6 and injuring 44, 8 seriously. The dead included 5 Israelis and an American tourist, Serina Sussman, 60. Both the Palestinian Liberation Organization (PLO) and the rival Fatah—Revolutionary Council claimed credit for the worst terrorist act in the city since 1979. Following the blast, the Israeli police arrested 41 suspects but by evening had released all but 4. The bus had stopped for a red light along Herzl Boulevard in Jewish west Jerusalem when the explosion blew the roof off of the packed bus and scattered debris for over 50 yards. A second bus, waiting behind the first, was also damaged by the explosion, and 5 of its passengers were injured. The bomb contained nails to cause maximum human injury. 83120601

December 7, 1983 — FEDERAL REPUBLIC OF GERMANY — The federal interior minister officially banned the neo-Nazi group, Action Front of National Socialists/National Activists (ANS/NA), headed by Michael Kuehnen.

December 7, 1983 — MOZAMBIQUE — In the suburbs of Maputo, a bomb blast injured two South Africans, asleep in bed. 83120701

December 9, 12, 20, 30, 1983 — ISRAEL — On April 9, 1984, Israeli police announced the arrest of four members — Amram Deri, Avraham Deri, David Deri, and Uri Ben-Ayoun — of the Terror against Terror (TNT) group, responsible for hand grenade attacks at 14 Christian and Moslem holy places throughout Jerusalem in December 1983. On December 9, two booby-trapped hand grenades were left on the steps of a Franciscan monastery, one was planted at a Greek Orthodox seminary, and one was lashed to a door of the Dormition Abbey. On December 12, three grenades were planted in Husan, an Arab village on the occupied West Bank. On December 20, two grenades detonated in El Azariya, seriously injuring an Arab. On December 30, grenades exploded near two mosques in Hebron. On November 21, 1984, all but Avraham Deri were sentenced to six years for planting the bombs. The three men also received three-year suspended sentences.

December 10, 1983 — UNITED KINGDOM — In an early morning blast, four soldiers at the Royal Artillary Barracks in the Woolwich district of London were slightly injured. The Scottish National Liberation Army claimed responsibility in a call to the PRESS ASSOCIATION and threatened further attacks. The Irish Republican Army also claimed credit. 83121001

December 11, 1983 — SPAIN — In Madrid, a bomb exploded in front of the United States embassy. No injuries or damage resulted from the explosion, attributed to Honduran guerrillas protesting United States presence in their country. 83121101

December 12, 1983 — COSTA RICA — In San Jose, police guarding the United States embassy repelled an armed attack by two men. No one was injured in the exchange, in which both assailants escaped. 83121201

December 12, 1983 — LEBANON — According to Beirut VOICE OF LEBANON, three British soldiers were briefly held by Amal members when their patrol entered the Harat Hurayk section of the city. 83121202

December 12, 1983 — KUWAIT — At 9:32 A.M., a lone man in a truck with explosives and gas cylinders plowed through a flimsy sheet-metal embassy gate, veered left, and detonated the explosives at the corner of the administration building of the United States embassy. The blast blew out windows, caused the collapse of the three-story structure, and started a large fire. Fifty-nine were injured and 4 killed, including a Syrian working at the embassy, a Kuwaiti visa applicant, the truck driver, and an unidentified person. Most of the injured were locally employed embassy staff and visa applicants.

At 10:00 A.M., a booby-trapped Buick parked in the employee parking lot exploded at the Kuwait International Airport, killing an Egyptian technician and injuring 6. The airport's telecommunications center and control tower were damaged by the blast.

At 10:45 A.M., a booby-trapped car parked next to the French embassy exploded in the suburb of Jabriyah. The blast blew up a protective wall but left most of the building intact. At least 3 people were injured.

Other blasts were directed at the Ash-Shu'aybah oil refinery, an American compound in Al-Bida', the Ministry of Electricity and Water, and an American compound in Salwa. In total, about 10 people were injured in the 4 attacks. A fifth bomb was defused near the Hawalli passport office in the Ar-Rumaythiyah suburb.

On December 14, Iraqi warplanes and long-range ground-to-ground missiles hit the Iranian cities of Dezful, Andimeshk, Bahbahan, Nahavand, and Rahmoroz as a reprisal for the Kuwaiti bombings, claimed by the pro-Iranian Islamic Jihad. Twenty-four were killed and 283 wounded in the air attack. Khomeini's regime condemned the murders and claimed no responsibility for the Shiite Moslems who blew up Kuwaiti targets.

On December 18, the Kuwaiti government accused 9 Iraqis and 3 Lebanese of the December 12 bombings. Ten of those accused were in custody and were identified as members of the Islamic Al Dawa party, a Shiite group with close ties to Iran and to the Hezbollah. Raad Akeel Badran, identified by prints from fingers severed in the blast, was the suicide bomber at the United States embassy. Another 7 suspects were arrested on December 27. By February, 21 suspects were held in connection with the bombings. On February 11, the State Security Court convened to try the 21 prisoners and 4 others in absentia. Table 4.1 lists the defendants' names (aliases), ages, nationalities, and sentences.

As of April 1987, none of the death sentences had been carried out. The 17 Kuwaiti prisoners have instead become important pawns in the game of international terrorism. Their release has been demanded on numerous occasions by the Islamic Jihad in return for Americans held captive in Lebanon in 1986; however, the Kuwaiti government repeatedly refuses to release them. 83121203–10

December 13, 1983 — FRANCE — Security was increased around potential terrorist targets, including the presidential palace in Paris. Recent attacks on French citizens and interests in Lebanon prompted the security measures.

Table 4.1. _Suspects in the December 12, 1983, Bombing in Kuwait_

Name	Age	Nationality	Sentence
1. Badir Ibrahim 'Abd ar-Rida	30	Iraqi	Death
2. Elias Fu'ad Sa'ib	23	Lebanese	Death
3. Ahmad 'Ali Husayn (Abu Haydar)*	?	Iraqi	Death
4. Mustafa Ibrahim Ahmad (Abu Zahra)*	?	Iraqi	Death
5. 'Abdil Husayn 'Aziz 'Abbas	28	Iraqi	15 years
6. Jamal Ja'afar Muhammad*	?	Iraqi	Death
7. 'Amir 'Abd az-Zahra Sulayman al-'Awad	22	Iraqi	Life
8. Husayn Qasim Hassan	27	Iraqi	Death
9. 'Adil 'Abd ar-Razzaq Shaykh Hadi	30	Iraqi	Life
10. Nosrallah Matuk Saywan	30	Iraqi	Life
11. Jabbar 'Abbas Jabbar	22	Iraqi	Life
12. Husayn al-Sayyid Yusif al Musawi	28	Lebanese	Life
13. 'Azzam Khalil Ibrahim	28	Lebanese	15 years
14. Ibrahim Sabah Frayhaj (Ahmad)	29	Iraqi	15 years
15. Ya'arib Faiq Mahdi	24	Iraqi	15 years
16. Hassan Flayj al-Hamad	26	Iraqi	Life
17. Sa'ad Yasin 'Abdallah al-Dhayabi	21	Kuwaiti	Life
18. Yusef Majid Wahib	21	Iraqi	10 years
19. 'Abdil Muhsin Rashash 'Abbas	20	Iraqi	5 years
20. Haytham Mahfuz 'Abd ak-Karim*	?	Iraqi	Acquitted
21. Nasir Matar Dahsh	25	No Nationality	5 years
22. Ahmad 'Abd ak-Karim Niimah (Kazim)	29	Iraqi	Acquitted
23. Sharif Mutlaq Nasir	44	No Nationality	Acquitted
24. 'Abd ar-Rida Dawud Madwah	53	Kuwaiti	Acquitted
25. 'Abd as-Samad Jawad 'Abdallah as-Saffar	32	Kuwaiti	Acquitted

*Still at large.

December 13, 1983 — LEBANON — A French paratrooper was killed while on patrol in Beirut. 83121301

December 13, 1983 — GUATEMALA — At 7:30 P.M., unidentified persons in vehicles sprayed machine-gun fire and hurled a fragmentation grenade at the Salvadoran embassy in Guatemala City. No one was injured and damage was minor in the attack later claimed by a left-wing clandestine group. 83121302

December 13, 1983 — UNITED STATES — In a phone call, the United Freedom Front warned a navy recruitment office in East Meadow, New York, of bombs hidden in attache cases. After clearing the building, police covered the two attache cases, which had been affixed to the east and west staircases, with blast-absorbing blankets. Minutes later the bombs exploded, causing heavy damage to the stairwells. The terrorist group's communique criticized United States intervention in South and Central America.

December 13, 1983 — SPAIN — In a phone call to a news agency in Barcelona, an anonymous caller claiming to represent the Islamic Jihad organization threatened further "violent acts over Europe" unless United States, French, Italian, and British peacekeeping forces were pulled out of Lebanon. 83121303

December 14–15, 1983 — LEBANON — Just before midnight, on December 14, 1983, a French paratrooper was killed by a shell near his observation post. On the morning of December 15, a second paratrooper was assassinated while emptying garbage cans. The assailants fled the scene in a car. In a third incident that day, three paratroopers were injured, one seriously, from shelling. 83121401, 83121501–02

December 15, 1983 — REPUBLIC OF SOUTH AFRICA — In a telex sent from its Lusaka, Zambia, office to the ASSOCIATED PRESS in Johannesburg, the African National Congress (ANC) took credit for three bombings to government offices in Johannesburg. The most serious blast heavily damaged the first four floors of a Foreign Ministry building and resulted in slight injuries to seven people. Three other bombs exploded near the beachfront in Durban, located three hundred miles southeast of Johannesburg. No one was injured in these blasts.

December 15, 1983 — COSTA RICA — Security was increased around the United States ambassador's residence in San Jose after two suspicious, hooded men were seen.

December 15, 1983 — LEBANON — Buildings in the vicinity of the headquarters of the British peacekeeping forces were hit by shells.

December 16, 1983 — COLOMBIA — Jaime Garces Rivera, the commander of the 8th Front of the Revolutionary Armed Forces (FARC), was killed by government troops in the municipality of Tambo in Cauca. Documents found on Rivera indicated that FARC "does not plan to lay down its arms or suspend kidnappings." Guerrilla activity increased after Rivera's death. In Yacopi jurisdiction, government troops killed Edelio Valencia, leader of the 11th Front of FARC. Following both actions, the government troops confiscated large amounts of military material.

December 17, 1983 — PAKISTAN — The Dir Police reported the arrest of a member of a new terrorist organization, Liyaqat, allegedly supervised by the Afghan intelligence agency. Twenty-five plastic explosive devices were also confiscated.

December 17, 1983 — EGYPT — In Alexandria, a youth hurled a Molotov cocktail at the Israeli consulate. No one was injured, and the youth was arrested. 83121701

December 17, 1983 — UNITED KINGDOM — At 12:44 P.M., the Samaritans, a charity organization, received the following message: "This is the IRA [Irish Republican Army]. Car bomb outside Harrods. Two bombs in Harrods. One in Oxford Street. One in Littlewood's [a department store], Oxford Street." At 1:21 P.M., a 25-pound bomb, planted in an Austin on Hans Crescent at the rear entrance of Harrod's, exploded as police approached. The blast killed 6, including Kenneth Salvesan, a 28-year-old American. Two police — Sgt. Noel May, 26, and Constable June Arbuthnot, 21 — were also killed. A time device set off the explosion, which damaged all five floors of Harrod's and sent a shower of glass fragments onto shoppers and passersby. Witnesses said that an eerie silence followed the blast as bleeding people walked around stunned. In addition to those killed, 90 were wounded, including 2 Americans — Mark A. McDonald and Rene White. The wounded included 77 civilians and 13 police. The other bombs claimed by the caller were a hoax to throw the police off.

On December 18, the Irish Republican Army apologized for the civilian deaths and said that the action was perpetrated by "volunteers without the authority of the high command." The communique promised that there would be no further incidents of its kind.

In March, Paul Kavanagh, a 29-year-old resident of Northern Ireland, was arraigned in Belfast for the bombing. On June 24, Natalino Christopher Francis Vella, 30, of Ireland was charged with plotting the bombing. 83121702

December 18, 1983 — ANGOLA — Eight Roman Catholic missionaries of various nationalities were captured by the National Union for the Total

Independence of Angola (UNITA) in Cacola. They were released April 26, 1984, along with 66 Portuguese and 15 Filipinos. 83121801

December 19, 1983 — REPUBLIC OF SOUTH AFRICA — Two explosions damaged the Port Natal Administration Board office in the black township of Kwa Mashu near Durban.

December 19, 1983 — FRANCE — In Bayonne, the Antiterrorist Liberation Group (GAL) took credit for the assassination of Ramaon Onaderra, a Spanish Basque refugee accused by GAL of being a militant of the Basque Fatherland and Liberty (ETA) terrorist group. Large street demonstrations protested the murder. 83121901

December 19, 1983 — FEDERAL REPUBLIC OF GERMANY — Four alleged members of the Red Army Faction were arrested along with documents detailing a planned bomb attack to a railway site in Ruesselsheim used for unloading NATO arms and munitions. Thirty-seven pounds of explosives were also confiscated during the Ruesselsheim arrest. 83121902

December 19, 1983 — TURKEY — In Izmir, a car packed with 25 containers of nitroglycerine was deactivated. The rental car had been parked on a median strip in a boulevard running past the NATO Atlantic Alliance complex and the French cultural center, some one hundred meters away. It had failed to explode, owing to a maladjusted detonator. Six months earlier, a Jordanian woman had leased the car from a Turkish rental agency but had never returned it. 83121903

December 20, 1983 — UNITED STATES — In an article published by the Institute for Foreign Policy Analysis, Neil C. Livingstone and Joseph D. Douglass warned that toxic and chemical terrorist attacks were more likely than nuclear ones. The article mentioned the Muharem Kurbegovic threats to assassinate a United States president with nerve gas and to explode a nerve gas device in the Capitol. Kurbegovic was arrested for the August 6, 1974, bombing of a terminal at the Los Angeles International Airport that killed 3 and injured 35.

December 20, 1983 — UNITED STATES — A federal judge in New York ruled that LAN-Chile Airlines be placed in receivership if it did not secure a $4 million bond owed by the Chilean government to the Letelier and Moffit families as damages and interest. Orlando Letelier, the Chilean ambassador to the United States, and Ronnie Moffit, his aide, died in a fiery car bombing on Sheridan Circle in Washington, ordered by the Chilean intelligence agency in September 1976. The families had won a $2.9 million judgment against the Chilean government in 1980, but the Chilean government refused to pay. On December 27, the airlines posted the $4 million bond. As of April 1987, the families have still failed to collect anything.

December 21, 1983 — LEBANON — At 7:30 P.M., a bomb exploded in the Pickwick Bar at the Marble Tower Hotel in west Beirut. Four people were killed and about a dozen injured in the blast at the bar, frequented by United States Marine and United States embassy personnel. No United States victims were reported. At 7:35 P.M., a pickup truck packed with 1½ tons of explosives pulled up to within 50 yards of the French peacekeeping force command post in east Beirut. The driver leaped out and ran to a waiting gray Volvo minutes before the massive explosion toppled a three-story apartment building nearby. A French paratrooper and 17 Lebanese civilians were killed; 90 people were wounded, including 16 French soldiers.

In a phone call to the Beirut office of AGENCE FRANCE-PRESSE, a man claiming to represent the Islamic Jihad said that the French and Americans had 10 days to leave Lebanon. "Otherwise we shall generate a real earthquake under their feet." The caller also claimed responsibility for the two bombings. Another caller, said to represent the Black Hand, took credit for the two bombings in a call to a right-wing radio station. The Black Hand was a previously unknown group. 83122101–03

December 21, 1983 — LEBANON — Gunmen in cars fired three rocket-propelled grenades and machine guns at French forces in Beirut's Al-Awza'i Street. No casualties were reported. 83122104

December 21, 1983 — TURKEY — In Istanbul, two gunmen overpowered a guard and hurled a bag of explosives into the fountain in front of the Iraqi consulate. Three persons were injured and the windows of nearby buildings broken by the blast. In Ankara, a car bomb exploded in a residential area and resulted in broken windows but no injuries. Prior to the explosion, Ahmed Ahkir Mansour, a Syrian, and Muhammed Muassir, an Iranian, were arrested near the car, which they had intended to move to the Iraqi embassy. This was revealed in a confession given under interrogation. An anonymous caller to the London office of AGENCE FRANCE-PRESSE claimed that the Islamic Dawa was responsible. 83122105–06

December 22, 1983 — GUATEMALA — The Armed People's Revolutionary Organization (ORPA), a left-wing group, claimed responsibility for an arson attack on the government's information office located in Guatemala City. No one was injured, but the building was a total loss.

December 22, 1983 — THAILAND — A bomb threat was received by the United States embassy in Bangkok. 83122201

December 22, 1983 — GUATEMALA — The United States embassy was evacuated following a telephone call warning of a powerful bomb. The call was a hoax. 83122202

December 23, 1983 — ZIMBABWE — In Matabeleland, insurgents attacked a white farming family and killed four. Nearby farmers, who had come to the family's aid, killed one of the fleeing rebels. The attack took place in the Kezi district, located about 50 miles south of Bulawayo.

December 23, 1983 — FRANCE — The Grand Vefour Restaurant, near the Palais Royale, was the scene of a terrorist bomb that injured 10 people, 1 seriously. Five Americans were among the wounded. 83122301

December 23, 1983 — LEBANON — Three members of the International Red Cross were injured by a land mine in the Kharroub region southeast of Beirut. The injured included two Swiss nationals and a Lebanese. 83122302

December 23, 1983 — MALTA — Esther Millo, Israel's acting charge d'affaires, narrowly escaped assassination when a lone gunman pulled up beside her car at a shopping center and fired five shots. 83122303

December 23, 1983 — CANADA — Police arrested 8 men who had been purchasing arms and ammunition in an alleged plot to arm a 20-man team to assassinate Guyanese president Forbes Burnham in a coup. 83122304

December 24, 1983 — GUATEMALA — During the evening hours, several men fired at the Nicaraguan embassy from a moving vehicle. A fragmentation grenade was also hurled at the embassy, located in Panama City. No injuries were reported. 83122401

December 25, 1983 — UNITED KINGDOM — A one- to three-pound bomb planted in a garbage bin in Orchard Street exploded, slightly injuring two and shattering nearby windows. Orchard Street is located between two large department stores on Oxford Street — Marks and Spencer, and Selfridges. The evening blast was first attributed to the Irish Republican Army, but later Habib Maamar, a 25-year-old Tunisian arrested in Paris in May 1986, confessed to the December 1983 bombing. Maamar claimed that he was paid three thousand dollars a month by a pro-Iraqi faction (Abu Ibrahim) of the Palestine Liberation Organization to bomb Israeli targets, including Marks and Spencer owned by Lord Sieff, an outspoken Zionist. He also confessed to the February 23, 1985, bombing of Marks and Spencer in Paris, which killed 1 and injured 14, and to the August 21, 1985, bombing of the Israeli Bank Leumi office in Paris. Large quantities of a plastic explosive, penthrite, were found at Maamar's Paris home. Naji Allush, known as Abu Ibrahim, denied the charges in Damascus. Allush is the secretary-general of the Arab Popular Liberation Movement. 83122501

December 26, 1983 — PERU — In Lima, five men hurled explosive devices at the Cuban embassy. No injuries resulted from the blasts, which were confined to the gardens in front. 83122601

December 27, 1983 — LEBANON — A member of the British peacekeeping force was injured from a dynamite blast. 83122701

December 28, 1983 — COLOMBIA — The Bogota home of Gregorio Infante, a retired colonel, was attacked by Shining Path members who stole several weapons from the colonel's collection. The colonel was not at home.

December 28, 1983 — FRANCE — In recent weeks, France continued its crackdown on members of the Basque Fatherland and Liberty (ETA) group. Spain had repeatedly accused France of providing ETA members with sanctuary in the French border towns of Hendaye, St. Jean-de-Luz, and Biarritz. France deported six ETA members to Panama the previous week and ordered another four to report to authorities in Paris.

The Antiterrorist Liberation Group (GAL) claimed to have assassinated Mikel Goikoetxea outside his home in St. Jean-de-Luz. Goikoetxea was thought to be an ETA hit man and was wanted in Spain for 27 murders. 83122801

December 29, 1983 — ANGOLA — The National Union for the Total Independence of Angola (UNITA) released 26 hostages, including 21 Portuguese, 1 Cape Verdian, 2 Spaniards, 1 Uruguayan, and 1 Brazilian.

December 29, 1983 — GUATEMALA — Nicaraguan ambassador Orlando Rojas Morales was given 48 hours to leave the country in a threatening note, written by the "Council of Commanders" of the Counterrevolutionary Solidarity (SC), an anti-Sandinist organization. 83122901

December 29, 1983 — SPAIN — In Madrid, Walid Jamal Balkiz and Ibrahim Subhi Mohammed Mamid, two Jordanian embassy employees, were attacked by a man with a machine gun. The assailant fled on foot after firing at the employees' car. Balkiz died and Mamid was seriously wounded. In an anonymous call to the AGENCE FRANCE-PRESSE in Paris, the Arab Revolutionary Brigades claimed credit for the attack. The Abu Nidal group uses the Arab Revolutionary Brigades name for many of its Europe attacks. 83122902

December 30, 1983 — FRANCE — Five Iranian students and an Iranian diplomat were expelled on allegations by French counterintelligence units that the six were trained terrorists. Within the preceding week, France also had expelled three Iranian diplomats and closed an Iranian cultural center. The Division of Territorial Surveillance, France's counterintelligence service, charged that between 150 to 300 trained Iranian militants operated in France posing as students. France felt especially vulnerable after its reprisal bombing on Islamic Amal militants in the Bekaa Valley, an attack that followed the Beirut bombing in which 58 French soldiers were killed. France also felt vulnerable because of the anti-Khomeini groups using the country as a sanctuary.

December 30, 1983 — ARGENTINA — The Captain Giachino National Command of the 2 April organization announced in a Buenos Aires communique that it had planted "a nuclear minibomb right in the heart of the city of the decadent and overbearing British empire." The communique threatened to set off the bomb on April 2, 1984, unless the British government began negotiations to return the Falklands. The threat was not taken seriously. 83123001

December 31, 1983 — GUATEMALA — In Guatemala City, the Counterrevolutionary Solidarity (CS) claimed responsibility for an attack on the Mexican embassy. Machine guns and explosives were used, but no injuries were reported. 83123101

December 31, 1983 — FRANCE — At 7:35 P.M., a bomb in a first-class car of the French TGV high-speed train, enroute from Marseilles to Paris, exploded killing 2 and injuring 11. A 3d person died later from his wounds. The blast occurred 120 miles north of Marseilles. About 25 minutes later, a powerful bomb left in a suitcase exploded at the Saint Charles Station in Marseilles. Two were killed and 35 wounded, some critically, in the explosion, which left a three-foot crater in the concrete floor. Six different groups claimed responsibility including the Islamic Jihad, the Arab Armed Struggle Organization, and the Occident (West) movement. In a letter sent to the AGENCE FRANCE-PRESSE office in Berlin, Carlos, the famed Venezuelan terrorist and member of the Arab Armed Struggle Organization, took credit for the bombings. Experts identified the handwriting as that of Illich Ramirez Sanchez (Carlos), who was believed to be in hiding in East Berlin. The true perpetrator remains unknown. 83123102–03

APPENDIX 1

Terrorist Groups

THE GROUPS appearing on this list are the names of organizations for which responsibility was claimed or attributed for specific terrorist actions. The inclusion of any given group should not be interpreted as an evaluation of that organization's goals or motivations. Many of the groups listed are cover names for organizations that may wish to deny responsibility for a particular action producing counterproductive results. In some cases, individuals falsely claim responsibility in the name of a group in order to tarnish the image of the group. Some groups have become governing bodies of nations. No attempt has been made to "break" these covers, and the names provided by the claimants have been accepted. Sources are often vague regarding the actual name of the organization responsible, or unclear about the amount of legally acceptable evidence pointing to responsibility. The names of the major suspects in such vague cases have been used.

An attempt has been made to have the initial three digits of the four-digit code follow the codings used for the nation (see Appendix 2) in which the group's members operate, or claim citizenship, where appropriate. For cases in which more than 10 groups have appeared in that nation, an attempt has been made to make the initial three digits as close as possible to that of the relevant nation code. Where useful, annotations about the group's characteristics have been made. Code 0003 was used for cases in which individuals or groups were seeking political asylum or other very specific goals and are not expected to engage in future attacks. Incidents engaged in by pathological individuals or groups are also included here where such attacks were initially treated by authorities as attacks by politically motivated terrorists.

We have included many groups that have operated from 1984 onward. Some groups operating after 1984 have not been included because, at the time of completing this volume, our coders have not entered them. The codebook will be updated periodically to include omitted groups and new

477

groups. We refer the reader to the current edition of the codebook for the most up-to-date list.

0002 criminals
0003 no group involved; not a group that will engage in terrorist activities again
0009 Organization of Struggle against World Imperialism
0010 Phalangist Security Group
0011 Squad of the Martyr Patrick Arguello
0012 Weatherman faction of the Students for a Democratic Society
0013 Moslem International Guerrillas
0014 VFVP LBF
0015 Islamic Liberation Organization
0016 Che Guevara Brigade
0017 International Revolutionary Front
0018 Pan Epirotic Federation of America and Canada
0019 International Che Guevara Organization
0020 United Freedom Front, United Freedom Fighters, United Freedom Federation
0021 Jewish Defense League
0022 Republic of New Africa
0023 Black Panther Party
0024 Revolutionary Force 7
0025 Jewish Defense League–Wrath of God
0026 Revolutionary Affinity Group 6
0027 Revolutionary Action Party
0028 Student Struggle for Soviet Jewry
0029 Black Revolutionary Assault Team
0030 White Panthers
0031 Jewish Armed Resistance
0032 indeterminate Black Power urban guerrillas
0033 indeterminate militant Jewish group
0034 Hungarian Peace and Freedom Fighters
0035 Jewish Armed Resistance Strike Movement
0036 Jewish Underground Army
0037 Red Guerrilla Family
0038 Jewish Armed Resistance Strike Force
0039 Jewish Armed Resistance Strike Unit
0040 New World Liberation Front
0041 Save Our Israel Land
0042 Hanafi Muslims
0043 National Socialist Movement, a neo-Nazi group
0044 Islamic Guerillas in America
0045 Iranian Liberation Army
0046 Iranian Free Army, an anti-Khomeini group
0047 Imperial Iranian Patriotic Organization
0048 People's Majority, an anti-Khomeini group

0049 Black Brigade, possibly Liberian exiles
0050 Ku Klux Klan
0051 Jewish Committee of Concern
0052 People's Temple
0053 New Jewish Defense League
0054 Revolutionary Communist Party (U.S.A.) Committee to Give a Fitting Welcome
0055 International Committee against Nazism
0056 Jewish Action Movement
0057 Iranian Student Association
0058 United Americans
0059 United Jewish Underground (UJU)
0060 indeterminate Puerto Rican terrorists
0061 Armed Commandos of Liberation
0062 MIRA
0063 Puerto Rican Resistance Movement
0064 Puerto Rican Liberation Front
0065 FALN, Armed Front for National Liberation
0066 Independence Revolutionary Armed Commandos
0067 Anti-Communist Alliance
0068 Machete Wielders, Macheteros
0069 Ramon Emeterio Betances Puerto Rico Independence Commandos, Manuel Rojas Luzardo International Solidarity Operation
0070 Organization of Volunteers for the Puerto Rican Revolution
0071 Puerto Rican Popular Army
0072 Armed Forces of Popular Resistance
0201 Quebec Liberation Front
0202 Canadian Hungarian Freedom Fighters Federation
0203 Direct Action, Action Directe
0371 Pedro Luis Boitel Command
0372 Pedro Ruiz Botero Commandos
0373 International Secret Revolutionary United Cells
0374 Anti-Castro Commandos
0375 CORU, Coordination of United Revolutionary Organizations
0376 Cuban Revolutionary Organization
0377 Secret Anti-Castro Cuban Army
0378 Brigade 2506
0379 Cuban Youth Group
0380 El Condor
0381 Cuban Power 76
0382 Youths of the Star
0383 El Alacran, The Scorpion
0384 Cuban Action Commandos
0385 Omega-7
0386 Movement for Cuban Justice
0387 Pragmatistas
0388 Cuban C-4 Movement

0389 Latin American Anti-Communist Army, Anti-Communist Latin American Army
0390 M-7
0391 Secret Organization Zero
0392 Abdala
0393 Secret Hand Organization
0394 Cuban Action
0395 Cuban Anti-Communist League
0396 FIN, Cuban Nationalist Front, National Integration Front
0397 Cuban National Liberation Front, FLNC
0398 Anti-Communist Commandos
0399 Young Cubans
0400 indeterminate Cuban group
0401 El Poder Cubano, Cuban Power
0402 Cuban Revolutionary Directorate
0403 indeterminate anti-Castro Cubans
0404 Alpha 66
0405 Second Front of Escambray
0406 Cuban Representation in Exile
0407 Secret Cuban Government
0408 Cuban Liberation Front
0409 JCN
0410 indeterminate Haitian exiles
0411 Coalition of National Liberation Brigades (anti-Duvalier)
0412 Haitian Coalition
0413 Hector Riode Group
0414 indeterminate Haitian (pro-Duvalier)
0420 indeterminate Dominican Republic exiles
0421 United Anti-Reelection Command (a Dominican group oppposed to President Balaguer's reelection)
0422 Dominican left-wing revolutionaries
0423 Dominican youths
0424 MDP Dominican Popular Movement
0425 Dominican leftists
0426 12th of January Liberation Movement
0541 Rastafarians
0651 Guadeloupe Liberation Army
0681 Caribbean Revolutionary Alliance
0701 Armed Communist League
0702 People's Revolutionary Armed Forces
0703 23rd of September Communist League
0704 Mexican People's Revolutionary Army
0705 People's Armed Command
0706 Leftist rural Acapulco guerrillas led by Genaro Vazquez Rojas
0707 People's Liberation Army
0708 FRAP (led by Lucio Cabanas)
0709 United Popular Liberation Army of America
0710 Armed Vanguard of the Proletariat

0711 National Independent Committee for Political Prisoners and Persecuted and Missing Persons
0712 FPDN, National Democratic Popular Front
0713 COCEI, Isthmian Labor, Peasant and Student Coalition
0851 Roque Dalton Command, a Honduran group
0852 Juan Rayo Guerrilla Group, a Honduran group
0894 Counterrevolutionary Solidarity
0895 National League for the Protection of Guatemala
0896 Pedro Diaz Command of the IXIM Revolutionary Movement of the People
0897 Guatemalan Labor Party, a communist-led group
0898 CUC, Committee for Peasant Unity of Guatemala
0899 Che Guevara Command of Guatemala
0900 indeterminate Guatemalan
0901 FAR, PGT/FAR, Revolutionary Armed Forces, Fuerzas Armadas Revolucionarias
0902 MR-13, Movimiento Revolucionario de 13 Noviembre
0903 GALGAS, Guatemalan Anti-Salvadoran Liberating Action Guerrillas
0904 EGP, Guerrilla Army of the Poor, People's Guerrilla Army
0905 Guatemalan Nationalist Commando
0906 Secret Anti-Communist Army
0907 Clandestine Rebel Armed Forces
0908 Maximiliano Hernandez Martinez Front, anti-communists
0909 FP-31, January 31 Popular Front, 31 January People's Front
0910 indeterminate Honduran Guerrillas
0911 FREPA, Patriotic Anticommunist Front
0912 URP, Revolutionary People's Union
0913 Popular Revolutionary Command Lorenzo Zelaya, Lorenzo Zelaya Revolutionary People's Command, Lorenzo Zelaya Revolutionary Front
0914 National Coordinating Board of Solidarity with the Salvadoran People
0915 Martyrs of La Talanquera
0916 Cinchonero National Liberation Front
0917 Federation of Secondary Students
0918 Honduran Anti-Communist Movement
0920 indeterminate El Salvadoran guerrillas
0921 ERP, Peoples Revolutionary Army
0922 FMLN, Faribundo Marti Liberation Labor Forces, Faribundo Marti National Liberation Forces
0923 White Warriors Union
0924 LP-28, 28 February Popular League
0925 PRTC, Central American Workers Revolutionary Party
0926 January 28 Popular Leagues
0927 FPL, People's Liberation Forces, Popular Liberation Forces
0928 FARN, Armed Forces of National Resistance, Maoist Armed Forces of National Liberation
0931 FSLN, Sandinist National Liberation Front
0932 Nicaraguan Anti-Communist Democratic Movement, International Movement to Save Nicaragua from Communism

0933 indeterminate Nicaraguan guerrillas
0941 Revolutionary Commandos of Solidarity
0942 Roberto Santucho Revolutionary Group
0943 Carlos Aguero Echeverria Command
0944 People's Vanguard
0951 Panamanian students
0952 Revolutionary Student Front
0953 Kuna Indians
0971 FDR, Revolutionary Democratic Front of El Salvador
0972 DRU, Salvadoran Unified Revolutionary Directorate
0973 BPR, Popular Revolutionary Bloc
0974 FAPU, United Popular Action Front
0994 People's Revolutionary Organization
0995 September 14 Workers Self-Defense Command
0996 Patriotic Liberation Front
0997 MAO, Worker's Self-Defense Movement of Colombia, Workers' Autode-
     fense Movement
0998 Colombian Indians
0999 Chilean Socialist Party
1000 indeterminate Colombian guerrillas
1001 The Invisible Ones
1002 ELN, National Liberation Army
1003 M-19, April 19 Movement
1004 Colombian students
1005 United Front for Guerrilla Action
1006 FARC, Revolutionary Armed Forces of Colombia
1007 Military Liberation Front of Colombia
1008 EPL, Popular Liberation Army
1009 Revolutionary Workers Party
1011 People's Revolutionary Army–Zero Point
1012 Bandera Roja, Red Flag
1014 National Liberation Armed Forces
1015 Group of Revolutionary Commandos–Operation Argimiro Gabaldon
1016 Luis Boitel Commando
1101 People's Progressive Party
1300 indeterminate Ecuadoran leftists
1301 Anti-Poncista group
1302 Ecuadoran students
1303 18 October Movement Astra Revolutionary Action Command
1304 Ruminahui Front of Solidarity with Central America and the Caribbean
1349 indeterminate Peruvian guerrillas
1350 Peruvian students
1351 MTR
1352 MANO, Movimiento Armada Nacionalista Organizado
1353 Condor
1354 Revolutionary Vanguard
1355 MIR, Movement of the Revolutionary Left

1356 Sendero Luminoso, Shining Path, Maoists Shining Path, a Maoist Red Flag breakaway
1357 Peruvian Anti-Communist Alliance
1358 MRTA, Tupac Amaru Revolutionary Movement
1400 indeterminate Brazilian extremists
1401 VPR, Popular Revolutionary Vanguard, Vanguarda Popular Revolucionaria
1402 MR-8, Revolutionary Movement of the 8th, Movimiento Revolucionario-8
1403 ALN, Action for National Liberation, Acao Liberation National
1404 VAR-Palmares, Armed Revolutionary Vanguard-Palmares
1405 Aurora Maria Nacimiento Furtado Command
1450 Bolivian peasants
1452 Bolivian dissidents
1453 Falange Socialista Boliviana, a rightist group
1454 Nationalist Commando
1501 MoPoCo, Popular Colorado Movement (a dissident faction of the Colorado Party of Paraguay)
1502 Political Military Organization
1503 Reorganization Committee of Revolutionary Front 17
1551 Proletarian Action Group
1552 Revolutionary Movement of the Left
1553 Chilean leftists
1554 MIR
1555 Revolutionary Action Group
1600 indeterminate Argentine leftists
1601 FAP, Peronist Armed Forces
1602 FALN, Argentine National Liberation Front
1603 MANO, Argentine National Organization Movement
1604 ERP, Ejercito Revolucionario del Pueblo
1605 Comite Argentino de Lucha Anti-Imperialisto
1606 Montoneros
1607 indeterminate Peronist guerrillas
1608 Descamisados Peronistas Montoneros
1609 ERP-August 22
1610 indeterminate Argentine guerrillas
1611 FAR, Revolutionary Armed Forces
1612 Frente de Liberation Nacionel del Vietnam del Sur
1613 Movemento Peronista
1614 Argentine students
1615 Maximo Mena Commando (a Peronist group)
1616 AAA, Argentine Anti-Communist Alliance
1617 indeterminate Argentine rightists
1618 Argentine National Social Front (a neo-Nazi group)
1619 Argentine Youth for Sovereignty
1620 2 April Group–Capt. Giacchino Command
1650 indeterminate Uruguayan guerrillas

1651 Tupamaros, MLN National Liberation Movement
1652 OPR-33, Organization of the Popular Revolution-33
1653 PCU
1654 Armed Popular Front, FAP
1655 Raul Sendic International Brigade
2000 indeterminate British guerrillas
2001 Black Liberation Army
2039 Catholic Reaction Force
2040 Irish Freedom Fighters
2041 IRA-Provos, PIRA, Irish Republican Army–Provisional Wing
2042 Sinn Fein
2043 UDA, Ulster Defense Association
2044 Red Flag 74
2045 Young Militants
2046 indeterminate Protestant militants
2047 UVF, Ulster Volunteer Force
2048 INLA, Irish National Liberation Army
2049 Bobby Sands Group
2050 indeterminate Irish guerrillas
2051 indeterminate Baader-Meinhof Group supporters
2061 Scottish National Liberation Army
2101 Dutch revolutionaries
2102 Revolutionary People's Resistance of the Netherlands
2103 People's League of Free Palestine, a Dutch group
2111 Direct Action, Section Belgium
2112 Black Lebanon
2113 Julien Lahaut Brigade
2114 Revenge and Freedom
2115 Andreas Baader Commando of the Red Army Faction
2116 CCC, Combatant Communist Cells
2121 October 18 Movement
2191 Corsican National Liberation Front
2192 Pasquale Paoli Unit of the Corsican Guerrillas and Partisans
2200 French students
2201 Movement of Youthward Brothers in War of the Palestinian People
2202 Masada–Action and Defense Movement
2203 Committee of Coordination
2204 Charles Martel Group
2205 We Must Do Something
2206 Group for the Defense of Europe
2207 Youth Action Group (a rightist organization)
2208 6th of March Group
2209 Front de l'Auto-Defense Juive
2210 International Solidarity
2211 indeterminate French Zionists
2212 indeterminate French rightists
2213 Avengers (composed of ex-WWII resistance fighters)
2214 Spanish deportees

2215 Action Front for the Liberation of the Baltic Countries
2216 Committee for Socialist Revolutionary Unity
2217 Solidarity Resistance Front
2218 New Order
2219 Red Army Faction of Southern France
2220 Andreas Baader Commando
2221 Direct Action, March 27–28 Direct Action Group, Action Directe (AD)
2222 Afghan Collective
2223 Jewish Brigade
2224 Palestine Resistance
2225 Autonomous Revolutionary Brigade
2226 Afghanistan Islamic Nationalist Revolutionary Council
2227 Gazi
2228 Assembly for Moral Order and Anti-Communist Youth
2229 Self-Defense Against All Authority
2230 National Youth Front, a right-wing group
2231 Militant Zionist Resistance Fighters
2232 Committee for the Safeguard of the Islamic Revolution
2233 Order and New Justice Cell of the Friends of Inspector Jacques Mazel
2234 Organization of European Nationalist Group
2235 National Revolutionary Movement, ultrarightists
2236 Basque Spanish Battalion (French ultrarightists)
2237 Pessah, Passover, a Jewish anti-Nazi group
2238 September France
2239 Bakunin Gdansk Paris Group, Bakunin-Gdansk-Paris-Guatemala-Salvador Group, Internationalist Hooligans-Group Bakunin-Gdansk-Paris-Guatemala-El Salvador
2242 Friends of Carlos
2243 Committee of Solidarity with Arab and Middle Eastern Political Prisoners
2244 Benchella Column
2245 French Revolutionary Brigades
2246 Organization Delta
2247 Talion Law
2248 Autonomous Intervention Collective against the Zionist Presence in France and the Israeli-Egyptian Peace
2249 GAL—Anti-terrorist Liberation Group
2251 Les Beliers (Swiss Jura-ists)
2252 Petra Kraus Group
2253 Swiss anarchists
2290 Iparretarrak
2291 Spanish National Association
2292 Spanish Armed Group
2293 Basque Justice
2294 Committee of Solidarity with Euzkadi
2295 Armed Revolutionary Groups
2296 Spanish-Catalan Battalion
2297 CAA, Autonomous Anti-Capitalist Commandos

2298 GRAPO, Anti-Fascist Resistance Group–October 1
2299 Juan Paredes Manot International Brigade
2300 indeterminate Basques
2301 ETA, Basque Nation and Liberation, Basque Fatherland and Liberty, Euzkadi Ta Azkatasuna
2302 indeterminate Spanish extremists
2303 Hammer and Sickle Cooperative
2304 MIL, Iberian Liberation Movement
2305 GARI, International Revolutionary Action Group
2306 Warriors of Christ the King, Cristo Rei Guerrillas
2307 Catalan separatists
2308 Nationalist Intervention Group (a rightist group)
2309 FRAP
2351 ARA
2352 Revolutionary Internationalist Solidarity
2353 Portuguese Liberation Army (a rightist group)
2354 Portuguese Anti-Communist Movement
2355 April 25 Popular Forces (FP-25)
2356 Zionist Action Group
2357 Action Group for Communism
2549 Venceremos Beginning of Autumn
2550 indeterminate West German leftists
2551 Baader-Meinhof Group, Red Army Faction
2552 2nd of June Movement
2553 International Anti-Terror Organization
2554 Holger Meins Kommando, Revolutionary Cell
2555 Baader Solidarity Group
2556 Holger Meins Brigade
2557 Ulrike Meinhof Commando
2558 Puig Antich–Ulrike Meinhof Commando
2559 Socialist Patients Collective
2560 Revolutionary Cell Brigade Ulrike Meinhof
2561 Military Sports Group Hoffman, a neo-Nazi group
2562 Brunswick Group, neo-Nazis
2563 Black Bloc, RAF supporters
2564 In the Heart of the Beast
2565 Revolutionary Cells
2566 Andreas Baader Brigade of the German Liberation Popular Front
2567 Robert E. D. Straker Commando of the Territorial Resistance Army
2901 Armed Secret Organization–Execution Group
2902 antigovernment Polish guerrillas
3051 Justice Guerrilla
3151 indeterminate Czechoslovakians
3251 Red Brigades
3252 Ordine Nero, Black Order (a fascist group)
3253 Armed Communist Formations
3254 Sardinian separatists

3255 Proletarian Internationalism, Communist Group of Proletarian Internationalism
3256 Armed Proletarian Power
3257 Italian neo-fascists
3258 indeterminate Italian leftists
3259 Combatants for Communism
3260 Prima Linea, Front Line
3261 Chaka II
3262 Armed Revolutionary Nuclei, a neo-fascist group
3263 GIP, Proletarian Internationalist Groups
3264 Veneto Communist Cells
3265 Extraparliamentary Group for Communism
3266 Nuclei Armati Comunista
3267 Groups of Internationalist Communists
3268 Communist Anti-Imperialist Movement
3269 Party of the Guerrilla
3270 PLO–Red Brigades
3271 Fighting Communist Formations
3272 Proletarian Squad
3273 Proletarian Justice, Proletarian Committee of Subversion for Better Justice
3274 Red Guerrilla
3275 Autonomous Workers Movement
3381 Maltese Liberation Front
3390 indeterminate Albanian guerrillas
3391 Anti-Communist Military Council
3392 Albanian People's Path
3393 Fides Besa Bes
3394 Albanian Autonomist Movement of Kosovo
3395 Albanian Croat HDP
3396 Red Front
3450 indeterminate Yugoslav/Croatian/Serbian militants
3451 Trotskyist Organization
3452 Young Croatian Republican Army
3453 Young Croatian Army for Freedom
3454 Croatian National Liberation Forces, Fighters for a Free Croatia
3455 Croatian Freedom Fighters
3456 OTPOR, resistance
3457 Commando of Croatian Revolutionaries in Europe
3458 Croatian Revolutionary Cell, Bruno Busic Department
3459 Croatian Revolutionary Army in Germany
3460 Croatian Intelligence Service
3461 SEPO, Freedom for the Serbian Fatherland
3486 Revolutionary People's Army
3487 Front for the Liberation of Northern Ipiros (MAVI)
3488 People's Authority
3489 People's Revolutionary Solidarity

3490 People's Struggle, Laikos Agonas
3491 People's Revolutionary Combat Group
3492 4 August National Organization
3493 AOI, Solidarity with the El Salvador People
3494 Revolutionary Greek Battalion
3495 Blue Archer, a right-wing group
3496 Greek Armed Group for the Support of the Northern Ireland Struggle
3497 Revolutionary Solidarity
3498 October-80
3499 Revolutionary Left (a Greek group)
3500 indeterminate Greek urban guerrillas
3501 Popular Revolutionary Resistance Group
3502 AAA, Independence-Liberation-Resistance
3503 EAN, Greek Anti-Dictatorial Youth
3504 National Youth Resistance Organization
3505 Greek People
3506 Patriotic Front
3507 Greek Militant Resistance
3508 Free Greeks (a rightist group)
3509 LAOS People Number One
3510 LAOS Number 13
3511 dissident Greek students
3512 People's Resistance Organized Army
3513 Popular Liberation Organized Army
3514 LAOS-11, Popular Liberation Sabotage Group-11
3515 Organization of November 17
3516 Union of Officers Struggling for the National Idea, Army Officers Representing the Free Greek Spirit
3517 ELA, Revolutionary Popular Struggle, Popular Revolutionary Struggle
3518 People's Front Initiative
3519 Autonomous Resistance, Avtonomi Andistasi
3521 EOKA-B
3522 National Patriotic Front M.P. 14/31
3601 Romanian agents
3651 Ukraine Liberation Front
3652 Etienne Bandera Ukrainian group, The Rat Pack
3653 Fils de Makhno, Sons of Makhno, Ukrainian anarchists
3654 Ukrainian nationalists
3655 15 October Commando, Ukrainian nationalists
3801 B-26
3951 indeterminate Icelandic
4381 Guinean agents
4821 Central African National Liberation Movement
4822 Central African Empire students
4830 indeterminate Chadian guerrillas
4831 FROLINAT, Chadian National Liberation Front
4832 FAN

4833 OLTIF, Organization for the Liberation of Chad from Imperialism and Fascism
4841 Congolese Armed Patriotic Group
4901 People's Revolutionary Party
4902 People's Army of the Oppressed in Zaire
5001 Uganda Freedom Movement
5002 indeterminate Ugandan guerrillas
5003 National Resistance Army
5101 Revolutionary Youth Movement of Tanzania
5201 Somali Liberation Front
5221 FLCS, Somali Coast Liberation Front
5222 Popular Liberation Movement
5223 National Independence Union
5300 indeterminate Ethiopian guerrilla group
5301 Ethiopian students
5302 Galla nationalists
5303 Tigre People's Liberation Front
5311 ELF, Eritrean Liberation Front
5312 ELF-GC, ELF-General Command
5313 Popular Liberation Forces
5314 ELF–Revolutionary Council
5391 FLEC, Front for the Liberation of the Enclave of Cabinda
5400 indeterminate Angolan guerrillas
5401 MPLA, Popular Movement for the Liberation of Angola
5402 UNITA, National Union for the Total Independence of Angola
5411 COREMO, Mozambique Revolutionary Council
5412 FRELIMO, Mozambique Liberation Front
5413 NRM, MNR, RENAMO, National Resistance Movement
5414 Quizumba-South African backed guerrillas
5520 indeterminate Zimbabwe guerrillas
5521 indeterminate Rhodesian nationalists
5522 ZIPRA/ZAPU, Zimbabwe African People's Union
5523 ZANU, Zimbabwe African National Union
5530 indeterminate Malawi agents
5601 ANC, African National Congress
5602 South African Agents
5651 SWAPO, South West Africa People's Organization
5701 LLA, Lesotho Liberation Army
5911 Seychelles Resistance Movement
6071 MPAIAC, Canary Islands Independence Movement, Movement for Self-Determination and Independence of the Canary Islands, Movement for the Autonomy and Independence of the Canary Island Archipelago
6072 Canary Islands Intelligence Service
6091 POLISARIO, Popular Front for the Liberation of Saguia el Hamra and Rio do Oro
6092 Mustafa el Wali Bayyid Sayed International Brigade
6151 Soldier of the Algerian Opposition

6152 United Liberation Front of New Algeria
6153 Islamic Jihad of Shaykh Sadiq al-Mundhiri
6161 Les Vivants
6162 Tunisian Revolutionary National Organization
6201 Libyan Free Unionist Officers
6202 People of Omar
6203 Libyan dissidents
6204 Libyan Agents
6205 Green Brigades
6251 Sudanese People's Liberation Army
6252 Liberation Front for Southern Sudan
6301 indeterminate Iranian guerrillas
6302 Iranian students
6303 IPS, Peoples Strugglers, Mujahiddin e Khalq
6304 Reza Rezai International Brigades
6305 National Front Forces of Iran
6306 Islamic Jihad Organization
6307 Fedaye Islam
6308 Iranian Amal Movement
6309 Political Organization of the Arab People, Arab People's Political Organization
6310 Arab Masses Movement, Arab People's Movement
6311 Movement of the Moslem Arab People Strugglers
6312 Martyr Muhyi a-Din an-Nasir Operation
6313 Group of the Martyr
6314 Al-Nasir Mojahedin Group
6315 Arab People's Mujahiddin Combatants Movement
6316 Iranian National Liberation Movement–Red June, Iranian Red June Organization
6317 Revolutionary Islamic Organization
6318 Guards of Islam, Guard Corps of Islam Group
6319 Forqan
6320 Azadegan, Freedom Seekers, Iranian monarchist exiles
6321 Peykar, Muslim Protest
6322 Feda'iye Khalq, Mujaheddin e Khalq
6323 Mujahidin, People's Fighters Organization
6324 Fedayen-e-Islam, led by Ayatollah Sadegh Khalkhali
6325 Moslem Liberation Front
6326 Aref Boluki Dynamite Group
6327 Martyrs of the Islamic Revolution
6328 Iranian intelligence, agents
6329 Islamic Revolutionary Movement, Free Islamic Revolution Movement
6330 Army for Iran's National Liberation
6331 Hezbollah
6332 indeterminate Shiite moslems
6400 indeterminate Turkish guerrillas
6401 TPLA, Turkish People's Liberation Army
6402 TPLF, Turkish People's Liberation Front

6403 Yanikian Commandos
6404 Turkish Revolutionary Youth Federation
6405 indeterminate Armenian nationalists
6406 Mayir Cayan Suicide Group
6407 Marxist group
6408 Slave Kortin Yanikiyan Group (an Armenian group)
6409 JCAG, Justice Commandos of the Armenian Genocide
6410 ASALA, Armenian Secret Army for the Liberation of Armenia
6411 New Armenian Resistance Group
6412 28 May Armenian Organization
6413 Acilciler, The Swift Ones
6414 Marxist-Leninist Armed Propaganda Union
6415 Anti-Camp David Front
6416 Sons of the Land
6417 THKPC, Turkish Peoples Liberation Party/Front
6418 Commando of Avengers of Armenian Genocide
6419 Avril Noir, an Armenian group
6420 Revolutionary Way, Dev Yol
6421 Organization of October 3, 3 October Armenian Movement
6422 Party of Kurdish Workers in Turkey
6423 Turkish People's Liberation Party Front Warriors
6424 Commandos of Retribution for the Armenian Genocide
6425 Turkish Islamic Revolutionary Army
6426 Organization for the Liberation of Armenia
6427 Armenian June 9 Organization, an ASALA wing
6428 Army for the Protection of Turkey's International Rights
6429 Orly Group, Orly Organization, an Armenian organization
6430 Dev Sol, Revolutionary Left, Devrimci Sol, Turkish Revolutionary Left
6431 Armenian Red Army
6432 Turkish Revolutionaries
6433 Avengers of the Armenian Genocide
6434 Front for the Liberation of Armenia
6435 Armenian Revolutionary Army (ARA)
6436 Brigades for the Liberation of the Turkish People
6437 Anti-Christian Turkish Liberation Front
6448 indeterminate Iraqi guerrillas
6449 Iraqi Agents
6450 Iraqi Communist Party
6451 Kurdish sympathizers
6452 Iraqi Baathists
6453 Free Iraq
6454 Mujahidin Iraqis, Iraqi Mujahedeen Movement
6455 Iraqi Mujahidin Islam
6456 Al Dawa, a clandestine Iraqi fundamentalist Moslem group
6457 Martyr Araef Basri Commando
6458 Revolutionaries of Mohammed Baqir as-Sadr
6459 Iraqi Strugglers' Movement
6460 Unified Kurdistan Socialist Party

6461 Army for the Liberation of Kurdistan
6462 Iraqi Liberation Army-General Command
6463 Iraqi Islamic Amal Organization
6464 Group of the Martyr Talid Shahim al-'Alubi, under command of the Special Operations Section of the Islamic Action Organization
6465 KDP, Kurdish Democratic Party
6466 Kurdish rebels
6511 Egypt of Arabism, Misr al-'Urubah
6512 Takfir wa Hijra, Repentant and Holy Flight
6513 Independent Organization for the Liberation of Egypt, Rejection Front for the Liberation of Arab Egypt, headed by Saadeddin Shazli
6514 Correct Course of Fatah, Al-Kat as-Sahih Lifatah, headed by Wadi Haddad
6515 indeterminate Egyptian guerrillas
6516 Egyptian Revolution
6520 indeterminate Syrian guerrillas
6521 Moslem Brotherhood
6522 Arab Revolution Vanguards Organization
6523 Combatant Avant-Garde, a Moslem Brotherhood faction headed by 'Adnan al-'Uklah
6524 Islamic Revolutionary Command
6525 Syrian Struggle Front
6526 'Alawite intelligence service
6588 Islamic Liberation Organization
6589 Lebanese Front for National Resistance
6590 Black Lebanon Organization
6591 indeterminate Followers of Musa as-Sadr
6592 Organization of France's Friends in Lebanon
6593 Progressive Socialists, Druze militia
6594 indeterminate Lebanese guerrillas
6595 Martyr Sa'd Sayil Group
6596 Armed Struggle Organization, Munazmat an-Nidal al-Musallah
6597 Moslem Holy Warriors
6598 Free Naserite Revolutionaries
6599 Liberal Nasserite Organization
6600 Holy War Organization, Al-Jihad al-Muqaddas
6601 Lebanese Socialist Revolutionary Organization, Shibbu Gang
6602 Lebanese Revolutionary Guard
6603 Lebanese Revolutionary Socialist Movement
6604 Revolutionary Arab Youth Organization
6605 Socialist Labor Party
6606 Lebanese leftists
6607 Phalange
6608 Sons of the South
6609 Lebanese Amal, Shiite militia
6610 Front for the Liberation of Lebanon from Foreigners, Front for the Removal of Foreigners from Lebanon
6611 Forces of Mojahedin, Forces of the Struggling Line, Mojahedin Fighters of the Ranks, Quwwat as-Saf al-Mujahid

6612 Martyr Abu Ja'far Group
6613 Arab National Organization
6614 Vanguards of Revolutionary Violence
6615 Eagles of the Revolution, Nusur ath-Thawrah
6616 'Ali Nasir Group
6617 United Southern Front
6618 Lebanese Communist Party
6619 Front for the Liberation of Ahwaz, a pro-Iraqi group
6620 Syrian Liberation Army
6622 Lebanese Red Brigades
6623 Organization of Holy Struggle
6624 Imam Musa as-Sadr Brigades, Imam as-Sadr Brigades
6625 Movement of Arab Revolutionary Brigades
6626 Revolutionary Lebanese Forces
6627 LARF, Lebanese Armed Revolutionary Factions,
     al-fas'il ath-thawriya al-musallahah al-Lubnaniyah
6628 Al Aqsa Group
6629 Lebanese Cedar Force to Free Lebanon from Lebanese Terrorists
6630 indeterminate Jordanian
6631 Jordanian National Liberation Movement
6632 Jordanian intelligence organization
6633 Jordanian Free Officers Movement
6634 MOUAB, Military and Revolutionary Committee of Jordan
6651 Palestine Revolutionary Movement
6657 Black September-June, Black September and June
6660 indeterminate Israelis
6661 Irgun Zevai Leumi
6662 Wrath of God
6663 Sons of Zion
6664 TNT, Terror Against Terror
6670 indeterminate Arab/Palestinian guerrillas
6671 PFLP, Popular Front for the Liberation of Palestine
6672 AOLP, Action Organization for the Liberation of Palestine
6673 Al Fatah
6674 BSO, Black September
6675 Organization for the Victims of Zionist Occupation
6676 Palestine Popular Struggle Front
6677 Nationalist Youth Group for the Liberation of Palestine
6678 National Organization of Arab Youth
6679 PFLP-GC, PFLP-General Command
6680 Organization of Victims of Occupied Territories
6681 Organization of the Sons of Occupied Territories, Sons of the Occupied
     Territory Organization
6682 7th Suicide Squad
6683 Eagles of the Palestinian Revolution, Red Eagles of the Palestinian Revo-
     lution
6684 Punishment Squad, Al Icab
6685 OANY, ANYOLP, Organization of Arab Nationalist Youth for the Liber-
     ation of Palestine

6686 PLO, Palestine Liberation Organization
6687 Al Saiqa, Thunderbolt
6688 PDFLP, Popular Democratic Front for the Liberation of Palestine
6689 PLA, Palestine Liberation Army
6690 Palestinian students
6691 Palestine Revolutionary Forces
6692 Sons of the Occupied Land
6693 Commando Muhammed Boudia
6694 Arab Communist Organization
6695 Arab Liberation Front
6696 Group of the Fallen Abd al Kadir al Husayni
6697 Arm of the Arab Revolution
6698 Palestine Rejection Front
6699 Abdel Nasser Movement
6701 Union of the Peoples of the Arabian Peninsula
6710 Voice of the Palestinian Revolution
6711 15 May Arab Organization, May 15 Arab Organization for the Liberation of Palestine
6712 Fatah–Revolutionary Council, Abu Nidal Group
6713 Al Asifah, headed by Abu Nidal
6714 Black June, headed by Abu Nidal
6715 Arab Revolutionary Army Palestinian Commando
6716 Organization of the Sons of Southern Lebanon
6717 Organization of the Sons of Palestine
6718 Rejection Front of Stateless Palestinian Arabs
6719 PFLP–Special Operations
6720 ARA, Arab Revolutionary Army
6721 Arab People, Ash-Shab al-'Arabi
6722 Black March Organization
6723 Organization of Avenging Palestinian Youth
6724 Organization of the Standard Bearers of Imam Musa as-Sadr
6725 Group for Martyred 'Isam as-Sartawi
6726 Movement for Rebuilding Fatah
6727 Islamic Revolutionary Guard
6801 Eagles of National Unity
6901 Group of Martyr Salah al-Bitar of the Arab Revolution Vanguards
6961 People's Liberation Army of Oman
6971 Islamic Front Against Heretics
7000 indeterminate Afghan mujahadeen guerrillas
7001 People's Mojahedin of Afghanistan
7002 Islamic Alliance for the Liberation of Afghanistan
7003 Islamic Society of Afghanistan
7004 Hezb-e Eslami, led by Yunus Khalis
7005 Jami'at-e Eslami
7006 Harakat-e Enqelabe Islami
7007 Afghan National Liberation Front
7008 Islamic Movement of Afghanistan

7101 Anti-Government Chinese
7131 World United Formosans for Independence
7311 North Korean agents
7321 Anti-US Suicide Action Squad, Revolutionary Party for Reunification
7322 Nagai-Gumu Gang, affiliated with the Yamaguchi-Gumi syndicate
7323 indeterminate South Koreans
7400 indeterminate Japanese extremists
7401 JRA, JURA, Japanese Red Army, Rengo Sekigun, United Red Army, Arab Red Army, Army of the Red Star
7402 Asia Corps, a right-wing group
7403 Kansai Regional Revolutionary Army
7407 Okinawa Liberation League
7501 indeterminate Kashmiri nationalists
7502 Dal Khalsa, Sikhs calling for Khalistan independence
7503 Free India Army, Free India Party, Indian Independent Forces, Azad Hind Sena
7504 Ananda Marg
7506 Universal Proutish Revolutionary Front
7507 indeterminate Sikh extremists
7651 Bangladesh students
7652 Pro-Mujib Force (led by Kader Sidiqui)
7653 JDS, National Socialist Party
7701 Al Zulfiqar
7751 Shan tribesmen
7752 Kachin Independence Army
7801 Tamil Liberation Tigers
8000 indeterminate Thai communists
8001 Pattani Liberation Front
8002 PULO, Pattani United Liberation Organization
8003 New Thai Leftist Front
8004 indeterminate Thai guerrillas
8111 Kampuchean guerrillas
8121 anticommunist Laotian guerrillas
8201 Malay-Arab group
8202 International Moslem Brotherhood Organization
8401 Kabataang Makabayan (Philippine leftist students)
8402 April 6 Liberation Movement
8403 Light a Fire Movement
8406 MNLF, Moro National Liberation Front
8407 NPA, New People's Army
8408 Filipino dissidents
8501 indeterminate Amboinese–South Moluccan exiles
8502 Indonesian Islamic Revolution Board
8503 Front for the Liberation of Aceh–Sumatra
8504 Darul Islam Holy War Command
8505 Irian Jaya (OPM)
8521 indeterminate Moluccan terrorists

9001 Australian socialist youth group
9301 Kanaka Liberation Front, Palika military wing, Kanaka (Native New Caledonian) Liberation Party, Army for the Liberation of New Caledonia
9998 irrelevant, inapplicable
9999 unknown

APPENDIX 2

Attributes of Terrorist Events, 1978–1987:
ITERATE 3 Data Codebook

The ITERATE project is an attempt to quantify data on the characteristics of transnational terrorist groups, their activities that have international impact, and the environment in which they operate. ITERATE 3 updates the coverage of terrorist incidents first reported in ITERATE 1 and 2, which can be obtained from the Inter-University Consortium for Political and Social Research, Box 1248, Ann Arbor, Michigan, 48106. ITERATE 3 is compatible with the coding categories used in its predecessors but includes new variables.

The working definition of international/transnational terrorism used by the ITERATE project is the use, or threat of use, of anxiety-inducing, extranormal violence for political purposes by any individual or group, whether acting for or in opposition to established governmental authority, when such action is intended to influence the attitudes and behavior of a target group wider than the immediate victims and when, through the nationality or foreign ties of its perpetrators, through its location, through the nature of its institutional or human victims, or through the mechanics of its resolution, its ramifications transcend national boundaries. International terrorism is such action when carried out by individuals or groups controlled by a sovereign state, whereas transnational terrorism is carried out by basically autonomous nonstate actors, whether or not they enjoy some degree of support from sympathetic states. "Victims" are those individuals who are directly harmed by the terrorist incident. While a given terrorist action may somehow harm world stability, citizens of nations must feel a more direct loss than the weakening of such a collective good.

The sources of the data can be found in Edward F. Mickolus (1980),

---

ITERATE 3 compiled by Edward F. Mickolus, Todd Sandler, and Jean Murdock.

Transnational Terrorism: A Chronology of Events, 1968–1979 (Westport, Conn.: Greenwood Press), and in the Introduction to this volume.

The datasets are available for personal computers that use MS-DOS. The data is stored as PC-FILE III.

The dataset consists of four parts. Nearly all incidents appear in the COMMON file, which the FATE, HOSTAGE, and SKYJACK files supplement. Some nonterrorist domestic skyjackings appear in the SKYJACK file and not in the COMMON file.

SUMMARY OF VARIABLES

List of Variables in COMMON File

INCIDENT CHARACTERISTICS

1. Date of start of incident — year
2. Date of start of incident — month
3. Date of start of incident — day
4. Incident code number
5. Location start
6. Location end
7. Scene of incident
8. Evidence of state sponsorship
9. Type of state sponsorship
10. Type of incident
11. Total number of nationalities involved in incident

TERRORIST CHARACTERISTICS

12. First group initiating action
13. Second group initiating action
14. Number of terrorist groups directly involved
15. Number of terrorists in attack force
16. Number of female terrorists in attack force
17. Number of nationalities of terrorists in attack force
18. First nationality of terrorists in attack force
19. Second nationality of terrorists in attack force
20. Third nationality of terrorists in attack force
21. Recidivists in attack force

VICTIM CHARACTERISTICS

22. Number of victims
23. Number of nationalities of victims
24. First victim's nationality
25. Second victim's nationality

26. Third victim's nationality
27. Number of United States victims
28. Type of United States victim
29. Type of immediate victim
30. Nature of victim entities

LIFE AND PROPERTY LOSSES

31. Total individuals wounded
32. Terrorists wounded
33. Foreign wounded
34. United States wounded
35. Government officials wounded
36. Total number of individuals killed
37. Terrorists killed
38. Foreign killed
39. United States killed
40. Government officials killed
41. Amount of damage
42. Type of weapon used

SUCCESS/FAILURE

43. Terrorist logistical success

List of Variables in FATE File

FATE OF TERRORISTS

1. Incident code/date
2. First fate of terrorists
3. Number of terrorists receiving first fate
4. Second fate of terrorists
5. Number of terrorists receiving second fate
6. Third fate of terrorists
7. Number of terrorists receiving third fate
8. Fourth fate of terrorists
9. Number of terrorists receiving fourth fate
10. Total number of terrorists arrested

EXTRADITION

11. Was extradition requested
12. Nation requesting extradition
13. Identity of nation receiving extradition request
14. Was extradition request granted

List of Variables in HOSTAGE File

TARGET OF TERRORIST DEMANDS

1. Incident code/date
2. Number of hostages
3. Number of hostages that escaped during the incident after being secured by terrorists
4. Target of demands 1
5. Target of demands 2
6. Target of demands 3
7. Number of governments upon whom demands were made
8. Were demands made upon host nation

NEGOTIATION BEHAVIOR

9. Demand #1: Media announcement
10. Demand #2: Political change
11. Demand #3: Non–Robin Hood ransom
12. Demand #4: Robin Hood ransom
13. Demand #5: Release prisoners
14. Demand #6: Safe haven for a destination
15. Demand #7: Safe passage out of the location
16. Demand #8: Other demands
17. Terrorist behavior in negotiations
18. Allowed sequential release of hostages
19. Allowed deadline to pass without engaging in action threatened
20. Number of deadlines where the threat was carried out

RESULTS OF NEGOTIATIONS

21. Terrorist negotiation success
22. Type of target negotiator
23. Number of target negotiators
24. Response of target
25. Amount of ransom paid
26. Source of ransom payment
27. Number of prisoners released
28. Ultimate destination of released prisoners
29. First hostage's fate
30. Second hostage's fate
31. Duration of incident in hours
32. Duration of incident in days

OTHER NATIONS INVOLVED IN INCIDENT

33. Number of nations denying safe haven request
34. First nation denying safe haven request

35. Second nation denying safe haven request
36. Number of nations granting safe haven request
37. First nation granting safe haven request
38. Second nation granting safe haven request
39. Number of nations with ancillary involvement in incident
40. First ancillary nation
41. Second ancillary nation

List of Variables in SKYJACK File

INCIDENT CHARACTERISTICS

1. Date of start of incident — year
2. Date of start of incident — month
3. Date of start of incident — day
4. Incident code number
5. Duration in hours

AIRLINE INFORMATION

6. Type of plane
7. Airline company

LOCATION OF INCIDENT

8. Flight plan embarkation point
9. Hijacker embarkation point
10. Flight plan end point
11. Hijacker desired end point
12. Number of stopovers and refuelings

NUMBER OF INDIVIDUALS INVOLVED

13. Crew members
14. Individuals on board plane
15. Hijackers
16. Number wounded
17. Hostages wounded
18. Hijackers wounded
19. Crew wounded
20. Number killed
21. Hostages killed
22. Hijackers killed
23. Crew killed
24. Damage to plane
25. Logistical success of hijacking incident
26. Negotiation success of hijacking incident
27. Type of weapon

DESCRIPTION OF VARIABLES

Description of Variables in COMMON File

INCIDENT CHARACTERISTICS

1. Date of start of incident — year

The beginning of the incident is considered to be the date at the scene of the incident in which it first became apparent to individuals other than the initiators that a terrorist event was taking place.
Values:
78   1978
79   1979
   .
   .
87   1987

2. Date of start of incident — month

See description for Variable 1.
Values:
01   January
02   February
   .
   .
12   December
99   Unknown month

3. Date of start of incident — day

See description for Variable 1.
Values:
01
   .
   .
31
99   Unknown day

4. Incident code number

A unique two-digit code number is assigned to each discrete incident that occurs on a given day. Specific incidents may thus be accessed by calling up the first eight digits of an entry for an incident.
Values:
00
01
   .
   .
99

5. Location start

This variable is coded according to the place name in which the incident first began. In the case of hijackings, the point of takeoff of the plane's hijackers is used. Letter bombs are coded at the place of mailing, if known. Facilities of international organizations, such as NATO or the United Nations, are considered to be on the soil of the host government as are foreign embassies.

Codes for nations and place names conform with the standard international relations archive country code developed by Bruce M. Russett, J. David Singer and Melvin Small (1968), in "National Political Units in the Twentieth Century: A Standardized List," *American Political Science Review* 62(3): 935–50. A few entries not relevant to the Russett et al. study have been added. Incidents have occurred in locations other than nation-states, including colonies, dependencies, in the air, and on the high seas.

The legal existence of certain of these "countries" is in dispute—in some cases armed conflict—and their use here is not meant to prejudge the merits of individual cases, nor to convey or withhold citizenship to members of separatist-oriented organizations. Some attacks are engaged in by residents of nations in which they are fighting to alter their citizenship (e.g., separatists or irredentists). While many of these attacks are considered to be domestic terrorism, such attacks are included if the terrorists traverse a natural geographical boundary to conduct attacks on the metropole, for example, Northern Irish attacks on the main British island, Puerto Rican attacks outside of the island, and attacks within Israel by Palestinian refugees. Attacks by exiles resident in but not citizens of a nation are also included, for example, South Moluccans in the Netherlands, Cuban exiles in the United States. Domestic attacks engaged in during the conduct of a civil war are not included.

Values:

002   United States
004   United Kingdom Virgin Islands
005   United States Virgin Islands
006   Puerto Rico
010   Greenland
011   Faeroe Islands
020   Canada
030   Bermuda
031   Bahamas
040   Cuba
041   Haiti
042   Dominican Republic
050   West Indies Federation
051   Jamaica
052   Trinidad and Tobago
053   Barbados
054   Dominica
055   Grenada
056   Saint Lucia
057   Saint Vincent
058   Antigua and Barbuda

059	Montserrat
060	Saint Christopher (Saint Kitts), Nevis
061	Anguilla
065	Guadeloupe
068	Martinique
070	Mexico
080	British Honduras
090	Guatemala
091	Honduras
092	El Salvador
093	Nicaragua
094	Costa Rica
095	Panama
096	Panama Canal Zone
099	Indeterminate Latin American nation
100	Colombia
101	Venezuela
110	Guyana, British Guiana
115	Suriname, Dutch Guiana
120	French Guiana
130	Ecuador
135	Peru
140	Brazil
145	Bolivia
150	Paraguay
155	Chile
160	Argentina
165	Uruguay
170	Falkland Islands, Malvinas
200	United Kingdom
201	Isle of Man
202	Guernsey and dependencies
204	Northern Ireland
205	Ireland
206	Scotland
210	Netherlands
211	Belgium
212	Luxembourg
219	Corsica
220	France
221	Monaco
223	Liechtenstein
225	Switzerland
230	Spain
231	Gibraltar
232	Andorra
235	Portugal
255	Federal Republic of Germany (West Germany)

265 German Democratic Republic (East Germany)
290 Poland
300 Indeterminate European nation
305 Austria
310 Hungary
315 Czechoslovakia
325 Italy
328 Vatican City
331 San Marino
338 Malta
339 Albania
345 Yugoslavia
350 Greece
352 Cyprus
355 Bulgaria
360 Romania
365 USSR
375 Finland
380 Sweden
385 Norway
390 Denmark
395 Iceland
400 Azores
401 Madeira Isles
402 Cape Verde
403 Sao Tome and Principe
404 Guinea-Bissau
411 Spanish Guinea
412 Rio Muni
413 Fernando Po
420 Gambia
432 Mali
433 Senegal
434 Benin
435 Mauritania
436 Niger
437 Ivory Coast
438 Guinea
439 Burkina Faso, Upper Volta
450 Liberia
451 Sierra Leone
452 Ghana
461 Togo
471 Cameroon
475 Nigeria
481 Gabon
482 Central African Republic
483 Chad

484   Congo-Brazzaville
485   Zaire
500   Uganda
501   Kenya
510   Tanzania
511   Zanzibar
515   Ruanda-Urundi
516   Burundi
517   Rwanda
520   Somalia
522   Djibouti, French Somaliland
530   Ethiopia
531   Eritrea
539   Cabinda
540   Angola
541   Mozambique
551   Zambia
552   Zimbabwe, Rhodesia
553   Malawi
560   Republic of South Africa
561   Transkei
565   Namibia, South West Africa
570   Lesotho
571   Botswana
572   Swaziland
580   Madagascar, Malagasy Republic
581   Comoros
585   Reunion
590   Mauritius
591   Seychelles
599   Indeterminate African nation
600   Morocco
605   Ifni
606   Spanish North African Presidios, Alhucemas, Ceuta, Charfarinas, Me-
      lilla, Penon de Velez
607   Canary Islands
609   Spanish Sahara, Western Sahara
615   Algeria
616   Tunisia
620   Libya
625   Sudan
630   Iran
640   Turkey
645   Iraq
646   Kurdistan
651   Egypt
652   Syria
660   Lebanon

663 Jordan
666 Israel
667 Indeterminate Arabs, Palestine
670 Saudi Arabia
678 Yemen
680 South Yemen, PDRY
690 Kuwait
692 Bahrain
694 Qatar
695 Dubai
696 Trucial Oman States
697 Abu Dhabi
698 Muscat and Oman
699 United Arab Emirates
700 Afghanistan
710 People's Republic of China
712 Mongolia
713 Taiwan, Republic of China
720 Hong Kong
721 Macao
731 North Korea
732 South Korea
740 Japan
741 Ryukyu Islands
750 India
760 Bhutan
761 Sikkim
765 Bangladesh
770 Pakistan
775 Burma
780 Sri Lanka, Ceylon
781 Maldive Islands
790 Nepal
800 Thailand
811 Cambodia, Khmer Republic, Kampuchea
812 Laos
815 Vietnam
816 North Vietnam
817 South Vietnam
820 Malaysia
830 Singapore
835 Brunei
840 Philippines
850 Indonesia
851 West Irian, Netherlands New Guinea
852 South Molucca
860 Portuguese Timor
900 Australia

910   Papua–New Guinea
920   New Zealand
925   Cook Islands
930   New Caledonia
935   New Hebrides
936   Vanuatu
940   Solomon Islands
950   Fiji
955   Tonga
960   French Polynesia, Oceania
980   United States Pacific Trust Territories
981   Marianas Islands
985   Guam
990   Western Samoa
991   American Samoa
995   NATO
996   International organizations
997   Unspecified foreign nations
998   Irrelevant
999   Unknown

6. Location end

The same three-digit nation code used for the previous variable (number 5). Letter bombings are coded as the location at which they were discovered by authorities. Hijackings are coded as the last point of landing of the aircraft while in control of the hijackers.

Values:
(see Variable 5)

7. Scene of incident

Values:
1   Home, base, or installation of victim
2   Nonresidential, nonvocational site of victim (includes street corners, markets, theaters, taverns, and hotels)
3   Office, place of employment of victim (includes embassies and consulates)
4   Motor vehicle
5   Aircraft
6   Ship
7   Train
8   Embarkation area
9   Other, unknown

8. Evidence of state sponsorship

Direct state sponsorship of an incident entails a nation-state aiding the terrorist attack force in planning or executing the incident. Aid could come in the form of financial support, weapons transported in the diplomatic pouch, reinforcements, and so on. Mere generalized training—rather than incident-specific coaching—of individuals who subsequently appear in an incident is not included.

Values:

1   Some evidence that the incident received state support
2   No apparent evidence of state support
9   Unknown

9. Type of state sponsorship

Values:

1   Direct support to terrorists in incident
2   Officially sanctioned participation of government personnel in incident
3   1 and 2 above
9   Irrelevant

10. Type of incident

Each incident is given one unique event-type code. In situations in which an event had characteristics of two event types, the event is categorized as the type of incident that occurred first, for example, an airline hijacking that becomes a barricade-and-hostage seizure is classified as a hijacking. Kidnapping involves the seizure of an individual and transportation of the hostage and the initiators to an underground hideout, where he is held during negotiations for his release. Barricade-and-hostage seizure operations involve the initiators taking over a site and seizing whatever hostages happen to be available. Negotiations for the release of the hostages are then conducted with the initiators themselves effectively being hostages. A nuclear-related incident involves the actual use of nuclear material, such as radioactive iodine, pollution via nuclear substances, or nuclear bombings. A bombing of a nuclear weapons storage facility or the bombing of a nuclear power plant is classified as a bombing.

Values:

01   Kidnapping
02   Barricade and hostage seizure
03   Occupation of facilities without hostage seizure
04   Letter or parcel bombing
05   Incendiary bombing, arson, Molotov cocktail
06   Explosive bombing
07   Armed attack employing missiles
08   Armed attack—other, including mortars, bazookas
09   Aerial hijacking
10   Takeover of nonaerial means of transportation
11   Assassination, murder
12   Sabotage not involving explosives or arson
13   Exotic pollution, including chemical and biological agents
14   Nuclear-related weapons attack
15   Threat with no subsequent terrorist action
16   Theft, break-in of facilities

17   Conspiracy to commit terrorist action
18   Hoax (e.g., claiming a nonexistent bomb)
19   Other actions
20   Sniping at buildings, other facilities
21   Shoot-out with police
22   Arms smuggling
23   Car bombing
24   Suicide car bombing

11. Total number of nationalities involved in incident

A value of 01 would mean that the incident did not fit the definition of transnational terrorism that was used as the selection criterion for the dataset. Involvement in an incident may include victimization, targeting, hosting, negotiating, providing/denying asylum, patronage of the incident, and other ancillary roles.

02   2 nationalities involved
.
.
98   98 or more nationalities involved
99   Unknown number of nationalities involved

TERRORIST CHARACTERISTICS

12. First group initiating action

The groups appearing on this list are the names of organizations for which responsibility was claimed or attributed for specific terrorist actions. The inclusion of any given group should not be interpreted as an evaluation of that organization's goals or motivations. Many of the groups listed are cover names for organizations that may wish to deny responsibility for a particular action producing counterproductive results. In some cases, individuals falsely claim responsibility in the name of a group in order to tarnish the image of the group. Some groups have become governing bodies of nations. No attempt has been made to "break" these covers, and the names provided by the claimants have been accepted. Sources are often vague regarding the actual name of the organization responsible, or unclear about the amount of legally acceptable evidence pointing to responsibility. The names of the major suspects in such vague cases have been used.

An attempt has been made to have the initial three digits of the four-digit code follow the codings used for the nation in which the group's members operate, or claim citizenship, where appropriate. For cases in which more than 10 groups have appeared in that nation, an attempt has been made to make the initial three digits as close as possible to that of the relevant nation code. Where useful, annotations about the group's characteristics have been made. Code 0003 was used for cases in which individuals or groups were seeking political asylum or other very specific goals and are not expected to engage in future attacks. Incidents engaged in by pathological individuals or groups are also included here where such attacks were initially treated by authorities as attacks by politically motivated terrorists. Code

9998 is used for the second entry in cases in which only one group took part in the action.

Values:
(see Appendix 1 for list)

13. Second group initiating action

Values:
(see Appendix 1)

14. Number of terrorist groups directly involved

Terrorists who are considered victims of attacks by other terrorist groups are not considered initiators for purposes of this entry and are not included in the tally.

Values:
01   1 group
  .
  .
8   8 groups
9   Unknown

15. Number of terrorists in attack force

The tally includes only those individuals who were publicly involved in the incident. Support staff who remained underground during the initiation of the incident are not counted. In cases of kidnapping, where a rotating staff of guards were employed who were not involved in the actual seizure of the victim, only the seizing individuals are tallied. Terrorists who are considered victims of attacks by other terrorist groups are not considered initiators for this variable and are not tallied. Terrorists whose release from prison was demanded and who joined the initiating group during the incident are not considered initiators and are not tallied.

Values:
01   1 individual
  .
  .
89   89 individuals
90   90 and above
99   Unknown

16. Number of female terrorists in attack force

Values:
01   1 female terrorist participated
  .
  .
97   97 women were involved
98   Unknown, but there were some women involved
99   Unknown if any women were involved

17. Number of nationalities of terrorists in attack force

Unknown planners of the action who remained underground during perpetration of the incident are not included. The nationality, rather than the base of operations of the terrorist group, is counted.

Values:

1　1 nationality

.

.

8　8 nationalities

9　Unknown

18. First nationality of terrorists in attack force

When a source refers only to the name of a domestic terrorist group, the perpetrators are assumed to have the nationality of the host nation. Perpetrators of telephoned threats are assumed to have only one nationality, although it may not be known.

Values:

(same as used in Variable 5)

19. Second nationality of terrorists in attack force

Values:

(same as used in Variable 5)

20. Third nationality of terrorists in attack force

Values:

(same as used in Variable 5)

21. Recidivists in attack force

This variable records the number of terrorists in the attack force who are known to have participated in other terrorist attacks.

Values:

00　None are known to have been a past participant

01　1 participated in a previous terrorist attack

.

.

97　97 have previously been in terrorist attacks

98　Number unknown, but some participated in other attacks

99　Unknown

VICTIM CHARACTERISTICS

22. Number of victims

Victims are those who are directly affected by the terrorist incident by the loss of property, lives, or liberty. This variable records the number of individuals directly and physically victimized in the attack.

Values:

000–997	Actual number of victims
998	Unknown, but some victims
999	Unknown if any individuals were victimized

23. Number of nationalities of victims

International organizations are considered to have a distinct international personality and are considered to be one nationality (rather than have 160 + nationalities, as would be the case for universal groupings).

Values:

01	1 nationality
.	
.	
98	98 nationalities
99	Unknown

24. First victim's nationality

Victims are those individuals who are directly harmed by the terrorist incident. While a given terrorist action may have deleterious effects upon world stability, citizens of a nation must feel a more direct loss than the diminishing of a collective good.

Values:
(same as used in Variable 5)

25. Second victim's nationality

Values:
(same as used in Variable 5)

26. Third victim's nationality

Values:
(same as used in Variable 5)

27. Number of United States victims

Values:

000–997	Actual number of American individuals victimized
998	Number unknown, but some Americans were victimized
999	Unknown if any Americans were victimized

28. Type of United States victim

Bombings of subsidiaries of United States corporations are considered to affect United States interests sufficiently to be coded 4.

Values:

1   Diplomatic
2   Military
3   Other United States government
4   Commercial, business
5   Other nonofficial, including tourist, missionary, student
8   Irrelevant, no United States victimization
9   Unknown, indeterminate

29. Type of immediate victim

The host government is the nation in which the action begins. All other nations are considered to be foreign countries. The bombing of an office of a corporation is considered to be psychological and directed at that corporation's officials and is coded as 5.

Values:

1   Host government officials
2   Foreign diplomats or official nonmilitary
3   Host government military
4   Foreign military
5   Corporation officials and employees
6   Prominent opinion leaders (e.g., newsmen)
7   Private parties, including tourists, missionaries, students
8   Suspected terrorists
9   Indeterminate

30. Nature of victim entities

Skyjackings negatively affect both property and people and are coded as 3. Bombings of facilities that injure people are coded 3. The bombing of a facility with no casualties is coded as an attack on the installation only.

Values:

1   People
2   Installations, property
3   Both people and property
9   Unknown

LIFE AND PROPERTY LOSSES

31. Total individuals wounded

Wounded include those who are reported to have been sufficiently harmed physically to have required medical attention. No distinction is made between those who are outpatients and those who are rescued from the critical list. Those who later die from their injuries are coded as killed, rather than wounded.

Values:

000   None injured

   .

   .

998   998 injured
999   Unknown, but individuals were injured

32. *Terrorists wounded*

Individuals who are nominally members of terrorist groups who were attacked by the initiators of the incident are not included in the tally.
Values:
00   None injured

   .

   .

98   98 injured
99   Unknown, but some terrorists were wounded

33. *Foreign wounded*

Only nonhost country victims are tallied herein. Domestic victims wounded can be calculated by subtracting this variable and terrorists wounded from the total number of individuals wounded.
Values:
000   None injured

   .

   .

998 998 injured
999   Unknown, but individuals were wounded

34. *United States wounded*

Values:
000   No American citizens were wounded
001   1 American citizen was wounded

   .

   .

997   997 Americans were wounded
998   Unknown number, but some Americans were wounded
999   Unknown if any Americans were wounded

35. *Government officials wounded*

Figure includes negotiators, police, and military.
Values:
000–997   Actual number wounded
998   Unknown number, but some were wounded
999   Unknown if any were wounded

36. Total number of individuals killed

Values:
000   None killed

.
.

998   998 killed
999   Unknown, but individuals were killed

37. Terrorists killed

Individuals who are nominally members of terrorist groups who were attacked by the initiators of the incident are not included in the tally.
Values:
00   None killed

.
.

98   98 killed
99   Unknown, but some terrorists were killed

38. Foreign killed

Only nonhost country victims are tallied herein. Domestic victims killed can be calculated by subtracting this variable and terrorists killed from the total number of individuals killed.
Values:
000   None killed

.
.

998   998 killed
999   Unknown, but individuals were killed

39. United States killed

Values:
000   No American citizens were killed
001   1 American citizen was killed

.
.

997   997 Americans were killed
998   Unknown number, but some Americans were killed
999   Unknown if any Americans were killed

40. Government officials killed

Figure includes negotiators, police, and military.
Values:
000–997   Actual number killed

998   Unknown number, but some were killed
999   Unknown if any were killed

41. *Amount of damage*

Values:
0   None
1   Slight — less than or equal to $10,000
2   Moderate — less than or equal to $100,000
3   High — less than or equal to $1 million
4   Severe — more than $1 million
9   Unknown, but damage reported

42. *Type of weapon used*

The most destructive weapon of all of those known to be in the possession of the perpetrators at the scene of the incident is noted.
Values:
1   Hoax, no weapons used
2   Nonexplosive, nonprojectile weapons, including knives
3   Handguns
4   Rifles, shotguns, or machine guns
5   Explosives, incendiaries
6   Missiles, other heavy projectiles
7   Other
9   Unknown

SUCCESS/FAILURE

43. *Terrorist logistical success*

Values:
0   Aborted by terrorists before initiation
1   Incident stopped by authorities at planning stage
2   Incident stopped by authorities at scene or on the way to scene, before initiation
3   Aborted by terrorists during event
4   Unsuccessful owing to faults or error by terrorists
5   Stopped by authorities at the scene after initiation
6   Apparently completed as planned
9   Unknown

Description of Variables in FATE File

The FATE list describes the disposition, when known, of the perpetrators of incidents noted in the COMMON file after the incident. The disposition of nonterrorist hijackers in the SKYJACK file is not included. The FATE list includes only those incidents in which the fate of at least one of the perpetrators was other than "escaped at the scene of the incident."

FATE OF TERRORISTS

1. Incident code/date

Values:
(The eight-digit number will be same as that used for incident date/code in its COMMON file entry.)

2. First fate of terrorists

Four possible fates of the terrorist perpetrators, as well as ancillary participants in the incident, may be included. Shoot-outs may be initiated by the perpetrators or by authorities. If the individual was killed resisting arrest, he will also be coded as dead via shoot-out. Codes 04 through 09 refer solely to the length of the sentence, rather than the portion served. None of these entries are subsets of previous entries. The Bangkok Solution refers to the agreement made by the four Black Septembrists who took over the Israeli embassy in Bangkok on December 28, 1972, and Thai officials, which allowed the terrorists safe passage from the scene in return for the release of their hostages and dropping of their other demands. This solution has subsequently been used successfully as a precedent for other negotiations.
Values:
01 Dead in shoot-out with police
02 Dead due to suicide at scene
03 Dead via the death penalty
04 Long jail term (greater than 5 years)
05 Long jail term, subject of demands in subsequent incident
06 Long jail term, freed due to demands in subsequent incident
07 Short jail term (5 years or less)
08 Short jail term, subject of demands in subsequent incident
09 Short jail term, freed due to demands in subsequent incident
10 Freed by court verdict
11 Escaped captors en route to prison or in prison
12 Freed via "Bangkok Solution"
13 Arrested, not brought to trial, freed by other than court verdict, escape, or demands in other incident
14 Escaped at scene of incident
15 Arrested, indeterminate treatment of case
16 Jailed, released (other than due to demands) before finishing term
17 Arrested in subsequent incident
18 Granted asylum
19 Received death penalty, sentence altered
20 Committed suicide in later confrontation
21 Sentenced to indeterminate term
22 Sentenced in absentia
23 Died at scene due to accident
24 Released due to turning state's evidence
25 Sentenced to death, execution of sentence indeterminate
26 Committed suicide in prison

27 Killed attempting prison escape
28 Committed to mental institution
29 Died in subsequent incident
98 Irrelevant, not applicable
99 Unknown, indeterminate

3. Number of terrorists receiving first fate

Values:
01–97 Actual number
98   Irrelevant, not applicable
99   Unknown, indeterminate

4. Second fate of terrorists

Values:
(same coding as Variable 2)

5. Number of terrorists receiving second fate

Values:
01–97 Actual number
98   Irrelevant, not applicable
99   Unknown, indeterminate

6. Third fate of terrorists

Values:
(same coding as Variable 2)

7. Number of terrorists receiving third fate

Values:
01–97 Actual number
98   Irrelevant, not applicable
99   Unknown, indeterminate

8. Fourth fate of terrorists

Values:
(same coding as Variable 2)

9. Number of terrorists receiving fourth fate

Values:
01–97 Actual number
98   Irrelevant, not applicable
99   Unknown, indeterminate

10. *Total number of terrorists arrested*

Individuals need not have been in the attack force to be included in this tally.
Values:
00–97   Actual number
98   Irrelevant
99   Unknown

EXTRADITION

11. *Was extradition requested?*

A formal extradition treaty need not exist for a state to attempt to obtain
extradition of any accused terrorists.
Values:
1   Request was made
2   Request was not made
8   Irrelevant, circumstances of case were such that request could not be made
9   Unknown

12. *Nation requesting extradition*

Only one nation requesting extradition can be entered. Cases of multiple extradition requests are rare, and are noted in the chronology.
Values:
(same as found in Variable 5 of COMMON file)

13. *Identity of nation receiving extradition request*

Values:
(same as found in Variable 5 of COMMON file)

14. *Was extradition request granted?*

Values:
1   Yes
2   No
8   Irrelevant, extradition request was not made
9   Unknown

Descriptions of Variables in HOSTAGE File

The HOSTAGE file lists characteristics peculiar to incidents involving the taking of
hostages, skyjackings, kidnappings, and takeovers of nonaerial means of transportation. Incidents that would have been hostage situations are included, although
hostages may have all died and/or escaped at the initial scene of the attack. The
nonterrorist hijackings included in the SKYJACK file are not included.

TARGET OF TERRORIST DEMANDS

1. Incident code/date

Values:
(The eight-digit number will be same as that used for incident date/code in its COMMON file entry.)

2. Number of hostages

Individuals who successfully escape their captors-to-be at the beginning of an attack are considered to have never been captured, and an entry of 000 appears. Those who escape after having been captured, or who are released during negotiations by their captors, are considered to have been hostages for part of the time, and are included in the tally. All passengers and crew members, save the initiating terrorists, in a skyjacking are considered hostages. Terrorists in a barricade-and-hostage situation, although unable to come and go freely, are not considered hostages. Terrorists whose release from prison was demanded, and who join the initiating group during the incident voluntarily, are not considered to be hostages and are not included in the tally.

Values:
000–998   Actual number of hostages
999   Unknown, indeterminate, although it is known that hostages were taken

3. Number of hostages that escaped during the incident after being secured by terrorists

Values:
000–997   Actual number
998   Unknown, but some known to have escaped
999   Unknown

4. Target of demands 1

This variable includes governments and other entities (corporations, private individuals, and even other terrorist groups). Whenever a specific entity was called upon to perform a specific task, whether it be to fly a plane to a new destination, pay a ransom, or release prisoners, an entity is coded.

Values (in addition to country codes used in Variable 5 of the COMMON file, the following entity codes are used):

007   Business, corporation
008   Family
009   Other organization
012   Individual, for example, pilot
013   Newspaper

5. *Target of demands 2*

Values:
(same as Variable 4 above)

6. *Target of demands 3*

Values:
(same as Variable 4 above)

7. *Number of governments/entities upon whom demands were made*

This variable includes governments and other entities (corporations, private individuals, and even other terrorist groups). Whenever a specific entity was called upon to perform a specific task, whether it be to fly a plane to a new destination, pay a ransom, or release prisoners, an entity is coded.
Values:
0–7 Actual number
8   Irrelevant, demands were not made
9   Unknown, but demands were placed upon some entities

8. *Were demands made upon host nation?*

The host nation is considered to be the location in which the incident began.
Values:
1 Yes
2 No
9 Unknown

NEGOTIATION BEHAVIOR

9. *Demand #1: Media announcement*

Values:
0 Terrorists did not demand media coverage
1 Newspaper statement
2 Radio statement
3 Television statement
4 Circulate propaganda statement, medium unspecified
5 Unknown as to exact type of medium
6 Mix of above
9 Unknown

10. *Demand #2: Political change*

Values:
1 Yes

2   No
9   Unknown

11. *Demand #3: Non–Robin Hood ransom*

A Robin Hood ransom is a philanthropic demand—the terrorist group does not directly receive the money or other item of value demanded. Herein, only the group's organization coffers receive the proceeds.

Values:

0000–9996	Actual amount in $10,000 intervals
9997	Amount greater than $99.96 million
9998	Unknown, but some ransom was demanded
9999	Unknown if any ransom was demanded

12. *Demand #4: Robin Hood Ransom*

A Robin Hood ransom is a philanthropic demand—the terrorist group does not directly receive the money or other item of value demanded. The group may specify the beneficiary.

Values:

0000–9996	Actual amount in $10,000 intervals
9997	Amount greater than $99.96 million
9998	Unknown, but some ransom was demanded
9999	Unknown if any ransom was demanded

13. *Demand #5: Release prisoners*

Values:

001–996	Actual number whose release was demanded
997	More than 996
998	Unknown, but some asked for
999	Unknown

14. *Demand #6: Safe haven for a destination*

Values:

1   Yes, demand was made
2   No, demand was not made
9   Unknown

15. *Demand #7: Safe passage out of the location*

Values:

1   Yes, demand was made
2   No, demand was not made
9   Unknown

16. Demand #8: Other demands

These demands do not include those items previously mentioned, as well as ransom payments or "creature comforts" during incidents, such as food, drink, blankets, and medicines for perpetrators and hostages.
Values:
1 Yes, demand was made
2 No, demand was not made
9 Unknown

17. Terrorist behavior in negotiations

Values:
1 Lessened one or more demands without increasing any
2 No changes in demands by terrorists
3 Replaced demands with others
4 Increased one or more demands without decreasing any
5 Mixed behavior—that is, increased one or more while decreasing one or more
8 Irrelevant, negotiations were not conducted
9 Unknown

18. Allowed sequential release of hostages

Values:
0–7 Actual number of times hostages released
8   Unknown, but some sequential release of hostages
9   Unknown

19. Allowed deadline to pass without engaging in action threatened

Values:
0–6 Actual number of deadlines allowed to pass
7   None, demandees conceded before deadline
8   Unknown, but at least one deadline set and allowed to pass
9   Irrelevant, no deadlines set

20. Number of deadlines where the threat was carried out

Values:
0–6 Actual number of deadlines following which terrorists followed through
7   None, demandees conceded before deadline
8   Unknown, but at least one deadline set and was followed by threatened behavior
9   Irrelevant, no deadlines set

RESULTS OF NEGOTIATIONS

21. Terrorist negotiation success

Values:
1 Received some of their demands
2 Received all of their demands
3 Received none of their demands
8 Irrelevant, no demands made
9 Unknown

22. Type of target negotiator

This variable refers to the identity of the individuals who conducted the negotiations with the terrorists in response to their demands. In cases where codings of 1, 2, and/or 3 may be applicable to the same individual, the lowest numerical value should be used. Category 6 includes clergymen, individuals with a great public following, newsmen, nongovernmental leaders, and even nominal terrorist groups who put pressure on the initiators to alter their behavior during the incident.

Values:
1 Host government official, including police
2 Victim government official
3 Foreign government official
4 Corporate official
5 Private parties, including family
6 Prominent opinion leader
7 Other
8 Irrelevant, negotiations were not established
9 Unknown, indeterminate

23. Number of target negotiators

Values:
1–7 Actual number
8 Irrelevant
9 Unknown, indeterminate

24. Response of target

The Bangkok Solution refers to the agreement made by the four Black Septembrists who took over the Israeli embassy in Bangkok on December 28, 1972, and Thai officials, which allowed the terrorists safe passage from the scene in return for release of their hostages and the dropping of their other demands. This outcome has subsequently been used successfully as a precedent for other negotiation situations.

Values:
1 Capitulation
2 Stalling, with compromise on demands
3 Bangkok Solution
4 No compromise, no shoot-out with the perpetrators

5   Shoot-out with the terrorists
6   Government doublecross
7   Massive nationwide search for terrorists, with no compromise or capitulation by government regarding terrorist demands
8   Irrelevant, negotiations were not established, no demands made, no direct confrontation engaged
9   Unknown, indeterminate

25. Amount of ransom paid

Include both types (Robin Hood and nonphilanthropic) of ransom paid.
Values:
0000–9997   Actual amount in increments of $10,000
9998   Unknown, but some ransom paid
9999   Unknown

26. Source of ransom payment

Values:
1   Government
2   Corporate
3   Family
4   Other, including public collections, private sources
5   No ransom paid
6   Indeterminate, but ransom paid
7   Indeterminate if ransom was paid
8   Irrelevant, no ransom demanded
9   Unknown

27. Number of prisoners released

Values:
000–996   Actual number
997   More than 996
998   Irrelevant
999   Unknown, but some prisoners were released

28. Ultimate destination of released prisoners

The stopping-over and refueling points of released prisoners is not included. Their quasi-permanent destination at the end of the incident is entered.
Values:
(same as those used in Variable 5 of COMMON file)

29. First hostage's fate

Cases in which hostages are released without the levying of demands are coded as 01.

Values:
01 No damage or casualties, hostages released, no target capitulation
02 No damage or casualties, hostages released, capitulation or compromise by targets
03 Victims killed, no target capitulation
04 Victims killed, capitulation or compromise by targets
05 Damaged material, no target capitulation
06 Damaged material, capitulation or compromise by targets
07 Victim killed while attempting escape after initial capture
08 Victim successfully avoided capture
10 Victim successfully avoided capture after incident began
11 Hostages killed in shoot-out
12 Hostages killed, no provocation, during negotiations
13 Hostages killed during negotiations, deadline had passed
14 Hostages rescued by authorities
15 Incident forestalled by authorities before initiation
98 Irrelevant
99 Unknown, indeterminate

30. Second hostage's fate

Values:
(same as for Variable 29 above)

31. Duration of incident in hours

Coding should be from the time hostages were seized to the time that hostages' ultimate fate was determined.
Values:
00–96 Actual hours
97 More than 96 hours
98 Irrelevant
99 Unknown

32. Duration of incident in days

See caveat for #31.
Values:
000–996 Actual number of days
997 More than 996 days
998 Irrelevant
999 Unknown

OTHER NATIONS INVOLVED IN INCIDENT

33. Number of nations denying safe haven request

Such nations refer to those suggested by any negotiator as a final destination for the perpetrators.

Values:

0–7   Actual number

8   Irrelevant

9   Unknown

34. First nation denying safe haven request

Values:

(same codes used in Variable 5 of COMMON file)

35. Second nation denying safe haven request

Values:

(same codes used in Variable 5 of COMMON file)

36. Number of nations granting safe haven request

Such nations are those willing to grant the terrorists safe haven in their territory, rather than those nations willing to allow the terrorists to leave their territory to reach a safe haven.

Values:

0–7   Actual number

8   Irrelevant

9   Unknown

37. First nation granting safe haven request

Values:

(same codes used in Variable 5 of COMMON file)

38. Second nation granting safe haven request

Values:

(same codes used in Variable 5 of COMMON file)

39. Number of nations with ancillary involvement in incident

Ancillary involvement refers to a relation to the event not previously mentioned elsewhere, for example, as target, victim, host, or breeder of the terrorists. Such ancillary involvement may include being a refueling point for the escape vehicle, the site of a ransom payment, an additional source of demands, a mediator, a negotiator, a covert initiator of the specific incident, and so on.

Values:

0–8   Actual number

9   Unknown

40. *First ancillary nation*

   Values:
   (same codes used in Variable 5 of COMMON file)

41. *Second ancillary nation*

   Values:
   (same codes used in Variable 5 of COMMON file)

Description of Variables in SKYJACK File

This file includes terrorist hijackings that appear in the COMMON file as well as hijackings engaged in by nonterrorists.

INCIDENT CHARACTERISTICS

1. *Date of start of incident — year*

   The beginning of the incident is considered to be the date at the scene of the incident in which it first became apparent to individuals other than the initiators that a hijacking was taking place.
   Values:
   78   1978
   79   1979
   .
   .
   .
   87   1987

2. *Date of start of incident — month*

   See description for Variable 1.
   Values:
   01   January
   02   February
   .
   .
   .
   12   December
   99   Unknown month

3. *Date of start of incident — day*

   See description for Variable 1.
   Values:
   01
   .
   .

31
99   Unknown day

4. Incident code number

A unique two-digit code number is assigned to each discrete incident that occurs on a given day. Specific incidents may thus be accessed by calling up the first eight digits of an entry for an incident. These eight digits link the SKYJACK file to the COMMON, FATE, and HOSTAGE files, where appropriate.
Values:
00
01
.
.
99

5. Duration in hours

Values:
00   Less than 1 hour
01–97   Actual hours
98   Unknown, but more than 1 hour
99   Unknown

AIRLINE INFORMATION

6. Type of plane

Values:
001   BAC-111
002   Twin-engined Malev
003   DC-3
004   DC-4
005   DC-10
006   DC-6, DC-6B
007   F-7
008   Catalina flying boat
009   Dakota
010   Piper Apache PA-10
011   Vickers Viscount
012   Constellation
013   YAK-12
014   Piper Apache PA-10
015   Ilyushin IL-14
016   VC-10
017   FH-227
018   DC-8
019   DC-9

020 B-720
021 Cessna 210
022 Antonov AN-2
023 Piper Apache PA-23
024 Antonov AN-24
025 HS-125 air taxi
026 YS-11 twin turboprop
027 Fokker F-27
028 Ilyushin 18
029 YS-11A
030 YAK-40
031 Viscount 810
032 Cessna 310
033 Cessna 150
034 Comet IV
035 Cessna 206
036 Cessna Skymaster 336
037 DH-114
038 A-300 Airbus
039 L-410
040 Cessna 9-passenger 402
041 C-141
042 Islander BN2A
043 Grumman Goose 73
044 Convair twin-engine VC-440
045 4-engined plane, not further identified
046 C-46
047 C-47
048 Hawker Siddeley twin-engined turboprop 748
049 L-1049 Super Constellation
050 TU-104
051 Lockheed Electra
052 Junkers 52
053 Beechcraft C-45
054 Ilyushin twin-engined 14
055 Beechcraft D-80
056 TU-134
057 DeHavilland Heron 157
058 Convair 580
059 Caravelle 50
060 CV-600
061 DeHavilland Twin Otter
062 Lockheed L-1011 TriStar
064 CV-640
065 Zlin crop duster
066 Saunders ST-27
067 SC-7
068 Aero Commander Hawk 681

070   Boeing 707
071   B-727
072   Cessna 172
073   B-737
074   B-747 jumbo jet
075   Trident
077   Cessna 177
078   AVRO 748
079   Piper Cherokee 140
080   Convair CV-880
081   Piper Commanche
082   Cessna 182
085   twin-engined Cherokee
086   F-862
087   Piper twin-engined Seneca
088   Electra L-188
089   Cessna 180
090   helicopter
091   Caravelle not further identified
092   twin-engined plane, not further identified
093   Viscount 4-engined turboprop
094   Fokker twin-engined plane
095   Beechcraft plane, not further identified
096   Piper twin-engined Navajo
097   Convair plane, not further identified
098   Convair 990
099   Piper twin-engined plane
103   B-3 military plane
130   C-130 military plane
999   Unknown

7. Airline company

Airlines appear by region, in the order in which they were first hijacked. (This variable includes the same information but is coded somewhat differently than its predecessors in ITERATE 1 and 2. ITERATE 2 codes appear to the right of the entries.) Firms that are not identified as being general aviation carriers fly regularly scheduled flights. Such American firms became subject to mandatory passenger screening in 1973.

The regional organization of this variable is:

000–199   United States companies
200–399   European companies
400–499   Middle Eastern companies
500–599   Latin American companies
600–699   Far East and Asian companies
700–799   Eastern Bloc companies

800–899   African companies
900–998   Other companies
999   Unknown

Specific Values:

000	National Airlines	027
001	Eastern Air Lines	028
002	PAC, Pacific Air Lines	029
003	Continental Air Lines	030
004	Pan American Airlines	031
005	American Aviation	035
006	local US	038
007	Hawaiian Airlines	040
008	Aloha Airlines	041
009	Crescent Airlines, US charter	048
010	Delta Airlines	049
011	Southeast Airlines	052
012	Northwest Orient Airlines	053
013	TWA, Trans World Airlines	054
014	Island City Flying Service, US charter	055
015	Naples Airlines, US charter	057
016	Key West Airlines, US charter	061
017	United Airlines	065
018	Northeast Airlines	072
019	Texas International	073
020	Caldwell Aviation Corporation, US charter	104
021	North Central Airways	105
022	American Air Lines	109
023	Allegheny Airlines	125
024	PRINAIR, Puerto Rican International Airlines	126
025	Western Airlines	130
026	American Air Taxi, US charter firm	131
027	private US plane	132
028	Hughes Air West	135
029	Piedmont Airways	137
030	Braniff	139
031	Big Brother, US general aviation firm	141
032	Wein Consolidated Salta	142
033	Pacific Southwest Airlines	148
034	SFO Helicopter Company, US general aviation	149
035	Mohawk Airlines	150
036	Chalk's Flying Service, US general aviation	152
037	Tortugas Airways, US general aviation firm	153
038	Puerto Rican commuter flight firm	156
039	Frontier Airlines	157
040	Alaska Airlines	158
041	Southern Airways	168

228	Air France	179
229	Irish Helicopters, Inc.	180
230	British Airways	183
231	Dundalk Aero Club, an Eire firm	190
232	Canadian Pacific Airlines	192
233	TAP, a Portuguese firm	205
234	Aer Lingus, an Eire firm	209
400	local Egyptian	043
401	El Al	056
402	Misrair, an Egyptian firm	080
403	Iranian National Airlines	112
404	Saudi Arabian Airlines	113
405	Air Algerie	119
406	Egyptian Airlines	122
407	Indian Airlines	128
408	ALIA, Royal Jordanian Airlines	140
409	Pakistan International Airlines	145
410	Al Yemda, a South Yemeni firm	166
411	MEA, Middle East Airways, an Egyptian firm	175
412	Yemen Airways	178
413	Air India	194
414	Libyan Arab Airlines	208
415	Air Kuwait	212
416	Iranian Air Force	
500	local Peruvian	001
501	Faucett, a Peruvian firm	002
502	local Bolivian	017
503	Cubana	019
504	local Haitian	021
505	Aerovias, a Cuban firm	022
506	Panair do Brazil	023
507	Cuban general aviation firm	024
508	AVENSA	033
509	Cuban military plane	039
510	Aerocondor, a Colombian firm	042, 046
511	AVIANCA	047
512	local Mexican	050
513	VIASA, Venezuelan Airlines	051
514	Island Flying Service, a Bahamas charter	058
515	Aeromaya, a Mexican firm	060
516	SEASA, a Mexican firm	062
517	CMA, a Mexican firm	064
518	ASPA, a Venezuelan firm	066
519	Ecuatoriana International	067
520	SAM, Sociedad Aeronautica de Medellin, Col.	068
521	local Venezuelan	069
522	Aeropostal, a Venezuelan firm	070

523	Ecuadorian Airlines	071
524	La Urraca, a Colombian firm	075
525	SAETA, an Ecuadorian firm	076
526	Mexicana de Aviacion	077
527	Nicaraguan Airlines	078
528	TAME, an Ecuadorian firm	081
529	SAHSA, a Honduran firm	082
530	Cruzeiro do Sul, a Brazilian firm	084
531	Aerotaxi Airlines, a Colombian charter	085
532	LANICA, Lancia, a Nicaraguan firm	086
533	VARIG, a Brazilian firm	087
534	Austral, an Argentine firm	089
535	LAN, a Chilean firm	090
536	Chilean Airlines	091
537	Mexican general aviation	092
538	LACSA, a Costa Rican firm	095
539	RAPSA, a Panamanian firm	097
540	Netherlands Antilles Airlines	098
541	British Honduran general aviation	101
542	Costa Rican National Airways	103
543	VASP, Viacao Aerea de Sao Paulo, a Brazilian firm	106
544	British West Indies Airlines, Trinidad and Tobago	107
545	Aeronaves de Mexico	116
546	Trans-Caribbean Airways	117
547	Aerovia Quisqueyana, a Dominican firm	127
548	Bolivian military plane	143
549	Arawak, a Trinidad and Tobago firm	144
550	Lloyd Air Boliviano	146
551	Alas Del Caribe Air, a Dominican firm	147
552	Jamaica Air Taxi, general aviation	154
553	Empress Ecuatoriana de Aviacion	161
554	Aero Opita Tao, Opita Air Taxi, Colombian	165
555	local Argentine	177
556	Air Jamaica	181
557	Aeropesca, a Colombian firm	182
558	Cessnica, a Colombian general aviation firm	185
559	Haiti Air Inter	200
560	Aces Airlines, Colombian general aviation	204
561	Ladeco, a Chilean firm	211
562	National Transport Enterprise, general aviation	
563	Salas Air Taxi, general aviation	
600	Cathay-Pacific	008
601	China National Aviation Corporation	011
602	PAL, Philippine Air Lines	015
603	Korean National Airlines, a South Korean firm	018
604	Trans-Australia	025
605	East-West Airlines, an Australian firm	088
606	JAL, Japan Air Lines	102

607	Ansett Airlines, an Australian firm	108
608	Air Vietnam, a South Vietnamese firm	114
609	All Nippon Airways	118
610	Bira Air Transport, Thai general aviation	124
611	Merpati Nusuntara Airlines, Indonesian firm	155
612	Royal Nepalese Airlines	173
613	Far Eastern Air Transport, a Taiwanese firm	191
614	Australian military plane	199
615	Thai Airways Company	213
616	Malaysian Airlines Systems	214
617	CAAC, Civil Aviation Administration of China	
700	local Romanian	003
701	local Czechoslovakian	004
702	local Yugoslavian	005
703	Soviet-Romanian Airways	006
704	local Bulgarian	007
705	local Hungarian	010
706	LOT, a Polish firm	012
707	local Polish	013
708	Yugoslavian National Airlines	014
709	CSA, Czechoslovakia National Airlines	016
710	Czech general aviation charter firm	020
711	local USSR	026
712	Interflug, an East German firm	100
713	Aeroflot	111
714	TAROM, a Romanian firm	123
715	Slovair, a Czech firm	159
716	Balkan Airlines, a Bulgarian firm	198
800	Nigerian Airlines	044
801	Ethiopian Airlines	079
802	Angolan Air Taxi, a general aviation firm	136
803	South African Airlines	162
804	East African Airways, a Kenyan firm	163
805	an Angolan charter firm	189
999	Unknown, indeterminate	099

LOCATION OF INCIDENT

8. Flight plan embarkation point

When it cannot be determined from sources where the flight began, the value for this variable will be identical to that used for the embarkation point of the hijacker.

Values:

(same country codes as used for Variable 5 in COMMON file)

9. Hijacker embarkation point

When it cannot be determined where the hijacker boarded the plane, the last known refueling/stopoff location for the flight is entered.
Values:
(same country codes as used for Variable 5 in COMMON file)

10. Flight plan end point

Takeovers of nonscheduled flights (i.e., planes being serviced on the ground, with no crewmen on board) are listed as ending in the country of takeover.
Values:
(same country codes as used for Variable 5 in COMMON file)

11. Hijacker desired end point

The location need not be identical to the name of the country at which the hijacker finally left the plane.
Values:
(same country codes as used for Variable 5 in COMMON file)

12. Number of stopovers and refuelings

This variable notes the number of stops between the point of hijacking and the end of the incident. In cases where the incident ended at a location considered by the hijacker to be a refueling point, rather than a point of his chosen embarkation, a value of 1 is added to the tally of previous stopovers.
Values:
0–8   Actual number
9   More than 8 stopovers

NUMBER OF INDIVIDUALS INVOLVED

13. Crew members

Crew members include stewardesses as well as pilots, copilots, and navigators. Planes that are on the ground being serviced have no crewmen on board.
Values:
00–98   Actual number
99   Unknown

14. Individuals on board plane

This figure includes hijackers, crewmen, passengers, sky marshals, and other personnel.
Values:
00–97   Actual number
98   More than 97
99   Unknown

15. Hijackers

Unarmed members of the hijackers' family, such as children, are not included in this tally. Accomplices on the ground who aid the hijackers in providing weapons, entry, and so forth, but do not participate in the attack, are also not counted.
Values:
00–98   Actual number
99   Unknown

16. Number wounded

Wounded includes those who are reported to have been sufficiently harmed physically to have required medical attention. No distinction is made between those who are outpatients and those who are rescued from the critical list. Those who later die from their injuries are coded as dying, rather than wounded. The tally includes police, crew, passengers, hijackers, and others.
Values:
00–96   Actual number
97   More than 96
98   Unknown, but some individuals were wounded
99   Unknown

17. Hostages wounded

Values:
00–96   Actual number
97   More than 96
98   Unknown, but some individuals were wounded
99   Unknown

18. Hijackers wounded

Values:
00–96   Actual number
97   More than 96
98   Unknown, but some individuals were wounded
99   Unknown

19. Crew wounded

Values:
00–96   Actual number
97   More than 96
98   Unknown, but some individuals were wounded
99   Unknown

20. Number killed

Values:

00–96   Actual number
97   More than 96
98   Unknown, but some individuals were killed
99   Unknown

21. Hostages killed

Values:

00–96   Actual number
97   More than 96
98   Unknown, but some individuals were killed
99   Unknown

22. Hijackers killed

Values:

00–96   Actual number
97   More than 96
98   Unknown, but some individuals were killed
99   Unknown

23. Crew killed

Values:

00–96   Actual number
97   More than 96
98   Unknown, but some individuals were killed
99   Unknown

24. Damage to plane

Values:
0   None
1   Slight—less than or equal to $10,000
2   Moderate—less than or equal to $100,000
3   High—less than or equal to $1 million
4   Severe—more than $1 million
9   Unknown, but damage reported

25. Logistical success of hijacking incident

Values:
1   Incident stopped by authorities at planning stage
2   Incident stopped by authorities at scene or on the way to scene, before initiation

3 Aborted by hijackers during event
4 Unsuccessful owing to faults or error by hijackers
5 Stopped by authorities at the scene after initiation
6 Apparently completed as planned
9 Unknown

26. *Negotiation success of hijacking incident*

Values:
1 Received some of their demands
2 Received all of their demands
3 Received none of their demands
8 Irrelevant, no demands made
9 Unknown

27. *Type of weapon*

The most destructive weapon of all of those known to be in the possession of the perpetrators at the scene of the incident is noted.
Values:
1 Hoax, no weapons used
2 Nonexplosive, nonprojectile weapons, including knives
3 Handguns
4 Rifles, shotguns, or machine guns
5 Explosives, incendiaries
6 Missiles, other heavy projectiles
7 Other
9 Unknown